In the first months of 1864, Ulysses S. [Grant] an inconclusive winter campaign in east Tennessee while keeping an eye on Washington, where Congress debated a bill to create the rank of lieutenant general intended for him. Even before the passage of the bill, Grant thought about matters of strategy and command organization. In earlier times, he had "abstained from suggesting what might be done in other commands than my own," but he no longer had this luxury. Grant tentatively suggested that Richmond, and the Confederate forces defending it, might be more vulnerable if approached from the south. At the same time, he recommended that U.S. forces should keep the pressure on in the west by advancing toward Atlanta. He also revived his idea of a campaign against Mobile.

Grant continued to ward off the entreaties of politicians while awaiting the expected call from Washington. He made it clear that "Every body who knows me knows I have no political aspirations either now or for the future." He understood that he could not be a successful military commander while entangled in politics. Grant also made it known that he could not "be induced to take an office which would require me to stay in Washington and command whilst the Armies were in the field."

The call came in March as Grant was ordered to the capital to accept the rank of lieutenant general, the first to hold such high rank since George Washington, and to take command of all the armies of the United States. Grant immediately plunged into planning a coordinated spring campaign. He wanted to exert pressure with all the forces at his disposal to make it impossible for the Confederates to shift troops from one theater to another. The documents reveal Grant's genius for planning war. He did not envision a Napoleonic war with one magnificent victory, but a total war using all the resources available to fight the enemy. Grant's war is the first modern war.

Despite his heavy military responsibilities, Grant continued to supervise the daily activities of his family, filling letters to his wife, Julia Dent Grant, with advice about family finances and the care of their four children. The two oldest boys should learn to speak German, he wrote, and the youngest, six-year-old Jesse, needed supervision in the Washington hotel where he "eats five or six times each day and dips largely into deserts."

Grant realized that his success would be determined in large measure by his relationships with the authorities at Washington and with his commanders in the field. He placed the west in the able hands of his trusted friend lished volumes of the Grant Papers, four books, among which is *The Personal Memoirs of Julia Dent Grant*.

DAVID L. WILSON, assistant editor of the Grant Papers, received his Ph.D. degree from the University of Tennessee. He is Adjunct Assistant Professor of History at Southern Illinois University, Carbondale. He has co-authored *The Presidency of Warren G. Harding* and edited *Ulysses S. Grant: Essays and Documents*.

The Grant Papers are published under the auspices of the Ulysses S. Grant Association and are sponsored by Southern Illinois University and the National Historical Publications and Records Commission.

THE PAPERS OF ULYSSES S. GRANT

THE PAPERS OF

ULYSSES S. GRANT

Volume 10: January 1–May 31, 1864

Edited by John Y. Simon

ASSISTANT EDITOR
David L. Wilson

─────

SOUTHERN ILLINOIS UNIVERSITY PRESS

CARBONDALE AND EDWARDSVILLE

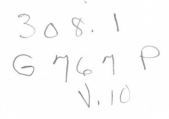

Library of Congress Cataloging in Publication Data (Revised)
Grant, Ulysses Simpson, Pres. U.S., 1822–1885.
The papers of Ulysses S. Grant.

Prepared under the auspices of the Ulysses S. Grant Association.
Bibliographical footnotes.
CONTENTS: v. 1. 1837–1861—v. 2. April–September 1861.
—v. 3. October 1, 1861–January 7, 1862.—v. 4. January 8–March 31,
1862.—v. 5. April 1–August 31, 1862.—v. 6. September 1–December 8, 1862.—v. 7. December 9, 1862–March 31, 1863.—v. 8.
April 1–July 6, 1863.—v. 9. July 7–December 31, 1863.—v. 10.
January 1–May 31, 1864.
1. Grant, Ulysses Simpson, Pres. U.S., 1822–1885. 2. United
States—History—Civil War, 1861–1865—Campaigns and battles
—Sources. 3. United States—Politics and government—1869–1877
—Sources. 4. Presidents—United States—Biography. 5. Generals—
United States—Biography. I. Simon, John Y., ed. II. Ulysses S.
Grant Association.
E660.G756 1967   973.8′2′0924   67–10725
ISBN 0–8093–0980–7 (v. 10)

To Bruce Catton (1899–1978)

Contents

Maps and Illustrations

Introduction

===

FOLLOWING THE BATTLE of Chattanooga (November 23–25, 1863), Ulysses S. Grant sent forces to relieve Knoxville, where Major General Ambrose E. Burnside had been besieged by Lieutenant General James Longstreet. Although General Braxton Bragg's Army of Tennessee had left Chattanooga in disorder, the need to send troops to Knoxville prevented Grant from launching an aggressive campaign into Georgia. Longstreet raised his siege upon learning that reinforcements were on the way, but he remained a menace in east Tennessee during the customary winter slackening of military action. Grant wanted to drive Longstreet away, but problems of supply and weather frustrated his efforts. Grant finally realized that Longstreet faced the same problems and once out of Tennessee might do more damage elsewhere.

The winter months of 1864 found Grant preparing for the inevitable spring campaign in Georgia. At the same time, he could not ignore the deliberations of Congress as it considered a bill to revive the rank of lieutenant general, intending it for Grant. In January, Grant and his staff mapped out grand strategy, forwarding suggestions to Major General Henry W. Halleck.

In late February, the lieutenant general bill passed, and President Abraham Lincoln called Grant to Washington to receive his commission and assume command of all the armies. Halleck immediately resigned his post of general-in-chief and was appointed Grant's chief of staff, a move which provided the U.S. Army with a modern command system, freeing Grant to take the field while Halleck dealt with administrative matters and implemented Grant's orders.

Grant decided to accompany the Army of the Potomac without superseding its commander, Major General George G. Meade, and planned a coordinated spring campaign of all the armies. Unless the armies moved together, Confederates could use interior lines to shift troops from one army to another to meet the greatest threat. Lincoln's response to the plan, "Those not skinning can hold a leg," so delighted Grant that he used it—without crediting the source—in his own correspondence. He soon learned that some commanders, notably Major Generals Nathaniel P. Banks, Benjamin F. Butler, and Franz Sigel, would let the legs slip from their grasp.

With the authorities in Washington supporting him, Grant still had to win the confidence of the Army of the Potomac, where his arrival caused little enthusiasm. By not bringing in victorious generals from the western armies and quietly conveying confidence in the eastern troops, Grant soon raised morale. Once the Army of the Potomac crossed the Rapidan in early May, it met Robert E. Lee's Army of Northern Virginia in a series of bloody battles beginning with the Wilderness and continuing at Spotsylvania and the North Anna. May ended with the armies massing for yet another encounter at Cold Harbor. Although Grant's army suffered heavy losses, he informed Washington that he proposed "to fight it out on this line if it takes all summer." This determination, somehow conveyed to the troops, seemed to create a new drive toward eventual victory. Analysis of Grant's success in May depends upon whether casualty figures or maps are examined; at awesome cost Grant pushed Lee back to Richmond.

When Grant assumed command of the Armies of the U.S., he ordered the commanders of the separate armies to send their reports and correspondence to headquarters in Washington. Much of this material, addressed to Halleck, was then copied and transmitted to Grant. Although Grant remained informed of the movements of each army, and issued orders on the basis of this information, correspondence not addressed to Grant has been excluded from this volume except when essential to an understanding of Grant's own letters. As Grant moved into Virginia, his correspondence increased in volume and significance, and Halleck's new position relieved Grant, then his editors and readers, of much routine army business. Top command also brought Grant his first printed stationery, and he usually remembered to cross out the heading when writing private letters. For the sake of economy this printed matter has not been reprinted.

We are indebted to W. Neil Franklin and Karl L. Trever for searching the National Archives; to Mary Giunta, Anne Harris Henry, and Sara Dunlap Jackson for further assistance in the National Archives; to Barbara Long for maps; to Fern L. Chappell, Sue E. Dotson, and Deborah Pittman for typing; to Harriet Simon for proofreading; and to Richard T. Boss, Susan Coggeshall, Karen Kendall, Patrick M. McCoy, Tamara Melia, and Patricia Lynn Walker, graduate students at Southern Illinois University, for research assistance.

Financial support for the period during which this volume was prepared came from Southern Illinois University and the National Historical Publications and Records Commission.

JOHN Y. SIMON

December 31, 1979

Editorial Procedure

1. Editorial Insertions

A.   Words or letters in roman type within brackets represent editorial reconstruction of parts of manuscripts torn, mutilated, or illegible.

B.   [...] or [— — —] within brackets represent lost material which cannot be reconstructed. The number of dots represents the approximate number of lost letters; dashes represent lost words.

C.   Words in *italic* type within brackets represent material such as dates which were not part of the original manuscript.

D.   Other material crossed out is indicated by ~~cancelled type~~.

E.   Material raised in manuscript, as "4th," has been brought in line, as "4th."

2. Symbols Used to Describe Manuscripts

AD	Autograph Document
ADS	Autograph Document Signed
ADf	Autograph Draft
ADfS	Autograph Draft Signed
AES	Autograph Endorsement Signed
AL	Autograph Letter
ALS	Autograph Letter Signed
ANS	Autograph Note Signed
D	Document
DS	Document Signed

Df	Draft
DfS	Draft Signed
ES	Endorsement Signed
LS	Letter Signed

3. *Military Terms and Abbreviations*

Act.	Acting
Adjt.	Adjutant
AG	Adjutant General
AGO	Adjutant General's Office
Art.	Artillery
Asst.	Assistant
Bvt.	Brevet
Brig.	Brigadier
Capt.	Captain
Cav.	Cavalry
Col.	Colonel
Co.	Company
C.S.A.	Confederate States of America
Dept.	Department
Div.	Division
Gen.	General
Hd. Qrs.	Headquarters
Inf.	Infantry
Lt.	Lieutenant
Maj.	Major
Q. M.	Quartermaster
Regt.	Regiment or regimental
Sgt.	Sergeant
USMA	United States Military Academy, West Point, N.Y.
Vols.	Volunteers

4. *Short Titles and Abbreviations*

ABPC	*American Book-Prices Current* (New York, 1895–)
CG	*Congressional Globe* Numbers following represent the Congress, session, and page.

J. G. Cramer	Jesse Grant Cramer, ed., *Letters of Ulysses S. Grant to his Father and his Youngest Sister, 1857–78* (New York and London, 1912)
DAB	*Dictionary of American Biography* (New York, 1928–36)
Garland	Hamlin Garland, *Ulysses S. Grant: His Life and Character* (New York, 1898)
HED	*House Executive Documents*
HMD	*House Miscellaneous Documents*
HRC	*House Reports of Committees* Numbers following *HED, HMD,* or *HRC* represent the number of the Congress, the session, and the document.
Ill. AG Report	J. N. Reece, ed., *Report of the Adjutant General of the State of Illinois* (Springfield, 1900)
Johnson, Papers	LeRoy P. Graf and Ralph W. Haskins, eds., *The Papers of Andrew Johnson* (Knoxville, 1967–)
Lewis	Lloyd Lewis, *Captain Sam Grant* (Boston, 1950)
Lincoln, Works	Roy P. Basler, Marion Dolores Pratt, and Lloyd A. Dunlap, eds., *The Collected Works of Abraham Lincoln* (New Brunswick, 1953–55)
Memoirs	*Personal Memoirs of U. S. Grant* (New York, 1885–86)
O.R.	*The War of the Rebellion: A Compilation of the Official Records of the Union and Confederate Armies* (Washington, 1880–1901)
O.R. (Navy)	*Official Records of the Union and Confederate Navies in the War of the Rebellion* (Washington, 1894–1927) Roman numerals following *O.R.* or *O.R.* (Navy) represent the series and the volume.
PUSG	John Y. Simon, ed., *The Papers of Ulysses S. Grant* (Carbondale and Edwardsville, 1967–)
Richardson	Albert D. Richardson, *A Personal History of Ulysses S. Grant* (Hartford, Conn., 1868)
SED	*Senate Executive Documents*
SMD	*Senate Miscellaneous Documents*
SRC	*Senate Reports of Committees* Numbers following *SED, SMD,* or *SRC* represent the number of the Congress, the session, and the document.
USGA Newsletter	*Ulysses S. Grant Association Newsletter*

Young	John Russell Young, *Around the World with General Grant* (New York, 1879)

5. *Location Symbols*

CLU	University of California at Los Angeles, Los Angeles, Calif.
CoHi	Colorado State Historical Society, Denver, Colo.
CSmH	Henry E. Huntington Library, San Marino, Calif.
CSt	Stanford University, Stanford, Calif.
CtY	Yale University, New Haven, Conn.
CU-B	Bancroft Library, University of California, Berkeley, Calif.
DLC	Library of Congress, Washington, D.C. Numbers following DLC-USG represent the series and volume of military records in the USG papers.
DNA	National Archives, Washington, D.C. Additional numbers identify record groups.
IaHA	Iowa State Department of History and Archives, Des Moines, Iowa.
I-ar	Illinois State Archives, Springfield, Ill.
IC	Chicago Public Library, Chicago, Ill.
ICarbS	Southern Illinois University, Carbondale, Ill.
ICHi	Chicago Historical Society, Chicago, Ill.
ICN	Newberry Library, Chicago, Ill.
ICU	University of Chicago, Chicago, Ill.
IHi	Illinois State Historical Library, Springfield, Ill.
In	Indiana State Library, Indianapolis, Ind.
InFtwL	Lincoln National Life Foundation, Fort Wayne, Ind.
InHi	Indiana Historical Society, Indianapolis, Ind.
InNd	University of Notre Dame, Notre Dame, Ind.
InU	Indiana University, Bloomington, Ind.
KHi	Kansas State Historical Society, Topeka, Kan.
MdAN	United States Naval Academy Museum, Annapolis, Md.
MeB	Bowdoin College, Brunswick, Me.
MH	Harvard University, Cambridge, Mass.
MHi	Massachusetts Historical Society, Boston, Mass.

MiD	Detroit Public Library, Detroit, Mich.
MiU-C	William L. Clements Library, University of Michigan, Ann Arbor, Mich.
MoSHi	Missouri Historical Society, St. Louis, Mo.
NHi	New-York Historical Society, New York, N.Y.
NIC	Cornell University, Ithaca, N.Y.
NjP	Princeton University, Princeton, N.J.
NjR	Rutgers University, New Brunswick, N.J.
NN	New York Public Library, New York, N.Y.
NNP	Pierpont Morgan Library, New York, N.Y.
NRU	University of Rochester, Rochester, N.Y.
OClWHi	Western Reserve Historical Society, Cleveland, Ohio.
OFH	Rutherford B. Hayes Library, Fremont, Ohio.
OHi	Ohio Historical Society, Columbus, Ohio.
OrHi	Oregon Historical Society, Portland, Ore.
PCarlA	U.S. Army Military History Institute, Carlisle Barracks, Pa.
PHi	Historical Society of Pennsylvania, Philadelphia, Pa.
PPRF	Rosenbach Foundation, Philadelphia, Pa.
RPB	Brown University, Providence, R.I.
TxHR	Rice University, Houston, Tex.
USG 3	Maj. Gen. Ulysses S. Grant 3rd, Clinton, N.Y.
USMA	United States Military Academy Library, West Point, N.Y.
ViHi	Virginia Historical Society, Richmond, Va.
ViU	University of Virginia, Charlottesville, Va.
WHi	State Historical Society of Wisconsin, Madison, Wis.
Wy-Ar	Wyoming State Archives and Historical Department, Cheyenne, Wyo.
WyU	University of Wyoming, Laramie, Wyo.

Chronology

JAN. 1.   USG at Knoxville planned a campaign in east Tenn.

JAN. 3.   USG at Strawberry Plains, Tenn., examining the position of C.S.A. Lt. Gen. James Longstreet.

JAN. 8.   USG at Barboursville, Ky., examining supply routes from Ky. into east Tenn.

JAN. 12.   USG returned to Nashville.

JAN. 16.   Longstreet moved toward Knoxville.

JAN. 19.   USG recommended a campaign in N.C. to cut C.S.A. supply lines to Richmond.

JAN. 21.   USG at Chattanooga.

JAN. 24.   USG ordered Maj. Gen. John A. Logan to make a reconnaissance in northern Ala.

JAN. 24.   USG left Chattanooga for St. Louis to visit his son, Frederick Dent Grant, then seriously ill.

JAN. 27.   USG arrived at St. Louis.

JAN. 27.   Maj. Gen. John M. Schofield assigned to command the Dept. of the Ohio in place of Maj. Gen. John G. Foster. Schofield assumed command on Feb. 9.

JAN. 29.   USG attended a banquet in St. Louis in his honor.

FEB. 1.   USG left St. Louis for Nashville.

FEB. 1.   President Abraham Lincoln ordered the draft of 500,000 men on March 10 to serve for three years or the duration of the war.

FEB. 3. Maj. Gen. William T. Sherman left Vicksburg with 26,000 men to destroy C.S.A. communications around Meridian, Miss., returning on March 4.

FEB. 4. USG arrived at Nashville.

FEB. 10. USG ordered Maj. Gen. George H. Thomas to prepare to move to Knoxville.

FEB. 12. USG issued regulations for the sale of cotton.

FEB. 12. USG suspended the campaign against Longstreet after consulting with Foster; instead, he ordered Thomas to make a demonstration toward Dalton, Ga.

FEB. 22. Thomas began a demonstration toward Dalton.

FEB. 22. U.S. cav. under Brig. Gen. William Sooy Smith defeated by C.S.A. Maj. Gen. Nathan B. Forrest at Okolona, Miss., after failing to connect with Sherman's expedition to Meridian.

FEB. 24. U.S. forces gained possession of Tunnel Hill, Ga.

FEB. 25. USG decided not to go to Chattanooga because of illness.

FEB. 26. Demonstration toward Dalton stopped by strong C.S.A. position at Buzzard Roost, Ga.

FEB. 29. Lincoln signed into law the bill reviving the grade of lt. gen. and nominated USG for that rank.

MAR. 1. A U.S. raid on Richmond led by Brig. Gen. Judson Kilpatrick and Col. Ulric Dahlgren failed, with Dahlgren being killed during the retreat.

MAR. 2. USG confirmed by the Senate as lt. gen.

MAR. 3. USG ordered to report in person to Washington.

MAR. 8. USG arrived in Washington accompanied by his oldest son Fred, and attended a reception at the White House.

MAR. 9. USG received his commission as lt. gen. in a ceremony at the White House.

MAR. 10. USG assigned to command the Armies of the U.S. He made a quick trip to see Maj. Gen. George G. Meade and the Army of the Potomac.

MAR. 11. USG started back to Nashville to wrap up affairs in the Military Div. of the Miss.

MAR. 12. Maj. Gen. Nathaniel P. Banks began the Red River Campaign.

MAR. 14. USG arrived at Nashville and ordered the 9th Army Corps to Annapolis, Md.

MAR. 17. USG issued General Orders No. 1, assuming command of the Armies of the U.S. with his hd. qrs. in the field.

MAR. 18. USG accepted a ceremonial sword presented by citizens of Jo Daviess County, Ill., and left Nashville for the East.

MAR. 18. Sherman assumed command of the Military Div. of the Miss.

MAR. 22. USG at Philadelphia.

MAR. 23. USG sat for photographer Mathew Brady in Washington.

MAR. 24. USG established hd. qrs. in the field at Culpeper Court-House, Va., with the Army of the Potomac, and started planning a coordinated spring campaign.

MAR. 24. Forrest again moved into west Tenn.

MAR. 26. Maj. Gen. James B. McPherson assumed command of the Army of the Tenn.

MAR. 28. USG at Washington.

MAR. 31. USG passed through Washington en route to Fort Monroe, Va.

APRIL 1. USG visited Maj. Gen. Benjamin F. Butler at Fort Monroe to consult about the spring campaign.

APRIL 4. USG returned to Washington.

APRIL 5. USG returned to Culpeper.

APRIL 7. Longstreet ordered to return to the Army of Northern Va.

APRIL 8. Banks defeated at the battle of Sabine Crossroads, La.

APRIL 12. C.S.A. forces commanded by Forrest captured Fort Pillow, Tenn., and Negro troops of the garrison were killed after the surrender.

APRIL 13. USG visited Maj. Gen. Ambrose E. Burnside and the 9th Army Corps at Annapolis.

APRIL 15. C.S.A. guerrillas attacked Bristoe Station, Va., shortly after USG's train passed by.

APRIL 15. USG decided to relieve Maj. Gen. Stephen A. Hurlbut at Memphis after learning of the capture of Fort Pillow, sending Maj. Gen. Cadwallader C. Washburn the next day.

APRIL 17. USG ordered a halt to the exchange of prisoners until C.S.A. authorities agreed to equalize the exchange and make no distinction "between white and colored prisoners."

APRIL 20. USG conferred with Lincoln in Washington.

APRIL 20. Plymouth, N.C., with 2,800 men captured by C.S.A. forces.

APRIL 22. USG decided to abandon Plymouth and Washington, N.C., unaware of the capture of Plymouth until April 24.

APRIL 22. USG requested the replacement of Banks, but for political reasons, Lincoln was unwilling to act.

APRIL 27. USG's forty-second birthday.

MAY 1. USG thanked Lincoln for his confidence and support.

MAY 4. The Army of the Potomac crossed the Rapidan River.

MAY 5–6. Battle of the Wilderness with heavy casualties suffered by both sides.

MAY 5. Butler landed his Army of the James at City Point and Bermuda Hundred, Va.

MAY 5. U.S. cav. began a raid against the Virginia and Tennessee Railroad from W.Va.

MAY 7. Sherman began to move toward Atlanta with more than 100,000 men.

MAY 8. The Army of the Potomac arrived at Spotsylvania Court-House only to find that C.S.A. forces had arrived first. Fighting began, continuing the next day.

MAY 10. C.S.A. forces repulsed a U.S. attack at Spotsylvania.

MAY 11. U.S. cav. commanded by Maj. Gen. Philip H. Sheridan mortally wounded C.S.A. Lt. Gen. James E. B. Stuart during the battle of Yellow Tavern, Va.

MAY 12. U.S. forces captured 4,000 C.S.A. troops at Spotsylvania during the battle of "Bloody Angle."

MAY 12. Sherman maneuvered C.S.A. forces out of Dalton.

MAY 13. USG continued shifting the Army of the Potomac.

MAY 14. Battle of Resaca, Ga., began, ending the following day with the withdrawal of C.S.A. forces.

MAY 15. Maj. Gen. Franz Sigel defeated by C.S.A. forces at New Market, Va.

MAY 16. USG again requested that Banks be removed from active command, unaware that Maj. Gen. Edward R. S. Canby had been sent to do so on May 7.

MAY 16. Butler retreated after the battle of Drewry's Bluff, or Fort Darling, Va., and was bottled up in Bermuda Hundred the following day by smaller C.S.A. forces.

MAY 18. After another assault failed at Spotsylvania, USG decided to shift his army southward.

MAY 19. C.S.A. forces repulsed in an attack on the U.S. right in the last engagement at Spotsylvania.

MAY 19. Maj. Gen. David Hunter replaced Sigel in command of the Dept. of W.Va.

MAY 23–26. Battle of North Anna fought by the Army of the Potomac.

MAY 25. Sherman stopped by C.S.A. forces at New Hope Church, Ga.

MAY 26. USG instructed Meade to withdraw from the North Anna to move to the right of the Army of Northern Va.

MAY 27. U.S. cav. occupied Hanovertown, Va.

MAY 28. The Army of Northern Va. approached Cold Harbor, Va.

MAY 31. USG shifted U.S. forces toward Cold Harbor.

The Papers of Ulysses S. Grant
January 1–May 31, 1864

To Maj. Gen. George H. Thomas

———

Knoxville [*January*] 1st 1864.

Maj. Gen Thomas

I arrived here yesterday morning   send forward all the supplies for Gen Foster with as little delay as possible, and clothing particularly   Keep a careful watch on the river between chickamauga & the Hiawassee to prevent interference with the steamboats.

U. S. Grant
Maj. Genl.

Telegram, copy, DNA, RG 393, Dept. of the Cumberland, Telegrams Received. *O.R.*, I, xxxii, part 2, 3. On Jan. 3, 1864, USG, Strawberry Plains, Tenn., telegraphed to Maj. Gen. George H. Thomas. "Send forward clothing for this command as fast as it arrives at Chattanooga. If you have clothing on hand that can possibly be spared, send it forward and deduct the same amount from that coming forward for Foster. Troops here are in bad condition for clothing and before making much advance must be supplied." Copies, DLC-USG, V, 34, 35; DNA, RG 393, Military Div. of the Miss., Letters Sent; *ibid.*, Dept. of the Cumberland, Telegrams Received. *O.R.*, I, xxxii, part 2, 19. On Jan. 5, Thomas, Chattanooga, telegraphed to USG. "Despatch of 3d Recd—Orders have already been given to despatch clothing as fast as it arrived—If contractors can be relied on the Rail road will be completed to Chattanooga by the middle of next week   I Can then put more steam boats on the river between here and Knoxville   Col Donaldson telegraphs me that has sent large quantitys of subsistence to Carthage for Foster & is ready to send stores to the mouth of Big South Fork if so ordered   Will you give them to him"   Telegram received, DNA, RG 393, Dept. of the Tenn., Telegrams Received; copies, *ibid.*, Military Div. of the Miss., Telegrams Received; *ibid.*, Dept. of the Cumberland, Telegrams Sent. *O.R.*, I, xxxii, part 2, 30. On the same day, Bvt. Lt. Col. James L. Donaldson telegraphed to USG. "Steamers are here with subsistence for Big South Fork   are these stores for Gen Foster and shall I send them on? If so I must get a Gunboat as convoy. Two steamers have discharged their freight at Carthage. These remain here to go up. Shall I send them also   There are only four hundred men at Carthage, and they do not know why supplies are sent there"   Copies, DNA, RG 393, Dept. of the Cumberland, Q. M. Dept., Telegrams Sent (Press); *ibid.*, Military Div. of the Miss., Telegrams Received. *O.R.*, I, xxxii, part 2, 32. On Jan. 8, Donaldson telegraphed to USG. "Have sent five steamers under convoy to the big south Fork one of which remains there for service. will attend to your order about the cargoes left at Carthage."

Copy, DNA, RG 393, Dept. of the Cumberland, Q. M. Dept., Telegrams Sent
(Press).

On Jan. 14, USG, Nashville, telegraphed to Brig. Gen. Grenville M. Dodge.
"How are the railroad bridges on your road progressing?" Copies, DLC-USG, V,
34, 35; DNA, RG 393, Military Div. of the Miss., Letters Sent. On the same day,
Dodge, Pulaski, Tenn., telegraphed to USG. "The bridges South of Duck River
are mostly completed   Duck River bridge will probably be done in three weeks
and by that time all the bridges will be completed to the junction   I am pushing
the work under my command as fast as possible"   Copies, *ibid.*, Telegrams Received; *ibid.*, 16th Army Corps, Left Wing, Telegrams Sent. *O.R.*, I, xxxii, part
2, 96. On Jan. 16, Dodge telegraphed to USG. "I have just returned for examination of work on Bridges from here to Decatur. All south of here will be done
Feby. 1st if weather holds good. Duck River is in Boomers hands—I put in ten
spans   he is putting in ten more. Have finished all bridges including the seven
North of Duck River to Elk River—No work is being done west of Huntsville and
there are four pretty large bridges to build"   Copies, DNA, RG 393, Military
Div. of the Miss., Telegrams Received; *ibid.*, 16th Army Corps, Telegrams Sent.
O.R., I, xxxii, part 2, 111. On Jan. 22 or 23, Dodge telegraphed to Lt. Col. Theodore S. Bowers. "I think something should be done to hurry up the Duck River
bridge—The workmen there claim it will take thirty days to put it in yet—They
could be at work on the trus by putting in a boat to hold one end now and not
wait for the Masonry to be finished—That could be going on at the same time—
Road has been finished to Duck River a week and bridge is not done there yet.
Mr. Boomer I believe is now in Nashville"   Copies (dated Jan. 22), DNA, RG
393, Military Div. of the Miss., Telegrams Received; (dated Jan. 23) *ibid.*, 16th
Army Corps, Left Wing, Telegrams Sent.

On Jan. 22, Jacob F. Guthrie, Mount Pleasant, Tenn., wrote to USG.
"Soldiers of the United States under command of Genl. Dodge at Lynnville Tenn
—have within the past few days pressed or taken by force, a number of negroe
slaves from this neighborhood for soldiers in the United States army—& have
done so against the consent of the slaves, taking the slaves without consulting the
wishes of the slaves   Among others they took two slaves belonging to me & in
my employment at the time   I am as My negroes are named Anthony & Finley—
I am advised that by the laws & orders of the United States there is no right to
take negroes for soldiers against thier will—I respectfully ask such redress as by
law I may or the said slaves may be entitled to & my neighbor Martin L. Stockard
Esq. is hereby appointed & empowered to act as my agent & attorney in the
premises—"   ALS, *ibid.*, Military Div. of the Miss., Letters Received. On Jan.
28, Dodge endorsed this letter. "Respectfully returned. These negroes were taken
to work on Rail Road repairs fortifications &c. No negro is put in the army against
his will, but where the service requires I often press them to work as above, and
it is in accordance with orders from Department and Military Division Mississippi, Commanders. We must do it   the people here would and will not, send
them." ES, *ibid.*

On Jan. 14, Thomas telegraphed and wrote to USG. "I am assured by the
Engineer of the Running Water Bridge that the road will be completed to this
place to day by 2 P. M.   Day before yesterday I telegraphed Col. Donaldson to
have trains loaded for this place and started from Nashville yesterday. We are
to day entirely out of forage and short of rations, the result of endeavoring to
supply Genl. Foster and ourselves by Steamboats. Now that the R. R. is finished
Mr. Anderson should be required to have as many trains running as can be put

on the Road—So far, instead of getting ahead, our supplies are decreasing. With the R. R. operated to its full capacity we certainly ought to accumulate supplies here and be able to give two or three Steamboats to Foster. I will write you at length to day." Copies, *ibid.*, Dept. of the Cumberland, Telegrams Sent; *ibid.*, Military Div. of the Miss., Telegrams Received. *O.R.*, I, xxxii, part 2, 88. "The Engineers on the Running Water Bridge have assured me that the R Road will be completed and in running order to this place to-day at 2 P. M.   General Crook reports that the Nashville and Decatur Road will be completed by the 15th February. In anticipation of the completion of the N & C Road I telegraphed Col Donaldson to have all the trains to come from Nashville to Bridgeport loaded for this place the first two with forage as our animals were entirely without food the next with provisions so that we could send some to General Foster. In this connexion I must say that I cannot possibly supply Genl Foster's *demands* and this command too, unless Mr Anderson does his share of the work. He ought to have had by this time something like two hundred or two hundred and fifty freight cars at Nashville with a corresponding number of motive power to put to work as soon as the Road was open, yet the depot at Bridgeport has never been properly supplied, but always out of, or short in, subsistence stores or forage. I have repeatedly urged him to exert himself,   His excuse is that the cars are not unloaded promptly on their arrival at Bridgeport and at Way Stations   In reply to enquiry on the subject of unloading cars Capt Le Duc asserts positively that with every obstacle thrown in his way by the R R Employees, compelling him to move every train from the main track and back by man or mule power he has managed to unload all the trains which have reached Bridgeport, and day before yesterday, when he made his report there were upwards of thirty empty freight Cars lying on the track, and had been there for several days. I have not heard yet that Mr Anderson has secured a sufficient construction and repair corps to keep his Road in order. His track Master, who has charge from Bridgeport here, called on me two weeks since for assistance to place the Road in condition to commence as soon as the R. Water Bridge was completed. I had previously ~~set~~ ordered a large detail of soldiers to work along the Road from here to Nashville so as to help Anderson and put the Road in order at once. Genl Slocum says he does not call on him for assistance nor say what he would like to have done. The Officer entrusted with the cutting of wood for the road between this & Bridgeport reports that he has over ~~fifty~~ forty thousand cords cut and that he can supply the road with wood until a corps of Wood cutters is hired by Mr Anderson. As yet I do not see that any steps have been taken either to get section hands or wood cutters, for this part of the Road, therefore infer from the unusual delay in geting the Road between Bridgeport and Nashville in order that but little has been done for that. But for the timely arrival of Col McCallum with something over two hundred of his men from Virginia (Army of Potomac) I doubt if the Bridge over Running Water would have been completed for ten days to come. Col McCallum informed me on his arrival that, on the receipt of Genl Meig's dispatch ordering him out here, he infered from the nature of the order that a strong corps of workmen was much needed. He therefore hired twelve hundred and was expecting their arrival early this week, but that Mr Anderson with relutance consented to take five hundred of them. I ordered him to put the other seven hundred to work on the North Western Road and complete it as rapidly as possible, and after repairing thoroughly this road as far to the rear as Nashville with the remaing five hundred and the bridge party of two (2) hundred which has been at work on the Running Water Bridge to commence work on the Road from here to Knoxville. After hearing Col McCallums report I determined to tellegraph to Genl Halleck the state of affairs and received in reply the accompanying tellegram, which will explain to you his position—I will direct him to call on you in Nashville and I feel confidant that you will feel satisfied that, if any body can help us out of this R. R difficulty he can. He is thoroughly practical and willing to obey orders and receive suggestions. Besides he fully comprehends all the difficulties in the way, as well as the magnitude of the undertaking, to supply by R. Road the force we are compelled to have at this point." ALS, DNA, RG 393, Military Div. of the Miss., Letters Received. *O.R.*, I, xxxii, part 2, 88–89. The enclosure is *ibid.*, p. 73.

On Jan. 15, 11:00 A.M., Maj. Gen. John G. Foster, Knoxville, telegraphed to USG. "The Strawberry plains bridge is completed also the ponton bridge at this place so that will stand I think   I am about commencing the bridge at this place on the piers of the Rail Road bridge   A Regement is ordered to Loudon to work on the Rail Road bridge at that place   No supplies have arrived for a week by the river—The bread rations are entirely exausted   I am forced to abandon all idea of active operations for the present and to place the army where it can live by foraging   The fourth Corps are now moving for Dandridge and the twenty third for Mossy Creek   Genl Sturgis with all the cavalry is in front of Dandridge, near Kimbers Cross roads—I propose to hold all the country & the forage in it on the South and East of The French Broad. As Longstreet has exhausted all the supplies in his vicinity and is now forced to send across the river for forage and grain I presume some portions of our forces will be in almost constant collision ~~with~~ if we succeed in holding as I expect Longstreet cannot long remain where he is   He is now building a ponton Bridge across the Nolechucky near Warrensburg" Telegram received, DNA, RG 393, Dept. of Mo., Telegrams Received; copy, *ibid.*, Military Div. of the Miss., Telegrams Received. *O.R.*, I, xxxii, part 2, 101.

To Julia Dent Grant

———

Knoxville Ten.
January 2d 1863. [*1864*]

DEAR JULIA,

Owing to the necessity of some supplies yet to come forward before an advance can be made by the Army here I may be detained here for a week yet. I do not think you need look for me back before the 15th, then it may be necessary for me to return here before the Winter is over. I very much fear the enemy intend holding a position in this country for the Winter and to make this the great battle field in the Spring. It has been as cold as Sacketts Harbor for the last two days so that I do not get out much. This is a very loyal place however and but for the inaccessibility of it I would bring you here and remain most of the Winter.

I have nothing special to write you and besides the mails are so irregular that I may beat this to Nashville now though I do not start for a week. Kisses for yourself and Jess.

ULYS.

ALS, DLC-USG.

To Maj. Gen. John G. Foster

Head Quarters, Mil. Div. of the Miss.
Near Maynardsville[1] Ten. Jan. 5th/64

MAJ. GEN. J. G. FOSTER,
COMD.G DEPT. OF THE OHIO,
GENERAL,

In conjunction with your move against Longstreet, when it is made, I think it will be advisable to send a Cavalry expedition against Abingdon and Saltville. Such an expedition should fit up at some place in Southeast Ky. and be prepared to start so as to co-operate with you, moving by the roads north of, and near to the Virginia line. The Tennessee troops now organizing in Kentucky[2] I think will be sufficient for this move. They could furnish you more assistance in this way than if directly with you.—Kautz[3] will be a most excellent officer to entrust this expedition to, and if selected had better begin at once organizing it.

I find that Wilcox has six batteries of Artillery, besides the captured pieces at Cumberland Gap. To move this a large number of additional horses will be required. If horses are brought here at this season of the year, (with the present scanty supply of forage, exposed in the open air, ~~and~~ with the very little attention they can receive whilst they and the men are in such a comfortless condition,) they would be mostly unfit for service by the time the roads are good in the spring. Under all the circumstances I think it advisable to get all the guns you can dispense with, this Winter, into fortifications and send the horses where they can be fed and recruited by spring. By selecting the best horses for the batteries you determine to keep in the field, enough might be got for any present movement.

Very respectfully
your obt. svt.
U. S. GRANT
Maj. Gen. Com

ALS, DNA, RG 94, War Records Office, Dept. of the Ohio. *O.R.*, I, xxxii, part 2, 27–28.

On Jan. 7, 1864, Maj. Gen. John G. Foster, Knoxville, telegraphed to USG. "I have received a communication from Gen'l Longstreet complaining of the secret circulation of the Presidents Proclamation and suggesting that any propositions &c should come to him. I accept in reply to his suggestion and enclose him twenty (20) copies of the proclamation and of the orders publishing the terms offered to deserters with the request that he will give them publicity among his officers and men—" Copy, DNA, RG 393, Military Div. of the Miss., Telegrams Received. On Jan. 26, Foster wrote to USG. "I have the honor to enclose herewith copies of the correspondence between General Longstreet and myself upon the subject of the Amnesty Proclamation." Copy, *ibid.*, Dept. of the Ohio, Letters Sent. For the enclosures, see *O.R.*, III, iv, 50–54; Lincoln, *Works*, VII, 153–54.

On Jan. 12, Foster twice telegraphed to USG, first at noon. "Two deserters from Barksdales old brigade have come in and given us full details of the enemys position strength and condition. Longstreets main body is between Morristown and Russelville with cavalry in front and at Kimbers Cross Roads   His strength is as I gave you when here Twenty six thousand men   forty thousand rations are issued daily   No reinforcements from Virginia   The bridge at Union nearly compleated, that at Carters station over the Watauga river is commenced. The condition of the enemy is in every way bad   They lack clothing, especially shoes rations and forage   The country in their vicinity for nearly twenty miles is nearly exausted   They have now to cross to the South of the French Broad for forage   The talk among the officers and men is that they will soon have to retreat to Bristol—Some Regimental commanders have not drawn tents expecting to move back in a week—Our own condition is worse by far than when you were here. Animals dying. Some clothing arrived   no forage by the last three last boats   We are now entirely destetute of bread   Bridge at Strawberry Plains crossed by train today   will be able to cross wagons on thursday   Shall move nearly all the force over to Dandridge to enable us to live   The movement is now in progress   Hope to get the Ponton bridge at this place done today   Shall go to Loudon tomorrow to hurry up the supplies of bread" "The cold weather & high rivers have made things worse   many animals are dying daily   the pontoon bridge at this place has been broken twice since you left by high water & floating ice   as soon as the bridge at Strawberry plains is done & weather moderates I shall move two corps to Dandridge to obtain forage & corn & wheat   everything is eaten out north of Holsten river   also nearly everything eaten up at Mossy creek   my move to the line of French broad river is therefore rendered imperative   some Q. m. stores have arrived but not in sufficient quantity   no rations by last boats   am entirely destitute of bread coffee & sugar   have teleghd these facts at to Gen Thomas   trust you will be able to raise the amt of supplies by river   the weather is intensely cold with one inch of snow on the ground"   Telegrams received, DNA, RG 393, Dept. of Mo., Telegrams Received; copies, *ibid.*, Military Div. of the Miss., Telegrams Received. *O.R.*, I, xxxii, part 2, 71–72.

1. Maynardville, Tenn., approximately twenty miles northeast of Knoxville on Bull Run Creek.

2. On Jan. 11, Brig. Gen. Alvan C. Gillem, Camp Nelson, Ky., wrote to USG. "There are at This place several detachments of Tennessee Cavalry recruits   They have not been mustered or the officers commissioned   Taking into consideration the condition of roads & scarcity of forage on road to East Tenn would it not be best take these recruits Nashville to organize arm & equip them   They are in destitute condition & can receive no bounty here   Gen Smith Ch'f of Cavalry thought it best organize them at Nashville & you give me authority to order them there but I have thought it best before moving them to consult you since you have been through East Tenn. Recruits can be brought to Nashville with greater facility in in the returning c[ars] than they can march to this place   Shall I take them to Nashville   Gov Johnson coincides with me in belief that it would be best for these troops organize in Tennessee—"   Telegram received, *ibid.*, Dept. of Mo., Telegrams Received; copy, *ibid.*, Military Div. of the Miss., Telegrams Received.

3. August V. Kautz, born in Germany in 1828, brought to Georgetown, Ohio, as a child, enlisted as a private in the Mexican War, graduated from USMA in 1852, and served on the Pacific Coast before the Civil War. As capt., 6th Cav., he fought with the Army of the Potomac until appointed col., 2nd Ohio Cav., as of Sept. 10, 1862. He was serving as president of a court-martial at Knoxville when USG suggested this new assignment. Andrew Wallace, *Gen. August V. Kautz and the Southwestern Frontier* (Tucson, 1967), pp. 43–44.

To Maj. Gen. Henry W. Halleck

Barboursville,[1] Ky. Jan'y 8. 1863. [*1864*]

MAJ. GEN. HALLECK
WASHINGTON. D. C.

Owing to the want of clothing, particularly shoes, in Foster's command, it is impossible to move more than sixty per cent of his men until they are supplied. Clothing is now on the way, and it is hoped will be in Knoxville within two one weeks from this time. I have directed Foster then to attack and drive Longstreet at least beyond Bull's Gap and Red Bridge.² In the meantime I have directed the 9th and 23d Corps to be pushed on to Moss Creek—the 4th Corps to Strawberry Plains, and the Cavalry to Dandridge³ to scout and forage south of French Broad, and threaten Longstreet's flank.

U. S. Grant
Maj Gen'l

LS (telegram sent), Michigan State Archives, Lansing, Mich.; telegram received, DNA, RG 107, Telegrams Collected (Bound). *O.R.*, I, xxxii, part 2, 43.

    1. Barboursville, Ky., approximately sixty-five miles north of Knoxville.
    2. Bull's Gap, approximately fifty miles northeast of Knoxville, where the East Tennessee and Virginia Railroad passes through the Bays Mountains, and Red Bridge, Tenn., twelve miles northwest of Bull's Gap.
    3. Dandridge, Tenn., approximately thirty miles east of Knoxville on the French Broad River.

To Maj. Gen. Henry W. Halleck

Nashville Tenn
Jany 13th 1864 11. a m

Maj Gen H. W. Halleck
Gen in Chief.

    If Gen Foster is relieved Gen McPherson or Gen Schofield would suit me to fill his place, but both are ranked by Generals already in the Department of the Ohio. I would recommend therefore the appointment of Gen W. F. Smith to Major General and rank dated back to his first appointment and he given the command. If it is in contemplation to give Gen Smith a higher command, either of the officers named or Gen Parke will suit me

U. S. Grant
Maj Genl Com'dg

Telegram received, DNA, RG 107, Telegrams Collected (Bound); copies, *ibid.*, Telegrams Received in Cipher; *ibid.*, RG 393, Military Div. of the Miss., Hd. Qrs. Correspondence; (incomplete) *ibid.*, RG 94, ACP, S327 CB 1864; DLC-John M. Schofield; DLC-USG, V, 40, 94. *O.R.*, I, xxxi, part 3, 571; *ibid.*, I, xxxii, part 2, 79–80. On Jan. 13, 1864, Maj. Gen. Henry W. Halleck wrote to USG. "I have just recieved your telegram recommending the appointment of

Brig Genl W. F. Smith to a Major Generalcy. Your former recommendation was submitted to the Secty of War and I think the appointment will be made as soon as there is a vacancy. Not only is there no vacancy now, but, by some error, *more* than the number authorised by law were made last summer, and some major Generals now in service must be dropt. Their names cannot be sent to the senate. I hope it may not be necessary to relieve Genl Foster, as he is a good officer and a *live* man. There are some doubts about Genl Schofie[ld's] confirmation. If ordered to your command, I think you will find him an able officer for any position. No change of commands will probably be made till the senate acts upon his case." ALS, DNA, RG 108, Letters Sent (Press). *O.R.*, I, xxxii, part 2, 80.

To Thomas E. Bramlette

Nashville January 13th 1864

GOVERNOR THOS E BRAMLETTE
FRANKFORT KY

I found your dispatch of January 6th at my Headquarters on my arrival here last night and in reply have the honor to inform you, that General Fosters orders to General Boyle do not contemplate the abandonment of Kentucky to the enemy, either in organized or guerrilla bands, but specially require a sufficient number of the troops now on duty in the State to be retained for the purpose of securing the safety of all important parts, as well as the security of our lines of communications. Kentucky is a portion of my command and shall receive hereafter as heretofore all the protection that my forces are capable of giving. In all the dispositions of troops that I may make, the importance of protecting her territory and securing her citizens from danger of internal disturbances will be kept steadily in view

But while busy with so many other matters of equal importance I am well aware that I may not be able to obtain a full understanding of all that concerns her interests, and have therefore to request that you will communicate frankly with me at all times upon any subject you may deem sufficiently important to demand my attention.

I regret exceedingly not having seen you as I passed thro. Frankfort, but I expect to be in Louisville next week and if possible will visit you at Frankfort. I desire to see you in person for the purpose of conferring more fully than is possible by letter upon the questions alluded to herein.

U S GRANT

Major General

Copies, DLC-USG, V, 34, 35; DNA, RG 393, Military Div. of the Miss., Letters Sent. *O.R.*, I, xxxii, part 2, 85–86. On Jan. 6, 1864, Governor Thomas E. Bramlette of Ky. had telegraphed to USG. "Genl Boyle has been ordered on 23d December by Maj. Gen'l Foster to send all organized troops in Ky. except small garrisson at Depots to Knoxville—This order takes the forces raised under Special Act for Ky. Defense will expose the State to desolation by home rebel and guerillas kept down by their presence, and will occasion the destruction of your Southern communications through Ky. by guerillas. The twelve months troops were all raised under the State defence, and to relieve other troops on that duty" Copy, DNA, RG 393, Military Div. of the Miss., Telegrams Received. *O.R.*, I, xxxii, part 2, 37. A petition to USG dated Jan. 6, signed by fifty-one members of the Ky. Legislature requested that Brig. Gen. Stephen G. Burbridge be assigned to command the Dept. of Ky. DS, DNA, RG 94, Generals' Papers and Books, Burbridge. A similar petition to USG of Jan. 12 had fifteen signatures. DS, *ibid.* An undated petition on the subject from Bourbon County, Ky., had thirty-four signatures. DS, *ibid.* On Jan. 19, Lt. Col. Theodore S. Bowers wrote to Burbridge. "I am directed by Major General U. S. Grant to acknowledge the receipt of your communication of date 18th inst and to respectfully say in reply, that the numerous petitions asking for your assignment to command in the State of Kintucky, have been referred to Maj Genl J G Foster com'dg Department of the Ohio for his action and that, he having appointed Brig Gen Jacob Ammen, who is your junior to the command of the District of Kentucky, it is not probable that he has any command to which he can assign you in his Dep't. I am directed to say further, that more General Officers having already been ordered to report to Gen Grant than he can provide with commands, he cannot at present apply to the Secretary of War to have you ordered to report to him for orders" Copies, DLC-USG, V, 34, 35; DNA, RG 393, Military Div. of the Miss., Letters Sent.

On Jan. 12, Bramlette wrote to USG. "I send you the accompanying correspondence &c, as due to you and to myself.—I would not interfere if [——] it with my ord[er] or movement of yours, for I assure you that my confidence in you judgement skill and prudence is such that I would act with confidence under any order emenating from you without pausing to investigate beyond its genuineness. I deem this necessary to avoid any mistaken judgement upon your part that I would meddle with movements planed by you. I will be my purpose at all times heartily and faithfully to cooperate in any way in my power with you in the execution of any of your plans. I regret exceedingly that you could not stay over at this place on your recent trip" ALS, *ibid.*, Letters Received. Bramlette enclosed a copy of his letter of Jan. 8 to President Abraham Lincoln protesting the movement of troops from Ky. to Knoxville. Copy, *ibid.* See Lincoln, *Works*, VII, 109, 134–35. On Jan. 15, USG telegraphed to Bramlette. "I have ordered General Foster to suspend his order for the removal of Kentucky troops until I can see you. I will be in Louisville next week, and if possible in Frankfort." Copies, DLC-USG, V, 34, 35; DNA, RG 393, Military Div. of the Miss.,

Letters Sent. On the same day, USG telegraphed to Maj. Gen. John G. Foster. "Suspend your order for the movement of 12 mos Kentucky men, until I can see Governor Bramlette which will be within a few days. This is not to effect the change you have made in the Commander of the District of Kentucky. Over one million rations will be sent to Big South Fork on first rise" Copies, *ibid.* *O.R.*, I, xxxii, part 2, 101–2. On Jan. 17, Foster telegraphed to USG. "dispatch recd I sent order some time since for the twelves months Ky. troops to remain in that state & so notified Gov Bramlette at the time" Telegram received, DNA, RG 393, Dept. of Mo., Telegrams Received; copy, *ibid.*, Military Div. of the Miss., Telegrams Received. *O.R.*, I, xxxii, part 2, 116.

On Jan. 20, 11:00 A.M., Foster telegraphed to USG. "The telegraph having reported that Gov Bramblette of Kentucky had reccommended the raising of State Troops for State defence I sent him the following telegram Knoxville 20 to Gov THOS BRAMBLETTE Louisville Ky. The telegraph announces that you have sent a message to the Legislature reccommending that troops be raised for State defence.—I regret ~~exceedingly~~ this step as I consider the precautions I have already taken and which were explained to you in my dispatch of Jan 9th ~~the~~ amply sufficient to guard against every emergency that may arise from Geurrillas, and Raids within the Borders of the state The defence of the State can best be made by this army in front the organization of Militia Regts will affect injuriously the reorganization and fitting up of the old regts that have reenlisted as veteran volunteers to provide however for the full protection of the state to allay all fears for the safety of Kentucky and thus render the raising of Militia Regts unnecessary I will send a Division of Cavalry into the Eastern part of the state as soon as the movement now in progress shall be completed which will be before the 15th of the next month signed J G FOSTER Maj Genl Comdg—The Div that I shall send is one of those whose horses are broken down it can be well mounted & reorganized at Camp Nelson" Telegram received, DNA, RG 393, Dept. of Mo., Telegrams Received; copies, *ibid.*, Military Div. of the Miss., Telegrams Received; *ibid.*, Dept. of the Ohio (Cincinnati), Telegrams Sent; *ibid.*, Dept. of the Cumberland and the Ohio (Nashville), Telegrams Sent. *O.R.*, I, xxxii, part 2, 159–60.

To Brig. Gen. Robert Allen

Nashville 14th January 1864

BRIG GENL ROBT. ALLEN Q M
LOUISVILLE KY

I have ordered the 13th Ohio Cavalry from Columbus Ohio to Nashville. Please direct the proper Quartermaster to furnish transportation to Louisville. I will not bring them further until navigation is opened to bring forage.

U. S. GRANT
Major General

Telegram, copies, DLC-USG, V, 34, 35; DNA, RG 393, Military Div. of the Miss., Letters Sent. On Jan. 14, 1864, USG telegraphed to Governor John Brough of Ohio. "order the thirteenth (13) cavalry to this place   I will direct the quartermaster at Louisville to furnish transportation"   Telegram received, AGO Records, Ohio Archives, Columbus, Ohio; copies, DLC-USG, V, 34, 35; DNA, RG 393, Military Div. of the Miss., Letters Sent. On the same day, Brough telegraphed to USG. "The ninth regt. of O. Cavalry is ready for the field   Gen'l Fry telegraphs it awaits your orders as to destination   we want the camp very much to equip the twelfth Cavalry   have you made any order in the matter or can you do so"   Copy, *ibid.*, Telegrams Received.

On Jan. 15, USG telegraphed to Brig. Gen. Robert Allen. "There are abundant rations here for one hundred days   You can use therefore transportation for forage to the exclusion of rations, until the rivers are navigable." Copies, DLC-USG, V, 34, 35; DNA, RG 393, Military Div. of the Miss., Letters Sent. *O.R.*, I, xxxii, part 2, 103.

To Maj. Gen. Henry W. Halleck

                                    Head Quarters Mil. Div. of the Miss.
                                    Nashville Ten. Jan.y 15th 1864
MAJ. GEN. H. W. HALLECK,
GEN. IN CHIEF, WASHINGTON D. C.
GENERAL,

I reached here the evening of the 12th on my return from East Tennessee. I felt a particular anxiety to have Longstreet driven from East Tennessee, and went there with the intention of taking such steps as would secure this end. I found however a large part of Foster's command suffering for want of clothing, especially shoes, so that in any advance not to exceed two thirds of his men could be taken. The difficulties of supplying them are such that to send reinforcements, for the at present, would be to put the whole on insufficient rations for their support. Under these circumstances I only made such changes of position of troops as would place Foster nearer the enemy when he did get in a condition to move, and would open to us new foraging grounds and diminish those held by the enemy. Having done this and seen the move across the Holston, at Strawberry Plains, commenced, I started on my return via Cumberland Gap, Barboursville, London[1] & Richmond[2] to Lexington Ky. The weather was intensly cold the thermometer standing a portion of the time below zero. But being desirous of seeing what portion of our supplies might be depended upon over that route, and it causing no loss of time, I determined to make the trip. From the personal inspection made I am satisfied that no portion of our supplies can be hawled by teams from Camp Nelson.[3] Whilst forage could be got from the country to supply teams at the different stations on the road some supplies could be got through in this way. But the time is nearly at an end when this can be done.

On the first rise of the Cumberland 1.200,000 rations will be sent to the mouth of the Big South Fork. These I hope teams will be able to take. The distance to hawl is materially shortened, the road is said to be better than that by Cumberland Gap, and it is a new route and will furnish forage for a time. In the mean time troops in East Tennessee must depend for subsistence on what they can get from the country, and the little we can send them from Chattanooga. The rail road is now complete into Chattanooga and in a short time, say three weeks, the road by Decatur & Huntsville will be complete. Steamers then can be spared to supply the present force in E. Ten. well and to accumulate a store to support a large army for a short time if it should become necessary to send one there in the Spring. This contingency however I will do every thing in my power to avert.

Two steamers ply now tolerably regularly between Chattanooga and Loudon. From the latter place to Mossy Creek we have rail road. Some clothing has already reached Knoxville since my departure. A good supply will be got there with all dispatch. These, if necessary, and subsistence can by possibility be obtained, I will send force enough to secure Longstreets expulsion.

Sherman has gone down the Miss. to collect at Vicksburg all the force that can be spared for a separate movement from the Miss. He will probably have ready by the 24th of this month a force of 20.000 men that could be used East of the river. But to go West so large a force could not be spared.

The Red River, and all the streams West of the Miss. are now too low for navigation. I shall direct Sherman therefore to move out to Meredian with his spare force, the Cavalry going from Corinth and destroy the roads East & South of there so effectually that the enemy will not attempt to rebuild them during the rebellion. He will then return unless the opportunity of going into Mobile with the force he has appears perfectly plain. Owing to the large number of veterans furloughed I will not be able to do more at Chattanooga than to threaten an advance and try to detain the force now in Thomas' front.

Sherman will be instructed, whilst left with large discretionary powers, to take no extra hazard of loosing his army, or of getting it crippled too much for efficient service in the Spring.

I look upon the next line for me to secure to be that from Chattanooga to Mobile, Montgomery & Atlanta being the important intermediate points. To do this large supplies must be secured on the Tennessee River so as to be independent of the railroads from here to the Tennessee for a conciderable length of time. Mobile would be a second base. The destruction which Sherman will do the roads around Meredian will be of material importance to us in preventing the enemy from drawing supplies from Mississippi and in clearing that section of all large bodies of rebel troops.

I do not look upon any points except Mobile in the South and the Tennessee in the North as presenting practicable starting points from which to opperate against Atlanta and Montgomery. They are objectionable as starting points, to be all under one command from the fact that the time it will take to communicate from one to the other will be so great. But Sherman or McPherson, one of whom would be entrusted with the distant command, are officers of such experience and reliability that all objection on this score, except that of enabling the two armies to act as one unit, would be removed. The same objection will exist, probably not to so great an extent however, if a movement is made in more than one column. This will have to be with an army of the size we will be compelled to use.

Heretofore I have abstained from suggesting what might be done in other commands than my own, in co-operation with it, or even to think much over the matter. But as you have kindly asked me in your letter of the 8th of Jan.y, only just received, ~~I will write~~ for an interchange of views on our present situation, I will write you again, in a day or two, going out side of my own operations.

I am General, very respectfully,
your obt. svt.
U. S. Grant
Maj. Gen.

ALS, DNA, RG 94, Letters Received, 2364M 1864. *O.R.*, I, xxxii, part 2, 99–101. On Jan. 8, 1864, Maj. Gen. Henry W. Halleck wrote to USG. "From the enclosed copy of a letter of instructions from Maj. Gen. Steele, and from the published orders issued by the Adjt General of the Army, you will learn that General Steele's command in the Dept of Arkansas has been placed under your orders. The main object in organizing the troops in the western theatre of war [into M]ilitary Departments [and placing] them under your orders, is to give you the general military control, and at the same time relieve you from the burthen of official correspondence and office duty. If the whole were organized into a single department under your immediate command, your time would be mostly taken up with the [details of] courts martial, furloughs, discharges, &c. &c. while the present arrangement enables you to give your full attention to military operations   In regard to General Banks' campaign against Texas, it is proper to remark that it was undertaken less for military reasons than as a matter of state policy. As a military measure simply, it perhaps presented less advantages than a movement on Mobile and the Alabama river, so as to threaten [the] en[e]my's interior lines and effect a diversion in favor of our armies at Chattanooga and in East Tennessee   But, however, this may have been, it was deemed necessary as a matter of political or state policy, connected with our foreign relations and especially with France and Mexico, that our troops should occupy and hold at least a portion of Texas. The President so ordered, for reasons satisfactory to him[self] and his cabinet, and it was, therefore unnecessary for us to inquire whether or not the troops could have been employed elsewhere with greater military advantage. I allude to this matter here, as it may have an important influance on your projected operations during the present winter   Keeping in mind the fact that Genl. Banks' operations in Texas, either on the Gulf coast or by the Louisiana frontier, must be continued during the winter, it is to be considered whether it will not be better to direct our efforts for the present to the entire breaking up of the rebel forces west of the Mississippi river, rather than to divide them by also operating against Mobile and Alabama. If the forces of Smith, Price and Magruder could be so scattered or broken as to enable Steele and Banks to occupy Red River as a line of defence, a part of their armies would probably become available for operations elsewhere   General Banks reports his present force as inadequate for the defence of his position and for operations in the interior; and General Steele is of opinion that he cannot advance beyond the Arkansas or Saline, unless he can be certain of cooperations and supplies on Red River. Under these circumstances it is worth considering whether such forces as Sherman can move down the Mississippi river should not cooperate

with the armies of Steele and Banks on the West side   Of course operations by
any of your troops in that direction must be subordinate and subsequent to those
which you have proposed for East and West Tennessee   I therefore present
these views at this time merely that they may receive your attention and consideration in determining upon your ulterior movements. If we can rely upon
what we see in the rebel newspapers and hear from Spies and refugees from
Richmond, the enemy is directing his attention particularly to the defense of
Georgia, in anticipation that your spring campaign will be directed on Atlanta.
In order to compensate for the loss of the Virginia and East Tennessee Rail-
Road, and for the possible capture by us of some point on their main Atlantic
route by Weldon & Charleston, the rebel government are working with great
diligence to complete the road from Danville, Va, to Greensboro N. C., by which
they will open a continuous interior line from Richmond to the Southwest. This
will enable them to transport troops and supplies from Virginia to Georgia, by
a short and safe route. It was hoped that when the season advanced so as to
prevent further operations by the Army of the Potomac, a portion of it could
be detached for service elsewhere. But so large a number have secured furloughs
for reenlisting in the veteran regiments that it is hardly possible at present to
make such detachments. Moreover, it is quite probable that a portion of the
Potomac river will be frozen over, and a bridge of ice thus formed from Virginia
to Maryland. If so, a large land force will be required to take the place of the
Potomac flotilla in preventing raids and contraband trade. As an interchange of
views on the present condition of affairs and the coming campaign will be advantageous, I hope you will write me freely and fully your opinions on these matters." ALS, DNA, RG 108, Letters Sent (Press). *O.R.*, I, xxxii, part 2, 40–42.

On Jan. 15, both Brig. Gen. William F. Smith and Brig. Gen. James H.
Wilson wrote lengthy letters to Asst. Secretary of War Charles A. Dana ex-
plaining and urging the plans discussed by USG in his letter to Halleck. ALS,
DLC-Edwin M. Stanton. See letter to Maj. Gen. Henry W. Halleck, Jan. 19, 1864.

On Sunday, Jan. 10, noon, Dana had telegraphed to USG. "I am authorized to say to you that just so soon as you deem everything to be safe in East
Tennessee you are authorized to move with such ~~force~~ troops as you think
necessary either against Mobile or any other place south of your present lines
that you may think it most advisable to attack   The question of safety in East
Tennessee is as you will observe left to your judgement and it is for you to
determine whether that safety is best obtained by wholly expelling Longstreet
or by leaving an army to observe & operate against him while you send or take
the main body of your command elsewhere—If you do not think Genl Foster can
be trusted to complete what is begun say so to me & I presume any change you
may deem needful may be made though I am not authorized to promise any
thing on that head. Please acknowledge the receipt of this despatch as that may
avoid the necessity of repeating it by a special messenger" Telegram received, DNA, RG 393, Dept. of Mo., Telegrams Received; copy, *ibid.*, Military
Div. of the Miss., Telegrams Received. *O.R.*, I, xxxii, part 2, 58. On Jan. 16,
USG telegraphed to Dana. "No despatch from you of last Sunday" Telegram
received (press), DNA, RG 107, Telegrams Collected (Bound); copies, *ibid.*,
RG 393, Military Div. of the Miss., Hd. Qrs. Correspondence; DLC-USG, V, 40,
94.

1. London, Ky., approximately twenty miles northwest of Barboursville,
Ky., and sixty-five miles southeast of Lexington.

2. Richmond, Ky., approximately sixty-five miles northwest of Barbours-ville and twenty miles southeast of Lexington.

3. Camp Nelson, Ky., approximately twenty miles southwest of Lexington on the Kentucky River.

To Maj. Gen. William T. Sherman

Head Quarters, Mil. Div. of the Miss.
Nashville Ten. Jan.y 15th 1864

Maj. Gen. W. T. Sherman,
Comd.g Dept. of the Ten.
Gen.

Enclosed I send you copy of a letter just received from Gen. Halleck,[1] one from him to Steele,[2] and my letter of this date to Halleck. The latter contains all the instructions I deem necessary to you in your present move. Your dispatch suggesting the move on Meredian is received and approved.[3] Nearly all the troops in Thomas' and Dodge's Commands, having less than one year to serve, have reinlisted and many of them been furloughed. This with the fact that Longstreet's presence in East Tennessee makes it necessary for me to keep always ready a force to meet him will prevent me doing much more than is indicated in my letter to Halleck. I will have however both Thomas & Logan ready so that if the enemy should weaken himself much in front they can advance. I see no special reason now for keeping up the force from Memphis to Corinth any longer. If you think proper therefore you may abandon the whole of that line. Should you do so order all the locomotives and cars on the road shipped to this place at once. Whilst you are at Vicksburg order the shipment of all cars that can be spared from that road also. One locomotive and ten cars is sufficient to keep there.

I am General, very respectfully
your obt. svt.
U. S. Grant
Maj. Gen. Com

ALS, DLC-William T. Sherman. *O.R.*, I, xxxii, part 2, 105.

On Jan. 4, 1864, Maj. Gen. William T. Sherman, Cairo, telegraphed to USG. "Arrived last night. Mississippi above frozen over but Ohio full and river below in good order   Railroad cars running very irregular from this late cold intense weather. Have seen Admiral Porter. Boats navigating the Miss. have not been disturbed of late and no apprehension felt on that score   Red river and Yazoo too low to admit of the movements on Shrevport and Grenada. But the season is otherwise favorable   I am satisfied we have men enough to take Shrevport if we can get up Red river which the Admiral thinks impossible   I will inspect Paducah tomorrow and Columbus next day then to Memphis. I will make all preparations for striking inland whenever the blow will be most effectual. There is no doubt the whole matter would be simplified if you had command of all the Mississippi valley below Cairo. I think if you were to name the subject to Gen'l Halleck that he would order it for its properly better known to him than any other   Admiral Porters Com'd extends to below New Orleans and ours should also. All is reported well and quiet below. Should you see cause to call for me at Huntsbille and Stevenson a dispatch sent me via Cairo would bring me as soon as Steamer could convey me." Copy, DNA, RG 393, Military Div. of the Miss., Telegrams Received. *O.R.*, I, xxxii, part 2, 24–25. On Jan. 6, Sherman telegraphed to USG. "I leave for Columbus and Memphis at four P. M. to day. Gen'l Wm S. Smith is supposed to be crossing the Tennessee to day—I will aim to reinforce him with Cavalry and with Infantry, occupy the attention of the enemy so as to enable him to reach Meridian and if possible Selma—The Yazoo and Red rivers are represented as too low to admit of navigation—There is no interuption to the boats on the Miss. at this time." Copy, DNA, RG 393, Military Div. of the Miss., Telegrams Received. *O.R.*, I, xxxii, part 2, 36.

On Jan. 19, Sherman, "Gunboat 'Silver Cloud'," wrote to USG. "I am now on my return to Memphis, which we shall reach tomorrow, the 20th, and if I find all things as I expect, shall start all hands by the 25th. The river is now clear of ice this far up, and we hope to find none this side of Memphis, but the water is from 12 to 20 feet lower than it was at the same period last year, and therefore to ascend Red River will be impossible. But the other trip will do more for our Dep't and your Army, and therefore I do not regret it. The Guerillas seem now to let the boats pass unmolested and so long as they do, we can afford to encourage the people to reoccupy their lands and resume their industrial pursuits. I found Gen'l McPherson at Vicksburg in fine health, his troops in like condition, only four per cent on the sick report. He has twenty one thousand effective men, so that he can take with him ten thousand and leave Vicksburg and Natches, the only points in his District fitted with stationary artillery, safe as against any probable danger. As near as I can ascertain, Genl Polk commands at Meridian with Loring at Canton, this Division has not over eight thousand men. Conscripts at Brandon and Enterprise.—Forest has North Mississippi, with not over two thousand five hundred irregular Cavalry—Cosby and Whitfield's Brigades are still watching on their old ground from Yazoo City, via Canton, Brownsville, Jackson, and Brandon to Port Gibson, a thin line of guards to prevent intercourse with Vicksburg.—Logan's old Command, now commanded by Wirt Adams is down behind Port Hudson and Baton Rouge, doubtless to prevent the people from becoming too familiar with the Yankees. I have one of my best Memphis female spies out, who will be back in time to let me know all we want. I observe that you were right in your calculations that

Longstreet would be reinforced in East Tennessee and will make a struggle for that Mountain Region. Halleck should compel a movement in North Carolina on Weldon and Raleigh if possible, which would in connection with active demonstrations against the Alabama border force the enemy to call back the reinforcements, or to allow these valuable districts to be overrun by us. If we could draw all of Lee's Army into East Tennessee they would be bound to go ahead or fall back. The Mountains on either flank will restrict their line of operations to the Railroad, and the Army that is on the defensive will have the advantage. I will write to Generals Logan and Dodge to hurry up the Railroad Repairs and I will try to be there in all February. The new fortifications of Vicksburg are nearly done, the redoubt at Mrs. Lums house being the only one incomplete. General McPherson tells me those at Natchez are equally well advanced" Copies (2), DLC-William T. Sherman. *O.R.*, I, xxxii, part 2, 146–47. A postscript: "Boat trembles, and my writing is more illegible than ever." does not appear in the copies.

On Jan. 20, Sherman, "Near Memphis," wrote to USG. "Gen McPherson at Vicksburg named to me what I had not heard that Gen Logan contemplated exchanging Corps with him. He also shwd me a letter he had written Gen Cullum in answer to one received, tellig him that parties had accused him of a leanig to the Secesh. I do think McPherson is too young and active to be kept at a Post like Vicksburg, and I will be perfectly willing to approve of a change that would take him to a more active field. Should this transfer be made I will yield to him with your concent the command of the 'Army in the Field' retaining the Departmt on the River. As to his leanig to the Secesh it is of course ridiculous nonsense. The young ladies that he naturally associates with have that leanig, but he has too much character to be swerved by such influences. I think I can keep up the Army in the Field to 25000 men and yet have enough left to hold the vital points on the Mississipi, as well as to stir up the inland Country from time to time to hold here a respectable force of the Enemy, and also give the inhabitants a chance to abandon the Confederacy. I will order Hurlbut to drop from his Return the troops detached to Steele, as they are lost to us." ALS, DNA, RG 393, Military Div. of the Miss., Letters Received. *O.R.*, I, xxxii, part 2, 157.

On Jan. 21, Sherman, Memphis, telegraphed to USG. "I am back from Vicksburg where I found all well—Will write you fully by mail. No firing on boats of late. Water very low for the season but river free of ice—Will be ready for the expedition by the Twenty Fifth (25). Enemy is scattered all over Mississippi and I think the movement indicated will clean them all out—" Copy, DNA, RG 393, Military Div. of the Miss., Telegrams Received. *O.R.*, I, xxxii, part 2, 169.

On Jan. 24, Sherman wrote to USG. "I have received at the hand of Colonel Duff your letter of the 15 inst, with copies of yours to Genl Halleck and those of General Halleck to you and Genl Steele. All these concur in their general plan, & my acts thus far are perfectly in accordance. The 16th Corps had become so domiciled at Memphis & along the Rail road that it is like pullig teeth to get them Started, but I think three Divisions, Veatch's Tuttles & A. J. Smiths will be embarked to day & tomorrow for the South. The Cavalry under Genl Wm Sooy Smith should also be ready tomorrow the day appointed, when I will start the former in the Boats already collected here for Vicksburg, and the latter by land in light order, for Pontotoc, Okalona, Meridian &c. As soon as the Cavalry is off I will haste for Vicksburg and with the Infantry & a sufficient force of Artilly *double* teamed will start for Black River, Jackson, Brandon and Meridian. I will use all caution and feel no doubt unless Johnston has caught wind of our movemt and brought an additional force frm Georgia which I do not believe. I have good scouts out & will know every thing in time. I believe that W Sooy Smith will have a force of Cavalry superior to that of Forest & Stephen Lee which is all that can meet him, and Genl Polk cannot have at Canton, Brandon & Meridian a force to meet me. Admiral Porter is hourly looked for, and I will confer with him. I will ask him to send a squadron of light draft Gunboats up the Yazoo & may send Hawkins up as far as Greenwood with orders if the opportunity offers to strike Grenada another blow. This would make a diversion, confuse the enemy, and demonstrate the value to us as a military Channel of the Yazoo. It may be that Forest will let Smith pass down & make a dash for Memphis. I leave Genl Buckland in command here, with about 3200 men. Those with the Fort will assume the Safety of the place, but in addition Gen Veatch under my orders has enrolled three Regmets of citizens to whom I will issue arms, partial clothig & ammunition, and have ordered the Quarter Master to Set aside for their use as armories Cotton Sheds which will make excellent Citadels or Block houses. The mayor & citizens offered me a dinner & I had to accept—I recall your experience and as the affair comes off tonight I will try to be cautious in any remarks I will be forced to make. I pity you when you will have to go back to the States for you will not be allowed to eat or sleep for the curious intrusion of the Dear People. Red River is still low, but should it rise by the time we get back from Meridian I will be tempted to help against Shreveport. Steele could move direct by land to Archadelphia & Fulton, Banks could regain Opelousas & Alexandria, the Admiral & I could pass Army up the River to Shreveport. This would be a connective movemt, but a little risky if Dick Taylor, Price & Magruder should unite, but the latter is supposed to be off in Texas, and the two latter dont seem to pull together. I will send you a Messenger the momnt I can after I reach Meridian. My supposition is that you will want Wm Sooy Smith with his cavalry back to Pulaski by March, and will keep that in mind as soon as he can be spared. I am much troubled by the promises we have made the veterans for the furloughs. All want the furlough at once. I doubt if 35 days will see any of them back   Once at home they will be beyond our reach and control." ALS, deCoppet Collection, NjP. *O.R.*, I, xxxii, part 2, 201–2.

On Jan. 30, Sherman, Vicksburg, wrote to USG. "Arrived last night. McPherson all ready. Hurlbut behind time. All things favorable thus far for movement on Meridian. General Banks sends an officer to engage for the Red River expedition twenty-five boats. He writes me on the faith of General Halleck that Steele and I are to co-operate with him. March 1 is as early as we should move on Shreveport, and the movements of Admiral Porter should control ours. Your orders are not specific that I should go up Red River after the Meridian movement. Please telegraph me, through Admiral Porter, your orders for myself and Steele." *Ibid.*, pp. 270–71; *O.R.* (Navy), I, xxv, 721.

1. See preceding letter.
2. *O.R.*, I, xxxii, part 2, 42–43.
3. On Jan. 12, Sherman, Memphis, telegraphed to Maj. Gen. Henry W. Halleck. "I think by the 24th I can make up a force of 20000 men to strike Meridian and it may be Selma. Infantry will move via Vicksburg, Jackson & Brandon.

Cavalry down the Mobile & Ohio road from La Grange meeting about Chunkey river   If you think we hazard too much you will have time to notify me by telegraph. I shall aim to reach Meridian by February Eighth at furthest. The attention of the enemy in front of Chattanooga should be occupied by a seeming move towards Rome by Thomas & Logan"   Copies, DLC-USG, V, 40, 94; DNA, RG 393, Military Div. of the Miss., Hd. Qrs. Correspondence; *ibid.*, Telegrams Received. *O.R.*, I, xxxii, part 2, 75. On Jan. 15, 3:45 P.M., the text of this telegram was telegraphed to USG "By order of the Secretary of War." On the same day, 11:30 A.M., Halleck had telegraphed to USG. "I have just recieved a telegram from Major Genl W. T. Sherman in regard to his proposed movements & the cooperation of Genls Thomas & Logan. I have directed him to telegraph directly to you on the subject." ALS (telegram sent), DNA, RG 107, Telegrams Collected (Bound); *ibid.*, RG 393, Military Div. of the Miss., Hd. Qrs. Correspondence; DLC-USG, V, 40, 94. *O.R.*, I, xxxii, part 2, 106.

On Jan. 17, Halleck wrote to USG. "Confidential. . . . It would seem from General Sherman's despatch to me, that he proposes to move with all his disposable force on Meridian and perhaps on Selma. Does he fully understand your plans, and is that a part of you proposed winter campaign? I have not so understood it. Moreover, I fear that Sherman's views are based upon the supposed condition of affairs in East Tennessee when he left Knoxville. I do not wish to change any instructions you may have given to him; I merely desire to call attention to Sherman's proposed movements in connection with the present position of the enemy and his probable operations this winter and the coming spring. The rebels seem to be making the most desperate efforts for the next campaign. Almost every man, of whatever age, capable of bearing arms, is being pressed into their ranks, and by spring their armies will be very considerably increased. Our people, on the contrary, are acting on the mistaken supposition that the war is nearly ended, and that we shall hereafter have to contend only with fragments of broken and demoralized rebel armies. Such is the tone of the public press and of the debates in Congress. The latter has been in session six weeks, and the draft bill has not yet passed the senate. Six weeks more may elapse before it becomes a law, and then it will require several months to execute it, and get the men ready for the field. It is, therefore, very probable that our military force in the spring may be relatively much smaller than it now is. Under these circumstances it seems very important that we should act with caution and keep our troops well in hand, so as to prevent the enemy from fighting us in detachments. General Banks represents the condition of affairs in his Department to be such as to require all the reenforcements that we can possibly send him. As soon as I found that he had divided his force by operating upon the Gulf coast, I urged that troops should be sent to him from South Carolina and that the attack on Charleston be abandoned. It was decided otherwise. My opinion has been, and still is, that all troops not required to hold our present positions in Virginia and on the Atlantic coast, should be sent to you and to General Banks for operations this winter, and as preparatory to a spring campaign. I I hoped that by this means Tennessee, Arkansas, Mississippi & Louisiana would be secured, and the rebel force in Texas be so reduced and hemmed in as to give us but little trouble hereafter. Our armies in the west and south could then have been so concentrated, or at least could have been so cooperated, as to inflict some terrible blows upon the rebels. But I fear that the unexpected condition of affairs in East Tennessee will prevent the accomplishment of these objects, or at least a part of them, this winter, and that we must soon prepare for a spring campaign. The furloughing of so many troops has greatly reduced our forces in the north, but I hope to send some more to General Banks. There, however, is much difficulty and delay in obtaining transportation by sea. This makes it still more important that the navigation of the Mississippi should be well protected, and that Sherman & Steele should so operate as to assist General Banks as much as possible. I leave it entirely to your judgement to determine how, and to what extent, such assistance can be rendered." LS, DNA, RG 393, Military Div. of the Miss., Miscellaneous Letters Received. *O.R.*, I, xxxii, part 2, 122–23.

To Maj. Gen. George H. Thomas

Nashville 15th January 1864

MAJOR GENERAL G. H THOMAS
CHATTANOOGA

Can you not order Gen Paine to the command of a Brigade in the front. He is entirely unfit to command a Post.[1] General Rousseau[2] will send you by mail some statements of, his administration of affairs. If nothing better can be done I advise that you send a Staff Officer to investigate fully and report upon his administration, and if then found advisable, I will relieve him.

U. S GRANT
Major General

Telegram, copies, DLC-USG, V, 34, 35; DNA, RG 393, Military Div. of the Miss., Letters Sent; *ibid.*, Dept. of the Cumberland, Telegrams Received. *O.R.*, I, xxxii, part 2, 103. On Jan. 15, 1864, 1:30 P.M., Maj. Gen. George H. Thomas telegraphed to USG. "I do not think it advisable for Genl. Paine to come to the front. His rank will entitle him to a Division, and if not placed in command according to rank I should have constant trouble with him. I think it better to have his conduct enquired into and his position fixed according to deserts" Copy, DNA, RG 393, Dept. of the Cumberland, Telegrams Sent; *ibid.*, Military Div. of the Miss., Telegrams Received. *O.R.*, I, xxxii, part 2, 103.

1. Brig. Gen. Eleazer A. Paine then and later commanded the post of Gallatin, Tenn. See *ibid.*, p. 268.
2. Lovell H. Rousseau, born in Ky. in 1818, moved to Ind. in 1840, where he gained admission to the bar in 1841, served in the legislature (1844, 1845, 1847–49), and served as capt. during the Mexican War. He moved to Louisville, Ky., in 1849 and continued his political activities, actively campaigning against secession. Commissioned col., 3rd Ky., as of Sept. 9, 1861, he was appointed brig. gen. as of Oct. 1, promoted to maj. gen. as of Oct. 8, 1862, and commanded the District of Nashville in Jan., 1864.

To Maj. Gen. Henry W. Halleck

Nashville Tenn
Jany 16th 1. P. M 1864

MAJ GEN H. W. HALLECK
GEN IN CHIEF

Longstreet is said to be moving towards Knoxville by the main Virginia road reinforced by one division from Ewells[1] Corps; another division expected.

I have advised Gen Foster to keep between Longstreet and Thomas and the latter to use every exertion to forward supplies.

The question of supplies makes it impossible to reinforce Foster where he now is and will I think defeat the enemy.

U. S. GRANT
Maj Genl

Telegram received, DNA, RG 107, Telegrams Collected (Bound); copies, *ibid.*, Telegrams Received in Cipher; *ibid.*, RG 393, Military Div. of the Miss., Hd. Qrs. Correspondence; DLC-USG, V, 40, 94. *O.R.*, I, xxxii, part 2, 109. On Jan. 18, 1864, Maj. Gen. Henry W. Halleck wrote to USG. "Your last telegram in regard to General Foster has caused new anxiety here in regard to our position in East Tennessee. As I have before remarked, the holding of that country is regarded by the President and Secty of war of the very greatest importance, both in a political and military point of view, and no effort must be spared to accomplish that object. While we hold Chattanooga (and it supposed that place will be rendered impregnable during the winter), and the passes of the mountain range which seperates East Tennessee from Georgia and North Carolina, the enemy cannot molest Kentucky or Tennessee except by wide flank marches through Alabama or Mississippi, and by the valley of Virginia, which would give us very great strategic advantage by enabling us to move on central and interior lines. Again, if we resume the offensive, we shall have the advantage of operating from a central position against their long line of defense and of selecting our point of attack. I fully agree with you in the great importance of being able in the next campaign to select our theatre of operations and fields of battle, instead of having them forced on us by the rebels. But we cannot do this unless we have the control of East Tennessee   I also fully agree with you that our greatest difficulty at present is to supply our troops in that country. Every possible effort should be made to increase the supplies at Chattanooga and to open and protect the line from that place to Knoxville. The project of General Burnside, adopted in part I understand by General Foster, to build a new rail road and to open new lines of communication with Kentucky across the mountains, does not seem to me to be feasible; at least it will not obviate the difficulty; for they roads cannot be built and opened in time to be of any use in this campaign or the next. General Thomas seems to fully appreciate the importance of increasing the means of transportation between Nashville and Chattanooga and thence to Knoxville, and Colo McCallum has full powers from the Secty of war to repair and improve these lines and to increase the rolling stock. The matter will also, no doubt, recieve your personal attention" ALS, DNA, RG 108, Letters Sent (Press). *O.R.*, I, xxxii, part 2, 126–27. On Jan. 24, Maj. Gen. George H. Thomas, Chattanooga, wrote to Brig. Gen. John A. Rawlins. "Colonel McCallum has just left for Knoxville to ascertain the condition of that railroad, and make arrangements to push forward the work as fast as possible. He will return by first boat, when I will give him your order. The working parties for repairing the Nashville and Chattanooga Railroad have been assigned their positions and will be at work as soon as possible." *Ibid.*, p. 195.

1. Richard S. Ewell, born in Georgetown, D. C., in 1817, USMA 1840, served in the Mexican War and resigned from the U.S. Army on May 7, 1861, holding the rank of capt. Appointed C.S.A. brig. gen. as of June 17 and promoted to maj. gen. as of Jan. 24, 1862, he lost a leg at the battle of Groveton, Va., on Sept. 29. Promoted to lt. gen. as of May 23, 1863, he succeeded Lt. Gen. Thomas J. Jackson in command of the 2nd Army Corps. He did not send reinforcements to Tenn.

To Maj. Gen. Henry W. Halleck

Nashville

2 P M—Jany 16th 1864—

MAJ. GENL. HALLECK

GENL IN CHIEF—

I would respectfully suggest the propriety of ordering such new troops as have been organized in the Western States to report to me for orders at once   I could replace Veterans with them and enable all reenlisted troops to take their furlough and return by Spring   They would also have better opportunities for drilling during the winter season in the South and would be improved by contact with old troops—

U. S. GRANT

Major. General

Telegram received, DNA, RG 107, Telegrams Collected (Bound); copies, *ibid.*, Telegrams Received in Cipher; *ibid.*, RG 393, Military Div. of the Miss., Hd. Qrs. Correspondence; DLC-USG, V, 40, 94. *O.R.*, I, xxxii, part 2, 109. On Jan. 17, 1864, 1:00 P.M., Maj. Gen. Henry W. Halleck telegraphed to USG. "As fast as new troops are organised they will be sent to the Depts where most needed at the time. A general order cannot be given before hand without interfering with the arrangements of the war Dept and the governors of states. Some troops are being raised for a special service or under promises to be sent to a particular corps or command." ALS (telegram sent), DNA, RG 107, Telegrams Collected (Bound); copies, *ibid.*, RG 94, Letters Received, 23A 1864; *ibid.*, RG 393, Military Div. of the Miss., Hd. Qrs. Correspondence; DLC-USG, V, 40, 94. *O.R.*, I, xxxii, part 2, 115. On Jan. 15, USG had telegraphed to Halleck. "Are the states of Ohio Iowa and Illinois still within my command? I do not ask the question because I desire they should be but because I do not know" Telegram received, DNA, RG 107, Telegrams Collected (Bound); copies, *ibid.*, RG 393, Military Div. of the Miss., Hd. Qrs. Correspondence; DLC-USG, V, 40, 94. On Jan. 16, 10:00 A.M., Halleck telegraphed to USG. "The state of Iowa is in Genl Pope's command; and the states of Ohio, Indiana & Illinois in Genl Heintzelman's command." ALS (telegram sent), DNA, RG 107, Telegrams Collected (Bound); copies, *ibid.*, RG 393, Military Div. of the Miss., Hd. Qrs. Correspondence; DLC-USG, V, 40, 94. *O.R.*, I, xxxiv, part 2, 95. On Jan. 27, 7:40 P.M., Secretary of War Edwin M. Stanton telegraphed to USG. "~~Your sending~~ Some apprehension being expressed that the armies in the West may be too much weakened by sending home ~~troops~~ the regiments that have re-enlisted it may be well to suggest that ~~the order of~~ this Department leaves it to the discretion of the Commanding General what proportion of troops shall be furloughed at any one time. You will therefore give instructions that will prevent the armies under your command from being reduced ~~too much~~ beyond what you consider safe. [P]ray let me hear how you find [y]our sons health" ALS (telegram sent), DNA, RG 107, Telegrams Collected (Bound); copies, *ibid.*, RG 393, Military Div. of the Miss., Hd. Qrs. Correspondence; DLC-USG, V, 40, 94. Printed as sent at 7:50 P.M., I, xxxii, part 2, 230. On Jan. 28, 9:00 A.M., USG, St. Louis, telegraphed to Stanton. "No more veterans are to be furloughed from the Dept. of the Cumberland, except as those now absent return:—from the Dept. of the Ohio, not until Longstreet is driven from Tennessee. My son has passed the crisis of his disease but is so much reduced that it will take months to restore him to his strength." Telegram received, DNA, RG 107, Telegrams Collected (Bound); copies, *ibid.*, RG 393, Military Div. of the Miss., Hd. Qrs. Correspondence; DLC-USG, V, 40, 94. *O.R.*, I, xxxii, part 2, 244.

By War Dept. General Orders No. 376, Nov. 21, 1863, vols. who reenlisted as veterans were given thirty-day furloughs before their original terms of service expired. On Dec. 11, Brig. Gen. Grenville M. Dodge, Athens, Ala., telegraphed to USG. "There is good deal of interest manifested just now in my com'd. in relation to reenlistments as Veterans   three fourths of several companies have agreed reenlist provided they can receive the benefits of General orders No. 376 H'd Qrs. War. Dept and I could send home under that order all reenlisting without decreasing my effective force more than fifteen hundred at any one time. I have no doubt I could send home some of those companies after they have been mustered out & in that it would save to the Govt. a large number of Veterans Soldiers in this command. I did not feel constrained to act under this order until I received instructions from you   The thirty days at home as company organization transportation free is very tempting to old soldiers   please advise—" Copy, DNA, RG 393, Military Div. of the Miss., Telegrams Received. On the same day, 7:00 P.M., USG telegraphed to Dodge. "Reenlist under General Orders 376, as you propose. General Sherman will be here in two or three days and will order the Furloughs in accordance with the provisions of the order" Copies, DLC-

USG, V, 34, 35; DNA, RG 393, Military Div. of the Miss., Letters Sent. On Dec. 14, Maj. Gen. James B. McPherson, Vicksburg, telegraphed to USG. "The fourteenth Wis Infty having reenlisted in a body I desire to send it on furlough in accordance with the orders. It will have an excellent effect on the command   I think three fourths of my command will reenlist." Copy, *ibid.*, Telegrams Received. On Dec. 21, USG telegraphed to McPherson. "Furlough the fourteenth 14   This & all regiments that reenlist as fast as you can spare them"   Telegram received, *ibid.*, 17th Army Corps, Telegrams Received (Unarranged); copies, *ibid.*, Military Div. of the Miss., Letters Sent; DLC-USG, V, 34, 35.

On Dec. 23, Brig. Gen. James H. Wilson, Chattanooga, telegraphed to USG, Nashville. "The question of reenlistments under the order for Veterans is attracting a good deal of attention here particularly as it is generally believed that the War. Dept. has decided to require the reenlistment of three fourths of the men borne on the rolls before allowing the priviliges set forth in the Gen'l order   wouldnt be well enough to telegraph at once for permission to construe the order to mean three fourths of the men present with the regt give the furlough for permission to recruit up request Govs to fill their regts by drafted men & if they do not reach the minimum to entitle to the regimental organization have them consolidated after the draft into battalions & if the battalions put together to form regts. This course promptly adopted will have 9 tenths of the able bodied men of the army with good organization whilst a strict adherence to the order will not obtain one regt in ten simply from the impracticability of getting at the men to know their feelings   I send this by telegraph because every moment is of the utmost importance." Telegram received (incomplete), DNA, RG 393, Dept. of the Tenn., Telegrams Received; copy, *ibid.*, Military Div. of the Miss., Telegrams Received. On the same day, Dodge, Pulaski, Tenn., telegraphed to Lt. Col. Theodore S. Bowers. "In the Veteran Regiments there are a large number of men who have been recruited in last year or 18 months. I understand that those men remain in the organization but do not go home and the men who have less than a year to serve but do not reenlist are the ones I transfur to other regts—Is this so?"   Copy, *ibid.* On Dec. 22, Governor Oliver P. Morton of Ind. telegraphed to USG. "The telegram just rec'd. to forward request to announce it to all concerned. 'Washington Dec 21st 1863. O. P. MORTON Gov. of Ind. The Secy. of War has ordered first that the term "three fourths" as used in connection with Veteran rights under existing orders is understood to mean three fourths of the organization serving and does not include men absent in prisons Gen. Hospitals &c. Second. that men belonging to Veteran regts. who have not served two years & consequently do not come within the limits of reenlistments will be permitted to go on furlough with the main body of the regt in case it gives [*goes*] as an organization provided they show their willingness to reenlist as soon as they come within the limits. The men however who come within the limits for recruiting & yet dicline to reenlist will not be granted furloughs. Third. That no volunteer recruit shall be rejected on account of hight who is five feet or over. Present regulations being thus modified. (Signed) JAS. B. FRY Pro. Marshal General. I will thank you to communicate the above provisions to Co'l. Wilder at Bridgeport or Huntsville and to all commanders having Ind. regts. serving under them." Copies, *ibid.*; (incomplete) Morton Papers, In. On Dec. 29, Maj. Gen. John A. Logan, Scottsville, Ala., telegraphed to Bowers. "Frequent enquiries are made if Infantry can reenlist as cavalry in the Veteran Corps service   if they can a considerable number will so enlist in the corps. Answer." Copies, DNA, RG 393, Military Div. of the Miss., Telegrams Received; *ibid.*, 15th Army Corps,

Telegrams Sent. On Jan. 1, 1864, Maj. Gen. Stephen A. Hurlbut, Memphis, telegraphed to USG. "I report that veteran regts have been in the field since receipt of late orders regarding reinlists of veteran vols & that the necessary papers for reinlistment have not been furnished in time for them to reinlist by Jany fifth, eighteen sixty four 1864 Troops on active service should have longer time" Telegram received, *ibid.*, Dept. of the Tenn., Telegrams Received; copies, *ibid.*, 16th Army Corps, Letters Sent; (misdated Dec. 1, 1863) *ibid.*, Military Div. of the Miss., Telegrams Received. On Jan. 14, Maj. Samuel Breck, AGO, telegraphed to USG. "Thirty one boxes blanks for the enlistments of Veterans Volunteers were forwarded yesterday to your address by Adams Express. More will be sent in a day or two." Copies, DLC-USG, V, 40, 94; DNA, RG 393, Military Div. of the Miss., Hd. Qrs. Correspondence.

On Jan. 12, McPherson telegraphed to USG. "No telegram of the ninth of Dec. from these secy of war calling for report of veterans mustered have been recd at these Head Qrs I have twenty four reg'ts of veterans over three fourths of each regt having enrolled themselves & they are being mustered in as fast as rolls can be procured five regts already mustered I am satisfied that I will have twenty six or twenty eight regts in my command of Veterans all of the regts that have served two years & upwards will reenlist with two or three exceptions the muster in rolls forwarded from the adjt Genls office Washington during the last three months on requisition from these Hd Qrs have never been recd—" Telegram received, *ibid.*, Dept. of the Tenn., Telegrams Received; copy (misdated Jan. 21), Military Div. of the Miss., Telegrams Received.

On Dec. 4, 1863, Maj. Thomas M. Vincent, AGO, wrote to USG giving authority to accept resignations of vol. officers provided that their final pay be withheld until the Pay Dept. gave proof that they were not indebted to the government. Copies, *ibid.*, Hd. Qrs. Correspondence; *ibid.*, Dept. of the Tenn., Unregistered Letters Received.

To Maj. Gen. John G. Foster

Nashville 16th January 1864

MAJ GENL J. G. FOSTER
KNOXVILLE

I am advised that Longstreet has been reinforced by a Division of Ewells Corps, and that another Division is expected Longstreet is said to be moving towards Knoxville by the main Virginia road. I could send you reenforcements but they cannot be subsisted. I think if this is true you had better keep your forces between Longstreet and Thomas. I will telegraph Thomas to make extra exertions to feed you.

U S GRANT
Major General

Telegram, copies, DLC-USG, V, 34, 35; DNA, RG 393, Military Div. of the Miss., Letters Sent. *O.R.*, I, xxxii, part 2, 109–10. On Jan. 15, 1864, 8:00 P.M., USG had telegraphed to Maj. Gen. John G. Foster. "As soon as you deem your position secure, order the Fourth Corps to return to Chattanooga. They will return the earliest and most practicable route, taking as much time for the march as the condition of the roads, men, and animals may be necessary." *Ibid.*, p. 102.

On Jan. 16, Foster telegraphed to USG. "I have the honor to report that on the 14th Genl. Vance—brother of Governor Vance, of N. C. with 300 Cavalry made a raid towards Severeville and captured a train of 23 wagons, sent out from Knoxville for forage—General Sturgiss immediately ordered Col. Palmer with the 15th Penn.—Anderson Cavalry, to persue them—He did so with such activity that he came up with the party as they had halted to feed—23 miles from Severeville, suprised them—recaptured all the wagons, drivers and animals, and in addition, a fine ambulance filled with Medical Stores—one hundred and fifty (150) saddle horses, and One hundred (100) Stand of arms—General Vance with his Adjutant General, and Inspector General were among the prisoners. The remainder of the rebel party broke and fled to the mountains—closely persued by the 'union home guards'—General Sturgis speaks in high terms of Col. Palmer's activity and skill—As he has exhibited on several occasions before. I recommend him for appointment as Brig. Genl.—and respectfully ask, that you endorse the recommendation as a reward for what Col. Palmer has done and as an incentive to other officers to imitate his example—" Copies, DNA, RG 393, Dept. of the Cumberland, Telegrams Sent; (2) *ibid.*, Dept. of the Ohio (Cincinnati), Telegrams Sent; *ibid.*, Military Div. of the Miss., Telegrams Received. *O.R.*, I, xxxii, part 1, 73–74. On Jan. 17, USG telegraphed to Maj. Gen. Henry W. Halleck. "On the fourteenth (14) instant Genl Vance made a raid towards Lenisville [*Sevierville*] and captured a train of twenty three (23) wagons He was promptly pursued by Colonel Palmer who recaptured the wagons and took one ambulance loaded with medicines one hundred and fifty (150) saddle horses and one hundred stand of arms. Vance his A. A. G. and Inspector General are among the prisoners captured" Telegram received, DNA, RG 107, Telegrams Collected (Bound); copies, *ibid.*, RG 393, Military Div. of the Miss., Hd. Qrs. Correspondence; DLC-USG, V, 40, 94. *O.R.*, I, xxxii, part 1, 73.

On Jan. 16, Foster telegraphed to USG. "General Sturgis occupied ~~the~~ Dandridge and the country for five miles in front on the 14th As soon as Granger arrives in support with the fourth and Twenty third Corps Sturges will push the enemy in front and occupy as far up the north bank of the River as possible I shall cross the fourth and twenty third Corps to the south side and occupy the entire country to the South and East of The French Broad River; This being done I shall make a threat with Cavalry on Longstreets rear These dispositions will give us good foraging ground where we can live for six weeks, and it also gives us an advantage in position I do not expect to hold it without some fighting." Telegram received, DNA, RG 393, Dept. of Mo., Telegrams Received; copy (dated Jan. 17), *ibid.*, Military Div. of the Miss., Telegrams Received. Dated Jan. 17 in *O.R.*, I, xxxii, part 2, 116. On Jan. 17, USG telegraphed to Foster. "Your dispatch of the 16th approved highly. Have you been able to drive the enemy from Jonesville?" Copies, DLC-USG, V, 34, 35; DNA, RG 393, Military Div. of the Miss., Letters Sent. *O.R.*, I, xxxii, part 2, 117. On Jan. 17, Foster telegraphed to USG. "The fourth and twenty third Corps are at Dandridge—The Enemy is in some force near Kimbers Cross roads Sturgis skirmished heavily with them yesterday   I shall cross all the infantry of these two corps to the south side of the French broad to obtain food and forage to keep Longstreets foragers out of that section and also to threaten his flank"   Telegram received, DNA, RG 393, Dept. of Mo., Telegrams Received; copy, *ibid.*, Military Div. of the Miss., Telegrams Received. *O.R.*, I, xxxii, part 2, 116.

To Maj. Gen. George H. Thomas

Nashville Jany 16th 12 30 a m [*1864*]

MAJ GENL THOMAS

Longstreet is said to be marching towards Knoxville.

Enemy reinforced by one Div from Ewells Corps with another expected.

I have advised Foster to keep his force between Longstreet and you.

Should he be forced back south of the Tenn it may become necessary to reinforce him from your command.

In that case I would fill the place of troops taken away from Maj Genl W T Shermans Command

Send Foster all the provisions you can.

The question of provisions alone may decide the fate of East Tenn

Maj Genl GRANT

Telegram received, DNA, RG 94, Generals' Papers and Books, George H. Thomas; copies, *ibid.*, RG 393, Dept. of the Cumberland, Telegrams Received; *ibid.*, Military Div. of the Miss., Letters Sent; DLC-USG, V, 34, 35. *O.R.*, I, xxxii, part 2, 110. On Jan. 16, 1864, Maj. Gen. George H. Thomas telegraphed to USG. "Your dispatch of 12. m. to day received. Will send all the provisions I can possibly spare without starving my own men. Will increase number of boats as soon as R. R. is in full operation   Have given directions about repairing the Hiawassee & Loudon bridges." Copies, DNA, RG 393, Dept. of the Cumberland, Telegrams Sent; *ibid.*, Military Div. of the Miss., Telegrams Received. *O.R.*, I, xxxii, part 2, 110.

Also on Jan. 16, USG wrote to Bvt. Lt. Col. James L. Donaldson. "please let me know if the cars have yet been sent through to Chattanooga with supplies. If not give directions at once to have the trains go to that place direct, with such QuarterMaster's, Company and Ordnance stores as are needed for the troops on duty there and in the vicinity. The boats for Genl. Foster should be loaded at Chattanooga instead of at Bridgeport as heretofore," LS, DNA, RG 393, Dept.

of the Cumberland, Letters Received. On the same day, Donaldson wrote to USG. "On my return from Levee, find your letter directing cars to go through to Chattanooga, and enquiring if any have already gone. The accompanying copy of telegram from my agent Bridgeport shows that three trains passed there for Chattanooga yesterday—By monday I think the road will be fully open, and in effective working condition—I am making my arrangements here accordingly—I propose going over the road On monday myself to see if I cannot stop thefts, and regulate matters out of gear at Bridgeport. I expect to meet Col Eastan at Bridgeprt and arrange with him about the Supplies for Fosters Army." ALS, *ibid.*, Military Div. of the Miss., Letters Received. The enclosure is *ibid.*

To Maj. Gen. George H. Thomas

Nashville 16th January 1864.

MAJ GENL GEO H THOMAS
CHATTANOOGA

It is impossible to spare Granger or Elliott from East Tennessee until Longstreet is driven out. It may be necessary soon to send additional troops there. I will write you more fully.

Orders are again received directing Crook to report to Kelly. Relieve him at once   Crooks Cavalry cannot be foraged at Huntsville.[1] It had better therefore be ordered to some point where they can get forage.

U S GRANT
Major General

Telegram, copies, DLC-USG, V, 34, 35; DNA, RG 393, Military Div. of the Miss., Letters Sent; *ibid.*, Dept. of the Cumberland, Telegrams Received. *O.R.*, I, xxxii, part 2, 110. On Jan. 15, 1864, 3:00 P.M., Maj. Gen. George H. Thomas telegraphed to USG. "The R. R. is now completed to this place and there is a prospect of getting some forage here. I would therefore like to have Elliotts Cavly, now in E. Tennessee, moved down to Charleston on the Hiawassee where he can procure some forage and with what he can get from here his horses can be kept in condition to demonstrate on the enemy's position at Dalton and completely occupy his attention. As soon as Granger's Command can be sent back other movements can be so made as to withdraw the enemy's attention from operations from the direction of Memphis or Vicksburg, should you contemplate making any from either." Copies, DNA, RG 393, Dept. of the Cumberland, Telegrams Sent; *ibid.*, Military Div. of the Miss., Telegrams Received. *O.R.*, I, xxxii, part 2, 102–3.

1. See letter to Edwin M. Stanton, Dec. 9, 1863.

To Maj. Gen. George H. Thomas

———

Nashville Tenn January 17th 64

MAJ GENL GEO H THOMAS
CHATTANOOGA

I return to you General Granger's reccommendations of Brig Genl Hazen to Maj General, without endorsement. I will state however that I look upon Hazen as among the first, if not the first entitled to promotion, and in sending on a list of reccommendations will be pleased to place his name as high on it as you choose to place it. My objection to endorsing this paper is, that it is calculated to forestall other Officers who will also be recommended for promotion.

After the recommendations for promotion have been sent in I will have no objection to then endorsing favorably Genl Hazen's seperate recommendation.

U S GRANT
Major General

Copies, DLC-USG, V, 34, 35; DNA, RG 393, Military Div. of the Miss., Letters Sent.

To Francis Southwick

———

Nashville Tennessee,
January 17th 1864

FRANCIS SOUTHWICK, ESQ.
ALBANY N. Y.
DEAR SIR:

Owing to my absence in East Tennessee your letter of the 17th of Dec. is only just laid before me.

If I had the time, and the facilities for getting facts not already known to myself, I would delight in giving you items for the biography of an officer so much to be admired as the late Maj. Gen.

C. F. Smith. I have neither the time nor the means however of doing so.—Gen. Smith left a very aged mother, and one or more daughters, residing, I believe, at the Capital of Md. He also left a wife, possibly with the younger children, residing in the City of New York.

Brig. Gen. Cullum, Chief Eng. on the staff of Maj. Gen. Halleck, I think, can give you all the facts & incidents of Gen Smith's life better than any other one.

> Your Truly
> U. S. GRANT

ALS, Morristown National Historical Park, Morristown, N. J.

To Maj. Gen. Henry W. Halleck

———

> Hdqrs Milty Div of the Miss.
> Nashville 18th Jan 1864

MAJ GEN H. W. HALLECK
GENL IN CHIEF
GENERAL

I would respectfully recommend for appointment as 2d Lieutenant in the regular Artillery or Infantry Henry A Ulffers & Otto H Matz.[1] They have served long and faithfully in the Army of the Tennessee as Civil Asst Engrs. They are men of education, skill and good character and will reflect credit on the service. These officers have served under my personal observation, and if appointed I would request that they be continued on duty in the Mil Divn. as acting Engineer Officers

> I am &c
> U. S GRANT
> Maj Genl.

Copies, DLC-USG, V, 40, 94; DNA, RG 393, Military Div. of the Miss., Hd. Qrs. Correspondence. On Jan. 25, 1864, Maj. Gen. Henry W. Halleck wrote to USG. "Your letter of the 18th recommending the appointment of H. A. Ulffers and O. H. Matz to the regular army is recieved. The law and regulations of the

War Dept. require that all vacancies in regular regiments be filled by the promotion of non-commissioned officers. If this rule were changed, such vacancies would all be filled by political appointments, and the non-commissioned officers of the army would have no chance of promotion. If the parties referred to can get appointments in volunteer regiments they can be retained by you on Engineer duty. Your application to the Governor of any of the Western states would undoubtedly secure their appointment." LS, *ibid.*, Letters Received.

On Jan. 18, USG telegraphed to Halleck. "I would like to have Captain Muhler [*Merrill?*] and Ruse [*Reese*] of the Engineers directed to report to me for assignment   The former as Chief Engineer of the Department of the Cumberland and the latter of Shermans"   Telegram received, *ibid.*, RG 107, Telegrams Collected (Bound); copies, *ibid.*, RG 393, Military Div. of the Miss., Hd. Qrs. Correspondence; DLC-USG, V, 40, 94.

1. Otto H. Matz, born in Prussia in 1830, was appointed chief architect of the Illinois Central Railroad (1854–57), and engaged in private practice in Chicago as an architect (1857–61). Working as an asst. topographical engineer in 1861, he served under Maj. Gen. John C. Frémont in Mo., and participated in the siege of Corinth, Miss., in 1862. Appointed maj., Ill. Vols., he was an engineer officer during the siege of Vicksburg. He returned to Chicago in 1864 to resume his architectural practice.

To Henry Wilson

Head Quarters, Mil. Div. of the Miss.
Nashville Ten. Jan.y 18th 1864,

HON. H. WILSON,
CHAIRMAN MIL. COM. U. S. SENATE,
SIR:

Permit me to address you, as Chairman of the Committee on Military Affairs, on a subject which I believe Conscientiously the welfare of the Country and best interests of the service are interested in. I want to speak in behalf of the confirmation of Gens. Sherman & McPherson[1] as Brigadiers in the regular Army. They are both men of the purest integrity and greatest capacity as soldiers. They are never found defending themselves against charges made through the press of the country, except by an untiring devotion to their duties. They are a class of General officers the country cannot well despense with. Either of them ~~are~~ is qualified to be trusted alone with our largest Armies. This is a quality not possessed by many even of our best soldiers. They are both, particularly McPherson, young enough to do the country service in future wars if we should be so unfortunate as to be involved in any within the next ten or twenty years.

There is one thing more I will say in favor of these two officers. They may be relied on for an honest and faithful performance of their duties regardless of what may be their private views of the policy pursued. Neither will they ever discourage, by word or deed, others from a faithful performance of their duties. In a word they are not men to discuss policy whilst their country requires their services.

Neither of these officers are aware that a word is being said in their favor and I know them well enough to assert that they would not ask the intervention of any one even if they knew, without it, they would be defeated in their confirmation.

> I have the honor to be
> Very respectfully
> your obt. svt.
> U. S. GRANT
> Maj. Gen.

ALS, DLC-USG. Maj. Gens. William T. Sherman and James B. McPherson were confirmed as brig. gens. U. S. A. on Feb. 29, 1864, to rank from July 4 and Aug. 1, 1863. On Jan. 18, 1864, USG again wrote to U.S. Senator Henry Wilson of Mass. "A uniform ambulance system in our armies is much needed and I deem that proposed in your bill (S. 30) sufficient for the needs of the service, subject of course to the modifications which experience may suggest." LS, IHi.

1. On Dec. 22, 1863, Maj. Gen. Henry W. Halleck had written to USG, the letter reaching USG on Jan. 18, 1864. "*Private* . . . I understand that an effort will be made to defeat, in the Senate, the nomination of McPherson, on the ground that he is semi secesh, &c. You know how absurd this is. The true course of the opposition is the jealousy of other officers who want the place, but who have not rendered half as good services. I dont think Mc. has a single friend or acquaintance in the Senate. I therefore suggest that you write to some of your friends on the subject." ALS, DNA, RG 108, Letters Sent (Press). See James Harrison Wilson, *The Life of John A. Rawlins* (New York, 1916), pp. 385–86. On Dec. 2, McPherson, Vicksburg, had written to USG. "Permit me to extend to you my heartfelt congratulations on your recent Victory over Bragg—and to hope that the same success may attend all your efforts until this Rebellion is completely crushed,   The details of the Battle are yet to come, but through Rebel sources I learn that your Victory was complete,   I received your letter and am under many obligations,   With regard to 'Coolbaugh' he was employed by me as

Agent at Corinth while I had charge of the Rail Roads, on the strength of excellent letters of recommendation from men of standing in Penn, & the North West—He brought some six thousand Dollars in money with him when he came to Corinth, and shortly after he entered the R. R. Office he asked me if he could purchase Cotton, I told him no, not as long as he remained in my Employ—That if he was not satisfied with his salary & position, and wanted to engage in Cotton Speculations he could resign and I would employ someone else, That I would not allow any man on the Roads to engage in any outside business if I knew it— And I am not aware that he ever bought one ounce of Cotton on his own or any other persons acc't,—Gov. Sprague's Agent, who was purchasing Cotton at Corinth & Vicinity, frequently left his money in the safe in the office, and on several occasions Coolbaugh paid over funds from this to parties from whom the Agent had purchased Cotton merely as a matter of accommodation, That he was acting as agent, or ever has acted as Agent I do not believe—He has been with me off and on, for nearly a year and a half, in the Field and in the office, and I have found in him a most Valuable and able assistant, Prompt, competent and energetic, I have never called upon him to perform any service, but what he did it well and quickly—If his being on my Staff compromises my *confirmation* as *Brig Genl U. S. A.* all I can say is let it do so, Conscious of having tried under all circumstances to do my duty to my Country, to the best of my ability, I shall let the matter take its own course, I certainly shall never dismiss a competent, Valuable Officer, who has shared with me the dangers of the campaign, *simply* because his being on my staff damages *my prospects*, though I would not retain him or any other officer *One moment*, if I thought they were *guilty* of any thing *wrong*, I have communicated to him the substance of the last part of your letter, and I do not think he will remain much longer My kindest regards to Rawlins & the other members of your staff" ALS, USG 3. Regarding the agent of Governor (later U.S. Senator) William Sprague of R. I., see *PUSG*, 5, 333*n*.

On Feb. 8, 1864, Brig. Gen. James H. Wilson, Washington, wrote to USG. "there are one or two little matters I wished to write to you about, but have delayed for want of time. In the first place you have probably not forgotten our conversations concerning Mr Washburn's active interest in your affairs and the view we took of the motive by which he was actuated. I find that neither of us was mistaken; and as I suspected he is doing your reputation no particular good— or rather I should say he's doing *you* no particular good. He is given credit for closer intimacy with you than he has any right to—and is now supposed to be a proprietary guardian of every matter that concerns you. I am not quite certain but that he has done some thing of this kind—Given assurances that you were no aspirant for political place—but as a sort of reward for your forbearance would like to be 'Lieut. General' I don't mention these matters to have you take any positive steps, but simply in order that you may be on your guard in future correspondence with him. This view of the case, is concurred in by Mr. Dana. In conversation with different public men I have found a sort of suspicion in one or two instances that Mr Washburn, as a shrewd politician, seeing the substantial popularty of yourself might not have been entirely disinterested in his advocacy. The Lieut. General bill will be amended in the Senate, by striking out the recommendation for your appointment and leaving the President to make his own selection. The result will be the same undoubtedly—while the freedom of the Presidential functions will in no way be interfered with. The original bill allowing the president to assign whoever he chooses to the command of the Army will still leave it possible for him to continue in the active command in the field. Mr.

Sprague, Senator from R. I. is the only opponent in the Senate Military Committee to the *new Grade*. Do you remember the story you heard of Coolbaugh's connection with him? I wonder if he was pleased with the amount of cooperation given him in your command, in the cotton trade? *Apropos* of Coolbaugh, I have just received a letter from Vicksburg with the following passage in it: 'I deem it my duty as a friend and classmate to put you on your guard against the machinations of Coolbaugh; he is your (*my*) *inveterate* enemy and has just told me "he had already invested ten thousand dollars to secure your rejection as Brigadier General—and had a *hundred thousand* ready for the same purpose if necessary." He has the key to every thing—*Money*.' That's quite refreshing isn't it? I never valued myself at half that rate and don't know but it would be a good investment to *sell* out. Some of your nominations have not been very favorably received—and in one or two instances it is thought you may have been deceived as to the real merits of the men. Should you wish to withdraw any recommendation it can be done in an informal way through Mr. Dana—Or if you prefer through me. I will hand any thing you may send, or communicate it to the proper persons. Our friend McClernand you know has been ordered to report to Banks for duty thro' the influence of Mr Trumbull. The president did it—and in opposition to the views of Mr Washburn—that too, just after he had assured the latter that he would not allow him to be put on duty any where. In subsequent explanation to Mr. W. the president said grave political considerations in Illinois had induced him to change his decision. What Twaddle! Genl Washburn will no doubt make application to be relieved of his command in the Gulf department. An impression here prevails among the government people that McClernand has political weight at home—I stated the truth of the case. The army of the Potomac *84000 strong* is on the move in conjunction with Butler from the White House on York River, against Lee not over 35000 strong; successful so far, but I suspect nothing serious is meant, for only 3 days' rations are taken. Sedgewick is in command and telegraphs he fears the movement is premature and will simply result in preventing the capture of the Enemy—by causing him to fall back out of reach. The command of the Army of the Potomac is not yet settled. The newspapers are beginning to stir up the matter and in the interest of the ideas you express. Mr. Dana thinks as I do that its agitation will do no harm but may result in real good. Mr. Lincoln seems to be the *hanging point* in the whole matter—he is slow as can be to move. but an attempt will be made to interest Greely and Bryant in whom he has great confidence. I am quite sure both their papers will go in favor of it.— I have been thinking a great deal of your spring movements and the more I think the more I become convinced that your true policy is to bend every effort towards a movement from the line of the Tennessee—It is a question of supplies and can probably be as well settled where you are as elsewhere. To go to Mobile involves chances of failure in the first step, and if successful, leaves you still at an immense distance from the real vital point point—with your forces scattered. Wouldn't it be better to bend all of your own effects in a united effort in a direct attempt, and leave Banks and the Coast forces of Butler & Gillmore, to make a diversion towards Mobile? It will require all possible exertion to get a store of supplies on the Tennessee to enable you to go forward with perfect assurance   Couldn't the Memphis & Charleston road, be used to assist in this as far east as Decatur? particularly inview of the fact that Sherman is to move his forces way into the interior of Alabama? It seems to me that by concentrating the forces of the Army of the Tennessee, not used now in forward movements along and south of this road, it might be kept in running order as far as Decatur till you got ready to move with your entire force. Then break it up and remove the rolling stock—or leave it for the enemy to do, just as might seem most advantageous. If the Army of the Tennessee could support itself that way temporarily a great advantage would be secured. The latest news from Richmond indicates the greatest despondency—but the scoundrels are working like beavers and no doubt will accomplish much towards filling up their ranks—and getting ready to give us a hard tug for it in the spring. Every body seems to look to you for our future success as for the past—no hope is entertained that the Army of the Potomac can or will do much. It *must* be regenerated—and have a new commander. Smith is the favorite and ought to be appointed. You cannot put yourself too decidedly on the record in regard to that point, and the necessity of coöperation now! I am getting along pretty well in my new position—and hope to introduce some good reform, if not efficiency of service into the Bureau. What I want now is a few honest cavalry officers, or civilians for horse inspectors. 11.500 horses were contracted for, on the 30th Ult for you—They will be received at St. Louis, Indianapolis, Chicago, Columbus—and forwarded as you request per telegram. Give my kindest regards to Mrs. Grant—Remember me kindly to Genl.s Rawlins & Smith, and all the staff. I heard Hillyer was in town a few days ago but he didn't call upon me. Hoping you wont find more in this letter than you wish to read," ALS, USG 3. See letters to Elihu B. Washburne, Dec. 12, 1863; to Barnabas Burns, Dec. 17, 1863. Regarding George Coolbaugh, brother of the prominent Chicago banker William F. Coolbaugh, see James Harrison Wilson, *Under the Old Flag* (New York and London, 1912), I, 236–37. Concerning his own nomination as brig. gen., Wilson evidently quoted a letter from Capt. John M. Wilson, also USMA 1860, on duty at the time in Memphis, Natchez, and Vicksburg.

To Maj. Gen. Henry W. Halleck

Confidential   Head Quarters, Mil. Div. of the Miss.
                                  Nashville Ten. Jan.y 19th 1864,
MAJ. GEN. H. W. HALLECK,
GEN. IN CHIEF OF THE ARMY,
WASHINGTON D. C.
GENERAL,

I would respectfully suggest whether an abandonment of all previously attempted lines to Richmond is not advisable, and in line of these one be taken further South. I would suggest Raleigh North Carolina as the objective point and Suffolk as the starting point. Raleigh once secured I would make New Bern the base of supplies until Wilmington is secured. A moving force of sixty thousand men would probably be required to start on such an expedition. This force would not have to be increased unless Lee should withdraw from his present position. In that case the necessity for so large a force on the Potomac would not exist.

A force moving from Suffolk would destroy first all the roads about Weldon, or even as far north as Hicksford. From Weldon to Raleigh they would scarsely meet with serious opposition. Once there the most interior line of rail way still left to the enemy, in fact the only one they would then have, would be so threatened as to force ~~enemy~~ him to use a large portion of his army in guarding it. This would virtually force an evacuation of Virginia and indirectly of East Tennessee. It would throw our Armies into new fields where they could partially live upon the country and would reduce the stores of the enemy. It would cause thousands of the North Carolina troops to desert and return to their homes. It would give us possession of many Negroes who are now indirectly aiding the rebellion. It would draw the enemy from Campaigns of their own choosing, and for which they are prepared, to new lines of operations never expected to become necessary. It would effectually blockade Wilmington, the port now of more value to the enemy than all the balance of their sea coast. It would enable operations to commence at once by removing the war to a more southern climate instead of months of inactivity in winter quarters. Other advantages might be cited which would be likely to grow out of this plan, but these are enough. From your better opportunities of studying the country, and the Armies, that would be involved in this plan, you will be better able to judge of the practicability of it than I possibly can.

I have written this in accordance with what I understood to be an invitation from you to express my views about Military operations and not to insist that any plan of mine should be carried out. Whatever course is agreed upon I shall always believe is at least intended for the best and until fully tested will hope to have it prove so.

> I am General, very respectfully
> your obt. svt.
> U. S. GRANT
> Maj. Gen.

ALS, Schoff Collection, MiU-C. *O.R.*, I, xxxiii, 394–95. An undated three and one-half page "Memorandum of a Campaign in N. C.," not in USG's hand, apparently served as the basis for this letter. The final paragraph was in USG's hand. "I have written this in accordance with what I understood to be an invitation from you to express my views about operations, and not to insist that any plan of mine should be carried out. Whatever is agreed upon I shall always believe is at least intended for the best, and, until tried will hope for the best." Oliver R. Barrett Sale, 1190, Parke-Bernet Galleries, Inc., Oct. 30-Nov. 2, 1950, no. 485. On Jan. 18, 1864, Lt. Col. Cyrus B. Comstock wrote in his diary: "Gen W. F Smith & I submitted Mem. to Gen. as to landing 60000 men at Norfolk or Newbern & operating against Rail R. south of Richmond & alternately against Raleigh & Wilmington." DLC-Cyrus B. Comstock.

To Maj. Gen. George H. Thomas

Nashville January 19th 1864

MAJ GENL GEO H THOMAS
CHATTANOOGA

Wilson is ordered to Washington in charge of Cavalry Bureau.[1] None of the officers named by you are among those awaiting assignment. I have asked for Ransom to be sent here. He has always proved himself the best man I have ever had to send on expeditions. He is a live man and of good judgement. He will not of course be sent to command Crooks Cavalry if you have an officer at the time who gives full satisfaction. I wish you would inform me from time to time the information obtained from scouts and deserters. Also send me Southern papers when you get them.

U S GRANT
Major General

Telegram, copies, DLC-USG, V, 34, 35; DNA, RG 393, Military Div. of the Miss., Letters Sent; *ibid.*, Dept. of the Cumberland, Telegrams Received. *O.R.*, I, xxxii, part 2, 141. On Jan. 16, 1864, 11:35 A.M., USG had telegraphed to Maj. Gen. George H. Thomas. "I have asked to have Genl Ransom ordered here to take Crook's place. You can therefore only make temporary arangements for a Commander to that Cavalry Division" Copies, DLC-USG, V, 34, 35; DNA, RG 393, Military Div. of the Miss., Letters Sent; *ibid.*, Dept. of the Cumberland, Telegrams Received. On the same day, Thomas telegraphed to USG. "Can you let me have Wilson to command Crook's Division I think he would like to come." Copy, *ibid.*, Telegrams Sent. On Jan. 18, USG telegraphed to Thomas. "General Wilson has been ordered to take charge of Cavalry Bureau and cannot therefore relieve Crook. I have asked for Ransom who is as fine an officer for the place as can be found in the service. If we get him however, it cannot be under twenty or thirty days." Copies, DLC-USG, V, 34, 35; DNA, RG 393, Military Div. of the Miss., Letters Sent; *ibid.*, Dept. of the Cumberland, Telegrams Received. *O.R.*, I, xxxii, part 2, 130. On Jan. 19, 11:00 P.M., Thomas telegraphed to USG. "I have no objection whatever to Genl. Ransom. My application for Wilson was made before I knew that you had applied for Genl. R. I have efficient Colonels Commanding Cavalry brigades and prefer keeping them to having Brigadiers who know nothing about Cavalry Service. I also prefer efficient Colonels to Command Infantry Brigades to Brigadiers who are of doubtful efficiency. I sent you a very interesting statement to day. Will send another tomorrow, made by an officer who came in this evening." Copies, DNA, RG 393, Dept. of the Cumberland, Telegrams Sent; *ibid.*, Military Div. of the Miss., Telegrams Received. *O.R.*, I, xxxii, part 2, 142.

On Jan. 17, USG telegraphed to Thomas. "Have you any Brigades to which you can assign Brigadier Generals? A number of Brigadiers have reported to me for assignment" Copies, DLC-USG, V, 34, 35; DNA, RG 393, Military Div. of the Miss., Letters Sent. On Jan. 18, Thomas telegraphed to USG. "I would like to know the names of the Brigadiers ordered to report to you, before I can decide whether I want any—If Brig. Genl. Harker, Kemmerling or Miller are ordered to report to you I would be glad to get them. I would also like to have Brig. Genl. Wilson for the Cavalry or Wilder if he has been promoted. The Colonels I have in command of Brigades are all efficient men & I would not care to exchange them for worthless Brigadiers." Copy, *ibid.*, Dept. of the Cumberland, Telegrams Sent. *O.R.*, I, xxxii, part 2, 131.

On Jan. 19, Brig. Gen. John A. Rawlins telegraphed to Thomas. "The following dispatch just recieved from Genl Dodge. 'Pulaski Jan 19th   Lt Col BOWERS, A A Genl. A force of mine started from six miles west of Florence yesterday. They found one reg't of Roddy's on this side of the Tennessee foraging. All reports of prisoners scouts and citizens, show that Roddy has and is building flats, hiding them in little Bear Creek, where he now has over twenty. Also in Spring and Town Creek, with one near Courtland. He has several in each of them creeks, and has been over two months building them. Roddy has about 1600 effective men. G. M. DODGE, B. G. You will direct Gen Crook to organize an expedition at once of efficient force, and proceed without delay by the most practicable route, and drive Roddy out from where he now is and destroy all boats and materials he can find, that might in any contingency be used by the enemy in crossing the Tennessee River." Copies, DLC-USG, V, 34, 35; DNA, RG 393, Military Div. of the Miss., Letters Sent. *O.R.*, I, xxxii, part 2, 142.

On Jan. 29, Brig. Gen. Grenville M. Dodge, Pulaski, Tenn., telegraphed to Lt. Col. Theodore S. Bowers. "The rebel conscription is driving to our lines a large number of Union men who furnished substitues and men who have always stood by us and kept out of rebel Army by taking to the mountains—They desire to go into our service and many prominent men among them think they can raise a regiment. Can you authorize me to enlist them and have a Regiment to be known as the 2d Alabama Cavalry—I raised and officered the 1st Alabama Cavalry. at Corinth now 800 strong and I have no doubt I can raise another—These men flock to my lines from this fact" Copy, DNA, RG 393, Military Div. of the Miss., Telegrams Received. *O.R.*, I, xxxii, part 2, 255–56. On the same day, Bowers telegraphed to Dodge. "You are authorized to Enlist and organize the Regiment proposed." Copy, Dodge Papers, IaHA. On Jan. 29, Dodge wrote to Bowers. "I am in receipt of your dispatch authorizing me to recruit and organize the 2d Alabama Cavalry and pursuant thereto have set the men to work. We will soon have a few companies. In order that the Regiment may start on a proper basis and have no trouble in being mustered as recruited, please forward me a written order: unless I have this I will have trouble with Mustering Officers, Paymasters &c. It will be necessary for me to appoint the Officers and they will then after being mustered get Commissions from the President. Put that authority in the order that will empower them to sign requisitions receipts &c as Officers." Copy, DNA, RG 393, 16th Army Corps, Left Wing, Letters Sent. On Jan. 30, Rawlins wrote to Dodge. "Your despatch suggesting the organization of a mounted force sufficient to hunt down and drive the enemy's Cavalry, now threatening our rail-roads in Middle Tennessee, to a point beyond any immediate apprehension of danger is approved of, but owing to the expedition already ordered and in motion our Cavalry and mounted force is so reduced that it will be difficult to get up a force strong enough to cross to the south side of the Tennessee at present. The enemy however must not be permitted to remain on this side. You will therefore collect and organize at once, under a competent officer, all the mounted men possible, of your command, for the purpose suggested in your dispatch and indicated above. The place for them to rendezvous and when & where to move, for the attainment of the desired object, will be left entirely to your own judgement and direction. A copy of your dispatch of the 19th inst., giving information obtained by the force of yours, from six miles west of Florence, the day before, was, on date of receipt, sent to General Thomas with the following directions—Viz.—'You will direct Gen. Crook to organize an expedition at once, of sufficient force, and proceed without delay by the most practicable route and drive Roddy out from where he now is, and destroy all boats and materials he can find, that might, in any contingency, be used by the enemy in crossing the Tennessee river.' No report has yet been had from General Crook. General W. S. Smith was to have moved from Memphis the 25th inst., via Okalona, with a large force of Cavalry; General Sherman moving at the same time, from Vicksburg eastward, a formidable force of all arms and General Logan has already thrown a pontoon bridge across the Tennessee river at Larkins Ferry, over which he will cross in a day or two at farthest, moving towards Rome with all his command, leaving only his rail-road gaurds behind. The forces at Chattanooga are not inactive. From all these expeditions and threatening movements it is hoped much will be accomplished and especially in forcing the Enemy back from within striking distance of our communications." LS, Dodge Papers, IaHA. *O.R.*, I, xxxii, part 2, 264–65. On Feb. 1, Dodge wrote to Rawlins. "I am in receipt of yours of Jan 30th, and so far as driving the enemy south of the Tennessee, I have anticipated your orders. The force sent by Gen Thomas struck the enemy on this side of Tennessee skirmishing with him down the bank, and returned to Huntsville, still leaving the enemy on this side of the River. I immediately fitted up what mounted men I could, preferring to take the chances of getting whipped in the offensive to standing here to be attacked at the pleasure of Roddy. This force moved out under Lieut. Col Phillips Thursday morning struck the enemy Friday morning and continued driving him Friday night. Johnson's Brigade of Roddy's Division recrossed to the south side of the river,—Col Phillips pursuing them so hard that he captured all their trains &.c. some 20. Mule teams, 200. head of Cattle and six hundred head of Sheep, and about 100. head of Horses and Mules. He also burned Foster's factory and Mill which had supplied them, this has cleared the north side of the river. The point we should in my opinion seize upon, as soon as possible and hold is Decatur   it is the best point to obtain information of movements of enemy's force, as well as for our Cavalry to operate from either south, east, or west, and I do not believe this line of communication can be successfully used unless that point is held. I notice what you say in relation to movements of Gen Sherman, telegraphs all news to me and explains the movements of troops—toward Mobile which I telegraphed you yesterday and today. There is no doubt but considerable force has gone in that direction. I think however only one Division and one Brigade have left Johnston. You are aware that I have guarded our line of communication for a long time and I trust when the Campaign opens, Gen Grant will see fit to allow me to take part in it. I am always willing and cheerfully acquiesce in any duties assigned me, but like all others, sometimes have a preference,   I trust you will not consider it as out of place for me to express the above wish,   I judge from your letter, that, the present movement is only temporary, the reports and movements of the enemy look as though Johnson were now south of the Etowah River"   Copies, DNA, RG 393, 16th Army Corps, Letters Sent; *ibid.*, Left Wing, Letters Sent. *O.R.*, I, xxxii, part 1, 120.

On Jan. 30, Dodge sent four telegrams to Bowers. "Two of my Scouts have just got in from Montgomery the other from Atlanta   both report movement and concentration of troops at Mobile—One from Atlanta says no troops have left Johnson but all commands scouting have been moved to Mobile as well as troops from Charleston and North Carolina"   "The Scout from Montgomery says that it was thought there that a movement was on foot from Memphis, Vicksburg and New Orleans against Mobile and it caused a good deal of excitement   whether the report was true or not it has caused a movement of troops there but when they left the force that had gone there was not large"   "One of my Scouts has returned from South side of River   he was at Corinth—it is evacuated and destroyed and Scouting party from Lees Cavalry was there"   "The Enemy in Colbert reserve and at Florence have been driven over the river   we captured several prisoners fifteen wagons and their teams from them"   Copies, DNA, RG 393, Military Div. of the Miss., Telegrams Received; *ibid.*, 16th Army Corps, Left Wing, Letters Sent. The first three are in *O.R.*, I, xxxii, part 2, 266–67. On Jan. 31, Rawlins telegraphed the last to Col. John C. Kelton. Telegram received, DNA, RG 107, Telegrams Collected (Bound); copies, *ibid.*, RG 393, Military Div. of the Miss., Hd. Qrs. Correspondence; DLC-USG, V, 40, 94.

On Feb. 1, Rawlins telegraphed to Maj. Gen. William T. Sherman. "Care General Reid Cairo Ills. who will forward this dispatch without delay to Genl Sherman at Memphis, Vicksburg, or wherever he may be. General Dodge's scouts just in from Montgomery Ala. and Atlanta reports concentration of troops at Mobile from Charleston and North Carolina. A scout from Selma says that one Division from Johnsons Army and Quarters Brigade, have moved west towards Mobile and Meridian, and that it was common talk that Johnson was to fall back behind the Etowah river. The movement of Genl Thomas on the 29th caused the enemy to fall back from Tunnel Hill. Logan has his bridge constructed and is moving across the river at Larkins Ferry, and from there will threaten Rome, while Genl Thomas keeps the attention of the enemy engaged in his front"   Copies, *ibid.*, V, 34, 35; DNA, RG 393, Military Div. of the Miss., Letters Sent. *O.R.*, I, xxxii, part 2, 310–11. On the same day, Rawlins also transmitted the information from Dodge to Thomas. Copies, DLC-USG, V, 34, 35; DNA, RG 393, Military Div. of the Miss., Letters Sent. *O.R.*, I, xxxii, part 2,

308–9. On Feb. 2, Rawlins telegraphed this information to Kelton. Telegram received, DNA, RG 107, Telegrams Collected (Bound); copies, *ibid.*, RG 393, Military Div. of the Miss., Hd. Qrs. Correspondence; DLC-USG, V, 40, 94. *O.R.*, I, xxxii, part 1, 117.

1. On Jan. 17, 1:00 P.M., Asst. Secretary of War Charles A. Dana telegraphed to USG. "Will it be practicable for you to spare Gen Wilson for a time to come here and get the Cavaly Bureau into order and honesty? Of course the Department will make no order which will deprive you of the services of such an officer without your full consent, but the necessity for him is very great and I know of no one else who can perform the duty as well as he. It is a question of saving millions of money and rendering the cavalry arm every where efficient. You can have him again as soon as he gets the machine in good working order, say in sixty days. If you spare him let him come directly. He will be appointed Chief of the Bureau. Please answer by telegraph" Copies, DLC-USG, V, 40, 94; DNA, RG 393, Military Div. of the Miss., Hd. Qrs. Correspondence. *O.R.*, I, xxxii, part 2, 115–16. On Jan. 18, 11:30 A.M., USG telegraphed to Dana. "I will order Genl Wilson at once. No more efficient or better appointment could be made for the place" Telegram received, DNA, RG 107, Telegrams Collected (Bound); copies, *ibid.*, RG 393, Military Div. of the Miss., Hd. Qrs. Correspondence; DLC-USG, V, 40, 94. *O.R.*, I, xxxii, part 2, 131.

To Maj. Gen. George H. Thomas

(Confidential) Head Quarters, Mil. Div. of the Miss.
Nashville Ten. Jan.y, 19th 1864

MAJ. GEN. G. H. THOMAS,
COMD.G DEPT. OF THE CUM.D
GENERAL,

Owing to the presence of Longstreet still in East Tennessee it will be impossible to attempt any movement from present positions whilst he remains. The great number of veteran volunteers now absent, and yet to be furloughed, will be another difficulty in the way of any movement this Winter. Sherman however will be able to collect about 20.000 men from that part of his command now along the Mississippi River available for a movement Eastward from Vicksburg. He expects to have these ready to start about the 24th inst. He will proceed eastward as far as Meredian at least and will thoroughly destroy the roads east & south from there, and if possible will throw troops as far east as Selma, or, if he finds Mobile so far unguarded as to make his force sufficient for the en-

terprise, will go there. To co-operate with this movement you want
to keep up appearances of preparation of an advance from Chattanooga. It may be necessary even to move a column as far as
Lafayette.[1] The time for this advance however would not be before the 30th inst. or when you might learn the enemy were falling
back,   Logan will also be instructed to move at the same time what
force he can from Belfontain towards Rome.

We will want to be ready at the earlyest possible moment in
the Spring for a general advance. I look upon the line for this
Army to secure in its next Campaign to be that from Chattanooga
to Mobile, Atlanta & Montgomery being the important intermediate points. I look upon the Tennessee River and Mobile as being the most practicable points from which to start, and to hold
as bases of supplies after the line is secured. I have so written to
the Gen. in Chief only giving my views more fully, and shall write
to him to-day giving my views of the co-operation we should have
from the Eastern Armies. I shall recommend that no attempt be
made towards Richmond by any of the routes heretofore operated
on, but that a moving force of sixty thousand men be thrown into
New Bern or Suffolk, favoring the latter place, and move out destroying the road as far towards Richmond as possible. Then move
to Raleigh as rapidly as possible, hold that point and open communication with New Bern, even Wilmington. From Raleigh the
enemy's most inland line would be so threatened as to force them
to keep on it a guard that would reduce their Armies in the field
much below our own. Before any part of this programme can be
carried out Longstreet must be driven from East Tennessee. To
do this it may be necessary to send more force from your command.
I write this to give you an idea of what I propose and at the same
time to hear such suggestions as you may have to propose.

> I am Gen very respectfully
> your obt. svt.
> U. S. GRANT
> Maj. Gen. Com

ALS, CSmH. *O.R.*, I, xxxii, part 2, 142–43. On Jan. 30, 1864, Maj. Gen. George
H. Thomas wrote to USG. "As I have seen you since the receipt of your letter

of the 29th [*19th*] inst, I deem it of but little consequence to make any reply to that portion referring to the movements of this Army and the Army of the Tennessee this Spring, as I fully concur with you in the view you take of the best moves for them to make. In reply to the latter portion of your letter, I would suggest, the landing of the Column at Smithfield and vicinity, marching from that point to Sussex Court House, thence to Hick's Ford, on the Petersburg and Roanoke R. R. and thence to Raleigh. By this route the Column would experience but little difficulty in crossing the Nottoway, Maherrin, and Roanoke Rivers and would also find large plantations well supplied with forage and cattle. The roads are also good and well watered. By the lower route or the one you propose the Column would encounter great difficulties in crossing all three of the above named streams because they are bordered by extensive and boggy Swamps. I will also suggest another route which perhaps might be better for a smaller force than either of the other two (say twenty thousand Infantry and ten thousand cavalry)—I would land at Winton on Chowan River, march thence to Northampton Court House & thence to Weldon. This is the shortest practicable route and only presents one difficulty that of crossing Roanoke river—There is still another route, Land at Washington march thence to Raleigh and from Raleigh to Weldon. The Roanoke is one of the finest streams in the country to cover the movements of an army." ALS, DNA, RG 393, Military Div. of the Miss., Letters Received. *O.R.*, I, xxxii, part 2, 264.

1. La Fayette, Ga., approximately twenty-five miles south of Chattanooga.

To Maj. Gen. Henry W. Halleck

Nashville Tenn
11 A. M January 20th 1864

MAJ GENL HALLECK
GENL IN CHIEF

Major General J G Foster is falling back from Dandridge towards ———¹ He can hold the place as long as supplies can be got to him—I shall go to Chattanooga and make every exertion for furnishing the supplies and will send reinforcements if necessary

Under existing circumstances I will not go to St Louis—²

U S. GRANT
Maj. Genl

Telegram received, DNA, RG 107, Telegrams Collected (Bound); copies, *ibid.*, Telegrams Received in Cipher; *ibid.*, RG 393, Military Div. of the Miss., Hd. Qrs. Correspondence; DLC-USG, V, 40, 94. *O.R.*, I, xxxii, part 2, 151.

1. "Knoxville" omitted. On Jan. 18, 1864, Maj. Gen. John G. Foster, Knoxville, telegraphed to USG. "Your telegram rec'd. Gen'ls Park and Granger have been forced to fall back from Danbridge before Longstreet. I shall concentrate on this place. It is impossible to retire further towards Gen'l Thomas without sacrificing one half of our artillery and Forces besides I look upon this point as of too much Value to be abandoned without a desperate fight—If we are besieged here a relieving force can advance up the Tennessee and be well supplied all the way to Loudon by Steamboats on that river—We have a rumor We have a rumor that John Morgan is advancing towards Marysville. I have ordered Gen'l Sturgis to meet him at the crossing of the Little Tennessee" Copy, DNA, RG 393, Military Div. of the Miss., Telegrams Received. *O.R.*, I, xxxii, part 2, 127. On Jan. 19, Foster telegraphed to USG. "The enemy does not press very favorably account of the roads which are very bad I am gathering in all the stores I can and can stand him out here for Ten (10) days more on horse flesh if necessary—Your telegram directing me to keep my army between those of Longstreet and Thomas does not as I understand mean to evacuate Knoxville. I cannot do that without a direct order" Copy, DNA, RG 393, Military Div. of the Miss., Telegrams Received. *O.R.*, I, xxxii, part 2, 138.

2. On Jan. 17, USG, Nashville, had telegraphed to Maj. Gen. Henry W. Halleck. "I am telegraphed from St Louis that my oldest son is lying ill of typhoid Pneumonia. Can I go to see him   answer" Telegram received, DNA, RG 107, Telegrams Collected (Bound). On Jan. 19, 9:10 P.M., Halleck telegraphed to USG. "You have the permission asked. Please keep up your telegraphic communication with East Tennessee." ALS (telegram sent), *ibid.*; telegram received, USG 3. On Jan. 20, Lt. Col. Theodore S. Bowers issued Special Orders No. 15 sending 1st Lt. William M. Dunn, Jr., to St. Louis "for the transaction of business specially confided to him by the Major General Commanding." Copy, DLC-USG, V, 38. Dunn escorted Julia Dent Grant from Louisville to St. Louis. John Y. Simon, ed., *The Personal Memoirs of Julia Dent Grant* (New York, 1975), p. 126.

To Maj. Gen. Henry W. Halleck

Nashville Tenn
Jany 20th 1864

MAJ GEN H W HALLECK
GENL IN CHIEF

I have ordered the cipher operator to give the Washington cipher to Col Comstock. The necessity of this I felt whilst in East Tennessee recieving dispatches I could not read until I returned The operator has received the following dispatch from Col Stager To Capt Bruch[1] Louisville

"Beckwith[2] must not instruct any one in the cipher An order will be issued and sent to you on this subject" I protest against Col Stagers interference I shall be as cautious as he possibly can that improper persons do not get the key to official correspondence

U. S GRANT
Maj Genl

Telegram received, DNA, RG 107, Telegrams Collected (Bound); copies, *ibid.*, RG 393, Military Div. of the Miss., Hd. Qrs. Correspondence; DLC-USG, V, 40, 94. *O.R.*, I, xxxii, part 2, 150. On Jan. 20, 1864, 2:30 P.M., Maj. Gen. Henry W. Halleck telegraphed to USG. "The Secty of War directs that you report by telegraph the facts and circumstances of the act of Lieut Col Comstock in requiring A. C Beckwith, telegraphic cipher clerk, to impart to him (Col Comstock) the secret cipher intrusted to said Beckwith for use exclusively in your correspondence ~~of Genl Grant~~ with the War Dept and Head Qrs of the Army." ALS (telegram sent), DNA, RG 107, Telegrams Collected (Bound); copies, *ibid.*, RG 393, Military Div. of the Miss., Hd. Qrs. Correspondence; DLC-USG, V, 40, 94. *O.R.*, I, xxxii, part 2, 159.

On Jan. 21, 1:10 P.M., USG telegraphed to Halleck. "I ordered Beckwith to give Col Comstock the key to Washington Cipher in order that I might have always someone with me who had it. Whilst at Knoxville I experienced the disadvantage of not having given such an order before. I would recommend that a cipher be used not known to Col Stager or any operators." Telegram received, DNA, RG 107, Telegrams Collected (Bound); copies, *ibid.*, RG 393, Military Div. of the Miss., Hd. Qrs. Correspondence; DLC-USG, V, 40, 94. *O.R.*, I, xxxii, part 2, 161. See letter to Maj. Gen. Henry W. Halleck, Feb. 4, 1864; diary of Cyrus B. Comstock, Jan. 21, 30, 1864, DLC-Cyrus B. Comstock.

1. Samuel Bruch, born in Ohio in 1831, became a telegrapher in 1851, and in the summer of 1861 was the chief operator for the South-western Telegraph Co. in Louisville. Appointed asst. superintendent of the military telegraph, he was nominated as asst. q. m. with the rank of capt. on Jan. 19, 1863, and confirmed on Feb. 19 to date from Aug. 8, 1862.

2. Samuel H. Beckwith enlisted as private, Co. F, 11th Ill., on July 30, 1861, participated in the battles of Fort Donelson and Shiloh, and often worked as an asst. telegrapher. By Sept., 1862, he was assigned to USG's hd. qrs. and was discharged from the 11th Ill. on Feb. 19, 1863, to continue his duties as telegrapher and cipher clerk with USG. On Nov. 8, USG wrote to Capt. Ocran H. Howard. "I would respectfully reccommend for appointment and commission in the Signal Corps. Mr. S. H. Beckwith, Telegraph Operator, to the rank of 1st Lieutenant. I am personally acquainted with Mr Beckwith, he having been on duty with me for more than a year as operator and cypher clerk and know him to be fully qualified for the position. I feel satisfied the service would be benefitted by his appointment." Copies, DLC-USG, V, 34, 35; DNA, RG 393, Military Div. of the Miss., Letters Sent; *ibid.*, RG 111, Letters Received. On Feb. 13, 1864, Howard favorably endorsed a copy of this letter. ES, *ibid.* Beckwith, however, continued as a civilian employee of the U.S. Military Telegraph.

See Beckwith's articles in New York *Sun*, April 6–27, 1913; *New York Times*, May 31, 1914. See also *HRC*, 55-2-1030; DNA, RG 15, Pension Record 659763.

To Maj. Gen. Henry W. Halleck

Head Quarters, Mil. Div. of the Miss.
Nashville Ten. Jan.y 20th 1864

MAJ. GEN. H. W. HALLECK,
GENERAL IN CHIEF, OF THE ARMY,
GENERAL,

From dispatches just received from General Foster the siege of Knoxville is about to be reniewed. It was a great oversight in the first place to have ever permitted Longstreet to come to a stop within the state of Tennessee after the siege was raised. My instructions were full and complete on this subject. Sherman was sent with force sufficient alone to defeat Longstreet, and notwithstanding the long distance his troops had marched proposed to go on and carry out my instructions in full. Gen. Burnside was sanguine that no stop would be made by the enemy in the Valley. Sherman then proposed to leave any amount of force Burnside thought might be necessary to make his position perfectly secure. He deemed two Divisions ample. These were left numbering about 11.000 men for duty, besides Elliotts Cavalry Division of about 3,000 present effective men. All this force is still with Foster.—I regretted from the start that Longstreet was permitted to come to a halt in the valley, but was in hopes the judgement of Gen. Burnside would prove correct. Gen. Wilson & Mr. Dana were both present at the interview between Gens. Sherman & Burnside on this subject and can give all the reasons assigned for the course pursued.—My official report will be accompanied by all the dispatches and orders given to Burnside & Sherman, but I write this now more particularly to show that the latter named officer is in no wise to blame for the existing state of affairs in East Tennessee. —I feel no alarm for the safety of East Tennessee, but the presence of Longstreet has been embarassing in forcing me to keep more troops there than would have been otherwise necessary, and in preventing other movements taking place. It has also taxed some of the most loyal people in the United States to support a cause they detest.

> I am General, very respectfully
> your obt. svt.
> U. S. GRANT
> Maj. Gen.

ALS, Schoff Collection, MiU-C. *O.R.*, I, xxxii, part 2, 149–50.

To Maj. Gen. George H. Thomas

Nashville January 20th 1864.

MAJOR GENERAL GEO H THOMAS
CHATTANOOGA

General Foster telegraphs that he is being forced back from Dandridge towards Knoxville. John Morgan is also said to be advancing from towards Johnstons Army. If Foster should be beseiged it will be necessary to send a force from Chattanooga to his relief. They can subsist on the country as far as the Hiwassee in such a contingency, and send forward to Loudon by boats all the supplies possible.

> U S GRANT
> Major General

Telegram, copies, DLC-USG, V, 34, 35; DNA, RG 393, Military Div. of the Miss., Letters Sent; *ibid.*, Dept. of the Cumberland, Miscellaneous Letters Received. Printed as sent at noon in *O.R.*, I, xxxii, part 2, 151.

On Jan. 20, 1864, USG twice telegraphed to Maj. Gen. John G. Foster. "I will go to Chattanooga and do all in my power to help you out, by pushing forward supplies and reenforcements if necessary" "Should you be beseiged in Knoxville I will strain every nerve to get sufficient force from Chattanooga to relieve you." Copies, DLC-USG, V, 34, 35; DNA, RG 393, Military Div. of the Miss., Letters Sent. *O.R.*, I, xxxii, part 2, 150, 151.

Also on Jan. 20, USG telegraphed to Brig. Gen. Robert Allen. "My visit to Louisville has to be deferred on account of news from the front, making it necessary for me to go there. Is it possible to get additional rolling stock forward? Foster must be supplied almost exclusively henceforth by this route." Copies,

DLC-USG, V, 34, 35; DNA, RG 393, Military Div. of the Miss., Letters Sent. *O.R.*, I, xxxii, part 2, 155. On Jan. 21, Allen, Louisville, telegraphed to USG. "There are Six locomotives & one hundred and fifty Cars at Jeffersonville which it has been impossible to get over the river. Not a moment will be lost in crossing them when the ice will permit   we hope in four or five days"   Copy, DNA, RG 393, Military Div. of the Miss., Telegrams Received.

On Jan. 20, Lt. Col. Theodore S. Bowers, Nashville, telegraphed to Col. Lewis B. Parsons. "Gen. Grant intended to start for Louisville today but has changed his mind and will go to chattanooga tomorrow"   Telegram received, Parsons Papers, IHi. On the same day, Parsons, Louisville, wrote to USG. "General Allen has shown me your dispatch relative to more Railroad Machinery. I enclose a copy of a report made by me, and a general order of the Quartermaster General's—an extract of which I have marked and which I beg you will peruse. I have as yet met no persons who did not concur in the propriety and expediency of my suggestions. I think I do not overestimate the importance of the subject. The amount to be expended is trifling compared with saving a delay of your Army for a week. May you not possibly require in the next six months ten (10) or twenty (20) Engines and three or four hundred (400) Cars. If so would it not be well to have them all ready, say at Indianapolis,—of good quality—so you can make them available in two days. I have taken no pains to get my suggestions carried into effect, but from the concurrence of better judges then I am, I think if the attention of the Sec'y of War or Quartermaster General was called to it they would at once direct Col. McCullum to put the thing in motion   If so it would in addition to other benefits relieve Railroads and the Quarter-masters Department of great and frequent annoyances. I was disappointed in learning you were not coming up here, as I desired to consult you relative to some plan of putting an effectual stop to frequent and gross impositions upon soldiers by Steamboats, and also as to a plan for regulating Pilots who are now demanding 400 & 500 Dollars per month each. I have sought to correct these difficulties without troubling you, but I believe nothing but military power can correct the evil." LS, DNA, RG 393, Military Div. of the Miss., Letters Received.

Also on Jan. 20, USG telegraphed to Maj. Gen. John A. Logan. "Build bridges from Huntsville to Decatur with all dispatch, using your Corps for the purpose. If you can impress Negroes for cutting wood, ties &c do so"   Copies, DLC-USG, V, 34, 35; DNA, RG 393, Military Div. of the Miss., Letters Sent. *O.R.*, I, xxxii, part 2, 154. See letter to Maj. Gen. John A. Logan, Jan. 24, 1864.

To Isaac N. Morris

Nashville Tennessee,
January 20 1864

Hon. I. N. Morris,
Dear Sir.

Your letter of the 29th of December I did not see until two days ago. I receive many such but do not answer. Yours however, is written in such a kindly spirit, and as you ask for an answer confidentially, I will not withhold it. Allow me to say however that I am not a politician, never was and hope never to be, and could not write a political letter. My only desire is to serve the country in her present trials. To do this efficiently it is necessary to have the confidance of the Army and the people. I know no way to better to secure this end than by a faithful performance of my duties. So long as I hold my present position I do not believe that I have the right to critizise the policy or orders of those above me, or to give utterance to views of my own except to the authorities at Washington, through the General in Chief of the Army. In this respect I know I have proven myself a "good soldier." In your letter you say that I have it in my power to be the next President! This is the last thing in the world I desire. I would regard such a consummation as being highly unfortunate for myself if not for the country. Through Providence I have attained to more than I ever hoped, and with the position I now hold in the Regular Army, if allowed to retain it will be more than satisfied. I certainly shall never shape a sentiment, or the expression of a thought with the view of being a candidate for office. I scarcely know the inducement that could be held out to me to accept office, and unhesitatingly say that I infinitely prefer my present position to that of any civil office within the gift of the people.

This is a private letter to you, not intended for others to see or read, because I want to avoid being heard from by the public except through acts in the performance of my legitimate duties.

I have the honor to be
Very respectfully
Your obdt servt
U S GRANT

Copies, USG 3; IHi. Isaac N. Morris, son of Jesse R. Grant's friend U.S. Senator Thomas Morris of Ohio, practiced law in Quincy, Ill., and served as Democratic U.S. Representative (1857–61). While promoting USG as a presidential prospect, Morris received a lengthy letter of Jan. 25, 1864, from Jesse Grant, which concluded: "I am fully satisfied that he would not be a candidate for the Presidency under any circumstances. He went into the Service avowedly to contribute his mite towards putting down this wicked rebellion without having any political ambitions after this was accomplished. He is now a Major General in the regular army, and will doubtless be placed at the head of it. And I believe that is the extent of his ambition." Jesse R. Grant, *In the Days of My Father General Grant* (New York and London, 1925), pp. 53–55. Other portions of this letter were incorporated verbatim in Morris's biography of USG, published anonymously in the Washington, D. C., *National Intelligencer*, March 21, 1864. On March 22, Morris wrote to USG. "I send you herewith a dozen papers containging my sketch of your life, character and services. You can have more if you desire them. My object in preparing the memoir was not to make it too long or too short, so that it would do you justice and could be read at one sitting without wearying. I have sent copies of the paper to your Father, Mother Lady, at St Louis, friends in Ohio &c. There are some typographical errors in the publication, and doubtless may be some in the details, but I hope you may find it in the main correct. I was as careful as my limited means of acquiring the facts, and time would allow. Gentlemen who have read the sketch seem highly delighted with it. If it needs any correcting please let me know   I wrote it because I had never met with any thing in print which I thought did you justice" ALS, USG 3. See letters to Jesse Root Grant, Feb. 20, March 1, 1864.

To Maj. Gen. Henry W. Halleck

Chattanooga Tenn
5 7 P M Jany 22/64

Maj Gen Halleck
Gen in Chief

   There is no objection to removing trade restrictions in all Kentucky East of the Tennessee River   I would advise no change in Tennessee until Longstreet is driven out. If Sherman Expedition proves successful I would then see no objection to the removal of restrictions [in] the whole state and in West Kentucky

U S Grant
Maj Genl

Telegram received, DNA, RG 107, Telegrams Collected (Bound); copies, *ibid.*, Telegrams Received in Cipher; (misdated Jan. 20, 1864) *ibid.*, RG 393, Military Div. of the Miss., Hd. Qrs. Correspondence; DLC-USG, V, 40, 94. *O.R.*, III, iv, 42. On Jan. 21, Maj. Gen. Henry W. Halleck telegraphed to USG. "The Secty of the Treasury proposes to remove restrictions on trade in Kentucky & part of Tennessee. I presume there is no objection in regard to Kentucky. Please report if in what part, if any, of Tennessee these restrictions can be removed with safety." ALS (telegram sent), DNA, RG 107, Telegrams Collected (Bound). *O.R.*, III, iv, 41. On the same day, 1:00 A.M., Maj. Gen. George H. Thomas, Chattanooga, telegraphed to USG. "Until the people of Tennessee by their voluntary act return to the Union, I do not think it prudent to remove the restrictions on trade at any point where trade is not at present permitted." Copy, DNA, RG 393, Dept. of the Cumberland, Telegrams Sent.

To Maj. Gen. Henry W. Halleck

Chattanooga Tenn
Jany 22nd 1864 8 P M

MAJ GEN H W HALLECK
GEN IN CHIEF

Genl Fosters last dispatch states that he thinks Longstreet has not been reinforced from Ewells corps   Foster is now withdrawing from Dandridge and Strawberry Plains to cross at Knoxville and move east on south side French Broad[1]—I have instructed him to get ready and attack as soon as possible.[2] With Anderson as Manager of Rail Road we can never accumulate supplies nor even supply full rations from day to day—[3]

U S GRANT
Maj Genl Comdg

Telegram received, DNA, RG 107, Telegrams Collected (Bound); copies, *ibid.*, Telegrams Received in Cipher; *ibid.*, RG 393, Military Div. of the Miss., Hd. Qrs. Correspondence; DLC-USG, V, 40, 94. *O.R.*, I, xxxii, part 2, 171–72.

1. On Jan. 20, 1864, Maj. Gen. John G. Foster, Knoxville, telegraphed to USG. "No evidence has reached me to prove that either Ewell or Hill A. P. have reenforced Longstreet although scouts and deserters report troops from both Corps. I cannot be convinced that that he has received anything but the 3rd Div. of his Corps. I am doubtful of his intention to attack us here. He will certainly meet with a defeat if he does. I am now moving Cav. up the south side of the French Broad River, to secure the forage grounds in that section. As soon as the Infantry can retire from strawberry Plains after first taking some of the bridges and sending the material here to be used in the bridge at this place I shall send the 4th Corps and the 23rd Corps to forage up the French Broad retaining the 9th Corps as garrison of this place Lenoir and Loudon" Copies (2), DNA, RG 393, Dept. of the Ohio (Cincinnati), Telegrams Sent. Printed as sent at noon in *O.R.*, I, xxxii, part 2, 151. On Jan. 21, Foster telegraphed to USG. "I sent an application for sick leave to Genl Halleck a few days since. I do not however wish to leave until everything is quiet" Telegram received, DNA, RG 393, Dept. of Mo., Telegrams Received; copies, *ibid.*, Military Div. of the Miss., Telegrams Received.
    2. See following telegram.

3. On Jan. 15, USG telegraphed to Maj. Gen. George H. Thomas. "Mr Anderson seems to be employed all his time about Louisville and away from where it seems to me, his duties are. If Col McCallum is a practical railroad man, I will appoint him to supersede Anderson, or place Gen Webster as General Superintendent of the Military Division and McCallum Superintendent for the Department of the Cumberland." Copies, DLC-USG, V, 34, 35; DNA, RG 393, Military Div. of the Miss., Letters Sent; (dated Jan. 16, 11:00 A.M.) *ibid.*, Dept. of the Cumberland, Telegrams Received. On Jan. 16, 2:00 P.M., Thomas telegraphed to USG. "Mr Anderson arrived here last night—I have had a conversation with him in which he has assured me that he has things as far advanced as is possible   I have told Col McCullum to call & see you as soon as he can get affairs in order here   He appears to me to be a practical Rail Road man   Since forwarding my report to you on the prospects of the road Genl Halleck has directed that a report be made to him before making any change"   Telegram received, *ibid.*, Dept. of the Tenn., Telegrams Received; copies, *ibid.*, Dept. of the Cumberland, Telegrams Sent; *ibid.*, Military Div. of the Miss., Telegrams Received. *O.R.*, I, xxxii, part 2, 111.

On Jan. 16, USG telegraphed to John B. Anderson. "Proper details of Cars must be made for supplying troops West of Stevenson. I have no disposition to take military control over railroad employees, but if a different spirit is not shown by them and more disposition to accomodate I will be compelled to do so and to punish some of them severely." Copies, DLC-USG, V, 34, 35; DNA, RG 393, Military Div. of the Miss., Letters Sent. On Jan. 19, Anderson telegraphed to USG. "Your dispatch recd. I have made provision for carrying all supplies loaded for Memphis and Charleston rail road. A conductor who acted badly was promptly discharged. If any neglect of duty on the part of any Employee of the Rail-road department is reported to me or to Mr. Thomson Supt. at Nashville it will be immediately corrected and the offending party discharged"   Copy, *ibid.*, Telegrams Received. On Jan. 24, Anderson telegraphed to USG. "Your dispatch rec'd. I will arrange with Co'l McCallum as to proper distribution of his force"   Copy, *ibid.*

On Jan. 24, 11:00 A.M., Maj. Gen. Henry W. Halleck telegraphed to USG. "The Secty of War authorises you to suspend or remove Mr. Anderson as supt of Railroads, if you deem it necessary for the public service. Your letter of the 15th is recieved. I will wait your next before answering." ALS (telegram sent), *ibid.*, RG 107, Telegrams Collected (Bound); copies, *ibid.*, RG 393, Military Div. of the Miss., Telegrams Received; *ibid.*, Hd. Qrs. Correspondence; DLC-USG, V, 40, 94. *O.R.*, I, xxxii, part 2, 192. On Jan. 25, 10:30 A.M., Secretary of War Edwin M. Stanton telegraphed to USG. "You are authorised to remove J B Anderson or any one else connected with rail road transportation whenever in your opinion the service will be improved and to appoint any one to their places who in your judgment will perform the service better." ALS (telegram sent), DNA, RG 107, Telegrams Collected (Bound). *O.R.*, I, xxxii, part 2, 213.

On Jan. 25, Brig. Gen. John A. Rawlins telegraphed to Thomas. "Please order Col D C McCallum Superintendent, Military Railroads here at once. Have him come up on to days train"   Copies, DLC-USG, V, 34, 35; DNA, RG 393, Military Div. of the Miss., Letters Sent. On the same day, Thomas telegraphed to Rawlins. "Co'l. McCallum has just left for Knoxville to ascertain the condition of that R. R. and make arrangements to push forward the work as fast as possible—He will return by first boat when I will give him your order—The

M & C R. R. have been assigned their positions and will be at work as soon as possible" Copy, *ibid.*, Telegrams Received. On the same day, Rawlins telegraphed to USG. "Co'l. McCullum has been ordered to report at once. Shall I assign him to duty when he arrives" Copy, *ibid.* On Jan. 25, USG, Louisville, telegraphed to Rawlins. "Make the order assigning McCallum and relieving the other, but do not do so until McCallum is ready to assume the duties   Ascertain when he can take charge." Copies, DLC-USG, V, 34, 35; DNA, RG 393, Military Div. of the Miss., Letters Sent.

On Jan. 28, Rawlins telegraphed to Thomas. "General Grant is authorized by the Secretary of War to relieve Mr Anderson in the superintendence of Military Rail roads and desires to do so by the appointment of Col McCallum   If he has not returned from Knoxville, can you not hasten him by sending the order directing him to report here, to Knoxville, and if so will you not please do it? I am directed to make the necessary order the moment he is ready to assume the superintendence of the roads." Copies, *ibid.* *O.R.*, I, xxxii, part 2, 248. On Feb. 1, Col. Daniel C. McCallum, Loudon, Tenn., telegraphed to USG. "Am here waiting boat   will report to you at Nashville as soon as possible" Copy, DNA, RG 393, Military Div. of the Miss., Telegrams Received. On Feb. 2, USG, Louisville, telegraphed to Rawlins. "Just arrived   will not go to Nashville until Friday unless absolutely necessary   has McCallum taken Charge of railroads yet. Dispatch me all important news." Copy, *ibid.* On Feb. 4, Lt. Col. Theodore S. Bowers issued General Orders No. 3 replacing Anderson with McCallum. Copies, DLC-USG, V, 14; DNA, RG 393, Military Div. of the Miss., General Orders. *O.R.*, I, xxxii, part 3, 329.

On Feb. 8, McCallum wrote to USG. "I have the honor to state that serious embarassment is caused by the absence of certain papers, and fact, in the posession of Mr J. B. Anderson late Genl. Manager of Railroads in the Mil. Div. of the Miss. I have not been able to ascertain the number of cars purchased, delivered, or in use, of contracts made for Rolling stock, and materials, and other information, upon which to base prompt action. I would therefore most respectfully ask the adoption, at the earliest practicable moment, of such measures, as will enable me to proceed understandingly." LS, DNA, RG 92, Military Railroads, Nashville, Letters Sent by McCallum (Press). On Feb. 9, USG telegraphed to Brig. Gen. Robert Allen. "Will you please have Mr Anderson railroad manager sent here to turn over to Colonel McCallum his books statements, contracts &c" Copies, DLC-USG, V, 34, 35; DNA, RG 393, Military Div. of the Miss., Letters Sent. On the same day, Allen telegraphed to USG. "Mr. Anderson is not in the City. I am told that he has gone to Washington" Copy, *ibid.*, Telegrams Received. On Feb. 12, USG telegraphed to Allen. "I understand J B Anderson is in Louisville   Please send him here to turn over to Col McCallum statements of contracts he has made. If he refuses, ask the Secretary of War to order him" Copies, DLC-USG, V, 34, 35; DNA, RG 393, Military Div. of the Miss., Letters Sent.

On Feb. 12, USG telegraphed to Halleck. "Col McCallum applies for Lt. Col. Wright Comd'g Ft. Woodbury Va. to assist him in railroad management. Can he be detailed?" Telegram received (dated Feb. 13), *ibid.*, RG 107, Telegrams Collected (Bound); copies (dated Feb. 12), *ibid.*, RG 393, Military Div. of the Miss., Hd. Qrs. Correspondence; DLC-USG, V, 40, 94. See *O.R.*, I, xxxii, part 2, 365. See also *ibid.*, pp. 420–21.

On Feb. 23, McCallum wrote to USG. "I take the liberty of enclosing herewith, copy of communication to the Secretary of War, which will explain itself, and permit me to add that I find myself here with heavy and daily increasing responsibilities, and without the facilities, requiring time to create, which ordinary foresight, and earnest effort should have secured long ago. I consider Mr Andersons connection with any Military Railroad, as nothing short of disaster to the country, and the cause." ALS, DNA, RG 393, Military Div. of the Miss., Letters Received. *O.R.*, I, xxxii, part 2, 454. McCallum enclosed a copy of a letter of Feb. 23 addressed to Stanton denouncing Anderson. Copy, DNA, RG 393, Military Div. of the Miss., Letters Received. Dated Feb. 20 in *O.R.*, I, xxxii, part 2, 454–55.

To Maj. Gen. John G. Foster

Chattanooga 22d January 1864

MAJ GENL J. G. FOSTER
KNOXVILLE

Facilities will be given you of getting supplies either by transferring boats to your Quartermaster or having them used for your benefit. Move forward and attack Longstreet as soon as you can and if more troops are required send to me for them. Do you not think it practicable to collect Wilcox's forces and move them by Jonesville[1] to Abingdon? If they could destroy the road from Abingdon to Saltville, it would be worth taking a great risk.

U. S. GRANT
Major General

Telegram, copies, DLC-USG, V, 34, 35; DNA, RG 393, Military Div. of the Miss., Letters Sent. *O.R.*, I, xxxii, part 2, 173, (misdated Jan. 24, 1864, 7:30 P.M.) 193. On Jan. 22, 3:30 P.M., Maj. Gen. John G. Foster telegraphed to USG. "Genl Sturgis who is with all the Cavalry opposite Dandridge reports the roads almost impassible and the forage nearly gone this side of Sevierville. These facts and the pressure of the enemy has forced me to order the Fourth Corps to march to protect the R R and Loudon and Kingston   The Twenty third Corps will be placed in town with the nineth in supporting distance   The enemy presses vigorously and is about seven miles from town. Our Drovers have cowardly abandoned their droves one of which three hundred cattle has already been captured   there is danger that a drove of two hundred hogs will also fall into their hands although I have sent active parties to endevor to save it. I am now satisfied that Longstreet has been considerably reinforced but not largely enough I think to warrant his renewing the seige of this place" Telegram received, DNA, RG 393, Dept. of Mo., Telegrams Received; copy, *ibid.*, Military Div. of the Miss., Telegrams Received. *O.R.*, I, xxxii, part 2, 173.

Also on Jan. 22, USG telegraphed to Foster. "Order down to report to General Thomas, the 15th Pennsylvania and 10th Ohio Cavalry. If more of Elliotts Cavalry can be spared send them." Copies, DLC-USG, V, 34, 35; DNA, RG 393, Military Div. of the Miss., Letters Sent.

On Jan. 24, Foster telegraphed to USG. "Your dispatch of the 22d is recd. also one without date ordering an advance. I have telegraphed the results of the past weeks movements. The whole force is now distributed to their positions to obtain forage and the rest which men and animals so much need. The roads are very bad and after a rain will become impassable—The animals are in a very bad condition; Very little of the Artillery can be taken forward at this time on a march—The bread thus far recd from Chattanooga has not amounted to one tenth of the rations. We now have only enough for the hospitals—I make the above representation in justice to the men who have already suffered much and would earnestly urge that they be allowed some weeks to rest" Copy, *ibid.*, Telegrams Received. *O.R.*, I, xxxii, part 2, 194.

1. Jonesville, Va., six miles north of the Tenn. border and approximately seventy miles northeast of Knoxville.

To Maj. Gen. Henry W. Halleck

Chattanooga Tenn
12 M Jany 24th 1864

MAJ GEN HALLECK
GEN'L IN CHIEF

I would respectfully ask authority to detail General Butterfield[1] [to] enlist and organize an [*African*] army Corps. Colored troops now raised in Tenn. can be taken as a commencement and from Tennessee Alabama and Georgia The balance can be raised

U. S GRANT
Major General

Telegram received, DNA, RG 107, Telegrams Collected (Bound); copies, *ibid.*, Telegrams Received in Cipher; *ibid.*, RG 393, Military Div. of the Miss., Hd. Qrs. Correspondence; DLC-USG, V, 40, 94. On Jan. 25, 1864, 3:50 P.M., Maj. Gen. Henry W. Halleck telegraphed to USG. "The organization of colored troops in the west is under the direction of Adjt Genl Thomas. The secty of war declines assigning Genl Butterfield for that duty. when regiments are organized and assigned to your command you can place them under any officer you deem proper." ALS (telegram sent), DNA, RG 107, Telegrams Collected (Bound); copies, *ibid.*, RG 94, Letters Received, 62A 1864; *ibid.*, RG 393, Military Div. of the Miss., Hd. Qrs. Correspondence; DLC-USG, V, 40, 94.

1. Daniel Butterfield, born in N. Y. in 1831, graduated from Union College in 1849. During the 1850s, he was superintendent of the eastern branch of the American Express Co. and col., 12th N. Y. Militia. Commissioned col., 12th N. Y., as of May 2, 1861, and appointed brig. gen. as of Sept. 7, maj. gen. as of Nov. 29, 1862, he participated in many battles of the Army of the Potomac as a div. and corps commander, was severely wounded during the battle of Gettysburg, and was chief of staff for Maj. Gen. Joseph Hooker during the battle of Chattanooga.

To Maj. Gen. John G. Foster

Chattanooga January 24th 1864.

MAJ GENL J. G. FOSTER
KNOXVILLE

Can you not now organize a Cavalry force to work its way past Longstreet south of him, to get into his rear, and destroy railroad and trains? Or cannot Wilcox do this from the North? Either this should be done, or battle given where Longstreet now is. Let me know what you think about this.

U S GRANT
Major General

Telegram, copies, DLC-USG, V, 34, 35; DNA, RG 393, Military Div. of the Miss., Letters Sent. Printed as sent at 3:00 P.M. in *O.R.*, I, xxxii, part 2, 193.
On Jan. 24, 1864, USG telegraphed to Maj. Gen. Henry W. Halleck. "Foster telegraphs that Longstreet is still advancing towards Knoxville I have directed him to [get] his cavalry to Longstreets rear [or] give battle if necessary I will send Thomas with additional troops [to] insure Longstreets being driven from the state" Telegram received, DNA, RG 107, Telegrams Collected (Bound); copies, *ibid.*, Telegrams Received in Cipher; *ibid.*, RG 393, Military Div. of the Miss., Hd. Qrs. Correspondence; DLC-USG, V, 40, 94. *O.R.*, I, xxxii, part 2, 192.
On the same day, USG telegraphed to Maj. Gen. John G. Foster. "I go north to night. Should you require aid either in troops or supplies, call on Genl Thomas and myself. Gen Thomas has instructions to supply you." Copies, DLC-USG, V, 34, 35; DNA, RG 393, Military Div. of the Miss., Letters Sent.
On Jan. 25, Foster telegraphed frequently to USG, first at 8:00 A.M. "Cumberland Gap is now garrissoned by three old regiments under Gen'l Gerrard—The nine months men of Gen'l Wilcox have gone in part and the remainder about going—Gen'l. Wilcox is on duty here in the 9th Corps. I will write to Gen'l. Gerrard and order him to make the move if practicable" At 8:30 A.M. "I will issue the orders for the 15th Penn. and the 10th Ohio Cavalry

—Col. Palmers with the 15th is now in the front engaged with the enemy and is valuable from his superior Knowledge of the Country the roads location of supplies—The Regiment can illy be spared at this time but will nevertheless be sent as soon as practicable in obedience to the order—" At 3:00 P.M. "Your Despatch of 3 P. M. on the 24th is received   I have directed General Sturgis to attempt the movement that you suggest but thus far he has found it impossible to execute it from the opposition met with and the worn down condition of his horses   I will now urge it again. I have also ordered Gen'l. Gerrard to attempt a raid from Cumberland Gap but this will be interrupted by the raid the Enemys Cavalry is now making on Tazwell. I do not think it practicable at this time to advance in force & attack Longstreet at Morristown"   Copies, *ibid.*, Telegrams Received. *O.R.*, I, xxxii, part 2, 208–10. At 10:00 P.M. "I regret to report that I am still suffering with my wounded leg & unable to take the field. The sooner I obtain relief by an operation the sooner I can return to active duty   Cannot I leave now for this purpose   Genl Parke will remain in Command"   Telegram received, DNA, RG 393, Dept. of Mo., Telegrams Received; copy, *ibid.*, Military Div. of the Miss., Telegrams Received. *O.R.*, I, xxxii, part 2, 208.

Also on Jan. 25, Maj. Gen. George H. Thomas telegraphed to USG. "The following dispatch recd. from Genl. Foster by telegraph—24. 11. a m   'The enemy has retired and I am now posting the tired troops in cantonment where they may rest a little before the Spring campaign. The Fourth Corps is ordered to hold Kingston. Loudon and half of the R. R. line to this place, with a brigade at Marysville to collect supplies &c. (Signed) J. G. FOSTER Maj. Genl.' I will push forward the work on the R. Rd. as rapidly as possible and also move up Stanley's Division to the position between Chickamauga and Hiawassee at once." Copies, DNA, RG 393, Dept. of the Cumberland, Telegrams Sent; *ibid.*, Military Div. of the Miss., Telegrams Received. *O.R.*, I, xxxii, part 2, 208.

After USG left Chattanooga, Foster continued to telegraph him there. Some messages were forwarded to Halleck by Brig. Gen. John A. Rawlins, who also answered Foster. Copies, DNA, RG 393, Military Div. of the Miss., Telegrams Received. *O.R.*, I, xxxii, part 1, 41–44, 130–31; *ibid.*, I, xxxii, part 2, 183–84, 217–18, 253, 271, 319. During this period, USG decided to relieve Foster. See telegram to Maj. Gen. Henry W. Halleck, Jan. 27, 1864.

On Feb. 28, Foster, Baltimore, wrote to USG. "Please to accept my hearty congratulations upon your promotion, which, the papers announce, has taken place. I beg to say that it will always give me pleasure to aid you in any way in my power. Although I was able to do very little in East. Tenn. in consequence of being hors-de-combat, yet I know that I can do good service when in proper trim. I have hopes of being able to return to duty in three or four weeks. Prof. Smith has not found it advisable to perform a surgical operation, and expects to reduce the inflamation in the knee-joint very soon. I shall be ready for anything and will cheerfully go wherever ordered, although I think that I can do better service in an expedition to move from the Coast into N. C., than in any other way. I wrote to Gen. Halleck, after I arrived, concerning this Project; but as soon as I learned that you had written, I sent a note of apology for thus volunteering suggestions. I am very anxious to obtain high rank in the Regular Army. I presume Gen. Sherman will fill the Major-Generalship that you vacate, for he certainly deserves it. This will make a vacancy in the Brigadiers. Cannot you render me the great favor to recommend me for the appointment? I would not ask it if I did not intend to deserve it. As I intend to remain in the service, always, promotion is very important to me, to give me rank after the war is over, and a sufficient support for my family." ALS, USG 3. On April 23, USG endorsed a letter in which Foster reported himself ready for duty. "Respy. returned to the Secretary of War. Gen'l Foster is a good officer, but I do not believe his health would permit him to perform active service in the field at present—Further all command to which his rank could entitle him are filled and the officers now on duty could not be displaced without detriment to the Spring Campaign. I would therefore recommend that General Foster be assigned to the first Department in the North that may become vacant." Copy, DLC-USG, V, 58.

To Maj. Gen. John A. Logan

Head-Quarters ~~Chief of Artillery~~, Mil. Div. of the Miss.
~~department of the cumberland~~.
Chattanooga Jan. 24th *1864.*

MAJ. GEN. J. A. LOGAN,
COMD.G 15TH A. C.
GENERAL,

General Sherman is collecting a force at Vicksburg with which to move Eastward. That force he expected to have assembled by this day, the 24th, and will move as soon as possible, say by the 28th or 30th. It will be necessary for Gen. Thomas and yourself to keep up a threatened advance on Rome with the view of retaining on this front as large a force of the enemy as possible. Gen. Thomas has his directions. You will push the work on your pontoon bridge with all dispatch. Collect such force as can be spared from the railroad, leaving that perfectly guarded however, and cross the river. From there use any Cavalry, ~~y~~ or Mounted Infantry, you may have in reconnoitering to the front, collecting information, a knowledge of the roads &c.—It is not expected to move forward at this time, but the movements of the enemy might change this. By a free interchange of information obtained by Gen. Thomas and yourself, and each reporting what you learn to me, an advance can be ordered if it should prove necessary. Should Gen. Thomas inform you at any time that he is going to make a reconnoisance to the front, and ask you to move in co-operation, do so without waiting further orders from Div. Hd Qrs. Report the fact however.

> I am Gen. very respectfully
> your obt. svt.
> U. S. GRANT
> Maj. Gen. Com

ALS, CtY. *O.R.*, I, xxxii, part 2, 198–99. See letter to Maj. Gen. William T. Sherman, Jan. 15, 1864.

On Jan. 23, 1864, Brig. Gen. John A. Rawlins, Chattanooga, had telegraphed to Maj. Gen. John A. Logan. "Where is your pontoon bridge, and what is the condition of the roads South of the river in the direction of Rome. Please answer to this place immediately." Copies, DLC-USG, V, 34, 35; DNA, RG 393, Military Div. of the Miss., Letters Sent. On the same day, Logan, Huntsville, Ala., telegraphed to Rawlins. "My ponton boats are up Mud Creek near Bellefonte. It has been impassible to get proper material to lay a bridge as yet. Am now having it sawed at Flint River. The roads South of Tenn River are represented as being in very bad condition   no forage south of the river for miles—Cavalry might by quick marches strike supplies within a day and a halfs march from river" Copy, *ibid.*, Telegrams Received. *O.R.*, I, xxxii, part 2, 189.

On Jan. 25, Logan telegraphed to Rawlins. "I will start on the line of R. R. to Scottsboro in the morning, have rec'd. Gen'l Grants conversation   how long will Gen'l Grant be at Chattanooga. Can I come through at once and see him on business directly connected with matters that are suggested in his communications   it will make no delay in preparations. Answer to this point and Scottsboro so that I may get it—"   Copy, DNA, RG 393, Military Div. of the Miss., Telegrams Received.

On Jan. 27, Rawlins telegraphed to Logan. "It is important that you commence your movement in pursuance of previous instructions at once   if you are likely to be delayed on account of lumber for your pontoon bridge send to Chattanooga ~~unless~~ where it can be obtained   shall have it rafted down. Sherman moved on the 25th inst   communicate freely with General Thomas   do you return to Scotts boro this Evening?   if so I will come out   Please answer" Telegram received, *ibid.*, RG 94, War Records Office, Dept. of the Tenn. *O.R.*, I, xxxii, part 2, 234.

On Jan. 29, Logan telegraphed to Rawlins. "The bridge is done and will move forward in a day or two" Copy, DNA, RG 393, Military Div. of the Miss., Telegrams Received. On the same day, Logan telegraphed to Lt. Col. Theodore S. Bowers. "The H'd Quarters of the Corps after to day will be moved to Huntsville. Dispatches for my Staff however will reach me at this point. I am just starting to Larkinsville Ferry which is off the road eight or ten miles   a courier is left here" Copy, *ibid.* On Feb. 1, Logan, Scottsboro, Ala., telegraphed to Bowers. "Expedition started from Larkins landing this morning   rebel Cavalry Heavy force removing from Vicinity of Rome in this direction" Copy, *ibid.* On Feb. 5, Logan telegraphed to Rawlins. "A portion of my forces under Brig Genl Morgan L. Smith advanced yesterday to Lebanon and Rawlinsville capturing about three officers and about 40 privates   many deserters are coming in daily for Refugees are crossing at Larkins Landing constantly. The country south to Coosa River is barren of any subsistence" Copy, *ibid.* On Feb. 6, Logan telegraphed to Rawlins. "Last night my troops under Gen'l M. L. Smith returned to the river having gone in the direction of Rome as far as they could on account of forage &c. They captured some 50 odd prisoners destroyed all the Nitre works at Rowlinsville. Wheelers force is at Gansden quiet. A force of the enemy have concentrated at Kingston & quite a number have passed through Montgomery to Mobile some 3 weeks since. There is no forage or subsistence after leaving the Tenn until you reach the Coosa. What is there is being removed as rapidly as possible. I have a force at the river and will send out again soon in that direction. I think the object has been accomplished however. I leave for Huntsville this morning and push the work on the road between Huntsville and Decatur as rapidly as possible. A great many Alabamians in the Country desire to enlist in the Ala. regt. they have shown themselves very useful men. If I had the Authority I could fill the regt. and use them to a good purpose. They are best Scouts I ever saw and know the Country well clear to Montgomery—My Veterans are very anxious to go home—Have heard nothing from Gen'l Thomas   I know nothing of his movements on the Lafayette road &c." Copies, *ibid.*; *ibid.*, 15th Army Corps, Letters and Telegrams Sent. *O.R.*, I, xxxii, part 2, 127–28. On the same day, Rawlins telegraphed to Logan. "You are authorized to enlist loyal Alabamians in the present Alabama Regiment for three years or during the war, and will so enlist them. Send the veteran regiments home as fast as you can. A more favorable time will not likely occur" Copies, DLC-USG, V, 34, 35; DNA, RG 393, Military Div. of the Miss., Letters Sent.

To Maj. Gen. George H. Thomas

Head Quarters, Mil. Div. of the Miss.
In the Field, Chattanooga Ten. Jan. 24th 1864.
MAJ. GEN. G. H. THOMAS,
COMD.G DEPT. OF THE CUM.D
GENERAL,

Should the advance of Longstreet upon Knoxville make reinforcements to Foster necessary send the remainder of the 4th Corps, except Artillery. I do not deem more Artillery necessary under any circumstances unless you should deem it advisable as a safe guard whilst on the march. Should the exigencies of Foster's position make more reinforcements necessary send such other troops as you can spare.

In case you are called on for troops to go into East Tennessee I wish you to take the command, in person, and on arrival at Knoxville to take command of all the forces. The condition Foster is now in makes it impossible for him to take the field, in justice to himself, and as I want Longstreet routed, and pursued, beyond the limits of the state of Tennessee, it is necessary to have a commander physically able for the task.

Troops starting from Chattanooga with three days rations in Haversacks will be able to make the trip to Loudon drawing the balance of their supplies from the country. Receips should be given in all cases where supplies are taken from loyal persons to enable them to get their pay in accordance with existing orders.

I wish to impress this fact: if further reinforcements are sent from here to East Tennessee Longstreet is to be driven beyond the reach of doing further harm in this state. Troops enough should go to secure this result. Should taking such a force weaken Chattanooga dangerously I will order such force from Logan's Command to this place as will secure it. In drawing troops from Chattanooga it would not be necessary to wait the arrival of their substitutes. The fact of them being on their way would be sufficient.

I would advise that immediate attention be given to preparations for moving troops so that they may be got off, if required, on the shortest possible notice.

> I am Gen. very respectfully
> your obt. svt.
> U. S. GRANT
> Maj. Gen. Com

ALS, USMA. *O.R.*, I, xxxii, part 2, 193–94.

On Jan. 25, 1864, Brig. Gen. John A. Rawlins wrote to Maj. Gen. George H. Thomas. "I am directed by the Major General commanding to send you the enclosed copy of letter from the General in Chief to him, relating to affairs in East Tennessee, and other points, touching the security of our position and future operations; and to say that you will relax no energy and spare no exertion in your preparations for moving a force into East Tennessee, sufficient with that now under Foster to give battle to, and defeat and drive Longstreet out of the State, no matter what news, short of the retreat of the enemy, you may have from Foster. Also, to invite your attention to that part of the letter of the General in Chief, where he speaks of the defences of Chattanooga, and to say that you will push forward these defenses to completion with all possible vigor. Further to say, that he goes to St Louis today but will be back this week, and any order, should one be necessary in the mean time, you may desire sent to General Logan, with a view to his cooperation with you in contemplated movements, I am directed to make on being advised of your wishes." LS, DNA, RG 94, War Records Office, Dept. of

the Cumberland. *O.R.*, I, xxxii, part 2, 207. For the enclosure, see telegram to
Maj. Gen. Henry W. Halleck, Jan. 16, 1864.

To Maj. Gen. Henry W. Halleck

———

Louisville Ky
Jany 25th 7.40 P. M. 1864

Maj Gen. H. W. Halleck
Gen-in-Chief

I left Chattanooga 6 30 P. M yesterday. Genl. Thomas has full
instructions to go in person to Fosters aid if necessary and in case
he does, not to leave until Longstreet is driven from Tennessee.

I go on tonight to St Louis. Will keep up telegraphic communication with my command and should Thomas go into East
Tennessee I will go immediately to Chattanooga. Thomas will be
ready to move his troops at once should the emergincy arise

U S Grant
Maj Genl

Telegram received, DNA, RG 107, Telegrams Collected (Bound); copies, *ibid.*,
Telegrams Received in Cipher; (misdated Jan. 26, 1864) *ibid.*, RG 393, Military
Div. of the Miss., Hd. Qrs. Correspondence; DLC-USG, V, 40, 94. Dated Jan. 25
in *O.R.*, I, xxxii, part 2, 207.

To Brig. Gen. Jacob Ammen

———

Louisville Jan 25th [*1864*] 7 00 P m

Genl Ammen

It is barely possible that communication may be cut between
you and Genl Foster—If so excersise your judgment as to the propriety of ordering the return of trains and droves now on their way
to Knoxville   Kentucky may also be threatened with a cavalry
raid   if so collect all the force you can, & get also what the governer ~~can spare~~ may be able to turn over to you and meet it   I do
not expect such a thing but Longstreet's present movements render
it possible

Communicate to me direct sending copy to Genl Foster any important information you may get of the enemy's movements or steps being taken by you to meet him

U S GRANT Maj Genl

Telegram received, DNA, RG 393, Dept. of Ky., Telegrams Received; copies, *ibid*.; (misdated Jan. 26, 1864) *ibid*., Military Div. of the Miss., Letters Sent; DLC-USG, V, 34, 35. Dated Jan. 25 in *O.R.*, I, xxxii, part 2, 207–8. Jacob Ammen, USMA 1831, older brother of USG's boyhood friend Daniel Ammen, resigned from the U.S. Army in 1837, then taught mathematics at various colleges before the Civil War. See *PUSG*, 2, 44*n*. He was appointed brig. gen. as of July 16, 1862. On Jan. 25, 1864, Ammen, Camp Nelson, Ky., telegraphed to USG. "Gen Fry's Command leaves Camp Dick Robinson in the morning via Somerset. Shall he be detained. No enemy reported yet in front—" Copy, DNA, RG 393, Dept. of Ky., Telegrams Sent.

On Feb. 7, Ammen wrote to USG. "Always willing to discharge to the best of my ability any duty assigned to me by my superior officers, I have neither sought nor declined any particular service. Ordered to the command of the District of Ky. Jan 6th 1864, and ordered January 25th 1864 by Sec. of War on Courtmartial at Cin. O. I have been absent from the District and may have to remain away some time yet—The command is an important one, and requires all the time of an officer—In my interview with Gen. Burbridge I have said to him, that I did not seek the particular decommand, and have no preference for it over others—" ALS, *ibid*., RG 94, Generals' Papers and Books, Ammen. On Feb. 14, USG telegraphed to Maj. Gen. John M. Schofield. "I have ordered Brig Genl Burbridge to Camp Nelson to command the District of Kentucky until relieved by Genl Ammen who is now on Court Martial duty. When relieved by Genl Ammen Genl Burbridge will report to me for assignment unless you have a place for him." Copies, DLC-USG, V, 34, 35; DNA, RG 393, Military Div. of the Miss., Letters Sent. *O.R.*, I, xxxii, part 2, 394. On Feb. 16, Lt. Col. Theodore S. Bowers wrote to Ammen. "Enclosed please find Special Order No 41. assigning General Burbridge to the command of the District of Northern Central Kentucky. The reason for such assignment was the uncertainty of the time you might be absent. When relieved from duty on Court Martial you will return to your District and relieve General Burbridge in its command" Copies, DLC-USG, V, 34, 35; DNA, RG 393, Military Div. of the Miss., Letters Sent. *O.R.*, I, xxxii, part 2, 410. See *ibid*., p. 401.

To Maj. Gen. Henry W. Halleck

St. Louis, Jan. 27th 1864

MAJ. GEN. H. W. HALLECK, WASHINGTON

Understanding that Gen. Schofield is ordered to report to me I would request that he be assigned to the Comd. of Dept. of the

Ohio and Gen. Stoneman to command of 23d Army Corps.[1] No objection to Gen. Foster but I fear if he does not attend soon to his wounded leg it will be too late and he is now entirely unfit for field duty.

U. S. GRANT

Maj. Gen.

ALS (telegram sent), DNA, RG 94, War Records Office, Dept. of the Cumberland; telegram received, *ibid.*, RG 107, Telegrams Collected (Bound). *O.R.*, I, xxxii, part 2, 229–30. On Jan. 27, 1864, Secretary of War Edwin M. Stanton telegraphed to USG. "Your telegram of this date to General Halleck has been just received. ~~General~~ According to your request General Schofield is assigned to the command of the Department of the Ohio and General Foster relieved, General Stoneman is assigned to the command of the twenty third Army Corps. The official orders will be transmitted tomorrow. ~~You~~ the General-in-Chief ~~being~~ having gone to his residence in the Country this evening. ~~You will please instruct your commanding~~" ALS (telegram sent), DNA, RG 107, Telegrams Collected (Bound); copies, *ibid.*, RG 393, Military Div. of the Miss., Hd. Qrs. Correspondence; DLC-John M. Schofield; DLC-USG, V, 40, 94. Printed as sent at 7:50 P.M. in *O.R.*, I, xxxii, part 2, 230. See telegram to Maj. Gen. Henry W. Halleck, Jan. 13, 1864. On Jan. 22, by AGO General Orders No. 28, Maj. Gen. William S. Rosecrans was assigned to command the Dept. of Mo., relieving Maj. Gen. John M. Schofield, assigned to report to USG. *O.R.*, I, xxxii, part 2, 182. On the same day, Schofield, Harrisburg, Pa., telegraphed to USG. "I am ordered to report to you for the purpose of relieving Gen. Foster if he is to be relieved and if he is not to be relieved for such duty as you may assign me—I shall join you as soon as I can return to St. Louis and turn over my present command." Copy, DNA, RG 393, Military Div. of the Miss., Telegrams Received. On Jan. 30, Schofield, St. Louis, wrote to USG. "Having turned over the Command of the Department of the Missouri to Major General Rosecrans in compliance with General Order No 38. current series from the War Department I have the honor to report to you for orders. Will you please give me an order for transportation for myself, four staff officers, six horses and baggage, from St Louis to Knoxville? Also, as I shall probably leave St. Louis before receiving the order of the President assigning me to the command of the Department of the Ohio, it will I presume be necessary for me to have your order to assume that Command on my arrival at Knoxville. I will be ready to start for Knoxville to morrow evening." Copy, *ibid.*, Dept. of Mo., Letters Sent. *O.R.*, I, xxxiv, part 2, 188. On Jan. 29, USG had telegraphed to Brig. Gen. John A. Rawlins. "Gen Schofield will go at once to Knoxville I prefer foster should remain until he arrives" Telegram received, DNA, RG 393, Dept. of the Tenn., Telegrams Received; copy, *ibid.*, Military Div. of the Miss., Telegrams Received. *O.R.*, I, xxxii, part 2, 253.

On Feb. 1, 12:30 P.M., Maj. Gen. Henry W. Halleck telegraphed to USG. "Genl Foster's condition is such that Genl Schofield must hasten to relieve him." ALS (telegram sent), DNA, RG 107, Telegrams Collected (Bound); copies, *ibid.*, RG 393, Military Div. of the Miss., Hd. Qrs. Correspondence; DLC-USG, V, 40, 94. *O.R.*, I, xxxii, part 2, 306. On the same day, Lt. Col. Theodore S. Bowers,

Nashville, telegraphed to Maj. Gen. John G. Foster. "Major General Schofield is by direction of the General in Chief en-route from St Louis to Knoxville to relieve you that you may take the benefit of your leave of absence" Copies, DLC-USG, V, 34, 35; DNA, RG 393, Military Div. of the Miss., Letters Sent. *O.R.*, I, xxxii, part 2, 306. On Feb. 3, Bowers issued Special Orders No. 29 assigning Schofield to relieve Foster. Copy, DLC-USG, V, 38. *O.R.*, I, xxxii, part 2, 322.

On Feb. 6, Schofield, Chattanooga, telegraphed to USG. "I am about to start for Knoxville have been detained here two days for a boat" Copy, DNA, RG 393, Military Div. of the Miss., Telegrams Received. *O.R.*, I, xxxii, part 2, 335. On Feb. 9, Schofield, Knoxville, telegraphed to USG. "I arrived here and assumed command this morning. I will report the condition of affairs as soon as possible." Copies (undated), DNA, RG 393, Dept. of the Ohio, Telegrams Sent; (dated Feb. 9) *ibid.*; *ibid.*, Military Div. of the Miss., Telegrams Received. *O.R.*, I, xxxii, part 2, 356. See telegram to Maj. Gen. John M. Schofield, Feb. 11, 1864.

1. George Stoneman of N. Y., USMA 1846, promoted to capt., 2nd Cav., as of March 3, 1855, was stationed at Fort Brown, Tex., on the eve of the Civil War. He was appointed brig. gen. as of Aug. 13, 1861, serving as chief of cav., Army of the Potomac, from Aug. 14 to March 10, 1862. Promoted to maj. gen. as of Nov. 29, he commanded the 3rd Army Corps, Army of the Potomac, during the battle of Fredericksburg and the Cav. Corps, Army of the Potomac, during a raid toward Richmond, April 13—May 2, 1863. He was chief of the Cav. Bureau from July 28 to Jan. 29, 1864. On Feb. 4, Bowers issued Special Orders No. 30 assigning Stoneman to command the 23rd Army Corps. Copy, DLC-USG, V, 38. *O.R.*, I, xxxii, part 2, 329.

To John O'Fallon et al.

St. Louis, Mo.
Jan.y 27th 1864,
COL. J. O'FALLON, HON. J. HOW, & CITIZENS OF ST. LOUIS,
GENTLEMEN,

Your highly complimentary invitation to meet "old acquaintances and to make new ones" at a dinner to be given by citizens of St. Louis, is just received.

I will state that I have only visited St. Louis on this occation to see a sick child. Finding however that he has passed the crisis of his disease, and is pronounced out of danger by his physician, I accept the invitation. My stay in in the City will be short, probably not beyond the 1st proximo. On to-morrow I shall be engaged. Any other day of my stay here, and any place selected by the Citizens of St. Louis, it will be agreeable for me to meet them.

I have the honor to be
very respectfully
your obt. svt.
U. S. GRANT
Maj. Gen. U. S. A.

ALS, MoSHi. On Jan. 27, 1864, John O'Fallon and fifty-five other citizens of St. Louis wrote to USG. "Your fellow citizens of St. Louis, in common with all loyal men of the Republic, have witnessed with the highest admiration your patriotic devotion, unsurpassed service and commanding success in the various military positions occupied by you from the commencement of the existing war. They remember the alacrity with which you sprung to arms at the first call of your country, placing yourself at its disposal to aid in suppressing this most unjustifiable and gigantic rebellion. As citizens of Missouri they can never forget the promptness and skill with which you aided in defending this State at the beginning of the conflict, when the means at the command of those in authority were wholly inadequate to the great work committed to them; and as citizens of the great Valley of the Mississippi, they owe you unbounded gratitude, not only for the first signal victories which, under your auspices, crowned our arms and thrilled the nation with joy, but also for those later and unparalleled triumphs which gave again freedom to western commerce, from the source of its great rivers to the Gulf. Not with more certainty is the indivisibility of the Mississippi Valley proclaimed by its geographical features, than by the devoted loyalty of the North West, which demands that from the Lakes to the Gulf, along its broad rivers and over its fertile plains, only one flag shall be known, and that the glorious banner of our Republic—'one and indivisable.' You have borne that flag victoriously with your heroic legions until the Mississippi goes 'unvexed to the sea'; and looking down from the mountain heights of Tennessee upon the States between you and the Gulf in one direction and the Atlantic in the other, you have, with the inspiration which the past glories of that State should ever arouse, made at Chattanooga a glorious response to that grand utterance of an immortal hero which crushed out incipient rebellion years gone by:—'The Federal Union: It shall be preserved.' As citizens of a Republic consecrated to constitutional liberty, and duly appreciating the destinies of the future for our own and other lands which hang upon the results of the present conflict, we glory in the brilliant deeds and unparalleled triumphs of yourself, officers and men. To you and the gallant soldiers whom you have led, a nation's honors and gratitude are due. In the name of ourselves and of St. Louis, we earnestly request that you will, before leaving this city, once your home, meet your fellow citizens at a public dinner, where old personal friendships may be renewed and new ones formed, and where congratulations over the successes of the past and the hopes of the future may be freely interchanged. We have the honor to be, with sentiments of profound regard," ALS, USG 3.

Two hundred fifty persons attended the dinner on Jan. 29 at the Lindell House, a lengthy affair with numerous speeches, toasts, and ceremonies. Called upon for a speech, USG said: "Gentlemen, in response, it will be impossible for me to do more than to thank you." *Missouri Democrat*, Jan. 30, 1864.

On the preceding evening, USG dined at the Planters' House, where a large crowd assembled for a serenade. USG responded: "Gentlemen: I thank you for this honor. I cannot make a speech. It is something I have never done, and never intend to do, and I beg you will excuse me." After continued calls for more, USG spoke again. "Gentlemen: Making speeches is not my business. I never did it in my life, and never will. I thank you, however, for your attendance here." *Ibid.*, Jan. 29, 1864.

To Maj. Gen. Henry W. Halleck

(Cypher) St. Louis Jan. 28th/64
MAJ. GEN. HALLECK WASHINGTON

Before leaving Chattanooga I directed one Div. to move between the Chicamauga & the Hewassee to cover the river and to be on the road if it should prove necessary to reinforce Foster. Thomas was to make a demonstration towards Dalton at the same time. These moves may induce the enemy to reinforce Johnston as his Army is rapidly dissolving by desertions. I also made arrangements for pushing through to Knoxville as many rations as possible to support reinforcements if they should have to go. A Cavalry raid in the direction named in your dispatch is almost impossible with the present state of the roads. Fearing it might be attempted however I directed Gen. Ammen before I left Ten. to watch closely and to collect the Ky. forces to meet it if attempted.

U. S. GRANT
Maj. Gen.

ALS (telegram sent), DNA, RG 94, War Records Office, Miscellaneous War Records; telegram received, *ibid.*, RG 107, Telegrams Collected (Bound). *O.R.*, I, xxxii, part 2, 244–45. See following telegram.

To Maj. Gen. George H. Thomas

(Cypher) St. Louis, Jan. 28th/64
MAJ. GEN. THOMAS, CHATTANOOGA TEN.

Gen. Hallect telegraphs that one Brigade left Ewells Corps on the 17th one the 20th to reinforce Longstreet or Johnston. If the former the moves indicated before I left should commence as soon as possible. Telegraph any information you have and what you are doing.

U. S. GRANT
Maj. Gen.

ALS (telegram sent), DNA, RG 94, War Records Office, Miscellaneous War Records; copies, *ibid.*, RG 393, Dept. of Mo., Telegrams Sent; *ibid.*, Dept. of the Cumberland, Telegrams Received; *ibid.*, Military Div. of the Miss., Letters Sent; DLC-USG, V, 34, 35. *O.R.*, I, xxxii, part 2, 247. On Jan. 28, 1864, 1:24 P.M., Maj. Gen. Henry W. Halleck telegraphed to USG. "Major Genl Sedgewick telegraphs that two brigades of Ewell's corps have left for Johnston or Longstreet, one on the 20th and one on the 25th. Adjt Genl Anderson telegraphs from Lexington of an expected raid by Morgan through Stone or Sounding Gap into Kentucky." ALS (telegram sent), DNA, RG 107, Telegrams Collected (Bound); copies, *ibid.*, RG 393, Military Div. of the Miss., Hd. Qrs. Correspondence; DLC-USG, V, 40, 94. *O.R.*, I, xxxii, part 2, 244. On the same day, 10:30 P.M., USG telegraphed to Brig. Gen. Jacob Ammen, Camp Nelson, Ky. "What do you hear of an attempted raid by way of Stone or Sounding Gap? What force can you collect to meet such raid if attempted?" ALS (telegram sent), DNA, RG 94, War Records Office, Miscellaneous War Records; telegram received, *ibid.*, RG 393, Dept. of Ky., Telegrams Received. *O.R.*, I, xxxii, part 2, 245. On Jan. 30, Capt. Alexander C. Semple, Camp Nelson, telegraphed to USG. "Your telegrame to Genl Ammen has been recd. and forwarded to him at Cincinnati to which place he has been ordered by the Secy of War as Pres'd't of a General Court Martial—" Copy, DNA, RG 393, Dept. of Ky., Telegrams Sent. On Feb. 1, Ammen, Camp Nelson, telegraphed to USG. "There is nothing further from the anticipated raid into Eastern Ky. Everything quiet at last accounts" Copy, *ibid.*

On Jan. 29, 8:00 P.M. and 9:00 P.M., Maj. Gen. George H. Thomas telegraphed to USG. "Your dispatch twenty Eighth 10.30 recd. Genl. Stanleys Division is now between Chickamauga and Hiawassa. Col. McCallum is at Knoxville looking into the condition of the R. Rd. which I will push forward as rapidly as possible. I have just made a demonstration toward Dalton and find affairs unchanged except two Brigades which are supposed to have gone to Mobile. I will push matters forward as fast as possible." "I telegraphed yesterday to Genl. Foster to know what he knew of the enemy's movements—He has not answered me yet, but the last news from him was that Longstreet was falling back. I expect Col. McCallum back tomorrow. He can probably give me some news. I sent an expedition to Dirttown last Friday and captured a home guard camp and over two hundred horses—Also a flag of truce to near Dalton—All we could learn was that troops had been sent off to Mobile. Genl. Palmer has just returned from Ringgold—He reports that he encountered the enemy's pickets and drove them into Tunnel Hill without much difficulty. I am trying to get up forage enough for a ten days expedition and if successful will make a strong demonstration on Dalton & Resaca, unless Longstreets movements compel me to go to East Tennessee." Copies, *ibid.*, Dept. of the Cumberland, Telegrams Sent; *ibid.*, Military Div. of the Miss., Telegrams Received. *O.R.*, I, xxxii, part 2, 253–54.

On Jan. 31, Brig. Gen. John A. Rawlins wrote to Thomas. "It is reported that Dalton is evacuated. Is it so? Please telegraph any information you may have relating to it, that General Sherman may be advised of the same." *Ibid.*, p. 276. On Feb. 1, Thomas telegraphed to Rawlins. "Dalton is not Evacuated   their position is very much the same as when you were here   I have directed Genl Rousseau to make the report you desire"   Telegram received, DNA, RG 393, Dept. of the Tenn., Telegrams Received; copy, *ibid.*, Military Div. of the Miss., Telegrams Received. Dated Jan. 31 in *O.R.*, I, xxxii, part 2, 276. On Jan. 31, Rawlins wrote to Thomas. "You will please direct General Rousseau to furnish a report to the Chief Engineer of this Military Division, at this place on the condition of the defenses within the limits of his District and particularly the defenses of Nashville, to know whether they are capable of standing a seige, and if the depots of supplies are properly covered from Artillery, fire and protected from assault, and also the same information with reference to the rail road bridge. Also, information as to whether any work is being done on the defenses here and what Artillery is in position and what is its character and the amount of ammunition and condition of same." Copies, DLC-USG, V, 34, 35; DNA, RG 393, Military Div. of the Miss., Letters Sent.

On Feb. 1, Thomas telegraphed to Rawlins. "The latest information I have is that the rebels have two regts Cavalry four regts. Infy. and three guns at or near Tunnel Hill. One Division between Tunnel Hill and Dalton. Three brigades and some other troops between Dalton and Tilton. Six pieces new Artillery just arrived at Dalton were being trained on the twenty eighth. No other Artillery there. Eighteen thousand rations are issued for all the troops in Dalton and Tunnel Hill. Four Div. have been sent down the R. R. to Mobile Ala. and Rome Ga. The pickets extend twelve miles north of Dalton in direction of Charleston. There are no troops east of Dalton   Gov. Brown has ordered all families dependant on the Govt. for supplies to move south of the Etowah River"   Copy, *ibid.*, Telegrams Received. *O.R.*, I, xxxii, part 2, 308.

To Abraham Lincoln

St. Louis, Mo.
January 31st 1864.

HIS EXCELLENCY, A LINCOLN
PRESIDENT OF THE UNITED STATES
SIR:

I would respectfully recommend 1st Lieut. B. M. Callender, 1st Mo. Light Artillery, for the position of Commissary of Subsistence.—Lt. Callender has proven himself a valuable officer. The time of his company expires some time in April next and he is desirous of continuing in the Army until the end of the War, hence this application.

I respectfully refer to the recommendation given Lt. Callender by Col. T. J. Haines, C. S. in a letter addressed to the Com.y Gen. of the Army, of Jan.y 26th 1864.

> I have the honor to be
> very respectfully, your obt. svt.
> U. S. GRANT
> Maj. Gen.

ALS, DNA, RG 94, ACP, C1471 CB 1864. The letter of Col. Thomas J. Haines is *ibid.* In a letter of March 6, 1864, from Maj. Franklin D. Callender to Maj. Gen. Henry W. Halleck urging the appointment of his brother, a copy of USG's letter was enclosed. *Ibid.* No appointment followed.

To Maj. Gen. William T. Sherman

———

St Louis, Mo. Jany 31st 1864.

MAJ GEN'L W. T. SHERMAN.
COM'DG DEPT OF THE TENN.
GEN'L:

I understand the authorities at Memphis, Tenn, have seized the little steamer "Wenona," to be used as a Picket Boat. If not absolutely necessary for the public service I wish you would order her release. I know the owner of the Wenona, and have for years, and if there is a person on the Miss. River who will conform to regulations and restrictions without watching, it is Mr. C. W. Ford, one of the owners of this Steamer. For this reason I would myself exempt his steamer from seizure if another could be got suitable for the purpose required.

I come here to see my oldest boy who has been dangerously ill of Typhoid Pneumonia. He is now regarded by his Physician as out of danger. I leave here this afternoon.[1]

> Yours Truly
> U. S GRANT.
> Maj Gen'l.

Copy, Parsons Papers, IHi.

1. On Saturday, Jan. 30, 1864, 7:00 P.M., USG telegraphed to Lt. Col. William L. Duff, Cairo, Ill. "Go to Louisville. I leave for there on Monday" Copy, DNA, RG 393, Dept. of Mo., Telegrams Sent. On Jan. 31, USG wrote to Jesse R. Grant. "I leave here for Nashville to-morrow. Cannot go home at present, in fact do not want to leave 'Dixie' again until the war is over. The attention I received whilst it is flattering, is to me very embarassing . . ." Oliver R. Barrett Sale, 1190, Parke-Bernet Galleries, Inc., Oct. 30–Nov. 2, 1950, no. 473. USG also discussed the illness of Frederick Dent Grant.

To William G. Eliot et al.

St. Louis, Mo, January 31, 1864.
DR. W. G. ELIOT, GEORGE PARTRIDGE AND OTHERS,
WESTERN SANITARY COMMISSION:
GENTLEMEN: Your letter of yesterday, requesting my presence at a general meeting of the loyal citizens of St. Louis on Monday evening, to make preparations for a "Grand Mississippi Valley Fair," for the benefit of the sick and wounded soldiers of the Western army, is before me. I regret that my already protracted stay in the city will prevent any longer delay from my public duties. I regret this, as it would afford me the greatest pleasure to advance, in any manner, the interests of a Commission that has already done so much for the suffering soldiers of our Western armies. The gratuitous offerings of our loyal citizens at home, through the agency of Sanitary Commissions, to our brave soldiers in the field, have been to them the most encouraging and gratifying evidence that whilst they are risking life and health for the suppression of this most wicked rebellion, their friends who cannot assist them with musket and sword are with them in sympathy and heart.

The Western Sanitary Commission have distributed many tons of stores to the armies under my command. Their voluntary offerings have made glad the hearts of many thousands of wounded and sick soldiers, who otherwise would have been subjected to severe privations. Knowing the benefits already conferred on the army by the Western Sanitary Commission, I hope for them a full and enthusiastic meeting to-night, and a fair to follow which will bring together many old friends who have been kept apart for the last three years, and unite them again in one common cause—that of their country and peace.

I am, gentlemen, with great respect, your obedient servant,

U. S. GRANT, Maj. Gen. U. S. A.

Missouri Democrat, Feb. 2, 1864. William G. Eliot, born in New Bedford, Mass., in 1811, graduated from Harvard Divinity School, and organized a Unitarian church in St. Louis, where he was a founder of Washington University. George Partridge, president of the Union Merchants' Exchange, had established a grocery business in Boston before moving to St. Louis about 1840, where he continued to deal in groceries and contributed $150,000 to Washington University. See *O.R.*, III, ii, 947.

To Julia Dent Grant

Louisville Feb'y 3d 1864

DEAR JULIA,

Owing to a break in the New Albany & Chicago rail-road I did not reach here until last night. This morning I called on Mr. Page's family.[1] Charles is quite unwell, confined to his bed. Disease more Hypocondria I think than anything els. I go to Nashville in the morning. Have no more peace here than in St. Louis. At Hd Qrs. I am constantly busy and as I get no rest away I do not know what I am to do. I believe I will move temporarily to some one company post out on the rail-road where no body lives and where but few people are to be seen.

If you will send to the Photograph establishment on the N. E. corner of 4th & Walnut you can get some of me that are probably better than any heretofore taken. If they are send me some of them.

Louisville on account of the Crittenden Court of Enquiry[2] is filled with Maj. Gens. I want to get away.—You will have no difficulty in going to Nashville by way of the river. Col. Myers, Quartermaster, came over here with me. On his return he will call on you and let you know that when you want to start he will pick out a good boat for you and see you safe aboard.—Jess' pony is all right. I will have it sent to wherever he is next summer.—Orvil, the goose, has bought Collins out and is of course tied to Galena.

No special news from the army in front. Kisses for you and the children. Tell Jess he may kiss the young ladies for me.

ULYS.

ALS, DLC-USG.

1. See letter to Samuel K. Page, [*Feb., 1864*].
2. Following the battle of Chickamauga, Maj. Gen. William S. Rosecrans relieved Maj. Gen. Thomas L. Crittenden, who was later exonerated by a court of inquiry. *O.R.*, I, xxx, part 1, 971–1004.

To Henry Wilson

Louisville Ky.
Feb.y 3d 186[4]

HON. H. WILSON,
CHAIRMAN COM. ON MIL. AFFAIRS,
UNITED STATES SENATE,
WASHINGTON CITY, D. C.
SIR:

Among the unemployed General Officers reported to the Senate my attention has been called to the name of Brig. Gen. Robt. Allen, Principal Quartermaster in the West. It is true General Allen has not had command of troops in the field, but his duties have been much more arduous, and much more important to the Government, than that of an Army Corps commander, and involving greater responsibilities. Gen. Allen exercises a supervising controll over a number of Commissioned officers, and Citizen employees of the Government, greater than that of any Corps Commanmander in the Army. His pecuniary responsibilities runs into Millions monthly. All his duties have been performed wi[th] a promptness and fidelity redounding to his credit and greatly to the interest of the public service and the Government. To have these duties to perform with less rank than Brigadier General would be hard indeed.

Allow me to ask your aid for the retention of Gen. Allen, with his present rank. If there was any pressident for it I would feel no hesitation in recommending him even for a grade higher. His duties, and the manner in which they have been performed both would, in that event, entitle him to it.

> I have the honor to be,
> with great respect
> your obt. svt.
> U. S. GRANT
> Maj. Gen. U. S. A.

ALS, ICarbS. On May 7, 1864, the U.S. Senate confirmed Robert Allen's appointment as brig. gen.

To Maj. Gen. Henry W. Halleck

Nashville Tenn
Feby 4th 1864.

MAJ GEN H W HALLECK
GEN IN CHIEF

Arrived here five 5 P. M today. Sherman leaves Vicksburg the 27th. Many troops have gone to Mobile, mostly from North Carolina and Charleston

> U. S. GRANT
> Maj Genl

Telegram received, DNA, RG 107, Telegrams Collected (Bound); copies, *ibid.*, RG 393, Military Div. of the Miss., Hd. Qrs. Correspondence; DLC-USG, V, 40, 94.

On Jan. 30, 1864, Brig. Gen. Hugh T. Reid, Cairo, telegraphed to USG. "General order number seventeen makes Illinois a part of the Northern Dept and Gen'l Heintzleman sends order here requiring reports to be made to him. Is it not the intention that the Post of Cairo should be excepted" Copy, DNA, RG 393, Military Div. of the Miss., Telegrams Received. On Feb. 4, USG telegraphed to Maj. Gen. Henry W. Halleck. "Cairo Ill and Jeffersonville Indiana bear such relations to each department of the Tennessee and Ohio that I respectfully request they be assigned accordingly" Telegram received (dated Feb. 5), *ibid.*, RG 107, Telegrams Collected (Bound); copies (dated Feb. 4), *ibid.*, RG 393, Military Div. of the Miss., Hd. Qrs. Correspondence; DLC-USG, V, 40, 94.

On Feb. 5, USG telegraphed to Halleck. "Gov Johnson is consolidating the Eighth and Tenth Tenn. Cavalry   The latter not yet mustered in   To facilitate

the consolidation I ask authority to muster out the Officers in excess of organization"   Telegram received, DNA, RG 107, Telegrams Collected (Bound); copies,
ibid., Military Div. of the Miss., Hd. Qrs. Correspondence; DLC-USG, V, 40,
94. On Feb. 6, Halleck telegraphed to USG. "You are authorized to muster out
officers made surplus by consolidating regiments. Application in regard to
Cairo & Jeffersonville will be submitted to the Secty of War." ALS (telegram
sent), DNA, RG 107, Telegrams Collected (Bound); copies, *ibid.*, RG 393, Military Div. of the Miss., Hd. Qrs. Correspondence; DLC-USG, V, 40, 94.

To Maj. Gen. Henry W. Halleck

Head Quarters, Mil. Div. of the Miss.
Nashville Ten. Feb. 4th 1864.

MAJ. GEN. H. W. HALLECK,
GEN. IN CHIEF, WASHINGTON,
GENERAL,

Your letter of the 22d of Jan.y, enclosing copy of Col. Stager's
of the 21st to you, is received. I have also Circular, or Order, dated
Jan.y 1st 1864, post marked Washington Jan.y 23d and received
on the 29th.

I will state that Beckwith is one of the best of men. He is competant and industrious. In the matter for which he has been discharged he only obeyed my order and could not have done otherwise than he did and remain. Beckwith has always been employed
at Hd Qrs. as an operator and I have never thought of taking him
with me, except when Hd Qrs. are moved. On the occation of my
going to Knoxville I received Washington dispatches which I
could not read until my return to this place. To remedy this for the
future I directed Col. Comstock to acquaint himself with this
Cypher. Beckwith desired, ~~in fact refused~~, to telegraph Col. Stager
on the subject before complying with my direction. Not knowing
of any order defining who and who alone could be entrusted with
the Washington Cypher I then ordered Beckwith to give it to Col.
Comstock and to inform Col. Stager of the fact that he had done so.
I had no thought in this matter of violating any order, or even wish,
of the Secretary of War. I could see no reason why I was not as
capable of selecting a proper person to entrust with this secret as

Col. Stager, in fact thought nothing further of the matter than that Col. Stager had his operators under such discipline that they were afraid to obey orders from any one but himself without knowing first his pleasure.

Beckwith has been dismissed for obeying my order. His position is important to him and a better man cannot be selected for it. I respectfully ask that Beckwith be restored.

When Col. Stager's directions were received here the Cypher had already been communicated. His order was signed by himself and not by direction of the Sec. of War. It is not necessary for me to state that I am no stickler for forms but will obey any order or wish of my superiors, no matter how conveyed, if I know, or only think, it comes from them. In this instance I supposed Col. Stager was acting for himself and without the authority or knowledge of any one els.

> I am Gen. very respectfully
> your obt. svt.
> U. S. GRANT
> Maj. Gen.

ALS, IHi. *O.R.*, I, xxxii, part 2, 323–24. See telegram to Maj. Gen. Henry W. Halleck, Jan. 20, 1864. On Feb. 4, 1864, USG telegraphed to Maj. Gen. Henry W. Halleck. "There is an entire mistake about Beckwiths position. He has given entire satisfaction and only obeyed my orders and not Col. Comstocks. My reason has been explained for giving that order. I respectfully ask that Beckwith be restored." ALS (facsimile), Samuel H. Beckwith, "Silhouettes by 'Grant's Shadow,'" *National Magazine* (Boston), XX, 5 (Aug., 1904), 573; telegram received, DNA, RG 107, Telegrams Collected (Bound). On Jan. 22, Halleck wrote to USG. "I enclose herewith a copy of a note from Col Stager in regard to his instructions to Mr. Beckwith respecting the new cipher. Your telegrams in regard to Lt. Col. Comstocks orders to Mr. Beckwith have been submitted to the Secty of War. It was known that the contents of telegrams communicated by means, of existing ciphers have been made public without authority. As these ciphers had been communicated to a number of persons, the Dept. was unable to discover the delinquent individual. To obviate this difficulty a new and very complicated cipher was prepared for communications between you and the War Dept., which, by direction of the Secty of War was to be communicated to only two individuals,—one at your Head Quarters and one in the War Dept. It was to be confided to no one else, not even to me or any member of my staff. Mr. Beckwith who was sent to your Head Quarters was directed by the Secty of War to communicate this cipher to *no one*. In obeying Col. Comstock's orders he disobeyed the Secty and has been dismissed. He should have gone to prison if Col Comstock had seen fit to put him there. Instead of forcing the cipher from him in violation of the orders of the War Dept, Col. Comstock should have reported the facts of the case here for the information of the Secty of War who takes the personal supervision and direction of the military telegraphs. On account of this ciphers having been communicated to Col Comstock, the Secty has directed another to be prepared in its place, which is to be communicated to no one, *no matter what his rank*, without his special authority. The Secty does not percieve the necessity of communicating a special cipher, intended only for telegrams to the War Dept., to members of your staff, any more than to my staff, or to the staff officers of other Genls commanding geographical Departments. All your communications with others are conducted through the ordinary cipher. It was intended that Mr. Beckwith should accompany you wherever you required him, transportation being furnished for that purpose. If by any casualty he should be seperated from you, communications could be kept up by the ordinary cipher, till the vacancy could be supplied. It is to be regretted that Col Comstock interfered with the orders of the War Dept. in this case. As stated in former instructions, if any telegraphic employee should not give satisfaction, he should be reported, and, if there be a pressing necessity, he may be suspended. But as the corps of telegraphic operators recieve their instructions directly from the Secretary of War, these instructions should not be interfered with except under very extraordinary circumstances, which should be immediately reported. . . . P. S. Col Stager is the confidential agent of the Secty of War, & directs all telegraph matters under his orders." LS, *ibid.*, RG 108, Letters Sent (Press). *O.R.*, I, xxxii, part 2, 172–73. Halleck enclosed a letter of Jan. 21 to him from Col. Anson Stager, superintendent, Military Telegraph. "I beg leave to offer the following in explanation of my message to Captain Bunch, referred to in Gen Grants communication of last evening. The information furnished me, led me to believe that the request of the Staff Officer for copy of the cipher was without Gen. Grants authority and, as a new cipher had been arranged expressly for Mr Beckwiths use at Genl Grants Headquarters, with the order of the Secretary of War, recently issued, that the operators for this duty should be held responsible for strict privacy in its use, I indited the message referred to, not thinking that it would come in conflict with General Grants orders, or wishes, the General having recently expressed his entire satisfaction with Mr. Beckwiths services. I am exceedingly mortified at the result, as my only desire was to furnish the most reliable means of communication to General Grant with the War Department. The new cipher was arranged with a view of being used by telegraph experts, and it is believed cannot be used with any success by others than telegraphers. A great number of errors have been made by Staff Officers working ciphers, owing to their lack of experience in telegraphic characters, and it is believed that greater accuracy can be secured by placing ciphers in the hands of experts, selected for this duty. The new cipher differs in many respects from those formerly used, and the one arranged for Gen Grant should not be known to any other party, hence my anxiety to keep it in Beckwiths hands. I sincerely regret that Gen Grant is led to believe that it is willful interference on my part." Copies, DLC-USG, V, 40, 94; DNA, RG 393, Military Div. of the Miss., Hd. Qrs. Correspondence. *O.R.*, I, xxxii, part 2, 161. On Jan. 1, Col. Edward D. Townsend, AGO, had issued unnumbered orders. "That the cipher books issued by the superintendent of Military Telegraphs, be entrusted only to the care of telegraph *experts*, selected for this duty by the superintendent of telegraphs, and approved and appointed by the Secretary of War, for duty at the respective Hd. Quarters of the Military Departments, and to accompany the Armies in the

Field. The ciphers furnished for this purpose are not to be imparted to any one, but will be kept by the operator to whom they are entrusted in strict confidence, and he will be held responsible for their privacy and proper use. They will neither be copied nor used by any other person, without special permission from the Secretary of War. Generals commanding will report to the War Department any default of duty, by the cipher operators, but will not allow any staff or other officer to interfere with the operators in the discharge of their duty." Copies, DLC-USG, V, 40, 94; DNA, RG 393, Military Div. of the Miss., Hd. Qrs. Correspondence.

On Feb. 10, 4:00 P.M., Halleck telegraphed to USG. "Mr. Beckwith has been restored. Capt Stokes will be made Qr Master with the rank of Lieut Col. Governors of states have no authority to furlough troops. Please report any cases that have occurred, and the Secty of War will so inform the Governors who have done so." ALS (telegram sent), *ibid.*, RG 107, Telegrams Collected (Bound); copies, *ibid.*, RG 393, Military Div. of the Miss., Hd. Qrs. Correspondence; (incomplete) *ibid.*, RG 94, Letters Received, 96A 1864; DLC-USG, V, 40, 94. *O.R.*, I, xxxii, part 2, 361. See *Memoirs*, II, 103–4. For James H. Stokes, see letter to Maj. Gen. Henry W. Halleck, Feb. 6, 1864. On Feb. 9, USG had telegraphed to Halleck. "There seems to be an impression among Governors of states that when troops return to the states to which they are acredited either [on] furlough or to Hospital they become subject to the order of Governors and can be furloughed by them—An inspection of some Hospitals just had shows that convalescents are promptly sent out but in many instances [are] furloughed by Governor." Telegram received, DNA, RG 107, Telegrams Collected (Bound); copies, *ibid.*, Telegrams Received in Cipher; *ibid.*, RG 393, Military Div. of the Miss., Hd. Qrs. Correspondence; DLC-USG, V, 40, 94.

To Maj. Gen. Henry W. Halleck

Nashville Tenn
Feby 6th 1864 3 30 P. M.

MAJ GEN H. W. HALLECK
GENL IN CHIEF

I am making every effort to get supplies to Knoxville for the support of a large force long enough to drive Longstreet out. The enemy have evidently fallen back with most of their force from Gen Thoma's front, some going to Mobile. Has there been any movement in that direction by our troops?

U S GRANT
Maj Genl Com'dg

Telegram received, DLC-Robert T. Lincoln; DNA, RG 107, Telegrams Collected (Bound); copies, *ibid.*, Telegrams Received in Cipher; *ibid.*, RG 393,

Military Div. of the Miss., Hd. Qrs. Correspondence; DLC-USG, V, 40, 94. *O.R.*, I, xxxii, part 2, 334. On Feb. 7, 1864, 12:30 P.M., Maj. Gen. Henry W. Halleck telegraphed to USG. "There has been no movement on Mobile, unless made by Genl Sherman." ALS (telegram sent), DNA, RG 107, Telegrams Collected (Bound); copies, *ibid.*, RG 393, Military Div. of the Miss., Hd. Qrs. Correspondence; DLC-USG, V, 40, 94. *O.R.*, I, xxxii, part 2, 348.

To Maj. Gen. Henry W. Halleck

Head Quarters, Mil. Div. of the Miss.
Nashville Ten. Feb.y 6th 1864.

MAJ. GEN. H. W. HALLECK,
GEN. IN CHIEF, WASHINGTON,
GENERAL.

Feeling satisfied that there was much useless extravigance in the Quartermaster's Dept. and having some cases reported to me of probable peculation, I applied to the Q. M. Gen. to detail an honest and experienced officer of the Dept. to ~~detail~~ inspect. His reply was that he had not such an officer available but for me to select one and order him on that duty. I, under this authority, detailed Capt. Jas. H. Stokes of the Chicago Board of Trade Battery, for this duty. The result has been already to find that Govt. is being constantly defrauded by those whos duty it is to protect and guard the public interest. The guilty parties will be relieved and brought to trial.

Capt. Stokes is an old officer of the regular army and also of the Q. M. Dept. He is eminently fitted for this duty though a very disagreeable one to him, and particularly so whilst occupying the grade of Capt. of Artillery. Gen. Thomas informed me some after my assumption of command of this Mil. Div. that he regarded Capt. Stokes as one of his most efficient officers and that he had recommended him for the position of Brig. General. I now would most heartily endorse that recommendation, and if it cannot be granted would ask that he be appointed ~~Chief~~ Q. M. of Vols. with the rank of Lieut. Col. I have no such staff officer and believe the law authorizes it.

I do not require a staff officer of the Q. M. Dept. for any other duty than that suggested by this letter. For the active duties within my command I have Gen. Allen, Cols. Myers and Donaldson, men eminently capable and far above suspicion. In deed I would prefer Capt. Stokes with rank to enable him to perform the duties assigned him, should report directly to Gen. Allen instead of me.

> I am General, very respectfully
> your obt. svt.
> U. S. GRANT
> Maj. Gen.

ALS, DNA, RG 94, 496 ACP 1872. *O.R.*, I, xxxii, part 2, 334–35. James H. Stokes of Md., USMA 1835, resigned in 1843 as capt. and q. m., then for a decade operated a glass factory. Employed by the Illinois Central Railroad before the Civil War, he aided in arming Ill. troops and was commissioned capt., Chicago Board of Trade Battery, as of July 31, 1862. On Feb. 2, 1864, Lt. Col. Theodore S. Bowers issued General Orders No. 2 assigning Stokes as inspector gen., Q. M. Dept. Copies, DLC-USG, V, 14; DNA, RG 393, Military Div. of the Miss., General Orders. See letter to Maj. Gen. Henry W. Halleck, Feb. 4, 1864.

On Jan. 17, USG telegraphed to Brig. Gen. Montgomery C. Meigs. "Can you send me at once an efficient and fearless Quarter Master. I wish for a rigid inspection of the accounts and administration of Disbursing and Depot Quarter Masters in the Department of the Cumberland" Telegram received, DNA, RG 107, Telegrams Collected (Bound); *ibid.*, RG 92, Consolidated Correspondence, Army of the Cumberland; copies, *ibid.*, RG 393, Military Div. of the Miss., Hd. Qrs. Correspondence; DLC-USG, V, 40, 94. *O.R.*, I, xxxii, part 2, 118. On Jan. 19, 2:00 P.M., Meigs telegraphed to USG. "For the special inspection you desire I recommend that you detail temporarily one of the following officers: Lieut. Col. E. Nigh, Chief Qr. Mr. 16th Army Corps, Memphis; Lieut. Col. J. Condit Smith, 15th Army Corps; Lt. Col. J. C. Easton, Army of Cumberland; or, if none of these can be detached for the time necessary, Capt. W. G. Le Duc, who is now Depot Quartermaster at Bridgeport, and who would perhaps be better fitted for inspection than for charge of that Depot. I have no officer available here whom I could recommend and detach for the duty." LS (telegram sent), DNA, RG 92, Miscellaneous Telegrams Sent (Press); *ibid.*, RG 107, Telegrams Collected (Unbound); copies, *ibid.*, RG 393, Military Div. of the Miss., Hd. Qrs. Correspondence; DLC-USG, V, 40, 94. *O.R.*, I, xxxii, part 2, 138.

On Jan. 25, Bvt. Lt. Col. James L. Donaldson, Nashville, wrote to Meigs concerning letters written by R. M. Horsley of Cincinnati to USG and to others accusing Capt. Thomas R. Dudley, q. m. at Bridgeport, Ala., of theft, and recommending Stokes to investigate. LS, DNA, RG 92, Consolidated Correspondence, Thomas R. Dudley. On Feb. 9, Maj. William R. Rowley, provost marshal, wrote to Lt. Col. Cyrus B. Comstock. "In compliance with your request, I have to some extent investigated the anonymous charges against Capt Thos. R. Dudley A. Q. M referred by you to me, and have the honor to report, that I have thus far been inable to learn of any criminality on the part of Capt Dudley except that of gross carelessness and neglect of business in leaving irresponsible and incompetent Employees to look after matters to which he should have given his personal attention thereby causing unecessary delay and confusion in his department, as well as loss to the Government. With regard to the Money which he is reported to have sent home to his Father, I am disposed to think that the amount is largely overestimated. His brother who was at one time a Sutler at Bridgeport, is I learn a man much given to boasting, and has undoubtedly in that caused suspicion to be directed towards the Captain." Copies, DLC-USG, V, 106; DNA, RG 393, Military Div. of the Miss., Provost Marshal, Letters Sent. On Feb. 11, Comstock telegraphed to Maj. Gen. George H. Thomas. "The Major General Comman'dg directs that you will arrest and securely hold Captain T. R. Dudley, Quartermaster at Bridgeport, charged with large frauds—" Copies, DLC-USG, V, 34, 35; DNA, RG 393, Military Div. of the Miss., Letters Sent. On the same day, Thomas telegraphed to USG. "Does the Maj. Genl. Comd'g. desire Capt. Dudley held at Bridgeport or sent to Nashville." Copy, *ibid.*, Dept. of the Cumberland, Telegrams Sent. On Feb. 14, Bowers telegraphed to Thomas. "The Major General Commanding desires that Captain Warren, A. Q. M. at Stevenson, be arrested and held under guard as soon as a Quartermaster can be sent to take possession of his money and papers. Col Donaldson has requested Col Eaton to send Captain Gilgore to relieve him. The officer sent should secure all vouchers as they may be important evidence. The Major General Commanding also desires that if it has not been done, Captains Dudley's papers also be secured at once" Copies, *ibid.* On Feb. 16, Bowers wrote to Thomas. "Herewith you will find charges against Capt T. R Dudley, A Q M. U. S. Vols. one copy of which you will please forward to Capt Dudley. You will please convene a Court as early as practicable for his tri[al]" Copies, *ibid.* On the same day, Thomas telegraphed to USG. "Capt. W. A. Warren A. Q. M. Stevenson, has been arrested & placed under guard.—all his property papers & money are under guard, all papers & money under Seal." Copies, *ibid.*, RG 94, Staff Papers, William A. Warren; *ibid.*, RG 393, Military Div. of the Miss., Telegrams Received. On Feb. 23, Bowers telegraphed to Thomas. "Herewith find copies of additional charges and specifications against Capt W. A Warren Asst Quartermaster U. S. V. one copy of which you will please deliver to Capt W. A court for his trial should be convened as early as practicable" Copies, DLC-USG, V, 34, 35; DNA, RG 393, Military Div. of the Miss., Letters Sent. On Aug. 14, following a court-martial, Capt. William A. Warren was restored to duty. *Ibid.*, RG 94, Staff Papers, Warren. Dudley was also restored to duty. *Ibid.*, RG 92, Consolidated Correspondence, Dudley.

On Feb. 19, 7:30 P.M., USG telegraphed to Maj. Gen. Henry W. Halleck. "Is there any way by which an Inspector may be authorized to send for persons and take evidence [i]n cases of suspected fraud against Government before charges are made   Such authority is much needed to [secu]re [a] thorough investigation of the Quartermaster Department." Telegram received, *ibid.*, RG 107, Telegrams Collected (Bound); copies, *ibid.*, Telegrams Received in Cipher; *ibid.*, RG 393, Military Div. of the Miss., Hd. Qrs. Correspondence; DLC-USG, V, 40, 94. *O.R.*, I, xxxii, part 2, 428. On Feb. 20, 1:00 P.M., Halleck telegraphed to USG. "I know of no law authorising an Inspector to send for persons & take evidence, unless such persons, not military, are willing to attend; but this difficulty can be avoided by the order of a Court of Inquiry by the President, of one or more members. If you want such a court, telegraph who you wish on it." ALS (telegram sent), DNA, RG 107, Telegrams Collected (Bound); copies, *ibid.*, RG 393, Military Div. of the Miss., Hd. Qrs. Correspondence; DLC-USG, V, 40, 94. *O.R.*, I, xxxii, part 2, 432. On Feb. 27, USG telegraphed to Halleck. "I would name Brig Genls R S. Granger and A. C Gillett [*Gillem*] as members of a Court of inquiry   Lieut Col J. H. Stokes Judge Advocate"   Telegram received, DNA, RG 107, Telegrams Collected (Bound); copies, *ibid.*, RG 393, Military Div. of the Miss., Hd. Qrs. Correspondence; DLC-USG, V, 40, 94. On Feb. 28, 11:45 A.M., Halleck telegraphed to USG. "Please state what kind of an order you wish for a court of Inquiry & what it is to inquire into." ALS (telegram sent), DNA, RG 107, Telegrams Collected (Bound); copies, *ibid.*, RG 393, Military Div. of the Miss., Hd. Qrs. Correspondence; DLC-USG, V, 40, 94.

To Maj. Gen. George H. Thomas

Nashville February 6th 1864.

MAJ GENERAL G. H THOMAS
CHATTANOOGA

Reports of Scouts make it evident that Johnson has removed most of his available force from your front, two Divisions going to Longstreet. Longstreet has also been reenforced by troops from the East. This makes it evident the enemy intend to secure East Tennessee if they can, and I intend to drive them out or get whipped this month. For this purpose, you will have to detach at least tenthousand men besides Stanley's Division. More will be better. I can partially releive the vaccum at Chattanooga by troops from Logans command. It will not be necessary to take Artillery or wagons to Knoxville, but all the serviceable Artillery horses should be taken, to use on Artillery already there. Six mules to each two hundred men should also be taken if you have them to spare. Let me know how soon you can start.

U S GRANT
Major General

Telegram, copies, DLC-USG, V, 34, 35; DNA, RG 393, Military Div. of the Miss., Letters Sent; *ibid.*, Dept. of the Cumberland, Telegrams Received. Printed as sent at 2:30 P.M. in *O.R.*, I, xxxii, part 2, 337. On Feb. 8, 1864, Maj. Gen. George H. Thomas telegraphed to USG. "Your dispatch of 2 P. M. Feby. Sixth was received that evening but only so much of it could be translated as to make me understand that I am expected to detach from my command ten thousand men in addition to Stanleys Division and to report when I can start. I can start a portion of the additional troops day after tomorrow but I do not see how they can be fed in an exhausted country until the R. R. is completed to Loudon. I am in hopes to get the R. R. completed and in operation to Loudon by Thursday next. These ten thousand should be replaced by troops from Logan's Command immediately, else the enemy might take advantage of my move towards Knoxville and attack and capture this place. It will require an entire Division to hold the R. R. secure from here to Loudon." Copies, DNA, RG 393, Dept. of the Cumberland, Telegrams Sent; *ibid.*, Military Div. of the Miss., Telegrams Received. *O.R.*, I, xxxii, part 2, 352. On Feb. 9, USG telegraphed to Thomas. "You will please answer my dispatch to you of the 6th" Copies, DLC-USG, V, 34, 35; DNA, RG 393, Military Div. of the Miss., Letters Sent. On the same day, Thomas telegraphed to USG. "I answered your dispatch yesterday in cipher and have ordered it repeated." Copies, *ibid.*, Telegrams Received; *ibid.*, Dept. of the Cumberland, Telegrams Sent.

On Feb. 6, Brig. Gen. John A. Rawlins wrote to Maj. Gen. John A. Logan, Huntsville, Ala. "From all the information that has come to these Headquarters the indications are, that the enemy has greatly weakened himself in front of Chattanooga by sending forces to Mobile, and it is also reported two Divisions to Longstreet to enable him to hold his position in East Tennessee. To counteract this latter movement and to successfully give battle to Longstreet Gen Thomas has been directed to detach at least ten thousand men besides Stanleys Division and poceed with them at the earliest practicable moment to Knoxville. To supply as far as possible the place of the troops thus withdrawn from Chattanooga you will at once order in readiness to move there on the receipt of orders all the available force of your command that can possibly be spared without endangering too greatly the railroad they are now guarding" Copies, DLC-USG, V, 34, 35; DNA, RG 393, Military Div. of the Miss., Letters Sent. *O.R.*, I, xxxii, part 2, 343. On Feb. 8, Logan telegraphed to Rawlins. "I have ten thousand sparing one large division   Will leave me with muskets about six having all the property of the Veterans gone to take care of. If I hold the line now occupied—Could not well spare more. Will have that many ready and if more will be required please indicate the number when it becomes necessary to send if it does become necessary." Copy, DNA, RG 393, Military Div. of the Miss., Telegrams Received.

On Feb. 7, Thomas telegraphed to Rawlins. "Information recieved from Scott as follows—two Companies of home guards in each County Decalb and Cherokee Alabama   in Cherokee Co four Companies third Confederate Cavalry which with Roddys force makes nearly 2.000—This force under Roddy made attack on U. S. force at Lebanon Decalb County last Wednesday morning   Rebels were Repulsed in Confusion & retreated towards ~~Gasdain~~ Gasden Ala   Reported that Wheeler is on his way to reinforce Roddy   U S Forces fell back to Sandy Mountain   took position on Salt peter Cave near Fort Pain & Captured a number of the Rebels   fifteen days since twenty Eight Pieces of artillery were moved from dalton to Rome   the Infantry is to be Mounted on artillery Horses & this with all the Cavalry is to form Junction with Longstreet & Raid through tennessee & Ky   Morgan was to assume Command of his Cavalry on third Inst & Raid through Middle Tennessee & Come out at Stevenson or Tullohoma   there are fifty three Engines on western & Atlantic Rail Road & four hundred Box Cars   the outer RailRoad Depot on N & C R R took fire & burned down at three (3) oclock this morning   loss the building & 20.000 overcoats   nearly everything else Saved   I have sent a Reconnoisance in direction of Dalton today   not yet returned—Cars running as far as Cleveland—" Telegram received, *ibid.*, Dept. of the Tenn., Telegrams Received; copy, *ibid.*, Military Div. of the Miss.,

Telegrams Received. *O.R.*, I, xxxii, part 2, 349. On the same day, Thomas tele-
graphed to Rawlins. "Scouts and deserters say Claborns Division at Tunn'l Hill
Andersons Breckenridges Stewarts at Dalton. Cheatburns ordered to Mobile—
Gen Johnson at Rome last Thursday. Breckenridges Div. under marching orders
for the past week—Grigsbys brigade of Cavalry sent to Decatur to recruit   all
Ky. Cavaly turned over to John Morgan who is at Decatur organizing his com'd.
—force about two thousand men   fight took place yesterday between 2d Ky—
Cavy. and third Ala. Cavy.   the former refused to reenlist as ordered   the latter
ordered to fire on them did so   Killed 3 wounding 5   Second Ky. returned the
fire killing and wounding 30 then dispersed. Ky. Candidate for Congress making
speeches through the army. Deserters six days from Meridian says Gen'l Sherman
marching on that place with 12.000 men   Frenches and Lorings Divisions retreating before him to Mobile"   Copy (misdated Jan. 8), DNA, RG 393, Military Div. of the Miss., Telegrams Received. *O.R.*, I, xxxii, part 2, 352–53.

To Col. William D. Mann

Headquarters Military Division of the Mississippi,
Nashville, Tenn.,
Feb. 6, 1864.

COLONEL W. D. MANN, SEVENTH MICHIGAN CAVALRY:

COLONEL: An examination of the cavalry and infantry accoutrements exhibited by you satisfies me that the change from the
old style is such as to warrant their adoption throughout the army
as fast as new accoutrements have to be supplied. I think no more
of the old should be made until yours are fully tested.

The improvements in the cartridge-box are undoubted, and
should be adopted at once.

The change in the belt, and the manner of carrying the knapsack and cartridge-box, I believe will demonstrate itself to be a
great improvement, and if it does not, the soldier will naturally
make the change in carrying these, suggested by experience.

Yours, etc.,
U. S. GRANT,
Major-General.

Colonel Mann's Infantry and Cavalry Accoutrements. . . . (New York, 1864),
p. 34. Born in Sandusky, Ohio, in 1839, William D. Mann operated a hotel in
Grafton, Ohio, before the Civil War. Commissioned col., 7th Mich. Cav., in 1862,
he fought at Gettysburg, and resigned early in 1864 to promote his accoutrements.

On June 24, USG wrote to Brig. Gen. George D. Ramsay. "I would respectfully recommend that the next twenty thousand Infantry, and Ten thousand Cavalry accoutrements purchased by the Ordnance Department be of the pattern invented by Col Wm D. Mann. I am very anxious to see these accoutrements fully tested. I am satisfied the manner of carrying the knapsack and haversack will prove a great relief to our soldiers and the extra quantity of ammunition carried in the cartridge box would have proven of emmince advantage in several engagements when I have Commanded. Specially is this true with the Cavalry arm of the service. Hoping that this improvement will receive a fair trial," Copies, DLC-USG, V, 45, 59, 67; DNA, RG 108, Letters Sent. See Andy Logan, *The Man Who Robbed the Robber Barons* (New York, 1965), pp. 78–79.

To Abraham Lincoln

Head Quarters, Mil. Div. of the Miss.
Nashville Ten. Feb.y 7th 1864

HIS EXCELLENCY, A. LINCOLN,
PRESIDENT OF THE UNITED STATES,
SIR:

I would respectfully recommend Maj. L. C. Easton,[1] Asst. Q. M. U. S. A. for promotion to the rank of Brig. Gen. of Vols.— Maj. Easton has served for more than twenty-five years in the regular army, and sustained during all that time the highest reputation for integrity and ability. As a disbursing officer I believe he has guarded the interests of the Government with all the zeal and all the watchfulness a careful man could bestow upon his private affairs. We have a few such men among our Disbursing Officers and I believe the responsibilities resting with them entitles them to promotion.

Although I have never conversed with Maj. Easton on the subject I believe he has the highest recommendations for the promotion here asked.

I have the honor to be,
with great respect,
your obt. svt.
U. S. GRANT
Maj. Gen. U. S. A.

ALS, DNA, RG 94, 831 ACP 1881. On March 4, 1864, President Abraham

Lincoln endorsed this letter. "Submitted to the Secretary of War, & General-in-Chief." AES, *ibid*. No appointment followed.

On Jan. 22, Alton R. Easton, Mo. inspector gen., St. Louis, wrote to USG asking that his brother, Lt. Col. Langdon C. Easton, be assigned as chief q. m. on USG's staff and recommended to Lincoln for appointment as brig. gen. ALS, MoSHi. On Feb. 7, USG wrote to Alton R. Easton. "Your letter of the 4th inst. is received, but not the letters and papers refered to in it. I cordially grant your request however of recommending your brother for promotion both for his services & merit and for the high esteem and obligations I feel towards you personally." ALS, *ibid*.

On Feb. 19, USG wrote to Maj. Gen. William S. Rosecrans. "Permit me to introduce to you Col. A. R. Easton, of the Staff of the Governor of the state of Mo. The Col. is the brother of Lt. Col. Langdon Easton, Chf Q. M. of the Army of the Cumberland, and an old particular friend of mine whilst I was a citizen of Mo. He is a gentleman who I have more cause to remember favorably than almost any other in the City of St. Louis.—As you will necessarily be favorably impressed with him, on acquaintance, it is only necessary for me to add that I will regard courtesies shown him as favors to myself." ALS, DNA, RG 109, Union Provost Marshals' File of Papers Relating to Individual Civilians.

1. Easton of Mo., USMA 1838, appointed capt. and asst. q. m. as of March 3, 1847; maj. and q. m. as of Aug. 3, 1861, in charge of the depot at Fort Leavenworth; and chief q. m., Army of the Cumberland, on Dec. 15, 1863, which provided the *ex officio* rank of lt. col.

To Maj. Gen. Henry W. Halleck

Nashville Tenn
Feby 8th 1864—10 30 a m

MAJ GEN H W. HALLECK
GEN IN CHIEF

Can troops be sent me to take the place of Veterans gone home and those still awaiting furloughs—If immediate furloughs could be given it would stimulate reenlistments—There is necessity for all the troops now in the field   Furloughs therefore can only be given as other troops arrive to take the place of those furloughed

U S GRANT
Maj Genl

Telegram received, DNA, RG 107, Telegrams Collected (Bound); copies, *ibid*., Telegrams Received in Cipher; *ibid*., RG 393, Military Div. of the Miss., Hd. Qrs. Correspondence; DLC-USG, V, 40, 94. *O.R.*, I, xxxii, part 2, 350. See letter to Maj. Gen. Henry W. Halleck, Feb. 4, 1864.

To Maj. Gen. Henry W. Halleck

———

Nashville Tenn
Feb 8th 1864

Maj Gen Halleck
Gen in Chf

Genl Foster telegraphs from Knoxville under date of yesterday that an expedition sent against Thomas[1] and his band of Indians and whites at Quallatown[2] has returned completely successful They surprised the town, killed & wounded [two] hundred & fifteen, took fifty prisoners, dispersed the remainder of the gang in the mountains—Our loss two killed & six wounded

U S Grant M G

Telegram received, DNA, RG 107, Telegrams Collected (Bound). This telegram virtually repeated a telegram of Feb. 7, 1864, from Maj. Gen. John G. Foster, Knoxville, to USG. Copies (2), *ibid.*, RG 393, Military Div. of the Miss., Telegrams Received. *O.R.*, I, xxxii, part 1, 159.

1. William H. Thomas, born in N. C. in 1805, established a successful trading post at Quallatown, N. C., in the late 1820s. He worked as agent and advisor to the Cherokee Indians who remained in N. C. after 1838, and served in the N. C. Senate during the 1850s. In 1862, he organized Thomas' Legion (69th N. C.), two cos. of which consisted of Cherokees. See Richard W. Iobst, "William Holland Thomas and the Cherokee Claims," in Duane H. King, ed., *The Cherokee Indian Nation: A Troubled History* (Knoxville, 1979), pp. 181–201; Nathaniel C. Browder, *The Cherokee Indians and Those Who Came After . . .* (Hayesville, N. C., 1973), pp. 227–36.

2. Quallatown, N. C., on the Oconalufte River, approximately fifty miles southeast of Knoxville.

To Brig. Gen. Montgomery C. Meigs

———

From Nashville *M.*
Dated, Feby 9 *1864.*

Gen M C Meigs Q M G.

The wagons and mules called for by Genl Thomas are More than can be required by the four (4) dept's. in my Command   in addition to what they have if furnished we could not supply them nor move with such a train   I will make an order regulating transportation in a few days

U. S. GRANT

Maj Genl

Telegram received, DNA, RG 92, Consolidated Correspondence, Army of the Cumberland; *ibid.*, RG 107, Telegrams Collected (Bound); copies, *ibid.*, RG 393, Military Div. of the Miss., Hd. Qrs. Correspondence; *ibid.*, Letters Sent; DLC-USG, V, 34, 35, 40, 94. *O.R.*, I, xxxii, part 2, 354. On Feb. 8, 1864, Col. Charles Thomas, deputy q. m. gen., wrote to USG. "The following is a copy of a telegram sent to your address this day: 'General Thomas has directed Col. Easton to call upon Colonel Donalson for three thousand (3000) more wagons and harness. four thousand (4000) more horses, twenty three thousand (23000) more mules, first cost four and a quarter millions—monthly addition to wages and forage, not less than half a million—Can so much be necessary—and where? On 30th September, exclusive of supply trains, the Army of Cumberland had in the front, twenty eight hundred wagons, sixteen thousand four hundred mules—Many thousand animals died, or were sent to the rear, but only a few hundred wagons, according to my information were lost or or destroyed. Eleventh and twelfth corps, joined with full quota of transportation, after the 30th September—On 31st Dec. Army of Cumberland reports twenty five hundred wagons (2500) and thirteen thousand mules unserviceable—(13000)   Is the Army of the Cumberland to be doubled in size? and if so, will not the troops ordered to it, bring their own transportation? Will a larger train than that which sufficed to move from Murfreesboro into Georgia be necessary in the new Campaign? and finally, can such a train live? I have communicated with Genl. Allen. Many mules were sent to Louisville, St Louis, and Mattoon to recruit— These should be drawn upon—All the best teams in Depot service should be sent to the field and replaced by reduced animals still capable of serving in the cities—This we do here, but it will be resisted by Quartermasters, wagon masters and teamsters in the depots, and will require your strong authority to compel— There should be two or three thousand fresh mules at Louisville, and several thousand recruited—I have called for reports by telegraph. To supply three thousand more wagons in any short time will be difficult. Are they really necessary? The Armies will not in all be numerically stronger than last spring, and three thousand wagons cannot have been lost or worn out. It is important to collect existing material for the new campaign, as far as possible, instead of purchasing anew—The expenses of the past six months, are much greater than ever before, and our appropriations are giving out—When should the new outfit start? To avoid consumption of supplies difficult to get to the front the animals should be held in the rear as long as possible—Not being advised of your present intentions as to movements, I am unable to give instructions—Do not allow any calls not really necessary. Our difficulties are for money rather than men.' " LS, DNA, RG 393, Military Div. of the Miss., Letters Received. The telegram sent the same day was signed by Brig. Gen. Montgomery C. Meigs. LS, *ibid.*, RG 92, Miscellaneous Telegrams Sent (Press); *ibid.*, RG 107, Telegrams Collected (Unbound); copies (misdated Feb. 3), *ibid.*, RG 393, Military Div. of the Miss., Hd. Qrs. Correspondence; DLC-USG, V, 40, 94.

On Feb. 9, USG telegraphed to Maj. Gen. George H. Thomas. "When the army moves in the Spring, it will have to be with less than half the transportation they have been heretofore accustomed to. Much of the additional transportation required, can be got by reducing that in the hands of the troops left in Depots on R. R. Duty. It will be impossible to subsist a large wagon train, and besides they will impede the progress of armies marching over the narrow and mountainous roads of the south." Copies, DNA, RG 393, Dept. of the Cumberland, Letters Received; *ibid.*, Telegrams Received; *ibid.*, RG 393, Military Div. of the Miss., Letters Sent; DLC-USG, V, 34, 35. *O.R.*, I, xxxii, part 2, 354–55. On the same day, Thomas telegraphed to USG. "Your telegram in reference to transportation, received. Col. Easton's estimate was made on the supposition that this army might be filled up to the maximum strength, but we shall need nearly all the horses estimated for, as the Cavalry has been on constant duty all Fall, and Winter, and is now almost entirely broken down. The estimate for mules can be reduced by dispensing with the greatest part of the transportation for troops at depots, and guarding Rail-Roads." Copies, DNA, RG 393, Dept. of the Cumberland, Letters Received; *ibid.*, Telegrams Sent; *ibid.*, Military Div. of the Miss., Telegrams Received. *O.R.*, I, xxxii, part 2, 355.

On Feb. 24, 3:30 P.M., Meigs telegraphed to USG. "Col Donaldson advises me that there is to be a heavy draft for mules & horses for the army of East Tennessee as well as for the army of the Cumberland & that he thinks there will be a short supply unless special effort is made. Will you advise me what number of animals are likely to be needed & when   Gen Allen will aid you by all means in his power & I will give any additional instructions needed—How many mules & horses artillery & Cavalry should be forwarded to Nashville & where can they best be procured—I have heard nothing from you since your despatch in relation to the heavy trains & twenty three thousand mules estimated for Army of the Cumberland which you & I thought to be excessive. Let me hear from you on this subject in time for action"   ALS (telegram sent), DNA, RG 107, Telegrams Collected (Unbound); copies, *ibid.*, RG 393, Military Div. of the Miss., Hd. Qrs. Correspondence; DLC-USG, V, 40, 94. On the same day, Col. Charles Thomas sent the same message to USG by mail. LS, DNA, RG 393, Military Div. of the Miss., Letters Received. Also on Feb. 24, Bvt. Lt. Col. James L. Donaldson wrote to USG. "The necessity for horses and mules for the front is a growing one, and I apprehend delays and embarrassments, if more energetic measures are not taken to hurry them forward. I respectfully Suggest that Genl Allen be instructed by telegram to send all the horses and mules he can without delay—Parties are now here from the front whom I cannot Supply, and I repeat my opinion already Expressed, that we Shall want all the mules and horses I have called for." ALS, *ibid.*, RG 92, Dept. of the Cumberland, Q. M. Dept., Letters Sent (Press).

On Feb. 25, 1:00 P.M., Meigs telegraphed to USG. "Capt Hall Asst Qur-Master Camp Nelsen Kentucky asks permission to purchase three thousand aged mules less than fourteen hands to enable him to send subsistence stores ~~from~~ by pack trains to Knoxville such mode of supply being ordered by ~~Comman~~ Major General commandig Department of Ohio. Purchase of mules below fourteen hands is prohibited & ~~if~~ by General instructions & if allowed ~~can lead~~ must lead to imposition. All our attempts to transport supplies by pack trains have proved most wasteful & costly failures   Is not the line of supply by Chattanooga sufficient & can any-thing but waste of money result from the attempt to pack via Cumberland Gap. Please give such orders as you find necessary & proper & advise this Department thereof." ALS (telegram sent), *ibid.*, RG 107, Telegrams Collected

(Unbound); copies, *ibid.*, RG 393, Military Div. of the Miss., Hd. Qrs. Correspondence; DLC-USG, V, 40, 94. *O.R.*, I, xxxii, part 2, 463. On the same day, Thomas sent the same message to USG by mail. LS, DNA, RG 393, Military Div. of the Miss., Letters Received. On the same day, USG telegraphed to Meigs. "I do not think it advisable to get up pack trains and will so instruct Genl Schofield The route by Chattanooga is the only reliable one for the supply of East Tennessee & neither requires pack animals or teams" Telegram received, *ibid.*, RG 92, Consolidated Correspondence, Army of the Cumberland; copies, *ibid.*, RG 393, Military Div. of the Miss., Letters Sent; DLC-USG, V, 34, 35; (misdated Feb. 28) *ibid.*, V, 40, 94; DNA, RG 393, Military Div. of the Miss., Hd. Qrs. Correspondence. Dated Feb. 25 in *O.R.*, I, xxxii, part 2, 463. Also on Feb. 25, USG telegraphed to Maj. Gen. John M. Schofield. "Captain Hall applies for authority to purchase 3000 pack mules. I am satisfied the route by Chattanooga will have to be relied on for supplying East Tennessee and that the fitting out of a pack train would be useless waste. When pack mules have to be resorted to it will be because wagons cannot be used. Then the team mules can be taken for that purpose." Copies, DLC-USG, V, 34, 35; DNA, RG 393, Military Div. of the Miss., Letters Sent. *O.R.*, I, xxxii, part 2, 463–64. On Feb. 26, Schofield telegraphed to USG. "Capt Hall has been directed to stop the purchase of mules for this Department as I have quite as many in Ky as I shall need the original order for a pack train was given for the advance which was proposed from here it would be very useful if I had it now but would take too long to get it here I propose to do the best I can without it" Telegram received (dated Feb. 27), DNA, RG 393, Dept. of the Tenn., Telegrams Received; copies, *ibid.*, Military Div. of the Miss., Telegrams Received; (2—dated Feb. 26) *ibid.*, Dept. of the Ohio, Telegrams Sent. Dated Feb. 26 in *O.R.*, I, xxxii, part 2, 473.

To Maj. Gen. Henry W. Halleck

Nashville Tenn
Feby 9th 1864 10 30 A M

MAJ GEN H. W. HALLECK
GEN IN CHIEF

The change of Rail Road manager has added Sixty (60) per cent to the freight carried;[1] this I hope will enable me soon to supply an army in East Tennessee sufficient to drive Longstreet out. The roads will be complete to Loudon tomorrow and to Stevenson via Decatur by monday[2] next

U S. GRANT
Maj. Genl

Telegram received, DNA, RG 107, Telegrams Collected (Bound); copies, *ibid.*,

Telegrams Received in Cipher; *ibid.*, RG 393, Military Div. of the Miss., Hd. **Qrs.** Correspondence; DLC-USG, V, 40, 94. *O.R.*, I, xxxii, part 2, 354.

    1. See telegram to Maj. Gen. Henry W. Halleck, Jan. 22, 1864, note 3.
    2. Feb. 15.

To Maj. Gen. Henry W. Halleck

Hd. Qrs. Mil. Div. of the Miss.
Nashville, Tenn. Feb. 9th, 1864

Respectfully forwarded and attention invited to Gen. Slocum's statements. The position occupied by Gen. Hooker is embarassing to the service and I think injurious. I am inclined rather to recommend that the 11th and 12th Corps be filled up from the new levies, to having them consolidated, but what to do with Gen. Hooker is the question. I have no command to give him at present. While the states North of the Ohio were in my command I recommended that they be called one district and Gen. Hooker placed in command.[1] They are now a separate Dept.

U. S. GRANT
Maj. Gen.

Copies, DLC-USG, V, 39; DNA, RG 393, Military Div. of the Miss., Endorsements; (typescript) Atwood Collection, InU. *O.R.*, I, xxxii, part 2, 315. On Feb. 2, 1864, Maj. Gen. Henry W. Slocum wrote a protest against the command of the 11th and 12th Corps by Maj. Gen. Joseph Hooker. *Ibid.*, pp. 313–14. Hooker's endorsement of Feb. 3 is *ibid.*, pp. 314–15. On Feb. 24, Maj. Gen. Henry W. Halleck wrote to USG. "Major Genl Slocum's letter of the 2d with your endorsement of the 9th, in regard to the anomalous position of the commands of the 11th & 12th corps, has been recieved and submitted to the Secty of War. This arrangement having been made directly by the President, I have no authority to effect any change." ALS, DNA, RG 393, Military Div. of the Miss., Letters Received. *O.R.*, I, xxxii, part 2, 455. See endorsement to Maj. Gen. Henry W. Halleck, Oct. 26, 1863.

    1. On Dec. 13, 1863, 1:30 P.M., USG telegraphed to Halleck. "Does the order defining limits of the Dept of the Ohio take the States of Ohio, Indiana and Illinois out of this Military Division   If not I would suggest Genl Hooker to command the District composed of these States" Telegram received, DNA, RG 107, Telegrams Collected (Bound); copies, *ibid.*, RG 393, Military Div. of the Miss., Hd. Qrs. Correspondence; DLC-USG, V, 40, 94. *O.R.*, I, xxxi, part 3, 397.

To Maj. Gen. George H. Thomas

————

Nashville February 9th 1864.

MAJOR GENERAL GEO H THOMAS
CHATTANOOGA

There are a large number of women here applying to go south. I have declined giving any more such permits   As it is rather desirable that all such should be where their affections are set, I propose giving notice through the papers setting a day when all who wish will be permitted to go and fix the point where they will be allowed to pass our lines. Let me know where and when they should be allowed to go.

U S GRANT
Major General

Telegram, copies, DLC-USG, V, 34, 35; DNA, RG 393, Military Div. of the Miss., Letters Sent. On Feb. 9, 1864, Maj. Gen. George H. Thomas telegraphed to USG. "I would propose Decatur Ala as the most suitable point for persons whose sympathies are with the south to pass through our lines   If they come this way we are compelled to use Govt transportation to them out of our lines   It is decidedly inconvient   The R R will be through to Louden on friday next"   Telegram received, *ibid.*, Dept. of the Tenn., Telegrams Received; copies, *ibid.*, Military Div. of the Miss., Telegrams Received; *ibid.*, Dept. of the Cumberland, Telegrams Sent.

Also on Feb. 9, USG telegraphed to Thomas. "Nashville being the base of supplies for these Armies large accession to present storage room will be required. I will give the necessary orders for this without sending thr'o you"   Copies, DLC-USG, V, 34, 35; DNA, RG 393, Military Div. of the Miss., Letters Sent.

To Brig. Gen. Alvin P. Hovey

————

Nashville February 9th 1864.

BRIGADIER GENERAL ALVIN. P. HOVEY
INDIANAPOLIS INDA

The early winter we have had betokens an early spring. I am very desirous of being ready to take advantage of the first dry roads to commense a campaign. Before I can start however many of our veterans must return, and the new levies brought into the field. Now General, my particular object in detailing you for the service you are now on, was to have some one who knew the importance of reorganization and discipline with the new troops from their enlistment. In this way I expected to have troops ready for duty from the moment they report for duty. I wish you would urge upon Governor Morton the importance of this and ask him for me to organize into Companies and Regiments all those who are to go into new regiments, and to detatch those who are destined to fill up old organizations at once. We will have some sharp fighting in the spring, and if successful, I believe the war will be ended within the year; if the enemy gain temporary advantage, the war will be protracted. I want ten thousand and more troops now badly. With such a number I could let my veterans go and could drive Longstreet out of East Tennessee. I wish you could prevail on the Governor to organize all the forces he has and send you here at once. I would keep the Division together and where by contact with old troops, they would improve more in one day, than in six where they are.

U S GRANT
Major General

Copies, DLC-USG, V, 34, 35; DNA, RG 393, Military Div. of the Miss., Letters Sent. *O.R.*, I, xxxii, part 2, 355. On Feb. 8, 1864, Brig. Gen. Alvin P. Hovey wrote to USG. "I recd an order on the 3rd inst from Maj Gen Heintzleman commanding the Northern Department a Copy of which is herewith enclosed—It gives me great pleasure to know that the change made in this Department will not seperate me from your command for I am more than willing to share your fortunes—We have in this state about 10,000 volunteers for the new regiments now under the commandants of the different rendousvous, but the Governor has not yet organized a single regiment although I have been promised for more than three weeks that it should be done immediately—The consequence is that the men are idle, without arms and I am afraid will become greatly demoralized unless they are soon brought under rigid discipline—The Governor does not seem to be alive to the necessity of thier early organization and I am fearful that his delay will prevent me from bringing them into the field prepared for your Spring Campaign. My object in writing to you is to have you write to myself or the Governor urging the early organization of these troops—There seems to be a general impression in the North that the rebellion is nearly over and I am afraid it will eventually result in injury to our cause—If you write to the Governor do not say that I have made this request—I have urged him now until I am sure he feels sore under my many importunities" ALS, DNA, RG 393, Military Div. of the Miss., Letters Received. See Charles M. Walker, *Hovey and Chase*. . . . (Indianapolis, 1882), pp. 112–14.

To Maj. Gen. George H. Thomas

Nashville February 10th '64.

MAJOR GENERAL GEO H THOMAS
CHATTANOOGA

Prepare to start for Knoxville on Saturday.[1] I will order Logan to send to Chattanooga, all the troops he can and still guard his line of road.[2] The number will probably be about 5000 men. One division of your command will have to move out to hold the road to the Hiwassee.

U. S. GRANT
Major General

Telegram, copies, DLC-USG, V, 34, 35; DNA, RG 393, Military Div. of the Miss., Letters Sent; *ibid.*, Dept. of the Cumberland, Telegrams Received. *O.R.*, I, xxxii, part 2, 359. On Feb. 10, 1864, Maj. Gen. George H. Thomas telegraphed to USG. "The engineer reports that he will have the Rail Road finished to Loudon on Friday next. As they are very much in need of supplies at Knoxville I think it will be best to allow time for an accumulation there, before the troops from here move up. I will try to provide for the defense of this place by placing a Division of Genl. Logan's Corps at Chickamauga Station and Davis's Division in front of Cleveland to cover the R. R. taking with me Stanley's Johnson's and Bairds Divisions. Will you order the Division of Logan's to move to this place as soon as possible." Copies, DNA, RG 393, Dept. of the Cumberland, Telegrams Sent; *ibid.*, Military Div. of the Miss., Telegrams Received. *O.R.*, I, xxxii, part 2, 360.

Also on Feb. 10, USG telegraphed to Thomas. "An officer having blanks &c for your Dept. is occupying a building much needed for Com'g Officer. Have you any objection to his being removed to an other building?" Copy, DNA, RG 393, Dept. of the Cumberland, Telegrams Received. On the same day, Thomas telegraphed to USG. "The building asked for by the commissary contains in additional to blanks & c all the records of the dept haad Qrs they are of too much Importance to be moved carelessly I should think he could afford to get another building" Telegram received, *ibid.*, Dept. of the Tenn., Telegrams Received; copies, *ibid.*, Dept. of the Cumberland, Telegrams Sent; *ibid.*, Military Div. of the Miss., Telegrams Received.

On Feb. 11, 11:30 A.M., USG telegraphed to Maj. Gen. Henry W. Halleck. "I expect to get off from Chattanooga by monday next a force to drive Longstreet out of East Tennessee. It has been impossible heretofore to subsist the troops necessary for this work" Telegram received, *ibid.*, RG 107, Telegrams Collected (Bound); copies, *ibid.*, Telegrams Received in Cipher; *ibid.*, RG 393, Military Div. of the Miss., Hd. Qrs. Correspondence; DLC-USG, V, 40, 94. *O.R.*, I, xxxii, part 2, 365.

1. Feb. 13.

2. On Feb. 10, USG telegraphed to Maj. Gen. John A. Logan, Huntsville, Ala. "Move to Chattanooga all the forces you can at once   The entire line of railroad must be guarded, but reduce the force to a minimum. Send no Artillery. Let it remain where it is." Copies, DLC-USG, V, 34, 35; DNA, RG 393, Military Div. of the Miss., Letters Sent. *O.R.*, I, xxxii, part 2, 362. On the same day, Logan telegraphed to USG. "Your despatch Just received. will be in motion by daylight in the morning. Shall I send Camp Garrison Equipage or do you desire them to get there as rapidly as possible, light. please answer at once—important." Copies, DNA, RG 393, Military Div. of the Miss., Telegrams Received; DLC-John A. Logan. Printed as sent at 6:00 P.M. in *O.R.*, I, xxxii, part 2, 362. On the same day, USG telegraphed to Thomas. "Orders have been given to Logan and he reports that he will move in the morning." Copy, DNA, RG 393, Dept. of the Cumberland, Telegrams Received. On Feb. 11, Logan telegraphed to USG. "Fourteen of my largest regiments of infantry from different commands along the line of R. R. started this morning at 7 Oclock for the place designated. I have sent Genl Matthies in Command, he being the only General Officer now in the Corps present except Division Commanders. if they are to remain at any given point I will leave him in Command, but if to go to the front I will send some one else and relieve him. You will please notify me if it becomes necessary to send some other officer" Copies, *ibid.*, 15th Army Corps, Letters Sent; *ibid.*, Military Div. of the Miss., Telegrams Received; DLC-John A. Logan. *O.R.*, I, xxxii, part 2, 370.

On Feb. 10, USG telegraphed to Brig. Gen. Grenville M. Dodge, Pulaski, Tenn. "Can you spare men from your command to hold Decatur and still hold the road? If so make immediate preparations to to do it." Copies, DLC-USG, V, 34, 35; DNA, RG 393, Military Div. of the Miss., Letters Sent. On Feb. 11, Dodge telegraphed to USG, then to Brig. Gen. John A. Rawlins. "I have just returned from opposite Decatur. Cars can run there as soon as Duck river bridge is done   Say next Wednesday. Not much done west of Huntsville: four pretty large bridges to build. I will get ready to move as suggested   I ought to have five or six regiments back now   The 2d and 7th Iowa's time is out also Fuller's Brigade from Ohio. If you could hurry up their return I would be strong enough. The Tennessee is fordable in two places and the Cavalry force has increased. I suspect that Davidson's division from Rome has been sent down into the valley. There was a Pontoon bridge in Nashville when I was there   can I have it:" "There is no guard at Duck river bridge. The nearest force is one company of mine stationed at Duck river station to guard my stores that arrive on cars: up to this time kept a good watch over it. My company will return in a day or two. It appears to me so important a work with the Pontoon bridge close by it: that the force at Columbia two and one half miles up the river should me moved down to it. I do not suppose you care about the towns   You know it is not in my command. I do not think it safe as now guarded" Copies, *ibid.*, Telegrams Received; *ibid.*, 16th Army Corps, Left Wing, Telegrams Sent. *O.R.*, I, xxxii, part 2, 369. On the same day, Lt. Col. Theodore S. Bowers wrote to Maj. Gen. Lovell H. Rousseau. "You will please direct Col Mizner to move a sufficient force from Columbia to Duck River bridge to guard it against all possible danger" Copies, DLC-USG, V, 34, 35; DNA, RG 393, Military Div. of the Miss., Letters Sent.

On Feb. 8, Dodge had telegraphed to Rawlins. "Mr. Boomer has commenced replacing the trestele bridges north of Duck river with truss bridges   a party of eight or ten men with three teams should be sent to his party with orders to send all the timber boats &c to the trestle bridge and put them in a safe place   unless this is done they will flow off down stream lost &c   if done in case of any raid the bridges are destroyed the trestles can again be put up and thus cause but little delay in running the road north of Duck River. There are seven of these bridges all good, strong, well framed trestles   when they get within my jurisdiction—I can save them if required" Copies, *ibid.*, Telegrams Received; *ibid.*, 16th Army Corps, Left Wing, Telegrams Sent.

On Feb. 23, Dodge wrote to Maj. Roswell M. Sawyer, adjt. for Maj. Gen. William T. Sherman. "I have the honor to report the duty performed by this command in repairing the Railroad from Nashville to Decatur. . . ." LS, *ibid.*, RG 94, Letters Received, 126T 1864. *O.R.*, I, xxxii, part 2, 451–52. On March 16, USG endorsed this letter. "Respectfully forwarded to the Headquarters of the Army Washington D. C." ES, DNA, RG 94, Letters Received, 126T 1864. On Feb. 26, Dodge wrote to Rawlins. "Several of the bridges that I have put in are very substantial ones, and I think are very safe and not liable to wash out: for instance; two of the Richland Creek bridges, the Elk river bridge &c. Some, I think would be best to have changed. I understand that Mr Boomer—has a contract to put in Howe's truss over all streams where it was formerly: and, if after inspection the bridges I speak of should be considered safe &c, and Mr Boomers contrac[t] allows: it appears to me that these truss bridges could be saved in store for future use. I write this from the fact that I believe an effort has been made to have the Road repaired, looking more to the benefit of the owners of the Road than of the service; at least in several cases it has looked so to me" Copies, *ibid.*, RG 393, 16th Army Corps, Letters Sent; *ibid.*, Left Wing, Letters Sent.

On Feb. 24, Logan wrote to Bowers. "I understand that Genl Thomas has not moved, and does not intend to. And I would therefore respectfully request that the troops on service from my command in that Department be ordered to return. As soon as they do return, I will be enabled to complete the Railroad to Decatur in a short time,   As it is, I cannot put the necessary force to work upon it,   I am however doing all I can towards it. I wish to remind you that including the force sent to Genl Thomas there are twenty-five Regiments of Infantry absent from the command, and in my judgement, considering all the circumstances, the greatest necessity exists for the immediate return of the Detachment herein referred to, which is now under the immediate command of Brig. Gen'l C. S. Matthias. A number of the Regiments under Gen'l Matthias are Veteran Regiments, and ought to be permitted to go home as soon as possible, unless the necessity for their remaining be greater than what I have intimated exists for their return. I hope you will order them back at once." Copy, *ibid.*, 15th Army Corps, Letters and Telegrams Sent. *O.R.*, I, xxxii, part 2, 461–62.

To Julia Dent Grant

[*Feb. 10, 1864*]

It looks now as if the Lieut. Generalcy bill was going to become a law. If it does and is given to me, it will help my finances so much that I will be able to be much more generous in my expenditures.

... I am very well and very busy preparing and moving troops. I shall probably leave next week for Chattanooga and Knoxville. ...

ULYS.

William Nelson sale, Anderson Auction Company, No. 1025, April 16, 17, 1914, p. 47.

To Maj. Gen. Henry W. Halleck

Nashville Tenn.
11 30 A m. Feb. 11, 1864.

MAJ GEN. H. W. HALLECK,
GENL-IN-CHF.

It is very important to secure the early return of veterans and the forwarding of new levies to the front to enable us to commence an early Spring Campaign. Cannot Governors of states send their newly enlisted men at once? They will become soldiers much quicker by contact with veterans than where they are & they could take the place of those still left who are entitled to furloughs.

U. S. GRANT
maj G[en.]

Telegram received, DNA, RG 107, Telegrams Collected (Bound); copies, *ibid.*, RG 393, Military Div. of the Miss., Hd. Qrs. Correspondence; DLC-USG, V, 40, 94. *O.R.*, I, xxxii, part 2, 369. On Feb. 11, 1864, 4:00 P.M., Maj. Gen. Henry W. Halleck telegraphed to USG. "Congress has been more than two months discussing the draft bill, and unless it soon passes we cannot fill up infantry regts in time to supply the place of furloughed men. Other armies are in the same or worse condition than yours." ALS (telegram sent), DNA, RG 107, Telegrams Collected (Bound); copies, *ibid.*, RG 393, Military Div. of the Miss., Hd. Qrs. Correspondence; DLC-USG, V, 40, 94. *O.R.*, I, xxxii, part 2, 369.

On Feb. 12, USG telegraphed to Halleck. "Are soldiers of the regular army who re enlist entitled to furloughs, and if so are they entitled to public transportation?" Telegram received, DNA, RG 107, Telegrams Collected (Bound); copies, *ibid.*, RG 94, Letters Received, 203M 1864; *ibid.*, RG 393, Military Div. of the Miss., Hd. Qrs. Correspondence; DLC-USG, V, 40, 94. On Feb. 13, 1:00 P.M., Col. Edward D. Townsend, AGO, telegraphed to USG. "Your telegram of twelfth (12th) instant received, I~~ am instructed to inform you that you are allowed to give~~ The same furloughs and transportation are to be given to re-enlisted regulars as ~~are allowed~~ to re-enlisted Volunteers." LS (telegram sent), DNA, RG

107, Telegrams Collected (Unbound); copies, *ibid.*, RG 94, Letters Sent; *ibid.*, RG 393, Military Div. of the Miss., Hd. Qrs. Correspondence; DLC-USG, V, 40, 94.

To Maj. Gen. John M. Schofield

By Telegraph from Nashville Feby 11th 186[4]
To MAJ GENL SCHOFIELD
COMDG D O

I deem it of the utmost importance to drive Longstreets out immediately so as to furlough the balance of our veterans and to prepare for a Spring Campaign of our own chosing instead of permitting the enemy to dictate it for us—Thomas is ordered to start ten thousand men besides the remainder of Grangers Corps at once —he will take no artillery but will take his artillery horses and three mules to one hundred men   He will probably start next Monday.[1]

U. S. GRANT
M Genl

Telegram received (incomplete), DLC-John M. Schofield; copies, DLC-USG, V, 34, 35; DNA, RG 393, Military Div. of the Miss., Letters Sent. *O.R.*, I, xxxii, part 2, 367.

On Feb. 10, 1864, Maj. Gen. John M. Schofield had telegraphed to USG. "I am compelled to send about four thousand mules to Kentucky to be recruited. They will soon starve to death if kept here. This Army is almost destitute of serviceable mules, and Artillery horses, and it would be impossible to support them here if we had them. No movement of this Army can be made within the next six or eight weeks except by Infantry alone and carrying their provisions. The Artillery cannot move until supplied with fresh horses and forage. Longstreets Army is in much the same condition as this. I have no fears for the safety of our present position in East Tennessee, and unless there are reasons for a speedy advance which I do not now understand, I think it would be unwise to attempt one for the present. If however it is deemed necessary to drive Longstreet out of East Tennessee now I believe it is possible to do it with ten thousand more Infantry than I now have. But it will have to be done slowly so that the rail-road can be used to supply the troops. Please inform me what you desire me to do under the circumstances I have stated." Copies, DLC-John M. Schofield; DNA, RG 393, Military Div. of the Miss., Telegrams Received. *O.R.*, I, xxxii, part 2, 359.

On Feb. 13, Schofield telegraphed to USG. "Your despatch of the 11th is received. I will make all possible preparations and as rapidly as possible   Can probably be ready by the time reinforcements arrive. Can you send me a light pontoon train? If the rivers rise it will be indispensible. I will try to take some Artillery. If the weather continues dry there will be no difficulty. If the rainy season sets in we may have to work slowly along the rail-road. I will have to use pack-mules to supply me from this place at least for a time. Forage as well as provisions will have to be sent here by rail. I will need fresh horses for nearly all the Artillery. Longstreet was moving in this direction from Morristown on the 11th. I have nothing later from him. I can not learn of his receiving any reinforcements." Copies, DLC-John M. Schofield; (incomplete) DNA, RG 393, Military Div. of the Miss., Telegrams Received. Incomplete in *O.R.*, I, xxxii, part 2, 384. On Feb. 16, Schofield received a telegram: "Following is the Divisio[n] of cipher that we could not decipher of thirteenth—To dictate for us   Thomas is ordered to start ten thousand men besides remainder Grangers ~~remainder~~ Corps at once   He will take no artillery but will take his artillery horses and three mules to one hundred men   he will probably start next monday monday" Telegram received, DLC-John M. Schofield.

1. Feb. 15.

To Maj. Gen. George H. Thomas

Nashville February 11th 1864. [*11:00* A.M.]

MAJ GENL GEO H THOMAS

CHATTANOOGA

Are not Steamers carrying rations to Loudon? Cannot rations enough be got ahead by Monday to warrant your starting? It is important to move without much preparation so as to get off before the enemy anticipate our movement and reenforce Longstreet.

U. S GRANT
Major General

Telegram, copies, DLC-USG, V, 34, 35; DNA, RG 393, Military Div. of the Miss., Letters Sent; *ibid.*, Dept. of the Cumberland, Telegrams Received. *O.R.*, I, xxxii, part 2, 365. On Feb. 11, 1864, 8:00 P.M., Maj. Gen. George H. Thomas telegraphed to USG. "Your despatch of 11 a m is recd. Both Rail Road and River are carrying subsistence and forage   The troops will be ready to move Saturday   there will be but a small garrison left here   Genl Foster will arrive in Nashville at 4 a. m. tomorrow" Telegram received, DNA, RG 393, Dept. of the Tenn., Telegrams Received; copies, *ibid.*, Dept. of the Cumberland, Telegrams Sent; (misdated Feb. 12) *ibid.*, Military Div. of the Miss., Telegrams Received. Dated Feb. 11 in *O.R.*, I, xxxii, part 2, 365–66.

Also on Feb. 11, USG telegraphed to Brig. Gen. Robert Allen. "Supplies are only reaching here to supply daily consumption. Cannot a large amount of Stores be forwarded while the river is navigable?" Copies, DLC-USG, V, 34, 35; DNA, RG 393, Military Div. of the Miss., Letters Sent. *O.R.*, I, xxxii, part 2, 366. On the same day, Allen, Louisville, telegraphed to USG. "We have shipped from this port and New Albany since the first of Feby. thirteen thousand Bbls of flour two Millions of pounds of Pork & Bacon half a million pounds of Bread Thirty two hundred tons of Hay—Thirty four thousand bushels of Corn Fifty thousand bushels of Oats all independent of Shipments by the Nashville R. R.— Three times this amount of grain is on the way from St. Louis and ports be- low   we have called into service every boat within our reach   with the boats returning from Nashville and such others as we may be able to procure—We hope to be able to transport half a million of bushels of grain and other stores in proportion within the next ten (10) days—Gen'l Banks & Gen'l Sherman have taken from us Thirty seven (37) first class boats with large amount of stores— whatever is possible will be done"   Copy, DNA, RG 393, Military Div. of the Miss., Telegrams Received. *O.R.*, I, xxxii, part 2, 366.

Also on Feb. 11, Bvt. Lt. Col. James L. Donaldson wrote to USG. "I have the honor to subm[it] a memorandum of the principal articles that have been required of me for equiping the Army for f[ield] operations. To be prepared to meet these several [de]mands. I have made requisitions on Brig. Genl. Ro[bert] Allen, copies of which are also enclosed. I think the demands for the Army of the Cumberland are in excess of what will be required, and for that reason do not deem it judicious to call for more than has already been asked of Genl. Allen—I do not believe in fact that he can give us what I have required, yet it is not safe to ask for less, in view of the necessities that must arise from the Army in East Tennessee, the 500 miles of rail road soon to be completed, the 15th Army Corps, the Tennessee troops, and the various Garrisons & Depots in the Department. If my views are approved, I respectfully Suggest that they be laid before the Quar- termaster General with such endorsement as you may be pleased to make for his information & action." LS, DNA, RG 393, Dept. of the Cumberland, Q. M. Dept., Letters Sent (Press). On the same day, Col. Lewis B. Parsons, Louisville, wrote to USG. "Gen Allen advises me of your dispatch as to forage—It is really only 11 or 12 days Since the Ice gorge broke so boats could get out at all   There were few boats here or at Cincinatti then, but they were scattered everywhere   Since then there have been loaded or are now loading very nearly 40 boats for Nash- ville—Some of these are now taking on board a second load from Evansville— Some 200.000 bushels of corn is coming or landing on the Illinois and other boats are being put into this service as fast as possible—With the present low stage of the river none but small boats can go over Harpeth Shoals—And the number of boats is now limited   We are trying to gather up barges and organize in all ways most effective and I am confident with a little rise in the river your levee will be soon covered with stores—I wish Gov Johnson North Fisher road could be pushed to completion more speedily, as we can easily send large boats to Reynoldsburgh at nearly all times—*It would be of immense service if done*"   ALS (press), Parsons Papers, IHi. On the same day, Parsons wrote again to USG. "I inclose copies of letters from Capt. Pennock and Lt. Shirk as to convoys of Two small Steamers—the 'Alone' and 'Convoy #2'—purchased by me on the order of the Q M General to be taken up to Chattanooga when the Tennessee rises, so they can pass over Harpeth Shoals. As Capt. Edwards, a q m at Bridgeport will be first advised of a rise of river, I have placed the boats subject to his order by telegraph or otherwise. Will you please forward Capt. Edwards such orders for escort and protection as may be deemed necessary, unless our Cavalry in that vicinity will be sufficient?" LS (press), *ibid.* Also on Feb. 11, Capt. Arthur Edwards, Bridgeport, telegraphed to USG. "The new Steamer Chickamauga 175 feet long 27 feet beam 4½ feet hold & 42 feet over all was launched this day at noon by lowering her into the Tenn. river with tackles without the least to her hull" Copy, DNA, RG 393, Military Div. of the Miss., Telegrams Received. On Feb. 16, Capt. Adam Badeau, Nashville, wrote to Parsons. "I am directed by Maj. Gen. Grant to acknowledge the receipt of your letter of Feby 11th, and in reply to state that the left bank of the Tennessee as far as Decatur will be occupied by him, before any rise occurs; and as soon as he is notified by telegraph or otherwise, of the arrival of the steamers 'Alone' and 'Convoy 2' at the Shoals, he will send escorts to convoy them up the river." ALS, Parsons Papers, IHi.

General Orders No. 5

Headquarters Military Division of the Mississippi
Nashville Tenn. Feby. 12, 1864.

GENERAL ORDERS, No. 5,

All persons not exempt from the Amnesty granted by the Proclamation of the President, dated December 8th, 1863, owning cotton and other Southern products, and residing in localities from where it would naturally or of necessity pass through Nashville, Tenn., to the North, may in pursuance of the "Additional Regulations of Trade" bring the same to Nashville for sale on his own account, in compliance with Trade Regulations, if he resides within the line of national military occupation; and where such owner lives beyond the lines of such military occupation he shall deliver the same to the Supervising Special Agent or Assistant Special Agent of the Treasury Department, at Nashville, as the case may be, to be sold for his benefit, in pursuance of said Treasury Regulations, on his compliance with the requirements of the same.

II ... Persons will not be allowed to go to the front nor to send agents there for the purpose of of purchasing cotton on pain of expulsion from the Military Division and forfeiture to the Government of all they have purchased.

III . . . Military railroads will charge ten cents per mile per bale for all cotton carried by them, and twenty five cents per ton per mile for all other freight carried for private citizens.

By order of Maj. Gen. Grant
T. S. BOWERS
Asst. Adjt. Genl

Copies, DLC-USG, V, 14; DNA, RG 393, Military Div. of the Miss., General Orders; (printed) *ibid.*, RG 366, Correspondence of the General Agent; *ibid.*, Printed Copies of Orders; USGA.

On Feb. 21, 1864, Maj. Gen. John A. Logan, Huntsville, Ala., telegraphed to Brig. Gen. John A. Rawlins. "I~~ have Construed~~, In construing order No 5. from Mil Div- Head Qrs. in reference to cotton, is it the proper constuction that the Producers, are the ones allowed to ship to Nashville? Or, does it admit of a more liberal construction? in my own mind I have concluded it meant producers but not wanting to do injustice if wrong I make this inquiry, and hope you will answer me, at once." ADfS, ICHi; copies, DNA, RG 393, 15th Army Corps, Letters and Telegrams Sent; *ibid.*, Military Div. of the Miss., Telegrams Received. On Feb. 23, Lt. Col. Theodore S. Bowers telegraphed to Logan. "Resident owners who have become possesed of the cotton prior to our occupation of the country and producers are the only ones embraced in the order   all speculators and purchasers are excluded"   Telegram received, DLC-John A. Logan; copies, DLC-USG, V, 34, 35; DNA, RG 393, Military Div. of the Miss., Letters Sent. On Feb. 25, Rawlins telegraphed to Logan. "you will please permit all cotton purchased under proper Treasury licence within your comman[d] & before the publica[tion] of your prohibitor[y] order to be shipped to Nashville by the purchaser or agent"   Telegram received, DLC-John A. Logan; copies, DLC-USG, V, 34, 35; DNA, RG 393, Military Div. of the Miss., Letters Sent. On the same day, Bowers wrote to Brig. Gen. Grenville M. Dodge repeating this message. LS, Dodge Papers, IaHA. On the same day, Logan telegraphed to USG. "I have not intended to prevent these men from shipping the cotton they purchased and paid for from Loyal men when transportation could be furnished,   we are now using all the cars allowed us on this road sending corn up the line for our annimals,   a great portion of the cotton claimed by these hungry speculators was purchased from the vilest rebels in this country, and some from agents of rebels in the army, the cotton belonging to rebel soldirs   this I have seized, and intend sending to Nashville on Govt. account. I think I understand the *ins* and *outs* here pretty well, and can and will deal justly in the premises,   I have no doubt, they all can show great injustice if we listen to their stories,   I will act in accordance to instuction & send the cotton forward as soon as can be done without injury to the service." ADfS, Logan Papers, IHi; copies, DNA, RG 393, 15th Army Corps, Letters and Telegrams Sent; *ibid.*, Military Div. of the Miss., Telegrams Received.

On Feb. 26, Logan telegraphed to Bowers. "I will call your attention to a contraband trade that is carried on from Shelbyville, Tenn. to this County. Wagon loads of boots shoes sugar, coffee and salt, are brought by and to the worst rebels in Limestone Co. and from there carried across the River to Rodey's

Command. This has been going on for some time. I am told that any man can go to Shelbyville, and get whatever is wanted, in fact, captured rebel letters show that the rebel troops across the River are being supplied bountifully in this way." Copies, *ibid. O.R.*, I, xxxii, part 2, 477–78.

On Feb. 25, Bowers issued General Orders No. 6. "Planters who have taken, or may hereafter take, the amnesty oath prescribed by the President of the United States, who are desirous of resuming the cultivation of their plantations, will be protected in so doing throughout this Military Division, and will be allowed to employ colored laborers in compliance with the rules and regulations established by the Supervising Agent of the Treasury Department. Negroes in the employ of the Government, and those hired by citizens, whether by order of the Treasury Department or otherwise, are exempted from conscription, and the registry of of the names of those employed by the Government with the proper offices and the contracts for hire with citizens will be sufficient evidence of such exemption, and will be so regarded by all persons. The State of Kentucky is hereby excepted from the operations of General Orders No. 4, of date, Nov. 5th, 1863, from these Headquarters" Copies, DLC-USG, V, 14; DNA, RG 393, Military Div. of the Miss., General Orders. *O.R.*, I, xxxii, part 2, 470. On Feb. 26, Logan telegraphed to Bowers. "A Major of colored troops is here with his party, capturing negroes with or without their consent. Many persons in this County have employed their negroes to make crops. They are being conscripted: Is this right? It will entirely stop the cultivation of farms that were being prepared for crops by loyal men. I desire you to telegraph me instructions in the premises, so that I may interfere in proper cases" Copies, DNA, RG 393, 15th Army Corps, Letters and Telegrams Sent; *ibid.*, Military Div. of the Miss., Telegrams Received. *O.R.*, I, xxxii, part 2, 477. On the same day, USG telegraphed to Logan. "Stop recruiting Officers impressing negroes who are employed in any way by the government or by persons now loyal to the Gov't We want to encourage to cultivation of the soil & all persons living in states declared free by the president can employ their negroes under Treasury regulations & the fact of such employment as protection against impressment" Telegram received, DLC-John A. Logan; copies, DLC-USG, V, 34, 35; DNA, RG 393, Military Div. of the Miss., Letters Sent; (misdated Feb. 29) *ibid.*, Cav. Corps, Letters Received. Dated Feb. 26 in *O.R.*, I, xxxii, part 2, 477. On March 2, USG telegraphed to Maj. Gens. George H. Thomas, Logan, and Dodge. "Whenever a negro is employed by Government in any capacity, he is to be exempted from conscription and any recruiting officers impressing such negroes will be arrested immediately" Copies, DLC-USG, V, 34, 35; DNA, RG 393, Military Div. of the Miss., Letters Sent.

On Feb. 14, Brig. Gen. Robert Allen telegraphed to USG. "I am informed that boats loaded from here with Government Stores are allowed to take return trips of private freights to Cincinatti & other points instead of returning to Evansville and points below here where we have very large quantities of forage for shipments to Nashville this naturally interferes with the arrangements I have made for forwarding supplies to your command will you please issue an order for bidding these shipments, and see that such orders are given boats leaving Nashville as will insure the movements of Government supplies" Copy, *ibid.*, Telegrams Received. On the same day, Bvt. Lt. Col. James L. Donaldson wrote to USG. "I have replied to Genl Allen's telegram in relation to freights per steamboats, from Louisville to Nashville and referred his communication to my transportation officer, who states the case very plainly in reply. It is enclosed. I shall give orders for all boats to return to Evansville, and points below Louisville for freight; but the difficulty is, we cannot control them except by chartering them by the day. At so much per hundred pounds, they will seek the best market they can find, and the only correction that suggests itself to me, under such a system, is, to give orders to impress the boats as they arrive at the various ports North, and compel them to take Government freights, to the exclusion of private." LS, *ibid.*, Dept. of the Cumberland, Q. M. Dept., Letters Sent (Press). On Feb. 19, Allen wrote to USG. "(Unofficial) . . . I am apprehensive, from the tenor of Col. Donaldson and Capt Winslow's letters that I have failed to make myself understood in the proposition to compel steamboats to go to particular ports for freight   I simply desired that for the present that boats after discharging at Nashville should not be permitted to take private freight on returns, as the bulk of our forage is at Evansville and other points below. I put up the price of freight so as to make the trip amply remunerative without any back cargo. I called the principal steamboat owners together, and submitted my rates to them and they expressed entire satisfaction   In fact I increased *twenty per cent* on Col. Parsons contract rates, and the cry of hardship is not worth a moments respect or consideration. If the boats are permitted to receive private freight, of course they must come here, to Cincinnatti and over Pittsburgh to discharge, whereas if they are turned back empty, they will go voluntarily to Evansville and the other points direct, from Nashville   I expect that by the increased sales of freight I have made this direct voyage lucrative. Of course if the boats are permitted to load on returning they would *make more* money, but if that were permitted I would not pay the present high price   It is true that the boats are not chartered and therefore not subject to military orders, and why Capt Winslow dwells on this I cannot understand. I have expressly told him that I do not want any *orders* given to the boats at all. I only for a limited time, want the shipment of private freight from Nashville prohibited. This done there will be no further trouble; the thing will regulate itself, for as I before stated, the boats will go without any prompting to where they know they can get freight the quickest, and that is to Evansville. I am writing now simply to let you understand this matter. Capt Winslow has signified that the private freight will now be stopped, but he does this with a bad grace, apparently thinking that he is doing some grievous private wrong, whereas the steamboat men are humbugging him beautifully   There is not an idle boat on any of the Rivers unless some have become idle by the obstructions of the ice which ~~has~~ is again ~~closed~~ in the Ohio between this and Cincinnatti, and in the upper Mississippi   Excuse my long letter, but the subject is one that gives me great concern" ALS, *ibid.*, Military Div. of the Miss., Letters Received. On Feb. 22, Bowers issued Special Orders No. 48 permitting express cos. to operate in USG's command, permitting merchants to send seed on the military railroads, and prohibiting the shipment of private freight by boat from Nashville. Copies, DLC-USG, V, 38; (incomplete) Parsons Papers, IHi. On March 16, USG endorsed a letter of Col. Daniel C. McCallum concerning the organization of a new express co. in USG's dept. "There is no necessity of increasing the present facilities given for expressing goods over Military R Rds. but what is now allowed can be well divided between rival companies and the troops be thereby benefitted" Copies, DLC-USG, V, 39; DNA, RG 393, Military Div. of the Miss., Endorsements.

To Maj. Gen. Henry W. Halleck

———

Head Quarters, Mil. Div. of the Miss.
Nashville Ten. Feb.y 12th 1864,

MAJ. GEN. H. W. HALLECK,
GEN. IN CHIEF, WASHINGTON,
GENERAL,

I have got Gen. Thomas ready to move with a force of about 14.000 Infantry, into East Tennessee to aid the forces there in expelling Longstreet from the state. He would have started on Monday next if I had not revoked the order. My reasons for doing this are these: Gen. Foster who is now, here (or only left this morning,) says that our possession of the portion of East Ten. is perfectly secure against all danger. The condition of the people within the rebel lines cannot be improved now after loosing all they had. Keeping Longstreet where he is makes more secure other parts of our possessions. Our men from scanty clothing and short rations are not in good condition for an advance. There are but very few Animals in East Tennessee in condition to move Artillery or other stores. If we move against Longstreet with an overwhelmming force he will simply fall back towards Va. until he can be reinforced or take up an impregnable position. The country being exhausted all our supplies will have to be carried from Knoxville the whole distance advanced. We would be obliged to advance rapidly and return soon whether the object of the expedition was accomplished or not. Longstreet could return with impunity on the heels of our returning column, at least as far down the valley as he can supply himself from the road in his rear. Schofield telegraphs to the same effect. All these seem to be good reasons for abandoning the movement and I have therefore suspended it. Now that our men are ready for an advance however I have directed it to be made, on Dalton, and hope to get possession of that place and hold it as one step towards a Spring campaign.

Our troops in East Tennessee are now clothed. Rations are also accumulating. When Foster left most of the troops had ten days supplies with 5000 barrels of flour and forty days meet in store and the quantity increasing daily.

> I am General, very respectfully
> your obt. svt.
> U. S. GRANT
> Maj. Gen.

ALS, Schoff Collection, MiU-C. *O.R.*, I, xxxii, part 2, 374–75. On Feb. 12, 1864, USG telegraphed to Maj. Gen. Henry W. Halleck. "Despatches just received from General Schofield and conversation with General Foster who is now here has determined me against moving immediately against Longstreet   I will write more fully   No danger whatever to be apprehended in East Tennessee"   Telegram received (misdated Feb. 13), DNA, RG 107, Telegrams Collected (Bound); copies (dated Feb. 12), *ibid.*, Telegrams Received in Cipher; *ibid.*, RG 393, Military Div. of the Miss., Hd. Qrs. Correspondence; DLC-USG, V, 40, 94. Misdated Feb. 13 in *O.R.*, I, xxxii, part 2, 384. On Feb. 17, Halleck wrote to USG. "Confidential . . . Your letter of the 12th inst is just received. I fully concur with you in regard to the present condition of affairs in East Tennessee. It certainly is very much to be regretted that the fatal mistake of General Burnside has permitted Longstreets army to winter in Tenn. It is due to yourself that a full report of this matter should be placed on file so that the responsibility may rest where it properly belongs. The condition of affairs in East Tennessee and the uncertainty of General Banks' operations in Texas and Louisiana have caused me to delay answering your former communication in regard to operations of the campaign. In one of these you suggest whether it might not be well not to attemp anything more against Richmond and to send a column of sixty thousand men into North Carolina   In the first place, I have never considered Richmond as the necessary objective point of the army of the Potomac; that point is *Lee's army*. I have never supposed that Richmond could be taken till Lee's army was defeated or driven away. It was one of Napoleon's maxims that an army covering a capital must be destroyed before attempting to capture or occupy that capital. And now how can we best defeat Lee's army; by attacking it between here and Richmond, on our shortest line of supplies and in such a position that we can combine our whole force, or by a longer line and with a force diminished by the troops required to cover Washington and Maryland? The movement through North Carolina, alluded to by you, and also one from Port Royal on Savannah and into Georgia, have been several times suggested here and pretty fully discussed by military men. It is conceeded by those suggesting these expeditions that neither of them can be safely undertaken with a less force than that estimated by you, viz, sixty thousand effective men. Some require a still larger force. If we admit the advantage of either of these plans, the question immediately arises, where can we get the requisite number of troops? There is evidently a general public misconception of the strength of our army in Virginia and about Washington. Perhaps it is good policy to encourage this public error. The entire effective force in the fortifications about Washington and employed in guarding the public buildings and stores, the aqueduct, and rail roads, does not exceed eighteen thousand men. We have a few thousand more in the convalescent and distribution camps, and in the cavalry and artillery depôts; but these are mostly fragments of organizations temporarily here for equipment and distribution, and could contribute very little to the defence of the place. This force is, therefore, less than one half of what General McClellan, and several boards of officers recommended as the permanent garrison. Considering the political importance of Washington and the immense amount of military stores here, it would be exceeding hazardous to reduce it still further. The effective force of the Army of the Potomac is only about seventy thousand. General Meade retreated before Lee with a very much larger force, and he does not now deem himself strong enough to attack Lee's present army. Suppose we were to send thirty thousand men from that army to North Carolina; would not Lee be able to make another invasion of Maryland and Pennsylvania? But it may be said that by operating in North Carolina we would compel Lee to move his army there. I do not think so. Uncover Washington and the Potomac river, and all the forces which Lee can collect will be moved north, and the popular sentiment will compel the Government to *bring back* the army in North Carolina to defend Washington, Baltimore, Harrisburg and Philadelphia. I think Lee would tomorrow exchange Richmond, Raleigh and Wilmington for the possession of either of the aforementioned cities. But suppose it were practicable to send thirty thousand men from Meade's army to North Carolina; where shall we get the other thirty thousand? We have there now barely enough to hold the points which it is necessary to occupy in order to prevent contraband trade. Very few of these would be available for the field. Maryland is almost entirely stript of troops, and the forces in Western Virginia are barely sufficient to protect that part of the country from rebel raids. The only other resource is South Carolina. Generals Foster and Gillmore were both of opinion at the commencement of operations against Charleston that neither that place nor Savannah could be taken by a land force of less than sixty thousand (60.000) men. A Large land and naval forces have been employed there for nearly a year without any important results. I had no faith in the plan at first, and for months past have ineffectually urged that ten or fifteen thousand men from Gillmore's command be sent against Texas or Mobile. And now these troops are sent upon an other expedition which, in my opinion, can produce no military result. I always have been, and still am opposed to all these isolated expeditions on the sea and Gulf coasts. It is true they greatly assist the Navy in maintaining the blockade and preventing contraband trade; but I think the troops so employed would do more good if concentrated on some important line of military operations. We have given too much attention to cutting the toe nails of our enemy instead of grasping his throat. You will percieve from the facts stated above that there are serious, if not insurmountable obstacles in the way of the proposed North Carolina expedition. Nevertheless, as it has much to recommend it, I shall submit it, with your remarks, to the consideration of the President and Sect'y of War, as soon troops enough return from furlough to attempt any important movement in this part of the theatre of war. Lee's army is by far the best in the rebel service, and I regard him as their ablest general. But little progress can be made here till that army is broken or defeated. There have been several good oportunities to do this, viz; at Antietam, at Chancellorsville, and at Williamsport in the retreat from Gettysburg. I am also of opinion that General Meade could have succeeded recently at Mine Run, had he persevered in his attack. The overthrow of Lee's army being the object of operations here, the question arises how can we best attain it? If we fight that army with our communications open to Washington, so as to cover this place and Maryland, we can concentrate upon it nearly all of our forces on this frontier; but if we operate by North Carolina or the peninsula, we must act with a divided army, and on exterior lines, while Lee, with a short interior line can concentrate his entire force upon either fragment. And yet, if we had troops enough to secure our position here, and at the same time to operate with advantage on Raleigh or Richmond, I would not hesitate to do so, at least for a winter or spring campaign. But our numbers are not sufficient, in my opinion, to attempt this, at least for the present. Troops sent south of James river cannot be brought back in time to oppose Lee, should he attempt a movement north, which I am satisfied would be his best policy. Our main efforts in the next campaign should unquestionably be made against the armies of Lee and Johnson. But by what particular lines we shall operate cannot be positively determined until the affairs of East Tennessee are settled, and we can know more nearly what force can be given to the army of the Potomac. In the mean time it will be well to compare views and opinions. The final decision of this question will probably depend, under the President, upon yourself. It may be said that if General McClellan failed to take Richmond by the Peninsular route, so also have Generals Burnside, Hooker and Meade failed to accomplish that object by the shorter and more direct route. This is all very true, but no argument can be deduced from this bare fact in favor of either plan of operations. General McClellan had so large an army in the spring of 1862 that possibly he was justified in dividing his forces and adopting exterior lines of operation. If he had succeeded his plan would have been universally praised. He failed, and so also have Burnside, Hooker and Meade on an interior route; but their armies were far inferior in number to that which McClellan had two years ago. These facts in themselves prove nothing in favor of either route and to decide the question we must recur to fundamental principles in regard to interior and exterior lines, objective points, covering armies, divided forces &c, &c,. These fundamental principles require, in my opinion, that all our available forces in the east should be concentrated against Lee's army. We cannot take Richmond (at least with any military advantage), and we cannot operate advantageously on any point from the Atlantic coast, till we destroy or disperse that army. And the nearer to Washington we can fight it the better for us. We can here, or between here and Richmond, concentrate against him more men than any where else. If we cannot defeat him here with our combined force, we cannot hope to do so elsewhere with a divided army. I write to you plainly and frankly, for between us there should be no reserve or concealment of opinions. As before remarked, I presume that, under the authority of the President the final decision of these questions will be referred to you. Nevertheless, I think you are entitled to have, and that it is my duty to frankly give my individual opinion on the subject. It will no doubt be received for what it may be intrinsically worth. I can ask or expect nothing more In regard to the operations of our western armies, I fully concur in your views; but I think the condition of affairs in East Tennessee, and west of the Mississippi river, will require some modification in your plans, or at least will very much much delay the operations of your proposed spring campaign. These, however, are delays and changes which neither of us could anticipate." LS, USMA. *O.R.*, I, xxxii, part 2, 411–13.

To Maj. Gen. John M. Schofield

By Telegraph from Nashville [*Feb.*] 12th *186*[*4*] 4 P M
To MAJ GENL SCHOFIELD COMDG
You need not attempt the raid with the the cavalry you now have
—If that in Ky can recruit up it may do hereafter to send it on
such an expedition—I have asked so often for a cooperation movement from the troops in West Virginia that I hardly expect to see
anything to help us from there—Genl Halleck says they have not
got men enough—Crook however has gone there and may undertake to strike the road about need [*New*] river
U S GRANT M Genl

Telegram received, DLC-John M. Schofield; copies, DLC-USG, V, 34, 35; DNA,
RG 393, Military Div. of the Miss., Letters Sent. *O.R.*, I, xxxii, part 2, 374. On
Feb. 11, 1864, Maj. Gen. John M. Schofield had telegraphed to USG: "Gen.l
Foster informed me that a raid upon Longstreet's rear had been projected,
through North Carolina, but its execution was suspended until my arrival   To
make that raid now would use up all my effective cavalry horses and leave me
destitute of cavalry. I think it would be better to organize the cavalry I know
have here in Kentucky, and send it through Pound Gap upon Longstreets rear.
If at the same time one could be made up the Kanawha Valley, and my force
here be ready to move at the same time we might hope for complete success.
Please inform me what you think should be and what can be done." Copies, DLC-
John M. Schofield; DNA, RG 393, Military Div. of the Miss., Telegrams Received. Printed as sent at 10:00 A.M. in *O.R.*, I, xxxii, part 2, 367.
On Feb. 12, 10:20 A.M., USG telegraphed to Schofield. "no movement will
be made aganst Longstreet at present   give your men and animals all the rest
you can preparatory for early operations in the Spring.—furlough all the veterans
you deem it prudent to let go"   Telegram received, DLC-John M. Schofield;
copies, DLC-USG, V, 34, 35; DNA, RG 393, Military Div. of the Miss., Letters
Sent. *O.R.*, I, xxxii, part 2, 374. On the same day, 11:30 A.M., Schofield telegraphed to USG. "If it is decided to advance from this point before the road will
admit of wagon transportation I can organize a train of pack mules sufficient to
supply the army from this place   It will take until the first of march & perhaps
longer to accomplish it   Ten Thousand additional Infy will be sufficient without artillery unless Longstreet should receive reenforcements—He has recd none
yet unless it be some cavalry from Georgia   He has the Rail Road in runing
order to Strawberry Plains   His main force is still in the vicinity of Morristown   His cavalry are foraging south of the French Broad. He shows no disposition to advance and I think is in no condition to do so." Telegram received
(incomplete), DNA, RG 393, Dept. of the Tenn., Telegrams Received; copies
(incomplete), *ibid.*, Military Div. of the Miss., Telegrams Received; DLC-John
M. Schofield. Incomplete in *O.R.*, I, xxxii, part 2, 374.

On Feb. 17, Schofield telegraphed to USG. "Your despatch of the 12th deferring movement was received yesterday. I will get my command in condition as rapidly as possible. Can you tell me about what time a movement will probably be made? My preparations will depend somewhat upon the length of time. It will hardly be safe for me to send off any veterans unless Genl Thomas can replace them by other troops. Longstreets cavalry is so much superior to mine that I have to keep the rail road strongly guarded by Infantry. I have telegraphed Genl. Thomas on the subject." Copies, DLC-John M. Schofield; DNA, RG 393, Military Div. of the Miss., Telegrams Received. *O.R.*, I, xxxii, part 2, 414.

On Feb. 12, Schofield telegraphed to USG. "Please inform me whether Genl Cox will be assigned to duty out of this Dept in accordance with Genl Fosters suggestion If he can be given a suitable Command I am willing on his account for him to go if not he can be of service to me here as inspector Gen'l" Telegram received, DNA, RG 393, Dept. of the Tenn., Telegrams Received; copies, *ibid.*, Military Div. of the Miss., Telegrams Received; (2) *ibid.*, Dept. of the Ohio, Telegrams Sent; DLC-John M. Schofield. On Feb. 17, Schofield telegraphed to USG. "I can make Gen Cox useful here but cannot give him a command nor other duty acceptable to him he desires a command in the field if one can be given him I reccommend that it be don" Telegram received (undated), DNA, RG 393, Dept. of the Tenn., Telegrams Received; copies, *ibid.*, Military Div. of the Miss., Telegrams Received; DLC-John M. Schofield. *O.R.*, I, lii, part 1, 521. On Feb. 22, Brig. Gen. Jacob D. Cox telegraphed to Rawlins. "By permission of Gen'l Schofield I respectfully inquire whether action has been taken by the Gen'l Com'dg upon Gen'l Schofields last dispatch in reference to myself." Copy, DNA, RG 393, Military Div. of the Miss., Telegrams Received. On Feb. 4, Cox had written to Maj. Gen. John G. Foster that he had been replaced by Maj. Gen. George Stoneman in command of the 23rd Army Corps and wanted to continue in active service. ALS, *ibid.*, Letters Received. On Feb. 5, Foster endorsed this letter. "Since Brig Gen Cox has been under my command, I have been impressed with his soldierly qualities, his thorough habits of discipline, and the skill and judgement displayed in his efforts to improve the discipline of the troops placed under him—Under him the 23d corps has continually improved. Owing to the number of absent regiments from the corps, it now consists of two small Divisions, in the field, both commanded by experienced officers, Brig. Gen Judah & Brig Gen Hascall. Under these circumstances, Gen. Cox's reluctance to dispossing either either of them, is very natural, and creditable—If therefore, Gen Grant, to whom this is respectfully referred, can assign Gen. Cox to command a Division in any other corps where a vacancy exists, he will, I am sure, subserve the public interests, and at the same time render a service to a meritorious officer—" AES, *ibid.*

To Maj. Gen. George H. Thomas

Nashville February 12th 1864

MAJ GENL GEO H THOMAS
CHATTANOOGA

Conversation with Genl Foster has undecided me as to the propriety of the contemplated move against Longstreet. Schofield telegraphs the same views. I will take the matter into consideration during the day after further talk with Foster and give you the conclusion arrived at. If decided that you do not go I will instruct Schofield to let Granger send off his veterans at once

Should you not be required to go into East Tennessee could you not make a formidable recconnoissance towards Dalton and if successful in driving the enemy out, occupy that place and complete the railroad up to it this winter

U. S GRANT
Major General

Telegram, copies, DLC-USG, V, 34, 35; DNA, RG 393, Military Div. of the Miss., Letters Sent; *ibid.*, Dept. of the Cumberland, Telegrams Received. *O.R.*, I, xxxii, part 2, 373. On Feb. 12, 1864, Maj. Gen. George H. Thomas telegraphed to USG. "I think an attack on Dalton would be successful if you will let me have the Div. of Logan's during the movement." Copies, DNA, RG 393, Dept. of the Cumberland, Telegrams Sent; *ibid.*, Military Div. of the Miss., Telegrams Received. *O.R.*, I, xxxii, part 2, 373.

On Feb. 12, USG telegraphed to Thomas. "No monthly returns have been received from the Department of the Cumberland since this Military Division has been established. No tri-monthlies have been received since the 10th December. I am required to furnish consolidated returns and reports to Washington and must have them from Department Commanders" Copies, DLC-USG, V, 34, 35; DNA, RG 393, Military Div. of the Miss., Letters Sent; *ibid.*, Dept. of the Cumberland, Telegrams Received. On the same day, Thomas telegraphed to USG. "Everything that can be done is being done to make up and forward the returns. The delay has been occasioned by the scattering of the troops, the discontinuing of the 20th and 21st Corps and the separating of the troops from their records. It has been impossible to get returns from the Cavalry for which we have been waiting. It is however promised tomorrow when I hope to forward the monthly for October." Copies, *ibid.*, Telegrams Sent; *ibid.*, Military Div. of the Miss., Telegrams Received.

Also on Feb. 12, USG telegraphed to Thomas. "There is an order in your Department proscriptive of one or more newspapers, and I believe also giving the vending of papers to a few persons. I would advise the revocation of such orders." Copies, DLC-USG, V, 34, 35; DNA, RG 393, Military Div. of the Miss.,

Letters Sent; *ibid.*, Dept. of the Cumberland, Telegrams Received. On the same day, Thomas telegraphed to Brig. Gen. John A. Rawlins. "I have Issued no orders proscriptive of any news papers & have no objection to any papers being sold here—The present system of furnishing the army with news papers is the most satisfactory that has yet been tried here   The person who sells them keeps a general assortment & is not permitted to sell for more than five cents except for periodicals & Pictorials"   Telegram received, *ibid.*, Dept. of the Tenn., Telegrams Received; copy, *ibid.*, Military Div. of the Miss., Telegrams Received. On Feb. 14, USG telegraphed to Thomas. "The orders alluded to were issued by Gen Rosecrans proscribing three or more papers circulated in the north. If I had reflecting I knew you had requested the selling of papers advantage for the soldiers. Rosecrans order has not been revoked." Copy, *ibid.*, Dept. of the Cumberland, Telegrams Received.

On Feb. 12, USG telegraphed to Thomas. "A dispatch of yesterday from Adjutant General Thomas advises against granting of passes promiscuously for citizens to go to the front. No passes are given from these Head-Quarters except in meritorious cases, and where I would deem it a hardship to refuse or delay. I did give a pass to two men on a letter from Speaker Colfax, when probably the object was business; in all other cases I believe such persons have telegraphed to the front and obtained passes." Copies, DLC-USG, V, 34, 35; DNA, RG 393, Military Div. of the Miss., Letters Sent; *ibid.*, Dept. of the Cumberland, Telegrams Received. On Feb. 11, Brig. Gen. Lorenzo Thomas, Chattanooga, had telegraphed to USG. "The arrival of Civilians at this point Coming here for no other object than their self aggrandizement is the Cause of much Annoyance at these Head Quarters. I have therefore to urge that no permits be given to citizens to come to this place unless by permission of Maj Genl Thomas or to such as have sick or wounded relations in Hospital or in such instance as you may have a personal Knowledge of their wants"   Telegram received, *ibid.*, Dept. of the Tenn., Telegrams Received; copies, *ibid.*, RG 94, Letters Sent by Gen. Thomas; *ibid.*, RG 393, Military Div. of the Miss., Telegrams Received.

On Feb. 12, USG telegraphed to Maj. Gen. George H. Thomas. "Col Mc-Callum reports that protection papers prevent his getting timber necessary for railroad purposes, along the line of the road. Please telegraph orders instructing Commanders from here to Bridgeport not to interfere with Col McCallum' men taking such timber as he may deem necessary, giving receipts however, where protection has been extended." Copies, DLC-USG, V, 34, 35; DNA, RG 393, Military Div. of the Miss., Letters Sent; (dated Feb. 13) *ibid.*, Dept. of the Cumberland, Telegrams Received. See *O.R.*, I, xxxii, part 2, 385.

To Maj. Gen. George H. Thomas

Nashville February 12th 64

MAJ GENL GEO H THOMAS
CHATTANOOGA

Logan with fifteen regiments is now on his way to Chattanooga.

This will enable you to move forward with all your effective force. Start at the earliest practicable moment. It will be well to keep up the idea among the officers and men that they are going into East Tennessee until they actually start. By this means the enemy may be deceived.

U. S GRANT
Major General

Telegram, copies, DLC-USG, V, 34, 35; DNA, RG 393, Military Div. of the Miss., Letters Sent; (dated Feb. 13, 1864, 10:00 A.M.) *ibid.*, Dept. of the Cumberland, Telegrams Received. Dated Feb. 13, 10:00 A.M., in *O.R.*, I, xxxii, part 2, 383. On Feb. 13, 8:00 P.M., Maj. Gen. George H. Thomas telegraphed to USG. "Your dispatch of 10. a. m. this day is received. I will start as soon as possible after the arrival of Genl. Logan's troops. Have received a rebel paper of the ninth to day which reports that Genl. Sherman occupied Jackson Miss. on the evening of the 5th. Enemy falling back across Pearl River. Cavalry under Lee and Ferguson on west side. Loring is moving from his position (not named) to concentrate his forces with those in front of Sherman. Cars running through to Loudon and telegraph will be finished by tomorrow night." Copy, DNA, RG 393, Dept. of the Cumberland, Telegrams Sent; (dated Feb. 14) *ibid.*, Military Div. of the Miss., Telegrams Received. Dated Feb. 13 in *O.R.*, I, xxxii, part 2, 384.

On Feb. 12, Thomas telegraphed to USG. "Will Logan's troops reach here by Monday. I shall have to take nearly every body away to make up ten thousand men, and therefore do not think it prudent to move before Logan's troops are near here." Copies, DNA, RG 393, Military Div. of the Miss., Telegrams Received; *ibid.*, Dept. of the Cumberland, Telegrams Sent. *O.R.*, I, xxxii, part 2, 372. On the same day, 3:20 P.M., USG telegraphed to Thomas. "Logans troops started yesterday morning   If I decide not to make the move at present into East Tennessee, I will turn them back unless you require them to aid in an advance on Dalton. (see my dispatch of this morning). Captain Dudley will be tried on serious charges and will be secured against absconding either at Bridgeport or Chattanooga." Copies, DLC-USG, V, 34, 35; DNA, RG 393, Military Div. of the Miss., Letters Sent; *ibid.*, Dept. of the Cumberland, Telegrams Received. Incomplete in *O.R.*, I, xxxii, part 2, 373. See letter to Maj. Gen. Henry W. Halleck, Feb. 6, 1864.

On Feb. 13, USG telegraphed to Maj. Gen. John A. Logan. "Halt your troops wherever you may be when this reaches you and await further orders. It is possible you will not be required at Chattanooga." Copies, DLC-USG, V, 34, 35; DNA, RG 393, Military Div. of the Miss., Letters Sent. *O.R.*, I, xxxii, part 2, 385.

On Feb. 14, USG telegraphed to Thomas. "Do you think it advisable for Logan to leave his trains at Stevenson, and send his baggage up by boats? If so advise him." Copies, DLC-USG, V, 34, 35; DNA, RG 393, Military Div. of the Miss., Letters Sent; *ibid.*, Dept. of the Cumberland, Telegrams Received. *O.R.*, I, xxxii, part 2, 390. On the same day, 3:00 P.M., Thomas telegraphed to USG. "As I am disirous of using a portion of Logans force in the movement on Dalton I think it will be better for his whole train to come here   As yet no one knows of the direction of the movement I therefore have great hopes of its success" Telegram received, DNA, RG 94, War Records Office, Military Div. of the Miss.; copies, *ibid.*, RG 393, Dept. of the Cumberland, Telegrams Sent; *ibid.*, Military Div. of the Miss., Telegrams Received. *O.R.*, I, xxxii, part 2, 389.

To John Brough

Nashville February 12th 64.

GOVERNOR (J) BROUGH OF OHIO
COLUMBUS OHIO

Your letter of the 8th inst, relative to the condition of the 3d Ohio Infantry Volunters, is just received. Suitable officers can be detailed from other Regiments to command that Regiment I will direct Genl Thomas to detail the Lieut Colonel of the 113th Ohio if practicable, and if not to take some other suitable officer from an Ohio regiment. If the men desire to reenlist under other officers than those they now have, I do not believe it can be legally done. But where there is one objectionable officer as in the case of the Captain now commanding the 3d Ohio, he can be easily disposed of by bringing him before an Examining Board. The places of those officers held as prisoners of War in the South cannot be filled.

U S GRANT
Major General

Copies, DLC-USG, V, 34, 35; DNA, RG 393, Military Div. of the Miss., Letters Sent. On Feb. 12, 1864, Governor John Brough of Ohio telegraphed to USG. "Has any order been issued upon my request to detail Officers to command the third Ohio V. I. if so who is appointed the Lt. Co'l of the Hundred thirteenth O. V. I. whom I accompanied is here on duty (detached) until the 25th inst. has been detailed if so shall he be sent forward" Copy, *ibid.*, Telegrams Received. On Feb. 13, USG telegraphed to Brough. "Gen Thomas has been directed to detail Lt Col one hundred thirteenth 113th to command third 3d Ohio if practicable if not to detail some other good field officer from an ohio regt I have answered your letter" Telegram received, AGO Records, Ohio Archives, Columbus, Ohio.

To Maj. Gen. George H. Thomas

———

Nashville, Tenn. Feby 13, 1864

MAJ. GEN. GEO. H. THOMAS
COMDG. DEPT. CUMBERLAND

Conversation with Foster who has had much better opportunity for knowing the exact state of affairs in East Tennessee satisfies me that all that could be accomplished by the proposed campaign there would not compensate for the hardships upon our men, and the disqualifying effects it would have upon them and our war material, for a spring campaign. All orders therefore for that campaign are revoked. As you have been preparing for a move however, I deem it advisable to make one to your immediate front. The object will be to gain possession of Dalton and as far south as possible. Should you succeed in gaining possession of Dalton, leave there, or at such advanced position as you think can be held, the force necessary for it. They will have to avail themselves of the resources of the country, for subsisting so far as it will supply them, and upon teaming from the nearest point of railroad accessible.

Gen. Logan is now on his way to Chattanooga with sixteen regiments of Infantry. This will enable you to take your whole effective force from Chattanooga. On your return to Chattanooga with a part of your forces, Logan can be relieved and allowed to return to his place on the line of the road between Stevenson and Decatur.

I mark out no line for you to pursue in this expedition, but if the enemy are not much more favorable in numbers than I believe them to be, I would feel no hesitation in marching past all the force they have at Tunnell Hill and Dalton and come in on the railroad to their rear with a force from sixteen to twenty thousand effective fighting men. The Cavalry on the Hiawasse can be ordered to move at the same time towards Spring place,[1] with directions to form a junction if possible

Telegraph in cipher the substance of the plan you adopt and send by mail copies of your orders.

> Very respectfully, &c,
> U. S. GRANT
> Major General

Copies, DLC-USG, V, 34, 35. On Feb. 15, 1864, Maj. Gen. George H. Thomas telegraphed to USG. "Your communication of the 13th by Genl. Elliott was received yesterday. Seven Regiments of Logan's force have arrived. Genl. Matthias reports that the remainder will reach here tomorrow. My plan was to place Matthias in reserve near Cleveland and march with Stanley's Division supported by two Brigades of Matthias on the road from Cleveland to Dalton and with the 14th. Army Corps take the direct road from here to Dalton, covering my advance and right flank with Cavalry. I have thought of the route you suggest, but find upon inquiry that the roads across the mountains are so difficult that they can hardly be considered practicable at this season of the year. I have been considerably embarrassed by having Genls. Stanley and Davis summoned before the McCook Court of Inquiry just at this time, but if it continues to rain through the day as it did all night I think nothing will be gained by starting just yet. In the mean time Stanley and Davis can get back, by Wednesday. Should the weather clear up however I will not wait. I intend to relieve as much of the Cavalry at Calhoun as I can with Infantry and send it (the Cavalry) towards Dalton, via Spring Place in cooperation with Stanleys force." Copy, DNA, RG 393, Dept. of the Cumberland, Telegrams Sent. *O.R.*, I, xxxii, part 2, 395.

1. Spring Place, Ga., ten miles east of Dalton.

To Maj. Gen. George H. Thomas

Nashville February 10th [*14*] 1864.

MAJOR GENERAL GEO H THOMAS
CHATTANOOGA

The Provost Marshal at Tullahoma is advertising cotton for sale. This is in violation of law and orders, which require such property to be turned over to the Treasury Dep't

> U S GRANT
> Major General

Telegram, copies (misdated Feb. 10, 1864), DLC-USG, V, 34, 35; DNA, RG 393, Military Div. of the Miss., Letters Sent; (dated Feb. 14) *ibid.*, Dept. of the Cumberland, Telegrams Received. On Feb. 14, Charles A. Fuller, Nashville, asst. special agent, Treasury Dept., had written to USG. "Your attention is respectfully called to the following 'Notice' as published in the Nashville Union of this date, viz: 'Notice—Eight thousand pounds of cotton will be sold at public sale, at Tullahoma, at 3 P. M., on Monday, the 15th inst   J C. WILLIAMS   Capt and Provost Marshal.' I know nothing more of the transaction referred to than what the 'Notice' itself discloses. If the Cotton offered for sale is 'Captured Cotton' or 'Abandoned Cotton' collected by the Military at Tullahoma, or even 'seized Cotton,' General order No 88 from the Hon. Secretary of War requires that the same be turned over to an Agent of the Treasury Department and disposed of in conformity to Treasury Regulations. Your authority is asked that the sale may be stopped, and that an order be issued requiring the Cotton to be turned over, &c   I hold myself in readiness to execute the receipts required by the Treasury Regulations and the Order of the Secretary of War." ALS, *ibid.*, Military Div. of the Miss., Letters Received. On Feb. 14, Maj. Gen. George H. Thomas telegraphed to USG. "The Cotton advertised for Sale in Tullahoma was taken in payment of Tax on Citizens of Lincoln County for murder of soldiers by Guerrillas pursuant to Gen. orders No 6 from these Head Quarters   Cannot the Cotton be sold for That purpose as advertised or how shall we proceed to get the Money for it"   Telegram received, *ibid.*, Dept. of the Tenn., Telegrams Received; copies, *ibid.*, Military Div. of the Miss., Telegrams Received; *ibid.*, Dept. of the Cumberland, Telegrams Sent. On the same day, Maj. Gen. Henry W. Slocum telegraphed to USG. "The Cotton was taken and avertised to be sold at public sale pursuant to Gen'l Orders number six Dept. of the Cumberland. I have ordered the sale stopped   the proceeds of the sale were directed in the order to be paid to proceed to realize any money from the Cotton—"   Copy, *ibid.*, Military Div. of the Miss., Telegrams Received. On the same day, USG telegraphed to Slocum. "The sale of cotton under the order you refer to is right   My dispatch was on the report of Treasury Agent supposing it to be confiscated by Government." Copies, DLC-USG, V, 34, 35; DNA, RG 393, Military Div. of the Miss., Telegrams Sent; (addressed to Thomas, dated Feb. 15) *ibid.*, Dept. of the Cumberland, Telegrams Received.

To Julia Dent Grant

Nashville Feb.y 14th/64

DEAR JULIA,

I have just rec'd a letter from Dr. Hewitt to you which I opened not noticing to whom it was directed. There is one from Hunt which I also enclose.

I am now occupying a room just across the street from the office where I am more comfortably fixed than I have been before during the War. The family where I board, and lodge, consists only of an elderly gentleman & his wife, son-in-law and his wife besides a young school Miss. The young lady goes to Mrs. Holcome,[1] sister of Dr. Steinhauer.[2] Mrs. H. sent me word by the young lady she would like to see me. I have not called however. I usually take a ride for an hour in the evening on horseback or in the buggy. This you know always keeps me feeling well. I drive my spotted horse or the one sent me by the Citizens of Ill.[3] always. They are both gentle and fine driving horses, the one last mentioned the best I ever drove. I think when the Spring Campaign opens I will send the spoted horse for you to keep. The one Orvil has I understand is unsafe to drive. He balks and sometimes after he gets a few miles from home refuses to go further. I send off my recommendations for promotion in a few days and Fred's will go at the same time. I make his however in a separate letter to the President. Unless a good many Generals are legislated out however I do not think any new generals will be made. Those whos names you see before the senate for confirmation are officers who were appointed months ago. I expect to go to the front about Wednsday. I am making important moves there. Shall not go with ~~my~~ the troops myself unless there should prove a necessity for it, but will be at Chattanooga so as to be ready to reach them in the shortest time if it should become necessary. If the move results in what I expect I will return to Nashville about the last of this month and remain until a Spring Campaign can commence. The time for that will depend on ~~the~~ how long the Spring rains continue. I think you may calculate on spending from about the 27th of this month to the 1st of April with me. You will be very comfortable however at Mrs. Dunlops so that you can come whenever you feel able to travel. I would advise you to come by boat. My best respects, you wont allow me to say love, to cousin Louisa,[4] and the young ladies. Kisses for yourself and the children. I have had one letter from you. I hope your eyes are better than when you wrote?

ULYS

ALS, DLC-USG.

1. Mrs. Emma Holcombe, head of the South Side Institute, Nashville, a school for young ladies. See Emma Holcombe to Governor Andrew Johnson,

Nov. 16, 1863, DLC-Andrew Johnson. On Dec. 14, 1863, USG had endorsed a letter in which Mrs. Holcombe asked permission to send clothing to her daughter through the lines. "Respectfully returned. I am acquainted with the parties and they are very worthy people, but to grant the within request would be to establish a precedent prejudicial to the interest of the service." Copies, DLC-USG, V, 39; DNA, RG 393, Military Div. of the Miss., Endorsements. USG lived in Nashville at the home of Daniel F. Carter, a banker. Henry McRaven, *Nashville: "Athens of the South"* (Chapel Hill, 1949), p. 95. For Carter, see Johnson, *Papers*, V, 412n.

2. See *PUSG*, 1, 45. USG spelled the name correctly.

3. On Dec. 11, USG had written to Orval Pool. "The very elegant horse presented me by the citizens of Gallatin, Pope, Saline and Hamilton counties, Illinois, reached me during the absence of General Wilson (at Knoxville) who was commissioned to make the presentation in the name of the citizens of the above named counties. Permit me, through you, to thank them for their present, which I accept as a token of their devotion to the Union, and as a very great compliment to me personally, as an agent of the loyal people in assisting in breaking down rebellion." *New York Herald*, Dec. 25, 1863. In his diary for Sept. 15, Lt. Col. James H. Wilson noted that he had written to his uncle Orval Pool, a leading merchant of southeast Ill., urging him "not to forget the horse for Genl Grant." Historical Society of Delaware, Wilmington, Del. See James Harrison Wilson, *Under the Old Flag* (New York and London, 1912), I, 7.

4. See letter to Louisa Boggs, March 18, 1864.

To Maj. Gen. Henry W. Halleck

Nashville Tenn
Feby 15th 10 A M 1864

MAJ GEN H. W. HALLECK
GEN IN CHIEF

Is Gen Banks preparing an expedition to go up Red River? boats seem to be assembling at New Orleans for that purpose. I ask because in that event it will not be necessary for me to send, as contemplated doing on Sherm[an]s return, to the Red River. Genl Thomas advances this morning

U. S. GRANT
Maj Gen Comdg

Telegram received, DLC-William T. Sherman; DNA, RG 107, Telegrams Collected (Bound); copies, *ibid.*, Telegrams Received in Cipher; *ibid.*, RG 393, Military Div. of the Miss., Hd. Qrs. Correspondence; DLC-USG, V, 40, 94; DLC-Andrew Johnson. *O.R.*, I, xxxii, part 2, 394; *ibid.*, I, xxxiv, part 2, 330.

On Feb. 16, 1864, 1:00 P.M., Maj. Gen. Henry W. Halleck telegraphed to USG. "According to Genl Banks last despatch (Feby 7th) Admiral Farragat was to threaten Mobile in order to draw the enemy from Sherman & Thomas. As soon as Sherman's present expedition is terminated (about the 1st of March), it was understood that he and Genl Banks would move up Red River to meet Steele's advance against Schreveport. This was Genl Banks plan, if Sherman & Steele could cooperate with him. Sherman had agreed, but Steele not yet heard from. The time of movement would depend upon Stage of water in Red River. It was understood that as soon as Steele and Banks had effected a junction on that River, Sherman's army could all be with drawn to operate east of the Mississippi. Will not the probable delay in expelling Longstreet from East Tennessee justify the adoption of this plan of Banks & Sherman? Banks reports his force too weak to advance without Sherman's aid." ALS (telegram sent), DNA, RG 107, Telegrams Collected (Bound); telegram received, DLC-William T. Sherman. *O.R.*, I, xxxii, part 2, 402; *ibid.*, I, xxxiv, part 2, 340–41.

To Maj. Gen. Henry W. Halleck

Nashville Tenn.

Feby 15th 1864 10 30 a m

MAJ GEN H W HALLECK
GEN IN CHIEF

If Gen Schofield is rejected I would prefer Maj Gen J. B Mc-Pherson to all others for his place. Gen P. H. Sheridan second, Gen. O. O. Howard third choice. I do not know Genl Stoneman's merits

U S GRANT
Maj Genl Com'dg

Telegram received, DNA, RG 107, Telegrams Collected (Bound); copies, *ibid.*, Telegrams Received in Cipher; *ibid.*, RG 393, Military Div. of the Miss., Hd. Qrs. Correspondence; DLC-USG, V, 40, 94. *O.R.*, I, xxxii, part 2, 394. On Feb. 14, 1864, 12:30 P.M., Maj. Gen. Henry W. Halleck had telegraphed to USG. "Recruiting officers & Provost Marshals have been directed to send recruits to their regiments as fast as collected, and also to send new regiments to the field as fast as organized. In case Genl Schofield should be rejected, who do you want to command his Dept? Name several to select from." ALS (telegram sent), DNA, RG 107, Telegrams Collected (Bound); copies, *ibid.*, RG 393, Military Div. of the Miss., Hd. Qrs. Correspondence; DLC-USG, V, 40, 94. *O.R.*, I, xxxii, part 2, 389. See telegrams to Maj. Gen. Henry W. Halleck, Jan. 13, 27, 1864.

To Brig. Gen. Robert Allen

Nashville February 15th '64

BRIG GENERAL R. ALLEN Q. M.
LOUISVILLE KY

If boats have gone to New Orleans to transport troops up Red River there is no necessity for others to be sent to Vicksburg. One expedition is sufficient. If Banks makes it Sherman will not. If Banks does not Sherman can get the transports sent to Banks. Advise the Quartermaster at St Louis not to send transports to Vicksburg unless there is a surplus

U. S. GRANT
Major General

Telegram, copies, DLC-USG, V, 34, 35; DNA, RG 393, Military Div. of the Miss., Letters Sent. On Feb. 12, 1864, Brig. Gen. Robert Allen wrote to USG. "I fear that the demands which Gen. Banks, or rather Gen. Bank's, subordinates, are making for transportation, will greatly embarrass us in our efforts to get Stores ahead at Nashville. Gen. Banks, himself only made requisitions on me for fifteen boats. I assented to his having twenty. These together with Seventeen previously given to Gen. Sherman, make a wide gap in our means, but I have just this moment received a dispatch from the Quarter Master, at St Louis, which reads as follows: 'Capt. Lewis, had special orders to provide transportation for the force of Gen. Banks, movement. He will take forty Steamers embracing many of the largest boats on the river. They have turned back the "Empress" from Memphis, unloading a full cargo of Sugar and molasses. Colonel Mac Pheely arrived with verbal orders to get boats for ten thousand men to be at Vicksburg by the 1st of March, to go to same place as Gen. Banks Troops. I presume that the movement is the same, and that the forty Boats now taking will lay at New Orleans until the 5th or tenth of March' Of the nature of these movements you, General, are likely informed. I know nothing about them, but if subordinate officers are allowed to come up the Rivers and sweep them of their boats without any calculation of actual wants, we will labor in vain to get any large supply of Stores in advance at Nashville. We are employing now all the boats on the Ohio and getting supplies as fast as possible with our means." LS, *ibid.*, Letters Received.

To Col. Henry R. Mizner

                                        Headqrs. Mil. Div. of the Mississippi
                                        Nashville. Tenn. Feby 15th, 1864

COLONEL H. R. MIZNER
COM'D'G U. S. FORCES
COLUMBIA. TENN
COLONEL:

Your dispatch of the 11th of December 1863, to Capt. T. C. Williams,[1] and one of January 16. 1864 to Capt. Polk,[2] together with Brig Gen. G. M. Dodge's explanation and remarks thereon, have reached these Headquarters. Your wholesale attack upon Gen'l Dodge, a gallant and superior officer, is uncalled for and improper. The authority you usurped to yourself in arresting officers acting under his orders, and outside of your guard lines, was unmilitary and in bad taste. The whole tenor of your dispatches show bad temper, and is calculated to create hostility of feeling between troops expected to co-operate with each other. Enclosed you will find copy of Gen. Dodge's explanation.

                                        U. S. GRANT
                                        Major Gen. U. S. A.

Copies, DLC-USG, V, 39; DNA, RG 393, Military Div. of the Miss., Endorsements; Dodge Papers, IaHA. In response to charges by Col. Henry R. Mizner, 14th Mich., Columbia, Tenn., that troops commanded by Brig. Gen. Grenville M. Dodge had plundered civilian property, Dodge telegraphed to Lt. Col. Theodore S. Bowers on Feb. 3, 1864, requesting an investigation. Copy, DNA, RG 393, Military Div. of the Miss., Telegrams Received. On Feb. 4, after receiving Mizner's charges, Dodge wrote at length to Bowers explaining that some property had been taken by "a gang" in the 18th Mo. but that most had been seized under orders and through necessity. Copies, *ibid.*, 16th Army Corps, Letters Sent; *ibid.*, Left Wing, Letters Sent. On Feb. 5, Mizner wrote to Dodge listing the persons plundered and property taken. ALS, Dodge Papers, IaHA. On Feb. 12, Dodge wrote to Bowers discussing in detail the case of Mrs. Brown. LS, DNA, RG 109, Union Provost Marshals' File of Papers Relating to Individual Citizens. On Feb. 17, Dodge telegraphed to Bowers. "One John D. Vance of 18th Mo Infty the leader of a gang of robbers and murderers has been tried, convicted and ordered to be shot. I respectfully request authority to carry sentence into effect. It is a just verdict and will have a good effect if promptly acted upon. He is a very bad man" Copies, *ibid.*, RG 393, 16th Army Corps, Left Wing, Telegrams Sent;

ibid., Military Div. of the Miss., Telegrams Received. On Feb. 18, Dodge telegraphed to Bowers details of Vance's criminality. Copies, *ibid.* On the same day, Bowers telegraphed to Dodge that the sentence required presidential approval. Copies, DLC-USG, V, 34, 35; DNA, RG 393, Military Div. of the Miss., Letters Sent.

1. Thomas C. Williams, capt., 19th Inf., adjt. for Maj. Gen. Lovell H. Rousseau.

2. Burr H. Polk, capt., 33rd Ind., as of Sept. 6, 1861, and adjt. as of March 11, 1863. On Jan. 15, 1864, USG telegraphed to Maj. Gen. Henry W. Halleck. "I respectfully request that the order accepting the resignation of Capt B. H. Polk A. A. G. be revoked. Please answer" Telegram received, *ibid.*, RG 107, Telegrams Collected (Bound); copy, *ibid.*, RG 94, ACP, P325 CB 1867. On Jan. 16, 3:10 P.M., Halleck telegraphed to USG. "Order accepting resignation of Capt Polk is revoked, as requested." ALS (telegram sent), *ibid.*, RG 107, Telegrams Collected (Bound); copies, *ibid.*, RG 393, Military Div. of the Miss., Hd. Qrs. Correspondence; DLC-USG, V, 40, 94. On Jan. 16, 4:00 P.M., Lt. Col. James A. Hardie telegraphed to USG. "The acceptance of the Resignation of Captain B. H. Polk, has been revoked." LS (telegram sent), DNA, RG 107, Telegrams Collected (Unbound). On March 20, Polk wrote to USG. "Major General Rousseau was kind enough to apply for my appointment as Major & A. A. G. which application has either been lost in the mails or overlooked by the War Department. If with your knowledge of my character as an officer, you could conscientiously ask my promotion and would spare the time to do it, I should never forget the favor, and always strive to merit the promotion I am sure your recommendation would secure me—" ALS, *ibid.*, RG 94, ACP, P325 CB 1867. On March 25, USG endorsed this letter. "The promotion of the within named officer is respectfully recommended." ES, *ibid.* Polk was confirmed as maj. on April 20. On April 21, 1865, Rousseau wrote to Secretary of War Edwin M. Stanton asking that Polk be promoted to lt. col. LS, *ibid.* On May 11, USG endorsed this letter. "Respectfully forwarded. I have no doubt but that Maj. Polk is in every way worthy of the promotion asked and if there is any law by which an Asst. A. G. can hold the rank of Lt. Col. whilst serving with less than a Corps Commander I would like to see the promotion given." AES, *ibid.* Polk was appointed bvt. lt. col. and col. as of March 13, 1865.

To Mary E. Duncan

Nashville Ten.
Feb.y 15th 1864.

MISS MARY DUNCAN,

Your letter to me and one to Mrs. Grant enclosing Photograph were received. Mrs. G. is in St. Louis and very much afflicted with her eyes. I forwarded your letter to her there.—I was very glad to hear from you and ever shall be. I have to much to do however to write long letters so you must excuse me.—After the War I hope to make a long visit to Galena and to meet all my old friends there again.

My best regards to all your family and to other friends in Galena.

Yours Truly
U. S. GRANT
Maj. Gen. U. s. a.

ALS, C. S. Bentley Pike, Chicago, Ill. See letter to Julia Dent Grant, May 3, 1861.

To Maj. Gen. Henry W. Halleck

By Telegraph from Nashville Tenn Feb 16 *1864* 6. P. M

To MAJ. GEN HALLECK WASHINGTON

Genl Allen telegraphed me that Genl Banks had taken large amount of Rive transportation to New Orleans preparatory to a move up Red River. Also that a Staff Officer was collecting transportation for Sherman for the same move. This was crippling us here for transportation and I stopped it.[1] I expected Sherman however to go to Shreveport in conjunction with Steeles movement if Banks had not the force to send. I would suggest that Sherman himself go in command of a part if his troops go

U. S. GRANT
Maj Gen

Telegram received, DLC-William T. Sherman; DNA, RG 107, Telegrams Collected (Bound); copies, *ibid.*, Telegrams Received in Cipher; *ibid.*, RG 393, Military Div. of the Miss., Hd. Qrs. Correspondence; DLC-USG, V, 40, 94; DLC-Andrew Johnson. *O.R.*, I, xxxii, part 2, 401; *ibid.*, I, xxxiv, part 2, 341. On Feb. 17, 1864, 12:30 P.M., Maj. Gen. Henry W. Halleck telegraphed to USG. "I have given no orders to Genl Sherman in regard to his movements, but requested him to communicate freely with Genls Banks & Steele in regard to concert of action. I presume, from Genl Banks despatches, that Genl Sherman proposes to go in person to assist in effecting a junction between Banks and Steele on Red River. By last dispatch he was waiting an answer from Steele. In regard to river transportation you will exercise your own discretion, giving them all you can spare." ALS (telegram sent), DNA, RG 107, Telegrams Collected (Bound);

telegram received, DLC-William T. Sherman. *O.R.*, I, xxxii, part 2, 410; *ibid.*, I, xxxiv, part 2, 351.

1. See telegram to Brig. Gen. Robert Allen, Feb. 15, 1864.

To Maj. Gen. John M. Schofield

Head Quarters, Mil. Div. of the Miss.
Nashville Ten. Feb.y 16th 1864

Maj. Gen. Schofield,
Comd.g Dept. of the Ohio,
Gen.

I telegraphed you some days ago that conversation with Gen. Foster had decided me not to make any push against Longstreet for the present. Also that you might now get off all the Veterans you think you can spare. At the same time every preparation should be made for as early a move in the spring as practicable. Clothing should be got for the men and all the rations accumulated possible. All new regiments you may receive during the Winter, as well as any old ones back in Ky. available for duty to the front, should be rendezvozed where they can be eazily provisioned and at the same time be on the road either to join the Army in the Field, or form a column to march into Western Virginia either by Pound or Stoney Gaps.[1]

There is probably such a force in South West Virginia as would prevent a Cavalry force penetrating by that route, unaided by Inf.y and Artillery. But it looks now to me as if a column should be pushed through by that, or one of those, routes in conjunction with an advance up Holsten Valley.

I have but little hope of Sturgis being able to reach Longstreets rear unaided. If he is preparing for it, as I understood from Foster he is, let him try. I suppose going without Infantry, or only a mounted force, he would go by Jonesville & Estellville?[2] This enterprise would be hazardous but would pay well if successful. The destruction of important bridges between Bristol & Saltville, and of the Saltworks there, would compensate for great risks.

Let me know what you think and wish in this matter so that I will know how to dispose of such new troops as I may intend to add to your command.

I am General, very respectfully your obt. svt.

U. S. GRANT

Maj. Gen. Com

ALS, DLC-John M. Schofield. *O.R.*, I, xxxii, part 2, 402. On Feb. 21, 1864, Maj. Gen. John M. Schofield telegraphed to USG. "I had not recieved your letter of the Sixteenth when I answered your despatch of the Eighteenth 18 & hence did not understand its full import will write you fully today The enemy retreated from Flat Creek yesterday after our reconnoisance I have not learned whether the recrossed the Holstein" Telegram received, DNA, RG 393, Dept. of the Tenn., Telegrams Received; copies, *ibid.*, Military Div. of the Miss., Telegrams Received; DLC-John M. Schofield. *O.R.*, I, xxxii, part 2, 440. On Feb. 22, Schofield wrote to USG. "Your letter of the 16th relative to the concentration of troops for the spring campaign did not reach me until yesterday. I have no doubt of the wisdom of the plan you suggest of sending a column from Ky. into West Virginia, provided my force here can be made strong enough with out the aid of the troops necessary to form that column. Its successful execution might fairly be expected to result in the destruction of Longstreets army. The best place of rendezvous for a force intended to join me here early in the spring is Carthage on the Cumberland. The road from that place to this is good, and troops can be supplied there by water. The proposed expedition from Kentucky should, in my opinion, move through Pound Gap to Estillville. A Cavalry force moving by that route with sufficient Infty. and artillery to force its way through and to cover the retreat of the cavalry after its work is finished, would probably accomplish, in conjunction with a force moving up the Holston valley, the full result desired. It does not appear to me that a force moving from Cumberland Gap could be expected to accomplish the same result. Yet it would be valuable in conjunction with my movement from this place in enabling me to turn the enemy's right and open communication with Cumberland Gap. It would not, however, be wise to sacrafice anything of the essential strength of this column for that purpose. I would rather rely upon a rapid movement of a powerful force from this point to turn the right of Longstreets present position than to divide the force in the manner proposed. If, instead of a movement from here upon the enemys right flank, any other be adopted, a detachment upon his right could be sent from here nearly as well as from Cumberland Gap. On the other hand, to place a force at or in rear of Cumberland Gap would probably be a wise precautionary measure against a movement by the enemy into Kentucky if he should be prepared for aggressive operations before we are. The road through Pound Gap is not so good as that through Cumberland Gap, but is quite practicable for Cavalry. It is barely passable for Artillery and wagons in the dry season. It would be late in the Spring before Infty and Artillery could move by either route. I am now compelled to use pack mules to supply the troops at Cumberland Gap from Camp Nelson. A force intended to move by either route should rendezvous at Camp Nelson. It could hardly start from that place before the first of May. This would delay the movement from this place until the 15th or 20th of May. My impression is that a force may be concentrated here (and supplied) sufficient to drive Longstreet out of the country at least a month earlier. If you can calculate with certainty upon giving me here a sufficient force to insure my success, I think it would be wise by all means to rendezvous a force of Infantry & Artillery at Camp Nelson for the purpose you suggest. But if there is any doubt of your ability to make this column strong enough to act independently of the other it would be better to concentrate the troops you propose to give me at Carthage. From that place they can be brought to this at any time I may require them. In view of the considerations I have presented, I must leave it to you General, to decide what course is to be pursued. At present I am entirely unable to determine what can be done by Sturgis' Cavalry. I am informed it is now scattered all over Kentucky and Sturgis gone north. I am making every effort to get it together and prepare it for service. I have very little information about the enemy force in South West Virginia and am not able to judge whether Cavalry alone would be able to penetrate to the rail road. If they did it would probably be much more difficult to get back after they had accomplished the work assigned them. I will write you more fully upon this matter as soon as I can get further information." LS, DNA, RG 94, War Records Office, Military Div. of the Miss. *O.R.*, I, xxxii, part 2, 446–47.

1. Stone Gap and Pound Gap, between Va. and Ky., approximately sixty and seventy miles northeast of Cumberland Gap.
2. Probably Esserville, Va., approximately fifteen miles south of Pound Gap and thirty miles northeast of Jonesville.

To Brig. Gen. Rufus Ingalls

Nashville, Ten.
Feb.y 16th 1864.

DEAR RUF,

Your very welcom letter was received by due course of Mail and read with great interest and full intention to answer it right off. But since that time I have been moving about so much that I have neglected it. I have often wished that I could have you here to run the machinery of your department. This was on account of old acquaintance however. The Quartermaster's Dept. here has been well and satisfactorily managed so far as the heads are concerned. I did once apply to have you sent here as chief[1] but it was thought you could not be spared from where you are. I have never had any cause of complaint either on account of deficiency in the Staff Deptmts or embarassments trown in the way by the Authorities at Washington. The fact is I believe complaints are generally made to shift responsibility of inaction from commanders to Staff

Departments or Washington Authorities. Of course I only speak for the West. I am thankful my lot has not been cast where I could judge for any other section.

I am begining now to make preparations for attack or defence when Spring opens. Two important expeditions are now out, one under Sherman and the other under Thomas, which, if as successful as I expect them to be will have an importan[t] bearing on the Spring Campaign.

This war has developed some of our old acquaintances much differently from what we would have expected. Fred. Steele, a good fellow always but you would have supposed not much more, is really a splendid officer and would be fully capable of the management of the Army of the Potomac or any of the Departments. Some who much would have been expected from have proven rather failures. This class I do not like to mention by name.

I believe Ruf. you are still leading a bachilor's life? Don't you regret it? Now I have four children, three boys and one girl, in whos society I feel more enjoyment than I possibly can with any other company. They are a responsibility giving much more pleasure than anxiety. It may not be too late for you yet.

My respects to such old acquaintances as are with you.

Yours Truly
U. S. GRANT

ALS (facsimile), Frank A. Burr, *Life and Deeds of General Ulysses S. Grant....* (Philadelphia, 1885), pp. 491–97.

1. See letter to Maj. Gen. Henry W. Halleck, April 8, 1863.

To Commander Daniel Ammen

Nashville Ten.
Feb.y 16th 1864,

DEAR AMMEN,

Your letter was duly received and advice fully appreciated, particularly as it is the same I would give any friend: i. e. to avoid all political entanglements. I have always thought the most slavish life any man could lead was that of a politician. Besides I do not believe any man can be successful as a soldier whilst he has an anchor ahead for other advancement. I know of no circumstances likely to arise which could induce me to accept of any political office whatever. My only desire will be, as it has always been, to whip out the rebellion in the shortest way possible and to retain as high a position in the Army afterwards as the Administration then in power may think me suitable for.

I was truly glad to hear from you. I was once on leave of absence at the same time you were and went from Clermont County to Cincinnati more to see you than for any other purpose   When I got there found you had gone to Ripley by river. I believe the last time we met was in Philadelphia, in /43. We have both grown older since though time sets very lightly with me. I am neither grey nor bald nor do I feel any different from what I did at twenty-five   I have often wished you had been selected to command the Mississippi Flotilla. I have no fault to find however with the Naval Officers who have co-operated with me. I think Porter, Phelps and some of the younger officers as clever men as I ever fell in with. I ~~certainly~~ cannot complain of them certainly for I believe I never made a request of them they did not comply with, no matter what the danger. I know I caused Porter to loose one Gunboat, against his judgement, and he never found fault.

Remember me to Mrs. Van Dykes family[1] and any other friends of mine in Cin. I will be very glad to hear from you again.

Yours Truly

U. S. GRANT

ALS (facsimile), Frank A. Burr, *Life and Deeds of General Ulysses S. Grant....* (Philadelphia, 1885), pp. 484–89. Daniel Ammen, USG's boyhood friend, passed midshipman, U.S. Navy, in 1842, and became commander in 1862, serving on the Atlantic Coast during the war. On Feb. 5, 1864, Ammen, Cincinnati, wrote to USG. "I will not suppose that you have forgotten me although more than twenty years have passed since we last met.—The recollections of boy hood are so strong that I remember as of yesterday many of our fishing and other excursions and can assure you that no one of all your acquaintances has looked with more pleasure at your rapid and well deserved advancement than myself. It is not flattery to say that your career has been most brilliant and that the hopes of a Nation rest far more on you than upon any other man. In common with all who desire the welfare of the Nation I trust and pray that the Future will add to your distinguished reputation, so that at the end of our troubles, the history of the world will show few who have performed so enviable or so distinguished a part. You would be spared this letter of congratulation however, did I not wish to express to you warmly my appreciation of the profound wisdom you have shown in avoiding making speeches and all political entanglements.—It is my earnest sense of how much depends upon you that induces me to express a wish that you may continue the wise and patriotic course you have adopted. Twenty seven years in the Naval service and a not inconsiderable intercourse with persons in political life at Washington, among them 'Jeff Davis' whom I knew very well, has impressed me that there are higher aspirations than political preferment; that the gratitude and love of a whole people and the record of a great and unselfish career are of far greater worth. I pray you then for the sake of our unhappy country, to continue steadfastly in the wise course you have adopted, and doubt not that with the blessings of Providence you will realize the hopes of a Nation and bring us again into a state of prosperity. I saw Capt De Camp of the Navy three weeks ago who spoke most kindly of you and of Mrs. Grant whom he knew in times past at St. Louis.—His brother I think was a particular friend and died in New York when you were present, of Cholera. I am now suffering with rheumatism and on leave, but trust soon to be able to go on blue water again. I trust that when peace and quiet is restored I shall have the pleasure of meeting you. Your relatives the Tweeds and indeed all the members of Mrs. Van Dykes family I see frequently; they are charming, particularly Miss Alice who is admired by all who know her. Believe me most truly your admirer and early friend" ALS, USG 3. On April 18, USG wrote: "Pass Comd.r. D. Ammen, U. S. N. to and from the Army of the Potomac free over Military rail-roads. Good until countermanded." ANS, Winterthur Manuscripts, Eleutherian Mills Historical Library, Greenville, Del. See Daniel Ammen, *The Old Navy and the New* (Philadelphia, 1891), pp. 383–85.

1. On July 10, 1863, Alice Tweed, Cincinnati, wrote to USG. "I take this opportunity to send to you by my Uncle, 'Augustus C Van Dyke' the very sincere congratulations of myself and mother for the unparalelled success you have met with, in taking the stronghold of the Confederacy. believe me we watch with the utmost interest your every act—and none more heartily rejoice in your success than our family—With highest considerations of regard, and prayers for your continued prosperity" ALS, USG 3.

To Maj. Gen. John M. Schofield

By Telegraph from Nashville [*Feb.*] 17 12.30 P M *186*[*4*]
To MAJ GENL SCHOFIELD

Can you not by proper disposition of your Cavalry and Grangers Corps prevent any raid on your Communications west of Knoxville? It is highly desirable Thomas should make a move for which he is now prepared and which will be prevented by reinforcing you—It is also desirable that the force at Knoxville should be kept at the lowest standard so as to accumulate supplies for a large force when needed—It is hoped Sherman & Thomas' movement will throw the enemy into a position which will leave your Army and Thomas to act more as a unit

U S Grant M G

Telegram received, DLC-John M. Schofield; copies, DLC-USG, V, 34, 35; DNA, RG 393, Military Div. of the Miss., Letters Sent. *O.R.*, I, xxxii, part 2, 414. On Feb. 17, 1864, Maj. Gen. John M. Schofield telegraphed to Maj. Gen. George H. Thomas. "Your despatch of 16th is just received—Longstreet remains with his infantry so far as I can learn, at Strawberry Plains New Market, & Dandridge, has made several demonstrations as if to cross at Strawberry Plains but has not crossed. He has sent Three brigades of cavalry from near Seveirville along the foot of Chilhowee mountains with the apparent intention of crossing the Little Tenn His Cavalry officers say, to make a raid upon the rail road in rear of Loudon and then move into Georgia The rivers have risen so much that I think McCooks will be able to prevent his crossing the Little Tennessee If you can leave Stanleys Division on the road I can do without other reenforcements until you can make your demonstration upon Dalton—I will have to retain the Veterans It is rumored in Longstreets camp that his main force is to move into Georgia by the route taken by The Three Cavalry brigades I think the Cavalry movement is all but will watch him closely" Telegram received, DNA, RG 94, War Records Office, Military Div. of the Miss.; copy, *ibid.*, RG 393, Military Div. of the Miss., Telegrams Received. Printed as sent at 8:00 P.M. in *O.R.*, I, xxxii, part 2, 415. This telegram was forwarded to USG.

On Feb. 18, USG telegraphed to Schofield. "I expect a division of about ten thousand (10000) men soon which I propose adding to your Dept where will you have them sent" Telegram received, DLC-John M. Schofield. On the same day, Schofield telegraphed twice to USG. "I can get along with what force I have including Grangers corps until Genl Thomas makes his move I did not know one was contemplated when I suggested that he should send more troops" "Can you tell me if an order has been issued to send the 9th Army Corps out of this Department or whether such an order is contemplated? It is important in connection with the furlough of the Veterans" Telegrams received, DNA, RG 393, Dept. of the Tenn., Telegrams Received; copies, *ibid.*, Military Div. of the Miss., Telegrams Received; DLC-John M. Schofield. The first is in *O.R.*, I, xxxii, part 2, 421. Also on Feb. 18, USG telegraphed to Schofield. "I know nothing of the ninth (9) Corps. leaving your Dept they cannot go if ordered until it is safe to relieve them—Let such a rumor make no difference in furloughing Veterans" Telegram received, DLC-John M. Schofield. On the same day, 8:30 P.M., Schofield telegraphed to USG and Thomas. "Perceived Longstreet moved his main Infy force from New Market towards Strawberry Plains yesterday morning I have nothing more definite" Telegram received, DNA, RG 393, Dept. of the Tenn., Telegrams Received; copies, *ibid.*, Military Div. of the Miss., Telegrams Received; DLC-John M. Schofield. *O.R.*, I, xxxii, part 2, 422.

On Feb. 18 or 19, Schofield telegraphed to USG and Thomas. "The belief is very general among citizens living within Longstreets lines that he is making some move toward Georgia. But I have not yet been able to get the facts in a reliable shape. The most reliable reports indicate that one division of Infantry and a considerable force of cavalry have gone in that direction. The Infantry is going up the French Broad. The Cavalry was to go down this side of the mountains and attempt to destroy the rail-road ~~this~~ below Loudon, before crossing the mountains into Georgia. They have failed to get across the Little Tennessee, and have probably taken the other route." Copies (dated Feb. 18), DNA, RG 393, Military Div. of the Miss., Telegrams Received; (dated Feb. 19) DLC-John M. Schofield. Dated Feb. 18, 1:00 P.M., in *O.R.*, I, xxxii, part 2, 422. On Feb. 19, 7:30 P.M., Schofield telegraphed to USG. "If the Division is coming from the North the best route is via Nashville   It is hardly possible to bring troops here through Kentucky at this season   From Nashville the best route is to Carthage by boat and thence via Montgomery and Winter Gap or they can march from Nashville by way of Sparta & Kingston. The road via Montgomery is the best   There is forage enough on either route unless it has been consumed recently"   Telegram received, DNA, RG 393, Dept. of the Tenn., Telegrams Received; copies, *ibid.*, Military Div. of the Miss., Telegrams Received; DLC-John M. Schofield. *O.R.*, I, xxxii, part 2, 428.

On Feb. 20, 10:00 P.M., Schofield telegraphed to USG. "I sent a cavalry division toward Strawberry Plains today. It met a force of Infantry from three thousand to five thousand strong on the East bank of Flat Creek—Nearly all Longstreets Infantry force appears to be near Strawberry Plains on either side of the river. And most of his cavalry South of the French Broad—I am at a loss to interpret his movements unless he meant to attack this place.—This he will hardly do unless, he has received reinforcements. I cannot learn of his having received any. I am prepared for him, and will try to be for ~~any~~ whatever he may attempt." Copies, DLC-John M. Schofield; DNA, RG 393, Military Div. of the Miss., Telegrams Received. *O.R.*, I, xxxii, part 2, 433. On the same day, Lt. Col. Cyrus B. Comstock, Knoxville, telegraphed to USG. "Reconnoisance of thousand men just returned report three thousand Rebel infantry at Flat Creek Three miles this side Strawberry Plains   at that point a Pontoon bridge across river is reported by Scouts and Citizens say Rail Road bridge is being repaired. . . . a Cavalry Scout across the river seeing a few men and followed them till he came upon Two brigades of Cavalry out Seiverville Road 5 Miles—It is hardly believed that Longstreet will attack Knoxville but nothing has been heard for a few days of his going through Smoky mountains"   Copy, DNA, RG 393, Military Div. of the Miss., Telegrams Received.

To Maj. Gen. George H. Thomas

Nashville noon 17th February 1864

MAJOR GENERAL GEO H THOMAS
CHATTANOOGA

Longstreet cannot afford to place his force between Knoxville and the Tennessee. If he does it will then be time to move against him. The work of a raid on the road can soon be repaired if it cannot be prevented. Make your contemplated move as soon as possible

U. S GRANT

Major General

Telegram, copies, DLC-USG, V, 34, 35; DNA, RG 393, Military Div. of the Miss., Letters Sent. *O.R.*, I, xxxii, part 2, 414. On Feb. 16, 1864, 12:00 P.M., Maj. Gen. George H. Thomas had telegraphed to USG. "I have just received a telegram from Genl. Schofield dated Feby. 14th. stating that he had reliable information that Longstreet had advanced to Strawberry Plains and had brought up Pontoon boats. Schofield thought that he might intend to make a cavalry raid to cut his communication with Loudon or that he might advance to attack Knoxville and asks me to send him reinforcements as early as practicable. What shall I do? If reinforcements are sent to Knoxville they will be detained there for the Winter and cannot make an advance on Longstreet until the Loudon and Strawberry Plains bridges are rebuilt. It will also become necessary to give up any demonstration against Dalton. But if Schofield can hold Knoxville the demonstration on Dalton can be made and I hope with success. Capt Gay just from Knoxville and gone to Nashville, does not mention such reports." Copies, DNA, RG 393, Dept. of the Cumberland, Telegrams Sent; *ibid.*, Military Div. of the Miss., Telegrams Received. *O.R.*, I, xxxii, part 2, 403. On Feb. 17, 5:00 P.M., Thomas telegraphed to USG. "Your despatch of this mornng received—I have had more obstacles to overcome than I had anticipated   I find it absolutely necessary to take artillery and for which I must have horses   I Cannot say positively what day I shall start but certainly by monday   The destination is not known as all think it is Schofield I am to reinforce   The Rebels have the same information from scouts   The heavy rain of sunday has raised the Chickamauga so it is not fordable   I also desire to have Genls Davis and Stanley back"   Telegram received, DNA, RG 94, War Records Office, Military Div. of the Miss.; copies, *ibid.*, RG 393, Dept. of the Cumberland, Telegrams Sent; *ibid.*, Military Div. of the Miss., Telegrams Received. *O.R.*, I, xxxii, part 2, 414.

On Feb. 18, Thomas telegraphed to USG. "I regret to be obliged to riport that I do not think I shall be able to take the field   The cold & damp weather having brought on an attack of neuralegia from which I suffer intensely   I am getting troops prepared as rapidly as possible & will send them out under Genl Palmer if you think it best"   Telegram received, DNA, RG 94, War Records Office, Military Div. of the Miss.; copies, *ibid.*, RG 393, Military Div. of the Miss., Telegrams Received; *ibid.*, Dept. of the Cumberland, Telegrams Sent. *O.R.*, I, xxxii, part 2, 421. On the same day, USG telegraphed twice to Thomas, the second time at 2:00 P.M. "By all means send the expedition. I think it of vast importance that it should move as easily [*soon*] as possible for the effect it will have in favor of Sherman, and also on affairs in East Tennessee. I regret you cannot go." "Please order Companies C. H. F and M. 5th Tennessee Cavalry from this place to join their regiment. Send the order to day by telegraph." Copies, DLC-USG, V, 34, 35; DNA, RG 393, Military Div. of the Miss., Letters Sent; *ibid.*, Dept. of the Cumberland, Telegrams Received. The first is printed as sent at 2:30 P.M. in *O.R.*, I, xxxii, part 2, 421. On the same day, Thomas telegraphed to USG. "Lieut Col Gelbrith Commanding Batallion 5th Tenn Cavalry five hundred men & one hundred & sixty mounted will order the mounted men to move out—The others as soon as horses can be obtained" Telegram received (dated Feb. 19), DNA, RG 393, Dept. of the Tenn., Telegrams Received; copies, *ibid.*, Military Div. of the Miss., Telegrams Received; (dated Feb. 18) *ibid.*, Dept. of the Cumberland, Telegrams Sent. Also on Feb. 18, USG telegraphed to Thomas. "Please direct Gen. Butterfield to report me in person without delay." Copy, *ibid.*, Telegrams Received.

On Feb. 19, Thomas telegraphed to USG. "Asst. Surg Jacob Keller 6th Mo. Vol. Infty. arrived here yesterday from Dalton. He was captured at Lebanon Ala. when Genl. Logan sent out an expedition towards Rome. He reports Claborne's Division at Tunnel Hill—Stewarts between Tunnel Hill and Dalton— Walker two miles out from Dalton towards Spring Place. Cheatham at Dalton and Stevenson and Bates to the west of Dalton two miles. He saw all of the Camps and estimates their force between thirty and forty thousand. He moreover states that no troops have been sent away Except one Brigade of Infty. which went to Rome about the first of this month." Copies, *ibid.*, Telegrams Sent; *ibid.*, Military Div. of the Miss., Telegrams Received. *O.R.*, I, xxxii, part 2, 429.

To Julia Dent Grant

Nashville Ten.
Feb.y 17th 1864

DEAR JULIA,

Two letters from you, and a Valentine from Jess I suppose, are just rec'd. I am glad to hear your eyes are getting better. If you and Fred can travel I think you had better take a steamer direct for this place. The Spring Campaign will open probably in the early part of Apl. after which there is no assurance when we will meet again. The passage of the Lieut. Gen. Bill, if it does pass, may effect a change however in this respect. With such a change it might be necessary for me to pass from West to East occationally when of course we would meet. I do not want you to repeat what I say on this subject.

Lagow had received notice of the acceptance of his resignation. I wrote to him however a friendly letter. I will direct Orvil to send back the horse he has to Lagow and will write to him that I have no means of keeping him. In that case I will send you *Hipa-drome* and you can get a nice carriage for four persons. He drives beautifully and is big enough for two horses. My horse presented by citizens of Southern Ill. drives most elegantly and is gentle enough for Jess to manage. I must find some person to send him to to keep during the next campaign. He is too fine to risk loosing. I presume not less than one thousand dollars was paid for him.

I dined the other day with Mrs. Dunlap. She is very anxious to see you back. I dont know but she wants to see Jess about as much as she does you. She certainly seems very fond of him. I write to you so often that, of course, I find but little to say. About your dream! in this case your dream certainly has gone by contrary. I never felt better nor looked better than I have all the time since my return from St Louis.

Love and kisses for yourself and the children   Love and kisses, or only best respects as you think best, to Cousin Louisa and the young ladies.

ULYS.

ALS, DLC-USG.

To Maj. Gen. William T. Sherman

Head Quarters, Mil. Div. of the Miss.
Nashville Ten. Feb.y 18th 1864

MAJ. GEN. W. T. SHERMAN,
COMD.G DEPT. OF THE TEN.
GENERAL,

Enclosed I send you copies of dispatches between Gen. Halleck and myself relative to a movement up Rid River on your return from your present expedition.[1] Whilst I look upon such an expedition as is proposed as of the greatest importance, I regret that any force has to be taken from East of the Miss. for it. Your troops will want rest for the purpose of preparing for a Spring Campaign and all the Veterans should be got off on furlough at the very earliest moment. This latter I would direct even if you have to spare troops to go up Red River.

Unless you go in command of the proposed expedition I fear any troops you may send with it will be entirely lost from further service in this command. This however is not the reason for my suggestion that you be sent. Your acquaintance with the country, and otherwise fitness, were the reasons.

I can give no possitive orders that you send no troops up the Red River, but what I do want is their speedy return if they do go, and that the minimum number necessary be sent.

I have never heard a word from Steele since his Dept. has been placed in this Military Division. Do not know what he proposes nor the means he has for executing. The time necessary for communicating between here and Vicksburg being so great you will have to act in this matter according to your own judgement simply knowing my views.

Is it possible that Banks will entrust such an expedition to the command of McClernand?[2] I have so little confidance in his ability to command that I would not want the responsibility of entrusting men with him, without positive orders to do so.

I send this by special Messenger who will await your return to Vicksburg and will bear any letters you may have for me.[3]

> I am General, Very Truly
> your obt. svt.
> U. S. GRANT
> Maj. Gen. Com

ALS, DLC-William T. Sherman. *O.R.*, I, xxxii, part 2, 424–25.

On Feb. 6, 1864, Maj. Gen. William T. Sherman, Jackson, telegraphed to USG through Brig. Gen. James M. Tuttle, Big Black River Bridge, Miss., who added the last two sentences. "Shermans command composed of McPherson and Hurlbuts Corps left Vicksburg on the third in two columns via Rail Road Bridge —At Messengers on the 4th McPherson met the enemy Wirt Adams Brigade and skirmished as far as Colton [*Bolton*]   on the 5th Hurlbuts column encountered Starks Brig of Cavalry at Davis plantation and drove it through Clinton towards Canton   same day McPherson encountered and drove Wirt Adams in and through Jackson—Sherman occupied Jackson on the 6th and will cross Pearl River & enter Brandon on the 7th & so on—He reports three small Brigades of Cavalry and Lorings Division of infantry to his front at or near Brandon   I sent forward your despatches last night but they failed to get through in consequence of Starks Brigade being in Shermans rear—My Division is here"   Telegram received (sent on Feb. 8, received Feb. 22), DNA, RG 94, War Records Office, Military Div. of the Miss.; copy, *ibid.*, RG 393, Military Div. of the Miss., Telegrams Received. Incomplete in *O.R.*, I, xxxii, part 2, 340.

On Feb. 27, Sherman wrote to Brig. Gen. John A. Rawlins. "I got in this moring from Canton where I left my army in splendid heart & condition. We reached Jackson Feb 6—crossed Pearl & passed through Brandon to Morton where the Enemy made despositions for Battle but fled in the night—pushed on over all obstacles & reached Meridian Feb 14. Gen Polk having a Railroad to assist him in his retreat, escaped across the Tombigbee on the 17th. We staid at Meridian a week and made the most complete destruction of Railroads ever beheld, South below Quitman, East to Cuba Station 20 miles, North to Lauderdale springs, and west all the way back to Jackson. I could hear nothing of the Cavalry force of Gen Wm Sooy Smith ordered to be there by February 10. I enclose by mail this with a copy of his instructions. I then began to move back slowly making a circuit by the North to Canton, where I left the Army yesterday in splendid condition. I will leave it there five days in hopes the Cavalry from Memphis will turn up, then I will have them come in. Banks writes he will be ready for his Red River trip March 5, and will want ten thousand men of me. I will run down to see him tonight, also admiral Porter who is near Red River. I know if we wipe out Shreveport as I have done Meridian you can safely call for twenty thousand men from here & Arkansas in all April. I will report fully by Mail. . . . P S. Gen Reid will telegraph the foregoing from Cairo, and send this the original and its enclosure by Mail." ALS, DNA, RG 393, Military Div. of the Miss., Letters Received. Incomplete in *O.R.*, I, xxxii, part 1, 173. On March 10, this message was sent by telegraph from Cairo, with Brig. Gen. Hugh T. Reid adding a postscript. "The army arrived at Vicksburg on the fourth." Telegram received, DNA, RG 107, Telegrams Collected (Bound); copy, *ibid.*, RG 393, Military Div. of the Miss., Telegrams Received. On March 8, USG, Baltimore, telegraphed to Lt. Col. Theodore S. Bowers. "Despatch me to washington first news from Sherman" Telegrams received (2), *ibid.*, RG 107, Telegrams Collected (Unbound); copy, *ibid.*, RG 393, Military Div. of the Miss., Telegrams Received. On March 10, Bowers telegraphed Sherman's message to USG. Telegram received (incomplete), *ibid.*, RG 107, Telegrams Collected (Bound). On March 11, Reid telegraphed to Bowers. "Gen'l Sherman arrived in person at Vicksburg Feby. 27th and left same day for New Orleans to see Gen. Banks Army arrived at Vicksburg March 4th in fine condition had but little fighting and destroyed Rail-roads generally. I forwarded Gen. Shermans dispatch to Gen'l Rawlins at Nashville and to Gen'l Grant at Washington by Telegraph last night also by mail to Nashville. Your dispatch of the 8th inst. recd" Copy, *ibid.*, RG 393, Military Div. of the Miss., Telegrams Received. *O.R.*, I, xxxii, part 3, 53.

On Feb. 25, 1:00 P.M., Brig. Gen. James H. Wilson wrote to USG. "having heard that notwithstanding your views to the contrary, orders had been issued requiring you to send Sherman and twenty thousand men West of the Mississippi to cooperate with Steele and Banks—I immediately took steps to ascertain the origin of the order. When I wrote to Capt. Badeau this morning, I thought the President had issued it—but I have just seen Mr. Dana who spoke to the President concerning it. The latter says, no such order or authority ever came from him and if any one has given it, he did it without consulting *him* in any manner shape or form! Mr. Dana don't think it at all probable *that you have received any such instructions.* This is rather remarkable—and certainly mystefies me somewhat. However, you know the *straight* of the story yourself and can tell better than any one who is right. If the president hasn't issued the order, and it didn't go through the War Department there's only one other competent authority. Things are some times done very strangely here—for instance a few days ago General Halleck wrote to Gillmore, reproving him for going to Florida without orders—whereupon Gen'l. Gillmore replies, enclosing a copy of his instructions sent direct from the President over and around every body! I understand that Mr. Lincoln's motive was to have such a movement made as would give Military control of Florida, and thus enable him to reëstablish State authority with as little delay as possible. From what I hear, there is a somewhat feverish anxiety on the part of the Government to bring back or reorganize the state governments in the conquered territory with as little delay as possible. This is a ruinous policy, if to enforce it they are compelled to divide our forces, while the enemy still confronts us in strong array. We must destroy his armies before we begin to reërect the broken machinery of the states by the exercise of military strength. It seems to me that Genl. Butler in command of conquered territory might do more than any else towards carrying out such a policy as seems to have been adopted. Won't Sherman be too far out of the way to be sent West of the river before spring? I think however General, that any fully matured line of policy that you may advise will be acquiesced in without questions, so it looks towards whipping the enemy—and destroying his power for offensive movements. Mr. Stanton is therefore very decidedly in favor of letting you alone. Should Schofield not be confirmed, there will be no difficulty in putting MacPherson in his place if you recommend it. I can't ascertain what the difficulty is, in Baly Smith's case—but suspect that there is a strong secret influence working against him. Who, or where this may be I have no means of ascertaining. There are now vacancies among the Major Generals—but the fact that six or seven nominations are waiting for confirmation may in some degree account for their not sending in Smith's name. If you would write Senator Wilson a letter it might help him. The winter is passing and no definite plan determined for the Spring Campaign. Something should be done soon or the rebels will get the start of us. The bill for Lt. General, will soon become a law, notwithstanding the opposition of the Rosecranz interests. Garfield has made a complete summer set since he was at Chattanooga. Mr. Dana says he was then open in the denunciation of Rosecranz for his conduct at Chicamauga—his course in congress is just the reverse. I think there will be no difficulty in my getting away from here by the middle of April, as I shall either have the machine in complete working order by that time, or have raised such a flutter among the patriotic contractors, as will cause Mr. Lincoln and Mr. Stanton to wish they had never heard of me. I'm having quite a struggle with Contractors now—but I think their *patriotism* will triumph, and cause them to sacrafice their interest to the welfare of the Country. Remember me kindly to Mrs. Grant." ALS, USG 3.

1. See telegrams to Maj. Gen. Henry W. Halleck, Feb. 15, 16, 1864.
2. On Feb. 18, Maj. Gen. Edward O. C. Ord wrote to USG. "I am about, loose again—McClernand is back—with an order or letter from Genl. Halleck to Genl. Banks—saying that if he Banks should place McCld. in command of the 13th Corps—it would be approved by the President—this is a double move and you can see by it that you must have one of your quiet smiles ready to meet attacks of, *enemies in the rear*, as cooly as you allways do those in front—I have nothing to complain of for I have been using every effort to get corps & all out of Genl Banks department and into yours—Sherman whom I met at Louisville promised to ask for me and part of my corps all of which has been lying idle now all winter—it is in splendid condition—Dana and Ransom—Division Commanders —are determined to quit rather than serve under Mc.   Lawler says I must try and get him away also—*all* the Corps Staff here will quit at least so they say— can you give me a command if I am sent to you—please look out for me as I shall

be along soon—and have recovered my health, and feel like whipping some body—good bye   my regards to all your staff—to Thomas—Wilson—Sherman if he is near—Genl Rawlins—Cols Lagow & Riggin—and others who know me—Genl. Banks is mad as the devil—so Stone says—at the *order* of which he is expected to assume the paternity—has not executed it yet—but of course he will have to—I am just back from Texas—and found the corps in lovely health—but nothing doing—it is the easiest place to take, going—"   ALS, USG 3.

3. On Feb. 21, Bowers issued Special Orders No. 47. "Major General Daniel Butterfield, Chief of Staff, to Major General Hooker, will proceed without delay to Vicksburg, Mississippi, with despatches from the General Commanding, to Major General W. T. Sherman, Commanding Army of the Tennessee. On the delivery of said despatches to General Sherman, he will report in person to these Headquarters." Copy, DLC-USG, V, 38. On Feb. 26, Maj. Gen. Daniel Butterfield, Memphis, telegraphed to USG. "Gen'l W. S. Smith returned here last night   had been to West Point Ala. which point he left twenty second   he reports a running fight for sixty miles back to Pontiac with Forrests Cavalry said to be reinforced by Lee, Numbering in all about six or seven thousand men   was successful in every encounter punishing the enemy severely except at Okalona where he drove them three times from the field with one regiment   when this regiment was withdrawn the enemy in heavy force fell upon a disorganized regiment inflicting heavy loss probably three hundred—Six prairie Howitzers were run into a ditch from which it was impossible to extricate them—The guns were then spiked Carriages were partially destroyed and abandoned to the enemy—The results of the raid were captured thirty five hundred horses and mules—fifteen hundred contrabands one hundred prisoners including a number of Officers   Col Forrest brother to rebel Gen. Forrest killed—destroyed two thousand bales Confederate Cotton two million bushels Corn thirty miles Rail Road and five bridges between Okalona and West Point. Over three thousand contrabands started to come in but many were unable to keep up with the Cavalry—Found abundance of supplies through the country   it was reported by rebel deserters that Gen'l Sherman took Meridian without opposition on the fifteenth—Polk falling back towards Demopolis and Selma and being reinforced by Johnsons Army—Gen'l Smith had no communication with Gen'l Sherman finding it impossible"   Copy, DNA, RG 393, Military Div. of the Miss., Telegrams Received. *O.R.*, I, xxxii, part 2, 478. On Feb. 29, Butterfield, Vicksburg, wrote to USG. "Just arrived—Sherman came in last night & left for Natchez Red River & New Orleans   Hurlbut & McPherson with commands at Canton waiting news of Smiths movements—under orders to remain until 3d & 4th unless they hear from Smith sooner—Have sent Hurlbut information of Smiths return—leave sealed copies of dispatches here in case Sherman passes me on river and go by fast boat to overtake him & deliver originals—I do so as I thinking you would desire him to have them before he completes arrangements with Banks. Col Chamberlain captured three weeks since at Skipworths Landing escaped near Greenwood on Yazoo and came in by transport & gun boats—arrived this noon—reports Capt Dent in hands of enemy one day behind him near Sunflower   Col Coats landed at Yazoo city 3. P. M 28th   Rebel pickets just entering outer works as Osbornes cavalry got possession—Skirmish & fighting took place—rebels driven back—our loss killed wounded & missing 20 to 25—Col Coats supposed it to be Forrests advance—was confident of holding position but feared Forrest would throw force to Liverpool on Yazoo—Coats did not know of our force at Canton—Information of above has been sent Hurlbut—"   ALS,

DNA, RG 393, Military Div. of the Miss., Letters Received. *O.R.*, I, xxxii, part 2, 499–500. On March 8, Sherman, "en route for Memphis," wrote to Rawlins. "I had the honor to receive at the hands of General Butterfield Gen Grants letter of February 18. I had returned from Meridian by the time I had appointed, but the condition of facts concerning the Red River Expedition being indefinite I took one of the Marine Boats, the Diana, and went down to New Orleans to confer with General Banks. En route I saw the Admiral & learned that he was ready and a large & effective Gunboat fleet would be at the Mouth of Red River ready for action Mch 5. At New Orleans I received the Generals letter with Enclosures and was governed by it in my interview with Genl Banks. Gen McClernand had been ingeniously disposed of by being sent to command in Texas. General Banks is to command in person taking with him 17000 of his chosen troops, to move by land from the end of the Opelousas Railroad, via Franklin, Opelousas and Alexandria; Steele is to move from Little Rock on Natchitoches: and he asked of me ten thousand men in boats to ascend Red River meeting him at Alexandria the 17th of March. I enclose Copies of General Banks letter to me and my answer, which was clear & specific. I have made up a Command of ten thousand men, 7500 of Hurlbut, and 2500 of McPherson. Gen A. J. Smith goes in command of the whole. Will be at the mouth of Red River by the 10th at farthest and at Alexandria, on the 17th. These ten thousand men are not to be gone over, 30 days, at the expiration of which time McPhersons quota will return to Vicksburg, and Hurlbuts quota will come to Memphis whence if all things remain as now I can bring them rapidly round to Savannah Tenn & so on to my Right flank near Huntsville. I think this will result as soon as the furloughed men get back. In as much as Genl Banks goes in person I could not with delicacy propose that I should command, and the scene of operations lying wholly in his Dept I deemed it wisest to send A. J. Smith and to return in time to put my Army in the Field in shape for the coming Spring Campaign. I have ordered five Regiments under Genl Veatch to join Dodge at once, and I feel sure I can safely draw A. J. Smiths Division of full five thousand men to the same point in April. McPherson & Hurlbut are both instructed to furlough their veterans at once and many Regiments are already off. I have inspected Natchez & Vicksburg & feel sure they can now be held safe with comparatively small Garrisons, and the River is patrolled by Gun-boats & the Marine Brigade. I will inspect Memphis, and in a few days will hasten to Huntsville to put myself in Command of my troops in that quarter & will be ready for work at once as I am in no manner fatigued. Indeed the men I took with me to Meridian are better fitted for war now than before we started. I send by Genl Butterfield my official Report, with copies of orders, letters &c giving you full information of all matters up to date." ALS, DNA, RG 393, Military Div. of the Miss., Letters Received. *O.R.*, I, xxxii, part 3, 40–41. Sherman's lengthy report was addressed to Rawlins. ADfS, InNd; copy, DLC-William T. Sherman. *O.R.*, I, xxxii, part 1, 173–79. On March 11, 8:00 P.M., Butterfield, Columbus, Ky., telegraphed to USG. "Left Gen. Sherman yesterday—command all safe in—total loss. K. W and M. only 170—The general result of his expedition including Smiths & Yazoo River movement about as follows.—150 miles rail road—67 Bridges—7000 feet trestle work—20 locomotive[s—] 28 cars —ten thousand bales cotton—several steam mills—over two million bushels corn completely destroyed—destruction of R. R. complete & thorough—captures of prisoners exceed all losses—upwards of eight thousand contrabands & refugees came in with various columns—Your dispatches by Capt. Badeau recieved by Sherman on 9th. Gen. Banks in person commands Red River expedition—Sherman sends A. J. Smith with ten thousand men to cooperate—expressly understood that they return in thirty days by which time McPherson's furloughed men return—Smiths meets Banks column at Alexandria on the 17th—I have despatches from Gen'l. Sherman he directs me to proceed & deliver them to you—Where shall I find you—please answer at Mitchell ~~Bud~~ if it will reach there by 4. P. M of the 12th after that Burnet House Cinncinatti" ALS (telegram sent), DNA, RG 107, Telegrams Collected (Unbound); telegram received, *ibid.*; *ibid.*, Telegrams Collected (Bound). Printed as sent from Cairo at midnight in *O.R.*, I, xxxii, part 3, 54.

To Maj. Gen. Henry W. Halleck

Head Quarters, Mil. Div. of the Miss.
Nashville Ten. Feb.y 20th 1864,

MAJ. GEN. H. W. HALLECK,
GEN. IN CHIEF OF THE ARMY,
GENERAL,

Understanding that a greater number of Brig. Gens. have been appointed than than can be confirmed by the Senate, I would respectfully state that the list of recommendations sent in by me was made up from those recommended by their Corps, or immediate, commanders. Being personally acquainted however with all those who have been so recommended I will now submit the list anew, giving their names in the order of my preference, taking into concideration services rendered, and fitness for the position;

1st Jno. A. Rawlins
2d Chas. R. Wood
3d Giles A. Smith
4th Jas H. Wilson
5th J. M. Corse
6th Alex. Chambers
7th Wm Q. Gresham
8th J. A. Maltby
9th M. F. Force
10th Edward Hatch
11th P. A. Cameron
12th J. R. Slack

13th J. B. Sanborn
14th T. Kilby Smith.[1]

I have the honor to be
very respectfully, your obt. svt.
U. S. GRANT
Maj. Gen.

P. S. The name of B. H. Grierson, which I see, after having this letter partly copied in the books, has been left out. He was appointed I believe without recommendation from me, and for most excellent services rendered. Whether his name should not come before any of those named in the foregoing list I respectfully submit.

U. S. G.

ALS, DNA, RG 94, ACP, G408 CB 1864. *O.R.*, I, xxxii, part 2, 432–33. On Feb. 27, 1864, Maj. Gen. Henry W. Halleck wrote to USG. "Your letter of the 20th with a list of recommendations for Brig. Genls is recieved and submitted to the Secty of war with my approval. I am not aware whose names were on the last list sent in by the Prest, to which you allude, not having seen it or been consulted in regard to it. I understand, however, indirectly that the nominations were made on the recommendations of Governors of states and not of the War Dept." ALS, Ritzman Collection, Aurora College, Aurora, Ill. *O.R.*, I, xxxii, part 2, 481.

1. On April 7, Secretary of War Edwin M. Stanton telegraphed to USG. "Is there any reason for not confirming T. Kilby Smith of Ohio for Brigadier" ALS (telegram sent), DNA, RG 107, Telegrams Collected (Bound). On the same day, 1:30 P.M., USG telegraphed to Stanton. "I know of no reason for withdrawing the name of Genl T K Smith   He is a gallant officer but I would place him last on the list recommended by me   If any names are to be withdrawn—I would ask to have them taken commencing at the foot of the list as arranged by me in my letter to Genl Halleck written late in February" Telegram received, *ibid.*; copies, *ibid.*, RG 108, Letters Sent; DLC-USG, V, 45, 59.

To Maj. Gen. John M. Schofield

By Telegraph from Nashville [*Feb.*] 21st [*20*] 1 P. M *1864*
To MAJ GENL. J. M. SCHOFIELD KNOXVILLE
Maj Genl. Geo. H. Thomas was expected to move towards Dalton one week ago, or Monday last at furtherest—Rains prevented

him. He will certainly move tomorrow. bear this in mind in the influence it will have on the enemy. watch him closely and if you can take any advantage of his movements do it. I do not think Longstreet should be allowed to quietly withdraw from Knoxville nor to come up and invest the place without opposition. Cause him all the annoyance you can either by demonstration or actual attack

U. S. GRANT
Maj. Genl.

Telegram received, DLC-John M. Schofield; copies (dated Feb. 20, 1864), DLC-USG, V, 34, 35; DNA, RG 393, Military Div. of the Miss., Letters Sent. *O.R.*, I, xxxii, part 2, 434. On Feb. 21, Maj. Gen. John M. Schofield telegraphed to USG. "I am watching Longstreet carefully and will avail myself of ~~any~~ every opportunity to strike him. My cavalry is far inferior to that of the enemy; and I have no portable bridge—Hence my movements have been very much restricted during the high water—I intended to attack the enemy on Flat Creek but he retreated after my reconnoisance of yesterday. I will have a bridge in a few days. Longstreet cannot intend to invest this place without he receive reinforcements. I think his movements clearly indicate that he expects reinforcements enough to enable him to do so. Genl. Thomas' movement may effect Longstreets. I will watch him closely, and do all I can, but it is impossible to do much under present circumstances. Indeed I have thought, as suggested in your dispatch of the 12th inst. that it was most important to prepare for future operations" Copy, DLC-John M. Schofield. *O.R.*, I, lii, part 1, 522–23. According to Schofield's register of letters received, USG wrote or telegraphed on Feb. 21: "What is latest information from Longstreet." DLC-John M. Schofield.

To Maj. Gen. George H. Thomas

Nashville February 20th 1864

MAJOR GENERAL GEO H THOMAS
CHATTANOOGA

Can you spare a pontoon bridge from Chattanooga to throw across the river at Decatur? If not, what objections to sending your reserve bridge train to Decatur. If required at Chattanooga afterwards, they can be towed up by our steamers or transports by rail as conveniently as from here. Answer

U. S GRANT
Major General

Telegram, copies, DLC-USG, V, 34, 35; DNA, RG 393, Military Div. of the Miss., Letters Sent; *ibid.*, Dept. of the Cumberland, Telegrams Received. *O.R.*, I, xxxii, part 2, 434. On Feb. 20, 1864, Maj. Gen. George H. Thomas telegraphed to USG. "I have no bridge here that I can spare at this time   The one you allude to can be spared for a short time   Please order it sent here as soon as it can be dispensed with" Telegram received, DNA, RG 393, Dept. of the Tenn., Telegrams Received; copies, *ibid.*, Military Div. of the Miss., Telegrams Received; *ibid.*, Dept. of the Cumberland, Telegrams Sent. *O.R.*, I, xxxii, part 2, 434.

On Feb. 21, 11:00 A.M., USG telegraphed to Thomas. "Do your troops move to morrow? It is important that at least a demonstration be made at once." Copies, DLC-USG, V, 34, 35; DNA, RG 393, Military Div. of the Miss., Letters Sent; *ibid.*, Dept. of the Cumberland, Telegrams Received. *O.R.*, I, xxxii, part 2, 442. On the same day, 4:00 P.M., Thomas telegraphed to USG. "Your dispatch of this morning received. The troops will move tomorrow morning by daylight. Have sent you a copy of my instructions to Genl. Palmer by courier this noon." Copy, DNA, RG 393, Dept. of the Cumberland, Telegrams Sent. *O.R.*, I, xxxii, part 2, 443.

On Feb. 22, 11:30 P.M., Thomas telegraphed to USG. "The following has been recd. from General Palmer at Ringgold 10 30 P. M. We have reliable information that Cheatham & Clebournes Div. have gone to Demopolis   Cleburne left yesterday   Genl Cruft is at Red Clay tonight & has pushed a reconnoissance towards Varnell station   Long has gone towards Dalton on the Spring place road with orders to push his reconnoissance as far as possible" Telegram received, DNA, RG 393, Dept. of the Tenn., Telegrams Received; copy, *ibid.*, Military Div. of the Miss., Telegrams Received. *O.R.*, I, xxxii, part 2, 444.

To Jesse Root Grant

Nashville Ten.
Feb.y 20th 1864

DEAR FATHER,

I have rec'd your letter and those accompanying; towit. Mr. Newton's[1] and I. N. Morris.' I may write to Mr. Newton but it will be differently from what he expects. I am not a candidate for any office. All I want is to be left alone to fight this war out, fight all rebel rebel oposition, and restore a happy Union, in the shortest possible time. You know, or ought to know, that the publick prints are not the proper mediums through which to let a personal feeling pass. I know that I feel that nothing personal to myself could ever induce me to accept a political office.

From your letter you seem to have taken an active feeling, to say the least, in this matter, that I would like to talk to you about. I could write but do not want to do so. Why not come down here and see me?

I did tell Julia to make a visit to Cincinnati, Batavia, Bethel and Georgetown.

ULYSSES,

ALS, PPRF.

1. Eben Newton, born in Conn. in 1795, moved to Ohio in 1814 and was admitted to the bar in 1823. He served in the Ohio Senate (1842–51, 1862–64), as Whig U.S. Representative (1851–53), and as president of the Ashtabula and New Lisbon Railroad (1856–59). See letter to Jesse Root Grant, March 1, 1864.

To Brig. Gen. Robert Allen

Nashville February 23d 1864

BRIG GENL ROBT ALLEN Q M
LOUISVILLE KY

I know nothing officially of a movement up Red River. The first thing to be thought of is supplying this Army   No boats will be taken to the detriment of procuring such supplies   The two thousand horses, mentioned in Capt Eddy's letter for Gen Sherman, you will send to Memphis.[1]

U. S GRANT
Major General

Telegram, copies, DLC-USG, V, 34, 35; DNA, RG 393, Military Div. of the Miss., Letters Sent. On Feb. 23, 1864, Brig. Gen. Robert Allen, Louisville, had telegraphed to USG. "I have received the following dispatch from Co'l McFeely dated St. Louis Feby. twenty second 22   I am instructed by Gen'l Sherman to make requisition for Steamboats to transport ten thousand troops with baggage &c up Red River   will you order the necessary transportation to be at Vicksburg March first. This in addition to the large amount of transportation furnished for Gen'l Banks   shall the Steamboats be sent—are the two thousand Cavalry required by Gen'l Sherman to be sent to Memphis"   Copy, *ibid.*, Telegrams Received. *O.R.*, I, xxxii, part 2, 449.

1. On Feb. 21, Allen telegraphed to USG. "I have a letter from Capt. Eddy dated Memphis Feby. fifteenth 15th in which he says Gen. Sherman orders two thousand 2,000 cavalry Horses to mount the dismounted Cavalry at Mem-

phis your orders are required" Copy, DNA, RG 393, Military Div. of the Miss., Telegrams Received. On Feb. 24, Allen telegraphed to USG. "Shall I send two thousand Cavalry horses to Gen'l Sherman before sending any Horses to Nashville. The Cavalry Bureau have but few horses on hand" Copy, *ibid. O.R.*, I, xxxii, part 2, 456. On the same day, USG twice telegraphed to Allen. "Forward horses to this place as rapidly as possible They are now much needed at the front. I will write to you as soon as I can ascertain about what will be required. In the meantime they cannot be sent too fast." "Send horses to Nashville first." Copies, DLC-USG, V, 34, 35; DNA, RG 393, Military Div. of the Miss., Letters Sent. On Feb. 28, USG telegraphed to Allen. "It will be impossible probably to supply the number of Artillery and Cavalry horses called for within this Military Division but I would suggest that now, all on hand be forwarded as rapidly as possible, to this place and others be procured and forwarded as fast as they can be purchased. I will order their distribution from here." Copies, *ibid. O.R.*, I, xxxii, part 2, 489.

On Feb. 21, Maj. Gen. George H. Thomas endorsed to USG a letter concerning horses requested by Governor Andrew Johnson of Tenn., requesting that the Dept. of the Cumberland have priority in receiving horses. *Ibid.*, p. 436.

To Maj. Gen. John M. Schofield

Nashville 11. A. M. 24th Feb. 1864

MAJOR GENERAL J. M SCHOFIELD
KNOXVILLE TENN

Should you discover by your movement on Strawberry Plains that the enemy has retreated eastward and is abandoning East Tennessee, push him as far as practicable with your whole force destroying effectually the railroads. Relieve Granger's troops to return to Chattanooga as soon as you ascertain the enemy is gone and cannot be overtaken by infantry. Shermans safety in Mississippi depends upon our efforts here. Thomas is moving with apparent success on Dalton.

U. S GRANT
Major General

Copies, DLC-USG, V, 34, 35; DNA, RG 393, Military Div. of the Miss., Letters Sent. *O.R.*, I, xxxii, part 2, 456.

On Feb. 23, 1864, Maj. Gen. John M. Schofield telegraphed three times to USG, first at 5:30 P.M., then at 11:00 P.M. "I have not yet learned whether Longstreet has moved any more of his main force. I am building a bridge as rapidly as possible will take advantage of any move he may make as soon as possible" "I have information which I believe reliable that Longstreet has retired from Strawberry Plains   He has also withdrawn his Cavalry from the south side of the French Broad—I shall march for Strawberry Plains with all my available force tomorrow morning leaving a sufficient garrisson for this place"   Copies, DNA, RG 393, Military Div. of the Miss., Telegrams Received. *O.R.*, I, xxxii, part 2, 449–50. "I sent a reconnoisance toward Sevierville under Genl Hascall and another toward Strawberry Plains under Col. Garrard on the 21st. Each had a skirmish with the enemy. Genl. Hascall captured nine prisoners and killed several of the enemy. He lost one man killed and several wounded. The enemy fell back and recrossed the Holston at Strawberry Plains, and the French Broad at Boyds Ferry—Longstreet has taken up his pontoon bridge at Strawberry Plains. A reconnoisance in force under Genl. Stoneman found no enemy south of the French Broad today." Copies, DLC-John M. Schofield; DNA, RG 393, Military Div. of the Miss., Telegrams Received. *O.R.*, I, lii, part 1, 524.

On Feb. 24, Schofield telegraphed to USG. "Longstreet destroyed the ferry-boat and completed the destruction of the Ral-Road bridge and retreated from this place yesterday. From the best information I can get he is moving rapidly towards Virginia or Georgia. As soon as I can cross the river I will push forward as far and rapidly as possible—His main force has gone towards Goldsboro   the indications are that his whole force is going up the French Broad." Copy, DNA, RG 393, Military Div. of the Miss., Telegrams Received. *O.R.*, I, xxxii, part 2, 456–57. A copy of this telegram went to Maj. Gen. George H. Thomas. On the same day, 7:00 P.M., Schofield telegraphed to USG. "Your despatch of 6 P. M. is just received—If Longstreet is leaving Tenn. with his whole force it will be impossible for me to overtake him. I will try to learn positively in time to let Grangers Corps join Genl. Thomas before Longstreet can reach Johnston. I will press forward here as rapidly as possible." Copies, DLC-John M. Schofield; DNA, RG 393, Military Div. of the Miss., Telegrams Received. *O.R.*, I, xxxii, part 2, 456. The last two sources refer to USG's telegram of 11:00 A.M.

To Maj. Gen. George H. Thomas

Nashville February 24th 1864

MAJOR GENERAL G. H THOMAS
CHATTANOOGA

Your dispatch received. Push the enemy as far as possible. If unable to carry Dalton, keep at least a heavy force threatening it so as to hold the enemy there. Shermans safety may be dependent upon your effort. Should you drive the enemy out of Dalton follow him as far as possible. If you have sufficiently recovered your health, I would like to have you go out to the front in person, if only to see the situation of affairs and return.

U. S. GRANT
Major General

Telegram, copies, DLC-USG, V, 34, 35; DNA, RG 393, Military Div. of the Miss., Letters Sent; (datelined 10:30 A.M.) *ibid.*, Dept. of the Cumberland, Telegrams Received. *O.R.*, I, xxxii, part 2, 458–59. On Feb. 24, 1864, 4:00 A.M., Maj. Gen. George H. Thomas telegraphed to USG. "Reports from the front just recd.   our skirmishers engaged the enemy for some four miles & drove them through tunnel hill on Doubl Quick   a mile beyond town they formed & brought up a Battery of artillery   Col Long went within three & one half miles of Dalton & Drove a regiment of Infantry out of winter Quarters   our main force encamped within 3 miles of tunell hill last night & will be on the Road Dalton tomorrow night"   Telegram received, DNA, RG 393, Dept. of the Tenn., Telegrams Received; copies, *ibid.*, Military Div. of the Miss., Telegrams Received; *ibid.*, Dept. of the Cumberland, Telegrams Sent. *O.R.*, I, xxxii, part 2, 458. On the same day, 9:00 P.M., Thomas telegraphed to USG. "Despatch from Tunnel Hill 4. P. M. says—We have just gained possession of Tunnel Hill Pass. Small loss. Dispatch from Col. McCook of Elliott's Cavalry reports having captured near Murphy N. C. five commissioned officers and sixty three men and burned five wagons. Fifteen of Thomas' North Carolina Indians came in and surrendered themselves to Col. McCook on the 22d. Your dispatch of 10 30 a. m. was not received until 5.30 P. M.   I have ordered the enemy to be pushed as you directed and shall start for the front in the morning." Copies, DNA, RG 393, Dept. of the Cumberland, Telegrams Sent; *ibid.*, Military Div. of the Miss., Telegrams Received. *O.R.*, I, xxxii, part 2, 459.

To Maj. Gen. Henry W. Halleck

Nashville Tenn
Feby 25th 1864. 1. P. M

MAJ GEN H W HALLECK
GEN IN CHIEF.

On the 23rd Genl Schofield telegraphed that he had good reason to believe Longstreet was leaving East Tennessee   He started immediately in pursuit since which I have heard nothing further from him. Gen Thomas force left Chattanooga last monday to demonstrate against Dalton to prevent forces being sent from there against Genl. Sherman—Our troops have Tunnel Hill   some prisoners wagons, &c have been captured from the enemy

U. S. GRANT

Telegram received, DNA, RG 107, Telegrams Collected (Bound); copies, *ibid.*, Telegrams Received in Cipher; *ibid.*, RG 393, Military Div. of the Miss., Hd. Qrs. Correspondence; DLC-USG, V, 40, 94. *O.R.*, I, xxxii, part 2, 462–63. On

Feb. 25, 1864, 8:00 P.M., USG telegraphed to Maj. Gen. Henry W. Halleck. "Genl Schofield has moved to Strawberry Plain and will follow Longstreet as soon as he can get over the river—He says information received says Longstreet was ordered back to Virginia, but do not know if this is the fact—Schofield will follow up vigorously and ascertain his movement as soon as possible" Telegram received (misdated Feb. 25, 1863), DNA, RG 107, Telegrams Collected (Bound); copies (dated 1864), *ibid.*, Telegrams Received in Cipher; *ibid.*, RG 393, Military Div. of the Miss., Hd. Qrs. Correspondence; DLC-USG, V, 40, 94. Printed as sent at 9:00 P.M. in *O.R.*, I, xxxii, part 2, 463.

To Maj. Gen. Henry W. Slocum

Nashville February 25th 1864

MAJOR GENERAL SLOCUM
TULLAHOMA TENN

During present operations at the front it is of the highest importance that Stevenson and Bridgeport be guarded vigilantly against a raid by the enemy. The fords in the river below Bridgeport should be well guarded. I wish you would go in person and make an inspection of those two posts. Go by to nights train if you receive this in time.

U. S. GRANT
Major General

Telegram, copies, DLC-USG, V, 34, 35; DNA, RG 393, Military Div. of the Miss., Letters Sent. On Feb. 26, 1864, Maj. Gen. Henry W. Slocum, Stevenson, Ala., telegraphed to USG. "I have sent guards to the fords mentioned in your dispatch—The field work at this place is a strong one & the troops both Infantry & artillery can be relied upon—I shall go to Bridgeport tomorrow" Telegram received, *ibid.*, RG 94, War Records Office, Military Div. of the Miss.; copy, *ibid.*, RG 393, Military Div. of the Miss., Telegrams Received. On Feb. 27, Slocum, Bridgeport, Ala., telegraphed to USG. "I find every thing at this post in good order The fords are well Guarded scouts are sent in every direction the field works are all garrisoned I think you can feel perfectly safe as to this post & stevenson" Telegram received, *ibid.*, RG 94, War Records Office, Military Div. of the Miss.; copy, *ibid.*, Military Div. of the Miss., Telegrams Received. *O.R.*, I, xxxii, part 2, 485.

To Maj. Gen. George H. Thomas

Nashville [*Feb.*] 25th 1864.

MAJ GEN. THOMAS

Mrs Colo. Sherman is here having come from Ill. to see her husband who is sick at Loudon. She desires a pass which she says has been refused by you, probably not knowing the circumstances. Please answer. Mrs. Sherman is a lady who has spent much time in our hospitals for the last year, and has passes from your predecessors to take her back to the eighty eighth Ill. Vols. the reg't of which her husband is Colonel.

U. S. GRANT,
Maj. General.

Telegram, copy, DNA, RG 393, Dept. of the Cumberland, Telegrams Received. Francis T. Sherman, born in Conn. in 1825, brought to Chicago in 1834, was mustered in as col., 88th Ill., on Aug. 27, 1862. He had married Eleanor N. Vedder in 1851. On Feb. 25, 1864, Maj. William McMichael, adjt. for Maj. Gen. George H. Thomas, telegraphed to Lt. Col. Theodore S. Bowers. "Dispatch just received from Maj. Gen'l Grant   Gen'l Thomas went to the front this morning—Co'l Shermans Application for a pass for Mrs. Sherman was presented to him by me and his instructions were to say that it could not be granted at present but would be as soon as affairs become settle—The application did not mention Co'l Shermans illnes nor do I think the General was aware of it." Copy, *ibid.*, Military Div. of the Miss., Telegrams Received. On Feb. 27, Thomas telegraphed to USG. "Mrs. Col. Sherman was refused a pass because I thought it not safe for a lady to be at the front. She has now however my permission to visit Loudon to attend on her husband"   Copy, *ibid.*, Dept. of the Cumberland, Telegrams Sent.

To Julia Dent Grant

Nashville Tennessee
Feb.y 25th 1864.

DEAR JULIA,

As I have heard indirectly that you would leave St. Louis on Wednsday next this will be the last letter I will write, unless I should hear from you again that you are not coming. I presume your letters all reach me. Three came at once last week. I had had two before that and one since from Louisa Boggs. You have had a terrible time with your eyes: I hope they have improved sufficiently to allow you to travel. It can only be about a month more that I can remain here with you. I did not go to the front as was anticipated but left Thomas to move his own forces. I have not been very well for the last three or four days but hope to be all right in a day or two. I have been taking quinine enough to make my head buz and now have taken a large dose of Blue Mass.[1] This I hope will be the last.

Kisses for the children and yourself, and remember me to all the household.

ULYS.

ALS, DLC-USG.

    1. A mercury compound used as a cathartic.

To Gen. Joseph E. Johnston

Head Quarters, Mil. Div. of the Miss.
Nashville Ten. Feb.y 26th 1864

GEN. J. E. JOHNSTON,
COMD.G C. S. FORCES, NORTHERN GA,
GENERAL,

I have learned,[1] do not know as to the reliability of my information, that J. T. Stancel, Jesse Grear & Robt. Waits, soldiers belonging to the 3d West Tennessee Cavalry, U. S. Service, are now confined at Atlanta Ga. charged with belonging to the C. S. Army.

I would state that these men have been for a long time in the Federal Army and are entitled to the same treatment as other prisoners of War. Of course I would claim no right to retaliate for the punishment of deserters who had actually been mustered into the Confederate Army, and afterwards deserted and joined ours. But I cannot agree that any wholesale Conscription act can cover as deserters persons who escape into our lines and join our service to avoid such conscription. Further, I would claim that persons who have been personally notified to report at a certain place by a certain time, for muster, and afterwards escaped to our service before obeying such summons, would be entitled to the protection of Government against trial, or rather I should say punishment, as deserters, if afterwards captured.

I believe General an examination into the cases herein refered to will show that they have never been sworn into the Confederate Army; that their services to the Government entitles them to the protection of that Government.

Believing fully that you are disposed to be governed by the laws of War, justice and humanity, I subscribe myself,

very respectfully
your obt. svt.
U. S. GRANT
Maj. Gen. U. S. A. Com

ALS, PPRF. *O.R.*, II, vi, 991. On March 9, 1864, Gen. Joseph E. Johnston, Dalton, Ga., wrote to USG. "I have had the honour to receive your letter of the 26th Ulto—& on inquiry have learned that J. T. Stancel & Jesse Green, claiming to belong to the 3d West Tennessee Cavalry U. S. Service, are now confined in Atlanta. The former is charged with 'violating his parole'—probably without foundation—the latter with 'desertion to the enemy.' There can be no conviction of this offence without full proof that the accused was a confederate soldier. Robt. Waits, also charged with deserting to the enemy, has escaped. As you justly believe that I am 'disposed to be governed by the laws of War, justice & humanity' I need not assure you that no prisoner in my power will suffer contrary to those laws." ALS, OClWHi. *O.R.*, II, vi, 1026.

1. On Feb. 21, 1st Lt. J. H. Shepherd, 9th Ky., wrote a letter received at USG's hd. qrs. on Feb. 26 concerning men of the U.S. Army imprisoned at Atlanta as deserters from the C.S. Army. DLC-USG, V, 37.

To Maj. Gen. John M. Schofield

Nashville 11.30 A M Feby [*26, 1864.*]

MAJ. GENL. SCHOFIELD

Your arrangements for following Longstreet will be satisfactory I do not suppose you will be able to overtake him unless it should be his desire to give battle the Great object to be gained is to secure East Tennessee from another invasion by this enemy if the rail road can be entirely destroyed up in Virginia it would but secure this. I am much in hopes an effort to do this will be made by troops from West Virginia—I have urged it & before sending Crook off to that Department talked to him my views   He expressed a strong conviction that he could accomplished all I asked   possibly such a move may now be making & that account for Longstreets present withdrawal   If this should be so it would then become advisable to push him from Knoxville as far & fast as possible & destroy the rail road close up to him   I would not advise any destruction of the rail road west of Bristol if that point & further East can be reached

U S GRANT

M Genl

Telegram received, DLC-John M. Schofield; copies, DLC-USG, V, 34, 35; DNA, RG 393, Military Div. of the Miss., Letters Sent. *O.R.*, I, xxxii, part 2, 472. On Feb. 25, 1864, Maj. Gen. John M. Schofield twice telegraphed to USG, first at 10:00 A.M. "Longstreet's whole army has gone as far back as Morristown & Greenville at least. A rebel captain who came in yesterday says Longstreet is ordered to Virginia. Some deserters also say the wagons were loaded for and ordered to Bristol, five days rations having been issued to the men. It is quite uncertain whether Longstreet is going to Georgia or Virginia, and not quite certain whether he is leaving Tenn. at all. I will probably know the facts as soon as I can possibly advance from this place." "I have not yet gained accurate information of the movements of Longstreet's Army beyond Greenville. The present appearance is that the most of it has gone toward Virginia. It will be impossible for me to move with any prospect of success before the 29th inst. Meanwhile I will know what disposition Longstreet has made of his army, and thus be able to judge what force I must take with me. I propose to take supplies with enough to carry me to the Watauga, and if possible to the Salt Works— Without this my work will not be complete. I think it is better to wait a few days to make these preparations than to move with only the three or four days rations which the men can carry. Please inform me whether this meets your views and wishes." Copies, DLC-John M. Schofield; DNA, RG 393, Military Div. of the Miss., Telegrams Received. *O.R.*, I, xxxii, part 2, 464.

On Feb. 26, 11:00 A.M., USG telegraphed to Maj. Gen. Henry W. Halleck. "Is there a move on foot from West Va on the Va. and Tenn R. R. If so it may account for Longstreets retrograde movement and would also make it important to follow him with rapidity from Knoxville" Telegram received, DNA, RG 107, Telegrams Collected (Bound); copies, *ibid.*, Telegrams Received in Cipher; *ibid.*, RG 393, Military Div. of the Miss., Hd. Qrs. Correspondence; DLC-USG, V, 40, 94. *O.R.*, I, xxxii, part 2, 473. On Feb. 27, 11:00 A.M., Halleck telegraphed to USG. "There is no immediate movement on foot in West Virginia towards Longstreet. Advices just recieved from Jacksonville, Florida, that Hardee with fifteen thousand men from Johnston's army defeated Genl Seymour near Baldwin on the 20th inst." ALS (telegram sent), DNA, RG 107, Telegrams Collected (Bound); copies, *ibid.*, RG 393, Military Div. of the Miss., Hd. Qrs. Correspondence; DLC-USG, V, 40, 94. *O.R.*, I, xxxii, part 2, 480.

On Feb. 26, Schofield telegraphed to USG. "My present impression is that Longstreet's main force has gone toward Virginia His cavalry and perhaps some Infantry having been sent to Georgia. He will doubtless leave a considerable force to defend the Salt Works, and can readily reinforce it from Virginia, unless the rebel Army there be occupied. If Genl. Meade can, at the proper time, occupy the attention of Lee's Army, I may be able to reach the Salt Works. I propose to go prepared to reach that place if possible At best it will exhaust all my resources and will be impossible without a diversion in Virginia—Please inform me what I may expect." Copies, DLC-John M. Schofield; DNA, RG 393, Military Div. of the Miss., Telegrams Received. *O.R.*, I, xxxii, part 2, 472.

To Brig. Gen. Stephen G. Burbridge

By Telegraph from Nashville [*Feb. 26,*] 1864
To GEN BURBRIDGE

Forward all troops from Louisville bound for the front with all rapidity inform the railroad Managers, the road must be used to the full extent of its capacity putting on extra trains & Stopping the travel of citizens over the road for the time being, if necessary Cars may taken from the Louisville & Lexington Road for this purpose

U. S GRANT
Maj Gen

Telegram received, DNA, RG 393, Dept. of Ky., Telegrams Received; copies, *ibid.*, Military Div. of the Miss., Letters Sent; DLC-USG, V, 34, 35. On Feb. 27, 1864, Brig. Gen. Stephen G. Burbridge, Louisville, twice telegraphed to USG. "Will forward by train today fifteen hundred troops. Can send forward as fast as troops can be assembled here. shall I send all troops belonging to. the Dept. of the Ohio to Nashville. Fourth Ky. Cavalry. hundred and fifty strong and sixth Ky. Cavalry five hundred strong are in Camp at Lexington Ky. waiting to be remounted. I have written to Maj. Gen'l Thomas this fact. Shall I order these two regts. to the front the eighteenth and twenty first Ky. Infantry will rendezvous and be ready for the field next week" Copy, DNA, RG 393, Military Div. of the Miss., Telegrams Received. "The R R can ship about five thousand troops per day if the cars are returned promptly from Nashville all troops will be sent forward as soon as the arrive" Telegram received, *ibid.*, RG 94, War Records Office, Military Div. of the Miss.; copies, *ibid.*, RG 393, Military Div. of the Miss., Telegrams Received; *ibid.*, Dept. of Ky., Telegrams Sent. *O.R.*, I, xxxii, part 2, 486. On Feb. 27, Brig. Gen. Robert Allen, Louisville, telegraphed to USG. "Two thousand men will leave for Nashville at 2 o'clock today   we can transport from three 3 to five thousand 5.000 men per day if they arrive" Copy, DNA, RG 393, Military Div. of the Miss., Telegrams Received. On March 1, Burbridge telegraphed to USG. "The 51st New York Veteran Vols arrived here this morning   The regiment belongs to the 9th Army Corps portions of which is now at Knoxville   Where shall this regiment be sent, and by what route   They have no orders" Copies, *ibid.*, Dept. of Ky., Telegrams Sent; (dated March 4) *ibid.*, Military Div. of the Miss., Telegrams Received.

General Orders No. 7

Headquarters Military Division of the Mississippi
Nashville, Tenn., Feby. 27th. 1864.
GENERAL ORDERS, No. 7.

The following named officers compose the Staff of the General Commanding, and will be obeyed and respected accordingly.

Brig. Gen. John A. Rawlins, Chief of Staff
Brig. Gen. Wm. F. Smith, Chief Engineer.
Brig. Gen. W. Sooy Smith, Chief of Cavalry.
Lieut. Col. T. S. Bowers, Assistant Adjutant General.
Lieut. Col. W. L. Duff, Chief of Artillery.
Lieut Col. C. B. Comstock Assistant Inspector General[1]
Major Wm. R Rowley, A. D. C. and Provost Marshal General;
Capt. Ely S. Parker, Assistant Adjutant General;
Capt. George K. Leet, Assistant Adjutant General;[2]
Capt. O. M. Poe, Assistant Chief Engineer;
Capt. B. P. Chenoweth, Acting Assistant Inspector General;
Capt. S. A. Stockdale, Assistant Provost Marshal General;
Capt. Adam Badeau, Additional Aid-de-Camp;[3]
Capt. P. T. Hudson, Aid-de-Camp;[4]
Capt. O. H. Ross, Aid-de-Camp[5]
Capt. Henry W. Janes, A. Q. M.;[6]
Lieut. H. N. Towner, Assistant Chief of Artillery;
Lieut. Wm. M. Dunn, Acting Aid-de-Camp.

By order of Maj Gen. Grant
T. S. BOWERS
Asst. Adjt. Gen'l.

Copies, DLC-USG, V, 14; DNA, RG 393, Military Div. of the Miss., General Orders; (printed) USGA. *O.R.*, I, xxxii, part 2, 486–87. On March 18, 1864, Lt. Col. Theodore S. Bowers issued Special Orders No. 1. "The following named Officers of the Staff of the Lieut. General commanding, will accompany him to Washington D. C:—Brig. Gen. John A. Rawlins, Chief of Staff Brig. Gen. W. F. Smith, Chief Engineer Lieut. Colonel T. S. Bowers, Assistant Adjutant General Lieut Colonel W. L. Duff, Aid-de-Camp Major W. R. Rowley, Aid-de-Camp Captain E. S. Parker, Assistant Adjutant General Captain George K. Leet, Assistant Adjutant General Captain Adam Badeau, Additional Aid-de-Camp Lieutenant William M. Dunn, Jr, Acting Aid-de-Camp Captain H. W. Janes, Assistant Quartermaster, U. S. Army, on duty as Staff Quartermaster, at these Headquarters, will proceed immediately to Washington, D. C., with the clerks, horses, baggage, office furniture, servants &c., belonging to these Headquarters. The Quartermaster's Department will furnish necessary transportation on Captain Janes' requisitions. Military authorities will afford him all necessary assistance for the execution of this order. . . . Brig. Gen W. F. Smith, Chief Engineer, being under orders to Washington, to save transportation, will turn over to the Quartermaster's Department, at Nashville, Tenn., his private horses, taking receipts therefor, on which receipts the Quartermaster's Department at Washington will issue to him, horses in lieu of those thus turned over. . . . S. H. Beckwith, Cipher Telegraph Operator, will accompany the Lieut. General commanding to Washington, D. C. Captain H. W. Janes Assistant Quartermaster, U. S. Army, will commute and pay to him, his transportation at military rates." Copies, DLC-USG, V, 57, 63.

On Feb. 4, Maj. Samuel Breck, AGO, wrote to USG. "I am instructed to direct you to furnish to this Depmt, at the end of each month, a report of the Officers serving on your Staff as required by General Orders 244 Series of '63 from this Office." Copy, DNA, RG 94, Enlisted Branch, Letters Sent. USG signed such a report, dated Nashville, Feb. 1. DS, *ibid.*, ACP, 4754/1885. On Feb. 16, 4:00 P.M., Breck telegraphed to USG. "Please forward to this Office, the Tri-Monthly Returns of your command, as soon as possible, giving on the back of the returns a list of your own Staff. No return of your Staff has been received since the organization of the Milt'y Division of the Mississippi, and it is desirable to know what officers are serving on it, that they may not be reported absent without leave, as the rules of this Office require, when officers are not heard from for many months." LS (telegram sent), *ibid.*, RG 107, Telegrams Collected (Unbound); copies, *ibid.*, RG 94, Enlisted Branch, Letters Sent; *ibid.*, RG 393, Military Div. of the Miss., Hd. Qrs. Correspondence; DLC-USG, V, 40, 94.

1. On Nov. 16, 1863, USG telegraphed to Maj. Gen. Henry W. Halleck. "I would respectfully recommend Capt C. B. Comstock Engineer Corps for promotion to Asst. Inspector General with the rank of Colonel vice J. H. Wilson promoted to Br. Genl." Telegrams received (2), DNA, RG 94, ACP, C860 CB 1863; *ibid.*, RG 107, Telegrams Collected (Bound); copies, *ibid.*, RG 393, Military Div. of the Miss., Hd. Qrs. Correspondence; DLC-USG, V, 40, 94. On the same day, USG telegraphed to Capt. Cyrus B. Comstock. "I have recommended you for the position of Asst Inspector Genl. of my Staff with rank of Lt. Col." Telegram received (press), DNA, RG 107, Telegrams Collected (Bound). Earlier on Nov. 16, Comstock, Washington, D. C., had telegraphed to USG. "Genl Foster has offered me a Lt Colonelcy on his staff I do not

wish to leave your staff if you wish to retain me under the changed circumstances   Genl Foster waits for my answer"   Telegram received, *ibid.*, RG 94, Generals' Papers and Books, Comstock; copy, *ibid.*, RG 393, Military Div. of the Miss., Telegrams Received. On Nov. 17, 10:00 A.M., Comstock telegraphed to USG. "If appointed inspector Genl on your staff the appointment will be accepted"   ALS (telegram sent), *ibid.*, RG 107, Telegrams Collected (Unbound); telegram received, *ibid.*, RG 94, Generals' Papers and Books, Comstock. Comstock served as asst. inspector gen., Military Div. of the Miss., from Nov. 19 to March 29, 1864, with his appointment announced on Dec. 9, 1863, by General Orders No. 8. Copies, *ibid.*, RG 393, Military Div. of the Miss., General Orders; DLC-USG, V, 14; (printed) USGA.

2. On Sept. 21, Brig. Gen. John A. Rawlins wrote to Col. John C. Kelton. "I would most respectfully recommend that Private George K. Leet of the Chicago Mercantile Battery be promoted to an Asst. Adjt. Genl. with the rank of Captain, and ordered to report to me. this appointment I most earnestly ask to be made as a reward of merit to a brave and accomplished soldier, as well as a recognition of the services of the enlisted men whose valor contributed to the recent successes of our arms, here. He was with his Battery at Chickasaw Bayou, in the attack on Vicksburg last Decr, in the Battles of Arkansas Post, Port. Gibson, Champion Hill, Black River Bridge, seige of Vicksburg, investment of Jackson Miss. in July last, in all of which he served faithfully and bravely. He was detached for duty as Clerk at these Head Quarters on the 28th of July last, and by his industry and ability has shown himself eminently fitted for the position for which he is hereby recommended." Copies, DNA, RG 393, Dept. of the Tenn., Hd. Qrs. Correspondence; DLC-USG, V, 6, 8, 24, 94. On the same day, USG endorsed this letter. "Respectfully forwarded to Head Quarters of the Army Washington D. C. All that is said of Private George K. Leet. by General Rawlins I heartily concur and for the reasons within stated earnestly ask his appointment"   Copies, *ibid.*, V, 25; DNA, RG 393, Dept. of the Tenn., Endorsements. Private George K. Leet was promoted to capt. to rank from Oct. 3.

3. On May 5, USG wrote to Brig. Gen. Lorenzo Thomas. "I have the honor to request that Capt. Adam Badeau, A. A. D. C. be ordered to report to me for duty on my staff." LS, *ibid.*, RG 94, ACP, 124G CB 1863. On the same day, Thomas endorsed this letter. "Respectfully submitted to the Secretary of War. This officer an additional A D. Camp is serving with General T. W. Sherman, and desires service elsewhere. He is represented as a good officer and an accomplished gentleman, and would be of great service on the staff of General Grant." AES (misdated June 5), *ibid.* USG's letter is in the hand of Lt. Col. James H. Wilson, who had urged USG to appoint Capt. Adam Badeau to his staff. Wilson, *Under the Old Flag* (New York and London, 1912), I, 190–92. Wounded before he received orders to join USG, Badeau recuperated until Feb., 1864.

4. On April 24, USG telegraphed to Maj. Gen. William T. Sherman. "Unless Genl Wm S Smith takes field with you order Capt Hudson to me"   Telegram received, DNA, RG 107, Telegrams Collected (Bound); copies, *ibid.*, RG 108, Letters Sent; *ibid.*, RG 393, Military Div. of the Miss., Letters Sent; DLC-USG, V, 40, 59, 94. On the same day, Sherman telegraphed to USG. "Capt Hudson has been ordered to report to you." Copies, *ibid.*, V, 94; DNA, RG 393, Military Div. of the Miss., Letters Sent. See *O.R.*, I, xxxiii, 820.

5. On March 31, Capt. Orlando H. Ross, Cincinnati, wrote to Thomas reporting that he was awaiting orders. ALS, DNA, RG 94, ACP, R449 CB 1864. On Aug. 31, Ross, Amelia, Ohio, wrote to Thomas tendering his resignation.

ALS, *ibid.* On Sept. 2, USG endorsed this letter. "Approved and respectfully forwarded." AES, *ibid.*

6. On Oct. 20, 1863, USG wrote to Secretary of War Edwin M. Stanton. "Captain Henry W. Janes, A Q M of Vols, is the name of the Officer I requested to have appointed to same position in regular Army. It will be a favor to me to have this appointment made." Copies, DLC-USG, V, 40, 94; DNA, RG 393, Military Div. of the Miss., Hd. Qrs. Correspondence. On Nov. 17, Capt. Henry W. Janes, Chattanooga, wrote to U.S. Representative Elihu B. Washburne noting that through USG's influence he had twice been promoted, from q. m., 55th Ill., to asst. q. m. of vols. and then to asst. q. m., U.S. Army, and requesting Washburne's aid in securing confirmation. ALS, DLC-Elihu B. Washburne. Janes's appointment, submitted on Dec. 31, was confirmed on March 18, 1864.

To Maj. Gen. Henry W. Halleck

Nashville Tenn
Feb 27th 1864 5 30 P M

Maj Gen H W Halleck
Gen in Chief

Your despatch of 1.30 P. M. to day received   Gen Thomas movement intended to keep force from leaving Johnston, has had the effect to bring back one division which had already started south   I feel that with a man like Sherman to command, he is in no great danger. He will find an outlet. [I]f in no other way he will fall back on Pascagoula and ship from there under protection of Farraguts fleet

U. S Grant Maj Gen

Telegram received, DNA, RG 107, Telegrams Collected (Bound); copies, *ibid.*, RG 393, Military Div. of the Miss., Hd. Qrs. Correspondence; DLC-USG, V, 34, 35. *O.R.*, I, xxxii, part 2, 481. On Feb. 26, 1864, 3:40 P.M. or 4:00 P.M., Maj. Gen. Henry W. Halleck had telegraphed to USG. "The 35th Wisconsin regt will be ready next week. It is also hoped that several Indianna regts will be ready. To what points do you wish them sent?" ALS (telegram sent), DNA, RG 107, Telegrams Collected (Bound); copies, *ibid.*, RG 393, Military Div. of the Miss., Hd. Qrs. Correspondence; DLC-USG, V, 40, 94. *O.R.*, I, xxxii, part 2, 473. On the same day, 11:00 P.M., USG telegraphed to Halleck. "I would like all troops for this Division ordered to this place. Gen Shermans movements may make it necessary to send other troops on to the Mississippi. If I learn of anything to show this I will telegraph you immediately" Telegram received, DNA, RG 107, Telegrams Collected (Bound); copies, *ibid.*, RG 393, Military Div. of the Miss., Hd. Qrs. Correspondence; DLC-USG, V, 40, 94. *O.R.*, I, xxxii, part 2, 473. On

Feb. 27, 1:30 P.M., Halleck telegraphed to USG. "The Wisconsin regt is ordered to Nashville as requested. Others will be so ordered as fast as reported ready, unless you should wish otherwise. Much anxiety is felt here about Sherman's movements. We have nothing official since the 8th   Rebel accounts represent his forces as far south as Quitman, but say nothing of any movement on Selma. It is reported that Johnston has ordered the evacuation of the part of Georgia north of Chattahoochee river." ALS (telegram sent), DNA, RG 107, Telegrams Collected (Bound); copies, *ibid.*, RG 393, Military Div. of the Miss., Hd. Qrs. Correspondence; DLC-USG, V, 40, 94. *O.R.*, I, xxxii, part 2, 481.

To Maj. Gen. George H. Thomas

Nashville 11.30 A. M. 27th February '64

MAJOR GENERAL G. H THOMAS
CHATTANOOGA

It is of the utmost importance that the enemy should be held in full belief that an advance into the heart of the south is intended until the fate of Sherman is fully known. The difficulties of supplies can be overcome by keeping your trains running between Chattanooga and your position. Take the depot teams at Chattanooga and Howards wagons. These can be replaced temporarily by yours returning. Veterans are returning daily. This will enable you to draw reenforcements constantly to your front. Can you not also take a Division of Howards Corps? Schofield is instructed to send Granger to you the moment it is to be safe without him.

U. S. GRANT
Major General

Telegram, copies, DLC-USG, V, 34, 35; DNA, RG 393, Military Div. of the Miss., Letters Sent; *ibid.*, Dept. of the Cumberland, Telegrams Received. *O.R.*, I, xxxii, part 2, 480. On Feb. 26, 1864, 7:30 A.M., Maj. Gen. George H. Thomas, Tunnel Hill, telegraphed to USG. "I arrived here last night. Davis and Johnson occupy the pass at Buzzards Roost. They have a force equal to theirs in their front who outnumber them in artillery. It is not possible to carry this place by assault. Genl. Palmer made the attempt to turn yesterday with Baird's and Crufts Division but was met by an equal force, exclusive of their cavalry, and in an equally strong position as at Buzzards Roost—After expending nearly all his ammunition he retired during the night to Catoosa Platform. Our transportation is poor and limited, we are not able to carry more than sixty rounds per man— Artillery horses so poor that Palmer could bring but sixteen pieces. The country is stripped entirely of subsistence and forage. The enemy's cavalry is much superior to ours. Prisoners taken yesterday report that a portion of Claborne's Division has returned. I will await the developments of this day and advise you further." Copies, DNA, RG 393, Dept. of the Cumberland, Telegrams Sent; *ibid.*, Military Div. of the Miss., Telegrams Received. *O.R.*, I, xxxii, part 2, 480.

On Feb. 27, 2:30 P.M., USG telegraphed to Maj. Gen. Henry W. Halleck transmitting Thomas's telegram of Feb. 26 and USG's reply. Telegram received, DNA, RG 107, Telegrams Collected (Bound); copies (misdated Feb. 28), *ibid.*, RG 393, Military Div. of the Miss., Hd. Qrs. Correspondence; DLC-USG, V, 40, 94. Dated Feb. 27 in *O.R.*, I, xxxii, part 2, 480. On the same day, 5:00 P.M., USG telegraphed to Halleck. "It is now known that General Thomas move has called back to Dalton at least Clayborns Division which had started for the South" Telegram received, DNA, RG 107, Telegrams Collected (Bound); copies, *ibid.*, RG 393, Military Div. of the Miss., Hd. Qrs. Correspondence; DLC-USG, V, 40, 94. *O.R.*, I, xxxii, part 2, 480.

Also on Feb. 27, USG telegraphed to Thomas. "In requesting you to have a colored regiment report to the Quartermaster at Nashville the removal of one from the North Western Railroad was not contemplated and you will therefore please suspend the order. If there are any other colored regiments available, one should be ordered to report to the Quartermaster here in place of the one whose movement is stopped." Copies, DLC-USG, V, 34, 35; DNA, RG 393, Military Div. of the Miss., Letters Sent; *ibid.*, Dept. of the Cumberland, Telegrams Received. On the same day, 10:00 P.M., Thomas telegraphed to USG. "Your two despatches of this date received. I have just returned from the front. My troops after ceaseless labor under the greatest embarrassment for want of transportation reached within three miles of Dalton, where they were received by the enemy strongly posted and in force fully equal to my own in Infantry. His Artillery and Cavalry was not only in better condition (as regards horses) but was at least two to our one in pieces and men. We found the Country entirely stripped of every thing like forage and our mules being in such poor condition that double the number of teams we now have could not supply the troops. I thought it best to come back to Ringgold, and if workmen can be found by Col. McCallum to go to work deliberately to repair the R. R. and advance as it progresses The present condition of the roads is not good and one day's rain would render the part across Chickamauga bottom impassable for loaded wagons. So it will be absolutely necessary to repair the Rail Road to supply the troops at Ringgold. The fact of working on the road would hold Johnston at Dalton unless he intended to leave under any circumstances. Howard's teams and the Depot teams at this place and Bridgeport are in no better condition than those belonging to the Divisions, all being composed of such mules as we have been able to keep up after a fashion during the Winter. Johnston has no idea of leaving Dalton until compelled, and having a force greater than what I now have under my immediate command I can not drive him from the place. If Longstreet has retired why can I not get Granger's two Divisions and my first Cavalry Division back? The little Cavalry I had on the expedition is completely worn down from constant work and for want of forage." Copies, *ibid.*, Telegrams Sent; *ibid.*, Military Div. of the Miss., Telegrams Received. See following telegram.

To Brig. Gen. William D. Whipple

Nashville 6. P. M. 27th February 1864.
BRIG GENL W. D. WHIPPLE CHIEF OF STAFF TO
MAJ GEN G. H THOMAS
CHATTANOOGA

Information has reached Washington that orders have been given for Johnston's Army to fall back. General Thomas should watch any such move, and follow it up closely. Cant you draw teams from Bridgeport and Stevenson to send supplies to the front? They have teams in great numbers at those places—Every energy should be exerted to get supplies and reenforcements, forward. Troops will leave here at the rate of two or three thousand a day for the front.[1] Many of them go to Chattanooga

U S GRANT
Major General

Telegram, copies, DLC-USG, V, 34, 35; DNA, RG 393, Military Div. of the Miss., Letters Sent; *ibid.*, Dept. of the Cumberland, Telegrams Received. *O.R.*, I, xxxii, part 2, 481–82. William D. Whipple of N. Y., USMA 1851, was appointed brig. gen. as of July 17, 1863. On Oct. 27, Whipple, Cincinnati, telegraphed to USG. "I am ordered by the Genl in chief to report to you for assignment   have you any orders for me at this point   shall I report to you in person." ALS (telegram sent), DNA, RG 94, War Records Office, Dept. of the Ohio; telegram received, *ibid.*, RG 393, Dept. of the Tenn., Telegrams Received. On Oct. 27, 5:00 P.M., USG telegraphed to Whipple. "Report here to Major General Thomas for duty." Copies, DLC-USG, V, 34, 35; DNA, RG 393, Military Div. of the Miss., Letters Sent. Whipple was assigned as adjt., Army of the Cumberland, Nov. 12, and chief of staff, Dec. 5. On June 10, 1864, Maj. Gen. William T. Sherman, Acworth, Ga., telegraphed to Maj. Gen. Henry W. Halleck. "Genl Thomas asks me to telegraph to you and Genl Grant to solicit your influence to procure the confirmation by the Senate of Brig Genl W D Whipple who is acting in the capacity of Thomas' Chf of Staff—I send by mail today Thomas' letter to me which recites the services of Genl Whipple far better than I could do"   Telegram received, *ibid.*, RG 107, Telegrams Collected (Bound). The letter from Maj. Gen. George H. Thomas is *ibid.*, RG 94, Letters Received, 1500W 1862. On Feb. 27, Whipple had telegraphed to Brig. Gen. John A. Rawlins. "The following dispatches were rec'd yesterday   Gen Thomas is absent at the front. As you from your position in Nashville can judge best as to whether the 12th regt Colored troops is needed most at Nashville or on the Northwestern railroad I submit the following dispatches for your orders in the case"   Telegram received, *ibid.*, RG 393, Dept. of the Tenn., Telegrams Received; copies, *ibid.*, Military Div. of the Miss., Telegrams Received; *ibid.*, Dept. of the Cumberland, Telegrams Sent. See preceding telegram.

1. On Feb. 28, Rawlins wrote to Bvt. Lt. Col. James L. Donaldson. "You will for the next three days send forward troops to the front to the exclusion if necessary of every thing else. There are now about three thousand men in the city to go forward." LS, DNA, RG 393, Dept. of the Cumberland, Letters Received.

To Maj. Gen. Francis P. Blair, Jr.

————

Nashville Tennessee,
Feb.y 28th 1864

My Dear General,

Your letter of the 16th inst. is but just received. It is on a subject upon which I do not like to write, talk, or think. Every body who knows me knows I have no political aspirations either now or for the future. I hope to remain a soldier as long as I live, to serve faithfully any and every Administration that may be in power, and which may be striving to maintain the integrity of the *whole Union*, as long as I do live.

However far the powers that be may choose to extend my authority I will always endeavor to realize their expectations of me. However much my command may be reduced I will serve with the same fidelity and zeal.

Under no circumstances would I use power for political advancment, nor whilst a soldier take part in politics. If, in the conventions to meet, one candidate should be nominated whos election I would regard as dangerous to the country, I would not hesitate to say so freely however. Further than this I could take no part. Admiral Porter in writing to Asst. Sec. Fox[1] has probably obtained his information from Sherman. Sherman knows my views exactly. On the subject of the Lieut. Generalcy however he has not exactly caught my idea. When the Bill reviving that grade was first proposed I did express doubts as to the effect such a measure might have on my infulance over those whom I might have to command, and who after all have all the fighting to do. Rather than to loose the least power to do good, towards crushing out the rebellion in the shortest possible time, I would prefer remaining as I am. I also stated that under no circumstances could I be induced to take an office which would require me to stay in Washington and command whilst the Armies were in the Field.[2]

I hope you will show this letter to no one unless it be the President himself. I hate to see my name associated with politics either as an aspirant for office or as a partizan.

Write to me again.

sincerely your friend
U. S. GRANT

ADfS (addressed to Maj. Gen. Francis P. Blair, Jr.), USG 3; ALS, Claude K. Rowland, St. Louis, Mo. On Jan. 31, 1864, Peter L. Foy, Post Office, St. Louis, wrote to Blair. "I have just heard that Haw. [*How*] put the question to Grant with whom he is quite intimate, whether he would consent to be a candidate for the Presidency. He answered that under no circumstances would he be a candidate in opposition to Lincoln. I think it well to let you know this at once, so that you may take it for what it is worth. My information did not come from Haw himself but from Bart Able. . . ." ALS, DLC-Robert T. Lincoln.

1. On Jan. 13, 1864, Rear Admiral David D. Porter, Cairo, wrote to Asst. Secretary of the Navy Gustavus V. Fox, Blair's brother-in-law. "Grant could not be kicked into the Presidency, he would not have it at 40,000 per year, he dont like anything but fighting and smoking, and hates politics as the devel does holy water—he dont want even to be a Lieut. General until the war is over. So having no aspirations of a political nature, he should have as big a command as he can manage, and the success of the next year depends on his having all the Mississippi—it is indeed a necessity." Bruce Catton, *Grant Takes Command* (Boston, 1969), p. 110.

2. USG added this sentence after preparing his draft.

To Maj. Gen. John M. Schofield

Nashville [*Feb.*] 28th. 10 30 a m

MAJ GENL J M SCHOFIELD

Whilst Gen Thomas is engaged in front of Dalton do not think it advisable for your force to go up the valley   there is a possibility of it becoming necessary to reinforce Gen Thomas with Maj Gen Gordon Grangers Corps   for the present push your Cavalry as close on to Longstreet as possible & learn all you can of his movement   be prepared to move yourself if circumstances should require it   there is no movement of troops in West Virginia nor on Patomoc

U S Grant M G

Telegram received, DLC-John M. Schofield. Dated Feb. 29, 1864, in *O.R.*, I, xxxii, part 2, 495. On March 1, 2:00 P.M., Maj. Gen. John M. Schofield, Morristown, Tenn., wrote to USG. "Your despatch of the 28th was not recd until this moment. I have accomplished all that is possible at this time and will act at once as directed in your despatch just received. Meanwhile I will watch the enemy and keep you informed of his movements. The present heavy rains will render it impossible for either him or me to do much for some time." ALS, DLC-John M. Schofield. On the same day, Schofield telegraphed to USG. "I pushed forward with my advance to this place yesterday. The remainder of my troops will come up today. The enemy is still in force on my front. Longstreet has sent no infantry away, unless it may be Ransoms Division. I have not been able to learn anything of that Division. I am not yet satisfied what the ultimate object of his late movements is—It has been raining heavily for two days and the roads are nearly impassable. It will be impossible to do much until I get the Rail road Bridge across the Holston"   Copies, *ibid.*; DNA, RG 393, Military Div. of the Miss., Telegrams Received. *O.R.*, I, xxxii, part 3, 3. Also on March 1, Brig. Gen. Edward E. Potter, Knoxville, chief of staff for Schofield, telegraphed to USG. "Gen'l Schofield is this night at Morristown   his cavalry force is small and probably not far in advance   My last dispatch from Gen'l S. was from New Market this morning. there is no later information as to Longstreets movements"   Copy, DNA, RG 393, Military Div. of the Miss., Telegrams Received.

On March 2, USG telegraphed to Maj. Gen. Henry W. Halleck. "Gen Schofield was at Morristown last night   No special information sent of Longstreets movements"   Telegram received, *ibid.*, RG 107, Telegrams Collected (Bound); *ibid.*, RG 393, Military Div. of the Miss., Hd. Qrs. Correspondence; DLC-USG, V, 40, 94.

Also on March 2, Schofield, New Market, Tenn., wrote to USG. "My latest information from Longstreet is up to the night of the 28th. That night Hoods Division encamped at Bull Gap, McClaws near Greenville and Johnsons near Chucky Bend—Ransom's Division had preceded McClaws by one days march   The greater part of Longstreets cavalry has gone up the French Broad. The advance of my Infantry is at Panther spring, four miles this side of Morristown. My cavalry has been as far up as Russellville and Chucky Bend where it met a superior force of rebel cavalry. I have Woods Division of Grangers Corps at this place from which I can quickly send it to Genl. Thomas if necessary. I will retain it here until I hear from you again. I will have the railroad bridge at Strawberry Plains rebuilt in about ten days. Then I can advance whatever the weather may be. Until then it will be impossible if we have any more rain. I will make all possible preparation. My cavalry is reduced to almost nothing and I could not

support more if I had it. I can not learn much of the enemys movements by the use of cavalry alone. My spies will be able to keep pretty close track of him."
ALS, DLC-John M. Schofield.

To Maj. Gen. George H. Thomas

Nashville 11. A. M. 28th Feb 1864

MAJOR GENERAL G. H THOMAS
CHATTANOOGA

General Schofield was notified as soon as it was reported that Longstreet was leaving East Tennessee, to return Grangers Corps the moment it was known to be safe to do so.

With the limited command now left to Schofield you will, with Granger returned, have to hold to Loudon. Send Logans troops back at the earliest moment you can dispense with them. Notify me when they start.

U. S. GRANT
Major General

Telegram, copies, DLC-USG, V, 34, 35; DNA, RG 393, Military Div. of the Miss., Letters Sent; *ibid.*, Dept. of the Cumberland, Telegrams Received. *O.R.*, I, xxxii, part 2, 490.

On Feb. 28, 1864, 8:45 P.M., Maj. Gen. George H. Thomas telegraphed to USG. "I propose to give Genl Schofield all the East Tenn. troops Infantry & Cavalry now in my ~~command~~ Department named Spears Brigade composed of the Thirty fifth and fifth East Tennessee infantry Second third and fifth Tennessee Cavalry They have been of no use to me, as their private interests have drawn them towards East Tennessee It has been impossible for me to get any returns from them & consequently I have been unable to make returns of my command as promptly as I wish" Telegram received, DNA, RG 393, Dept. of the Tenn., Telegrams Received; copies, *ibid.*, Military Div. of the Miss., Telegrams Received; *ibid.*, Dept. of the Cumberland, Telegrams Sent.

On Feb. 29, USG telegraphed to Maj. Gen. John A. Logan. "Your troops with Thomas have been ordered back Send such orders to them at Stevenson as you want to give. Is it not better that the veterans among them should leave from there?" Copies, DLC-USG, V, 34, 35; DNA, RG 393, Military Div. of the Miss., Letters Sent.

To Maj. Gen. George H. Thomas

Nashville February 28th 1864.

MAJ GENERAL GEO H THOMAS
CHATTANOOGA

Between this time and the commencement of the active spring campaign it will be necessary to get new guards for the road from Columbia to Stevenson via Decatur so as to relieve Sherman's force for the field. Guarding that line protects the other to a great extent and will of course enable you to reserve many of your present railroad guards. Make an estimate as soon as you can of the force that can be got in the way here suggested and what new force in addition will be required to enable you to keep your present organization in the field.

U. S. GRANT
Major General

Telegram, copies, DLC-USG, V, 34, 35; DNA, RG 393, Military Div. of the Miss., Letters Sent; *ibid.*, Dept. of the Cumberland, Telegrams Received. *O.R.*, I, xxxii, part 2, 490. On Feb. 28, 1864, Maj. Gen. George H. Thomas twice telegraphed to USG, the second time at 9:00 P.M. "Genl. Butterfield by my direction has recently examined the line between here, and Nashville, and reports that he thinks six thousand men will be sufficient to guard that line, two Regiments of which force should be Cavalry. From what I know of the road between Nashville, and Decatur, two thousand Infy, and two thousand Cavalry will be sufficient to protect that line. One Thousand Infantry will be sufficient to protect the line from Athens to Stevenson. Possibly both lines of communication can be guarded by Six Thousand Infantry, and Two Thousand Cavalry, a great portion of which should be made up from the local militia of Tenn. or troops organized especially for the preservation of order in the State. I believe, if I can commence the campaign with the 14th, and 4th Corps in front with Howard's Corps in reserve, that I can move along the line of the R. R., and overcome all opposition as far at least as Atlanta. I should want a strong Division of Cavalry in Advance. As soon as Capt. Merrill returns from his reconnoisance along the R. R. lines, I can give you a definite estimate of the number of troops required to guard the bridges along the road." Copies, DNA, RG 393, Dept. of the Cumberland, Telegrams Sent; *ibid.*, Military Div. of the Miss., Telegrams Received. *O.R.*, I, xxxii, part 2, 489. "I have caused a thorough examination of the Rail Road between this and Tunnell Hill to be made— The officer reports that with four hundred of Col. McCallums construction corps the road can be put in complete running order in six weeks from the time they commence   Genl Baird is now at Ringgold and the whole of the road in his rear is protected so this party can commence work immediately   The road from Cleveland to Dalton can be finished in a week provided we can get the necessary rails" Telegram received, DNA, RG 393, Dept. of the Tenn., Telegrams Received; copies, *ibid.*, Military Div. of the Miss., Telegrams Received; *ibid.*, Dept. of the Cumberland, Telegrams Sent. *O.R.*, I, xxxii, part 2, 489–90.

To Brig. Gen. Lorenzo Thomas

Nashville, Tenn., Feb. 29th *1864.*

To The Adjutant General of the Army,
Washington D. C
General:

Enclosed herewithe please find communication, of date February 13th 1864. from the office of Commissary General of Subsistence.[1]

In answer thereto I would respectfully state that from the time I assumed command of the "District of South East Missouri," in September 1861, to the 31st day of January 1864, I have ordered the commutation of rations for clerks (detailed men) at my Head Quarters. Under paragraph 1218 "Revised Army Regulations," 1861, I never doubted my authority when my Head Quarters were established in a City, and when in the field the reason for such an order seemed so much greater that I had no thought but the commutation would be allowed, and never having had one returned until within the last month, I had supposed my action was approved of. True, I had seen the "Regulations" sometime after their publication however, that commutation of rations would not be allowed at points where rations could be drawn, but this was not the ground for my action, it was the impracticability of their cooking them, their whole time being required in the discharge of their clerical duties. I am sure the business of my several commands and the good of the service has been greatly facilitated by the ordering of the commutations herein referred to.

In consideration of the facts here stated I would respectfully ask that such authority be granted me as will cover all orders for commutation of rations, that I have heretofore made, and save me from the operation of paragraph 1007, "Army Regulations" 1861, and also continue the ordering of the same for the clerks at my Head Quarters.

> I have the honor to be, General,
> Very respectfully
> Your obt. svt.
> U. S. GRANT
> Maj. Gen. U. S. A.

LS, DNA, RG 94, Letters Received, 308M 1864. On March 12, 1864, Brig. Gen. Edward R. S. Canby endorsed this letter. "The authority asked for is granted. By order of the Secretary of War." ES, *ibid.*

1. On Feb. 13, Brig. Gen. Joseph P. Taylor, commissary gen., wrote to Brig. Gen. John A. Rawlins. "It appears from Capt E. T. S. Schenck's account for July 1863 that, by order of Maj Genl U. S. Grant, certain enlisted men were paid 75 cents per diem for commutation of rations, while on duty at Head Quarters Department of the Tennessee as clerks, mail agents, &c. Similar disbursements were made by other officers doing duty in the Subsistence Dept with troops under the General's command. Such Commutation, not being Authorized by the Regulations, is chargeable, under Par 1007 Army Regs 1861, to the officer ordering it. Please request the General to forward to this office, such special authority relating to these cases as may have been given him, in order that disallowances for such commutations may be avoided." LS, *ibid.*

To Maj. Gen. Henry W. Halleck

Nashville Tenn
Monday Feb 29th 64 6 P M

MAJ GEN H W HALLECK
GEN IN CHIEF

My last advices from Gen Schofield are dated twenty sixth (26th)   Longstreet seems to be going into Virginia,   Possibly some Infantry and Cavalry have gone South into Georgia

Gen Schofield could not follow farther than Strawberry Plains except with Cavalry, because every step took him from his supplies whilst Longstreet was falling back on his—The Cavalry was directed to follow up and observe movement. I did not like either to move a force East whilst our Army near Dalton were engaged with Enemy. Gen Thomas remained near Dalton as long as he could supply himself. He is back now to Ringgold where he hopes to be able to haul supplies until the RailRoad can be completed to him

As soon as Schofield is heard from I will telegraph—

U S GRANT
Maj Genl

Telegram received, DNA, RG 107, Telegrams Collected (Bound); copies, *ibid.*, RG 393, Military Div. of the Miss., Hd. Qrs. Correspondence; DLC-USG, V, 40, 94. *O.R.*, I, xxxii, part 2, 495. This telegram reached Washington on March 3, 1864, 2:30 A.M. On Feb. 29, 3:30 P.M., Maj. Gen. Henry W. Halleck telegraphed to USG. "Have you any further information of Longstreet's retreat. Please keep us advised here, as far as possible, of his movements." ALS (telegram sent), DNA, RG 107, Telegrams Collected (Bound); copies, *ibid.*, RG 393, Military Div. of the Miss., Hd. Qrs. Correspondence; DLC-USG, V, 40, 94. *O.R.*, I, xxxii, part 2, 494.

Also on Feb. 29, USG telegraphed to Maj. Gen. John M. Schofield. "What is your latest information from Longstreets movements   how far up the valley has our cavalry been able to go" Telegram received, DLC-John M. Schofield; copies, DLC-USG, V, 34, 35; DNA, RG 393, Military Div. of the Miss., Letters Sent. *O.R.*, I, xxxii, part 2, 494.

To Maj. Gen. John M. Schofield

Nashville February 29th 1864

MAJOR GENERAL J M SCHOFIELD
KNOXVILLE

Farmers in East Tennessee should be encouraged to cultivate all the grain they can the coming season. Quartermasters may sell them what can be spared for such purposes, and seed of all kinds will be permitted to pass over the roads. Orders were issued from these Headquarters on the 22d permitting merchants to bring grain and grass seed to Nashville for sale to citizens of Tennessee for such purposes.

U. S. GRANT
Major General

Telegram, copies, DLC-USG, V, 34, 35; DNA, RG 393, Military Div. of the
Miss., Letters Sent. *O.R.*, I, xxxii, part 2, 494. On Feb. 26, 1864, Maj. Gen.
John M. Schofield telegraphed to USG. "I think it would be wise to send here
ten thousand bushels of Oats to the farmers for Seed. it is the only method by
which we can get forage here in the summer. the farmers have the money to pay
for the Oats   please inform me if this can be done"   Telegram received, DNA,
RG 393, Dept. of the Tenn., Telegrams Received; copies, *ibid.*, Military Div. of
the Miss., Telegrams Received; (2) *ibid.*, Dept. of the Ohio, Telegrams Sent.
O.R., I, xxxii, part 2, 473.

To Maj. Gen. George H. Thomas

Nashville February 29 '64

MAJ GENL GEO H THOMAS
CHATTANOOGA

What is to prevent the troops commencing immediately the
work of reconstruction on the railroad from Chattanooga to
Dalton?

The 10th Illinois Veterans are now here on their way to the
front. There has always been difficulty between this Regiment and
General Morgan since his promotion out of it. The good of the
public service will be subserved by attaching this regiment to
some other Division than that to which it now belongs. General
Morgan I always regarded as a superior officer whilst he was with
me but after an officers promotion from a regiment it has been my
policy to seperate his command from that regiment   Upon promotion being made after the fall of Fort Donelson I adopted this
rule and believe it a good one. In the present case I know that it
will relieve feelings that have existed more than a year.

U. S. GRANT
Major General

Telegram, copies, DLC-USG, V, 34, 35; DNA, RG 393, Military Div. of the
Miss., Letters Sent; (entered as two separate telegrams) *ibid.*, Dept. of the
Cumberland, Telegrams Received. *O.R.*, I, xxxii, part 2, 496. On Feb. 29, 1864,
Maj. Gen. George H. Thomas telegraphed to USG. "General Morgan has so constantly and faithfully devoted himself to his old Brigade, and so often expressed
the desire to me to keep it entire and as it was originally organized, and is withall
so entirely devoted to his duties that I dislike to change his command. I have generally adopted the plan suggested by you in other cases, but have not in his case

for the above reasons." Copy, DNA, RG 393, Dept. of the Cumberland, Telegrams Sent.

On Feb. 8, USG wrote to Governor Richard Yates of Ill. "Your letter of the 2d inst. relative to the assignment of the 10th Ill. Vol. Inf.y to another command when it returns to the field is just received. I have been aware for some time of the feeling of Col. Tilson towards Gen. Morgan and regarded the good of the service as requiring their separation and had determined to effect it when this regiment again returns to duty. All Col. Tilson has to do is to report to me, by letter or otherwise, when he is ready to return to duty and I will assign where he can render good service with his regiment and where he will be under a competant commander." ALS (facsimile), Yates Papers, IHi. On Feb. 6, Lt. Col. William L. Duff wrote a similar letter to John Wood, Quincy, Ill., former governor of Ill. Copy, DNA, RG 393, Military Div. of the Miss., Letters Received. On Feb. 25, Col. John Tillson, 10th Ill., Quincy, telegraphed to USG. "As directed in your letters to Govr'ns Wood & Yates I report that my Regiment is ordered and leaves for Nashville via Louisville on Friday twenty sixth 26th at Nine 9 A. M. will reach Nashville about Monday next." Copy, *ibid.*, Telegrams Received.

On March 20, Tillson wrote to U.S. Senator Lyman Trumbull of Ill. "I have just learned that Genl Grant has gone to Washington   I suppose that the more important matters on his mind prevented him fulfilling his promise to me . . ." ALS, DLC-Lyman Trumbull. On March 29, Tillson telegraphed to USG. "No changes have been made in assignment   I write you today" Telegram received, DNA, RG 107, Telegrams Collected (Bound).

On July 6, USG endorsed a letter of Col. Charles M. Lum, 10th Mich., and others protesting the assignment of Brig. Gen. James D. Morgan to command their brigade. "Respectfully referred to Maj. Gen W. T. Sherman Comd'g Military Division of the Miss—Gen. Morgan entered the service in this Regiment, and on his promotion Col. Tillson succeeded to the Colonelcy of it. Unpleasant relations have existed for a long time between these officers, on being apprized of which, I addressed a communication to Maj Gen Thomas in form of a request, which I trusted would have the effect of an order, asking that this Reg't. might be transferred out of Gen Morgans command, feeling that the good of the service would be promoted thereby. But the change was not made. I therefore direct that the Reg't. be transferred from the Army of the Cumberland to one of the other Armies of your command—" ES, *ibid.*, RG 393, Military Div. of the Miss., Letters Received. On July 26, Thomas endorsed this letter. "Respectfully returned to Maj. Gen. Sherman. In my opinion there is no military reason why this Regiment should be transferred from Gen. Morgan's command. The Regiment is perfectly satisfied with being in his Brigade. He is a kind, judicious, and meritorious officer, never asking indulgences and never making complaints, and as far as I have been a[b]le to judge always discharging his duty with the strictist impartiality and kindly feeling toward his subordinates. This application seems to have been made by Col. Tilson who is a captain in the Regular army to gratify a personal pique, and he appears to have endeavored to use political and family influence to obtain his wishes, both of which are highly unbecoming an officer of the Regular Army. These are the reasons why I have declined to grant this application heretofore. I did not consider the request of Lieut. Gen. Grant as an order, or I should have obeyed it at once. As the order of the Lieut. General Commanding directs a transfer from the Army of the Cumberland, it is out of my power to execute it. And I respectfully request that some other Regiment, in justice to this Army, be assigned to take the place of this." ES, *ibid.*

To Maj. Gen. George H. Thomas

Nashville February 29th 1864.

MAJOR GENERAL GEO H THOMAS
CHATTANOOGA

I have not heard from Schofield since the 26th. He was directed to relieve Granger as soon as it was know that Longstreet had gone beyond striking distance. Telegraph Schofield what orders to give Granger when relieved. McCooks[1] cavalry I expect is now far up the Holston.

U. S. GRANT
Major General

Telegram, copies, DLC-USG, V, 34, 35; DNA, RG 393, Military Div. of the Miss., Letters Sent; *ibid.*, Dept. of the Cumberland, Telegrams Received. *O.R.*, I, xxxii, part 2, 496. On Feb. 29, 1864, Maj. Gen. George H. Thomas twice telegraphed to USG, the second time at 11:00 P.M. "I have given orders for Genl Matthias to rejoin his command   He will start tomorrow—Has Genl Schofield been directed to relieve Genl's Granger & McCook and send them to me? I wish to place Grangers troops in front of Cleveland protecting the road from there to Loudon one or two regiments of McCooks Cavalry at Calhoun to prevent any flank movement of the enemy from Dalton in that direction   The balance of his troops to cover & observe our front—I have been making arrangements today to commence the reconstruction of the Rail Road between this & Dalton"   Telegram received, DNA, RG 393, Dept. of the Tenn., Telegrams Received; *ibid.*, Military Div. of the Miss., Telegrams Received; *ibid.*, Dept. of the Cumberland, Telegrams Sent. *O.R.*, I, xxxii, part 2, 497. "Col. McCooks Cavalry is now on the Little Tennessee out at Madisonville. He reports to Genl. Elliott that he will be out of forage in ten days. His services are much needed in my front—I can have him foraged at Cleveland." Copy, DNA, RG 393, Dept. of the Cumberland, Telegrams Sent.

On March 1, Thomas telegraphed to USG. "I will have four hundred men at work on the R. R. between here, and Ringold tomorrow. The reconnoisance towards Dalton demonstrated that the enemy was still there in force. I have since heard from different sources (all confirmatory) that Johnston had received orders to retire behind the Etowah, and send reinforcements to Selma, or Mobile. One informant, Browns reports that some of the troops had already started, but that our demonstration has brought them back. He is now in Dalton, and will report to me immediately any changes Johnston makes. I have signified to Genl. Schofield my willingness to transfer to him all the East Tennessee troops under my command, if he will release the Fourth Corps, and McCook's Division of Cavalry. I am entirely crippled for want of Cavalry. I am pushing forward the works for the defences of the R. R. between this and Nashville. When they are completed, I am in hopes I can order to the front, Howard's entire Corps, and perhaps a part of Slocum's. Did you place Genl. Hovey in command of the District of Kentucky? If so, I think Genl. Johnson would like to exchange duties with him." Copies, *ibid.*; *ibid.*, Military Div. of the Miss., Telegrams Received. *O.R.*, I, xxxii, part 3, 5. On the same day, Thomas wrote to USG. "Sometime last winter you mentioned in conversation that you would send General Hovey to report to me, and I think I saw it announced afterwards in the papers that he had been placed in command of the district of Indiana. My object in writing this is to propose an exchange of Genl R. W Johnson for him as from what you told me in the conversation alluded to I infered that Genl Hovey would prefer duty in the field to such duty as superintending the Recruiting service &c. I think Johnson would like to be placed on such duty. I have also received a proposition from a man (who from all I can learn of him) is reliable to burn the Bridge over the Etowah for thirty thousand dollars in Confederate money. I have but ten thousand but will be obliged if you will send me twenty thousand more if you have it. I think it will be well spent if we can get that bridge destroyed   No further movements of the enemy observed to-day. I have received additional confirmation that the recognisance has brought back all the troops which had left Dalton. Mrs Dr. Gordan of Lafayette informs me that she saw two cars of wounded going south." ALS, DNA, RG 94, War Records Office, 16th Army Corps. *O.R.*, I, xxxii, part 3, 4.

1. Edward M. McCook, born in Ohio in 1833, moved to Colo. during the gold rush and practiced law, serving in the Kan. Territorial Legislature (1859). Commissioned 2nd lt., 1st Cav., as of May 8, 1861, he was appointed maj., 2nd Ind. Cav., as of Sept. 29, and promoted to col. as of April 30, 1862. In Feb., 1864, he commanded the 1st Div., Cav. Corps, Army of the Cumberland.

To Brig. Gen. Stephen G. Burbridge

By Telegraph from Nashville [Feb. 29] 1864

To GENL BURBRIDGE

I think all work by negroes upon Rail Roads in Ky ought to cease   I have referred to the Dept commander to know what is being done and to order the revertion of the impending order if negroes are being employed at public expense to carry on the work. I refer your despatch to Genl Schofield[1]

U S GRANT
Maj Genl

Telegram received, DNA, RG 393, Dept. of Ky., Telegrams Received; copies, *ibid.*, Military Div. of the Miss., Letters Sent; DLC-USG, V, 34, 35. *O.R.*, I, xxxii, part 2, 497–98. On Feb. 29, 1864, Brig. Gen. Stephen G. Burbridge telegraphed

to USG. "In impressing negroes for labor on military roads in this state it is necessary to Employ Citizens for the purpose of Enrolling and Collecting the negroes
in each county   Will you authorize the payment of these citizens at rates in no
case to exceed five dollars per diem"   Copy, DNA, RG 393, Dept. of Ky., Telegrams Sent. On March 1, Burbridge telegraphed to USG. "Every Regiment arriving at this City from Nashville bring with them from twenty to seventy five
able bodied contrabands   Cannot these negroes be taken and turned over to the
Nashville R R Co to cut fire wood for these use of the road   The Superintendent
of the road reports that unless something is done at once the road will be unable
to comply with the government demand for transportation"   Copies, *ibid.*; *ibid.*,
Military Div. of the Miss., Telegrams Received. On the same day, Burbridge
wrote to USG. "I telegraphed you a few days since in reference to the impressment of negroes in this state for labor on military roads. Under the order of
impressment made by Maj. Gen'l. Burnside last fall, a number of negroes are
still kept [at] work [in] various parts of the State, under citizen overseers, whom
the Q. M. Dept. now refuses to pay as they were not taken up on their Rolls as
employees of the Q. M. Dept. . . . The people of that portion of the state in which
the road will pass are very anx[ious] to hire their negroes to the R. R. Co. in
preference to hiring them to the Gov'mt with the uncertainty of Pay. I consider
the early construction of this road of great importance to the Government & the
work can be done without any expense on the part of the government, the rail
road Company only asking the assistance of the military authorities in procuring
the Negro[es] to perform the labor. I enclose for your consideration a copy of a
communication from Brig Genl Wilson to Maj Genl Schofield on the subjec[t]
also copies of letters from Hon. Jas Guthrie Prest. and Geo McLeod Esq Chief
Eng. of the L & N. R. R. Co. in reference to the road, also copy of Maj Genl.
Burnside's order in reference to the impressment of negroes"   LS (partly illegible), *ibid.*, Dept. of Ky., Letters Sent (Press). On March 4, Lt. Col. Theodore S. Bowers telegraphed to Burbridge. "Negroes belonging to Regts passing
through Louisville cannot be detained"   Telegram received, *ibid.*, Telegrams
Received.

On Feb. 23, J. M. Nash, superintendent of railroad repairs, Military Div.
of the Miss., wrote to Adna Anderson, superintendent of military railroads, Military Div. of the Miss. "A negro pressing or conscripting party have taken nearly
all the negro force from the T. and A. R. Rd., between Columbia and Duck River.
In the gang now here in town there is about Fifty, mostly Wood choppers, some
Track-men and other kind of Laborers,   they report they were brought here
against their will and ask to be released that they may return to their former
occupation   they are now under guard on Church street near the depot"   Copy,
ibid., Dept. of the Cumberland, Records of Colored Troops. On Feb. 24, USG
endorsed this letter. "Respectfully forwarded to Brig. Gen. L. Thomas, Adjutant
General of the Army, with the request that if the conscripting of Negroes is not
consistent with his orders, that the within named Negroes be returned to work
on the rail roads. No orders directing conscription of Negroes in Tennessee have
been received at these Head Quarters"   ES, *ibid.* On Feb. 25, Brig. Gen. Lorenzo
Thomas endorsed this letter. "As recruiting officers show no discretion and take
~~from~~ negroes from employments necessary to carry on the operations of the government, my orders are revoked   The negroes referred to within will be returned"   AES, *ibid.*

1. On Feb. 27, USG wrote to Maj. Gen. John M. Schofield. "If there are any existing orders of the Department of the Ohio authorizing any expenditure by the United States of money in the construction of railroads in the State of Kentucky you will at once revoke them as there are no railroads now in process of construction in Kentucky, which would probably be finished in time to be of service in a military way. A copy of an order from Gen Burbridge is herewith enclosed for your information" Copies, DLC-USG, V, 34, 35; DNA, RG 393, Military Div. of the Miss., Letters Sent. Entered as written by Bowers, *ibid.*, Dept. of the Ohio, Register of Letters Received.

To Brig. Gen. William Sooy Smith

Nashville February 29th 1864.
BRIG GENL W. S. SMITH COMDG CAV: EXP. MEMPHIS
CARE GEN REID COMDG POST, CAIRO ILLS.

Move out again immediately and push towards a junction with Sherman until you know he has struck a safe lodgement somewhere. If you hear of his arrival at Jackson Miss, or any point on Pearl River south of there, you may regard him as safe and return. Take as many men as can possibly go.

U. S GRANT
Major General

Telegram, copies, DLC-USG, V, 34, 35; DNA, RG 393, Military Div. of the Miss., Letters Sent. *O.R.*, I, xxxii, part 2, 500. On Feb. 28, 1864, Brig. Gen. Hugh T. Reid wrote to USG. "Genl. W. S. Smith, went as far South as West Point, Mississippi, at which point and at Okalona, had severe fights with forces of Forrest Chalmers & Roddy, fell back fighting to the Tallahatchie, and thence, without fighting to Memphis said to have taken three hundred prisoners, and to have destroyed much corn, cotton and Rail Road" Copy, DNA, RG 393, District of Columbus, Telegrams Sent. *O.R.*, I, xxxii, part 2, 492.

In the opening months of 1864, Brig. Gen. William Sooy Smith, chief of cav., Military Div. of the Miss., frequently communicated with USG and his staff, sometimes at great length. See *ibid.*, 20, 22, 49, 75–76, 123–24, 326–27, 370; *ibid.*, I, xxxii, part 1, 254. Smith's lengthy report of the Meridian expedition, printed *ibid.*, pp. 254–60, was also addressed to Brig. Gen. John A. Rawlins. Copy, DNA, RG 393, Military Div. of the Miss., Chief of Cav., Letters Sent.

To Samuel K. Page

[*Feb., 1864*]

MR. PAGE,

DEAR SIR:

Your letter requesting a pass for Chas. & Edward to visit these Hd Qrs. is just received and I hasten to comply with your request. I regret that I am not keeping house so as to entertain them myself but I will do all I can to make their time pass pleasantly. At present I am boarding with a private family just over the stre[et] from my office and have but a single room. Mrs. Grant however may be here before they arrive in which case I go to another place, still a private family, but where there are no other boarders and where there is plenty of room. I can then take them in and make them comfortable. Write to me in advance, or telegraph, when they start so that I can meet them at the cars.—If Julia should be here why not let "sis," (I dont know her name) come along?—Julia is still suffering from her eyes. My kindest regards to all your family.

Yours Truly

U. S. GRANT

ALS, ICHi. On Feb. 15, 1864, Samuel K. Page, Louisville, had written to USG. "My Son Charles is yet confined to his room. he is very feeble his doctors recommend a change as soon as his health will allow it, I therefore will ask the favour of sending to me a pass for Charles A Page & Edward. W. Page to come to your head Quarters. I do think a change will help him. he is now near 4 weeks confined, and I think of he was weighed this day he would not weigh 60#. My own health is good and the balance of the family" ALS, USG 3. For information on the Page family, see letter to Julia Dent Grant, April 3, 1862.

To Thomas E. Bramlette

Nashville March 1st 1864.

GOVERNOR T. E BRAMLETTE

FRANKFORT KEY

The memorial of the Senators and Representatives of the Counties of Graves, Hickman, Fulton, McCracken, Bullard Marshall and Calloway, to have the State of Kentucky placed in one District or Department in order to insure greater uniformity in orders throughout the State so far as they relate to citizens and the elective franchise, with your endorsement thereon, is received.

The Department of Tennessee was established by order of the War Department and the limits prescribed by the great natural boundaries of the Tennessee, Ohio and Mississippi Rivers with special regard to the best interests of the public service

There are no reasons stated in said memorial which should induce a change in those boundaries so as to attach that part of the State of Kentucky west of the Tennessee river to the Department in which the remainder of the State is comprised. The placing of territory belonging to different Departments into one District, even were it admissable under "Regulations" and "orders" would necessarily beget confusion, in the Commander of such District having to obey the orders of, and report to, several Department Commanders.

The uniformity of the exercise of the elective franchise throughout the State of Kentucky will not here after be interfered with by military orders while the State remains in my command. It is a matter purely civil and with which the military have nothing to do, except when called on to protect the citizens from violence in the exercise of it under the laws prescribed by the State.

Instructions in accordance herewith will be given to Commanders of troops and Districts in the State of Kentucky.

U. S. GRANT
Major General

Copies, DLC-USG, V, 34, 35; DNA, RG 393, Military Div. of the Miss., Letters Sent. *O.R.*, I, xxxii, part 3, 7–8.

On March 1, 1864, Governor Thomas E. Bramlette of Ky. telegraphed to USG. "The law passed by the Kentucky legislature giving loyal men an action against disloyal men for injuries by rebel guerillas does not cover past injuries. I therefore withdraw objections to the enforcement of the Military assessment for past injuries—Co'l Hicks will no doubt exercise a sound discretion in executing it" Copy, DNA, RG 393, Military Div. of the Miss., Telegrams Received.

On March 8, Bramlette telegraphed to USG. "Unless otherwise ordered, General Ammen will take command in Kentucky so soon as relieved from court-martial at Cincinnati. He does not desire the command, and I deem it important to our condition that General Burbridge be retained in command in Kentucky.

I have telegraphed Major-General Schofield, and hope the order may be made to keep General Burbridge in command." *O.R.*, I, xxxii, part 3, 39. On March 14, 9:00 P.M., USG, Nashville, telegraphed to Maj. Gen. John M. Schofield. "General Burbridge seems to be doing so well in Kentucky that I think he had better be retained permanently in the command of the District. Genl Ammen can be assigned to the command intended for Burbridge" Copies, DLC-USG, V, 34, 35, 45, 59; DNA, RG 108, Letters Sent; *ibid.*, RG 393, Military Div. of the Miss., Letters Sent. *O.R.*, I, xxxii, part 3, 68.

On March 15, Brig. Gen. Stephen G. Burbridge, Frankfort, telegraphed to USG. "We came to Frankfort tonight. We have spent the night with the Govenor a Proclamation from him will appear in the morning which will quiet the People. Everything about it is right and we can say of Kentucky, 'all is ~~right~~ well.' There need be no fear now about the Enrollment." Telegram received, DNA, RG 108, Letters Received; copy, *ibid.*, RG 393, Military Div. of the Miss., Letters Received.

On Feb. 23, Brig. Gen. Hugh Ewing, Lancaster, Ohio, wrote to USG. "My leave expires tomorrow but I have not yet received the order appointing me in command of the Louisville District—I will await it here by telegraph or letter— My Mother was burried today My Father, Mrs Sherman & family send their compliments to yourself & Mrs Grant" ALS, *ibid.*, RG 94, Generals' Papers and Books, Ewing. On Feb. 29, Lt. Col. Theodore S. Bowers issued Special Orders No. 55 assigning Ewing to command at Louisville. Copy, DLC-USG, V, 38. *O.R.*, I, xxxii, part 2, 501.

On March 4, Bowers wrote to Schofield. "For the better order and efficiency of the troops in the District of Kentucky, you will organize them into two Divisions. Those at Louisville and guarding the line of the Louisville and Nashville railroad south through the State of Kentucky and all west of said road to constitute one division. Those east of said Railroad & Louisville to constitute the other. The former to be commanded by Brig Genl Hugh Ewing with his Hd Qtrs on the line of said railroad about midway between Louisville and the southern boundary of the District; The Commanding Officer of the latter to have his Hd Qtrs with his troops. The senior officer of the troops garrisoning Louisville, to be the Commander of the Post of Louisville and he will be instructed to furnish the requisite number of men to Lieut Col J. H Hammond, commanding depot for drafted men, to guard said depot and also to go forward with the men to their regiments. The Commanding officer of the District of Kentucky will make his Hd Qtrs at Lexington or Camp Nelson, that he may properly watch over the line in that direction. This change is necessary from the fact that officers in Kentucky heretofore have many of them seemed to desire to make a luxury of their position instead of rendering service to the Government." Copies, DLC-USG, V, 34, 35; DNA, RG 393, Military Div. of the Miss., Letters Sent; (incomplete) *ibid.*, RG 94, War Records Office, Dept. of the Ohio. *O.R.*, I, xxxii, part 3, 14– 15. See *ibid.*, p. 75.

On March 16, Col. James B. Fry, provost marshal gen., telegraphed to USG. "The Secretary of War directs me to say that he thinks it will be well to leave General Burbridge in Command in Kentucky, unless you see some reason for not doing so." ALS (telegram sent), DNA, RG 107, Telegrams Collected (Bound); telegram received, *ibid.*, RG 108, Letters Received. On the same day, Bowers telegraphed to Burbridge. "Schofield was directed to change Ewings order. Orders will be sent by next mail—let Ewing await them" Telegram received, *ibid.*, RG 393, Dept. of Ky., Telegrams Received.

To Jesse Root Grant

Nashville Ten.
March 1st 1864,

DEAR FATHER,

Your letter enclosing one from Mr. Newton was received by due course of mail.[1] No letter from I. N. Morris accompanied however. I had previously ~~written~~ rec'd a letter from him, Morris, and answered,[2] but the answer may not have been received when he wrote to you.—I cannot write to Mr. Newton on the subject he asks, nor to any one. I have no ambition outside of my profession and in that only to see our arms every where successful.

Fred. is now with me quite recovered. The Drs. said he would not be strong enough to send to school before next Fall and for that reason I brought him here to spend a few weeks. The balance of the family are all well.

Rains have set in here which will probably make any military movements impossible for some weeks. In that event I do not look upon a visit home for a few days as improbable. A few days absence throws me back in correspondence terribly but so far as Military command goes, in these days of telegraph & steam, I can command whilst traveling and visiting about as well as by remaing here.

Remember me to all at home.

ULYSSES

ALS, IHi.

1. See letter to Jesse Root Grant, Feb. 20, 1864. On Feb. 11, 1864, Eben Newton, Columbus, Ohio, wrote to USG. "I have been a long time acquainted with your father, and on intimate terms, and there fore make more free with you. I have observed your course since you entered the army, and if there is one trait more than another I admire, it is the indifference with which you treat the public demonstrations in relation to yourself. In times like this, if there is one man occupying a high position in the Nation, who can pursue steadily and laboriously his duty without aspiring to the Presidency, he ought to be styled a public benefactor. I am exceedingly anxious that the public mind should not be diverted from Mr Lincoln while he is President, and the great measures which he puts forth for the suppression of the rebellion. If we permit ourselves to be divided up into factions, we certainly weaken our power to accomplish the

object we are striving for, and strengthen the hands and encourage the hearts of our enemies. It has been said that you wish for no office, except it was supervisor of high ways in your own town. It was said in yesterdays Commercial with perfect certainty, that you were not, nor would not be a candidate for the Presidency. If you feel at liberty to express yourself freely upon these subjects, you will do yourself a high honour, and the country a great service. I write as an ardent and admiring friend, having a deep solicitude for the interest of our country" ALS, USG 3.

2. See letter to Isaac N. Morris, Jan. 20, 1864.

To Maj. Gen. George H. Thomas

Nashville March 2d 1864

MAJOR GENERAL G. H THOMAS
CHATTANOOGA

I have directed Schofield to send the Cavalry you [*ask*] for if possible.[1] The Cavalry with Smith have returned to Memphis and may be looked for in your Department soon. I shall recommend the merging of the Department of the Ohio into that of the Cumberland if Schofield is not confirmed.

Hovey is not assigned to the command of Kentucky.[2]

U S GRANT
Major General

Telegram, copies, DLC-USG, V, 34, 35; DNA, RG 393, Military Div. of the Miss., Letters Sent; *ibid.*, Dept. of the Cumberland, Telegrams Received. *O.R.*, I, xxxii, part 3, 11.

1. On March 2, 1864, noon, USG telegraphed to Maj. Gen. John M. Schofield. "If you can possible dispense with cavalry order them to report by telegraph to Maj Gen Geo H. Thomas for orders   Genl Thomas is very much in want of their services" Telegram received (undated), DLC-John M. Schofield; copies (dated March 2), DLC-USG, V, 34, 35; DNA, RG 393, Military Div. of the Miss., Letters Sent. *O.R.*, I, xxxii, part 3, 9. On the same day, 9:45 P.M., Schofield telegraphed to USG. "Your despatch of 12 M today is recd. I have ordered one brigade of Cavalry to report to Maj Genl. Thomas. It is now between the Little Tennessee & the Hiawassee   It is nearly half the effective cavalry I now have." Copy, DLC-John M. Schofield.

2. See telegram to Maj. Gen. George H. Thomas, Feb. 29, 1864.

To Maj. Gen. George H. Thomas

———

Nashville March 2d 1864.

MAJOR GENERAL G H THOMAS
CHATTANOOGA

I have just learned from what I believe to be reliable authority that Johnston has 37000 Infantry at and about Dalton   Your movement no doubt had the effect to hold them there. I have directed Gen Allen to forward as rapidly as possible horses, mules and wagons. We must equip the best we can and do without what cannot be got. Reduce the transportation at all depots and railroad stations to the lowest possible. Substitute poor animals for their fat ones. Dismount the Quartermasters orderlies and employees, infantry officers and all unauthorized persons at any stations, and take their horses to mount the Cavalry. There is a new strong Cavalry regiment here which I will send to Dodge, but which will be left as guard for the road between here and Decatur.[1]

U. S. GRANT
Major General

Telegram, copies, DLC-USG, V, 34, 35; DNA, RG 393, Military Div. of the Miss., Letters Sent; *ibid.*, Dept. of the Cumberland, Telegrams Received. Printed as sent at 11:00 A.M. in *O.R.*, I, xxxii, part 3, 10–11.

1. On March 3, 1864, USG wrote to Brig. Gen. Grenville M. Dodge. "When will you be ready to occupy Decatur? I have ordered a Regiment of Cavalry over 900 strong to report to you." Copies, DLC-USG, V, 34, 35; DNA, RG 393, Military Div. of the Miss., Letters Sent.

To Maj. Gen. John M. Schofield

———

By Telegraph from Nashville [*March*] 4th. 10 a m *1864*
To MAJ GENL JNO M SCHOFIELD

Your force being inferior to that of Longstreet it will not be advisable to push him so as to bring on an engagement. take up all the ground eastward however as fast as you can without an unequal battle   If you should be compelled to fall back do all the damage you can to the Rail Road. Keep Genl. Thomas advised of the movement of the enemy during my absence.

U. S. GRANT
Maj. Genl.

Telegram received, DLC-John M. Schofield; copies, DLC-USG, V, 34, 35; DNA, RG 393, Military Div. of the Miss., Letters Sent. *O.R.*, I, xxxii, part 3, 14. On March 4, 1864, Maj. Gen. John M. Schofield telegraphed to USG. "I have no additional information of a positive character about Longstreets movements. His recent movements if any have been very slow and do not indicate an intention to abandon East Tenn. Possibly he may have sent away some of his Infantry since the 28th I am satisfied he had not previous to that time. The possession of the crossing at Strawberry Plains removes to a great extent the difficulty of advancing at this season. If I had the necessary force I could advance as soon as the R. R. bridge is completed with a fair prospect of ending the campaign in East Tenn. in a short time. The Division you proposed to send me would no doubt be sufficient. If practicable I think it should be sent at once" ALS (telegram sent), DLC-John M. Schofield; copies, *ibid.*; DNA, RG 393, Military Div. of the Miss., Telegrams Received. *O.R.*, I, xxxii, part 3, 14.

On March 5, Schofield telegraphed to USG. "Since sending my despatch of yesterday I have learned that Genl. Thomas has returned to Chattanooga. If it is now practicable for him to send me the force necessary to drive Longstreet out of Tenn I think it may be done without delay. I will probably have the R. R. bridge at Strawberry Plains completed by the time his troops can reach that place We will then be able to supply our troops without serious difficulty." Copies, DLC-John M. Schofield; (2) DNA, RG 393, Military Div. of the Miss., Telegrams Received. *O.R.*, I, xxxii, part 3, 20. On March 7, Lt. Col. Cyrus B. Comstock, Cincinnati, telegraphed to Schofield. "Lieutenant General Grant directs me to say, that troops can not be spared from Chattanooga. That you should keep Longstreet as far up the valley as you can, destroying the railroad near him if he advances." Copies, DLC-USG, V, 34, 35; DNA, RG 393, Military Div. of the Miss., Letters Sent. *O.R.*, I, xxxii, part 3, 32. On March 5, USG, Cave City, Tenn., had telegraphed to Lt. Col. Theodore S. Bowers. "Order Col Comstock to join me at Cincinnati or elsewhere as soon as possible" Telegram received, DNA, RG 393, Dept. of the Tenn., Telegrams Received; copies, *ibid.*, Military Div. of the Miss., Letters Sent; *ibid.*, Telegrams Received.

To Maj. Gen. William T. Sherman

Nashville Tennessee,
March 4th 1864.

DEAR SHERMAN,

The bill reviving the grade of Lieut. Gen. in the Army has become a law and my name has been sent to the Senate for the place.[1]

I now receive orders to report to Washington, *in person*, immediately,[2] which indicates either a confirmation or a likelyhood of confirmation. I start in the morning to comply with the order but I shall say very distinctly on my arrival there that I accept no appointment which will require me to make that city my Hd Qrs. This however is not what I started out to write about.

Whilst I have been eminently successful in this War, in at least gaining the confidence of the public, no one feels more than me how much of this success is due to the energy, skill, and harmonious puting forth of that energy and skill, of those who it has been my good fortune to have occupying a subordinate position under me. There are many officers to whom these remarks are applicable to a greater or less degree, proportionate to their ability as soldiers, but what I want is to express my thanks to you and McPherson as *the men* to whom, above all others, I feel indebted for whatever I have had of success. How far your advice and suggestions have been of assistance you know. How far your execution of whatever has been given you to do entitles you to the reward I am receiving you cannot know as well as me. I feel all the gratitude this letter would express, giving it the most flattering construction.

The word *you* I use in the plural intending it for Mc. also. I should write to him, and will some day, but starting in the morning I do not know that I will find time just now.

Your friend

U. S. GRANT

Maj. Gen.

ALS, DLC-William T. Sherman. *O.R.*, I, xxxii, part 3, 18. On March 10, 1864, Maj. Gen. William T. Sherman, "Near Memphis," wrote to USG a letter headed "(Private and Confidential)." "I have your more than kind and characteristic letter of the 4th—I will send a copy to General McPherson at once. You do yourself injustice and us too much honor in assigning to us so large a share of the merits which have led to your high advancement. I know you approve the friendship I have ever professed to you, and permit me to continue as heretofore to manifest it on all proper occasions. You are now Washington's legitimate successor and occupy a position of almost dangerous elevation, but if you can continue as heretofore to be yourself, simple, honest, and unpretending, you will enjoy through life the respect and love of friends, and the homage of millions of human beings that will award to you a large share in securing to them and their descendants a Government of Law and Stability. I repeat you do General Mc-

Pherson and myself too much honor. At Belmont you manifested your traits, neither of us being near—at Donelson also you illustrated your whole character. I was not near, and Gen'l McPherson in too subordinate a capacity to influence you. Until you had won Donelson, I confess I was almost cowed by the terrible array of anarchial elements that presented themselves at every point, but that victory admitted the ray of light which I have followed ever since   I believe you are as brave, patriotic, and just, as the great phototype Washington—as unselfish, kindhearted and honest, as a man should be, but the chief characteristic in your nature is the simple faith in success you have always manifested, which I can liken to nothing else than the faith a Christian has in a Savior. This faith gave you victory at Shiloh and Vicksburg. Also when you have completed your best preparations you go into Battle without hesitation, as at Chattanooga—no doubts —no reserve, and I tell you that it was this that made us act with confidence. I knew wherever I was that you thought of me, and if I got in a tight place you would come if alive   My only points of doubt were in your knowledge of Grand Strategy and of Books of Science and History. But I confess your common sense seems to have supplied all these. Now as to the future. Dont stay in Washington. Halleck is better qualified than you are to stand the buffets of Intrigue and Policy. Come out West, take to yourself the whole Mississippi Valley. Let us make it dead sure, and I tell you the Atlantic slope and Pacific shores will follow its destiny as sure as the limbs of a tree live or die with the main trunk. We have done much, but still much remains to be done. Time and times influences are all with us. We could almost afford to sit still and let these influences work. Even in the Seceded States your word now would go further than a Presidents Proclamation or an Act of Congress. For Gods sake and for your Countrys sake come out of Washington. I foretold to Gen'l Halleck before he left Corinth the inevitable result to him, and I now exhort you to come out West. Here lies the seat of the coming Empire, and from the West when our task is done, we will make short work of Charleston, and Richmond, and the impoverished coast of the Atlantic"   Copy, DLC-William T. Sherman. *O.R.*, I, xxxii, part 3, 49.

1. On Feb. 26, U.S. Representative Elihu B. Washburne telegraphed to USG. "The Leutenant Gen[er]al Bill has passed both Houses of Congress to-day. The appointment will probably be made early next week." LS (telegram sent), DNA, RG 107, Telegrams Collected (Unbound). On Feb. 29, President Abraham Lincoln wrote to the U.S. Senate. "I nominate Ulysses. S. Grant, now a Major General in the Military service, to be Lieutenant General in the Army of the United States." ALS, *ibid.*, RG 46, McCook Collection. On the same day, 12:30 P.M., Secretary of War Edwin M. Stanton telegraphed to USG. "I have directed that Nashville be put in direct Telegraphic communication at eight (8) oclock tonight. please come into Telegraph office at that hour. I desire to communicate with you." Telegram received, *ibid.*, RG 107, Telegrams Collected (Bound); copies, *ibid.*, RG 393, Military Div. of the Miss., Hd. Qrs. Correspondence; DLC-USG, V, 40, 94. *O.R.*, I, xxxii, part 2, 494. On the same day, 4:00 P.M., USG telegraphed to Stanton. "Dispatch received. Will be at Telegraph office at appointed time," Telegram received, DNA, RG 107, Telegrams Collected (Bound); copies, *ibid.*, RG 393, Military Div. of the Miss., Hd. Qrs. Correspondence; DLC-USG, V, 40, 94. *O.R.*, I, xxxii, part 2, 494.

On March 1, Maj. Gen. Henry W. Halleck wrote to USG. "Your promotion to the lieut Generalcy, which I presume will be immediately made, will create a vacancy of major General in the Regular Army. There are plenty of applicants for it, and these applications will be accompanied by much political intriguing and wire-pulling. In my opinion the place should be given to W. T. Sherman or G. H. Thomas—to the former I would say decidedly if he succeeds in his present expedition. A recommendation from you, strongly urged by the military authorities here, may be able to overcome the political influences that will be brought to bear in favor of others. I hope you will give the matter your early consideration. Your letter in regard to McPherson assisted us very much and he was confirmed yesterday." Copy, DNA, RG 108, Letters Sent. USG was confirmed as lt. gen. on March 2.

2. On March 3, 3:30 P.M., Halleck telegraphed to USG. "The Secty of War directs that you will report in person to the War Dept as early as practicable considering the condition of your command. If necessary you will keep up telegraphic communication with your command while en route to Washington." ALS (telegram sent), *ibid.*, RG 107, Telegrams Collected (Bound); copies, *ibid.*, RG 94, 165A 1864; *ibid.*, RG 393, Military Div. of the Miss., Hd. Qrs. Correspondence; DLC-USG, V, 40, 94. *O.R.*, I, xxxii, part 3, 13. On March 4, 11:00 A.M., USG telegraphed to Halleck. "I will leave Louisville on Monday for Washington" Telegram received, DNA, RG 107, Telegrams Collected (Bound); copies, *ibid.*, RG 393, Military Div. of the Miss., Hd. Qrs. Correspondence; DLC-USG, V, 40, 94. *O.R.*, I, xxxiii, 638. Also on March 4, USG telegraphed to Maj. Gen. John M. Schofield, Maj. Gen. George H. Thomas, Maj. Gen. John A. Logan, and Maj. Roswell M. Sawyer, adjt. for Sherman. "I shall leave to morrow morning for Washington but shall keep up communication with my Headquarters here, by telegraph, All information of the movements of the enemy, as well as matters affecting the command that require my action, you will telegraph here that I may get them. Should a movement of the enemy be made in force against any part of our line, and cooperation of troops of different Departments be deemed necessary, Major Genl G. H Thomas will command during such movements." Telegram received (garbled), DLC-John M. Schofield; copies, DLC-USG, V, 34, 35; DNA, RG 393, Military Div. of the Miss., Letters Sent; *ibid.*, Dept. of the Cumberland, Telegrams Received. *O.R.*, I, xxxii, part 3, 17.

On March 6, 11:30 A.M., Halleck telegraphed to USG, Cincinnati. "The Secty of War directs me to say to you that your commission as Lieut. Genl. is signed and will be delivered to you on your arrival at the War Dept. I sincerely congratulate you on this recognition of your distinguished and meritorious services." ALS (telegram sent), DNA, RG 107, Telegrams Collected (Bound); telegram received, USG 3. *O.R.*, I, xxxii, part 3, 26.

On March 3, Lt. Col. James A. Hardie, AGO, wrote to USG stating that his commission as lt. gen. was enclosed. DS, DNA, RG 94, ACP 4754/1885. Hardie may have erred: USG's commission as maj. gen. was signed on March 3, his commission as lt. gen. on March 4. The commissions are reproduced in William H. Allen, *The American Civil War Book and Grant Album* (Boston and New York, 1894). See letter to Brig. Gen. Lorenzo Thomas, July 18, 1863. Furthermore, Lincoln presented USG with his commission as lt. gen. in Washington. See Speech, March 9, 1864. On March 9, USG signed his oath of office as lt. gen. DS, DNA, RG 94, ACP 4754/1885.

To Maj. Gen. William T. Sherman

Nashville, Tenn., March 4th *1864*

MAJ. GEN. W. T. SHERMAN,
COMD.G DEPT. OF THE TEN.
GENERAL,

You will be able better than me to judge how far the damage you have done the rail-roads about Meredian will disable the enemy from sending an Army into Mississippi and West Tennessee with which to operate on the river: also what force will now be required to protect and guard the river. Use the negroes, or negro troops, more particularly for guarding plantations and for the defence of the West bank of the river. Make but little calculation on their services East of the river. The Artillerests among them of course you will put in fortifications, but most of the Infantry give to Hawkins to be used on the West bank. Add to this element of your forces what you deem an adequate force for the protection of the river, from Cairo down as far as your command goes, and extend the command of one Army Corps to the whole of it. Assemble the balance of your forces at, or near, Memphis and have them in readiness to join your column on this front in their Spring Campaign. Whether it will be better to have them march, meeting supplies sent up the Tennessee to East Port, or whether they should be brought round to the latter place by steamers can be determined hereafter. Add all the forces now under Dodge to the two Corps, or to one of the two Corps, you take into the field with you.

Forces will be transfered from the Chattanoog[a] and Nashville road to guard all the road now protected by your troops. If they are not sufficient enough will be taken from elswhere to leave all yours for the field.

I am ordered to Washington but as I am directed to keep up telegraphic communication with this command, I shall expect in the course of ten or twelve days, to return to it.

Place the Marine Brigade under the command of the Corps

Commander left on the Miss. river. Give directions that it be habitually used for the protection of leased plantations[1] and will not pass below Vicksburg nor above Greenville except by order of the Corps Commander, or higher authority.

> I am General, very respectfully your obt. svt.
> U. S. GRANT
> Maj. Gen. Comd.g

ALS, DLC-William T. Sherman. *O.R.*, I, xxxii, part 3, 19. On March 4, 1864, Lt. Col. Theodore S. Bowers issued Special Orders No. 59 sending Capt. Adam Badeau as bearer of dispatches from USG to Maj. Gen. William T. Sherman. Copy, DLC-USG, V, 38. See *O.R.*, I, xxxii, part 3, 19. On March 7, Badeau, Memphis, telegraphed to Bowers. "Shermans force is back safe at Vicksburg without important fighting. Sherman himself has gone to New Orleans some of his troops are at Memphis going home to veteranize. I learn this from Gen'l Buckner commanding at Memphis. He got it unofficial yesterday" Copy, DNA, RG 393, Military Div. of the Miss., Telegrams Received.

On March 10, Sherman, "on board Westmoreland near Memphis," wrote to USG. "Capt Badeau found me yesterday on board this Boat and delivered his despatches I had anticipated your orders by ordering Veatchs Division of Hurbuts corps at once to Dodge via the Tennessee River, and had sent A. J. Smith up Red River with 10.000 men to be absent not over 30 days when I designed Smiths Divn. of about 6000 men also to come round. We must furlough near 10000 men, and by the time they come back, the Red River trip will be made and I can safely reinforce my army near Huntsville with 15000 veterans. I send you by General Butterfield full details of all past events, and dispositions which will meet your approval. As to the negros, of course on arrival of Memphis I will cause your orders to be literally executed. A Clamor was raised by lessees by my with drawal of Osband (400) from Skipwiths, and Genl Hawkins Brigade (2100) from Goodrich's. I transferred them to Haines Bluff to operate up Yazoo, and the effect was instantaneous. Not a shot has been fired on the River since, I also designed to put a similar force at Harrisonburg to operate up the Washita which would secure the West Bank from Red River to Arkansas. Admiral Porter has already driven the Enemy from Harrisonburg so that project is immediately feasable. I assert that 3000 men at Haines Bluff and 3000 at Harrisonburg would more effectually protect the Plantation Lessees than 50000 men scattered along the shores of the Mississipi. You know the Geography so well that I need not demonstrate my assertion. I understand Genl Lorenzo Thomas has passed down to Vicksburg and am sorry I did not see him, but as soon as I reach Memphis today I will send orders below and show him how much easier it will be for us to protect the Mississipi by means of the Yazoo and Washita Rivers, than by merely guarding the Banks of the Mississipi. After awaiting to observe the effect of recent changes I will hasten round to Huntsville to prepare for the Big fight in Georgia. Fix the time for crossig the Tennessee & I will be there." ALS, *ibid.*, Letters Received. *O.R.*, I, xxxii, part 3, 50.

On March 2, 12:30 P.M., USG had telegraphed to Maj. Gen. Henry W. Halleck. "News from the South shows that Sherman divided Palkes [*Polk's*] force and followed south twenty five or thirty miles, then went East to Demapalis. Eight days ago, he was back at Meridian no doubt having [des]troyed Rail road connections with the State of Mississippi completely" Telegram received, DNA, RG 107, Telegrams Collected (Bound); copies, *ibid.*, RG 393, Military Div. of the Miss., Hd. Qrs. Correspondence; DLC-USG, V, 40, 94. *O.R.*, I, xxxii, part 3, 8.

On March 13, Brig. Gen. Hugh T. Reid, Cairo, telegraphed to Bowers. "Dispatch from Gen Grant to Gen. Sherman from Pittsburg yesterday forwarded to him last at Memphis where he now is." Copy, DNA, RG 393, Military Div. of the Miss., Telegrams Received. On March 14, Reid telegraphed to USG. "Your dispatch of today rcvd Dispatch from Pittsburg to Genl Sherman rcvd on the twelfth (12) and forwarded to him same day at Memphis where he now is he will be here in a day or two & will be notified as you direct" Telegram received, *ibid.*, RG 108, Letters Received; copies, *ibid.*, RG 393, Military Div. of the Miss., Telegrams Received; *ibid.*, Dept. of Ky., District of Columbus, Telegrams Sent. On March 16, in a telegram to "Comdg Officer," Reid quoted USG's telegram of March 14. "Notify Gen Sherman on his arrival to proceed to Cincinnati & await me if He reaches Cairo before saturday" Telegram received, DLC-William T. Sherman. On March 16, Reid telegraphed to USG. "Genl Sherman arrived here at three this moning and left immedeatly on the train for Louisville to which place I have sent to him your dispatch, from Louisville as I did not see him." Copy, DNA, RG 393, Dept. of Ky., District of Columbus, Telegrams Sent.

1. On Feb. 16, 3:30 P.M., Halleck telegraphed to USG. "It is deemed important by the Government that leased plantations on the Mississippi river recieve due protection and the Secty of War desires that Genl Elliot's Marine brigade be assigned to that service. It is understood that it has been so assigned temporarily by Genl Sherman." ALS (telegram sent), *ibid.*, RG 107, Telegrams Collected (Bound); copies, *ibid.*, RG 94, Vol. Service Div., Letters Received, E27 (VS) 1863; *ibid.*, RG 393, Military Div. of the Miss., Hd. Qrs. Correspondence; DLC-USG, V, 40, 94. *O.R.*, I, xxxii, part 2, 407. See *ibid.*, p. 488.

To Maj. Gen. George H. Thomas

Nashville March 4th 1864

MAJ GENERAL G. H THOMAS
CHATTANOOGA

You will have to watch the movements of the enemy closely in front. Should Longstreet join Johnston they will likely attack your advance. At present most of Longstreets force is up Holston Valley I have directed Schofield to keep you advised of the movements of the enemy.

U S GRANT
Major General

Telegram, copies, DLC-USG, V, 34, 35; DNA, RG 393, Military Div. of the Miss., Letters Sent; (marked 10:00 A.M.) *ibid.*, Dept. of the Cumberland, Telegrams Received. Printed as sent at 10:00 A.M. in *O.R.*, I, xxxii, part 3, 17. On March 4, 1864, 12:00 P.M., Maj. Gen. George H. Thomas telegraphed to USG. "Your two dispatches of this date are just recd. The information I get from the front to day is that Johnston's Infy. about 30.000. strong still remains in Dalton, and as yet no changes have been made in his transportation—that is, his transportation being sent to the rear before the reconnoissance from this Post was made, has not returned to Dalton. Deserters say that it was understood in the army that they would fall back and that the movements had already commenced, but the troops were all ordered back, Johnston supposing we had advanced against Dalton in full force—. Not having brought back his transportation makes me believe he will fall back yet, but I am nevertheless taking every precaution to get the earliest information should he advance against me. None of Longstreet's troops have joined him as yet." Copies, DNA, RG 393, Dept. of the Cumberland, Telegrams Sent; *ibid.*, Military Div. of the Miss., Telegrams Received. *O.R.*, I, xxxii, part 3, 17–18.

On March 5, Lt. Col. Theodore S. Bowers, Nashville, telegraphed this text, except for the first sentence, to USG at Louisville. Also telegraphed to USG by Bowers was a telegram of March 4 from Brig. Gen. Grenville M. Dodge, Athens, Ala., to USG. "I have been ready to cross the river for a week, but the rail road smashing up, prevents me from getting boats and bridge stuff. I will try and get over with what boats I have got in a day or two. The enemys pickets the river strongly from Florence to Trianna and boats going over sloals will be in great danger unless I could accompany them from South Side with troops. The river will have to raise at least ten feet yet before boats can get over shoals. Inform me about what time boats will reach Florence so I may be there." Copy, DNA, RG 393, Military Div. of the Miss., Letters Sent. On March 6, USG, Louisville, telegraphed to Bowers. "Condense information from the front so as to give me only important matter during my absence   Give the walker House up to Owner   The Officers now there can make arrangements with Mr Walker to stay with him or not as they like"   Telegram received (month omitted), *ibid.*, Dept. of the Tenn., Telegrams Received; copy, *ibid.*, Military Div. of the Miss., Telegrams Received.

On March 5, Thomas telegraphed to Brig. Gen. John A. Rawlins. "The enemy advanced a Brigade of Cavalry early this morning on Col. Harrison's pickets 39th Ind. Mtd. Infy., at Wood's gap in Taylor's Ridge, and drove them back towards Lee &. Gordon's Mills. The enemy then fell back through Gordon's gap, as reported by General Baird from Ringgold. A scout just from Dalton reports Johnston has been reenforced by ten thousand men from South Carolina, and by Roddy, and he believes he contemplates a forward movement." Copies, *ibid.*; (entered as sent March 6, "12. M.") *ibid.*, Dept. of the Cumberland, Telegrams Sent. Dated March 5 in *O.R.*, I, xxxii, part 3, 21–22.

To Brig. Gen. Grenville M. Dodge

Nashville March 4th 1864.

Brig General G M Dodge
Pulaski Tenn.

The Tennessee is now up so that an attempt will be made to get steamers above Muscle Shoals. Should they succeed in getting up be prepared to convoy them. One steamer can be retained for your purposes, should they get above.

U S Grant
Major General

Telegram, copies, DLC-USG, V, 34, 35; DNA, RG 393, Military Div. of the Miss., Letters Sent. *O.R.*, I, xxxii, part 3, 18. On March 4, 1864, USG telegraphed to Rear Admiral David D. Porter, Mound City, Ill. "Captain Edwards reports the Tennessee up and rising so rapidly that he thinks boats may now be taken over Muscle Shoals" Copies, DLC-USG, V, 34, 35; DNA, RG 393, Military Div. of the Miss., Letters Sent. On the same day, USG telegraphed to Brig. Gen. Robert Allen, Louisville. "The Tennessee is high and rising. I have telegraphed Admiral Porter to try and run Muscle Shoals with the boats for the upper river" Copies, *ibid.* *O.R.*, I, xxxii, part 3, 14.

On March 6, Brig. Gen. Grenville M. Dodge, Athens, Ala., telegraphed to Brig. Gen. John A. Rawlins. "The Tennessee is rising rapidly a Regt. of mounted Infy. went to Florence to-day to come up with boats I think by tomorrow or next day boats can get over shoals troops are passing through Montgomery daily going to Atlanta" Copy, DNA, RG 393, Military Div. of the Miss., Telegrams Received. *O.R.*, I, xxxii, part 3, 30.

On March 11, Dodge, Pulaski, Tenn., telegraphed to Lt. Col. Theodore S. Bowers. "Is there any necessity keeping troops at Florence any longer waiting for boats to go up over the Shoals? The River is now so low it will be impossible for them to get over until a heavy rise comes" Copies, DNA, RG 393, 16th Army Corps, Left Wing, Telegrams Sent; *ibid.*, Military Div. of the Miss., Telegrams Received.

On March 8, Dodge, Decatur, Ala., telegraphed to Rawlins. "We occupied this place at daylight and we hold it" Copy, *ibid.* *O.R.*, I, xxxii, part 3, 38. On March 11, Dodge telegraphed to Bowers. "After taking Decatur I pushed my forces out under Lt: Co'l. Phillips he captured Courtland driving the enemy out and followed them up crossing the the mountains captured Moulton. we took a number of Prisoners a large amount of stores and a large quantity of Artillery and rifle amunition also one hundred sacks of Salt Stock &c" Copy, DNA, RG 393, Military Div. of the Miss., Telegrams Received; *ibid.*, 16th Army Corps, Left Wing, Telegrams Sent. *O.R.*, I, xxxii, part 1, 492. On the same day, Bowers telegraphed the substance of this message to USG. Telegram received, DNA, RG 107, Telegrams Collected (Bound).

Speech

[*March 9, 1864*]

I accept the commission with gratitude for the high honor con-
fered.

With the aid of the noble armies that have fought on so many
fields for our common country, it will be my earnest endeavor not
to disappoint your expectations. I feel the full weight of the responsibilities now devolving on me and know that if they are met
it will be due to those armies, and above all to the favor of that
Providence which leads both Nations and men.

AD, DLC-USG, I, C. USG spoke in response to President Abraham Lincoln.
"The nation's appreciation of what you have done, and its reliance upon you for
what remains to do, in the existing great struggle, are now presented with this
commission, constituting you Lieutenant General in the Army of the United
States. With this high honor devolves upon you also, a corresponding responsibility. As the country herein trusts you, so, under God, it will sustain you. I
scarcely need to add that with what I here speak for the nation goes my own
hearty personal concurrence." AD, USG 3. Lincoln, *Works*, VII, 234.

On March 10, 1864, Lincoln wrote to USG. "Under the authority of the act
of Congress to revive the grade of Lieutenant General in the United States Army,
approved February 29th 1864, Lieutenant General Ulysses S. Grant, U. S. Army,
is assigned to the command of the armies of the United States." LS, USG 3. *O.R.*,
III, iv, 160–61. On the same day, 1:40 P.M., Secretary of War Edwin M. Stanton
telegraphed to USG. "Pursuant to the authority of the Act of Congress approved
February 29th 1864, the President, by Executive order of this date, has assigned
to you the command of the Armies of the United States." ALS (telegram sent),
DNA, RG 107, Telegrams Collected (Bound). *O.R.*, I, xxxiii, 663.

On March 9, Maj. Gen. Henry W. Halleck wrote to Stanton, sending a
copy to USG. "Under the provisions of the Act of April 4th 1862, which authorizes the President to assign to command officers of *the same grade*, without regard to *seniority* of *rank*, the undersigned, a Major General, was assigned, in
July 1862, to the command of the land forces of the United States. Since that
time the higher grade of Lieutenant General has been created, and the distinguished officer promoted to that rank has received his commission and reported
for duty. I, therefore, respectfully request that orders be issued placing him in
command of the Army and relieving me from that duty. In making this request
I am influanced solely by a desire to conform to the provisions of the law, which,
in my opinion, impose upon the Lieutenant General the duties and responsibilities
of General in Chief of the Army" LS, DNA, RG 108, Letters Received. *O.R.*,
III, iv, 160. On March 12, Col. Edward D. Townsend issued AGO General
Orders No. 98 relieving Halleck as gen. in chief and assigning him as chief of
staff, announcing USG's assignment to command the armies of the U.S., and
placing Maj. Gen. William T. Sherman in command of the Military Div. of the
Miss. and Maj. Gen. James B. McPherson in command of the Dept. and Army of

the Tenn. *Ibid.*, I, xxxii, part 3, 58; *ibid.*, III, iv, 172; (incomplete) *ibid.*, I, xxxiii, 669. See telegram to Maj. Gen. John M. Schofield, March 17, 1864.

On March 9, M. J. McCrickett, asst. superintendent, military railroads, telegraphed to USG. "Your dispatch just received. A special car will be attached to the nine forty five (9.45) A M train as you direct. Can send you by special train at that time if you desire it. Please answer tonight." Telegram received (press), DNA, RG 107, Telegrams Collected (Bound). On March 10, USG wrote to Stanton. "I start in the 9.45 a m train for the Army of the Potomac. Will return to-morrow evening." ALS, *ibid.*, RG 200, Stanton Papers.

Also on Thursday, March 10, Lincoln telegraphed to USG. "Mrs. L. invites yourself and Gen. Meade to dine with us Saturday evening—Please notify him, and answer whether you can be with us at that time." ALS (telegram sent), *ibid.*, RG 107, Telegrams Collected (Bound). Lincoln, *Works*, VII, 235. On the same day, USG telegraphed to Lincoln. "Genl Meade and Myself accept your kind invitation to dine with Mrs Lincoln on saturday." Telegram received, DLC-Robert T. Lincoln; DNA, RG 107, Telegrams Collected (Bound). USG, however, later decided to return west and missed the dinner. *New-York Tribune*, March 14, 1864. On March 8, forty-eight prominent citizens of New York City, headed by William B. Astor, wrote to USG inviting him to be their guest "at some period during your stay at the East." DS, USG 3. USG answered the letter, probably on March 11. "In reply Gen. Grant says, while highly appreciating the kind tender of the hospitalities of the city, he will not be able to accept of them. 'My duties,' he adds, 'call me immediately to the West, for which I start by the most expeditious route this evening. For that part of your letter complimentary to myself, accept my thanks and receive my assurance that all in my power will be done that your expectations may be realized. The men and money you patriotically offer for the war are all that will be required to insure its early termination in the reëstablishment of the whole Union, stronger than it has ever been.' " *New-York Tribune*, March 14, 1864.

To Maj. Gen. John M. Schofield

Washington, March 10th 1864.

MAJ. GEN. J M. SCHOFIELD COMDG. DEPT. OF OHIO
KNOXVILLE, TENNESSEE

Prepare your team mules for pack animals so that you can, when the roads get sufficiently good, drive the enemy out of East Tennessee. It will not be necessary to bring your animals to the front, where feed is hard to procure, until you know, you want them.

The troops of which I wrote you, will be new Indiana troops.

U S GRANT
Lieut. Gen.

Telegram received, DNA, RG 107, Telegrams Collected (Unbound); copies, *ibid.*, RG 108, Letters Sent; DLC-USG, V, 45, 59. *O.R.*, I, xxxii, part 3, 47.

On March 9, 1864, Lt. Col. Theodore S. Bowers had telegraphed to Maj. Gen. John M. Schofield. "Maj Genl U. S Grant direct by telegraph that you dismount your mounted infantry armed with Cavalry arms as fast as their horses and arms are required for the Purpose of equiping Cavalry troops for service. This as rendered necessary from the impossibility of procuring horses and arms for the Cavalry arm of the service, and necessity of getting it ready for service without delay" Telegram received, DNA, RG 393, Dept. of the Ohio, Telegrams Received. On the same day, Bowers telegraphed the same message to Maj. Gen. William T. Sherman and to Maj. Gen. George H. Thomas. Telegram received (addressed to Sherman), *ibid.*, RG 94, War Records Office, Dept. of the Tenn. *O.R.*, I, xxxii, part 3, 46. See *ibid.*, p. 53.

To Henry Wilson

QMrGenls office
Washington March 11th/64

HONL HENRY WILSON
U. S. SENATE
CHAIRMAN OF THE MILITARY COMMITTEE

The Quartermasters Department suffers for want of a more perfect organization in the field and at the Depots; some organization which will confer upon officers rank commensurate with the importance and extent of their duties is greatly needed.

Good officers who have gained experience, labored much and successfully for the public service after waiting in expectation that congress would provide the way to recognize such service, are resigning in disappointment.

I understand that the Quartersmaster General has prepared a bill providing a remedy by a larger organization, I commend it to your attention and hope that it will become a law.

Much depends upon keeping up the efficiency of this corps, whose labors are heavier, and whose rewards have been lighter, than those of their comrades in others Departments.

With great respect
your obt. svt.
U. S. GRANT
Lt. Gen. U S A.

LS, James S. Schoff, New York, N. Y. Copies and related documents indicating lobbying by Brig. Gen. Montgomery C. Meigs are in the Robert C. Schenck Papers, OFH.

To Edwin M. Stanton

From Pittsburgh, *M.*
Dated, March 12 *1864.*

HON E. M. STANTON.

Sherman has sent ten thousand (10000) men under A. J. Smith up Red River to co-operate with Banks on Schrivport. Banks commands in person. Shermans expedition was eminently successful I will be in Nashville on Tuesday.[1]

U. S. GRANT.
Lt Genl

Telegram received, DNA, RG 107, Telegrams Collected (Bound); copies, *ibid.*, RG 108, Letters Sent; *ibid.*, RG 393, Military Div. of the Miss., Hd. Qrs. Correspondence; DLC-USG, V, 40, 45, 59, 94; DLC-Andrew Johnson. *O.R.*, I, xxxii, part 3, 58.

1. March 15, 1864.

To Edwin M. Stanton

Nashville Tenn
Mch 14 1864 8 30 P M

HON. EDWIN M STANTON
SECY OF WAR

Genls Curtis and Blunt[1] desire a transfer of a portion of Steele's force and territory to the Department of Kansas,
    I think such a change decidedly undesirable

U S GRANT
Lt Genl

Telegram received, DNA, RG 107, Telegrams Collected (Bound); copies, *ibid.*, RG 108, Letters Sent; *ibid.*, RG 393, Military Div. of the Miss., Hd. Qrs. Correspondence; DLC-USG, V, 40, 45, 59, 94. *O.R.*, I, xxxiv, part 2, 602. On March 18, 1864, 3:30 P.M., Secretary of War Edwin M. Stanton telegraphed to USG. "This Department will not transfer troops from General Steeles Command unless at your request." ALS (telegram sent), DNA, RG 107, Telegrams Collected (Bound).

On March 11, Brig. Gen. John M. Thayer, Fort Smith, Ark., telegraphed to USG. "Gen'ls Curtis & Blunt are making an effort to have the Western tier of Counties of Arkansas set off to the Dept. of Kansas. If they should succeed it would take away all the old troops of the Country which are now in Dept. of Ark. If they can't get the tier of counties they will try to get the tier of Counties they will try to get a part of the troops. I would respectfully ask that you would advise the War Dept. against any such changes. Please excuse me for sending dispatch to you directly" Copy, *ibid.*, RG 393, Military Div. of the Miss., Telegrams Received. *O.R.*, I, xxxiv, part 2, 566. See *ibid.*, pp. 576, 617–18, 621, 631–32, 751.

1. James G. Blunt, born in Maine in 1826, graduated from Starling Medical College, Columbus, Ohio, in 1849, then practiced medicine in Ohio and Kan. Territory, where he became involved in antislavery activity as an ally of John Brown. Entering the Civil War as lt. col., 3rd Kan., Blunt was appointed brig. gen. as of April 8, 1862, and promoted to maj. gen. as of Nov. 29. In March, 1864, he commanded the District of the Frontier.

To Maj. Gen. Henry W. Halleck

Nashville Tenn
March 14 1864 8 P M

MAJ GEN H W HALLECK

All is quiet on this front. Schofield telegraphs from Morristown that he is running cars to that place—The enemy occupy Bulls Gap in some force   They have certainly sent a division of Cavalry into Georgia and a division of Infantry into Virginia

U S GRANT
Lt Genl

Telegram received, DNA, RG 107, Telegrams Collected (Bound); copies, *ibid.*, RG 108, Letters Sent; *ibid.*, RG 393, Military Div. of the Miss., Hd. Qrs. Correspondence; DLC-USG, V, 40, 45, 59, 94; DLC-John M. Schofield. *O.R.*, I, xxxii, part 3, 66. On March 12, 1864, Maj. Gen. John M. Schofield, Morristown, Tenn., telegraphed to Maj. Gen. George H. Thomas and to Brig. Gen. John A. Rawlins. "I have the bridge at Strawberry Plains completed & the cars running to this place   My troops are much improved in condition & effective strength. The enemy occupies Bull's Gap & Lick Creek in some force. Longstreet has certainly sent a Division of Cavalry to Georgia & some Infantry to Virginia. How

much, I do not positively know. I do not believe his force is much if at all su-
perior to mine. I expect to know soon." Copies, DLC-John M. Schofield; DNA,
RG 393, Military Div. of the Miss., Telegrams Received. *O.R.*, I, xxxii, part 3,
58–59. On March 19, 11:00 A.M., Maj. Gen. Henry W. Halleck telegraphed to
USG. "From all information recieved, it is thought that Longstreet is now with
Lee, and that some movement will soon be made." ALS (telegram sent), DNA,
RG 107, Telegrams Collected (Bound); telegram received, *ibid.*; *ibid.*, RG 108,
Letters Received. *O.R.*, I, xxxiii, 699. See *ibid.*, pp. 688–89.

To Maj. Gen. Nathaniel P. Banks

Head Quarters of the Army
In the Field, Nashville Ten.
March 15th 1864

MAJ. GEN. N. P. BANKS,
COMD.G DEPT. OF THE GULF,
GENERAL,

Enclosed herewith I send you copy of Gen. Orders No (1)
assuming command of the Armies of the United States.[1] You will
see from the order it is my intention to establish Head Quarters,
for the present, with the "Army of the Potomac."

I have not yet fully determined upon a plan of campaign for
this Spring but will do so before the return of our Veteran troops
to the field. It will however be my desire to have all parts of the
Army, or rather all the Armies, act as much in concert as possible.
For this reason I now write you.   I regard the success of your present move as of great importance in reducing the number of troops
necessary for protecting the navigation of the Mississippi River.
It is also important that Schrievesport should be taken as soon as
possible. This done send Brig. Gen. A. J. Smith, with his command, back to Memphis as soon as possible[.] This force will be
necessary for movemen[ts] East of the Mississippi. Should you
find that the taking of Schrievesport will occupy ten to fifteen days
more time than Gen. Sherman gave his troops to be absent from
their command you will send them back at the time specified in

~~Sherman's~~ his note of the   of March,[2] even if it leads to the abandonment of the main object of your expedition. Should your expediti[on] prove successful, hold Schrievesport, and the Red River, with such force as you may deem necessary, and return the balance of your troops to the neighborhood of New Orleans.

I would not, at present, advise the abandonment of any portion of territory now held, West of the Mississippi, but commence no move for the further acquisition of territory, unless it be to make that now ours ~~earlyer~~ more easily held. This of course is not intended to restrain you from making any disposition of your troops, or going anywhere, to meet and fight the enemy wherever he may be in force. I look upon the conquering of the organized armies of the enemy as being of vastly more importance than the mere acquisition of their territory. It may be a part of the plan for the Spring campaign to move against Mobile. It certainly will be if troops enough can be obtained to make it without embarassing other movements. In this case New Orleans will be the point of departure for such an expedition.

There is one thing General I would urge, and do not know but you have already adopted, and that is of supplying your Army, as far as possible, from the country occupied. Mules, horses, forage and provisions can be paid for, where taken from persons who have taken the Amnesty oath prescribed by the President, if the oath be taken before the loss of property, with both economy and convenience.

I have directed Gen. Steele to make a real move, as suggested by you, instead of a demonstration as he thought advisable.

> I am Gen. very respectfully
> your obt. svt.
> U. S. GRANT
> Lt. Gen. Com

ALS, DLC-Nathaniel P. Banks. *O.R.*, I, xxxiv, part 2, 610–11; (incomplete) *ibid.*, I, xxxiv, part 1, 203.

1. See telegram to Maj. Gen. John M. Schofield, March 17, 1864.
2. March 4. *O.R.*, I, xxxiv, part 2, 494.

To Maj. Gen. John M. Schofield

Nashville March 15, 11.30 A. M '64

MAJOR GENERAL J. M SCHOFIELD
KNOXVILLE TENN

Six new regiments of infantry are ready to be sent to you as soon as transportation can be furnished.[1] Will you have them in Tennessee or in Kentucky and order troops forward from the latter State? There are also five regiments of Cavalry, all ready, except mounting, which you can have if you require them.

Send the 9th Corps without its transportation.[2]

U S GRANT
Lieut General

Telegram, copies, DLC-USG, V, 34, 35, 45, 59; DNA, RG 108, Letters Sent; *ibid.*, RG 393, Military Div. of the Miss., Letters Sent. *O.R.*, I, xxxii, part 3, 76. On March 15, 1864, Maj. Gen. John M. Schofield, Morristown, Tenn., telegraphed to USG at 7:00 P.M. and 8:00 P.M. "The Ninth Corps will be sent at once as ordered—I hope troops will be sent me with as little delay as practicable   The enemy is still in my immediate front in superior force"   "I want the six infantry regiments here in Tennessee   I do not want the Cavalry now because I can not forage it but would like to have it ordered to report to Brig Genl Sturgis at Mount Sterling Kentucky   are the regiments new or old"   Telegrams received, DNA, RG 108, Letters Received; copies (the second misdated March 11), *ibid.*, RG 393, Military Div. of the Miss., Telegrams Received; DLC-John M. Schofield. *O.R.*, I, lii, part 1, 533.

On March 17, Schofield telegraphed to USG. "The Ninth (9) Corps having been sent away I propose to furlough the remaining Veterans of Woods Division   The number of men will be not more than fifteen hundred (1500)   Please inform me whether you approve this proposition"   Telegram received, DNA, RG 108, Letters Received; copy, DLC-John M. Schofield. On the same day, USG telegraphed to Schofield. "I approve of your furloughing veteran Volunteers as fast as they can be spared." Copies, DLC-USG, V, 34, 35; DNA, RG 393, Military Div. of the Miss., Letters Sent; *ibid.*, Dept. of the Ohio, Telegrams Received.

1. On March 14, USG telegraphed to Governor Oliver P. Morton of Ind. "Can the new Indiana regiments under Gen. Hovey be forwarded soon. I am making changes in location of troops in anticipation of their early arrival"   Copy, Morton Papers, In. On March 15, Morton telegraphed to USG. "I transferred six Regiments of Infantry to Gen Hovey yesterday which will leave here the moment transportation can be furnished   I have five regiments of cavalry waiting for horses." Copy, *ibid.*; DNA, RG 393, Military Div. of the Miss., Telegrams Received. *O.R.*, I, xxxii, part 3, 79. On March 17, USG telegraphed to Morton. "When the Indiana troops are ready, please send them to Louisville. The cavalry

I will send to Mt Sterling Ky, and the Infantry to Knoxville Tenn, via Chattanooga." Copies, DLC-USG, V, 34, 35, 45, 59; DNA, RG 108, Letters Sent; *ibid.*, RG 393, Military Div. of the Miss., Letters Sent; Morton Papers, In.

2. On March 14, 8:30 P.M., USG telegraphed to Schofield. "Order the 9th Army Corps to Annapolis Md as soon as possible. This will necessarily make your operations defensive, until you can have forces forwarded to you. I have expected 10 000 Indiana troops before this which will go to your Department when they do arrive." Copies, DLC-USG, V, 34, 35, 45, 59; DNA, RG 108, Letters Sent; *ibid.*, RG 393, Military Div. of the Miss., Letters Sent. *O.R.*, I, xxxii, part 3, 68. On the same day, USG telegraphed to Maj. Gen. Ambrose E. Burnside. "I have ordered the Ninth Corps from Knoxville to Annapolis and requested the Secretary of War to direct the veterans to rendezvous at that place. Please send this order to all regiments of the corps about to return to the field." *Ibid.*, p. 67. On the same day, Burnside, New York City, telegraphed to USG. "The Eighth 8 Regt Mich Vols belonging to the Ninth 9 Corps has just started from Furlough for East Tenn   would it not be well to stop it if the corps is to concentrate at Annopolis   all of my new troops are concentrating there as they are formed" Telegram received, DNA, RG 108, Letters Received; copy, *ibid.*, RG 393, Military Div. of the Miss., Telegrams Received. Also on March 14, 8:30 P.M., USG telegraphed to Maj. Gen. Henry W. Halleck. "I will order what remains in the field of the Ninth Corps to Annapolis Md as soon as they can go— Please direct the veterans of that Corps to assemble at the expiration of their leave at the same place—" Telegram received, *ibid.*, RG 107, Telegrams Collected (Bound); copies, *ibid.*, RG 94, Vol. Service Div., Letters Received, A189 (VS) 1864; *ibid.*, RG 108, Letters Sent; *ibid.*, RG 393, Military Div. of the Miss., Hd. Qrs. Correspondence; DLC-USG, V, 40, 45, 59, 94. *O.R.*, I, xxxii, part 3, 67.

On March 15, Burnside telegraphed to USG. "Would it not be will for Benjamin's Batty to leave their twenty pounder parrotts in Knoxville   the co can be entirely refilled at Anappolis   in fact the guns horses & harness of all the batteries can be left if necessary & be supplied at annapolis—" Telegram received, DNA, RG 108, Letters Received; copies, *ibid.*, RG 393, Military Div. of the Miss., Telegrams Received; *ibid.*, 9th Army Corps, Telegrams Sent. On the same day, USG telegraphed to Burnside. "Leave the 20 pdr Parrotts of Benjamins Battery at Knoxville and the horses and harness of the same. Also the horses and harness of all the other Batteries belonging to the 9th Corps. They can be replaced at Annapolis" Copies, DLC-USG, V, 34, 35, (undated) 45, 59; DNA, RG 108, Letters Sent; *ibid.*, RG 393, Military Div. of the Miss., Letters Sent. *O.R.*, I, xxxii, part 3, 74. Also on March 15, Burnside telegraphed to USG. "If possible will you please allow Genl. Parke to report to me here at once, and let the officer next in command bring on the corps—He would be of much assistance here." Copy, DNA, RG 393, 9th Army Corps, Telegrams Sent. On March 16, USG wrote to Burnside. "General Parke is ordered to report to you in person immediately." *O.R.*, I, xxxii, part 3, 80; *ibid.*, I, xxxiii, 685.

On March 26, 2:30 P.M., Halleck telegraphed to USG. "There are many individuals of regts belonging to 9th Army Corps still in the west, now on furlough in the different States. If those regts are to be brought to Annapolis, would it not be well to order all such persons to rendezvous at Annapolis?" ALS (telegram sent), DNA, RG 107, Telegrams Collected (Bound); telegram received, *ibid.*; *ibid.*, RG 108, Letters Received. On the same day, USG telegraphed to Col. Edward D. Townsend. "Publish an order directing all furloughed men of the ninth (9) Army Corps at the expiration of their furloughs to rendezvous at Annapolis Md" Telegram received, *ibid.*, RG 107, Telegrams Collected (Bound); *ibid.*, RG 94, Letters Received, 227A 1864. On March 27, Townsend telegraphed to USG. "Your cipher despatch of five p m yesterday received. The order is sent to the associated press." ALS (telegram sent), *ibid.*, RG 107, Telegrams Collected (Unbound); copy, *ibid.*, RG 94, Letters Sent. See *O.R.*, I, xxxiii, 752.

On March 26, USG telegraphed to Halleck. "Please order Maj. Gen. C. C. Washburn to the command at Annapolis until permanently assigned." ALS (telegram sent), DNA, RG 107, Telegrams Collected (Unbound); telegram received, *ibid.*; *ibid.*, RG 94, Letters Received, 266A 1864. See *O.R.*, I, xxxiii, 753.

To Maj. Gen. Frederick Steele

By Telegraph from Nashville Tenn
Mch 15th 1864
5.30 P M—

To—MAJ GEN STEELE,

Move your force in full co-operation with Genl N. P. Banks attack on Shreveport, a mere demonstration will not be sufficient— Now that a larger force has gone up Red River it is necessary that Shreveport and the Red River should come into our possession

U. S. GRANT
Lieut Gen'l

Telegram received, DNA, RG 94, War Records Office, Dept. of Ark.; copies, *ibid.*, RG 108, Letters Sent; *ibid.*, RG 393, Dept. of Mo., Telegrams Sent; *ibid.*, Military Div. of the Miss., Letters Sent; DLC-USG, V, 34, 35, 45, 59. *O.R.*, I, xxxiv, part 2, 616. On March 15, 1864, 10:30 A.M., Maj. Gen. Henry W. Halleck telegraphed to USG. "A despatch just recieved from Genl. Banks dated March 6th. He expects to effect a junction with Sherman's forces on Red River by the 17th. He desires that positive orders be sent to Genl Steele to move in conjunction with them for Red River, with all his available force. Sherman and Banks are of opinion that Steele can do much more than make a mere demonstration, as he last proposed. A telegram from you might decide him. Veterans of 9th Corps ordered to Annapolis." ALS (telegram sent), DNA, RG 107, Telegrams Collected (Bound); telegram received, *ibid.*, RG 108, Letters Received. *O.R.*, I, xxxiv, part 2, 609–10.

On March 10, Maj. Gen. Frederick Steele, Little Rock, wrote to USG. "I intended to have written you a letter to-day to send by your aide, but I unexpectedly received dispatches from Sherman and Banks in regard to the expedition against Shreveport, which I have been answering. They are both mistaken in regard to the strength of my command and also in regard to the situation of affairs in my department. I will send you copies of my letters to Banks on the subject. I have been intending to write you for a long time, but you do not appear to have any local habitation. The forces under Banks will make Kirby Smith run without a battle. From what I can learn through people returning to their homes within my lines Kirby and all his friends are prepared to leave for parts unknown. I shall move by way of Washington with all my available force to co-operate with Banks. I cannot spare from the line of the Arkansas more than about 7,000 of all arms. Holmes' command will break up and attempt raids in my rear." *Ibid.*, pp. 546–47. On March 12, 3:00 P.M., Steele telegraphed to USG. "General Banks with Seventeen thousand troops and ten thousand 10,000 of Gen'l Sherman will be at Alexandria on the seventeenth 17th inst. This is more than, or equal for everything Kirby Smith can bring against him   By holding the line of the Arkansas Secure I can Soon free this state from armed rebels. General Sherman insists upon my moving upon Shreveport to cooperate with the above mentioned force with all my effective force. I have prepared to do so against my own judgment and that of the best people here. The roads are most if not quite impracticable   The Country is destitute of provisions on the route, we Should be obliged to take   I made proposition to Genl Banks to threaten the enemy's flank & rear with all my Cavalry, go to make a feint with infantry on the Yorktown road. I yielded to Genl Sherman & Genl Blunt So far as this plea is concerned. Genl Blunt wished me to move by Monroe to Red River. S͟t͟ Genl. Sherman wants me to go by Camden & Overton to Shreveport. The latter is impracticable and the frontier plan would expose the line of the Arkansas & Missouri to Cavalry raids. Holmes has a large mounted force. I agreed to move by Arcadelphia or Hot Springs, and Yorktown to Shreveport. I can move with about seven thousand (7000) including the frontier. Our Scouting parties frequently have Skirmishes with detached parties all over the state and if they Should form on my rear in considerable force, I Should be obliged to fall back to Save my depots &c. Please give me your opinion immediately as I shall march tomorrow or next day. Genl Curtis & Genl Blunt are trying to have the frontier Counties of Arkansas transferred to the Depot of Kansas. The people of Arkansas protest against it"   Telegram received, DNA, RG 108, Letters Received; copy, *ibid.*, RG 393, Military Div. of the Miss., Telegrams Received. Printed as addressed to Halleck in *O.R.*, I, xxxiv, part 2, 576. On March 14, 2:00 A.M., USG telegraphed to Steele. "Maj Gen W. S. Sherman is now commander of the Military Division of the Mississippi   you will therefore treat his request in regard to your cooperation with Maj Genl N P Banks accordingly"   Telegram received, DNA, RG 94, War Records Office, Dept. of Ark.; copies, *ibid.*, RG 108, Letters Sent; *ibid.*, RG 393, Military Div. of the Miss., Letters Sent; DLC-USG, V, 34, 35, 45, 59. *O.R.*, I, xxxiv, part 2, 603.

On March 13, 12:30 P.M., Halleck telegraphed to USG. "Genl Steele telegraphs that Banks with Seventeen thousand & Sherman with ten thousand move from Alexandria on Schreveport, & wish him to cooperate. He says he can go with seven thousand effective, but objects to the movement on account of bad roads & guerrillas, and prefers to remain on the defensive line of the Arkansas. I have replied that he should cooperate with Banks & Sherman unless you direct otherwise. His objections on account of guerrillas threatening his rear will apply equally to an advance at any time into the enemy's country." ALS (telegram sent), DNA, RG 107, Telegrams Collected (Bound); telegram received, *ibid.*, RG 108, Letters Received. *O.R.*, I, xxxiv, part 2, 581–82. On March 14, 8:00 P.M., USG telegraphed to Halleck. "I received dispatch from Gen Steele at Louisville identical with the one you received, and replied to it substantially the same" Telegram received, DNA, RG 107, Telegrams Collected (Bound); copies, *ibid.*, RG 108, Letters Sent; *ibid.*, RG 393, Military Div. of the Miss., Letters Sent; DLC-USG, V, 34, 35, 45, 59. *O.R.*, I, xxxiv, part 2, 602.

Also on March 14, USG wrote to Steele introducing T. Dean, "a loyal Citizen of Cincinnati . . . who goes into your Dept. on some business of his own . . . I speak for him such facilities as will enable him to transact all legitimate business." C. A. Stonehill, Inc., Thirteenth Cooperative Catalogue . . . [1970], p. 33.

On March 18, Steele twice telegraphed to USG, the second time at 6:00 P.M. "I respectfully request that the following veterans be ordered to return as soon as possible for the defence of the line of the Arkansas viz: 12th Mich Infantry, 10th Illinois Cavalry 3d Iowa Cavalry, 9 Companies 54th Illinois Infantry, 25th Ohio Battery, 3d Iowa Battery, Battery K 1st Missouri Light Arty— 2 Companies 62d Illinois Infantry, 2 Companies 9th Wisconsin Infantry 4 Companies 3d Minnesota Infantry, 2 Compani[es] 18th Illinois Infantry and one Company 43d Illinois Infantry The 77th Ohio Infantry has just returned Pine Bluff is now threatened by a Considerable force fifteen hundred of which is Dockerys Brigade of Vicksburg and Port Hudson parolled prisoners" ALS (telegram sent), DNA, RG 107, Telegrams Collected (Unbound); copy, *ibid.*, RG 393, Military Div. of the Miss., Letters Received. *O.R.*, I, xxxiv, part 2, 646. "Your telegram of the 15th received It is probable that the Enemy will make a stand at Alexandria, I propose to Concentrate my forces at Archadelphia about ten thousand strong—Move from there on Camden and open Communication back to Pine Bluff, and then move on Shreveport in time to Co-operate with Banks at that point My Cavalry have not had a remount for a year Many of them are dismounted, and most of the horses on hand are in poor Condition, the same is the Case with most of the batteries Transportation in same Condition, I shall move as stated and do the best I possibly Can, Please send Copy of this to Sherman" ALS (telegram sent), DNA, RG 107, Telegrams Collected (Unbound); telegram received, DLC-William T. Sherman. Incomplete in *O.R.*, I, xxxiv, part 2, 646.

To Brig. Gen. Robert S. Granger

Head Quarters of the Army
In the Field, Nashville March 15th/64

BRIG. GEN. R. S. GRANGER,
COMD.G U. S. FORCES,
NASHVILLE TEN.
GEN.

An inspection of the "Home for Refugees" ordered by me shew the inmates to be in a suffering condition and subjected to all Kinds of impositions from heartless soldiers and Government employees.

An extension of premisis and the guardianship of humane and honest persons seems to be required for their relief. I would suggest that either more buildings, or soldiers Barracks, be given for their use, and that a permanent guard, under an officer selected for his intelligence and efficiency be detailed.

I enclose with this the report of Col. Duff, who made the inspection, refered to, Any thing you may desire to do for the benefit of these people I will approve of.

> Very respectfully
> your obt. svt.
> U. S. GRANT
> Lt. Gen. U. S. A. Com

ALS, PHi. Robert S. Granger of Ohio, USMA 1838, served in the Mexican War, was captured by C.S.A. forces in Tex. on April 27, 1861, and paroled (not to serve within C.S.A. lines through Aug., 1862), and promoted to maj., 5th Inf., as of Sept. 9, 1861. Appointed brig. gen. as of Oct. 20, 1862, he was assigned to command at Nashville on Dec. 18, 1863. On March 15, 1864, Lt. Col. William L. Duff wrote to USG. "By your order I have this day visited and inspected the building known as the Medical University in this city used as a temporary home for Union refugees. I also visited the Hospital for sick children of refugees No 14 Spruce Street In the first named building, while the Government supplies bountifully commissary stores, necessary for the subsistence of the objects of its charity—their condition is bad from the following causes. 1st. There is no fence round the lot to keep out unauthorized persons, and the inmates, many, of whom, are young girls are thus exposed to insult and annoyance from a class of men to be found both amongst soldiers and citizens, so lost to all sense of decency and morality, that the desolate condition of these poor unfortunates, is no protection from their base designs, upon their means, as well as upon their morals. 2nd. There are not separate dormitories for single men and women. 3rd. The practice of issuing rations to individuals, and to small messes, is very wasteful, and could be remedied by the employment of a person or persons to cook for all the inmates, thus saving in commissary stores, more than enough to make up the expenditure, necessary to be incurred by the QuarterMasters Department 4th. There is no commissioned Officer in charge, with proper authority to compel obedience to such rules, as may be established to give information to refugees, as to routes, to see that they are not preyed upon, or the women insulted by wicked and designing persons, and that the little specie funds which many of them possess, are exchanged at its market value for currency instead of their being swindled out of it, as they now are, to keep a proper register of names, date of arrival & departure deaths &c. to prevent the indiscriminate admission of visitors, and generally to exercise such control over the institution as that its object may not be perverted, but that the greatest amount of good may be done at the least possible expense 5th. There is no separate quarters for the guard detail who are at present quartered in the house. The Hospital for children No 14 Spruce Street, is entirely insufficient for the object in view, Mrs Harris and

Mrs McGinnis who have been giving, most kindly and disinterestedly their personal attention to this benevolent object, make valuble suggestions, and as these ladies are not extravagant in their ideas at all, but only propose, what I cannot but consider absolutely necessary, I beg respectfully to suggest that a competent commissioned Officer be detailed to superintend the preperation of this refuge, and the future conduct of it, and that he be instructed to avail himself of the practical experence of these ladies, as well as that of Miss Huey, a lady at present employed by private benevolence to exercise some care over these poor people." LS, DNA, RG 109, Union Provost Marshals' File of Papers Relating to Two or More Civilians. On April 4, Maj. Gen. William T. Sherman endorsed a letter of Granger in reply to USG's letter. "If the Governor of Tennessee, has a home for refugees, we should not—the Military, is simply designed to fill blanks in Government, not otherwise provided for." Copy, *ibid.*, RG 393, Military Div. of the Miss., Endorsements.

On March 16, Lt. Col. Theodore S. Bowers issued Special Orders No. 70. "The Quartermaster's Department will provide transportation to all Union Refugees from the Revolted States to such point on the Ohio River, between Cincinnati and Cairo as they may select, on requisition for transportation approved by the authority of the Military Governor of the State. Notice that such transportation will be furnished will be posted conspicuously about the Refugees' Home, and such other places as will give publicity to this Order." Copies, DLC-USG, V, 38; DLC-Andrew Johnson.

To T. Lyle Dickey

Nashville, Tenn.
March 15, 1864

The position I am now placed in I feel will prove a trying one, but by having an eye to duty alone I shall hope to succeed. Placed in command of all the Armies as I have been it will be necessary for me to have an office and an A. A. Gen. in Washington, but I will not be there. I shall have Hd. Qrs. in the field and will move from one Army to another so as to be where my presence seems to be most required . . . Sherman succeeds me to the command of this Military Division and McPherson succeeds him to the Comd. of the Dept. of the Ten. Neither could be in better hands, . . .

Anderson Galleries, Sale No. 1583, May 9–11, 1921, p. 38. On Feb. 29, 1864, T. Lyle Dickey, Ottawa, Ill., wrote to USG. "Allow me to congratulate you upon the magnificent success which has thus far crowned your military operations—& express my earnest wish & confident hope that it may ever be thus where you have control. Permit me also to declare my great gratification that your services are appreciated by the country & have been recognised by the Government in your promotion to the distinguished rank of Lieut. General—No man in this broad land feels more joy in your prosperity or a more sincere desire for your ~~well-being~~ well-being and happiness—It is perhaps wrong that I should claim even so much of your time—as is necessary to read this letter—when matters of moment so much more essential ~~demand~~ demand your attention—but I hope that this may fall into your hand at some juncture when it will not interfere with duty—From the day when I parted with you at Youngs Point last March I have watched your path with intense interest—& again & again have wished that I could have remained with you—As long as I live I know that I will look back, upon the months which I spent at your Head Quarters with pleasure & pride . . . The strangest thing on earth to my mind is the pertinacity of the President in his endeavour to make a great man of McClernand—McClernand said—(I am told) in a speech in Chicago that Generals like poets—were *born* not *made*—I am sure *he* will have to be '*born again*' before *he* will ever be a General worth shooting—My highest regards if you please to Gen Rawlins, Col Bowers & others of the old family—I will never forget Rawlins old toast of the 'Army of the Tennessee'—that it was. 'wedded to victory' &c—I would be very glad to hear from you under your own hand—but occupied as you are, I ought not & will not ask it—" ALS, USG 3.

To Maj. Gen. George H. Thomas

Nashville March 16th 64. 7. P. M.

MAJOR GENERAL G. H THOMAS
CHATTANOOGA

From your despatch of yestarday[1] and also one from Genl Logan,[2] it looks as though the enemy was preparing for a move against our line of communication east of Chattanooga and it may be west of there also. You will therefore if you have not already done so, place heavy guards upon the important railroad bridges both East and West of Chattanooga, so that they cannot without a severe battle destroy them. This should be attended to without delay.

U. S GRANT
Lieut General

Telegram, copies, DLC-USG, V, 34, 35, 45, 59; DNA, RG 108, Letters Sent; *ibid.*, RG 393, Military Div. of the Miss., Letters Sent; *ibid.*, Dept. of the Cumberland, Telegrams Received. *O.R.*, I, xxxii, part 3, 80. On March 16, 1864, Maj. Gen. George H. Thomas twice telegraphed to USG, first at 10:30 P.M. "Your dispatch of 7 P M Rec'd. I think the Disposition I have made are such as will meet any emergency that will arise of the kind you mention." "The following despatch from one of my most reliable scouts 'Tuesday A. M.   Just from Dalton   total force of enemy forty five thousand (45000)   Hoods Corps four (4)

Divisions   Stevenson left wing six Thousand (6000)   Breckenredges old Div
now Bates left centre being the smallest (4000) four Thousand Stewarts Division
Wells centre   Hindmans Division right wing   Beaurgards Corps four Divisions   Clebournes Division left wing largest five Thousand (5000)   Cheathams
Division right wing   other Division on RailRoad   dont know whose   all in
camp   Field artillery plenty small size   Roddy about Varnells station force
2000   Wheeler in front eleven thousand (11000)   Total Cavalry Twelve to
fourteen Thousand—wagons about five hundred   They do not draw full rations
commissary stores at Resacca and Calhoun   I think the estimate of Cavalry too
high although they have been reinforced to some extent since our reconnois-
cance" Telegrams received, DNA, RG 108, Letters Received; copies, *ibid.*, RG
393, Dept. of the Cumberland, Telegrams Sent; (2nd) *ibid.*, Military Div. of
the Miss., Telegrams Received.

On March 17, 10:30 A.M., USG telegraphed to Thomas. "Commence moving
the surplus troops you have, on the line of the Nashville and Chattanooga road
to the Columbia and Decatur road so as to relieve the troops now there to be
moved to the front. There is now on the road a regiment of Cavalry well mounted
and over 1100 strong, and two regiments of colored troops that will be left."
Copies, DLC-USG, V, 34, 35, 45, 59; DNA, RG 108, Letters Sent; *ibid.*, RG
393, Military Div. of the Miss., Letters Sent; *ibid.*, Dept. of the Cumberland,
Telegrams Received. *O.R.*, I, xxxii, part 3, 84.

On March 23, Thomas telegraphed to USG. "Since telegraphing you regarding the State of my command I sent Gen Ellicott to Nashville to ascertain the
wants & condition of the Cavalry. He informs me that there are at that place
forty nine hundred (4900) men for duty at that place exclusive of Gen. Gilloms
Tennessee regiments and only eight hundred (800) horses there and the following ordnance Stores required in addition to what are there—2600 Sabres 3900
Carbines—3600 saddles. I spoke to Capt Baylor my Cheif of Ordnance concerning this a few days since and he showed me an answer by telegram on the subject
from Chief of Ordnance which Stated that arms would be furnished as soon as
could be procured but that they were not to be had"   Telegram received, DNA,
RG 107, Telegrams Collected (Bound); (dated March 24) *ibid.*, RG 108, Letters Received; copy (dated March 23), *ibid.*, RG 393, Dept. of the Cumberland,
Telegrams Sent. *O.R.*, I, xxxii, part 3, 121.

1. On March 14, USG telegraphed to Thomas. "Do your troops occuppy the
same line now they did when you telegraphed me their position last. I shall leave
here about the last of the week and should like to be posted as to present position
of both armies before I go." Copy, DNA, RG 393, Dept. of the Cumberland,
Telegrams Received. *O.R.*, I, xxxii, part 3, 67. On March 15, Thomas telegraphed to USG. "My troops Occupy essentially the same position as when I
telegraphed last. Information regarding the Enemy locates Hardees Corps on the
road from Dalton to Cleveland & Hindmans Corps on the rail road between
Dalton & Tunnell Hill   His Cavalry is at Tunnell Hill & on the Lafayette
road   I am still very deficient in the latter arms & artillery horses notwithstanding all the Exertions of myself & Col Donaldson   The rail road will be finished
to Ringgold by the end of this week" Telegram received, DNA, RG 108, Letters
Received; *ibid.*, RG 393, Military Div. of the Miss., Telegrams Received; *ibid.*,
Dept. of the Cumberland, Telegrams Sent. *O.R.*, I, xxxii, part 3, 72.

2. On March 14, Maj. Gen. John A. Logan, Huntsville, Ala., telegraphed to
Lt. Col. Theodore S. Bowers. "I have information reliable that all the rebel troops

sent in the direction of Sherman and Mobile, have returned to Dalton, and all the squads, Home Guards &c except picquets on the river are ordered there save three Regiments of Infantry that are moving in the direction of Decatur. The enemy are certainly concentrating for some purpose." Copies, DNA, RG 393, 15th Army Corps, Telegrams Sent; *ibid.*, Military Div. of the Miss., Telegrams Received. *O.R.*, I, xxxii, part 3, 69.

To Maj. Gen. Henry W. Halleck

Nashville Tenn.
9.30 P. M. Mar. 17. 1864.

MAJ GEN HALLECK,
CHF OF STAFF—

According to the returns I saw in Washington it looked to me that troops could be taken from Gen. Rosecrans instead of more being required. No horses have been taken from troops already mounted by my order or with my knowledge. I will telegraph orders to correct any further interference with horses or troops for Gen Banks.[1]

U. S. GRANT
Lt. Gen.

Telegram received, DNA, RG 107, Telegrams Collected (Bound); copies, *ibid.*, RG 108, Letters Sent; *ibid.*, RG 393, Military Div. of the Miss., Hd. Qrs. Correspondence; DLC-USG, V, 40, 45, 59, 94; DLC-Andrew Johnson. *O.R.*, I, xxxiv, part 2, 635. On March 17, 1864, 2:30 P.M., Maj. Gen. Henry W. Halleck telegraphed to USG. "The furloughed regiments from Dept of the South are ordered to rendezvous here. Genl Rosecrans asks for four regiments of cavalry & one or two regts of Infantry to be sent to Missouri. Genl Banks reports that the 12th Ill. cavalry ordered to his Dept have been dismounted at St Louis & the horses sent to your orders; & that other horses collected there for his command have been diverted. I fear these diversions may interfere with his movemts." ALS (telegram sent), DNA, RG 107, Telegrams Collected (Bound); telegram received, *ibid.*, RG 108, Letters Received. *O.R.*, I, xxxiv, part 2, 634–35.

On March 16, 12:30 P.M., Halleck telegraphed to USG. "The furloughs of veteran regiments from Dept of the South (Hilton Head) are about to expire. If it is proposed to bring any troops north from that Dept for the coming campaign, Should not these regiments be retained in order to avoid double transportation?" ALS (telegram sent), DNA, RG 107, Telegrams Collected (Bound); telegram received, *ibid.*, RG 108, Letters Received. *O.R.*, I, xxxv, part 2, 20. On the same day, 7:00 P.M., USG telegraphed to Halleck. "To avoid double transportation I desire the veteran regiments from the Dept of the South rendezvoused at some point from whence they can be moved with facility either to the Army of the Potomac, or to Hilton Head as may be required." Telegram received, DNA, RG 107, Telegrams Collected (Bound); copies, *ibid.*, RG 94, Vol. Service Div., A204 (VS) 1864; *ibid.*, RG 108, Letters Sent; *ibid.*, RG 393, Military Div. of the Miss., Hd. Qrs. Correspondence; DLC-USG, V, 40, 45, 59, 94. *O.R.*, I, xxxv, part 2, 20. On March 14, 3:30 P.M., Halleck had telegraphed to USG. "Genl Curtis applies to retain the 7th Kansas now on furlough, in his Dept. Numerous other applications of same kind have been made. I will order every furloughed regiment back to its former command, till you direct otherwise." ALS (telegram sent), DNA, RG 107, Telegrams Collected (Bound); telegram received, *ibid.*, RG 108, Letters Received. *O.R.*, I, xxxiv, part 2, 606.

1. On March 17, USG telegraphed to Brig. Gen. John W. Davidson, St. Louis. "If the 12th Illinois Cavalry are in St Louis mount them and forward them to Gen Banks without delay. It is complained that this Regiment has been dismounted and the horses sent here, and also other horses for the Gulf Department diverted." Copies, DLC-USG, V, 34, 35, 45, 59; DNA, RG 108, Letters Sent; *ibid.*, RG 393, Military Div. of the Miss., Letters Sent. *O.R.*, I, xxxiv, part 2, 638.

To Maj. Gen. John M. Schofield

Nashville Mar 17th 12 M [*1864*]

FOR GEN SCHOFIELD—I have had an inspection made of Camp Nelson & Mt Sterling[1]

It shows a wasteful extravagance there and also that the points are badly selected—It seems to me that Camp Nelson should be broken up entirely and the public property issued where it will be of service. I would suggest that B. Genl. Cox,[2] or some other intelligent officer be sent into that part of Kentucky with authority to make such changes as the public good may seem to demand— The troops should watch closely an advance of the enemy from Western Virginia.

As soon as I return to the East[3] I will try to get up an expedition from Western Virginia to move on to the R. Rd. to the rear of Breckenridge.

I have ordered the new cavalry to Mt Sterling as you request— Cannot Cumberland Gap be supplied from Knoxville better than as now supplied—

U. S. GRANT

Telegram received, DNA, RG 393, Dept. of the Ohio, Telegrams Received; copies, *ibid.*, Military Div. of the Miss., Letters Sent; *ibid.*, RG 108, Letters Sent; DLC-USG, V, 34, 35, 45, 59. *O.R.*, I, xxxii, part 3, 83–84. On March 17, 1864, 11:00 P.M., Maj. Gen. John M. Schofield, Morristown, Tenn., telegraphed to USG. "I will send Genl Cox to Camp Nelson to attend to affairs in that part of Kentucky as you suggest   while compelled to remain on the defensive I will distribute my force North of the Holston so as to hold the valleys between that River and Cumberland Gap so as to guard as far as possible against any movement into Middle Tennessee   I will be able to meet any movement into that state from West Virginia   Cumberland Gap can I think be better supplied from Knoxville for a time at least—I will so order"   Telegram received, DNA, RG 108, Letters Received; copy, DLC-John M. Schofield. *O.R.*, I, xxxii, part 3, 84. On March 15, Lt. Col. James H. Stokes, Nashville, wrote to Brig. Gen. John A. Rawlins reporting in detail his inspection of Camp Nelson. *Ibid.*, pp. 77–79.

Also on March 15, Schofield had written to USG two lengthy letters concerning his situation. Copy, DLC-John M. Schofield; (2nd) ALS, DNA, RG 94, War Records Office, Dept. of the Ohio. *O.R.*, I, lii, part 1, 531–33.

On March 17, USG telegraphed to Schofield. "Order the battalion of the ninth 9th Ohio cavalry now with you to join the regiment at Huntsville via Chattanooga"   Copy, DNA, RG 393, Dept. of the Ohio, Telegrams Received.

Also on March 17, USG telegraphed to Schofield, Maj. Gen. George H. Thomas and Maj. Gen. John A. Logan his General Orders No. 1. "In pursuance of the following order of the President: . . . I assume command of the Armies of the United States. Head Quarters will be in the field, and, until further orders will be with the Army of the Potomac. There will be an Office Head Quarters in Washington, to which all official communications will be sent except those from the Army where Head Quarters are at the date of their address." Telegram received, *ibid.*; copies, *ibid.*, Dept. of the Cumberland, Telegrams Received; (printed) *ibid.*, RG 94, Generals' Papers and Books, U. S. Grant. *O.R.*, I, xxxii, part 3, 83. On the same day, USG telegraphed to Schofield, Thomas, and Logan. "Maj Genl Sherman has been assigned to the command of this military division & having arrived at Nashville this evening hereafter all official communications communicate to him—"   Telegram received, DNA, RG 393, Dept. of the Ohio, Telegrams Received; copy, *ibid.*, Dept. of the Cumberland, Telegrams Received. *O.R.*, I, xxxii, part 3, 85.

1. Mount Sterling, Ky., on the Lexington and Big Sandy Railroad, approximately thirty miles east of Lexington.

2. Jacob D. Cox, born in Montreal, Canada, in 1828, apprenticed briefly in law in New York City (1842–44), worked two years in the office of a banker, graduated from Oberlin College in 1851, and began to practice law in Warren, Ohio, in 1853. Strongly antislavery, he helped to organize the Republican Party in Ohio and was elected to the Ohio Senate in 1859. Appointed brig. gen. as of May 17, 1861, he commanded the 9th Army Corps at the battle of Antietam. Relieved from command of the 23rd Army Corps on Feb. 10, 1864, he served temporarily as act. chief of staff in the field for Schofield. See telegram to Maj. Gen. John M. Schofield, Feb. 12, 1864.

3. On March 19, U.S. Representative Elihu B. Washburne, Washington, telegraphed to USG. "Please telegraph me precisely when you will reach here. Have made very favorable arrangements for your family at Willards." ALS

(telegram sent), DNA, RG 107, Telegrams Collected (Unbound). On the same day, 2:00 P.M., USG, Elizabethtown, Ky., telegraphed to Washburne. "Will reach there Tuesday evening" Telegram received, *ibid.*, Telegrams Collected (Bound). On March 22, USG, Philadelphia, telegraphed to Washburne. "I leave here in the eleven P. M. train." Telegram received, DLC-Elihu B. Washburne. On the same day, USG telegraphed to Secretary of War Edwin M. Stanton. "I leave here at eleven (11) tonight." Telegram received, DNA, RG 107, Telegrams Collected (Bound).

Speech

[*March 18, 1864*]

GENTLEMEN: Permit me through you, to return to the Board of Supervisors and people of Jo Daviess county, sincere thanks for this beautiful and valued sword. Say to them that I accept it, not so much as a mark of esteem to myself, as an evidence of their devotion to their country, and their appreciation of the progress towards a final triumph, marked by the unbroken series of successes in every battle named upon it, from Belmont to Chattanooga, and I will use it in the maintenance of our nationality, liberty and law so long as the Government and armies repose confidence in me, and an armed foe to these exists. Say further to them that the support they have given me through evil as well as good report, has been to me a solace, and [is] remembered with gratitude, and that, as in the past, the successes of the brave armies which it has been my fortune to command justified that support, so in God I trust, the continued successes of our armies in the future may justify its continuance.

Galena Weekly Gazette, March 29, 1864. On Sept. 15, 1863, U.S. Representative Elihu B. Washburne laid before the Board of Supervisors, Jo Daviess County, Ill., "Petitions numerously signed by Citizens of Jo Daviess County praying that the County present to Major Genl. U. S. Grant, with a Sword, as a testimonial of his eminent services in the present War . . ." DS (by Richard Seal, county clerk), DLC-Elihu B. Washburne. On the same day, the board unanimously appropriated $1,000 for such a sword and appointed a committee to present it and a parchment record of the board's proceedings to USG. DS, *ibid.*; (incomplete) *The History of Jo Daviess County Illinois,* . . . (Chicago, 1878), p. 417. See *Galena Weekly Gazette*, Nov. 24, 1863. On Oct. 3, Brig. Gen. John A. Rawlins, Vicksburg, wrote to Washburne enclosing "a list of the principal battles in which General Grant has been, in this and the Mexican War. The dates of some I am unable to give, not remembering them nor having a history at hand to which to refer. . . ." LS, DLC-Elihu B. Washburne. This list was evidently based on an undated list prepared by USG; with certain names and dates inserted or corrected and with the battle of Chattanooga added, it was inscribed on the scabbard of the sword. D, _ibid._; ADf, deCoppet Collection, NjP. See letter to Elihu B. Washburne, Dec. 2, 1863; _Jo Daviess County_, pp. 417–18; John Y. Simon, ed., _The Personal Memoirs of Julia Dent Grant_ (New York, 1975), p. 128. On Jan. 25 and Feb. 1, 1864, Charles K. Rogers, New York City, formerly of Galena, wrote to Washburne regarding the manufacture of the sword by the Ames Manufacturing Co., Chicopee, Mass. ALS, DLC-Elihu B. Washburne. See letter to Elihu B. Washburne, Dec. 12, 1863. On Feb. 27, Washburne telegraphed to USG. "Where will you be in ten days or two weeks from this time? I go to Galena early next week, family sick. I̶ a̶m̶ Jo Daviess sword done and here. It is magnificent." ALS (telegram sent), DNA, RG 107, Telegrams Collected (Unbound). On the same day, USG telegraphed to Washburne. "Cant say where I will be ten days hence   probably here"   Telegram received, DLC-Elihu B. Washburne. Shown in New York City, put on exhibit in the office of the speaker of the U.S. House of Representatives on Feb. 29, and sent to Galena, the sword was carried to Nashville by Stephenson T. Napper and Halstead S. Townsend for the Jo Daviess County board. Rogers to Washburne, Feb. 23, 1864, ALS, _ibid._; P. J. Staudenraus, ed., _Mr. Lincoln's Washington: Selections from the Writings of Noah Brooks_ . . . (New York, 1967), p. 288; _Galena Weekly Gazette_, April 5, 1864. On Feb. 5, USG had written a note. "Mr. Chas. K. Rodgers, a loyal citizen of New York, is authorized to visit these Hd Qrs, at any time suiting his pleasure. Provost Marshal will issue the proper passes." ANS, Mrs. George B. Post, Long Island, N. Y. For the presentation speech, and accounts by Napper and Rogers of the presentation visit, see _Galena Weekly Gazette_, April 5, 1864; Rogers to Washburne, April 15, 16, 1864, ALS, DLC-Elihu B. Washburne. On March 18, USG wrote to Maj. Gen. George H. Thomas introducing the committee members, who planned to visit Chattanooga. Stan. V. Henkels Catalogue 1379, Oct. 15, 1925, p. 14. The sword is pictured in Lawrence A. Frost, _U. S. Grant Album_ (Seattle, 1966), p. [147].

To Louisa Boggs

Nashville, Tenn., March 18, 1864.

DEAR COUSIN:

I will take advantage of Fred's return to St. Louis to send you one hundred dollars for the use of the children in paying board, buying clothing or anything else you may think proper.

Julia will go with me to Washington but will not probably remain over three or four weeks. She will then make her home with her father so as to be near the children in future. If I am so situated that Julia and the children can join me during vacation, I will have them do so and would like you to come with them.

Fred will give you all the news.

Yours truly,

U. S. GRANT.

Topeka State Journal, April 22, 1905.

To Edwin M. Stanton

From Culpeper C. H[1] M.
Dated, Mch. 24 *1864.*

HON E M STANTON

I would like to have Genl L C Hunt's[2] orders changed and have him ordered to report to me for special duty.

I want him to make an inspection of the Department of Mo and Kansas with the view particularly of ascertaining if transportation & artillery horses cannot be taken from them to supply Troops taking the field & also to enable me to form a judgment if some of the Troops cannot be spared   When the duty is performed I will assign him. Genl. Hunt is now here, and can be reached by telegraph to my Hd Qrs.

U. S. GRANT.

Lt. Genl.

Telegram received, DNA, RG 107, Telegrams Collected (Bound); copies, *ibid.*, RG 108, Letters Sent; DLC-USG, V, 45, 59. On March 10, 1864, USG telegraphed to Brig. Gen. Lewis C. Hunt. "If relieved from duty, come to Washn. by the twelfth (12)   answer." Telegram received (press), DNA, RG 107, Telegrams Collected (Bound). Probably on March 11, Hunt's brother, Brig. Gen. Henry J. Hunt, telegraphed to USG. "Genl L. C. Hunt left for Washington this morning   a despatch to Genl Casey would reach him immediately on his arrival at that place" ALS (telegram sent—undated), *ibid.*, Telegrams Collected (Unbound). On March 14, Hunt, Washington, telegraphed to USG. "Your telegram to New Haven failed to reach me.—Arrived here, and found you gone—Will await your return, or Orders.—" ALS (telegram sent), *ibid.*; telegram received, *ibid.*, RG 108, Letters Received. On March 24, Lt. Col. Theodore S. Bowers issued Special Orders No. 2 sending Hunt to make the inspection USG wanted. Copies, DLC-USG, V, 57, 62. *O.R.*, I, xxxiv, part 2, 718. On March 26, USG telegraphed to Hunt, "Care Gen H J Hunt." "If Lewis Hunt has not yet left for the west please send him to my HdQrs" Telegram received, DLC-Henry J. Hunt. On April 19, Hunt, Springfield, Mo., sent an inspection report to Lt. Col. Cyrus B. Comstock, which USG endorsed on May 2. "Respy. referred to Maj General H. W. Halleck, Chief of Staff and commended to his attention." Copy, DLC-USG, V, 58. *O.R.*, I, xxxiv, part 3, 226–27. On April 29, Hunt, St. Louis, reported to Comstock on his inspection of Jefferson City. LS, DNA, RG 108, Letters Received. On May 6, Hunt, Fort Leavenworth, Kan., reported to Comstock. *O.R.*, I, xxxiv, part 3, 487–88.

On March 23, Maj. Gen. Henry W. Halleck telegraphed to Maj. Gen. George H. Thomas, by direction of USG, ordering Maj. Gen. Philip H. Sheridan to Washington. *Personal Memoirs of P. H. Sheridan* (New York, 1888), I, 339. On March 24, USG telegraphed to Secretary of War Edwin M. Stanton. "I would respectfully suggest that the order relieving Gen. Pleasanton from duty here and sending him to the Department of the Missouri be made at once. I will then direct Gen. Meade to place the senior officer of the Cavalry Corps in command of it until Gen. Sheridan arrives." Telegram received, DNA, RG 107, Telegrams Collected (Bound); copies, *ibid.*, Telegrams Collected (Unbound); *ibid.*, RG 108, Letters Sent; DLC-USG, V, 45, 59. *O.R.*, I, xxxiii, 721. On the same day, Stanton telegraphed to USG. "The orders you requested are issued. Nothing new has reached the Department from any quarter today. ~~I see that Gen Sigel offers to send you Major Rucker of Crooks Staff His Statements are to be received with great caution.~~" ALS (telegram sent), DNA, RG 107, Telegrams Collected (Bound). On April 1, Comstock telegraphed to Maj. Gen. John M. Schofield. "Lieut. Gen. Grant desires that if he has not already started, that Gen. Sheridan be directed to report at Gen. Grants Headquarters in person without delay for duty" Telegram received (torn), *ibid.*, Telegrams Collected (Unbound); copies, DLC-USG, V, 45, 59; DNA, RG 108, Letters Sent.

On March 23, Comstock telegraphed to Maj. Gen. George G. Meade. "Lt Gen Grant requests that you will send a strong Company of Cavalry to Culpeper C H to report to him for escort duty on his arrival there which will be tomorrow" Telegram received, *ibid.*, RG 94, War Records Office, Army of the Potomac. On the same day, 12:30 P.M., Brig. Gen. John A. Rawlins telegraphed to Meade. "Lieut. General Grant will be at Culpepper by tomorrow morning's train and will at your earliest convenience thereafter, desire to see your troops; not in review but simply drawn up in line, in front of, or near, their respective Corps Encampments." LS (telegram sent), *ibid.*, RG 107, Telegrams Collected (Bound); telegram received, *ibid.*; *ibid.*, RG 94, War Records Office, Army of the Potomac. *O.R.*, I, xxxiii, 718.

1. Culpeper Court-House, Va., on the Orange and Alexandria Railroad, approximately sixty miles southwest of Washington, D. C.

2. Hunt, USMA 1847, promoted to capt., 4th Inf., as of May 23, 1855, appointed col., 92nd N. Y., and severely wounded during the battle of Fair Oaks, Va., May 31, 1862. Appointed brig. gen. as of Nov. 29, he was in charge of the draft rendezvous at New Haven, Conn., from July, 1863, until March, 1864.

To Maj. Gen. Henry W. Halleck

Culpepper C. H. Va
Mar. 24th 1864

MAJ GEN H W HALLECK
CHIEF OF STAFF

Will you please send me a map with lines marked showing the territory now occupied by our forces. Also a copy of the returns of the Army you showed me. If practicable to spare them from their present stations three 3 regiments of Heavy Artillery, (one (commanded by Col Tidball[1] to be one of them) could be advantageously used with the Army of the Potomac

U S GRANT
Lt Genl

Telegram received, DNA, RG 107, Telegrams Collected (Bound); copies, *ibid.*, Telegrams Collected (Unbound); *ibid.*, RG 108, Letters Sent; DLC-USG, V, 45, 59. *O.R.*, I, xxxiii, 721. On March 24, 1864, Maj. Gen. Henry W. Halleck wrote to USG. "I send herewith, by special messenger, a synopsis of last returns of the Army; also copy of the Map which we had before us the other day. The red lines show approximately our lines of defense at the beginning of the Rebellion, and at the present time; the blue the various proposed ways of shortening them." ALS, DNA, RG 108, Letters Sent (Press). *O.R.*, I, xxxiii, 721. On March 26, 12:15 P.M., Lt. Col. Cyrus B. Comstock telegraphed to Maj. Gen. George G. Meade. "Lieut Gen Grant wishes to obtain if practicable a Map showing the position of the troops and picket lines of the A of P." Telegram received, DNA, RG 94, War Records Office, Army of the Potomac. On the same day, 12:30 P.M., Meade telegraphed to Comstock. "A map giving the information required by your telegram will be sent by orderly during the course of today.—" ALS (telegram sent), *ibid.*, RG 107, Telegrams Collected (Unbound). On the same day, Comstock wrote to Maj. Gen. William T. Sherman. "A paper map of the United States with two red lines and one blue line, is sent you by mail to-day by direction of General Grant. One red line indicates the front occupied by us at the beginning of the war, the other the front now occupied by us. The blue line indicates lines and fronts which it is proposed to occupy" Copies, DLC-USG, V, 45, 59; DLC-William T. Sherman; DNA, RG 108, Letters Sent. On April 5, Sherman wrote to Comstock. "Your letter of March 26th came to me on the 2nd Inst, and the mail brought me the Map yesterday. The parcel had evidently been opened, and the Postmaster had marked some additional postage on it. I will cause enquiries to be made lest the map has been seen by some eye intelligent enough to read the meaning of the blue and red lines. We cannot be too careful in these matters. That map to me contains more information and ideas than a volume of printed matter. Keep your retained copies with infinite care, and if you have occasion to send out to other Commanders any more, I would advise a special Courier. From that Map I see *all*, and glad am I that there are minds now at Washington able to devise, and for my part if we can keep our councils I believe I have the men and ability to march square up to the position assigned me, and to hold it. Of course it will cost us many a hard day, but I believe in fighting in a double sense, first to gain physical results, and next to inspire Respect on which to build up our Nation's Power. Of course General Grant will not have time to give me the details of movements East, and the *times*, concurrent action is the thing. It would be wise that the General through you or some educated Officer should give me timely notice of all contemplated movements with all details that can be foreseen. I now know the results aimed at. I know my base, and I have a pretty good idea of my Lines of operation. No time shall be lost in putting my forces in Mobile condition, so that all I ask is notice of *time* that all over the Grand Theatre of War there shall be simultaneous action. We saw the beauty of time in the Battle of Chattanooga, and there is no reason why the same harmony of action should not pervade a continent. I am well pleased with Captain Poe, and would not object to half a dozen thoroughly educated young Engineer Officers." Copy, USG 3. *O.R.*, I, xxxii, part 3, 261–62. The map is described *ibid.*, p. 261*n*, and reproduced in *O.R.* (Atlas), CXXXV-A.

On March 24, 3:45 P.M., Halleck telegraphed to USG. "Genl Burnside asks to have the 2d Ohio cavalry, now at Cincinati, & not mounted, ordered to his camp at Annapolis. This is a veteran regiment which formerly belonged to the Army of the Ohio. Shall they be so ordered?" ALS (telegram sent), DNA, RG 107, Telegrams Collected (Bound); telegram received, *ibid. O.R.*, I, xxxii, part 3, 135. On the same day, USG telegraphed to Halleck. "There is quite as much Cavalry with the Dept. of the Ohio as can be kept equipped and fed without the 2nd Ohio I see therefore no objection to its being ordered to Annapolis" Telegram received, DNA, RG 107, Telegrams Collected (Bound); copies, *ibid.*, RG 108, Letters Sent; DLC-USG, V, 45, 59. *O.R.*, I, lii, part 1, 536.

Also on March 24, USG telegraphed to Halleck. "I would like to have Gen. Segel directed to relieve Wheaton's Brigade, 6th A. C. and it ordered here. If Terry's Brigade is not absolutely needed at Sandusky I would like to have it also. According to my recollection of the forces in Gen. Hentzleman's Dept. he can easily spare troops from other places to take their place." ALS (telegram sent), DNA, RG 107, Telegrams Collected (Unbound); telegram received, *ibid.*, Telegrams Collected (Bound). *O.R.*, I, xxxiii, 721. On March 25, 11:30 A.M., Halleck telegraphed to USG. "Genl Sigel has been directed to return to the Army of the Potomac Wheaton's Brigade, and Genl Heintzelman has also been directed to return Terry's brigade." ALS (telegram sent), DNA, RG 107, Telegrams Collected (Bound); telegram received, *ibid.*; *ibid.*, RG 108, Letters Received. *O.R.*, I, xxxiii, 734.

1. John C. Tidball, born in Va., appointed from Ohio, USMA 1848, was promoted to capt., 2nd Art., as of May 14, 1861, and served in the Army of the Potomac until appointed col., 4th N. Y. Art., as of Aug. 28, 1863. For his transfer from the defenses of Washington to the art. brigade, 2nd Corps, Army of the Potomac, see *ibid.*, p. 760.

To Edwin M. Stanton

In field Culpepper C. H. Va March 25 1864.
HON E M. STANTON WASHINGTON D. C.

I would respectfully nominate the following officers for members of my staff, to wit:

Lieut. Col. C. B. Comstock Asst. Inspector General to be senior Aide with rank of Lieut. Col.

Captain Horace Porter Ordnance Department, to be aide with rank of Lieut. Col.

Major F. T. Dent, 4th U. S. Infantry to be aide with rank of Lieut. Colonel

Lieut. Col. W. L. Duff, 2nd Illinois Artilliry to be Asst. Inspector General vice Comstock appointed aide

Major Wm. R. Rowley Aide-de-camp to be private Secretary with rank of Lieut. Colonel

Captain Adam Badeau A. A. D. C. to be private Secretary with rank of Lieut. Colonel

I would be pleased if these appointments could be made at once, so as to enable me to announce my staff in orders.

U S GRANT
Lieut. Gen.

Copies, DLC-USG, V, 45, 59; DNA, RG 108, Letters Sent. On March 26, 1864, Secretary of War Edwin M. Stanton telegraphed to USG. "All the Staff appointments you ~~ordere~~ requested were ordered today. Tomorrow morning I shall probably send Mr Dana to confer with you on some matters." ALS (telegram sent), *ibid.*, RG 107, Telegrams Collected (Bound). On the same day, Col. Edward D. Townsend telegraphed to USG. "The Secretary of War approves the selection of officers for your personal Staff in your letter of twenty fifth instant —Under the ~~Aet~~ law you have the right to appoint four Aides and two Military Secretaries with rank of Lieutenant Colonel and they need not be nominated to the Senate or Commissioned by the President—Do you wish the officers to be ordered to report to you by this office?" ALS (telegram sent), *ibid.*, Telegrams Collected (Unbound); copy, *ibid.*, RG 94, Letters Sent. On the same day, USG telegraphed to Townsend. "Please order Maj. Dent and Capt Porter to report to me. All the others named ~~by me~~ for my staff are now with me." ALS (telegram sent), *ibid.*, RG 107, Telegrams Collected (Unbound); telegram received, *ibid.*, Telegrams Collected (Bound); *ibid.*, RG 94, Letters Received, 256A 1864.

On March 25, Brig. Gen. John A. Rawlins issued Special Orders No. 3. "Captain George K. Leet, Assistant Adjutant General, on the Staff of the Lieut.

General commanding, is hereby assigned to duty in Washington. D. C., and will have charge of the Office of Headquarters Armies of the United States, established there." Copies, DLC-USG, V, 57, 62.

On March 29, President Abraham Lincoln telegraphed to USG. "Capt. Kinney, of whom I spoke to you as desiring to go on your Staff, is now in your camp [i]n Company with Mrs. Senator Dixon. Mrs. Grant and [I] and some others agreed last night that I should, by this despatch, kindly call your attention to Capt. Kinney." ALS (telegram sent), DNA, RG 107, Telegrams Collected (Bound). Lincoln, *Works*, VII, 272. On the same day, USG telegraphed to Lincoln. "Your dispatch suggesting Capt. Kennedy for a staff appointment just recd. I would be glad to accommodate Capt. Kennedy but in the selection of my staff I do not want any one whom I do not personally know to be qualified for the position assigned them." ALS (telegram sent), DNA, RG 107, Telegrams Collected (Unbound); telegrams received (2), *ibid.*, Telegrams Collected (Bound); DLC-Robert T. Lincoln. On the same day, USG telegraphed to Maj. Gen. Henry W. Halleck. "Please have the order published announcing my staff as recommended in my letter to the Sec'y of War substituting Lt Col O. E. Babcock, for Capt H. Porter, this still leaves one vacancy, which I will be glad to give Porter, when he can be spared from his present duties, also order Maj Gen. C. C Washburn, to report to Gen Burnside, to Command a Division of the 9th Corps." Telegram received, DNA, RG 94, ACP, G178 CB 1864; *ibid.*, RG 107, Telegrams Collected (Bound); copies, *ibid.*, RG 108, Letters Sent; DLC-USG, V, 45, 59. Also on March 29, AGO General Orders No. 126 announced USG's staff. Printed, NjP. *O.R.*, I, xxxiii, 757.

On March 25, USG telegraphed to Stanton. "For the sake of uniformity would it not be better that all my dispatches be directed to the Chief of Staff of the Army? I will be governed in this matter entirely by your direction." ALS (telegram sent), DNA, RG 107, Telegrams Collected (Unbound); telegram received, *ibid.*, Telegrams Collected (Bound). On the same day, 2:15 P.M., Stanton telegraphed to USG. "It would certainly for several reasons be [b]etter to address your communications [to] the Chief of the Staff of the [A]rmy except where you desire [to] communicate with me directly. Where my directions are needed he will communicate with me." ALS (telegram sent), *ibid. O.R.*, I, xxxiii, 728.

On March 25, 2:15 P.M., Stanton telegraphed to USG. "If you have no objection I propose to forbid all newspaper telegraphic communications between here Your Head Quarters and all use of the telegraph save for military purposes." ALS (telegram sent), DNA, RG 107, Telegrams Collected (Bound). *O.R.*, I, xxxiii, 728. On the same day, USG telegraphed to Stanton. "I have no objection to prohibiting the use of telegraph lines here by newspaper correspondents, on the contrary I think it very strongly advisable." Telegram received, DNA, RG 107, Telegrams Collected (Bound); copies, *ibid.*, RG 108, Letters Sent; DLC-USG, V, 45, 59.

On April 6, USG wrote to Halleck. "I desire you to have announced in orders from the Adjutant Generals Office the following named officers as composing my Staff in the field: Brig. Gen. Jno. A Rawlins, Chief of Staff   Lieut. Col. T. S. Bowers, Assistant Adjutant General   Lieut. Col. C. B. Comstock, Senior Aid-de-Camp   Lieut. Col. O. E. Babcock, Aid-de-Camp   Lieut. Col. F. T. Dent, Aid-de-Camp   Lieut. Col. Horace Porter, Aid-de Camp   Lieut. Col. W. L. Duff, Assistant Inspector General   Lieut. Col. W. R. Rowley, ~~Private~~ Secretary   Lieut. Col. Adam Badeau ~~Private~~ Secretary   Captain E. S. Parker, Assistant Adjutant General   Captain, George K. Leet, Assistant Adjutant General in charge of office at Washington   Captain P. T. Hudson, Aid-de Camp   Captain H. W. Janes, Assist Quartermaster on special duty at Head quarters   1st Lieut. W. M. Dunn Jr. 83d Indiana Vols, Acting Aid-de-Camp"   LS, DNA, RG 94, Letters Received, 294A 1864. See *O.R.*, I, xxxiii, 820.

On March 7, a group of prominent citizens of Delaware County, Ind., wrote to Lincoln recommending Thomas J. Brady, formerly col., 117th Ind., for a position on USG's staff. LS, DNA, RG 107, Applications. On April 6, USG endorsed this letter. "Respectfully returned, with the information that my Staff has been made up." ES, *ibid.*

To Maj. Gen. Henry W. Halleck

Culpepper March 25th 1864.

MAJ. GEN. HALLECK, CHIEF OF STAFF OF THE ARMY
WASHINGTON D. C.

Gen. Sigel[1] telegraphs to V. K. Whaley[2] to ascertain whether 20th & 21st Pa Cavalry have been ordered to his Dept. That they properly belong to him & are ready to come and for him to see that they receive the order.

I know no reason why these two regiments should not be ordered to the Dept. of West Va but it is time Gen. Sigel should learn to carry on his official correspondence through the proper channels and not through members of Congress. Please call his attention to the fact that improper official correspondence will not be tolerated in future.

U. S. GRANT
Lt. Gen.

ALS (telegram sent), DNA, RG 107, Telegrams Collected (Unbound); telegram received, *ibid.*, Telegrams Collected (Bound). *O.R.*, I, xxxiii, 734. On March 25, 1864, Lt. Col. Cyrus B. Comstock telegraphed to Maj. Gen. Franz Sigel. "A dispatch from V. K. Whaley, from you in reference to 20th Pennsylvania Cavalry, has been sent to these Headquarters   The Commanding General directs me to ask who V. K. Whaley is" Copies, DLC-USG, V, 45, 59; DNA, RG 108, Letters Sent. *O.R.*, I, xxxiii, 735. On the same day, Sigel telegraphed to Comstock. "K. V. Whaley is a citizen of West Virginia & Member of the House of Representatives." ALS (telegram sent), DNA, RG 107, Telegrams Collected (Unbound). *O.R.*, I, xxxiii, 735.

Also on March 25, 4:00 P.M., Maj. Gen. Henry W. Halleck telegraphed to USG. "Col Mudd reports his regt. Second Ill cavalry, part at New Orleans, part at Memphis, & remainder on furlough at Springfield wants it united. Shall this be done, & if so, where?" ALS (telegram sent), DNA, RG 107, Telegrams Collected (Bound); telegram received, *ibid.* On the same day, USG telegraphed to Halleck. "Col Mudds regiment should be united under Banks." Telegram received, *ibid.*; *ibid.*, RG 94, Vol. Service Div., A236 (VS) 1864; copies, *ibid.*, RG 108, Letters Sent; DLC-USG, V, 45, 59.

On the same day, USG telegraphed to Halleck. "I would recommend that Gen Newton be ordered to report to Gen. Sherman and Gen. Sykes to Gen. Curtis." ALS (telegram sent), DNA, RG 107, Telegrams Collected (Unbound); telegram received, *ibid.*, Telegrams Collected (Bound). *O.R.*, I, xxxiii, 730. See *ibid.*, p. 722.

Also on March 25, USG telegraphed to Halleck. "Please have an order published requiring all General officers to send to these Head Quarters a full list of all staff officers and acting staff officers serving with them" LS (telegram sent), DNA, RG 107, Telegrams Collected (Unbound); telegram received, *ibid.*, Telegrams Collected (Bound).

1. Sigel, promoted to maj. gen. as of March 21, 1862, and assigned to command the Dept. of West Va. on Feb. 29, 1864. See *O.R.*, I, xxxiii, 618.

2. Kellian V. Whaley, born in N. Y., educated in Ohio, entered the lumber business in Ceredo, Va. He served as a Republican U.S. Representative from Va. (1861–63) and from West Va. (1863–67).

To Maj. Gen. Henry W. Halleck

Head Qrs in the feild
Culpepper Va. 4. P. M
Mar. 25th 1864

MAJ. GEN H W HALLECK
CHIEF OF STAFF.

I sent a letter to Genl Banks before leaving Nashville directing him to finish his present expedition and assemble all his available force at New Orleans as soon as possible and prepare to receive orders for the taking of Mobile. If Shreveport is carried about eight thousand (8000) troops can be spared from Steele and Rosecrans to join Banks & if more is necessary to insure success against Mobile they can be taken from Sherman. I would prefer Gilmore[1] to act entirely on the defensive at Charleston and hold all the spare force he has in readiness for orders   I will want him to cooperate with this Army against Lee. I would like it if the Secy of the Navy would order two of the Ironclads from Charleston to report to Admiral Farragut with instructions to the latter not to attack until the army is ready to operate with him

U S GRANT
Lt Genl

Telegram received, DNA, RG 107, Telegrams Collected (Bound); copies, *ibid.*, RG 108, Letters Sent; DLC-USG, V, 45, 59. *O.R.*, I, xxxiii, 729; *ibid.*, I, xxxiv, part 2, 721. On March 25, 1864, 2:00 P.M., Maj. Gen. Henry W. Halleck had telegraphed to USG. "Genl Gillmore reports that, if he is to act only on the defensive, he can spare from seven to eleven thousand troops from the Dept of the South to operate elsewhere. Admiral Farragut reports that with his present fleet and two or three Iron-clads from Charleston he can take Mobile, if a land force can be sent to hold it. The troops in Dept of the South are not fully supplied with transportation for operating in the interior of the country." ALS (telegram sent), DNA, RG 107, Telegrams Collected (Bound); telegram received, *ibid.*, RG 108, Letters Received. *O.R.*, I, xxxiii, 729. On March 26, noon, Halleck telegraphed to USG. "Orders sent to Genl Gillmore to hold his troops in readiness. I have also seen the Asst Secty of the Navy as you requested about Iron clads. Recent advices from Mobile represent that harbor defenses have been greatly increased. I think another regiment of heavy artillery can very soon be organized & sent to the front, if desired. Genl Augur will visit you to-morrow" ALS (telegram sent), DNA, RG 107, Telegrams Collected (Bound); telegram received, *ibid.*, RG 108, Letters Received. *O.R.*, I, xxxiii, 741.

On March 25, 11:30 A.M., Halleck telegraphed to USG. "The chief of Artillery reports that 1,800 men can be immediately spared from the defences of Washington, and it remains to be determined whether they shall be organized into field batteries or sent to the field as heavy artillery. Either will be done as you direct." ALS (telegram sent), DNA, RG 107, Telegrams Collected (Bound); telegram received, *ibid.*; *ibid.*, RG 108, Letters Received. *O.R.*, I, xxxiii, 729. On the same day, USG telegraphed to Halleck. "send the Heavy Artiellery as they are. There is Light Artillery sufficient with the Army." ALS (telegram sent), DNA, RG 107, Telegrams Collected (Unbound); telegram received, *ibid.*, Telegrams Collected (Bound). Printed as received at 2:00 P.M. in *O.R.*, I, xxxiii, 729. On the same day, 3:30 P.M., Halleck telegraphed to USG. "Two regiments of heavy Artillery numbering about ~~3~~ three thousand men are ordered to Army of the Potomac and will leave as soon as they can be replaced by men from other forts. Please direct Genl Meade to telegraph Genl Augur where they are to ~~stop~~ land." ALS (telegram sent), DNA, RG 107, Telegrams Collected (Bound); telegram received, *ibid.*; *ibid.*, RG 108, Letters Received. *O.R.*, I, xxxiii, 730. Also on March 25, USG telegraphed to Maj. Gen. George G. Meade. "Two regiments of heavy artillery numbering about three thousand men will be sent to you. Telegraph Gen Augur where you will have them" Telegram received, DNA, RG 94, War Records Office, Army of the Potomac; *ibid.*, RG 107, Telegrams Collected (Unbound); copies, *ibid.*, RG 108, Letters Sent; DLC-USG, V, 45, 59; Meade Papers, PHi.

On March 25, USG telegraphed to Maj. Gen. Christopher C. Augur. "If the Brigade of the Pa Reserves now at Alexandria can possibly be spared from their present duty order them to join their Div. in the field." ALS (telegram sent), DNA, RG 107, Telegrams Collected (Unbound); telegram received, *ibid.*, Telegrams Collected (Bound); *ibid.*, RG 94, War Records Office, Washington. *O.R.*, I, xxxiii, 733. On the same day, Augur telegraphed to USG. "There are but two regiments of the brigade of Penn Reserves at Alexandria or in the Dept. and they cannot be spared unless other troops take their place. They are the only troops there except a small District regt. for guards &c of all the public property there. They could be relieved by Invalid troops." ALS (telegram sent), DNA, RG 107, Telegrams Collected (Unbound). On the same day, Lt. Col. Cyrus B. Comstock twice telegraphed to Augur. "Lt Gen Grant desires that if the Penna regts referred to in your telegram of today can be relieved by Invalid troops to be obtained from Col Fry, it be done." Telegram received (press), *ibid.*, Telegrams Collected (Bound); copies, *ibid.*, RG 108, Letters Sent; DLC-USG, V, 45, 59. "Lt Genl Grant requests that you will come down & see him the first day that you can be spared from Washn." Telegram received, DNA, RG 94, Generals' Papers and Books, Augur. On March 26, Comstock telegraphed to Augur. "Lt Gen Grant will go to Washn. tomorrow, Sunday & would like to see you at Willards." Telegram received, *ibid.*, U. S. Grant; *ibid.*, RG 107, Telegrams Collected (Bound). On Aug. 26, Augur telegraphed to USG. "Col Fry will take immedite steps to replace the two Rgts of Penn reserves at Alexandria by invalid regts. I will come down myself tomorrow, Sunday." ALS (telegram sent), *ibid.*, Telegrams Collected (Unbound).

1. Quincy A. Gillmore of Ohio, USMA 1849, promoted to capt., Corps of Engineers, as of Aug. 6, 1861, assisted in the capture of Fort Pulaski, Ga., on April 11, 1862, and was appointed brig. gen. shortly afterward. Promoted to maj. gen. as of July 10, 1863, he commanded the 10th Army Corps and the Dept. of the South in March, 1864.

To Julia Dent Grant

Culpepper C. H. Va
March 25th 1864

Dear Julia,

I arrived here yesterday well but as on my former trip brought wet and bad weather. I have not been out of the house today and from appearances shall not be able to go out for several days. At present however I shall find enough to do in doors. From indications I would judge the best of feelings animate all the troops here towards the changes that have been made.—I find mails follow me up with remarkable promptitude. More letters reach me than I can answer.—I hope you have entirely recovered? It is poor enjoyment confined to bed in Washington.—There is one thing I learned in Washington just on leaving that wants attending to. You know breakfast lasts from early in the morning until about noon, and dinner from that time until night. Jess runs about the house loose and seeing the guests at meals thinks each time it is a new meal and that he must necessarily eat. In this way he eats five or six times each day and dips largely into deserts. If not looked after he will make himself sick.—Have you heard from Fred.? No doubt he got home safely. I shall go down to Washington on Sunday.[1] You need not mention it however.—I have sent in my recommendations for staff appointments placing Fred's name among them. I will know by to-morrow if they are approved. No doubt they will be however. I have put in the name of Capt. H. Porter, a very valuable regular officer, about such as Comstock, and still left one vacancy so that if Wilson should fail in his confirmation I can appoint him. I do not apprehend however any danger of his confirmation.

Kisses for yourself & Jess.

ULYS.

ALS, DLC-USG.

1. On March 26, 1864, USG telegraphed to Secretary of War Edwin M. Stanton. "I will see you in Washington tomorrow Sunday" Telegram received, DNA, RG 107, Telegrams Collected (Bound).

To Maj. Gen. William S. Rosecrans

In field, Culpepper C H. Va. March 26th 1864.
MAJ. GEN W. S. ROSECRANS COM'D'G. DEP'T. MO.
ST. LOUIS, MO.

It is desirable that as large force be brought into the field in the spring campaign as possible. To do this the garrisons for holding territory acquired and where there are no organized bodies of the enemy threatening, must be reduced to the smallest number possible necessary for the end to be accomplished   Between the

Department of the Missouri and any considerable force of the enemy, Steeles Army now intervenes. There is therefore in the Department nothing but irresponsible squads of guerellas and restless and dissatisfied Citizens to guard against. It looks to me as if a force consisting mostly of light cavalry, unencumbered with transportation and surplus equipage was the most needed for this purpose. An examination of the last return furnished by you shows that you have already a large preponderance of mounted troops, and if you deemed necessary I think two more regiments of cavalry can be added to that you already have. With such an addition to your mounted force you ought by judicious posting of your troops to spare from 5. to seven thousand of your present effective infantry, for service elsewhere. You are therefore directed to take immediate steps to collect all the infantry you can spare, not less than five thousand effectives, if your command has not been much reduced since last return, at St Louis or some other point convenient to the Mississippi river, where they can be embarked at short notice for any point to which they may be ordered. Report to these Headquarters by telegraph the number of troops you will be able to spare and the time when you will have them ready to embark and from what point. Such troops as you select to be sent to the field will bring with them their transportation, camp and garrison equipage

U S GRANT Lieut. Gen

Copies, DLC-USG, V, 45, 59; DNA, RG 108, Letters Sent; Rosecrans Papers, CLU. *O.R.*, I, xxxiv, part 2, 740–41.

On March 22, 1864, Maj. Gen. William S. Rosecrans wrote to USG. "I have sent Major Bond A. D. C. with a letter to General Halleck to see about my Provost Marshal General. I give him this note to you that he may answer any questions you may desire about the condition of affairs in this Dept. and about the changes and measures proposed here for the good of the service. I have directed him to say that the season is so far advanced that it is very desirable to have the policy for the coming summer at once marked out." Copy, DNA, RG 393, Dept. of Mo., Letters Sent. *O.R.*, I, xxxiv, part 2, 694–95.

On April 4, 11:30 P.M., Rosecrans telegraphed to USG. "Only four ~~regts~~ regiments of Volunteer one of state militiaa and six Companyies Colored recruits infantry in this Department One of these regiments ~~are~~ is guards of Alton prison One and the militia guard the interior fortified depots Pilot Knob Rolla and Warrensburg. Only two here at St. Louis twelve Hundred men Could not spare them without other troops. Very sorry have written you fully" ALS (telegram sent), DNA, RG 107, Telegrams Collected (Unbound); telegram received, *ibid.*, Telegrams Collected (Bound); *ibid.*, RG 108, Letters Received. *O.R.*, I, xxxiv, part 3, 42. On April 6, Rosecrans wrote to USG. "Your letter of the 26th Ult was handed me by General Hunt. I enter warmly into your views of brnging all our available force into the field in the coming campaign. My regret is that I shall not be able to give you much assistance from this Department. You will see by the accompanying 'Tri monthly for March 31' that our force here consists of Four Regiments U. S. Vol. Infantry; six comps Colored recruits   One Regiment M. S. Militia Infy,   Seven Regiments M. S. Vol Cavalry   Nine Regiments M. S. M Cavalry, & One Regiments Heavy Artillry not full   Of these four regiments of Vol. Infantry one whose term expires in June next, is the prison guard at Alton, two guard this City and the depots and landings here, the remaining one with the Militia infantry guard the fortified depots and some important R. R. Bridges in the interior. The existence of secret rebel organization diffused through the State a feverish state of public mind from apprehension of bushwhacking and rebel raids when the leaves come out, joined the magnitude of our interests in the depots here render it in my opinion inexpedient to with draw the infantry from those interior posts or greatly to reduce the force now on guard duty in this City. The total available infantry,—only three regiments, some two thousand effectives, could only be spared by replacing them with dismounted cavalry. Considering the additional expense and inferior discipline and efficiency for this kind of service would this be advisable? As to our Cavalry:—Were the M S. M converted into U. S. Vols or were the organized rebel and guerrilla force in Northern Arkansas driven out we would have more than sufficient. And when public confidence and tranquillity is once fully established the piotcting force could be still further reduced. But at present it is a matter of high public interest that the inhabitan[ts] should feel sufficiently secure to put in there spring crops. I respectfully recommend 1. That you spare two or three good cavalry rgiments to this Dept   2. That I receive authority to organize such of the M S M cavalry are willing to enlist in the U S. Vol. or Veteran Service and to consolidate and use or Muster out the remainder as may seem best. 3. If Genl Steele cannot do it that this Department be permitted to occupy the northern tier of counties in Arkansas and to establish a post at Pocahontas supplied by steamboat up White River having a gunboat for convoy until we get rid of the rbels there. These measure will enable me soon to rduce the force needed to get some troops available for outside service. Accompany is the Chf Qur Mr'ss Report of transportation sent with the tri monthly for your information"   ALS, MH. *O.R.*, I, xxxiv, part 3, 62. Entered as written on April 5 in DNA, RG 393, Dept. of Mo., Letters Sent. See telegram to Maj. Gen. William S. Rosecrans, April 9, 1864.

On April 11, Rosecrans telegraphed to Brig. Gen. John A. Rawlins. "If the Genl. in chief acedes to my views of allowing two good disciplined regiments of cavalry from without the state for this Department ask him to to please let me have the 2dnd Iowa and 3d Michigan—The 7th Kansas is a good fighting regiment but would be less likely to answer our purpose here"   ALS (telegram sent—dated April 12), DNA, RG 107, Telegrams Collected (Unbound); telegram received, *ibid.*, Telegrams Collected (Bound); *ibid.*, RG 108, Letters Received. *O.R.*, I, xxxiv, part 3, 136.

To Maj. Gen. William T. Sherman

By Telegraph From Culpepper March 26th 10. P. M. [*1864*]
To GENL SHERMAN NASHVILLE
AND COMMANDING OFFICER. MEMPHIS.

Forest should not be allowed to get out of the trap he has placed Himself in at Paducah. Send Grierson with all your Cavalry with orders to find and destroy him where ever found. If Genl Sherman has sent instructions they will govern.

U. S. GRANT
Lt Genl

Telegram received, DNA, RG 107, Telegrams Collected (Bound); *ibid.*, RG 393, 16th Army Corps, Miscellaneous Papers; copies, *ibid.*, RG 108, Letters Sent; *ibid.*, RG 393, Military Div. of the Miss., Telegrams Received; DLC-USG, V, 45, 59. *O.R.*, I, xxxii, part 3, 155. On March 27, 1864, Maj. Gen. William T. Sherman, Scottsboro, Ala., telegraphed to USG. "Your despatch recd. I had already ordered Veach with five (5) Regiments who was at Paducah last night to hurry up the Tennessee and strike inland to intercept Forrest also that Grierson should follow and attack Forrest no matter what the odds. I have with Mc person [*McPherson*] been examining our bridges at Decatur & Larkins. Tonight I go to Chatanooga, and tomorrow to Knoxville. I will be at Nashville in three days with a full knowledge of all matters pertaining to this army." Telegram received, DNA, RG 108, Letters Received. *O.R.*, I, xxxii, part 3, 165.

On March 28, 4:00 P.M., Sherman, Chattanooga, telegraphed to USG. "I am here, all well, no change in the attitude of things since you left. I had made orders as to Forrest which if executed with rapidity & energy should result in the dispersion or distruction of his forces." Telegram received, DNA, RG 107, Telegrams Collected (Bound); copies, *ibid.*, RG 393, Military Div. of the Miss., Letters Sent; DLC-USG, V, 94. *O.R.*, I, xxxii, part 3, 171. On the same day, midnight, Sherman telegraphed to USG. "Forrest is reported to have crossed the Tennessee eastward at Eddysville. I do not believe it but I have ordered him to be pursued from all points and if true I have no doubt his force will be broken up and destroyed. I wish you would as soon as possible name the Generals and Staff Officers to be assigned to me. I can place them better now than at a later period. Gen Reynolds has notified me that he has a sixty days leave from the War Department of which he proposes to avail himself now and that he is willing to give up his corps. I would therefore ask that a new corps commander be appointed for the 4th Corps. I will go up to Knoxville tomorrow to see Genl Schofield after which I can complete the organization and distribution of the whole command. The Enemy to our front and up the Tennessee seems inactive and I have no apprehension of any movement into East Kentucky and as soon as our furloughed men are back will be ready to test them on their own ground   Genl McPherson and I have inspected the whole line from Decatur to Chattanooga and have settled down to the conclusion that Decatur and Stevensonville are the true offensive points on the Tennessee. McPherson returns to Huntsville tonight" Telegram received, DNA, RG 107, Telegrams Collected (Bound); *ibid.*, RG 108, Letters Received; copies, *ibid.*, RG 393, Military Div. of the Miss., Letters Sent; DLC-USG, V, 94.

Also on March 28, 10:30 P.M., USG telegraphed to Sherman. "Cannot Steamers be used to supply our troops between Bridgeport and Lookout? And again to supply Knoxville from Chattanooga? If so it would enable you to accumulate supplies at the latter place." Telegram received, DNA, RG 107, Telegrams Collected (Bound); copies, *ibid.*, RG 108, Letters Sent; *ibid.*, RG 393, Military Div. of the Miss., Letters Sent; DLC-USG, V, 45, 59. *O.R.*, I, xxxii, part 3, 171. On March 29, 10:00 P.M., Sherman, Knoxville, telegraphed to USG. "Steamboats run regularly from Bridgeport to Chattanooga and from Chattanooga to Knoxville. Stores are rapidly accumulating at Chattanooga and Knoxville and I will push them still more rapidly. Longstreet is leaving East Tennessee for Virginia and the secessionists also are going south showing it to be a permanent abandonment   Gen Schofield has a much smaller command than I supposed, but he will push beyond Bulls Gap to develope the truth of the reports. Shall I order him to take up rails on the Rail Road so as to enable me to draw a part of his command to Genl Thomas when the time comes to move against Johnston? I shall stay here all day tomorrow and would like to hear from you before I return to Nashville." Telegram received, DNA, RG 107, Telegrams Collected (Bound); *ibid.*, RG 108, Letters Received; copies, *ibid.*, RG 393, Military Div. of the Miss., Letters Sent; DLC-USG, V, 94. *O.R.*, I, xxxii, part 3, 178. On March 31, USG telegraphed to Sherman. "I would destroy the rail-road as far to the East of Knoxville as possible. It is a good plan to ~~make the country to be held~~ concentrate all the forces you can wher fighting is expected and make all other territory necessary to hold defensible for the smallest possible number of troops." ALS (telegram sent), USMA; telegram received, DNA, RG 94, War Records Office, Dept. of the Cumberland; *ibid.*, RG 107, Telegrams Collected (Bound). *O.R.*, I, xxxii, part 3, 213. On the same day, 9:00 P.M., Sherman, Chattanooga, telegraphed to USG and Brig. Gen. Lorenzo Thomas. "Am just down from Knoxville   Longstreet is doubtless moving out of East Tennessee for Virginia   Schofield will occupy Bulls Gap with Infantry and feel up the Valley with Cavalry   Forrest was badly worsted at Paducah and is still between the Tennessee and Mississippi   I hope to catch him and break him up   Veatch is near Purdy with Infantry & Griersons cavalry is operating from Memphis   I will go to Nashville tomorrow where I can better direct the movement   All well here" Telegram received, DNA, RG 108, Letters Received; copies, *ibid.*, RG 393, Military Div. of the Miss., Letters Sent; DLC-USG, V, 94. *O.R.*, I, xxxii, part 3, 199–200.

On April 2, Sherman twice telegraphed to USG, the second time at 11:00 A.M. "Forrest is reported between Paducah and Jackson Tenn   I have posted Veatch with his five (5) regts. at Purdy and have ordered Hurlbut to move from Memphis with all his available forces towards the Hatchie   We will watch the Tennessee and Cumberland rivers and try and collect a force of veterans at Columbus to move against him direct   If I had a good bold officer at Columbus I would be better satisfied" Telegram received, DNA, RG 107, Telegrams Collected (Bound); copies, *ibid.*, RG 393, Military Div. of the Miss., Letters Sent; DLC-USG, V, 94. *O.R.*, I, xxxii, part 3, 230. "I am just back, having passed over my whole front, and spent a day with all my Army Commanders, possessing myself of the information necessary to act with inteligence. The problem of supplies is the most difficult. The Roads can now supply the daily wants of the Army, but does not accumulate a surplus, but I think by stopping the carriage of cattle and men and by runing the cars on the circuit from Nashville to Stevenson and Decatur it can be done with the present cars and locomotives. The superintendent of Railroads here, Mr Anderson, The Quarter Master Col Donaldson & myself will determine tonight. I find too many citizens and private freight along the Road, which are utterly inconsistent with our military necessities at this time. I will aim to accumulate in all april at Decatur & Chattanooga a surplus of seventy days provision and forage for one hundred thousand men." ALS (telegram sent), War Library and Museum, Military Order of the Loyal Legion, Philadelphia, Pa.; telegram received, DNA, RG 107, Telegrams Collected (Bound). *O.R.,* I, xxxii, part 3, 220. Secretary of War Edwin M. Stanton answered the second telegram. *Ibid.*

To Maj. Gen. Henry W. Halleck

Head Qrs. of the Army, In Field
Culpepper C. H. Va. March 28th/64

MAJ. GEN. H. W. HALLECK,
CHIEF OF STAFF OF THE ARMY,
WASHINGTON D. C.
GENERAL,

The batteries called for by Gen. Burnside had better be furnished in the way you suggest: that is to assign them to his Corps but leave them where they now are until his Corps is moved into the field.[1] They can then be ordered directly to the point where they will be wanted.

The order drafted by you is herewith returned with the request that it be published.[2]

I have ordered Gen. W. F. Smith to report to me in Washington City on Thursday next.[3] This order was given with the view of having him assigned to the command of the 10th Army Corps. I do not care however about the order being made, assigning him, until after he reports.

I think Gen. Wilson should be relieved from duty in the Cavalry Beauro as soon as it is possible to find an officer to sucseed him.[4] I can not suggest an officer to take his place.

In the Campaign which it is desirable to commence as soon as our veterans returns it is important to have some one near Banks who can issue orders to him and see that they are obeyed. This will be specially important if a move is made against Mobile as I now calculate upon. How to effect this I do not see unless all the territory embraced in the Depts. of the Mo. Kansas, the Arkansas and the Gulf are formed into a Military Div. Who to place in command of it I do not know. Of the four Dept. Commanders Steele would be by far the best, and would do very well. He has not got with him however a single General officer who I would like to trust alone with a command. The best suggestion I could make would be to promote Dodge for Steeles command. I wish you would think of this matter and give me your views.

> I am Gen. very respectfully
> your obt. svt.
> U. S. GRANT
> Lt. Gen. Com

ALS, Schoff Collection, MiU-C. *O.R.*, I, xxxiii, 752–53.

1. On March 26, 1864, Maj. Gen. Henry W. Halleck wrote to USG. "Major Genl Burnside has applied for six batteries now at Artillery Depot in this city to be assigned to his Army corps and sent to Annapolis. As these batteries are under drill and instruction here, and have quarters, I think they should remain till Burnside's corps is ordered to the field. If sent to Annapolis, barracks or tents must be provided for them there. Moreover, they may be very useful here in case of a raid on the city or across the Potomac. They will be kept in readiness to join Genl Burnside the moment he starts for the field. I think this arrangement far preferable to sending them at present to Annapolis. I think some measures should be adopted to prevent officers from corresponding with Members of Congress, Members of the Cabinet &c., on military affairs, without going through the proper military channels. A large portion of the time here and at the War Dept is taken up with these indirect applications for transfers, leaves of absence, promotions &c. The Secty of War is disposed to put a stop to this, by arresting every officer guilty hereafter of the offence. I enclose a draft of a Genl Order on this subject for your consideration." ALS, DNA, RG 108, Letters Received. *O.R.*, I, xxxiii, 741.

2. See *ibid.*, pp. 769–70.

3. March 31. On March 28, USG telegraphed to Maj. Gen. William F. Smith. "Report to me in Washington on next Thursday." ALS (telegram sent), DNA, RG 107, Telegrams Collected (Unbound); telegram received, *ibid. O.R.*, I, li, part 1, 1153. On March 18, 5:00 P.M., USG had telegraphed to Secretary of War Edwin M. Stanton. "I see it stated that Genl Smith has been nominated

for Major General Regular Army, on my recommendation. It was for Volunteer Service I recommended. My choice would be for Gen Sherman to recieve the other, or leave it open for competition" Telegram received, DNA, RG 107, Telegrams Collected (Bound); copies, *ibid.*, RG 108, Letters Sent; DLC-USG, V, 45, 59. In fact, Smith had been nominated to replace USG as maj. gen. of vols.

4. On April 6, USG telegraphed to Halleck. "Is Genl Wilson to come here? If he can be spared from the Cavalry bureau he is much wanted to command a Cavalry division I would like to know the decision of the Secy. of War in this matter as soon as possible so that the Cavalry command can be arranged" Telegram received, DNA, RG 107, Telegrams Collected (Bound); copies, *ibid.*, RG 108, Letters Sent; DLC-USG, V, 45, 59. *O.R.*, I, xxxiii, 809. See *ibid.*, p. 816. On April 7, Stanton telegraphed to USG. "General Wilson is relieved from the cavalry bureau and ordered to report to you." ALS (telegram sent), DNA, RG 107, Telegrams Collected (Bound). See letter to Maj. Gen. Ambrose E. Burnside, April 5, 1864.

To Maj. Gen. Edward O. C. Ord

Confidential—   Head Quarters of the Army, In Field,
                                           Culpepper C. H. Va. March 29th 1864
MAJ. GEN. E. O. C. ORD,
GENERAL,

In the expedition to start from Beverly Va,[1] and which you have been selected to command, the main object will be to destroy the East Ten. & Va. rail-road so that it can be of no further use to the enemy during the rebellion. Anything else that can be accomplished in the way of destroying what may be made useful by the enemy in prolonging the War will be well. Unless something should transpire to change present plans you will move, when directed to do so, by the most practicable route for Covington Va.[2] thence to the eas[i]est point of access ~~to~~ on the rail-road above alluded to. Gen. Crook will move about the same time from Charleston Va. striking for Saltville Va. and will work from that point Eastward to form a ~~connection~~ junction with you.—You may find it necessary to fall back from the line of the rail-road, to your former base, either in consequence of the difficulty of procuring supplies or by the movements of the enemy, especially Longstreet's or Breckenridges command. Not being able to communicate freely either with your Dept. Commander, or with these Hd Qrs. the necessity for such a move you will have to be the judge of. However, as there will be an advance attempted both East and West of you it is expected that you will find no difficulty in moving Eastward to Lynchburg,[3] and possibly, by subsisting upon the country for a time, establish a base of supplies on the James River. In case of this much success you will make no backward movement, at least not without further orders.

The Iron works at Fincastle[4] are of much importance to the enemy whilst they hold the part of the state in which they are located,   If therefore you find it necessary to fall back, and it is practicable to do so, destroy them beyond all repair.

This is not given as possitive official instructions, not having been given through the Dept. Commander. But it is the substance of what I now think will be your instructions, sent at the proper time, and in the proper manner, and is given in order that you may devote as much time as possible in obtaining a knowledge of the country over which you will have to operate.

> I am Gen. very respectfully
> your obt. svt.
> U. S. GRANT
> Lt. Gen.

ALS, Ord Papers, CU-B. *O.R.*, I, xxxiii, 758.
On March 14, 1864, Maj. Gen. Edward O. C. Ord, Louisville, telegraphed to USG. "Am ordered here to report to Washington   Can you send me orders" Telegram received, DNA, RG 107, Telegrams Collected (Bound). On March 14, Ord telegraphed to USG. "if you desire it I will follow you today   I reported to you by telegraph on the tenth 10th to Washington" Telegram received, *ibid.*, RG 108, Letters Received; copy, *ibid.*, RG 393, Military Div. of the Miss., Telegrams Received. On the same day, USG telegraphed to Ord. "Remain in Louisvill until I return"   Telegram received, Ord Papers, CU-B. On March 22, Ord telegraphed to USG. "Am without orders, Would rather have no Corps with you than one away." Telegram received, DNA, RG 107, Telegrams Collected (Bound). On March 23, USG telegraphed to Ord. "Report to me here for assignment." ALS (telegram sent), *ibid.*; telegram received, *ibid.*; Ord Papers, CU-B. On March 27, USG telegraphed to Capt. Alexander B. Sharpe, adjt. for Ord. "Where will a dispatch reach Genl Ord   answer immediately." Telegram received (press), DNA, RG 107, Telegrams Collected (Bound). On March 28, USG telegraphed to Ord, Louisville. "Report to me in person & without delay at

this place." Telegram received (press), *ibid.*; copies, DLC-USG, V, 45, 59; DNA, RG 108, Letters Sent.

On March 30, Ord wrote to USG. "On the way up Genl Crook stated to me very earnestly—that if Sigel had these 'instructions he'd be sure to blow and I said crook will fail' if he does—; as the success of an important expedition, in the commanders opinion would thus fail—I said to Genl C— I would telegraph you in the morning and ask if the command for Genl C could not be sent him by so many words & nothing said as to its probable route—I will take the risk—Lt. Col Painter hands you this   he wants to go with me & I want him—can he be ass in same manner as Majr Seward was—I telegraphd to day—will leave for Cumberland this P M—and if nothing reaches me there by telegraph from you directing otherwise will present the instructions to Genl. S—   I am sorry Genl Crook did not speak before I left so that if you thought proper Genl S could have been telegraphd accordingly—" ALS, *ibid.*, Letters Received. On the same day, 9:00 A.M., Ord telegraphed a similar message to USG. Telegram received, *ibid.*; *ibid.*, RG 107, Telegrams Collected (Bound). On the same day, 1:20 P.M., USG telegraphed to Ord. "Whilst Genl Sigel commands a department he will have to be treated with confidence—You will therefore deliver the letter addressed to him on your arrival—" Telegram received, Ord Papers, CU-B; DNA, RG 107, Telegrams Collected (Bound); copies, *ibid.*, RG 108, Letters Sent; DLC-USG, V, 45, 59. Printed as sent at 1:00 P.M. in *O.R.*, I, xxxiii, 770.

On April 9, Ord, Cumberland, Md., wrote to USG. "when on leave (sick) last winter I discovered (made an invention of,) what I think a matter of too much moment to delay putting in practice applied for caveat, and now want to experiment a few weeks—this raid of a Brigade can I find be managed as well or better by Averill, (whom I would have to follow) as by myself   Sigel is as jealous as the devil at my having come here, and I really think on that account that Averell will do *better* than I can—and I would give my right arm to carry out my discovery   you may think I want to get to some easy place—but I hope now that I tell you what the matter is you will let me go to Wheeling or some place where they have Shops &c for a couple of months—I intended telling you all this General but I thought when you gave me my orders that my services might be really necessary—and then I feared you might misunderstand me— loafing around here—for Sigel has taken the entire management of the organization upon himself—I have had time to think over the whole subject—I think my first duty is to pursue my discovery *other duties permitting*   You see general where my heart is, and you see I am running the risk of losing professional distinction to follow its desire—If you read the enclosed letter to Secty Stanton you will see what I was about willing to sacrifice to my invention—but I dont think Stanton cares enough for me to bother about it, hence I concluded to write to you —please destroy the letter to Stanton—and if you still want me to go on the raid— it is all right—" ALS, DNA, RG 108, Letters Received. On April 19, Lt. Col. Theodore S. Bowers issued Special Orders No. 15. "Major General E. O. C. Ord, U. S. Volunteers, is hereby relieved, at his own request, from duty in the Department of West Virginia, and will repair to Wheeling, Va., and there await further orders." Copies, DLC-USG, V, 57, 62. *O.R.*, I, xxxiii, 911. See telegram to Maj. Gen. Franz Sigel, April 17, 1864. On May 23, Ord wrote to Secretary of State William H. Seward that he had requested to be relieved because he believed that the expedition would lead to "failure, and defeat" after Sigel refused to furnish the necessary men and supplies. Ord did not mention his invention. Copy, DLC-Robert T. Lincoln.

1. Beverly, West Va., approximately one hundred miles west of Culpeper Court-House, Va.
2. Covington, Va., the western terminus of the Virginia Central Railroad, approximately seventy miles south of Beverly.
3. Lynchburg, Va., at the junction of the Virginia and Tennessee, Orange and Alexandria, and Petersburg and Lynchburg railroads, approximately ninety-five miles west of Petersburg and sixty miles southeast of Covington.
4. Fincastle, Va., approximately thirty-five miles west of Lynchburg.

To Maj. Gen. Franz Sigel

In field, Culpepper C. H. Va, March 29th 1864
MAJ. GEN. FRANZ SIGEL
CUMBERLAND, MD.

My object in ordering Gen. Crook here was with a view of learning from him the character of the country and roads in West Virgina, and to determine the practicability of ordering a cooperative movement from your Department, in connection with other movements, which will take place from other Departments. Whilst the long line of railroad you have to guard may require all the force you have, as opposing Armies now stand, for a movement towards the enemy, it looks to me that almost everything except a small force judiciously distributed for the protection of the most important bridges, might be spared. I would direct therefore that you collect at Beverly all the force you can spare, not less than eight thousand infantry, three batteries of Artillery and fifteen hundred picked cavalry, to make a southward move. This force is to be exclusive of that now commanded by Gen. Crook.

The concentration of this force at Beverly, should commence at once and when ready reported to me by telegraph. I will direct the date of their departure here after and the point at which they will strike making this movement simultaneous and cooperative with movements elsewhere. Troops should be required to travel as light as possible, and to live off the country where it can be done. In this latter case however *indiscriminate marauding should be avoided. Nothing should be taken not absolutely necessary for the troops, except when captured from an armed enemy.* Impressments should all be made under orders from the Commanding Officer and by a disbursing Officer. Receipts should be given for all property taken, so that the loyal may collect pay, and the property be accounted for.

Maj. Gen. E. O. C. Ord is ordered to report to you to be assigned to the command of the expedition.

Gen. Averill being acquainted with the country through which your forces will operate, I would suggest that he command the cavalry part of the expedition in person.

Every facility should be given to Gen. Ord to accumulate at Beverly all the supplies and equipments needed by him. I would suppose that ten days supply for his command would be required. If you have a pontoon train that too might be wanted with the expedition. You will give your own directions in this matter however, and will no doubt see that the proper supply of war munitions, pioneer tools &c. are sent.

Gen. Crook will be held in readiness to move at the same time with Gen. Ord, throwing his infantry south to hold the enemy from coming through the mountain gaps which they now hold, whilst with his cavalry, he makes his way through the East Tennessee and Virginia railroad and destroys it. His route probably should be left to himself. After striking the road he should however move eastward, destroying the railroad as he moves, and join Gen. Ord. Once united this force will be sufficient to choose their own route and time for returning to their base, or for executing such orders as may hereafter be given.

I have ordered two more regiments of cavalry to report at Charlestown, Va., and if I can will order infantry to report for the protection of the railroad. I do not see now where infantry is to come from, but will keep this in mind if it can be got

U. S. GRANT. Lieut. Gen.

Copies, DLC-USG, V, 45, 59; (2) Sigel Papers, OClWHi; DNA, RG 108, Letters Sent. *O.R.*, I, xxxiii, 765–66. See preceding letter.

On March 24, 1864, Lt. Col. Cyrus B. Comstock telegraphed to Maj. Gen. Franz Sigel. "Lt Genl Grant desires that if he can be spared for a few days Gen Crook be directed to report in person to Genl Grant at this place." Telegram received, DNA, RG 107, Telegrams Collected (Bound). On the same day, Sigel telegraphed to Comstock. "Gen Crook can be spared at present but it will take at least five (5) days to reach Culpepper   He being at Charleston Major Rucker of his staff is here—Is thoroughly acquainted with that Country and can give you valuable information   If you desire, I will send him with some papers prepared by me at once and will also direct Gen Crook to report to you if you deem best"   ALS (telegram sent), *ibid.*, Telegrams Collected (Unbound); telegram received, *ibid.*, Telegrams Collected (Bound). *O.R.*, I, xxxiii, 725. On the same day, 10:00 A.M., Comstock telegraphed to Sigel. "Lt Genl Grant requests that Gen Crook report to him without delay bringing the papers & information referred to in your Telegram of today"   ALS (telegram sent), DNA, RG 107, Telegrams Collected (Unbound); telegrams received (3), *ibid.*, Telegrams Collected (Bound). On March 25, 9:27 A.M., Sigel telegraphed to Comstock. "Your dispatch received and Gen Crook informed"   ALS (telegram sent), *ibid.*, Telegrams Collected (Unbound). See *O.R.*, I, xxxiii, 750.

On March 29, USG telegraphed to Maj. Gen. Henry W. Halleck. "Please order the 8th Ohio Cav.y Veterans Col. S. A. Gilbert Commanding to report to Gen. Crook at Charleston Va. I would like to have one other regiment at least ordered to the same place, say one of the regiments applied for a few days since by Gen. Sigel." ALS (telegram sent), DNA, RG 107, Telegrams Collected (Unbound); telegram received, *ibid.*, Telegrams Collected (Bound).

On March 31, Sigel telegraphed to USG. "Maj. General Ord has arrived. I will send report by ~~letter~~ messenger." Copy, *ibid.*, RG 393, Dept. of West Va., Letters Sent. *O.R.*, I, xxxiii, 778.

On March 31, Sigel wrote to USG. "I have the honor to acknowledge the receipt of your letter of the 29th inst. Maj. General Ord tells me, that he will leave to night. I take ~~A~~ opportunity ~~to~~ of sending you such information as I think most necessary and important. I also enclose a report, stating the condition of affairs here. This report was written before your letter of the 29th inst. was received. On the 2d page of this report, addressed to the Adj. General, you will find the total strength of the troops in this Department. Since that time ~~Wheaton~~son's brigade has left, also the 18th Connecticut and three ~~N~~ Maryland regiments are under Orders to be furloughed but have been stopped. There is no difficulty in regard to the Artillery an[d] Cavalry, but if I send 8000 Infantry to Beverly, hardly a man will be left to guard the Railroad and to protect New Creek, Cumberland and Harper's Ferry. According to a careful calculation about 6500 infantry can be sent to Beverly and they will be put in motion immediately. There will then remain within this Department 7 regts. of infantry, to be disposed of as follows: One regt (the 6th Va.) on the Railroad from Parkersburg to Oakland with a small reserve at Clarksburg. This regiment was raised under the proviso, to guard the Railroad and was never in the field   The 2 Md, Potomac Home Brigade, from Oakland to Cumberland. The 23d Illinois—Col. Mulligan's old regt., the remnants of the Irish Brigade', 454 men, at New Creek. One regiment, the 54th Pa, which was never in the field and in battle, from Cumberland to Hancock, with a small reserve at Cumberland. Two regiments (1 Md., Potomac Home Brigade and 2d Md. Eastern Shore, from Hancock to Frederick and Monocacy. One regt, the 34th Mass. at Harpers ferry. The ~~3~~ three Md. Rgts. mentioned have been ordered on furlough by the War department to be present at the Md. election, on the 6th of April. I have stopped them and would like to be informed whether they have to be furloughed or not. It was the wish of the Secretary of War, that they should be at their resp. places of election ~~on~~ three days before the 6th. I would respectfully suggest, that General Sullivan at Harpers Ferry be informed by Telegraph, whether the regiments can leave or not." Copy, Sigel Papers, OClWHi. See *O.R.*, I, xxxiii, 762–65.

To Col. Edward D. Townsend

Head Quarters In the Field,
Culpepper C. H. Va. March 30th/64

COL. E. D. TOWNSEND,
A. ADJ. GEN. OF THE ARMY,
WASHINGTON D. C,
COLONEL;

Your dispatch asking me to look over the Register and suggest the names of Brig. Gens. to be dropped, or mustered out of service, is rec'd. The following are names only of those personally known to my self as being unsuited for their positions; towit: W. R. Montgomery, Willis A. Gorman John Cook, N. B. Buford, Mason Brayman, T. T. Garrard and G. W. Deitzler. On their general reputation I would add very largely to this list, and if desired will do so. But I would suggest that Dept. Commanders be called on for the same suggestion I am now asked to make.

Very respectfully
your obt. svt.
U. S. GRANT
Lt. Gen.

ALS, CSmH. On March 29, 1864, Col. Edward D. Townsend wrote to USG. "The Secretary of War requests you will look over the Register and suggest names of Brigadier Generals who should be mustered out of service as such." LS (telegram sent), DNA, RG 107, Telegrams Collected (Unbound); copy, *ibid.*, RG 94, Letters Sent. On Sept. 1, 1863, Brig. Gen. William R. Montgomery wrote to Brig. Gen. John A. Rawlins asking to be assigned to command at Cairo. *O.R.*, I, xxx, part 3, 278–79. On Sept. 21, Rawlins endorsed this letter. "Respectfully referred to Major Genl. S. A. Hurlbut who will if he deems it best assign Genl. Montgomery to the command of the Post of Cairo, providing Genl. Montgomery will consent to report, and receive orders from the District Commander" Copies, DLC-USG, V, 25; DNA, RG 393, Dept. of the Tenn., Endorsements. *O.R.*, I, xxx, part 3, 278–79. Montgomery, USMA 1825, had been assigned to await orders at Cairo on March 2. After serving on a military commission at Memphis, he resigned as of April 4, 1864. Of the other brig. gens., Willis A. Gorman was

mustered out on May 4; John Cook, Napoleon B. Buford, and Mason Brayman
were mustered out on Aug. 24, 1865; Theophilus T. Garrard was mustered out
on April 4, 1864; and George W. Deitzler resigned as of Aug. 27, 1863.

To Maj. Gen. Henry W. Halleck

Culpepper, Va
March 30, 1864 10 P M

MAJ. GEN H W HALLECK
CHF-OF-STAFF

I think it advisable that Governors of States & Commanders of
all northern Departments be notified to forward to the field all recruits, new organizations, and all the old troops it is possible to
spare from their Dept. with the greatest dispatch   They can strip
their Departments to the lowest number of men necessary for the
duty to be performed. All veterans should return to the command
to which they belonged except when specially ordered otherwise—
All recruits and new organizations from Ohio and States East of
it, I would advise ordered to assemble at Washington and those
from States west of Ohio to be rendezvoused at Louisville—This
of course would not apply to recruits raised for particular Corps—

U S GRANT
Lieut Genl

Telegram received, DNA, RG 107, Telegrams Collected (Bound); copies, *ibid.*,
RG 108, Letters Sent; DLC-USG, V, 45, 59. *O.R.*, I, xxxiii, 770.
   On March 30, 1864, USG telegraphed to Maj. Gen. George G. Meade. "Are
the recruits for the 2d Corps coming forward? Gen. Hancock should urge them
up as rapidly as possible. ~~and~~ If any order is necessary for this let me know and
I will have it published." ALS (telegram sent), DNA, RG 107, Telegrams Collected (Unbound); telegram received, *ibid.*, RG 94, War Records Office, Army
of the Potomac. On March 31, Meade telegraphed to USG. "I have telegraphed
to Hancock & will let you know the result in the morning when I meet you at the
cars." ALS (telegram sent), *ibid.*, RG 107, Telegrams Collected (Unbound);
copy, Meade Papers, PHi.
   On March 30, USG telegraphed to Maj. Gen. Henry W. Halleck. "I will be
in Washington tomorrow on my way to Norfolk   Please notify the Quarter
master to have the steamer ready to leave the wharf at five (5) P. M." Telegram
received, DNA, RG 107, Telegrams Collected (Bound); copies, *ibid.*, RG 108,
Letters Sent; DLC-USG, V, 45, 59. *O.R.*, I, xxxiii, 770. On the same day, Halleck telegraphed to USG. "The 'City of Albany' steamer will be at foot of Sixth
Street at five P M to-morrow." ALS (telegram sent), DNA, RG 107, Telegrams

Collected (Bound); telegram received, *ibid*. On March 31, Brig. Gen. John A. Rawlins wrote to U.S. Representative Elihu B. Washburne. "The Genl is here and goes to Genl Butlers Head Quarters this P. M. on steamer City of Albany from foot of Sixth Street at 5 oclock ~~P. M.~~ You will therefore if you have not changed your mind which he hopes you have not please meet him there. 'Come dont fail' " ALS, DLC-Elihu B. Washburne.

On March 30, Halleck telegraphed to USG. "Gov. Bramlet asks to have that part of Kentucky west of the Tenn. River added to the Dept of the Ohio. Do you approve that arrangement?" ALS (telegram sent), DNA, RG 107, Telegrams Collected (Bound); telegram received, *ibid*.; *ibid*., RG 108, Letters Received. On the same day, USG telegraphed to Halleck. "I will leave the matter of changing the limits of the Department of the Ohio entirely to Gen. Sherman now that the three armies are operating in the same field—I see no objection to the state of Kentucky being all within either one of the departments—" Telegram received, *ibid*., RG 107, Telegrams Collected (Bound); copies, *ibid*., RG 108, Letters Sent; DLC-USG, V, 45, 59. *O.R.*, I, lii, part 1, 538.

To Maj. Gen. William T. Sherman

Culpeper C. H.
11 30 P m March 30th 1864

MAJ GENL. W. T. SHERMAN—
NASHVILLE

General F. P. Blair will be assigned to the seventeenth (17) Corps and not the fifteenth (15)[1]—Assign General Joseph Hooker subject to the approval of the President to any other Corps command you may have and break up the animosity[2] of one General commanding two (2) Corps—

U. S. GRANT
Lieut. Genl. Comdg

Telegram received, DNA, RG 107, Telegrams Collected (Bound); copies, *ibid*., RG 108, Letters Sent; *ibid*., RG 393, Military Div. of the Miss., Letters Received; DLC-USG, V, 45, 59, 94. *O.R.*, I, xxxii, part 3, 191.

1. On March 15, 1864, President Abraham Lincoln telegraphed to USG. "Gen. McPherson having been assigned to the command of a Department, could not Gen. Frank Blair without difficulty or detriment to the service, be assigned to command the Corps he commanded a while last Autumn? ~~without~~" ALS (telegram sent), DNA, RG 107, Telegrams Collected (Bound). Lincoln, *Works*, VII, 248. On March 16, 10:00 A.M., USG telegraphed to Lincoln. "Gen Logan commands the Corps referred to in your dispatch. I will see Gen. Sherman within a few days & consult him about the transfers and answer." Telegram received, DNA, RG 107, Telegrams Collected (Bound). On the same day, 7:15 P.M., USG

telegraphed to Maj. Gen. Francis P. Blair, Jr. "Why not the seventeenth the command of which is now vacant instead of the fifteenth Corps" Telegram received, *ibid.*; *ibid.*, Telegrams Collected (Unbound); copies, *ibid.*, Military Div. of the Miss., Letters Sent; DLC-USG, V, 34, 35. *O.R.*, I, xxxii, part 3, 81. On March 17, USG telegraphed to Lincoln. "Genl Sherman is here. He consents to the transfer of Gen Logan to the Seventeenth Corps and the appointment of Gen F. P. Blair to the Fifteenth Corps—" Telegram received, DNA, RG 107, Telegrams Collected (Bound). On March 26, Maj. Gen. John A. Logan, Huntsville, Ala., telegraphed to Brig. Gen. John A. Rawlins. "I am informed that it is contemplated to change my command to the seventeenth Corps. I hope this may not be done   I am now it the field with my corps fully organized and ready for any thing   The seventeenth will be to reorganize. I do not desire the change at this late date   Hope earnestly that it will not be made." Telegram received, *ibid.*, Telegrams Collected (Unbound); copy, *ibid.*, RG 393, 15th Army Corps, Letters Sent. On March 28, Logan wrote a similar letter to Lincoln. ALS, James S. Schoff, New York, N. Y.

On April 9, 10:00 P.M., USG telegraphed to Maj. Gen. Henry W. Halleck. "Will you please ascertain if Genl F. P. Blair is to be sent to Genl Sherman; if not an army Corps commander will have to be named for the 15th Corps. I would much sooner have Genl Hunter or Buell at Memphis than Hurlbut and Gen Sherman is not willing to try Hurlbut in the field again." Telegram received, DNA, RG 107, Telegrams Collected (Bound); copies, *ibid.*, RG 108, Letters Sent; DLC-USG, V, 45, 59. *O.R.*, I, xxxii, part 3, 304. On April 24, Col. Edward D. Townsend telegraphed to USG. "By order of the President Major General F. P. Blair has been assigned to command the seventeenth Army Corps—in General Orders number one hundred seventy eight (178)" ALS (telegram sent), DNA, RG 107, Telegrams Collected (Unbound). See *HED*, 38-1-80; *SRC*, 38-1-84. See also telegram to Maj. Gen. William T. Sherman, April 8, 1864.

2. The word is "anomaly" in USG's letterbooks.

To Maj. Gen. Nathaniel P. Banks

Washington March 31st 1864

MAJ. GEN. N. P. BANKS
COMD.G DEPT. OF THE GULF,
GENERAL:

In addition to the directions sent you by Lieut. Towner,[1] for immediate concentration at New Orleans of all the forces you can spare from the defence of your Dept. preparatory to a move against Mobile, I would now add the following:

1st   If sucsessful in your expedition against Schrieveport that you turn over the defence of the Red River to Gen. Steele and the Navy.[2]

2d   That you abandon Texas entirely with the exception of your hold upon the Rio Grande. This can be held with four thousand men if they will turn their attention immediately to fortifying their positions, ~~and~~ At least one half of the force required for this service might be taken from the colored troops.

3d   By properly fortifying on the Miss. River the force to guard it, from Port Hudson to New Orleans, can be reduced to ten thousand men, if not to a ~~much~~ less number. Six thousand men would then hold all the rest of the territory necessary to hold until active operations can again be resumed West of the river.—According to your last returns this would give you a force of over thirty thousand effective men with which to move against Mobile. To this I expect to add five thousand men from Missou[ri.] If however you think the force here stated too small to hold the territory regar[ded] as necessary to keep possession of I would say concentrate at least twenty-five thousand men of your present comman[d] for operations against Mobile. With these and such additions as I can give you from elswhere ~~loose~~ no time in making a demonstration to be followed by an attack, upon Mobile.

Two or more Iron Clads ~~have been~~ will be ordered to report to Admiral Farrigut. This gives him a strong Naval fleet with which to co-operate. You can make your own arrangements with the Admiral for his co-operation and select your own line of approach. My own idea of the matter is that Pascagoula should be your base, but from your long service in the Gulf Dept. you will know best about this matter.

It is intended that your movements shall be co-operative with movements of Armies elswhere and you cannot now start too soon. All I would now add is that you commence the concentration of your forces at once. Preserve a profound secrecy of what you intend doing and start at the earliest possible moment.

> I am General, very respectfully
> your obt. svt.
> U. S. GRANT
> Lt. Gen. Comd.g

ALS, DLC-Nathaniel P. Banks. Incomplete in *O.R.*, I, xxxiv, part 1, 11; *ibid.*, I, xxxvi, part 1, 15; *ibid.*, I, xxxviii, part 1, 4. On April 13, 1864, Maj. Gen. Nathaniel P. Banks, Grand Ecore, La., wrote to USG. "I had the honor to transmit to you at Washington, a report of recent operations in this Department. We have been compelled to act under circumstances of great difficulty, which have materially affected the course of events; but I trust that the results may meet with your approval. An immediate advance will be made upon the objective point of the expedition—Shreveport. In my conversation with General Sherman at New Orleans, I stated that I hoped to complete our operations within thirty days after reaching Red River at Fort DeRussy or Alexandria, which we should accomplish by the 15th ~~and~~ or 17th of March. I am still of opinion that this would have been accomplished except for the unavoidable delays that have been occasioned by the low stage of water in the Red River, and the very great difficulty of maintaining our communications on that line. My instructions however, were from Major General Halleck, who directed me to move upon Shreveport, and informed me that Generals Sherman and Steele, would co-operate with me in that view. No limitation of time was placed upon the movement, although it was expected to be accomplished with the least possible delay. I had the honor to receive from you a communication, to which a reply was forwarded on the 26th of March, by Lieutenant Towner. You instructed me in that communication that if the expedition could not be accomplished within ten or fifteen days of the time designated by General Sherman, the command of General Smith would be ordered to return to Vicksburg, even should it occasion the abandonment of the chief object of the expedition. The time specified I understand to be the 15th or 17th of the month; and I have hopes that within ten or fifteen days of that time our object will be accomplished, when General Smith will return. I have the honor to suggest however, that at this time his departure will affect other interests besides that of the possession of Shreveport. A large fleet of gunboats and transports, are in the upper river, which can not possibly descend below Alexandria on account of the falling water. I have in my immediate front, an army of twenty-five thousand men, among them some of the best troops of the rebel government, and commanded by distinguished and desperate officers. The withdrawal of General Smith's command from my forces at this time, places me at their mercy, and the army under my command. It will lead to the sacrifice of the army and the navy, as well as the abandonment of the expedition. My judgment is against it, and I can not believe that were the circumstances known to the government at Washington, that it would be insisted upon. Admiral Porter agrees with me fully in this view. I need not say that at the earliest moment when it may be done consistent with the safety of the army and navy, I shall execute the orders in relation to General Smith's return; until then, I hope he may be allowed to ~~ret~~ operate with us. The rebel army on the Red River, comprises the whole forces of the Trans-Mississippi Department, except a small number on the coast of Texas, under Magruder. If this organized force is destroyed, it can never be replaced. I regard that result as certain to be accomplished if our movement is not interrupted. This will enable you to throw all the forces now occupied in the Department of the Gulf as well as a large portion of those in Arkansas, and Missouri, to the support of the armies east of the Mississippi. If this expedition is abandoned without the destruction of the organized forces of the enemy now in our front, it will leave the Red River in his possession, and enable him constantly to threaten the navigation of the Mississippi. An army of twenty-five thousand (25,000) men holding possession of the Red River, makes the free navigation of the Mississippi a matter of perpetual uncertainty. This ought not to be. Its destruction is a work of certainty, requiring but small force and a short time, and will contribute greatly to the success of the cause of the Government, if accomplished without unnecessary delay. I await instructions from you upon this point with anxiety, promising that no unnecessary detention of the command of General Smith will be made." LS, DNA, RG 94, War Records Office, Union Battle Reports. *O.R.*, I, xxxiv, part 1, 186–87. On April 26, USG endorsed this letter. "Respectfully forwarded to the Secretary of War for the information of the President" ES, DNA, RG 94, War Records Office, Union Battle Reports. On April 13, Banks addressed to USG a lengthy report of the Red River campaign. LS, DNA, RG 94, War Records Office, Union Battle Reports; copies (3, dated April 14), DLC-Nathaniel P. Banks. *O.R.*, I, xxxiv, part 1, 181–85.

1. 2nd Lt. Horatio N. Towner, 2nd Ill. Light Art. See General Orders No. 7, Feb. 27, 1864.

2. On April 6, 9:30 A.M., USG telegraphed to Maj. Gen. William T. Sherman. "I have directed Gen. Banks to turn over the defense of the Red River to Gen. F. Steele and the Navy. Please give Gen. Steele such directions as you may think necessary to carry out this direction." Copies, DLC-USG, V, 45, 59, 94; DNA, RG 108, Letters Sent; *ibid.*, RG 393, Military Div. of the Miss., Letters Sent. *O.R.*, I, xxxiv, part 3, 56, 76. On April 8, Sherman wrote at length to Brig. Gen. John A. Rawlins acknowledging USG's telegram and outlining his plans for the future. *Ibid.*, pp. 85–86.

To Maj. Gen. Benjamin F. Butler

(Private & Confidential)[1]

Head Quarters of the Army, In Field
Fortress Monroe Va Apl. 2d 1864

MAJ. GEN. B. F. BUTLER,
COMD.G DEPT. OF VA & N. CAROLINA,
GENERAL,

In the spring campaign, which it is desirable shall commence at as early a day as practicable, it is proposed to have co-operative action of all the Armies in the field as far as this object can be accomplished. It will not be possible to unite our Armies into two or three large ones, to act as so many units, owing to the absolute necessity of holding on to the territory already taken from the enemy. But, generally speaking, concentration can be practically effected by Armies moving to the interior of the enemy's country from the territory they have to guard. By such movement they interpose themselves between the enemy and the country to be guarded, thereby ~~by~~ reducing the numbers necessary to garrison important points and at least occupy the attention of a part of the enemy's force if no greater object is gained.

Lee's Army, and Richmond, being the greater objects towards which our attention must be directed in the next campaign it is desirable to unite all the force we can against them. The necessity for covering Washington, with the Army of the Potomac, and of covering your Dept. with your Army, makes it impossible to unite these forces at the beginning of any move. I propose therefore what comes nearest this of anything that seems practicable. The Army of the Potomac will act from it present base, Lee's Army being the objective point. You will collect all the force from your command, that can be spared from Garrison duty, I should say not less than twenty thousand effective men, to operate on the south side of James River, Richmond being your objective point.—To the force you already have will be added about ten thousand men from South Carolina under Maj. Gen. Gilmore who will command them in person. Maj. Gen. W. F. Smith is ordered to report to you to command the troops sent into the field from your own Dept.

Gen. Gilmore will be ordered to report to you at Fortress Monroe, with all his troops on transports, by the 18th inst. or as soon thereafter as practicable. Should you not receive notice by that time to move you will make such disposition of them, and your other forces, as you may deem best calculated to deceive the enemy ~~of~~ as to the real move to be made.

When you are notified to move take City Point[2] with as much force as possible. Fortify, or rather intrench, at once and concentrate all your troops for the field, there, as rapidly as you can.

From City Point directions cannot be given at this time for your further movements. The fact that has already been stated, that is, that Richmond is to be your objective point, and that there is to be co-operation between your force and the Army of the Potomac must be your guide. This indicates the necessity of your holding close to the south bank of the James River as you advance.

Then should the enemy be forced into his intrenchments in Richmond the Army of the Potomac would follow and by means of transports the two Armies would become a unit. All the minor details of your advance are left entirely to your direction. If however you think it practicable to use your Cavalry south of you so as to cut the rail-road about Hicksford, about the time of the general advance, it would be of imense advantage.

You will please forward for my information at the earlyest practicable day all orders, details and instructions you may give for the execution of this order.

> I am Gen. very respectfully
> your obt. svt.
> U. S. Grant
> Lt. Gen Com

ALS, DLC-USG, I, B. *O.R.*, I, xxxiii, 794–95; *ibid.*, I, xxxiv, part 1, 12; *ibid.*, I, xxxvi, part 1, 15–16; *ibid.*, I, xxxviii, part 1, 5.

On April 2, 1864, 11:00 A.M., USG, Fort Monroe, telegraphed to Maj. Gen. Henry W. Halleck. "I should have been in Washington today but for a Storm [still] raging to such an extent as [to] make navigation in the Chesapeake [un]safe. I leave here as soon as the storm subsides" Telegrams received (2), DNA, RG 107, Telegrams Collected (Bound); *ibid.*, Telegrams Collected (Unbound). Printed as sent at 11:30 A.M. in *O.R.*, I, xxxiii, 790.

On April 3, Maj. Gen. Benjamin F. Butler wrote to USG. "Referring to a conversation that we had at my office I have the honor to request that you will order to report to me for duty Brig. Genl's Hazen and Neal." Copy, DNA, RG 393, Dept. of Va. and N. C., Letters Sent. On April 5, USG telegraphed to Butler. "Gen. W. T. H. Brooks an officer Gen. Smith thinks most highly of has been ordered to report to you—If Neil can be spared I will send him also.—" Telegram received, DLC-Benjamin F. Butler; (2) DNA, RG 107, Telegrams Collected (Bound); *ibid.*, Telegrams Collected (Unbound); copies, *ibid.*, RG 108, Letters Sent; DLC-USG, V, 45, 59. On the same day, USG telegraphed to Maj. Gen. George G. Meade. "Can you spare Gen Neill from your command? If so I want to order him to Gen Butler to command of a division" Telegram received, DNA, RG 94, War Records Office, Army of the Potomac; copies, *ibid.*, RG 108, Letters Sent; DLC-USG, V, 45, 59; Meade Papers, PHi. Probably on April 5 (misdated April 4), Meade telegraphed to USG. "I should be very sorry to lose Genl. Neill, he is one of my best brigade Commanders—I would prefer to transfer Maj. Genl. Birney—or Brig Genls. Ricketts or Prince.—" ALS (telegram sent), DNA, RG 107, Telegrams Collected (Unbound). Also on April 5, Lt. Col. Cyrus B. Comstock telegraphed to Meade. "Lt. Gen. Grant desires to know if you need a division commander—if so Gen. Crittenden will be ordered to report to you." ALS (telegram sent), *ibid.*, RG 108, Letters Sent by Comstock. On the same day, 6:00 P.M., Meade telegraphed to Comstock. "I do have no infantry Division vacant, but desire Division Commanders for the Cavalry—I would prefer seeing Lt. Genl. Grant which I will do tomorrow, before he decides on any.—" ALS (telegram sent), *ibid.*, RG 107, Telegrams Collected (Unbound); copy, Meade Papers, PHi.

On April 8, Butler telegraphed to USG. "Please order Col. Hiram Burnham 6th Maine, whose name is now before the senate for appointment as a Brigadier to ~~order~~ me to take ~~to me~~ a Brigade & also Genls Hazen & Niel if possible." Telegrams received (2), DNA, RG 107, Telegrams Collected (Unbound); ADfS, DLC-Benjamin F. Butler. On the same day, 9:00 P.M., USG telegraphed to Butler. "General W. H. T. Brooks a reliable Division Commander has been ordered to you. Hazen nor Neil can be spared from where they are without injury to the Service. I will find out if Colonel Burnham can go and if so send him" Telegram received, *ibid.*; DNA, RG 107, Telegrams Collected (Bound); copies, *ibid.*, RG 108, Letters Sent; DLC-USG, V, 45, 59. Also on April 8, Butler wrote to USG. "Wincoop's Regiment of Cavalry, stationed at Harrisburg I understand, commanded by a very excellent officer, is now full, and I respectfully ask that it may be ordered to this Department. I also desire that you will order me a first class Brig. General for a Cavalry Officer. I have none in my Department, and referring to my conversation with you as to a Cavalry movement, you will see the necessity. I ask that Lt. Col. Bowen, A. A. General, now with the 9th Army Corps, be ordered to report to me for duty with General Smith, provided General Burnside offers no objection. I am afraid that there may be some hitch in transportation in view of that which has been sent to General Gilmore, and the delay getting off from New York, and also because the sea-going vessels drawing 15 feet will be hardly able to ascend the bars of York River and the Pamunky with 9 ft. of water, but will endeavor to do everything I may to remedy the evil. I beg leave to call your attention to the substance of a telegram forwarded you today with regard to the detail of Col. Hiram Burnham to take charge of a Brigade, and also beg leave to refer to Generals Hazen and Neal. General Brooks has been ordered to report here, but has not yet done so, and in view of what has taken place probably will not do so. For this reason I press the applications for Generals Hazen and Neal. If General Brooks should be confirmed as Major General, he would rank General Smith, which I suppose was not your intention, but I understand that his name has been withdrawn." *Private and Official Correspondence of Gen. Benjamin F. Butler . . .* (n. p., 1917), IV, 42. On April 9, USG telegraphed to Meade. "Has Col Burnham been appointed a Brig Gen and can you spare him. Gen Butler applies for him." Telegram received, DNA, RG 94, War Records Office, Army of the Potomac; copy, Meade Papers, PHi. On the same day, 1:30 P.M., Meade telegraphed to USG. "The Secretary of War on the 3rd inst advised me that Col. Burnham 6th Maine, had been that day nominated as Brig Genl—He cannot be appointed till he is confirmed. Altho' there are twenty one brigades in this Army commanded by Cols— I am willing Col Burnham should be transferred if the exigencies of the public service require it" ALS (telegram sent), DNA, RG 107, Telegrams Collected (Unbound); copies, *ibid.*, RG 393, Army of the Potomac, Telegrams Sent; Meade Papers, PHi.

On April 12, Butler telegraphed to USG. "Dont think me importunate but for the good of the Service Can you not send me Brig Gen J. H. Wilson now of the Cavalry Bureau as chief of Cavalry to lead our expedition." ALS (telegram sent), DLC-Benjamin F. Butler; telegram received, DNA, RG 107, Telegrams Collected (Bound). *O.R.*, I, xxxiii, 850. On the same day, USG twice telegraphed to Butler, at 1:30 P.M. and 11:00 P.M. "Gen. Burnham is ordered to report to you. Gen. Brooks will be there also. Williams has not the rank for the command you suggest. It will be impracticable to give you either Neill or Hazen. If possible to give you a Cavalry Commander I will accommodate you." ALS (telegram sent), DNA, RG 107, Telegrams Collected (Bound); telegram received, *ibid.* *O.R.*, I, xxxiii, 850. "General Wilson has been assigned and commands a Division of Cavalry with the Army of the Potomac. He reported there for duty today. If I can send you General Rucker now doing Qr. Master duty I will send him, or substitute him for Wilson, and send the latter" Telegram received, DLC-Benjamin F. Butler; copies, DNA, RG 108, Letters Sent; DLC-USG, V, 45, 59. See *O.R.*, I, xxxiii, 851, 862. On April 14, Maj. Gen. William T. Sherman telegraphed to USG. "Gen Hazen is here—says W. F. Smith was promised a Division. Of course if Hazen is to be advanced I will heartily agree, but not otherwise,—without orders, he will have his old brigade, in Howards Corps." Telegram received, DNA, RG 107, Telegrams Collected (Bound); *ibid.*, RG 108, Letters Received. *O.R.*, I, xxxii, part 3, 352. On the same day, 11:00 P.M., USG telegraphed to Sherman. "Gen. Hazen has been applied for but I have declined transfering him." ALS (telegram sent), DNA, RG 107, Telegrams Collected (Bound); telegram received, *ibid.*; DLC-Benjamin F. Butler. On April 13, Butler telegraphed to USG. "I have no objections to General Rucker. Believe him to be a good Officer but for our expedition would prefer General Wilson a younger man. I have no Cavalry Officer—it is of the last importance that I have one at once." ALS (telegram sent), *ibid.*; telegram received, DNA, RG 107, Telegrams Collected (Bound). *O.R.*, I, xxxiii, 862. On the same day, 10:30 P.M., USG telegraphed to Butler. "I can send you Col. Kautz to command your Cavalry Div. He is a good Cavalry officer. Do you want him sent?" ALS (telegram sent), DNA, RG 107, Telegrams Collected (Bound); telegram received, *ibid.*; DLC-Benjamin F. Butler. *O.R.*, I, xxxiii, 862. On April 14, 9:30 P.M., Butler telegraphed to USG. "Col. Kauts is a most excellent officer but all my Cavalry Colonels rank him. No officer ordered here has as yet reported." ALS (telegram sent), DNA, RG 107, Telegrams Collected (Unbound); LS, *ibid.*; telegram received, *ibid.*, Telegrams Collected (Bound). *O.R.*, I, xxxiii, 865. Also on April 14, USG telegraphed to Brig. Gen. John A. Rawlins. "If Brig. Gen. Burnham has not been ordered to Gen Butler order him to report there at once. I will not be able to go out to-day." ALS (telegram sent), DNA, RG 107, Telegrams Collected (Bound); telegram received, *ibid.*

On April 16, USG telegraphed to Maj. Gen. Ambrose E. Burnside. "If you can Spare. Col Bowen order him to Genl. Butler to report to Genl. W. F Smith for duty" Telegram received, *ibid.*, Telegrams Collected (Unbound); *ibid.*, Telegrams Collected (Bound); copies, *ibid.*, RG 108, Letters Sent; DLC-USG, V, 45, 59. On April 17, Burnside telegraphed to USG. "Will order Col Bowen to genl Butler for Gen Smith at once. The order in reference to Veteran regts. has not reached me yet." Telegram received, DNA, RG 107, Telegrams Collected (Bound). On April 18, USG telegraphed to Burnside. "What order in relation to veteran regts is it that you refer to?" Telegram received (press), *ibid.* On the same day, Burnside telegraphed to USG. "I mean the Veteran Regts from Dept of the south now at home & in washn." Telegram received, *ibid.*, Telegrams Collected (Unbound).

1. Not in USG's hand.
2. City Point, Va., the eastern terminus of the Petersburg and Lynchburg Railroad, ten miles northeast of Petersburg on the James River.

To Brig. Gen. Lorenzo Thomas

Washington, D. C., Apl. 4th *1864.*

ADJ. GEN. OF THE ARMY,

The President consents to the following changes being made in the Mil. Div. of the Miss. towit:

The 11th & 12th Army Corps to be consolidated and called the 1st Army Corps, Maj. Gen. J. Hooker to command.

Maj. Gen. G. Granger to be relieved from command of the 4th A. C. and Maj. Gen. Howard appointed to the command.

Maj. Gen. Schofield to be appointed to command the 23d A. C.

Maj. Gen. Slocum will report to Gen Sherman for assignment, and Maj. Gen. Stoneman to Gen. Schofield. Gen. Granger will report by letter to the A. G. of the Army by letter.

> Very respectfully
> your obt. svt.
> U. S. GRANT
> Lt. Gen. Com

ALS, CSmH. *O.R.*, I, xxxii, part 3, 246–47.

On April 2, 1864, Maj. Gen. William T. Sherman had telegraphed to USG. "After a full consultation with all my Army Commanders I have settled down to the following conclusions, to which I would like to have the Presidents Consent before I make orders— 1st Army of the Ohio. Three Divisions of Infantry to be styled the 23rd Corps, Maj Gen Schofield in Command. One Division of Cavalry, Maj Gen Stoneman,—to push Longstreets forces well out of the valley, then fall back breaking Railroad to Knoxville to hold Knoxville & Loudon & be ready by May 1, with 12000 men to act as the Left of the Grand Army. 2nd. Gen Thomas to organize his Army into three Corps. The 11th and 12th to be United under Maj Genl Hooker, to be composed of four Divisions. The Corps to take a new title viz one of the series now vacant. Genl. Slocum to be transfered East, or assigned to some local command on the Mississipi. The 4th Corps Granger, to remain unchanged, save to place Genl Howard in command. The 14th Corps to remain the Same. Genl Palmer is not equal to such a command, and all parties are willing that Genl Buell or any tried soldier should be assigned. Thomas to guard the Lines of communication, and have by May 1, a command of 45,000 men for active service, to constitute the Centre. 3rd. Gen McPherson to draw from the Mississipi the Divisions of Crocker & Leggett now en route, mostly of veterans on furlough, and of A. J. Smith now up Red River, but due on the 10th inst out of that expedition, and to organize a force of 30000 men to operate from

Larkinsville or Guntersville as the Right of the Grand Army. His Corps to be commanded by Logan, Frank Blair and Dodge. Hurlbut will not resign and I know no better disposition of him than to leave him at Memphis. I propose to put Newton when he comes at Vicksburg. With these changes this army will be a Unit in all respects, and I can suggest no better. I ask the Presidents consent and ask what title I shall give the new Corps of Hooker, in place of the 11th and 12th consolidated. The lowest number of the Army Corps now vacant will be most appropriate. I will have the Cavalry of the Dept of the Ohio reorganized under Stoneman at or near Camp Nelson, and the Cavalry of Thomas, at least one Good Division under Garrard at Columbia." ALS (telegram sent), Schoff Collection, MiU-C; telegram received, DNA, RG 107, Telegrams Collected (Bound). *O.R.*, I, xxxii, part 3, 221. See following letter.

To Maj. Gen. William T. Sherman

Private & Confidential

Washington, D. C., Apl. 4th *1864.*

MAJ. GEN. W. T. SHERMAN,
COMD.G MIL. DIV. OF THE MISS.
GENERAL,

It is my design, if the enemy keep quiet and allow me to take the initiative in the Spring Campaign to work all parts of the Army to-gether, and, somewhat, towards a common center. For your information I now write you my programme as at present determined upon.

I have sent orders to Banks, by private messenger, to finish up his present expedition against Schrievesport with all dispatch. To turn over the defence of the Red River to Gen. Steele and the Navy and return your troops to you and his own to New Orleans. To abandon all of Texas, except the Rio Grande and to hold that with not to exceed four thousand men. To reduce the number of troops on the Miss. to the lowest number necessary to hold it and to collect from his command not less than twenty-five thousand men. To this I will add five thousand from Mo. With this force he is to commence operations against Mobile as soon as he can. It will be impossible for him to commence too early.

Gilmore joins Butler with ten thousand men and the two operate against Richmond from the south side of James River.[1] This will give Butler thirty-three thousand men to operate with, W. F. Smith commanding the right wing of his forces and Gilmore the left wing. I will stay with the Army of the Potomac increased by Burnsides Corps of not less than 25.000 effective men, and operate directly against Lee's Army wherever it may be found. Sigel collects all his available force in two columns, one under Ord & Averell to start from Beverly Va. and the other under Crook to start from Charleston on the Kanawphy to move against the Va. & Ten. rail-road. Crook will have all Cavalry and will endeavor to get in about Saltville and move East from there to join Ord. His force will be all cavalry whilst Ord will have from ten to twelve thousand men of all arms. You I propose to move against Johnston's Army, to break it up and to get into the interior of the enemy's country as far as you can, inflicting all the damage you can against their War resources.

I do not propose to lay down for you a plan of Campaign but simply to lay down the work it is desirable to have done and leave you free to execute in your own way. Submit to me however as early as you can your plan of operation.

As stated Banks is ordered to commence operations as soon as he can. Gilmore is ordered to report at Fortress Monroe by the 18th inst, or as soon thereafter as practicable. Sigel is concentrating now. None will move from their places of rendezvous until I direct, except Banks. I want to be ready to move by the 25th inst, if possible. But all I can now direct is that you get ready as soon as possible   I know you will have difficulties to encounter getting through the mountains to where supplies are abundant, but I believe you will accomplish it.

From the expedition from the Dept. of West Va. I do not calculate on very great results. But it is the only way I can take troops from there. With the long line of rail-road Sigel has to protect he can spare no troops except to move directly to his front. In this way he must get through to inflict great damage on the enemy, or the enemy must detach from one of his armies a large force to prevent it. In other words if Sigel cant skin himself he can hold a leg whilst some one else skins.[2]

> I am General, very respectfully your obt. svt.
> U. S. GRANT
> Lt. Gen.

ALS, DLC-William T. Sherman. *O.R.*, I, xxxii, part 3, 245–46. On April 9, 1864, 10:30 P.M., Maj. Gen. William T. Sherman telegraphed to USG. "Your letters of April 4th are this moment recieved and suit me exactly   I will write fully   All is well with me and I will be on time any how." Telegram received, DNA, RG 107, Telegrams Collected (Bound); copies, *ibid.*, RG 393, Military Div. of the Miss., Letters Sent; DLC-USG, V, 94. *O.R.*, I, xxxii, part 3, 305. On April 10, Sherman wrote to USG. *"Private & Confidential* . . . Your two letters of April 4 are now before me, and afford me infinite satisfaction. That we are now all to act in a Common plan, Converging on a Common Center looks like Enlightened War. Like yourself you take the biggest load and from me you shall have thorough and hearty cooperation. I will not let side issues draw me off from your main plan in which I am to Knock Joe Johnston, and do as much damage to the resources of the Enemy as possible. I have heretofore written to Genl Rawlins and Col Babcock of your staff somewhat of the method in which I propose to act. I have seen all my army, Corps and Division Commanders and have signified only to the former, viz Schofield, Thomas and McPherson, our general plans, which I inferred from the purport of our conversation here and at Cincinati. First I am pushing stores to the Front with all possible despatch, and am completing the organization according to the orders from Washington which are ample & perfectly satisfactory. I did not wish to displace Palmer, but asked George Thomas to tell me in all frankness exactly what he wanted. All he asked is granted and all he said was that Palmer *felt* unequal to so large a Command and would be willing to take a Division provided Buell or some tried & experienced soldier were given the Corps. But on the whole Thomas is now well content with his command, so are Schofield & McPherson. It will take us all of April to get in our furloughed veterans, to bring up A. J. Smiths command, and to collect provisions and cattle to the Line of the Tennessee. Each of the three armies will guard by detachmts of its own their Rear communications. At the signal to be given, by you, Schofield will leave a select Garrison at Knoxville & Loudon and with 12000 men drop down to Hiwassee & march on Johnstons Right by the Old Federal Road. Stoneman now in Kentucky organizing the Cavalry forces of the Army of the Ohio, will operate with Schofield on his left front, it may be pushing a select body of about 2000 Cavalry by Ducktown on Elijay & towards Athens. Thomas will aim to have 45000 men of all arms and move straight on Johnston wherever he may be, fighting him cautiously, persistently and to the best of advantage. He will have two Divisions of Cavalry to take advantage of any offering. McPherson will have nine Divisions of the Army of the Tennessee if A. J. Smith get in—in which case he will have full 30000 of the best men in America. He will cross the Tennessee at Decatur and Whitesburg march towards Rome and feel for Thomas. If Johnston fall behind the Coosa, then McPherson push for Rome, and if Johnston then fall behind the Chattahoochie as I believe he will, then Mc-

Pherson will cross and join with Thomas. McPherson has no cavalry, but I have taken one of Thomas' Divisions, viz Garrards, 6000 strong, which I now have at Columbia mounting equipping and preparing. I design this Division to operate on McPherson's Right Rear or Front according as the enemy appears. But the moment I detect Johnston falling behind the Chattahoochee I propose to cast off the Effective part of this Cavalry Division after crossing Coosa, straight for Opelika, West Point, Columbus or Wetumpka, to break up the Road between Montgomery and Georgia. If Garrard can do this work good he can return to the main army, but should a superior force interpose, then he will seek safety at Pensacola, and join Banks, or after Rest act against any force that he can find on the East of Mobile, till such time as he can reach me. Should Johnston fall behind Chattahoochee I would feign to the Right but pass to the Left and act on Atlanta or ~~to~~ on its Eastern communications according to developed facts. This is about as far ahead as I feel disposed to look, but I would ever bear in mind that Johnston is at all times to be kept so busy that he cannot in any event send any part of his command against you or Banks. If Banks can at the same time carry Mobile and open up the Alabama River he will in a measure solve the most difficult part of my problem, *Provisions*. But in that I must venture. Georgia has a million of Inhabitants. If they can live we should not starve. If the enemy interrupt my communications I will be absolved from all obligations to subsist on our own resources, but feel perfectly justified in taking whatever & whereever I can find. I will inspire my command if successful with my feeling that Beef & Salt are all that is absolutely necessary to Life & parched Corn fed General Jacksons Army once, on that very ground.—" ALS, PHi. *O.R.*, I, xxxii, part 3, 312–14.

1. On April 4, Maj. Gen. Henry W. Halleck wrote for USG to Maj. Gen. Quincy A. Gillmore concerning this move. ALS, DNA, RG 108, Letters Sent (Press). *O.R.*, I, xxxv, part 2, 34.
2. See Tyler Dennett, ed., *Lincoln and the Civil War in the Diaries and Letters of John Hay* (New York, 1939), p. 179; *Memoirs*, II, 143.

To Maj. Gen. William T. Sherman

Washington, D. C., Apl. 4th *1864.*

MAJ. GEN. W. T. SHERMAN,
COMD.G MIL. DIV. OF THE MISS.
GENERAL.

Most of the changes asked for by you, in your command have been made. The 11th & 12th Corps will be consolidated and the new Corps formed from them called the 1st Maj. Gen. Hooker to command. Schofield is assigned to the command of the 23d Corps which will embrace all the troops in his Dept. You can order such of them to the front to take the field as you deem best. Howard is assigned to the command of the 4th Corps.

I suggested Slocum to command the district of Vicksburg because there is such a large proportion of colored troops in that District, ~~and~~ (more will be constantly organizing,) and Slocum will take an active interest in this work which the President & Secretary of War fear Newton[1] will not. I do not join in this fear but have not had the oportunity of hearing Gen. Newton's views on the subject. He is evidently a Soldier and a Soldier does not consult his own views of policy when orders from his superiors intervene.

General Palmer will not be releived from the command of the 14th Corps at present. Indeed you have no officer of the rank of Maj. Gen. who could replace him. I think you will find Palmer a prompt, brave and hard working Corps commander.

> I am Gen. very respectfully
> your obt. svt.
> U. S. GRANT
> Lt. Gen.

ALS, DLC-William T. Sherman. On April 4, 1864, 8:00 P.M., USG telegraphed to Maj. Gen. William T. Sherman. "The 11th & 12th Corps will be consolidated ~~and~~ into the 1st Corps Hooker commanding. Howard will command the 4th Corps, Schofield the 23d. Relieve Granger assign Slocum to command Vicksburg District and Newton to a Division or wherever else you think best." ALS (telegram sent), DNA, RG 107, Telegrams Collected (Bound); telegram received, *ibid.*; DLC-William T. Sherman. *O.R.*, I, xxxii, part 3, 247. On April 5, 10:00 A.M., Sherman telegraphed to USG. "Despatch of yesterday received— The change will be made forthwith and will reconcile all conflicting interests that it is worth while to notice—All well with us   Schofield is working up the valley cautiously and dispositions are complete to make Forrest pay dear for his foolish dash at Paducah. I wrote very fully yesterday to Genl Rawlins"   Telegram received, DNA, RG 108, Letters Received; *ibid.*, RG 107, Telegrams Collected (Bound). *O.R.*, I, xxxii, part 3, 261. On April 4, Sherman had written at great length to Rawlins. ALS, Schoff Collection, MiU-C. *O.R.*, I, xxxii, part 3, 247–49.

1. John Newton of Va., USMA 1842, was promoted to maj., Corps of Engineers, as of Aug. 6, 1861, appointed brig. gen. as of Sept. 23, and promoted to maj. gen. as of March 30, 1863. He participated in numerous battles with the Army of the Potomac as a div. and corps commander, and was assigned to command the 2nd Div., 4th Army Corps, Army of the Cumberland, on April 16, 1864. *Ibid.*, p. 384.

To Maj. Gen. Franz Sigel

Washington, D. C., April 4th *1864*.

GEN SIGEL, CUMBERLAND VA.[1]

Your letter of the 2d received.[2] It will be early enough for troops to reach Beverly by the 15th inst. This will enable many of your absentees to return ~~and~~ in time for the proposed move.

All communications addressed to the Adj Gen of the Army Washington are immediately forwarded to me when important for my information or action. Whilst I am in immediate telegraphic communication there is no objection however to communicating with me direct in such matters as you deem necessary.

U. S. GRANT
Lt. Gen

ALS (telegram sent), DNA, RG 107, Telegrams Collected (Bound); telegram received, *ibid. O.R.*, I, xxxiii, 799. On April 4, 1864, 5:30 P.M., Maj. Gen. Franz Sigel telegraphed to USG. "Your despatch of today in regard to the movement of troops is received. I will act according to your instructions given in the telegram" Telegram received, DNA, RG 107, Telegrams Collected (Bound). *O.R.*, I, xxxiii, 799.

1. Cumberland, Md., on the Baltimore and Ohio Railroad, approximately ninety miles northwest of Washington, D. C.
2. On April 2, Sigel wrote to USG. "I have the honour to submit the following report The two *Maryland regiments at Harpersferry having been furloughed on the 29th as* General Sullivan informs me, there can be assembled at Beverly only 5.635 men inf.try leaving six Regiments on the Rail Road from Parkersburg to Monocacy, some of them very small which is the minimum number necessary to gaurd the road as may be seen from three letters of Genl. Sullivan which I send enclosed. The following regiments are left on the road. The 6th Va. from Parkersburg to Oakland with a small reserve at Clarksburg. This regt. was raised and organized under the proviso to gaurd the Rail Road and was never in the field. *There are 28 Blockhouses on that line.* The 23rd Illinois, Col: Mulligan's old regt. the remnant of the Irish Brigade, from Oakland to New Creek with reserve at New Creek. The 54th Penna. from Cumberland to Hancock, reserve at Cumberland This regt. was never in the field. The 116 Ohio from Hancock to Harpersferry. The 123rd Ohio from Harpersferry to Monocacy Bridge. The 34th Massachusetts at Harpersferry & Maryland Hights. The following regiments are in motion or preparing to move. The 1st Va. (arrived at Webster) 700. offs. & men effective The 10th Va. (at Beverly) 500. offs. & men effective The 11th Va. (en route from Clarksburg & Bulltown to Beverly) 707. offs. & men effective The 12th Va. (Cumberland, will embark to morrow) 700. offs. & men effective The 14th Va. (Just arrived at New

Creek from Burlington) to be embarked to Webster 602. offs. & men effective   The 15th Va. (Sir John's Run, will embark to morrow) 800. offs. & men effective   The 3rd & 4th Penna. (To move from Harpersferry under Genl. Sullivan to night or to morrow morning) 850. offs. & men effective   The 28th Ohio (at Beverly) 360. offs. & men effective (of this regt. 258 men have left on Veteran furlough the 24th of last month. I would propose that this regt. may be retained for the present if possible)   The 2nd Maryland (at New Creek but many on furlough   This regt. cannot leave New Creek before the 7th or 8th) 416 offs. & men effective   Total effective force of Infantry 10 Regiments 5.635 offrs. & men efficient   The Infantry will be under the command of Genl. Sullivan the senior Genl. Officer in this Department and will be formed into two or three Brigades. The Artillery is prepared and will be at Beverly at the same time. Genl. Averell is informed in regard to the Cavalry and written Orders were sent to him yesterday. Transportation, provisions, ambulance corps, Engineer tools & a small pontoon train will be ready and every effort made to have the troops properly equipped & provided. All the troops & trains *will start from the two points Webster and* Clarksburg. I would respectfully request to be informed to whom I shall send my letters & telegrams in regard to the movements of the enemy & of our own troops, if they are not in answer to your direct communications. I was instructed by Major Kelton A. A. Genl. to send my communications to the Adjutant Genl. of the Army, but I confess that I am anxious to know the name of the officer at Washington, to whom confidential despatches and letters have to be sent by me at the present time so that there may be no delay and confusion. I am perfectly satisfied with whatever instructions may be given me in this matter, but as there might exist some misunderstanding on my part I feel it my duty to apply to you to be made aware of your wishes"   Copies (2), Sigel Papers, OClWHi. *O.R.,* I, xxxiii, 790–92. On April 4, 12:45 P.M., USG telegraphed to Brig. Gen. Jeremiah C. Sullivan. "The Maryland troops furloughed by orders from Washington can be allowed to go if they will return to Harpers' Ferry by the 10th inst. Inform Gen Sigel of this dispatch" ALS (telegram sent), USMA; telegram received, DNA, RG 107, Telegrams Collected (Bound). *O.R.,* I, xxxiii, 800.

To Maj. Gen. Franz Sigel

Washington, D. C. April 4th 1864.

MAJ. GEN. FRANZ SIGEL
COM'D'G. DEP'T. W. VA. CUMBERLAND, MD.

I my letter of instructions for organizing an expedition from your Department for the purpose of cutting the Virgina and Tennessee railroad, I find the route by Covington, and the number of troops of each arm to be sent, on limited information of the country to be traversed and on examination of your last returns. I understood the best and most accessible south were from Covington.

If this is not the case I do not insist upon the route but only upon the work to be done.

If you can increase the cavalry force to go with the expedition do so.

As the first part of the route to be traveled by this expedition is through a country which will furnish but little subsistence or forage, a larger train will have to accompany it than I designed. This will be pretty well exhausted of supplies before reaching Lewisburg,[1] where the country becomes rich, and the most of it can be returned to Beverly under an escort of say eight hundred to one thousand men which will have to be detached from the expedition for that purpose.

This expedition being cooperative with movements made by other Armies, cannot leave Beverly until the other Armies are ready to leave also. I am now satisfied preparations cannot be made elsewhere before the 20th inst.,   You may understand then you have until the 20th to concentrate your forces.

It is possible the expedition with Generals Ord and Averill may have to return to you by the way of the Shenandoah Valley. To provide against this contingency you should collect any available force you may have at a convenient point from which to march on Staunton[2] to meet them. Should you find it necessary to go to Staunton you will want to take as large a supply train as you can, to not only provide for the troops you take with you, but to feed those you go to meet. Please consult Gen. Averill as to the most practicable routes for accomplishing the object to be obtained and advise with me by telegraph and letter of your conclusions

U. S. Grant, Lieut. Gen'l.

Copies, DLC-USG, V, 45, 59; DNA, RG 108, Letters Sent; (2) Sigel Papers, OClWHi; Sigel Papers, NHi. *O.R.*, I, xxxiii, 798–99. On April 8, 1864, Maj. Gen. Franz Sigel telegraphed to USG. "I had an interview with Gens Ord and Averell last night. All preparations are going on according to your wishes expressed in your letter of the 4th inst. I will send written report this evening to Washington, to be forwarded to you." ALS (telegram sent), DNA, RG 393, Dept. of West Va., Letters Sent (Press); telegram received, *ibid.*, RG 107, Telegrams Collected (Bound). *O.R.*, I, xxxiii, 823.

1. Lewisburg, West Va., about seventy-five miles southwest of Beverly, and twenty-five miles west of Covington, Va.

2. Staunton, Va., in the heart of the Shenandoah Valley on the Virginia Central Railroad.

To Henry Wilson

Washington, D. C., April 4, 1864.

HON. H. WILSON, CHAIRMAN COM. MILITARY AFFAIRS:

SIR—I would most respectfully, but earnestly, ask for the confirmation of Brigadier-General John A. Rawlins by your honorable body. General Rawlins has served with me from the beginning of the rebellion. I know he has most richly earned his present position. He comes the nearest being indispensable to me of any officer in the service. But if his confirmation is dependent on his commanding troops, he shall command troops at once. There is no department commander, near where he has served, that would not most gladly give him the very largest and most responsible command his rank would entitle him to.

Believing a short letter on this subject more acceptable than a long one, I will only add, that it is my earnest desire that General Rawlins should be confirmed: that if he fails, besides the loss it will be to the service and to me personally, I shall feel, that by keeping with me a valuable officer, because he made himself valuable, I have worked him an injury.

With great respect, your obedient servant,
U. S. GRANT, Lieutenant-General U. S. A.

Henry Coppée, *Grant and his Campaigns: A Military Biography* (New York, 1866), p. 458. On April 9, 1864, Lt. Col. Theodore S. Bowers wrote to U.S. Representative Elihu B. Washburne. "The interest I feel in the confirmation of Gen. Rawlins, not only from personal feelings to him, but from considerations of the highest importance to Gen. Grant and to the country, will I trust be accepted by you as an apology for intruding this letter upon your attention.—I see by the papers that the Senate makes confirmations every few days, and I have become apprehensive that Gen. Rawlins' case will be postponed, until finally the number of Brigadier Generals allowed by law will have been made, and he thus go by default. Gen. Grant has written to Senators Wilson and Hale that Rawlins is in dispensible to him, and urging as a personal favor that he be confirmed. The great difficulty in the way, I apprehend, is the prejudice against confirming officers on staff duty. But could the Senate be made to realize the facts—that Rawlins has been *in the field* since Sept. 1861—that he was chief of Staff while A. A. G. with the rank of Major and Lieut. Colonel—that he was Grant's associate and adviser in all his battles and Campaigns—that he was promoted after the seige of Vicksburg, for signal services in the field—that he has done more actual work than any Staff Officer in the Service—that Grant has always had a smaller number of officers on his Staff than any Major General in the Army, as reports on file in the War Office will prove—that Meade, Hooker, Rosecrans, Thomas and other commanders have all had, and most of them now have Major Generals as Chief's of Staff, while Grant only asks for a Brigadier General as such as Commander of all the Armies,—I think the objection or prejudice would fall to the ground in this case. Of Rawlins work, ability and intense patriotism I need say nothing to you who know him so well. Firmly impressed with the conviction that Gen. Rawlins confirmation is a matter of vital importance to the success of our arms, I beg of you, as the most influential man in Congress to spare no effort to secure his confirmation. If you secure this, it will be second in importance to the signal service you rendered the country in calling Grant to the command of all our Armies, and I believe as firmly that Grant's Spring Campaign will vindicate your judgment and sagacity, as that the American people will manifest their appreciation of the services you have rendered the country. I presume Gen. Rawlins has talked to you fully on the subject. I know that he has the most unreserved confidence that you will render him all assistance in your power. But I could not resist my inclination to make this appeal to you." ALS, DLC-Elihu B. Washburne. On April 10, Lt. Col. William R. Rowley wrote to Washburne. "I have been watching the Washington papers for some time with a great deal of interest hoping to see a notice of Rawlins' Confirmation as a Brigadier And seeing so many notices of the confirmation of others has induced me to think there must be a screw loose somewhere.—You know of how much importance I have always considered it to be to keep Rawlins with the General. Although a friend of Rawlins as you are aware it is not from motives of friendship that I would urge upon you not to lose sight of the matter   I fully believe that it is vital importance to the country that the confirmation be made   It is unnecessary for me to particularize as I have talked with you on the subject   I have written to Capt Stockdale a[t] Nashville and he will hunt Mr Clark & stir him up. Bowers who is shortly going to Nashville will also bear it in mind. No News from the front." ALS, *ibid.* On April 12, Capt. Ely S. Parker also wrote to Washburne urging the confirmation of Rawlins. ALS, *ibid.*

On April 10, USG telegraphed to Maj. Gen. Richard J. Oglesby. "Did you hand senators Wilson and Hale the letters handed you to give by Gen Rawlins   Please answer" Telegram received (press), DNA, RG 107, Telegrams Collected (Bound). On April 11, Oglesby telegraphed to USG. "The letters to Senators Wilson and Hale were handed to them before noon of the day on which I received them from Genl Rawlins." ALS (telegram sent), *ibid.*, Telegrams Collected (Unbound).

On April 1, the U.S. Senate confirmed the nomination of Rawlins as brig. gen., but Senator James R. Doolittle immediately moved to reconsider. On April 14, Doolittle withdrew his motion and Washburne telegraphed to Rawlins. "You have been confirmed this day." Telegram received, *ibid.*

To Maj. Gen. Ambrose E. Burnside

In field, Culpepper C. H. Va., April 5st 1864.

MAJ. GEN. E. A. BURNSIDE
COM'D'G, 9TH ARMY CORPS

Your letter of yesterday, enclosing copy of your letter of the 26th of January to the Secretary of War, was received this morning just as I was leaving Washington, and so short a time before leaving that I did not get to read it until my arrival here

The plan of operations for this spring campaign I fixed upon almost immediately on assuming command of the Army and I yet see no reason to change. It does not embrace the movements proposed in your letter to the Secretary of War. If it did your request for the return of troops formerly belonging to the 9th Army Corps would be immediately complied with. I may yet be able to return them to the 9th Army Corps but it can only be after they meet in the field. The Artillery for your command will be taken from the defenses of Washington, where they are now well quartered and provided for. To move them to Annapolis from which place they would have again to be moved so soon, could not compensate by any benefits to arise from it for the inconvenience of such a transfer, to say nothing of the expenses it would put the Goverment to.

I cannot make clear to you the reasons why your requests for transfer of troops cannot be immediately granted without giving you the plan of operations which I propose and for which most of the preparatory instructions have already gone out. When we meet I will take great pleasure in communicating to you fully (as it will be my duty to do in view of the part you are expected to take) what is to be done.

I wish you to get forward to Annapolis by the 20th inst. all the force you can and be in readiness to move at a days notice with whatever force you may have at any time after that.

I have appointed Col. Babcock,[1] an Aide of my Staff but have not been able to communicate the fact to him. If you know where he is, please order him to report to me

U. S. GRANT Lieut. Gen.

Copies, DLC-USG, V, 45, 59; DNA, RG 108, Letters Sent. *O.R.*, I, xxxiii, 807–8. On April 4, 1864, Maj. Gen. Ambrose E. Burnside, New York City, wrote to USG. "I beg to enclose to you a copy of letter sent in January last to the Secretary of War.—not knowing if you had seen the letter, and in view of the fact that the 9th Army Corps including the old 3d Division will probably be & below in a few days concentrated at Annapolis & below with a strength of Forty Thousand (40.000) or more men I deem it not improper to send it for your consideration—Some of the regiments of the old 3d Division, are now in the Department of the South, and I would respectfully suggest that some of the old regiments that were with me in North Carolina, and now on furlough from the Department of the South Should be ordered to take their place in the 3d Division—The 24th Mass, and the 11th Conn are the two regiments which I would like to have report instead of the 117th and 103d & 3d New York now on Folly Island—The 3d Division can be concentrated at Norfolk or such other point as you may think desirable, and would by this arrangement be composed of the following regiments   The 8th, 11th, 15th, 16th & 21st. Conn,   The 10th & 13th New Hampshire—   The 4th Rhode Island—now in Genl Butlers command   The 89th New York now on furlough   If orders could be issued for concentrating this Division, it would to some extent increase enlistments in the different regiments—I am interesting myself in the recruiting as if the order had already been issued—I made the application for the increased artillery to Gen Halleck, and suppose it has been laid before you—It would seem advisable that the batteries should be ordered to report to the Headquarters of the Ninth Corps at Annapolis —It might be advisable to concentrate the 3d Division in North Carolina if it is decided that the future operations of the Corps are to be in that Section—I send this by Lt Van Vliet of my Staff—"   ALS, DNA, RG 108, Letters Received. *O.R.*, I, xxxiii, 803.

On April 6, USG telegraphed to Maj. Gen. Henry W. Halleck. "If Gen Burnside [is] in Washington send him here. If he is not in Washington do you know whether he will be there within a day or two?" Telegram received, DNA, RG 107, Telegrams Collected (Bound). *O.R.*, I, xxxiii, 809. On the same day, Halleck twice telegraphed to USG. "Genl Burnside has an appointment with me to-morrow morning, when I will send him to You, as directed." "The 3d New Jersey cavalry [now] arriving at Annapolis is asked for by Genl Burnside. [It] was intended for Army of the Potomac. Which shall have it? Please answer as soon as possible." ALS (telegrams sent), DNA, RG 107, Telegrams Collected (Bound); telegrams received, *ibid.* On the same day, Lt. Col. Cyrus B. Comstock telegraphed to Halleck. "Gen Grant desires that the 3rd New Jersey Cavalry be given to Genl. Burnside—He also wishes that the 6th Ohio Cavalry and the 20th Penn. Cavalry be mounted equipped and sent to Western Virginia as rapidly as possible." ALS (telegram sent), *ibid.*, RG 108, Letters Sent by Comstock; telegram received, *ibid.*, RG 107, Telegrams Collected (Bound).

On April 7, 9:30 A.M., USG telegraphed to Halleck. "If Gen. Burnside has not started here he need not come but in that case notify him to be in readiness to leave Annapolis with whatever command he may have at the shortest notice after the 20th inst. I have written to the General in answer to his communication sent by Lieut. Van Vleet. Enjoin secrecy about divulging the time of expected movement from Annapolis or even that troops are to move from there at all." Telegram received, *ibid.*; copies, *ibid.*, RG 108, Letters Sent; DLC-USG, V, 45, 59. *O.R.*, I, xxxiii, 815. On the same day, 1:00 P.M., Halleck telegraphed to USG. "Genl Burnside left unexpectedly last night. Your message will be sent to him in cipher as soon as he can be found. Genl Wilson has been relieved, and troops ordered as directed. Genl Sigel asks that a regiment of heavy artillery be sent from Baltimore to garrison Harpers Ferry. Shall it be done?" ALS (telegram sent), DNA, RG 107, Telegrams Collected (Bound); telegram received, *ibid.*; *ibid.*, RG 108, Letters Received. *O.R.*, I, xxxiii, 815. Halleck's telegram is misquoted in James Harrison Wilson, *Under the Old Flag* (New York and London, 1912), I, 359.

On April 7, 8:00 P.M., USG telegraphed to Halleck. "Please order a regiment of heavy artillery from Baltimore Md to Harpers Ferry to garrison the latter place" Telegram received, DNA, RG 94, Letters Received, 295A 1864; *ibid.*, RG 107, Telegrams Collected (Bound); copies, *ibid.*, RG 108, Letters Sent; DLC-USG, V, 45, 59. *O.R.*, I, xxxiii, 816. On April 8, Halleck endorsed this telegram. "Adjt Genl will issue the order by telegraph to Genl Wallace" AES, DNA, RG 107, Telegrams Collected (Bound). On the same day, Comstock telegraphed to Maj. Gen. George G. Meade. "Lieutenant General Grant desires me to say that Gen. Wilson will be sent to you to take one of your cavalry divisions" Copies, DLC-USG, V, 45, 59; DNA, RG 108, Letters Sent. See *O.R.*, I, xxxiii, 851.

On April 14, Maj. Gen. Philip H. Sheridan wrote to Brig. Gen. John A. Rawlins. "General Wilson having been directed to report to me, I am very much embarrassed in his assignment to the Third Cavalry Division of the Cavalry Corps, as General Kilpatrick, commanding that division, ranks him. General Kilpatrick is anxious to be transferred to the West; is it possible to do so?" *Ibid.*, p. 862. On April 15, 10:00 A.M., Brig. Gen. James H. Wilson, Culpeper, telegraphed to Sheridan. "Genl Grant hasn't returned yet, will be back this afternoon—Genl. Rawlins says no doubt he will make the order we wish. Suppose you make my order and send it over." ALS (telegram sent), DNA, RG 107, Telegrams Collected (Unbound); telegram received, *ibid. O.R.*, I, xxxiii, 872. On the same day, Lt. Col. Theodore S. Bowers issued Special Orders No. 12. "Brig. Gen. J. Kilpatrick, U. S. Volunteers, is hereby relieved from duty in the Army of the Potomac, and will report in person, without delay, to Major General W. T. Sherman, commanding Military Division of the Mississippi, for orders." Copies, DLC-USG, V, 57, 62. *O.R.*, I, xxxii, part 3, 375.

1. Orville E. Babcock of Vt., USMA 1861, appointed 2nd lt., Corps of Engineers, as of May 6, 1861, was appointed lt. col. of vols. as of Jan. 1, 1863. Assigned as chief engineer, 9th Army Corps, on Feb. 6, he served under Burnside until appointed lt. col., U.S. Army, as of March 29, 1864, and assigned to USG's staff. See letter to Edwin M. Stanton, March 25, 1864.

To Maj. Gen. Henry W. Halleck

Culpeper C. H. Va
April 6th 1864

MAJ. GENL HALLECK
CHIEF OF STAFF—

The 1st & 3rd Corps having been merged into other Corps with the possibility of being filled up hereafter & restored to their corps organization—I would like to have the number of Hookers Corps changed to the 20th Corps   If this change is authorized please notify Sherman by telegraph—It will cause dissatisfaction to give No. 1. to any other but the old Corps having that number to retain—No 11 or 12 will probably have the same effect with those losing their number

U. S. GRANT
Leiut Genl

Telegram received, DNA, RG 107, Telegrams Collected (Bound); copies, *ibid.*, RG 94, Letters Received, 288A 1864; *ibid.*, RG 108, Letters Sent; DLC-USG, V, 45, 59. *O.R.*, I, xxxii, part 3, 270. On April 6, 1864, Maj. Gen. Henry W. Halleck telegraphed to USG. "Genl orders No 144 have been corrected from First to Twentieth Army Corps. I have so telegraphed to Genl Sherman." ALS (telegram sent), DNA, RG 107, Telegrams Collected (Bound); telegram received, *ibid.*

To Maj. Gen. Franz Sigel

Culpepper C. H
April 6th 1864

MAJ GENL SIGEL
CUMBERLAND MD.

If the enemy move against any part of your line, as your information would indicate they intend, the concentration you are making would enable you to meet them successfully. Of course in such a case you would take such a force as you deemed necessary regardless of any expedition ordered from here when no advance of the enemy was contemplated. Your forces would be accomplishing at home the greatest advantage expected from them by moving south if the enemy do attack you in force, that is they would divide him

U S GRANT
Lt Gen'l

Telegram received, DNA, RG 107, Telegrams Collected (Bound); copies, *ibid.*, RG 108, Letters Sent; Sigel Papers, OClWHi; DLC-USG, V, 45, 59. *O.R.*, I, xxxiii, 812. On April 6, 1864, 8:00 P.M., Maj. Gen. Franz Sigel telegraphed to USG. "Your letter of the 4th of April is received through Maj. Gen'l Ord, also your Telegram of today. I have no information of important movements of the enemy and every thing is going on well in regard to the movement of our troops. I will send report in writing with some suggestions I think necessary. I made an application to the Adjutat General, to have the regiment of heavy Artillery now at Baltimore transferred to this Department, to occupy Harpers Ferry, at least temporarily so that more infantry from there can be made available for the field. I also requested the Governor of West Va to call out part of the State Militia, to take care of the R. Road and will report the result." LS, DNA, RG 393, Dept. of West Va., Letters Sent (Press); telegram received, *ibid.*, RG 107, Telegrams Collected (Bound). *O.R.*, I, xxxiii, 812. On April 8, Sigel wrote to USG. "I have the honor to acknowledge your letter (of 4th of April) handed to me by Maj. General Ord, also a telegram from Culpepper, dated the 6th of April. To come to a clear understanding in regard to my instructions and future action, I take leave to recapitulate the main points, contained in the letters and the telegram. In your first letter, dated March 29, you only mention two movements, one under General Ord and Averell and a cooperative movement under Gen. Crook, the two columns to unite after a certain periode and to return to their base or to operate in such a way, as you may direct. You also state the number of troops for the expedition under General Ord to be 8000 inf 1500 cavalry and 3 batteries   In the second letter (of the 4th of April) you do not change the original plan in regard to Gen's. Ord and Crook, but you say, that in addition to the two movements a third movement should be executed. You say, that I should collect any aɴvailable force, I may have, and a large provision train and march towards or to Stanton, to meet Gen's Ord and Crook, in case Gen. Ord and Averell should find it necessary to return by the way of the Shenandoah. In your Telegram of the 4th, based on some information in regard to movements of the enemy, you say, that in case of an attack, I should meet it with such forces as I might deem necessary, regardless of any expedition ordered from you, but you also express the opinion that a moᵥvement South would be advantageous, as it would divide the enemy's forces.—This is essentially very true, but in the interview with Genl's Ord and Averell the question arose, whether it would be advisable to divide our forces into three different parts for the purpose of a simultaneous aggressive movement and I objected to it for several reasons, but Gen. Averell thought, that we could not bring a large train from Beverly across the mountains and it was therefore finally understood, that a third force should be collected at a convenient point or two points (Romney and Harpers Ferry) with some infantry and all the cavalry which would be left behind by Gen. Averell and which could possibly be mounted and armed. This force should move as a kind of reserve with a large provisions—and forage train some time after the expedition of Gen'l. Ord had started from Beverly. It was also understood, that the cavalry force of Gen'l. Averell, destined to accompany the expedition, should be increased from 1500 to 2000 picked men. Under these suppositions I am now acting and whilst the greater part of the troops for the expedition of General Ord are concentrated at Grafton and Webster and those of General Averell at Martinsburg, preparing to move rapidly to Beverly at the proper time (to be there on the 18th or 19th I will do my best to bring together a small force with the necessary trains mentioned. Should during this periode of concentration and preparation any movement of the enemy take place, we could from our positions meet him on any point between Clarksburg and Harpersferry, or march against his flank and rear. Within the next ten days it will also been seen, how many troops return, how much cavalry can be mounted and what the intentions of the enemy are. I will also have more accurate information in regard to the roads, bridges etc., and report by Telegraph and letter. In the map which I send to you, all the principal roads in West Va are marked with red ink. It will be seen, that there are two good roads leading off South of Beverly to Stanton and Warmsprings, one across Cheat mountain where the enemy has an abandoned fort, and one by Huntersville to Warmsprings. It seems to me that Warmsprings is a point of great importance, because it threatens Stanton and all the enemys forces in the lower Shenandoah valley and defends the road from Louisewisburg to Beverly." Copy, Sigel Papers, OClWHi.

To Maj. Gen. William T. Sherman

Culpeper Va
7 30 a m [P.M.] Apl 7th 1864

Maj. Gen Sherman
Nashville—

I have ordered all the troops that can be spared from the states west of the Ohio to be sent to you—You can send them to Genl Steele or where you think best   Genl Rosecrans reports he can send no troops   I have an inspector there however to see   If possible I will send Genl Steele some from there   I will make provision at Pensacola for supplying a Cavalry force[1]

U. S. Grant
Lieut Genl Comdg

Telegram received, DNA, RG 107, Telegrams Collected (Bound); copies, *ibid.*, RG 108, Letters Sent; *ibid.*, RG 393, Military Div. of the Miss., Letters Sent; DLC-USG, V, 45, 59, 94. *O.R.*, I, xxxii, part 3, 280; *ibid.*, I, xxxiv, part 3, 75.

On April 7, 1864, 10:00 A.M., Maj. Gen. William T. Sherman telegraphed to USG. "I will instruct Steele. Shreveport is the Grand doorway to Texas, and the Key of the entire southwest. Alexandria is next. To hold both Steele will want all the available troops now in Kansas and Missouri. I had sent for my 10,000 under A. J. Smith to return to Vicksburg, & then up Yazoo to Grenada. We must do this to counteract the effect of our Cavalry weakness as against Forrest, and I suppose you will want Banks to turn his whole attention against Mobile. In time we should have a Brigade & depot of suppies at Pensacola, a point I propose to reach by a Raid aimed at West Point & Columbus, Georgia, at some future day. I think you should give Steele all the troops in Kansas & Missouri, leaving Rosecrans & Curtis to manage the Militia & Civil matters." ALS (telegram sent), CLU; telegram received, DNA, RG 108, Letters Received; (illegible) *ibid.*, RG 107, Telegrams Collected (Bound). *O.R.*, I, xxxiv, part 3, 75. On the same day, 7:00 P.M., USG telegraphed to Sherman. "Do you think it will pay to send troops to Grenada at this late day? Unless Smith has already started I think that his force had better be got at once where it can operate with one of the main armies" Telegram received, DNA, RG 107, Telegrams Collected (Bound); copies, *ibid.*, RG 108, Letters Sent; *ibid.*, RG 393, Military Div. of the Miss., Letters Sent; DLC-USG, V, 45, 59, 94. *O.R.*, I, xxxii, part 3, 280. On April 8, 3:30 P.M., Sherman telegraphed to USG. "It is not too late to bring A. J. Smiths Division out of ~~Tennessee to~~ Red River to Join McPherson by the Mississippi and Tennessee instead of by Grenada As soon as I learn what force can be sent to Steele from states west of Ohio I will order them Have you ordered Genl Banks to come away with his troops or does he leave any subject to Steeles orders? & how many? Genl Steele reported to me that he had only about Seven thousand to take with him ~~from~~ of his own & that his Cavalry and artillery were very bad" Telegram received, DNA, RG 107, Telegrams Collected (Bound); *ibid.*, RG 108, Letters Received. *O.R.*, I, xxxii, part 3, 289–90; *ibid.*, I, xxxiv, part 3, 85.

1. On April 7, 7:30 P.M., USG telegraphed to Brig. Gen. Montgomery C. Meigs. "Please make provision at Pensacola Florida for five thousand (5000) cavalry for twenty (20) days. The first of May will be early enough for it to be there" Telegram received, DNA, RG 92, Consolidated Correspondence, Telegrams; *ibid.*, RG 107, Telegrams Collected (Bound); copies, *ibid.*, RG 108, Letters Sent; DLC-USG, V, 45, 59. On April 8, 3:30 P.M., Meigs telegraphed to USG. "I have today ordered forty thousand bushels of grain and seven hundred tons of hay from Eastern Ports to Pensacola under sealed orders—First shipment to be made by steam to arrive by ~~10th tenth M~~ first (1st) May All by tenth (10th). Also sent by Mississippi & Atlantic orders to Col. Holabird Chief Quarter Master New Orleans to send a cargo of forage from New Orleans to Pensacola to be there by 1st first May to meet any contingency" LS (telegram sent), DNA, RG 107, Telegrams Collected (Unbound); telegram received, *ibid.*, RG 108, Letters Received; ADf, *ibid.*, RG 92, Consolidated Correspondence, Telegrams. *O.R.*, I, xxxii, part 3, 300. On April 7, 7:30 P.M., USG telegraphed to Maj. Gen. Christopher C. Augur. "Please provide by the 1st of May supplies at Pensacola, Fla., for five thousand extra men for thirty days" Copies, DNA, RG 108, Letters Sent; DLC-USG, V, 45, 59. Also on April 7, 8:00 P.M., USG telegraphed to Brig. Gen. Joseph P. Taylor, commissary gen. "Please provide by first (1st) of May supplies at Pensacola for five thousand (5.000) Extra men for thirty 30 days" Telegram received, DNA, RG

107, Telegrams Collected (Bound); *ibid.,* RG 192, Letters Received. On April 8, 9:00 A.M., USG telegraphed to Sherman. "I have directed twenty days forage & provisions extra to be at Pensacola by first of May" Telegram received, *ibid.,* RG 107, Telegrams Collected (Bound); copies, *ibid.,* RG 108, Letters Sent; *ibid.,* RG 393, Military Div. of the Miss., Letters Sent; DLC-USG, V, 45, 59, 94. *O.R.,* I, xxxii, part 3, 288.

On Sept. 8, Meigs wrote to USG. "I have the honor to enquire whether the forage sent to Pensacola, by your Orders, last Spring, may be now Ordered Elsewhere." LS, DNA, RG 108, Letters Received. On Sept. 10, 6:30 P.M., USG telegraphed to Meigs. "The forage ordered to Pensacola last spring will not now be required there. It. may be ~~sent~~ used where you deem best." ALS (telegram sent), CSmH; telegram received (at 10:20 P.M.), DNA, RG 92, Consolidated Correspondence, Grant; *ibid.,* RG 107, Telegrams Collected (Bound). On the same day, 6:30 P.M., USG telegraphed to Brig. Gen. Amos B. Eaton, commissary gen. "Com.y stores ordered to Pensacola last spring in anticipation of the possibility of some of Gen. Sherman's raids being compelled to put in there will not now be wanted. The stores will be subject to your orders." ALS (telegram sent), CSmH; telegram received (at 10:20 P.M.), DNA, RG 92, Letters Received; *ibid.,* RG 107, Telegrams Collected (Bound).

To Maj. Gen. Henry W. Halleck

Culpepper C. H. Va
April 8th 3 30 P. M 1864

MAJ GEN H. W. HALLECK
CHIEF OF STAFF.

My letter to General Burnside gives no plan but simply requires him to be ready to move any time he may be notified after the 20th instant with whatever force he may then have. I will not want more transportation than you notified me the Qr Master ~~General~~ could spare from Washington. A few Ferries may be required to take up the James.

The order for publication for the removal of Sutlers was without my knowledge and has not my approval.[1]

U. S. GRANT Lt Genl

Telegram received, DNA, RG 107, Telegrams Collected (Bound); copies, *ibid.,* RG 108, Letters Sent; DLC-USG, V, 59. *O.R.,* I, xxxiii, 821. On April 8, 1864, 2:00 P.M., Maj. Gen. Henry W. Halleck telegraphed to USG. "Genl Burnside has just returned from New York where he recieved your despatch. I have directed him to go to Annapolis, to execute your orders. The secty of war suggests that no more of your plans be communicated to Genl B. than may be necessary.

Please remember that Genl Meigs will require some days notice, if he is to supply more transportation than he has on hand" ALS (telegram sent), DNA, RG 107, Telegrams Collected (Bound); telegram received, *ibid. O.R.*, I, xxxiii, 821.

1. Also on April 8, 11:30 A.M., Halleck telegraphed to USG. "Genl Patrick has here for publication an order that all sutlers leave the Army of the Potomac by the sixteenth. Will [not] this give notice of your intended movements? The Secty of war [has stopped] it till we learn whether it has your sanction. [Regt] of heavy Artillery ordered [to] Harpers Ferry." ALS (telegram sent), DNA, RG 107, Telegrams Collected (Bound); telegram received, *ibid. O.R.*, I, xxxiii, 820–21.

To Maj. Gen. Henry W. Halleck

Culpeper C. H. Va
8 30 P. m. Apl 8th 1864

MAJ GENL HALLECK
It is the intention to operate up the James River as far as City Point and all the Cooperation the Navy can give us we want—Two of the Iron Clads are wanted as soon as they can be got ~~ready~~ You will know how to communicate our wants to the Secretary of the Navy

U. S. GRANT
Lieut Gen. Comdg

Telegram received, DNA, RG 107, Telegrams Collected (Bound); copies, *ibid.*, RG 45, Miscellaneous Letters Received; *ibid.*, Area Files; *ibid.*, RG 108, Letters Sent; DLC-USG, V, 59; DLC-Gideon Welles. *O.R.*, I, xxxiii, 821; *O.R.* (Navy), I, ix, 611. See *ibid.*, pp. 584–85, 611.

To Maj. Gen. Ambrose E. Burnside

Culpepper C H
April 8th 1864 8. P M

MAJ. GEN BURNSIDE
WASHINGTON.
Artillery and transportation will be furnished you from Washington and will be sent from there to your corps in the field. You

need not look after 3rd division for the present. I have written to
you directing my letter to Annapolis. I will be in Annapolis about
the middle of next week.

U. S. Grant
Lt Genl

Telegram received, DNA, RG 107, Telegrams Collected (Bound); copies, *ibid.*,
RG 108, Letters Sent; DLC-USG, V, 59. *O.R.*, I, xxxiii, 820. On April 8, 1864,
Maj. Gen. Ambrose E. Burnside telegraphed to USG. "W̶i̶l̶l̶ h̶u̶r̶r̶y̶ a̶s̶ m̶u̶c̶h̶ a̶s̶
p̶o̶s̶s̶i̶b̶l̶e̶ Will make concentration i̶f̶ p̶o̶s̶s̶i̶b̶l̶e̶—Guns and horses were left in
East Tennessee—We have no transportation—Am I to look after 3d division—
I̶f̶ Are the 24th Mass and 10th Conn to come to me—If you wish I can be at
your Head Qrs in the morning" ALS (telegram sent), DNA, RG 107, Telegrams Collected (Unbound); telegram received, *ibid.*, RG 108, Letters Received. On April 9, Burnside telegraphed to USG. "Despatch received. have
given necessary orders. I go north tonight to hurry up m̶y̶ new regiments. Will
be here Thursday or earlier if you desire. A telegram sent here will follow me
promptly" Telegram received, *ibid.*, RG 107, Telegrams Collected (Bound);
ibid., Telegrams Collected (Unbound). *O.R.*, I, xxxiii, 834.

On April 8, 7:30 P.M., USG telegraphed to Maj. Gen. Henry W. Halleck.
"Special Order *135* transfers Battery C. 1st Rhode Island Artillery to Gen Burnside. this is one of the Batteries retained in the Army of the Potomac in the
reorganization and unless there is the necessity for it it ought not to be transferred. There is no necessity at all events for sending it back to Washington even
if it is transferred to Gen Burnside—Burnside will not require transports to
move his command" Telegram received, DNA, RG 107, Telegrams Collected
(Bound); copies, *ibid.*, RG 108, Letters Sent; DLC-USG, V, 59. *O.R.*, I, xxxiii,
821–22.

On April 9, Halleck telegraphed to USG. "A veteran Maryland Infantry
regiment belonging to the 12th corps (Slocum's) has been detained in Baltimore
a few days for a special purpose. If it is intended to bring more troops from the
west here or to West Virginia, it would save transportation to take this one.
Genl Burnside will be given another battery in place of that now in the Army of
the Potomac." ALS (telegram sent), DNA, RG 107, Telegrams Collected
(Bound); telegram received, *ibid.*; *ibid.*, RG 108, Letters Received. On the same
day, USG telegraphed to Halleck. "Give the veteran regiments of the 12th
(Slocum's) Corps, to Burnside. You may replace it in the 12th Corps by an Ohio
regiment, if you can." Copies, DLC-USG, V, 45, 59; DNA, RG 108, Letters
Sent.

On April 11, Burnside, Providence, R. I., telegraphed to USG. "Will probably get all new E̶n̶g̶l̶a̶n̶d̶ regiments from New England off this week. If I
am at Annapolis on Thursday will I be in season to meet you?" Telegram received, *ibid.*, RG 107, Telegrams Collected (Bound). *O.R.*, I, xxxiii, 838. On
the same day, 1:30 P.M., USG telegraphed to Burnside. "I will be at Annapolis Wednesday" Telegram received, DNA, RG 107, Telegrams Collected
(Bound). *O.R.*, I, xxxiii, 838.

On April 10, 1:00 P.M., USG telegraphed to Brig. Gen. Rufus Ingalls.
"Will there be a chance of going into the city to-morrow" Copies, DLC-USG,

V, 45, 59; DNA, RG 108, Letters Sent. On the same day, Capt. Luther H. Peirce, asst. chief q. m., wrote to USG. "It is thought the trains will run on time tomorrow   Will answer as soon as receive definite information. Do you want a special train? If so please state time." ALS, *ibid.*, RG 107, Telegrams Collected (Unbound). On the same day, USG wrote to Peirce. "If the train can be sent as well as not at 4 p. m. to-morrow I will go on it." AL, Connecticut State Library, Hartford, Conn.

On April 14, 2:25 P.M., USG telegraphed to Burnside. "I find the great majority of troops being drawn from the Northern states by the system of inspection established are men who belong to different regiments already in the field. The number therefore to be attached to your Corps will be less than I calculated." ALS (telegram sent), DNA, RG 107, Telegrams Collected (Bound); telegram received, *ibid.* O.R., I, xxxiii, 864.

To Maj. Gen. William T. Sherman

Culpepper Va
Apl 8th 1864 9 30 P M

GEN SHERMAN
NASHVILLE TENN

As I notified you before leaving Nashville I believe the rebels will attempt a raid into Kentucky by the way of Pound Gap or that vicinity, as soon as they can travel. From information just received at Washington Longstreets force may be added to Breckenridge's, to make this so formidable as to upset offensive movement on our part. By vigilance in South East Kentucky, which [I] know you are wide awake to the necessity of, such a raid can be made disastrous to the rebels, and still leave us free to act offensively from Chattanooga. If Forrest succeeds in getting his force out of Kentucky and West Tennessee, do you not think a bolder commander than Genl Hurlbut will be required for holding the Mississippi firmly.—

U. S. GRANT
Lt Gen'l

Telegram received, DNA, RG 107, Telegrams Collected (Bound); copies, *ibid.*, RG 108, Letters Sent; *ibid.*, RG 393, Military Div. of the Miss., Letters Sent; DLC-USG, V, 45, 59, 94. *O.R.*, I, xxxii, part 3, 288. On April 9, 1864, Maj. Gen. William T. Sherman telegraphed to USG. "Your dispatch of yesterday is received   I have Stoneman now in East Kentucky with all the Cavalry of the army of the Ohio   Genl Schofields troops are at Bulls Gap and I have no indications of an invasion of Kentucky from Pound Gap. That road is very long and very bad   Forrest will escape us—Veatch went to Waverly and came away without orders because he could hear nothing of Forrest   We will want a bolder man than Hurlbut at Memphis   Why not send Buell—Should any force come into East Kentucky would it not be checkmated by a comparitively small force sent to the Mouth of Big Sandy to march by Louisa and Prestonburg—In the mean time I am collecting everything with Genl Schofield, Gen. Thomas & McPherson to act offensive south of the Tenn. I will continue to draw here all detachments & furloughed men   I am also endeavoring to accumulate surplus stores to the front which would enable me to move troops rapidly by R. Road   McPhersons two divisions will soon begin to arrive at Cairo from their furloughs." Telegram received, DNA, RG 107, Telegrams Collected (Bound); *ibid.*, RG 108, Letters Received. *O.R.*, I, xxxii, part 3, 305. On the same day, 10:30 P.M., USG telegraphed to Maj. Gen. Henry W. Halleck. "Genl Sherman thinks Hurlbut not bold enough to retain at Memphis, I will think over the matter and suggest some one to take his place, but in the meantime do not know where to send Hurlbut. How ~~will~~ would he do to command at Charleston during Gillmore's absence?" Telegram received, DNA, RG 107, Telegrams Collected (Bound); copies, *ibid.*, RG 108, Letters Sent; DLC-USG, V, 45, 59. *O.R.*, I, xxxii, part 3, 304–5. See telegram to Maj. Gen. William T. Sherman, March 30, 1864. On April 11, 2:30 P.M., Halleck telegraphed to USG. "The secty of war has no information in regard to Genl Blair's case. Genl Hurlbut has not sufficient military experience for so important a command as the Dept of the South. I will write you in regard to this matter and also in regard to Genls Buell & Hunter. The 36th Ohio ordered as directed." ALS (telegram sent), DNA, RG 107, Telegrams Collected (Bound); telegram received, *ibid.*; *ibid.*, RG 108, Letters Received. *O.R.*, I, xxxv, part 2, 48; (incomplete) *ibid.*, I, xxxii, part 3, 322. On the same day, Halleck wrote to USG. "I regard our establishments at Morris Island, Hilton Head and on the Sea Islands of immense importance. As soon as Gillmore leaves the Rebels will probably attack one or more of these places. To defend them properly we want a general there of experience and military education. My own opinion of Genl Hurlbut has been favorable, but I do not deem him equal to the command of the Dept of the south, with its diminished forces. Genl Hatch is hardly the man for the place, but probably he is the best that can now be spared from the field. I would like very much to see Buell restored to a command, and have several times proposed him to the War Dept., but there has been such a pressure against him from the west, that I do not think the Secretary will give him any at present. I think Genl Hunter would not accept any command under McPherson, or if he did, trouble would follow. He is even worse than McClernand in creating difficulties. If you had him in the field under your immediate command, perhaps things would go smoothly. Before acting on Genl Hunter's case, it would be well for you to see his correspondence while in command of a Dept." ALS, DNA, RG 108, Letters Sent (Press). *O.R.*, I, xxxii, part 3, 322–23; *ibid.*, I, xxxv, part 2, 48.

On April 14, Sherman wrote to Brig. Gen. John A. Rawlins. "I send you a parcel of papers of latest dates from the South. You will find them interesting. One set of my former scouts is just in from Memphis having come from Memphis Holly Springs, Pontotoc, Aberdeen, Columbus Miss Selma, Montgomery, *Opelika*, West Point & Columbus Geo.—thence back to Selma and up the Rail road to

Talladega Jacksonville & Blue Mountain. The Enemy is collecting at a place near Centreville a camp to which Lorings Division is to come from Demopolis.— This force will be *behind* the Coosa, and is clearly designed by Johnston to watch McPherson as he advances against Rome. Forest still is up between the Tennessee & Mississipi & is reported today crossing the Tennessee at Hamburg, also attacking Columbus. I admire his great skill but he cant do that. I am willing he should continue to attack our posts, and he may also cross the Tennessee. We have plenty of stores here, also pushing them to the Front fast as possible. I will not let Forest draw off my mind from the Concentration going on. Longstreet is represented still up about Bristol & Abingdon, but I do not believe he will move into Kentucky by Pound Gap—Road too bad & long   He may send some Cavalry in, but he dont probably know that he cant interrupt our communications, because if the Louisville Road is reached by a dash we are not disturbed, and then to git out would be a question. All well with us. I await McPhersons two Divns on furlough and A. J. Smith from Red River." ALS, DNA, RG 108, Letters Received. *O.R.*, I, xxxii, part 3, 350–51. The enclosures are *ibid.*, pp. 351–52.

To Maj. Gen. George G. Meade

Head Quarters of the Army, In Field,
Culpepper C. H. Va. Apl. 9th/64

Maj. Gen. Geo. G. Meade,
Comd.g Army of the Potomac,
General,

For your information, and as instructions to govern your preparations for the coming campaign, the following is communicated confidentially for your own perusal alone.

So far as practicable all the Armies are to move together and towards one common center. Banks has been instructed to turn over the guarding of the Red River to Gen. Steele and the Navy. To abandon Texas, with the exception of the Rio Grande, and to concentrate all the force he can, not less than 25.000 men, to move on Mobile. This he is to do without reference to any other movements. From the scattered condition of his command however he can not possibly get it together to leave New Orleans before the 1st of May if so soon. Sherman will move at the same time you do, or two or three days in advance, Jo Johnston's Army being his objective point and the heart of Georgia his ultimate aim. If sucsessful he will secure the line from Chattanooga to Mobile, with the Aid of Banks.

Sigel cannot spare troops from his Army to reinforce either of the great Armies but he can Aid them by moving directly to his front. This he has been directed to do and is now making preparations for it. Two Columns from his command will move south at the same time with the general forward move, one from Beverly from ten to twelve thousand strong under Maj. Gen. Ord, the other from Charleston Va. principally Cavalry, under Brig. Gen. Crook. The former of these will endeavor to reach the Va. & Ten. rail-road about south of Covington and if found practicable will work Eastward to Lynchburg and return to its base by way of the Shanandoah Valley or join you. The other will strike at Saltville Va. and come Eastward to join Ord. The Cavalry from Ord's Command will try to force a passage southward, if they are sucsessful in reaching the Va & Ten. rail-road, to cut the main lines of road connecting Richmond with all the south & southwest.

Gilmore will join Butler with about 10.000 men from South Carolina. Butler can reduce his garrisons so as to take 23.000 men into the field directly to his front. This force will be commanded by Maj. Gen. W. F. Smith. With Smith and Gilmore Butler will seize City Point and operate against Richmond from the south side of the river. His movement will be simultaneous with yours.

Lee's Army will be your objective point. Wherever Lee goes there you will go also. The only point upon which I am now in doubt is whether it will be better to cross the Rapidann above or below him. Each plan presents great advantages over the other with corresponding objections. By crossing above Lee is cut off from all chance of ignoring Richmond and going North on a raid. But if we take this route all we do must be done whilst the rations we start with holds out. We separate from Butler so that he cannot be directed how to cooperate. By the other route Brandy Station can be used as a base of supplies until another is secured on the York or James River.

These advantages and objections I will talk with you more fully than I can write them.

Burnside with a force of probably 25.000 men will reinforce you. Immediate on his arrival, which will be shortly after the 20th inst. I will give him the defence of the road from Bull Run as far south as we wish to hold it. This will enable you to collect all your strenth about Brandy Station and to the front.

There will be Naval co operation on the James River and transports and Ferries will be provided so that should Lee fall back into his intrenchments at Richmond Butler's force and yours will be a unit, or at least can be made to act as such.

What I would direct then is that you commence at once reducing baggage to the very lowest possible standard. Two wagons to a regiment of five hundred men is the greatest number that should be allowed for all baggage exclusive of subsistence stores and Ordnance stores. One wagon to Brigade and one to Division Hd Qrs. is sufficient and about two to Corps Hd Qrs.

Should by Lee's Right flank be our route you will want to make arrangement for having supplies, of all sorts, promptly forwarded to White House on the Pamunkey. Your estimates for this contingency should be made at once. If not wanted there there is every possi probability they will be wanted on the James River or elswhere.

If Lee's Left is turned large provision will have to be made for Ordnance stores. I would say not much short of five hundred rounds of Infantry Ammunition would do. By the other, half the amount would be sufficient.

I am General, Very respectfully
your obt. svt.
U. S. GRANT
Lt. Gen.

ALS, Meade Papers, PHi. *O.R.*, I, xxxiii, 827–29. On April 17, 1864, Maj. Gen. George G. Meade wrote to USG. "I desire to report that, in conformity with my construction of your confidential letter of the 9th ins't. the following instructions have been given by me: —The Commissary Department, through its chief at these Head-quarters, has been notified that, at the close of the present month, or early in the next, there will be required one million of rations, on shipboard, in suitable vessels for being taken up the Pamunkey, or James river, as may be required, and, in advance of more specific instructions, Fortress Munroe has been designated as a proper point of assemblage. The Quarter Master Department has been notified, that, at the same time and place, forage, and other supplies furnished by that Department will be required. The Ordnance Department has been notified to have in similar readiness one hundred rounds of artillery ammunition per gun, and one hundred rounds of small-arm per man. The Engineer Department has been instructed to have the siege trains [now at Washington] in readiness for shipment, and such engineering tools and other supplies [in addition to those carried with the army] as would be required in the event of laying siege to Richmond. A special communication has been made to you in reference to the artillery for a siege train, in case one should be required before Richmond. The Medical Department has been notified, that, in addition to the supplies now in depot at Alexandria, and which will be kept there as long as the Orange and Alexandria railroad can be used, medical supplies for some 12000 wounded should be held in readiness on shipboard, to be thrown up the Pamunkey, or James, as circumstances may require. It is proper to observe, in connection with this duplication of reserve medical supplies, that, in case a battle is fought within communicating distance of the Orange and Alexandria railroad, the supplies at Alexandria can be thrown forward, but, if a rapid movement is made across the country, and a battle fought in the vicinity of Richmond, these supplies would have to be drawn from some other point; and the time which it would take after the battle occurs, to transfer from Alexandria to this point, and the consequent suffering that might ensue, justify, in my judgment, this duplication of *battle reserve supplies*, and their being held in readiness at some point nearer than Alexandria. The foregoing arrangements and instructions are based on the the contingency of the enemy's falling back without giving battle. Each Department has been notified to look to the Quarter Master Department for intimation of the period when the different supplies ordered should be sent to any particular point. For an immediate movement the following instructions have been given:—The Ordnance Department notified to have in readiness to issue, at short notice, one hundred and fifty rounds small-arm ammunition; fifty rounds to be carried on the person, and one hundred in supply train. The Subsistence Department, to have on hand for issue, sixteen days marching rations; four of salt meat and twelve of beef on the hoof;—six days to be carried on the person [*three* full rations in *havresacs*, and *three* small rations in *knapsacks*]; the balance in supply trains.—. The Quarter Master Department to have ten days full allowance of grain for all animals.—. The Medical Department to be prepared to send the sick, at short notice, to the rear, and to have all necessary field hospital supplies on hand.—. These preliminary instructions being given, it will require from *three* to *four* days notice to issue, and load supply trains, and prepare the army to move at an hours notice. This communication is respectfully submitted, that you may be fully advised of the steps I have taken, and that my attention may be called to the fact, in case I have done *more*, or *less*, than is expected and required of me" Copy (with bracketed material), Meade Papers, PHi. *O.R.*, I, xxxiii, 889–90. On March 30, 1880, Meade's son George wrote to Col. Robert N. Scott. ". . . You will also note that the letter of Genl. Meade to Genl. Grant—Apl 17th 1864—is not signed & is not in his own handwriting—I believe it to be a copy by Col. Wm. Day—or Col. Theo. Lyman—now of Boston,—after a more careful examination I ~~bel~~ am more inclined to think it the latter." ALS, DNA, RG 94, War Records Office, Letters Received.

To Maj. Gen. William S. Rosecrans

Culpeper C. H. Va
10 30 P m Apl 9th 1864

MAJ GEN ROSECRANS
[ST. LOUIS] MISSOURI

I see it will not do to take Infantry from your dept. If necessary for you [to] station troops in Arkansas for [the] protection of Missouri do it. The States Militia with their consent [can] be organized into U. S. Vol. Infy but not into Cavalry without *Special* authority from the War Dept. I cannot send more Cavalry to you [now] I will refer your recommendation for mustering militia into U. S. service & consolidating and mustering out such as will not accept such service—to the secy of War

U. S GRANT
Lt Genl

Telegram received, DNA, RG 107, Telegrams Collected (Bound); copies, *ibid.*, RG 108, Letters Sent; *ibid.*, RG 393, Dept. of Mo., Telegrams Received; DLC-USG, V, 45, 59; Rosecrans Papers, CLU. *O.R.*, I, xxxiv, part 3, 106. On April 9, 1864, USG wrote to Secretary of War Edwin M. Stanton. "In a letter of date April 6th, just received from Maj. Gen. W. S. Rosecrans, Com'd'g Department of the Missouri, he makes, among others, the following recommendation, which I respectfully submit to you: 'That I receive authority to organize such of the Missouri State Militia Cavalry as are willing to enlist in the United States Volunteer or Veteran service, and to consolidate and use or muster out the remainder as may seem best.' " LS, DNA, RG 94, Vol. Service Div., Letters Received, M2520 (VS) 1863.

To Maj. Gen. William T. Sherman

Culpeper C. H. Va.
10 30 P M April 9th 1864

MAJ GEN W. T. SHERMAN
NASHVILLE—

I have no objection to your proposed march of A. J. Smith across from Grenada All I want is all the troops in the field that can be got in for the Spring Campaign   I do not think any more Generals will be sent to you unless you want Milroy[1] McCook or Crittenden

U S. GRANT
Lieut Genl

Telegram received, DNA, RG 107, Telegrams Collected (Bound); copies, *ibid.*, RG 108, Letters Sent; *ibid.*, RG 393, Military Div. of the Miss., Letters Sent; DLC-USG, V, 45, 59, 94. *O.R.*, I, xxxii, part 3, 305. Earlier on April 9, 1864, 12:30 P.M., USG telegraphed to Maj. Gen. William T. Sherman. "Gen Banks is ordered to take all his troops with him and to turn over the defense of Red River to Gen. Steele and the Navy—One Regiment and a part have been ordered to Gen. Steele at Little Rock and the thirty fifth Wisconsin Regiment is subject to your orders"   Copies, DLC-USG, V, 45, 59, 94; DNA, RG 108, Letters Sent; *ibid.*, RG 393, Military Div. of the Miss., Letters Sent. *O.R.*, I, xxxii, part 3, 306. On April 8, USG telegraphed to Maj. Gen. Henry W. Halleck. "Are any regiments of Cavalry either new or old in the Western states unassigned   I wish to have two (2) or three (3) regiments sent to Genl Steele at Little Rock"   Telegram received, DNA, RG 107, Telegrams Collected (Bound); copy, *ibid.*, RG 108, Letters Received. *O.R.*, I, xxxiv, part 3, 89. This telegram was drafted on April 7, apparently by Lt. Col. Cyrus B. Comstock. Copies, DNA, RG 94, War Records Office, Dept. of the Cumberland; *ibid.*, RG 108, Letters Sent; DLC-USG, V, 45, 59. On April 8, 4:00 P.M., Halleck telegraphed to USG. "The 35th Wisconsin Infantry Regt. a new organization, was ordered to Louisville or Nashville under your general instructions. By some misunderstanding by Col Fry, it was also ordered to Annapolis. As orders conflicted, it was not moved. To which place shall [it] be sent? The 9th Iowa & a fractional Ill regt of cavalry have been ordered to Little Rock. I hope to get one or two more ready soon   The delay is for want of horses." ALS (telegram sent), DNA, RG 107, Telegrams Collected (Bound); telegram received, *ibid.* On the same day, 7:30 P.M., USG telegraphed to Halleck. "The 35th Wisconsin may be ordered to Sherman   Notify Sherman, however, to send the order for it as he may wish to send it to Steele, now that he has been directed to take the Red river into his command." Copies, DLC-USG, V, 45, 59; DNA, RG 108, Letters Sent. The telegram received was addressed to Secretary of War Edwin M. Stanton. *Ibid.*, RG 107, Telegrams Collected (Bound). *O.R.*, I, xxxiv, part 3, 88.

1. Robert H. Milroy, born in 1816 in Ind., graduated from Norwich University in 1843, served as capt., 1st Ind., in the Mexican War, then practiced law. Appointed col., 9th Ind., as of April 27, 1861, brig. gen. as of Sept. 3, and maj. gen. as of Nov. 29, 1862, his military career effectively ended after a disastrous defeat at Winchester, Va. (June 14-15, 1863). On March 17, 1864, Milroy, Rensselaer, Ind., wrote to USG. "Pardon my seeming disregard of military etiquette in addressing you directly,   Having been exiled from duty near nine months & not recollecting the name of your A. A. Gnl. is my apology. I desire, in common withe the loyal people of the U. S. to express to you my great pleasure & congratulation on your well merited promotion & assignment to the chief command of our armies, and I ask the honor & the privalege of reporting to you for assignment to duty. Although I had a military education, I am not a

professional soldier, & only entered the service of my country to assist in her salvation and my most earnest desire is to be on active duty, while her danger lasts. Prior to being deprived of command & placed in arrest, I had not been away from my command a day from the beginning of the war, and I have not been informed, & have never yet been able to learn, why I was so deprived of com.d & placed in arrest, and the Court of Inquiry convened by order of the President, was unable, after a months of close examination, to ascertain any reason for my painful treatment. But these are things of the past, & the mighty future demands the attention of all, and I most respectfully ask General, that you will try me—try me where there is danger and hard fighting to be done, and if I fail, then have me shot. It is not for me to suggest a command. I will gladly perform any duty to which you may assign me, but, I hope you will pardon me for saying I would prefer a cavalry com.d   I have not the honor of being known to you General, & should you think it worth while to make any inquiry about me, I would respectfully refer you to Maj: Gnls. Reynolds, Segil, Fermont, Schenck, Pope Shurze & Wallace—Brig. Gnls. Kelley, Waggoner, McLean, Tyler & Elliott—& Cols. Wilder, Straight & others with whom I have served in the present war & the war with Mexico." ALS, NHi. On April 8, 8:15 P.M., Lt. Col. Adam Badeau telegraphed to Maj. Gen. George G. Meade. "Lt. Gen. Grant desires to know if you know Gen. Milroy, and if he is fit to command a division of cavalry" ALS (telegram sent), PCarlA; telegram received, DNA, RG 94, War Records Office, Army of the Potomac. On the same day, 8:30 P.M., Meade wrote to Badeau. "I have no personal knowledge of Genl. Milroy—From report I should not judge him qualified to command a Division of Cavalry   I have assigned Genl. Torbert to the Cavalry, who with Genl Wilson will fill my divisions—" ALS, *ibid.*, RG 107, Telegrams Collected (Unbound); copy, Meade Papers, PHi.

To Maj. Gen. Franz Sigel

Culpepper Va
Apr. 11th 1864

Maj Gen F. Sigel
Cumberland

I have directed the 36th Ohio to be ordered to Genl Crook.[1] If I can send you an Engineer Officer in place of Lt Meigs I will do so,[2]

If one is not sent exercise your own judgement about letting him go into the field

U. S. Grant
Lt Genl

Telegram received, DNA, RG 107, Telegrams Collected (Bound); copies, *ibid.*, RG 108, Letters Sent; Sigel Papers, OClWHi; DLC-USG, V, 45, 59. Printed as sent at 10:30 A.M. in *O.R.*, I, xxxiii, 839. On April 11, 1864, Maj. Gen. Franz

Sigel telegraphed to USG. "Your dispatch in regard to the thirty sixth (36th) Ohio and Lieut Meigs is received" ALS (telegram sent), DNA, RG 107, Telegrams Collected (Unbound); copy, Sigel Papers, OClWHi. *O.R.*, I, xxxiii, 840.

1. On April 4, Brig. Gen. George Crook, Charleston, W. Va., telegraphed to USG. "I visited Marrietta Ohio. The thirty sixth (36) regt O. V. I. on veteran furlough at that place agree to the condition we were speaking of Their furlough is up on the nineteenth (19) inst. I need at least one (1) more Infy regiment. Will you please order it at once. I have just learned that the eighth (8) O. V. C. and the twentieth (20) Pa Vols are not mounted yet nor fully equipped yet." Telegram received, DNA, RG 107, Telegrams Collected (Bound); *ibid.*, Telegrams Collected (Unbound). *O.R.*, I, xxxiii, 802. On April 10, Crook sent a similar telegram to Sigel, which Sigel transmitted to USG on the same day, 12:30 A.M. Telegram received (dated April 11), DNA, RG 107, Telegrams Collected (Bound); copy (dated April 10), *ibid.*, RG 393, Dept. of West Va., Letters Sent (Press). Dated April 11 in *O.R.*, I, xxxiii, 842. On April 11, USG telegraphed to Maj. Gen. Henry W. Halleck. "Please order the 35th Ohio Veteran Infantry now at Marietta Ohio on furlough to join Genl Crook at Charleston Virginia by the 22nd of this month" Telegram received, DNA, RG 94, Vol. Service Div., Letters Received, A288 (VS) 1864; *ibid.*, RG 107, Telegrams Collected (Bound); copies, *ibid.*, RG 108, Letters Sent; DLC-USG, V, 45, 59.

2. On April 9, 5:30 P.M., USG telegraphed to Sigel. "Can you not spare Lieut. Meigs of the Engineers for the field this spring detailing an officer to take his place Perhaps another officer can be sent you" Telegram received, DNA, RG 107, Telegrams Collected (Bound); copies, *ibid.*, RG 108, Letters Sent; Sigel Papers, OClWHi; DLC-USG, V, 45, 59. On April 10, Sigel telegraphed to USG. "Your dispatch in regard to Lieut. Meigs received. He is just now in Baltimore to make arrangements for some Engineer work, but is expected to be back tomorrow, I will send him to you at such time as you want him to report. I will make application for another engineer officer, as there is no officer here whom I can detail. I have sent written report and maps to Washington in the evening of the 9th inst. I could not telegraph sooner because the wires were down" Telegram received, DNA, RG 107, Telegrams Collected (Bound); copies, *ibid.*, RG 393, Dept. of West Va., Letters Sent (Press); Sigel Papers, OClWHi. Printed as received at midnight in *O.R.*, I, xxxiii, 836. On the same day, 6:00 P.M., USG telegraphed to Sigel. "You misunderstood my dispatch in regard to Lieut Meigs, I do not want him here but Gen Averill regards him as a very valuable officer in the field and I wanted to know if you could send him with Genl's Ord and Averill by detailing another officer to take his place or would you require an Engineer Officer sent to you to enable you to spare him?" Telegram received, DNA, RG 107, Telegrams Collected (Bound); copies, *ibid.*, RG 108, Letters Sent; Sigel Papers, OClWHi; DLC-USG, V, 45, 59. On the same day, 9:30 P.M., Sigel telegraphed to USG. "Your dispatch in regard to Lieut Meigs is received I can send him with Genls Ord and Averell although I am sorry to lose him from my Staff as he is familiar with all the work in progress and in contemplation, and is a disbursing Officer. I believe that the interests of the service require a regular Engineer Officer to take his place" Telegram received, DNA, RG 107, Telegrams Collected (Bound); copies, Sigel Papers, OClWHi; (dated April 9) DNA, RG 393, Dept. of West Va., Letters Sent (Press). Dated April 9 in *O.R.*, I, xxxiii, 831–32. See telegram to Maj. Gen. George H. Thomas, Oct. 19, 1863.

To Maj. Gen. William S. Rosecrans

(Cypher)   Apl. 12th *1864*

~~Maj. Gen.~~

MAJ. GEN. ROSECRANS, ST. LOUIS MO.

Your report of transportation shows over sixteen hundred teams in the Dept. It is impossible to supply the necessary transportation for the Armies in Tennessee in time for spring operations. Can you not send the mules of five hundred of your teams to Louisville at once? Send all you can.

U. S. GRANT

Lt. Gen.

ALS (telegram sent), DNA, RG 107, Telegrams Collected (Bound); telegram received (at 2:00 P.M.), *ibid.*; Rosecrans Papers, CLU. Printed as sent at 2:00 P.M. in *O.R.*, I, xxxiv, part 3, 145. On April 12, 1864, Maj. Gen. William S. Rosecrans telegraphed to USG. "~~Your des~~ I can & will send all mules ~~to~~ I can to Louisville. The reason why so much transportation is used is that we have ~~t~~ so much hauling, for example—from Rolla to Springfield all supplies have to be waggoned one hundred & sixty miles" ALS (telegram sent), DNA, RG 107, Telegrams Collected (Unbound); telegram received (dated April 13), *ibid.*; *ibid.*, Telegrams Collected (Bound); *ibid.*, RG 108, Letters Received. *O.R.*, I, xxxiv, part 3, 145.

On April 9, 10:30 P.M., USG telegraphed to Brig. Gen. Robert Allen. "The whole of transportation on hand in the Dept of Missouri shows sixteen hundred and fifty (1650) teams besides Ambalances Of this number they ought to spare five hundred (500) at least if you want that elsewhere." Telegram received, DNA, RG 107, Telegrams Collected (Bound); copies, *ibid.*, RG 108, Letters Sent; DLC-USG, V, 45, 59. *O.R.*, I, xxxiv, part 3, 106. On April 11, Allen, Louisville, telegraphed to USG. "We want all the mules that can be obtained from all sources Have wagons Enough—" Telegram received, DNA, RG 107, Telegrams Collected (Bound).

On April 25, Rosecrans telegraphed to USG. "Col. Myers reports that fifteen hundred and twenty Mules can be spared from ~~thes~~ Department transportation. Many of these must be replaced as soon as the wants at Nashville are supplied. In ten days from ~~May 1~~ April 21st Col M will have shipped to Nashville four 4 thousand 4000 Mueles, and six hundred 600 Artillery horses." LS (telegram sent), *ibid.*, Telegrams Collected (Unbound); telegram received, *ibid.*, Telegrams Collected (Bound); *ibid.*, RG 108, Letters Received. *O.R.*, I, xxxiv, part 3, 283.

To Maj. Gen. Franz Sigel

Cypher   Apl. 12th *1864* [*1:30* P.M.]
MAJ. GEN. SIGEL, CUMBERLAND VA.

Your letter received. Will not a week or ten days good weather make the programe laid out in my previous instructions practicable. The route you now suggest, that is by sending the whole force to Gauly Bridge[1] to start was my idea exactly simply consulting the map without any personal knowledge of the country to be traversed. Consultation however with officers who had been in the country induced me to give the instructions I did. The late rains has so far set back offensive operations that we can change plan if found necessary any time in the next ten days.

U. S. GRANT
Lt. Gen

ALS (telegram sent), DNA, RG 107, Telegrams Collected (Bound); telegram received, *ibid. O.R.*, I, xxxiii, 845. On April 11, 1864, Maj. Gen. Franz Sigel telegraphed at length to USG about problems presented by impassable roads near Beverly. Telegram received (dated April 12), DNA, RG 107, Telegrams Collected (Bound); copy, Sigel Papers, OClWHi. Dated April 12 in *O.R.*, I, xxxiii, 844–45. On the same day, 7:00 P.M., Sigel telegraphed to USG. "Your despatch of today is received   I will continue in making all dispositions necessary to carry out your programme. According to it there would be only three 3 regiments of Infantry left besides the rest of Averills Cavalry to defend or move up the Shenandoah Valley. Ten 10 would go with Genl Ord. Six 6 with Genl Crook besides the thirty sixth Ohio and four 4 would be posted on the line of Balto & Ohio Rl. Rd. from Monocacy to Parkersburg amongst them two Maryland and one Virginia regiment raised for local defense and necessary to guard our stores and depots and to load and unload trains"   Telegram received, DNA, RG 107, Telegrams Collected (Bound); copy, Sigel Papers, OClWHi. *O.R.*, I, xxxiii, 845–46. See following telegram.

1. Gauley Bridge, West Va., at the confluence of the Gauley and Kanawha rivers, approximately twenty-five miles southeast of Charleston.

To Maj. Gen. Franz Sigel

———

Annapolis Md
April 13th 1864 *10. a. m.*

MAJ GEN FRANZ SIGEL
CUMBERLAND MD.

Your despatch of yesterday is received and is satisfactory. A movement up Shenandoah Valley, if necessary to make it, will not require much more than an escort for the wagon train. I have directed a regiment of Heavy Artillery to be sent to you from Baltimor which I do not see enters into your calculations of forces. In addition to this I may in case of an urgent necessity be able to send you say four (4) more ~~Inf~~ regiments of Infantry from Washington when the time for moving arrives

U S. GRANT
Lt General

Telegram received, DNA, RG 107, Telegrams Collected (Bound); copies, *ibid.*, RG 108, Letters Sent; Sigel Papers, OClWHi; DLC-USG, V, 45, 59. *O.R.*, I, xxxiii, 858. On April 13, 1864, 2:00 P.M., Maj. Gen. Franz Sigel telegraphed to USG. "Your dispatch of today is received. The arrival of the regiment of Heavy Artillery at Harpers Ferry was reported to me yesterday" Telegram received, DNA, RG 107, Telegrams Collected (Bound); copies, *ibid.*, RG 393, Dept. of West Va., Letters Sent; Sigel Papers, OClWHi. *O.R.*, I, xxxiii, 858.

To Maj. Gen. Henry W. Halleck

———

Culpeper C. H.
5 40 P M Apl 15th 1864

MAJ. GEN H W HALLECK
CHIEF OF STAFF—

If there is no special reason for retaining the Eighth (8) Illinois Cavalry in Washington send it to the front   It is one of the best regiments for the field—

If Cavalry is necessary for Washn. take the 27th New York now at Giesboro Point—

U. S. Grant
Lieut. General

Telegram received, DNA, RG 107, Telegrams Collected (Bound); copies, *ibid.*, RG 108, Letters Sent; DLC-USG, V, 45, 59. On April 16, 1864, 3:30 p.m., Maj. Gen. Henry W. Halleck telegraphed to USG. "Only four companies of the 8th Ill. cavalry are mounted. No twenty seventh N. Y. at cavalry depot. The twenty second N. Y. is there, but not mounted, the Army of the Potomac taking every horse as fast as we get one. The fraction of the 8th Ill mounted is the only cavalry for picket [and scout] duty, & the only one acquainted with the country." ALS (telegram sent), DNA, RG 107, Telegrams Collected (Bound); telegram received, *ibid.*; *ibid.*, RG 108, Letters Received. *O.R.*, I, xxxiii, 879.

On April 25, Brig. Gen. John A. Rawlins telegraphed to Maj. Gen. Philip H. Sheridan. "The Genl has asked twice to have the 8th Ill Cav ordered here but has been answered both times that it cannot be spared from Washn hence it has not been ordered to you" Telegrams received (2), DNA, RG 107, Telegrams Collected (Unbound); copies, DLC-USG, V, 45, 59; DNA, RG 108, Letters Sent. *O.R.*, I, xxxiii, 972. See *ibid.*, pp. 963, 985.

To Maj. Gen. William T. Sherman

Culpepper Va
Apl 15th 1864—8 P M

Maj Gen W T Sherman—
Nashville Tenn

Forrest must be driven out, but with a proper commander in West Tennessee there is force enough there now. Your preparations for the coming campaign must go on, but if it is necessary to detach a portion of the troops intended for it, detach them, and make the campaign with that much fewer men—

Relieve Gen Hurlbut,[1]—I can send Genl Washburn, a sober & energetic Officer, to take his place,   I can also send you Genl L. G. Hunt to command District of Columbus—Shall I send Washburne? Does Hurlbut think if he moves a part of his force after the only enemy within two hundred miles of him that the post will run

off with the balance of his force? If our men have been murdered after capture retaliation must be resorted to promptly—
U S Grant
Lt Genl

Telegram received, DNA, RG 107, Telegrams Collected (Bound); copies, *ibid.*, RG 108, Letters Sent; *ibid.*, RG 393, Military Div. of the Miss., Letters Sent; DLC-USG, V, 45, 59, 94. *O.R.*, I, xxxii, part 3, 366. On April 15, 1864, 9:00 A.M., Maj. Gen. William T. Sherman, Nashville, telegraphed to USG. "General Brayman reports from Cairo the arrival of fifty wounded white soldiers from Fort Pillow and that the place was attacked on the 12th fifty white soldiers Killed and one hundred taken prisoners and Three hundred blacks murdered after surrender   I dont know what these men were doing at Fort Pillow   I ordered it to be abandoned before I went to Meriden and it was so abandoned   Genl Hurlbut must have sent this garrison up recently from Memphis   So many men are on furlough that Grierson & Hurlbut seem to fear going out of Memphis to attack Forrest   I have no apprehensions for the safety of Paducah Columbus or Memphis but without drawing from Dodge I have no force to send over there and dont want to interrupt my plans of preparation for the grand object of the spring campaign   I expect McPhersons two Divisions from Vicksburg to rendezvous at Cairo from furlough about the twentieth & I ~~will~~ look for A. J. Smith up daily from Red River   Whenever either of these commands arrive I can pen Forrest up but it will take some time to run him down   Do you want me to delay for such a purpose or shall I go on to concentrate on Chattanooga? I dont know what to do with Genl Hurlbut   I know that Forrest could pen him up in Memphis with twenty five hundred men although Hurlbut has all of Griersons cavalry and the citizen militia Three thousand   If you think I have time I will send a Division from Dodge to Purdy & order A J Smith as he comes up to strike inland to Bolivar Jackson &c & come across by land to the Tennessee river   This may consume an extra two weeks   Corse was at Vicksburg ready to start up ~~Tennessee~~ Red river the eighth"   Telegram received, DNA, RG 107, Telegrams Collected (Bound); *ibid.*, RG 108, Letters Received. *O.R.*, I, xxxii, part 3, 367.

Also on April 15, 3:40 P.M., Secretary of War Edwin M. Stanton telegraphed to USG. "The Rebels have captured [F]ort Pillow, sacked Paducah again and have demanded surrender of Columbus which has not yet been given up. The slaughter at Fort Pillow is great. The news came first by way of Cairo but I telegraphed Nashville & the operator confirms the news"   ALS (telegram sent), DNA, RG 107, Telegrams Collected (Bound). *O.R.*, I, xxxii, part 3, 367. On the same day, USG telegraphed to Stanton. "Have you seen shermans despatches of today to me—if not I will forward them to you" Telegram received, DNA, RG 107, Telegrams Collected (Bound). *O.R.*, I, lii, part 1, 546. On the same day, 10:30 P.M., Stanton telegraphed to USG. "I have seen General Shermans despatch which arrived after my telegram to you. Another has reached here from Admiral Pennock which I have directed to be forwarded to you. The substance is the same ~~but with m~~ as Shermans but with fuller particulars. I will give Col Kautz the Brigadier certificate and send him to Fortress Monroe immediately. General Brooks left Pittsburg for Fortress Monroe yesterday." ALS (telegram sent), DNA, RG 107, Telegrams Collected (Bound). *O.R.*, I, xxxii, part 3, 366.

On April 15, 3:00 P.M., Capt. Alexander M. Pennock, Cairo, had telegraphed to Secretary of the Navy Gideon Welles news of the raid of C.S.A. Maj. Gen. Nathan B. Forrest. Telegram received, DNA, RG 108, Letters Received. *O.R.* (Navy), I, xxvi, 215–16.

Also on April 15, 8:30 P.M., USG had telegraphed to Maj. Gen. Henry W. Halleck. "Please ask the Secretary of War to give Col Kautz certificate of appointment as Brigadier General and order him to report to Maj Gen Butler to command his cavalry" Telegram received, DNA, RG 107, Telegrams Collected (Bound); copies, *ibid.*, RG 108, Letters Sent; DLC-USG, V, 45, 59. *O.R.*, I, xxxiii, 877. On the same day, Stanton telegraphed to USG. "General Brooks reports that he is going immediately to General Butler." ALS (telegram sent), DNA, RG 107, Telegrams Collected (Bound).

1. On April 16, noon, Sherman telegraphed to Maj. Gen. Stephen A. Hurlbut. "There has been marked timidity in the management of affairs since Forrest passed north of Memphis. Lt Genl Grant orders me to relieve you. You will proceed to Cairo and take command there. Leave for the present, Genl Buckland to defend Memphis and district. His Brigade with Griersons cavalry can and should hunt up Forrest and whip him." Telegram received, *ibid.*, RG 393, 16th Army Corps, Letters Received; copies, *ibid.*, Letters Sent; *ibid.*, RG 107, Letters Received from Bureaus. *O.R.*, I, xxxii, part 3, 381–82. On April 18, Hurlbut wrote to Stanton requesting a court of inquiry. ALS, DNA, RG 94, Letters Received, 385H 1864. *O.R.*, I, xxxii, part 3, 405–6. On April 30, Halleck endorsed this letter to USG, who endorsed it on May 2. "Respectfully returned. It is not consistent with the interests of the public service to convene the Court of Inquiry demanded by Maj. Gen. S. A. Hurlbut. Whether his course was 'timid' or not, it has been unsatisfactory. The propriety of releiving a subordinate officer when it is believed that some other officer can act more efficiently is beyond question, and it is not necessary or proper to assign specific reasons for such change, or to convene a Court to determine whether injustice has been done the officer so relieved." ES, DNA, RG 94, Letters Received, 385H 1864. *O.R.*, I, xxxii, part 3, 406. See *ibid.*, p. 397; *ibid.*, I, xxxix, part 2, 3–4.

To Maj. Gen. Franz Sigel

Culpeper C. H. Va. Apl 15th 1864.

MAJ GEN. F. SIGEL.
COMD'G DEPT WEST VA.

I send with this Lieut Col Babcock, of my Staff, to consult with you in person in reference to the preparations for the approaching campaign. I will state that the instructions which I communicated to you were based upon such information as is given by the maps, and as could be obtained by inquiries—from those who had previously been over the country. The point to be attained was marked in my instructions. That is, in the spring campaign it is desirable to bring into the field all the troops possible. From the extended line you have to guard, no troops can be taken from you, except to act directly from your line toward the enemy. In this way you must occupy the attention of a large force, (and thereby hold them from reinforcing elsewhere) or must inflict a blow upon the enemies resources, which will materially aid us. This being the object, it is not necessary that the exact line marked out by me should be followed. It was selected with the view of keeping your present line covered. If this can be equally well done by starting from Gauley Bridge, I have no objections to that route.

The concentration preparatory to starting—should go forward with all expedition, so that the two columns sent by you can be started by the 23rd inst, if called on to do so. I will give the signal from here for starting from Beverly, or Gauley as the case may be. It is now pretty certain that the enemy, suspecting a move up the Shenandoah Valley, have established a considerable force at Staunton to meet you. This may be, however, a cover for a formidable movement of the enemy by that route, northward. This you will want to watch closely, and report any information you may obtain. Confer freely with Col Babcock, and whilst he remains with you, let us settle, unalterably, the line to be pursued by your forces. Of course I do not intend you to understand that Col Babcock will give you orders in this matter, but by a personal interview the best thing to do can be arrived at, and by telegraphing to me, it can be adopted.

U S. GRANT
Lieut Genl.

Copies, DLC-USG, V, (misdated April 18, 1864) 45, 59; DNA, RG 108, Letters Sent; Sigel Papers, OCIWHi; Sigel Papers, NHi. O.R., I, xxxiii, 874. On April 17, Maj. Gen. Franz Sigel telegraphed to USG. "Lieut. Col. Babcock has arrived here and delivered to me your letter. I will consult with him and then report again." Copy, Sigel Papers, OCIWHi.

To Edwin M. Stanton

From Culpepper C. H.
Dated, Apr 16 [*1864*]

HON E. M. STANTON.

The only objection to West Kentucky being placed under Gen. Burbridge, is that it belongs to a different dept from the balance of the state. One (1) officer cannot well make returns, and reports to two (2) Depts and it would not be advisable to add that part of Ky to the Dept of the Ohio. In consequence of the weakness exhibited by the commander of West Ky, I expect to send another General there, and the one (1) I have selected ranks above Burbridge, the matter has now as much as he can attend to well.

U. S. GRANT.
Lt Genl

Telegram received, DNA, RG 107, Telegrams Collected (Bound); copies, *ibid.*, RG 108, Letters Sent; DLC-USG, V, 45, 59. *O.R.*, I, xxxii, part 3, 384. On April 16, 1864, 1:15 P.M., Secretary of War Edwin M. Stanton telegraphed to USG. "Governer Bramlette is extremely anxious to have the Western Counties of Kentucky included in the Same command as the remainder of the State, so that the whole State may be under command of General Burbridge. Is there any objection to the change being made" ALS (telegram sent), DNA, RG 107, Telegrams Collected (Bound). *O.R.*, I, xxxii, part 3, 384.

To Maj. Gen. Henry W. Halleck

Culpepper Va
April 16th 1864

MAJ GEN H W HALLECK
CHF OF STAFF

Genl Butler is absolutely without a cavalry commander, and I can think of no one available equal to Kautz—Cannot Gen J. W Davidson or some officer of less rank, now that the duties of the cavalry Bureau have been changed, do the duties as well.

I think Washburn, whilst he could not command an Army as

well would fill the place at Memphis better than Genl Pope   He is full of energy and will follow instructions—I think probably the Heavy Artillery with Gen Wallace had better remain with him— They answer there as a reserve to send to Genl Sigel, Washington, or almost any place in case of necessity—

U S GRANT
Lt Gen

Telegram received, DNA, RG 107, Telegrams Collected (Bound); copies, *ibid.*, RG 108, Letters Sent; DLC-USG, V, 45, 59. Printed as sent at 6:00 P.M. in *O.R.*, I, xxxiii, 879–80. On April 16, 1864, 12:50 P.M., Maj. Gen. Henry W. Halleck telegraphed to USG. "Col Kautz will be sent to Genl Butler if you deem him more useful there than here in charge of cavalry Bureau. There is no competent person here to take his place, and the difficulty of getting horses is daily increasing. Could you not employ Genl Pope to advantage on the Miss. river? He is anxious for active employment. There is a regiment of heavy artillery in Baltimore, drilled as infantry, fifteen hundred strong, which could be sent to the field, if you think it can be spared from Genl Wallace's command. His last returns give his effective force Six thousand seven hundred. Since then twelve hundred have been sent to Harpers ferry." ALS (telegram sent), DNA, RG 107, Telegrams Collected (Bound); telegram received, *ibid.*; *ibid.*, RG 108, Letters Received. *O.R.*, I, xxxiii, 879.

To Maj. Gen. Henry W. Halleck

Culpepper Va.
Apl 16th 1864

MAJ GEN HALLECK
CHF OF STAFF

Please ask the President to authorize the transfer of Fort Smith and the Indian Territory to the Department of the Arkansas

There is every reason why this territory and the State of Arkansas should be under one man, and that man in the field

In case this change is made I wish Genl Blunt ordered back to report to Gen Curtis

U S GRANT
Lt Genl

Telegram received, DNA, RG 107, Telegrams Collected (Bound); copies, *ibid.*, RG 108, Letters Sent; DLC-USG, V, (misdated April 18, 1864) 45, 59. *O.R.*,

I, xxxiv, part 3, 178. On April 15, Maj. Gen. Henry W. Halleck wrote to USG. "Confidential. . . . I enclose herewith a telegram just received from General Kimball, comd'g' at Little Rock. When the Departments of Kansas and Arkansas were formed, I advised that the Indian Territory, west of the latter state should be included in that Department inasmuch as it must be defended by General Steele's army, and recieve all supplies through Little Rock and Fort Smith. The Sec'y of War concurred with me in opinion; but the President on the urgent solicitation of Senator Lane and others directed that the Indian Territory and Fort Smith be assigned to General Curtis' command. General Blunt who seems to be a very quarrelsome man and against whom there are very serious accusations, was sent by General Curtis to command that district. Since then there has been much difficulty and confusion, which may produce some serious results. I see no way of avoiding these evils but to attach Fort Smith and the Indian Territory to the Department of Arkansas and send General Blunt back to Kansas to report to Genl Curtis. If you concur in this view & will write to that effect to the Sec'y of War, I think the President will consent to the change   Colonel Marcy, Inspector General, has just reported that General Rosecrans has in the Dep't of Mo. 16824 troops present, exclusive of some 2,000 enrolled militia, and that there are not more than 2,000 armed rebels in the entire Department, and that these are in small guerrilla bands concealed in the woods. Occasional raids from these men cannot be prevented by any number of troops. Colonel Marcy recommends that five thousand men be sent from General Rosecrans' command into the field. This will leave some twelve or fourteen thousand men to contend with some two thousand guerrillas! He is of opinion that even more can be spared, if those left in the state should be properly organized and distributed. Nothing, however, but a peremptory order from you will ever get any troop out of Missouri. . . . P. S. You will remember that in addition to Col Marcy's estimates an additional regiment of cavalry was given to General Rosecrans a few day ago" LS, DNA, RG 108, Letters Received. *O.R.*, I, xxxiv, part 3, 160–61. On April 16, President Abraham Lincoln endorsed USG's telegram. "Let it be done." *Ibid.*, p. 178.

To Maj. Gen. Henry W. Halleck

Culpeper Va.
7 P m April 16th 1864

Maj Genl H W Halleck
Chief of Staff

Please order General C. C. Washburn to proceed at once to Memphis and relieve Genl Hurlbut in command of district of West Tennessee General Hurlbut to report from Cairo by letter to the Adjutant General at what point orders will reach him   I do not want W. assigned to command of sixteenth (16) Army Corps but

will leave Genl Dodge to command that portion in the field   Gen
Crittenden may be ordered to report to General Burnside

U. S. Grant

Lt Gen Comdg

Telegram received, DNA, RG 94, Letters Received, 341A 1864; *ibid.*, RG 107, Telegrams Collected (Bound); copies, *ibid.*, RG 108, Letters Sent; DLC-USG, V, 45, 59. On April 17, 1864, USG telegraphed to Maj. Gen. Henry W. Halleck. "Has Genl Washburne been ordered to Memphis? I think it important that Hurlbut should be relieved without delay"   Telegram received, DNA, RG 107, Telegrams Collected (Bound); copies, *ibid.*, RG 108, Letters Sent; DLC-USG, 45, 59. On the same day, 2:00 P.M., Halleck telegraphed to USG. "Genl Kautz ordered to Fort Monroe, Washburne to Memphis, Crittenden to Burnside. Fort Smith & Indian Territory added to Dept of Arkansas, & Genl Blunt ordered to Genl Curtis. [An] Infantry regt organized from 2d Penn Heavy Artillery for Genl Burnside. Will write you to-day [about] others. Messenger from Genl [Gillmore] just arrived with list [of] regts to be left in Dept of [the] South; he wishes those on that list now here to be sent south immediately. Shall I so order? He hopes to have from seven to ten thousand at Fort Monroe by the [20th], if weather should favor. Shall those parts of his troops which are not to remain in the Dept of the south be sent to meet him at Fort Monroe, or wait here till he arrives there himself? A naval officer in North Carolina [writes] that rebel troops from the south are being concentrated at Weldon & Richmond, the military [having] taken possession of all rail roads. It is reported that all males capable of bearing arms are being conscripted [in] the Shenandoah valley and concentrated at Luray, and that wagon trains are transporting all forage & provisions from that valley to Lee's Army." ALS (telegram sent), DNA, RG 107, Telegrams Collected (Bound); telegram received, *ibid.*; *ibid.*, RG 108, Letters Received. *O.R.*, I, xxxiii, 887; (incomplete) *ibid.*, I, xxxiv, part 3, 192. On the same day, 6:00 P.M., USG telegraphed to Halleck. "Send detachments belonging to regts to remain in the Dept of the South back to their regts, all other troops belonging to Gen Gillmore's forces send to him as soon as notice is received of his arrival at Ft. Monroe." Telegram received, DNA, RG 107, Telegrams Collected (Bound); copies, *ibid.*, RG 108, Letters Sent; DLC-USG, V, 45, 59. *O.R.*, I, xxxv, part 2, 57.

   An undated telegram from Maj. Gen. Ambrose E. Burnside to USG was probably sent about this time. "If ~~interest~~ Washburn is ordered to Memphis— Would be glad to have no general officer ordered to report who ranks Potter—if interest of service permits—" ALS (telegram sent), DNA, RG 107, Telegrams Collected (Unbound). Another undated telegram from Burnside to USG may have been sent about April 18. "When I telegraphed you this morning I did not know of the existence of order for Genl Crittenden to report—The only objection I have to him is that he ranks Parke ~~and will be in command of every thing~~" ALS (telegram sent), *ibid.* See *O.R.*, I, xxxiii, 913.

   On April 17, USG telegraphed twice to Halleck, the second time at 5:30 P.M. "If the 6th Minn. has not recd orders please order it immediately to its place with the Army of the Potomac." "Gen Crook informs me that the 8th Ohio Cavalry is ordered to West Va to be mounted & equipped—Can it not be mounted

& equipped at Camp Dennison at once & forwarded to Charleston W Va?" Telegrams received, DNA, RG 107, Telegrams Collected (Bound); copies, *ibid.*, RG 108, Letters Sent; DLC-USG, V, 45, 59. On April 15, Brig. Gen. George Crook had telegraphed to USG. "I just learn that the Eigth (8) Ohio Cavy. is not yet mtd. or Equipped & that it will be sent to west Va. to be mounted   If such is the case it will not be ready for service for one month yet   will you have it Mtd & Equipped in Ohio   It is now in Camp Dennison   I fear I will not get near the number of mounted force you intended I should have. No reinforcements have reached me yet"   Telegram received, DNA, RG 107, Telegrams Collected (Unbound). *O.R.*, I, xxxiii, 876. On April 18, 3:00 P.M., Halleck telegraphed to USG. "The 8th Ohio cavalry was ordered to be mounted & equipped at Camp Dennison & *then* sent to Genl Crook. The cavalry Bureau has been directed to do this at once. Genl W. S. Smith at Nashville has called on Genl Davidson for thirty thousand cavalry horses. Such requisitions cannot possibly be filled. On the 28th of March Genl Pope asked for a delay in sending the 6th Minn. to Army of the Potomac for reasons given. I will immediately send you a copy of [his] letter, or will make the order peremptory, if you say so. Pope's force against Indians is very small." ALS (telegram sent), DNA, RG 107, Telegrams Collected (Bound); telegram received, *ibid. O.R.*, I, xxxiii, 897.

To Maj. Gen. Benjamin F. Butler

(Confidential)   Head Quarters Armies in the Field
                                        Culpepper C. H. Va. Apl. 16th 1864

MAJ. GEN. B. F. BUTLER,
COMD.G DEPT. OF VA. & N. C.
GENERAL,

I have just this moment received your letter of the 15th of Apl. brought by the hands of Maj. Gen. W. F. Smith.

You are entirely right in saying there should be but one movement made south of James River. At no time has more been intended.

I went to Fortress Monroe for the express purpose of seeing you and telling you that it was my plan to have the force under you act directly in concert with the Army of the Potomoc, and, as far as possible, towards the same point. My mind was entirely made up what instructions to give and I was very much pleased to find that your previously conceived views exactly coincided.

All the forces that can be taken from the coast have been ordered to report to you at Ft Monroe by the 18th inst, or as soon thereafter as possible. What I ask is that with them, and all you can concentrate from your own command, you seize upon City Point and act from there looking upon Richmond as your objective point. If you can send Cavalry to Hicksford and cut the rail-road connection at that point it is a good thing to do. I do not pretend to say how your work is to be done but simply lay down what, and trust to you, and those under you, for doing it well.

Keep what vessels may be necessary for your operations. No supplies are going to N. Carolina except such as may be necessary for the troops there. I presume the call for vessels is in consequence of the preparations ordered for supplying our Armies after a new base is ~~supplied~~ established. The Q. M. did not know where they were to go but that he was to have supplies afloat and supposed they were for N. Carolina. I hope this delusion will be kept up, both North & South, until we do move.

If it should prove possible for you to reach Richmond so as to invest all on ~~on~~ the South side of the river, and fortify yourself there, I shall have but little fear of the result.

The rains have now continued so long that it will be impossible to move earlier than the 25th so I will set that date for making your concentration. All men afloat could then be sent up York River, as you proposed, to conceal our real design if ~~y~~ we were not then ready to move.

> I am Gen. Very Truly
> Your obt. svt.
> U. S. GRANT
> Lt. Gen.

ALS, DLC-Benjamin F. Butler. *O.R.*, I, xxxiii, 885–86. On April 15, 1864, Maj. Gen. Benjamin F. Butler, Fort Monroe, Va., telegraphed to USG. "Will you remain long enough in Washington for General Smith or my Chief of Staff to see you upon business" LS (telegram sent), DLC-Benjamin F. Butler; DNA, RG 107, Telegrams Collected (Unbound); telegram received (dated April 14), *ibid.*; *ibid.*, Telegrams Collected (Bound). On the same day, 11:00 P.M., USG, Culpeper, Va., telegraphed to Butler. "Did not receive your cipher of this morning until I arrived here" Telegrams received (3), *ibid.*; DLC-Benjamin F. Butler. Also on April 15, Butler wrote to USG. "Unofficial . . . You dealt so kindly with the suggestions as to the movements which I desired should be made from Fortress Monroe up the James and upon Richmond, and shew so much consideration for the views I ventured to express, that it has occurred to me possibly you might in some slight degree have bent your plan of Campaign to meet those views and wishes, although perhaps the inclination of your more matured judgement would lead you to prefer a movement through North Carolina of which you at first spoke. Specially has this thought pressed itself upon my mind since I have been called upon to furnish transportation for *two millions and a half* of rations to North Carolina which inclines me to believe that a movement is intended in that direction. If this be so, as I have a very strong opinion that but one co-operative movement with the Army of the Potomac should be made on the South of the James, and fearing lest a desire to oblige me might possibly in some degree have swayed your judgement, I take leave to say to you that any disposition of the troops under my command will be most agreable to me, which shall in your opinion subserve the public service; so that if you think it best to have my troops for the North Carolina movement do not regard in the least degree my supposed wishes—or position as I shall be most happy to cooperate most heartily in any of your movements. I pray you General take this note in the exact spirit in which it is meant. I believe fully that but one movement (and that the one I indicated) South of the James with all the concentrated forces, that can be spared able to fight *Lee* in the field if we can get men enough—or if not, as near it as we can, is feasible and so believing I do not for a moment desire that any thought of myself, or of its effects upon the extent of my command should stand in the way of such concentration, whenever it shall be thought best. This besides being a duty is at least but a just return for the kind consideration you have shown me. I have possessed General Smith with my views as well upon the subject of the movement as upon the number of troops which can be spared from my lines for the purpose and beg to refer you to him for any explanations you may desire" ADf, *ibid.*; copy, USG 3.

To Maj. Gen. William S. Rosecrans

Culpepper Va.
April 16th 1864 2 P M

MAJ GEN. W. S. ROSECRANS
ST LOUIS MO.

Send at once all all the force you can to Cairo to report to the Commanding Officer then to be used against Forrest. Send either Cavalry or Infantry   Take that nearest the river and replace what you send away by troops from the interior. Answer what you can do

U. S. GRANT
Lt General

Telegram received, DNA, RG 107, Telegrams Collected (Bound); copies, *ibid.*, RG 108, Letters Sent; *ibid.*, RG 393, Dept. of Mo., Telegrams Received; DLC-USG, V, 45, 59; Rosecrans Papers, CLU. *O.R.*, I, xxxiv, part 3, 184. Also on

April 16, 1864, 10:30 P.M., USG telegraphed to Maj. Gen. William S. Rose-crans. "Send the 12th Missouri 9th Iowa and 13th Illinois Cavalry to Cairo with-out delay   You can replace as many of them as you require about St Louis from other parts of your Command"   Telegram received, DNA, RG 107, Telegrams Collected (Bound); copies, *ibid.*, RG 108, Letters Sent; *ibid.*, RG 393, Dept. of Mo., Telegrams Received; DLC-USG, V, 45, 59; Rosecrans Papers, CLU. Printed as sent at 10:30 A.M. in *O.R.*, I, xxxiv, part 3, 184. On April 17, 11:00 A.M. and 5:30 P.M., Rosecrans telegraphed to USG. "By having authority ap-parently not mine under existing orders from the War Dept to use to use the dismounted dismounted Cavalry at depot for guards at St. Louis, and 9th Iowa Cavalry ordered to Little Rock, can send two Regts of Infantry and one of Cavalry, and 17th Ill Cav Col Beveridge now at St. Charles Ill for which Iowa I am an applicant—Chalmers & the rebs rebs wish to steal and prevent planting West in West Kentucky & West and Tennessee. The intention of thes rebels in Northern Arkansas and of the guerillas and with a powerful armed secret organi-zation here, is to do the same in Missouri, and the time of the advent advent of their operations is at hand. For which reason no moves of troops from the in-terior, Should to increase increase the feeling of insecurity here should if pos-sible be made from the interior until planting planting is over. planting is over. a power Secret organizing to unrest throughout the state   Please if you approve send orders at once about using the 9th Iowa & 17th Ill Cavalry and as to the & the the dismounted Cavalry from the depot"   "The 9th Iowa will be sent as ordered. The 12th twelfth Missouri and thirteenth Iow Illinois Cavalry can fol-low but they are not mounted nor have we any other mounted troops within one hundred and twenty miles of St. Louis   judging from the last news and of the rebels going south from Ft Pillow and the tenor of your dispatch I shall await your orders before sending forward foot troops." ALS (telegrams sent), DNA, RG 107, Telegrams Collected (Unbound); telegrams received, *ibid.*, Telegrams Collected (Bound); *ibid.*, RG 108, Letters Received. *O.R.*, I, xxxiv, part 3, 197–98. The second is *ibid.*, I, xxxii, part 3, 396. On April 18, 7:00 P.M., USG tele-graphed to Rosecrans. "You can use dismounted cavalry for guards at depots   Re-tain the Ninth Iowa and send the two Regts of Infantry and any other troops you can to Cairo without delay"   Telegram received, DNA, RG 107, Telegrams Col-lected (Bound); copies, *ibid.*, RG 108, Letters Sent; *ibid.*, RG 393, Dept. of Mo., Telegrams Received; DLC-USG, V, 45, 59; Rosecrans Papers, CLU. *O.R.*, I, xxxiv, part 3, 215.

To Maj. Gen. William T. Sherman

Culpeper C H. Va
7 P M April 16th 1864

MAJ. GENL SHERMAN
NASHVILLE—

Genl Washburn is ordered to Memphis General Hurlbut re-lieved   I will order Hunt or Prince[1] to command over Brayman

Washburn will obey your instructions and establish no posts except where you order them

U. S. GRANT
Lieut. Genl

Telegram received, DNA, RG 107, Telegrams Collected (Bound); copies, *ibid.*, RG 108, Letters Sent; *ibid.*, RG 393, Military Div. of the Miss., Letters Sent; DLC-USG, V, 45, 59. *O.R.*, I, xxxii, part 3, 382. On April 16, 1864, 10:30 A.M., Maj. Gen. William T. Sherman, Nashville, had telegraphed to USG. "Send Washburne to Memphis and I would be glad to have Hunt at Columbus   In making up our fighting force we have left inferior officers on the river. Hurlbut has full ten thousand (10,000) men at Memphis but if he had a million he would be on the defense. The force captured & butchered at Fort Pillow was not on my returns at all. It is the first fruits of the system of trading posts designed to assist the loyal people of the interior. All these stations are a weakness and offer tempting chances for plunder   In a day or so there ought to be enough of McPhersons troops at Cairo to clean out Forrest without materially delaying our concentrating along the front." Telegram received, DNA, RG 107, Telegrams Collected (Bound); *ibid.*, RG 108, Letters Received. *O.R.*, I, xxxii, part 3, 382. On the same day, 10:30 P.M., USG telegraphed to Sherman. "I have ordered Genl Rosecrans to send to Cairo all the forces he can—Specifying three (3) regts. that must be sent. You can have them used against Forrest." Telegram received, DNA, RG 107, Telegrams Collected (Bound); copies, *ibid.*, RG 108, Letters Sent; (dated April 17) *ibid.*, RG 393, Military Div. of the Miss., Letters Sent; DLC-USG, V, 45, 59, (dated April 17) 94. Dated April 17 in *O.R.*, I, xxxii, part 3, 385; (dated April 16) *ibid.*, I, xxxiv, part 3, 183.

1. Henry Prince of Maine, USMA 1835, promoted to 1st lt., 4th Inf., as of July 7, 1838, was severely wounded during the Mexican War. Appointed brig. gen. as of April 28, 1862, captured during the battle of Cedar Mountain, Va., on Aug. 9, he served after Dec. in N. C. and with the Army of the Potomac. See telegram to Maj. Gen. William T. Sherman, April 18, 1864.

To Jesse Root Grant

Culpepper C. H. Va.
Apl. 16th 1864

DEAR FATHER,

Your letter enclosing one from young Walker asking for duty on my staff during his suspension is received.[1] It is the third letter from him on the same subject. Of course I cannot gratify him. It would not be proper. It would be changing punishment into reward.

I gave the President the other day Mary's husbands address and asked for him a "Hospital Chaplaincy" at Nashville.[2] He immediately sent for his Private Sec. to have him ascertain if there was such a vacancy and to have Mr. Cramer's appointment made out if there was. The Sec. happened to be out at the time however so he promised as soon as he came in it should be attended to.

Julia will start West in a few days and will stop at Covington on her way. She will remain at the house I purchased from Judge Dent until such time as she can join me more permanently. It is her particular desire to have Jennie go to St. Louis with her to spend the Summer. I hope she can and will go.

It has rained here almost every day since my arrival. It is still raining. Of course I say nothing of when the Army moves or how or where. I am in most excellent health and well pleased with appearances here. My love to all at home.

ULYSSES

ALS, deCoppet Collection, NjP.

1. John P. Walker of Ohio, USMA 1866, was suspended from USMA Jan. 19–Sept. 1, 1864. On April 29, USG telegraphed to Secretary of War Edwin M. Stanton. "Cadet Walker who has been suspended from West Point as a punishment is here and desires to see service on the Staff of some General. His suspension being intended as a punishment I have declined to give such ~~an order~~ authority without refering the matter to you." ALS (telegram sent), Albany Institute of History and Art, Albany, N. Y.; telegram received, DNA, RG 107, Telegrams Collected (Bound). On Oct. 13, 1865, Walker wrote asking pay for the period of his suspension. *Ibid.*, RG 108, Register of Letters Received. On Oct. 16, USG endorsed this letter. "Respectfully forwarded to the *Secretary of War*. It is believed that the suspension and turning back of a cadet at West Point is entirely analogous to the suspension of an officer from Command and promotion, and that unless the sentence in the case specify the loss of pay, that Cadet Walker is entitled to it" Copy, *ibid.*

2. On Oct. 27, 1863, USG's sister Mary married Michael John Cramer, born in Schaffhausen, Switzerland, in 1835. After graduating from Ohio Wesleyan in 1860, Cramer served as pastor to a Methodist church in Cincinnati until appointed hospital chaplain as of June 30, 1864.

To Maj. Gen. Nathaniel P. Banks

———

Head Quarters, Armies in the Field
Culpepper C. H. Va. Apl. 17th 1864

MAJ. GEN. N. P. BANKS,
COMD.G DEPT. OF THE GULF,
GENERAL,

Owing to the difficulty of giving possitive instructions to a distant commander respecting his operations in the field, and being exceedingly anxious that the whole Army should act nearly as a unit, I send Maj. Gen. Hunter, an officer of rank and experience, bearer of duplicate copy of instructions sent you of the 31st of March, together with writen instructions ~~to~~ for Gen. Hunter's guidance in your, and his interview.

It is not intended that Gen. Hunter shall give orders, in my name, further th[an] the instructions addressed to him are such orders but to express more fully my views th[an] I can well do on paper, and to remain with you until such time as you will be able to say definitely at what tim[e] you will commence your movement against Mobile.

In your letter of the 1st of April brought by Lt. Towner you, in anticipation of the enemy falling back from Schre[ve]port, propose a movement through Texas in pursuit of him. You had not, when this letter was written, receiv[ed] my instructions of the 31st of March. [I] hope ~~that letter~~ those instructions reached you before such a movement was commenced. I would much rather the Red River expedition had never been began than that you should be detained one day after the 1st of May in commencing your movement East of the Miss.

Hoping that Gen. Hunter will find you back at New Orleans with the work of concentration commenced, I remain

Very respectfully
your obt. svt.
U. S. GRANT
Lt. Gen Com

P. S. If you have commenced to move from Schrieveport to the interior of Texas, or away from the Red River in any directi[on], retrace your steps. On receipt of this, no matter what you may have in contemplation, commence your concentration, to be follow[ed] without delay by your advance on Mobile.

U. S. GRANT
Lt. Gen.

ALS, DLC-Nathaniel P. Banks. *O.R.*, I, xxxiv, part 3, 191–92. On April 17, 1864, Maj. Gen. Nathaniel P. Banks, Grand Ecore, La., wrote, then telegraphed to USG. "The campaign upon which we have entered has already developed several features of great importance. First; The enemy regards the possession of Shreveport as a point vital to the existance of the Trans-Mississippi Army and will fight to maintain its possession with all their forces and great desperation. Second; It has changed their operations from an offensive to a defensive character. It is unquestionable that they had intended to make an invasion of Missouri which they hoped would have disturbed the arrangement of troops east of the Mississippi. By this movement we have defeated that expectation and hold their full strength for the defense of their position, relieving entirely Missouri and Arkansas. Third; The co-operation of Steele upon the line on which he is moving renders us no assistance whatever. We should have but one column and one line and with his forces there would be no obstacle to our progress. Fourth; The low stage of water in the Red River deprives us substantially of the assistance of the Gunboats, leaving us to depend entirely upon the strength of our land force, with very little aid even of water transportation. These considerations together show that the campaign is of greater importance than was generally anticipated at its commencement, and also that ~~its~~ with ~~a~~ concentration of forces success is within our reach. I have drawn from my Department all the men that can be spared which gives me at the outside twenty thousand (20,000) bayonets. The junction of Steele's forces would give me all the strength I need. Governor Hall of Missouri, who is here, and who accepts the idea I have presented that this campaign is a defense of Missouri represents that there is a large unoccupied force in Missouri and Kansas from which ten thousand (10,000) men could be spared without detriment to the public service. I earnestly represent the increased importance of this campaign; the impossibility of withdrawing from it without the sacrifice of the Navy in the present state of the navigation; the fact that it has changed the operations of the enemy from an offensive to a purely defensive attitude; that it is a protection to Missouri and Arkansas, as well as Louisiana; and ~~a~~ the certainty of its immediate and successful terimnation as reasons why the forces west of the Mississippi as far as possible upon this line and with this column. If the rebel army under Smith is destroyed no other can be re-organized and the defense of these states can be safely left to the people themselves in a great measure; The whole available force of the union army being turned in the course of the season to the assistance of the troops east of the Mississippi. Unless this army be dispersed or destroyed it will require all our forces and more to protect these states. I regard it as of the highest importance in the changed as-

pect of affairs that this concentration should be made. I enclose herewith a statement of the garrisons in my Department with the number of men at each and ~~the~~
suggest that the forces are not too large for the defense of the coast which they
hold." Copies, DNA, RG 94, War Records Office, Union Battle Reports; DLC-
Nathaniel P. Banks. Printed with additional text in *O.R.*, I, xxxiv, part 1, 187–88.
"I send by mail today a dispatch the substance as follows—The enemy will defend Shreveport to the last extremity—while I threaten it they will abandon all
ideas of threatening Arkansas and Missouri—Steele does not co-operate with me
when moving on a different line. I request to be reinforced by Steele & his co-
operating force & also by troops from Missouri or Kansas that I may advance
immediately upon Shreveport—In this manner I shall defend Arkansas and Missouri and prevent offensive operations by the enemy in those states—while I shall
live upon & exhaust one of their most fertile regions a region that they must hold
or their army must cease to exist—This campaign cannot be abandoned without
abandoning the navy and permitting the invasion of Missouri" Telegram received, DNA, RG 107, Telegrams Collected (Bound); copy, *ibid.*, RG 393, Dept.
of the Gulf, Letters Sent. *O.R.*, I, xxxiv, part 1, 187.

On April 18, Banks telegraphed to USG. "The rebel army of the west, twenty
five thousand (25,000) strong, is in our front. The withdrawal of my command
without the destruction or dispersion of this force, will enable them to commence offensive operations in Missouri, Arkansas or Louisiana, or against each
of these States successively. It will require the whole force, more than a hundred
thousand strong, west of the Mississippi, to defend these states against the suc-
cessive attacks of this force, and it will be difficult to concentrate any considerable force from the army on the Mississippi for operations against Mobile, with
such an active and powerful enemy in our rear. The destruction or dispersion of
this army, the desolation of the country it occupies, and the destruction of its land
or water transportation, will make it impossible for a reorganization or any
movement against the States, bordering upon the Mississippi, and enable a strong
force of our troops to commence an immediate and successful campaign against
Mobile. This result is certain to be accomplished within thirty days, if only a
portion of Steeles command could operate with me upon this line, independent of
the river and of the Navy. This campaign is not of my suggestion, but its results
are so much more important than I first thought, and so certain to be attained,
that I hesitate to withdraw my forces without positive orders, and I send this
despatch by telegraph, knowing that a reply can be telegraphed me in return,
without delay. Important as the campaign is, I would not embarass the greater
operations of the army in the east." Copies (3), DLC-Nathaniel P. Banks. *O.R.*,
I, xxxiv, part 1, 189.

On April 19, 10:30 P.M., Secretary of War Edwin M. Stanton telegraphed
to USG. "The following despatches have just been received. They ~~are all~~ com-
prise all the intelligence we have had from General Banks. You have probably
maps that show the position of Mansfield ~~a short distance~~ south west of Shreveport and about half way between that place and Nachitoches. Grand Ecore is a
short distance north of Nachitoches." ALS (telegram sent), DNA, RG 107, Telegrams Collected (Bound). *O.R.*, I, xxxiv, part 3, 220. The enclosures are printed
ibid. On April 20, 10:35 A.M., Stanton telegraphed to USG. "Detailed telegraphic
reports from Chicago which you will see in this mornings Chronicle represent
General Stone to have been in command as Chief of Banks Staff at the time of
Banks disaster and that the operation was against the remonstrance of General

Ransom who is badly wounded." ALS (telegram sent), DNA, RG 107, Telegrams Collected (Bound). *O.R.*, I, xxxiv, part 3, 235.

On April 30, Banks wrote at great length to USG reporting his campaign. *Ibid.*, I, xxxiv, part 1, 189–92. On May 4, Banks, Alexandria, La., wrote to USG. "Major General Hunter left on the 30th of April for your Headquarters. No material change has occurred since his departure. The enemy is hovering about Alexandria in considerable force, chiefly Cavalry. There is every reason to believe that he will concentrate the whole of his strength here, including Price's and Magruder's forces, for the purpose of capturing or destroying the fleet, and crushing our army. He can muster for this purpose forty thousand (40.000) men. Considering the magnitude of the stake at issue, it is impossible to doubt that he will make every exertion to effect this purpose. Our Officers and soldiers who have escaped from the enemy, report this as the current topic of conversation, and it is confirmed also by deserters. No invasion of Missouri or Arkansas is probable while this state of things continues. Five or ten thousand of the unemployed forces in these States, should be sent to aid us in this contingency. There are nine gunboats above the rapids, constituting the essential part of Admiral Porter's fleet. We have commenced a dam across the river, with every prospect of success, which will enable us to float the boats below the Bar. Its construction will occupy ten days. The work is progressing very rapidly. Should it fail however, the safety of the fleet must depend upon the army, and it should be made strong enough to meet and destroy the enemy if he concentrates here. The army is in fine condition and excellent spirits. It numbers including Cavalry about thirty thousand (30.000) men, in better condition than at any period in this campaign, and as soon as the fleet is relieved, will be ready to move to any point of action, without the loss of time in reorgainzation." Copies (2), DLC-Nathaniel P. Banks. On May 7, Banks telegraphed to USG. "The dam will be completed tomorrow 9th inst and the gunboats relieved. We shall then move immediately for the Mississippi" Telegram received, DNA, RG 107, Telegrams Collected (Bound).

To Maj. Gen. Benjamin F. Butler

In field Culpeper C. H. Va. Apr. 17th 1864

MAJ. GEN. B. F. BUTLER,
COM'D'G DEPT. VA. & N. C.
FORTRESS MONROE, VA.
GENERAL:

Your report of negotiations with Mr. Ould,[1] Confederate States Agent, touching the exchange of prisoners, has been referred to me by the Secretary of War, with directions to furnish you such instructions on the subject, as I may deem proper.

After a careful examination of your report, the only points on which I deem instructions necessary, are—

1st.: Touching the validity of the paroles of the prisoners captured at Vicksburg and Port Hudson.

2nd.: The status of colored prisoners.

As to the *first*. No Arrangement for the exchange of prisoners will be acceeded to that does not fully recognize the validity of these paroles, and provide for the release to us, of a sufficient number of prisoners now held by the Confederate Authorities to cancel any balance that may be in our favor by virtue of these paroles. Until there is released to us an equal number of officers and men as were captured and paroled at Vicksburg and Port Hudson, not another Confederate prisoner of war will be paroled or exchanged.

As to the *second*. No distinction whatever will be made in the exchange between white and colored prisoners; the only question being, were they, at the time of their capture, in the military service of the United States. If they were, the same terms as to treatment while prisoners and conditions of release and exchange must be exacted and had, in the case of colored soldiers as in the case of white soldiers.

Non-acquiescence by the Confederate Authorities in both or either of these propositions, will be regarded as a refusal on their part to agree to the further exchange of prisoners, and will be so treated by us.

> I am General
> Very Respectfully
> Your Obt. Servant
> U. S. GRANT
> Lieut. General

LS, DLC-Benjamin F. Butler. *O.R.*, II, vii, 62–63. For a statement by Brig. Gen. John A. Rawlins that he had prepared this letter, see James Harrison Wilson, *The Life of John A. Rawlins* (New York, 1916), p. 418. On April 14, 1864, 11:00 A.M., USG had telegraphed to Maj. Gen. Benjamin F. Butler. "Your report respecting negotiations with Commissioner Ould for the exchange of prisoners of War has been refered to me for my orders. Until examined by me and my orders thereon are received by you decline all further negotiations." ALS (telegram sent), DNA, RG 107, Telegrams Collected (Bound); telegram received, *ibid.*; DLC-Benjamin F. Butler. *O.R.*, II, vii, 50. On the same day, Secretary of

War Edwin M. Stanton wrote to USG. "The accompanying report of Major-General Butler in respect to his regulations with Mr. Ould, touching the exchange of prisoners, is referred to you, together with the report therein of Major-General Hitchcock, commissioner of exchange. You will please give to Major-General Butler such instructions on the subject as in your judgment shall be proper." *Ibid.*, p. 46. Butler's report is *ibid.*, pp. 29–34.

Also on April 14, Butler wrote to USG. "I have the honor to enclose official copies of the correspondence between Gen. Pickett Comd'g. Confederate Forces District of North Carolina and General Peck Comd'g. U. S. Forces in said District, relative to the execution of certain prisoners belonging to the Second North Carolina Regiment. Many of these men were conscripted by the rebels—All of them were citizens of the United States who owed their allegiance to our Government. If misguided they forfeited their allegiance, repented and returned to it again   they have only done their duty and in my judgment are to be protected in so doing. I do not recognize any right in the rebels to execute a United States Soldier, because either by force or fraud, or by voluntary enlistment even he has been once brought into their ranks and has escaped therefrom. I suppose all the rights they can claim as belligerents is to execute one of the deserters from their Army while he holds simply the character of a deserter during the he has renounced his allegiance and before he has again claimed that protection and it has been accorded to him. Thereby no law of nations and by no belligerent rights have the rebels any power over him other than to treat him as a prisoner of War if captured. I would suggest that the Confederate Authorities be called upon to say whether they adopt this act and that upon their answer such action may be taken as will sustain the dignity of the Government and give a promise to afford protection to its citizens." Copy (undated), DNA, RG 393, Dept. of Va. and N. C., Letters Sent. *O.R.*, I, xxxiii, 865–66. See *ibid.*, pp. 866–70.

On April 15, Maj. Gen. Ethan Allen Hitchcock wrote to USG. "I have the honor to enclose herewith the statement signed by Col. Hoffman, which was directed to be prepared by the Secretary of War, in your presence last evening; and beg leave to explain, that the last formal declaration of exchange of prisoners, which was agreed to by both of the Agents, was dated June 8, 1863, and was published in General Orders No. 167. At that time, Col. Ludlow was our Agent of Exchange, and the declaration left us indebted to the rebels in officers and men reduced to privates, by rates agreed upon in the Cartel—12.794 men. Since the date of that declaration, the rebels have delivered to us 18.485 men,—making our total indebtedness 31.279. Since the declaration referred to, and soon after it, the tables were turned by the Capture of Vicksburg and Port Hudson, which brought the rebels largely indebted to us; in addition to which, there had been delivered, rebel prisoners by us, up to July 25—1863, 8.359 men, and after that date, 7.191, which, added to the Vicksburg and Port Hudson prisoners, makes a total of 65.182. Sometime in July—1863, Mr. Ould, without any conference or agreement with our Agent, Col. Ludlow, announced a declaration of exchange in favor of Lieu-Gen. Pemberton, and a few other officers of high rank, which Col. Ludlow protested against and refused to recognize, because it was contrary to usage, and, because we had no rebel officers of equivalent grades in our hands, to be exchanged for them; and it was supposed that Mr. Ould acquiesced in the protest,—but he subsequently reaffirmed this declaration. Col. Ludlow was relieved from duty as Agent of Exchange, and was Succeeded by Gen. Meredith. Not long afterwards, Mr. Ould renewed his mode of action, without any conference or agreement with Gen. Meredith, and made an arbitrary declaration of exchange, in favor of a considerable portion of the Vicksburg prisoners, without stating any definite number, but defining them by certain commanders and corps, which, we ascertained, included a large excess over the number of Federal troops who had been captured by the rebels, had been returned to us, and were on parole waiting to be exchanged. Notwithstanding the irregularity of this proceeding on the part of Mr. Ould, his conduct left us no alternative, but to make a declaration of exchange, in favor of a portion of the Federal paroled prisoners in our hands, and a declaration was made,—extending to 23.056. We were then in hopes that irregular declarations would not be repeated by Mr Ould;—but we were disappointed. between 19.814 (rebel troops on parole) and 8.223 (Federal troops on parole), being a claim to 11.591 (vide page 2—Statement), which number, in fact, should be added to the 23.213, to show the total indebtedness of the rebels to us. In a recently written letter from Mr. Ould, addressed to myself, dated Richmond, Va., Jan—27—1864, which fell into the hands of Gen. Butler, but which was never communicated to me, though acted upon by Gen. Butler without my knowledge, Mr. Ould assumes to dismiss this whole matter in a single sentence,—as if all his business with Gen. Meredith had been conducted with due regard to propriety, and without being questioned by Gen. Meredith; upon which he does not propose, but declares that 'on the 1st of Feb'y I shall declare all officers and soldiers who have been delivered at City Point at any time prior to Jan. 1. 1864, exchanged. You can make a similar notice as to those who have been delivered to you.' This extraordinary letter appears (and this is more extraordinary than the letter itself) to have been accepted by Gen Butler as a sufficient explanation of past differences of opinion; and declarations of exchange were made by Gen Butler and Mr. Ould, although they were not then in official communication with each other. The declaration, however, which was made by Gen. Butler was suspended by order of the Secretary of War, immediately on its receipt. I did not advise or suggest this suspension, and knew nothing of it until after it was done, although, had I been consulted I should have advised it, as it seemed to me to ignore entirely our just claims upon the rebels, for more federal prisoners than all they then held in Southern prisons. If to insist upon our just claims in this matter, has seemed to operate unfavorably upon our officers and men in Southern prisons, by subjecting them to cruel hardship, the imposition of which is a disgrace to the rebel authorities, it should be considered, on the other hand, that to allow the rebel Agent undisputed licence in his proceedings, not only puts in jeopardy all hope of just action from him in the future, but has thrown into the rebel ranks full twenty if not twenty five thousand men, who ought to be on parole, to ~~to~~ *fight* Federal troops, whose lives are thus exposed individually, while the public cause is also endangered—points which are undoubtedly entitled to the protection of the government. I can make no objection to a Surrender of this claim on our part, if my superiors deem it proper, but, as the Commissioner for the Exchange of Prisoners, I deem it my duty to express my convictions as to matters of fact, and principles involved in this business—" LS, DNA, RG 108, Letters Received. *O.R.*, II, vii, 53–54. See *ibid.*, pp. 55–56. Misdated April 16 in W. A. Croffut, ed., *Fifty Years in Camp and Field: Diary of Major-General Ethan Allen Hitchcock, U. S. A.* (New York and London, 1909), pp. 460–61.

On April 17, USG telegraphed to Stanton. "Has Col Hoffman prepared a statement of the prisoners of war paroled & delivered to the enemy for whom we have rec'd no equivalent? I want it to accompany directions to Gen Butler on the exchange question" Telegram received, DLC-Ethan Allen Hitchcock; copies,

DNA, RG 108, Letters Sent; DLC-USG, V, 45, 59; USG 3. On the same day, Hitchcock telegraphed to USG. "Col. Hoffman's Statement, to gether with an explanatory letter from myself, was mailed for you yesterday and I hope will safely reach you if it has not already." ALS (telegram sent), DNA, RG 107, Telegrams Collected (Unbound). Also on April 17, USG wrote to Butler. "Enclosed you will please find statement of Federal and Rebel Prisoners of War dilivered since last declaration, together with explanatory letter of Maj. Gen. E. A. Hitchcock Commissioner for exchange of prisoners." LS, DLC-Benjamin F. Butler. *O.R.*, II, vii, 62. On the same day, USG wrote to Stanton. "I have the honor herewith to enclose for your information a copy of my letter of instructions to Maj. Gen. B. F. Butler, com'd'g. Department of Virginia and North Carolina, touching the exchange of prisoners." Copies, DLC-USG, V, 45, 59; DNA, RG 108, Letters Sent; USG 3. *O.R.*, II, viii, 810.

On April 20, Butler telegraphed to USG. "Instructions in regard to exchange of prisoners received and will be implicitly followed. I assume however that they are not intended to interfere with the special exchanges of sick and wounded prisoners on one side and the other, now going on" DfS, DLC-Benjamin F. Butler; DNA, RG 107, Telegrams Collected (Unbound); telegram received, *ibid.*; *ibid.*, Telegrams Collected (Bound). *O.R.*, II, vii, 76. On the same day, 9:30 P.M., USG telegraphed to Butler. "Receive all the sick and wounded the Confederate Authorities will send you but send no more in exchange." ALS (telegram sent), DNA, RG 107, Telegrams Collected (Bound); telegram received, *ibid.*; *ibid.*, Telegrams Collected (Unbound); DLC-Benjamin F. Butler. *O.R.*, II, vii, 76.

1. Robert Ould, born in D. C. in 1820, graduated from the College of William and Mary in 1842, and practiced law in D. C. (1842–61). C.S.A. asst. secretary of war from Jan. until March, 1862, he was appointed agent for exchange of prisoners in July.

To Maj. Gen. David Hunter

Culpepper C. H. Va., April 17th 1864.

MAJ. GEN. D. HUNTER.
U. S. VOLS.

In giving the instructions to Maj. Gen. N. P. Banks, a copy of which accompanies this, the design was to impress upon the General particularly two points; 1st the importance of commencing operations at the very earliest possible moment against Mobile, so that his movement may serve as cooperation with those of the other Armies in the field. 2d That he should take with him the greatest number of troops possible from his command

In fixing the Rio Grande as the only point in Texas to retain possession of, I do not intend to take from him all discretion about what should be held. If there should be any point on the Gulf easily defended against largely superior forces, which in the opinion of Gen. Banks, it would give us great advantages in future operations to retain possession of, then he can hold such place. The same rule must apply in fixing garrisons for holding the Mississippi river. Gen. Banks can tell much better from where he is, than I can from here, what points are necessary to hold, and what is necessary to hold them.

Referring to Gen. Banks letter of the 2d of April, to Maj. Gen. Halleck, giving the strength of garrisons at the different points held by him, to wit: Rio Grande 3000, Matagorda Bay 3277, Pensacola 900, Key west 791, New Orleans 1125, Baton Rouge 1565, Plaquermine 620, and Port Hudson 9409, it looks to me that all might be taken from Matagorda, or two thousand, if the place is of such importance that it should be held,   from Baton Rouge, one half might be taken, and seven thousand might be taken from Port Hudson. This is my judgment from here.

It is of the 1st importance that we should hold Red river. This you will observe, I have turned over to Gen. Steele, in order that Gen. Banks might have a greater number of troops to move with. If however Gen. Steele has not with him the necessary force to leave for this purpose, Gen. Banks will have to supply the deficiency, until reinforcements can be got to Gen. Steele. Already several regiments have gone to Little Rock to reinforce him, probably two thousand men, and when some troops ordered from St. Louis to West Ky, get through with the work of of driving Forrest from the State, they can too be sent. The whole reinforcements for Gen. Steele, however, cannot be relied on at over five thousand men. Fort Smith and the Indian Territory having been added to the Dept of the Ark. may give Gen. Steele sufficient additional troops, as to materially strengthen him also.

Gen. Banks has always been very vigilant in the organization of Colored Troops. It is to be hoped that his expedition up Red River will give a large number of recruits of this class. All acquired in this way, however being without organization or discipline could not be counted as so many men for defense of garrison   Three of them though migh count equal to one veteran soldier in fixing the number to leave behind at any one place.

All plans for the attack on Mobile, are left to Gen. Banks. He will make his own arrangements for getting supplies of all descriptions. With movements to take place elsewhere, it is not at all probable that the enemy can make any effort at raising the siege, if Mobile is once invested. Should the place be difficult to take from the number of troops held to defend it, the success of holding them there will be great. You will remain with Gen. Banks until his move from New Orleans is commenced, and a landing effected at Pascagoula, or such place as may be selected for the base from which to draw the supplies. When this is secured, bring to me wherever I may be, such report of operations as Gen. Banks may then wish to forward.

Write to me fully how you find matters immediately on your first interview with Gen. Banks.

U. S. Grant
Lieut. Gen.

Copies, DLC-USG, V, 45, 59; DNA, RG 108, Letters Sent. *O.R.*, I, xxxiv, part 3, 190–91.

On April 15, 1864, 10:00 A.M., Maj. Gen. William T. Sherman, Nashville, telegraphed to USG. "I have dispatch from Little Rock of April 7th 10th giving dates from Gen Steele of April 7th at Camden. We had had considerable skirmishing in all of which he was successful and had halted and sent back to Pine Bluff for provisions & ammunition. It seems to me his movement is very slow and he may be so late in reaching Red River as to keep Genl Banks & A. J. Smith away behind time"   Telegram received, DNA, RG 107, Telegrams Collected (Bound). *O.R.*, I, xxxiv, part 3, 160. On the same day, 11:00 P.M., USG telegraphed to Maj. Gen. Henry W. Halleck. "Please send Genl Hunter to me report to me. From the last dispatches from Maj Gen Banks I fear he is going to be late in his Spring movement, and I am desirous of sending an Officer of rank with duplicate of his orders, and with further instructions"   Telegram received, DNA, RG 94, Letters Received, 531A 1864; *ibid.*, RG 107, Telegrams Collected (Bound); copies, *ibid.*, RG 108, Letters Sent; DLC-USG, V, 45, 59. *O.R.*, I, xxxiv, part 3, 160. On April 16, 11:00 A.M., Halleck telegraphed to USG. "Genl Hunter ordered as directed. Despatch from Genl Banks dated second inst. at Alexandria, says Admiral Porter went up Red River that day, the gunboats having been detained at the rapids by low water. Hopes to reach Shreveport by the tenth. Sigel says Genl Averell with two thousand cavalry is moving from Martinsburg to Webster & Clarksburg. Two regiments of Gillmore's command have reached Fort

Monroe, viz [Fourth] New Hampshire & eighth Maine. Genl Butler has [asked] for two more batteries which will be ordered to him to-day. I will send you copy of Genl Banks letter." ALS (telegram sent), DNA, RG 107, Telegrams Collected (Bound); telegram received, *ibid.*; *ibid.*, RG 108, Letters Received. *O.R.*, I, xxxiii, 878; *ibid.*, I, xxxiv, part 3, 169. See *ibid.*, I, xxxii, part 3, 397.

On April 28, Maj. Gen. David Hunter, Alexandria, La., wrote to USG. "I have the honor to report that I arrived here yesterday morning, in eight and a half days from Washington. I immediately had an interview with Gen. Banks, and delivered him your communications. I regret very much to find affairs here in a very complicated, perplexing and precarious situation. You have of course had the particulars of the fights. The situation at present is this; we have some six, eight or ten gun boats, among them two Monitors, above the Rapids, with no possibility of getting them out. The whole question is then reduced to this— shall we destroy the gun boats, or lose the services, at this critical period of the war, of the twenty thousand men necessary to take care of them. My opinion is of course to destroy the boats. Why this expedition was ordered I can not imagine. Gen. Banks assures me it was undertaken against his opinion and earnest protest. The result is certainly a very sad one.—I shall communicate, from day to day, any thing of interest which may occur," ALS, Gratz Collection, PHi. *O.R.*, I, xxxiv, part 3, 316.

On May 2, Hunter, New Orleans, wrote to USG. "You told me to write you fully with regard to affairs in this department. I may write too freely, but where great and vital interests are at stake you must excuse me if I am very free. Knowing that your time is very precious, I shall briefly state the conclusions to which I have arrived: First. The Department of the Gulf is one great mass of corruption. Cotton and politics, instead of the war, appear to have engrossed the army. The vital interests of the contest are laid aside, and we are amused with sham State governments, which are a complete laughing-stock to the people, and the lives of our men are sacrificed in the interests of cotton speculators. Second. The vicious trade regulations, or the vicious administration of them, have filled the enemy's country with all kinds of goods except military supplies, and these they have been smart enough to capture. If this course is continued we cannot look for a speedy termination of the war. Third. The best interests of the service require that General McPherson, or some other competent commander, should be sent immediately here. Port Hudson and Natchez are both threatened, and unless prompt action is immediately taken we shall lose the navigation of the Mississippi. General Banks has treated me with great politeness and kindness, and I regret greatly to say anything prejudicial to him as a soldier or a gentleman, but a strong sense of an important duty compels me to speak. The most intelligent of the officers of the army and navy will, I think, fully concur in all I have said. General Banks has not certainly the confidence of his army." *Ibid.*, p. 390.

To Maj. Gen. George G. Meade

Culpepper C. H. Va. Apl. 17th/64

MAJ. GEN. MEADE,
COMD.G ARMY OF THE POTOMAC,
GENERAL,

Should a siege of Richmond become necessary siege guns, ammunition and equipments can be got from the Arsenal at Washington, and Fortress Monroe, very rapidly. Every preperation is made for all classes of transportation by water so that these things can be directed to any point, by water, we may require them. Once at the nearest landing, with the means of transportation with an army, they can be readily moved to any point inland they may be wanted. The means of maning Heavy Artillery is always at hand with an Army as well as the means of constructing batteries.

I will take advantage of Gen. Hunt's[1] suggestions as to the proper officer to get the siege train ready, and, to a great extent, his suggestions as to the number Calibre &c. of guns necessary for it.

I am General, very respectfully
your obt. svt.
U. S. GRANT
Lt. Gen. Com

ALS, Meade Papers, PHi. *O.R.*, I, xxxiii, 889. On April 16, 1864, Brig. Gen. Henry J. Hunt, chief of art., Army of the Potomac, wrote at length to Maj. Gen. Andrew A. Humphreys proposing a siege train. *Ibid.*, pp. 880–81. On the same day, Maj. Gen. George G. Meade endorsed this letter. "Respectfully forwarded to the lieutenant-general commanding. The within paper has been prepared under my instructions by the chief of artillery, Army of the Potomac, in anticipation of the contingency of having to besiege Richmond. To carry out the project will require an additional force of heavy artillery, either one or two regiments, the commanding officer of which should at once commence the preparation and accumulation of the materials here indicated. The detail of this force will require the orders of the lieutenant-general commanding, for which purpose this communication is transmitted. No orders have been given from these headquarters." *Ibid.*, I, li, part 1, 1158.

1. Hunt, born in Mich., and appointed from Ohio, USMA 1839, served in

the Mexican War, and was promoted to maj., 5th Art., as of May 14, 1861. An art. officer with the Army of the Potomac, he was appointed brig. gen. as of Sept. 15, 1862, and became chief of art. in June, 1863.

To Maj. Gen. Franz Sigel

Culpepper Va
April 18th [17] 1864 12-midnight

MAJ GEN F SIGEL
CUMBERLAND MD

Maj Gen Ord has been relieved from duty at his own request Send Gen Averill in command of the Expedition already directed or go yourself, as you deem most advisable   Should you go it will be necessary to leave an Officer in whose judgement you can place the greatest reliance to command every thing you leave behind.

U S GRANT
Lt Genl

Telegram received, DNA, RG 107, Telegrams Collected (Bound); copies (dated April 17, 1864, 12:00 P.M.), *ibid.*, RG 108, Letters Sent; Sigel Papers, OClWHi; DLC-USG, V, 45, 59. Printed as sent at 12:00 P.M. in *O.R.*, I, xxxiii, 893.
   On April 17, 2:30 P.M., Maj. Gen. Franz Sigel, Cumberland, Md., telegraphed to USG. "The following telegram from Gen. Crook is just received 'Reports corr[obo]rated by s[evera]l deserters state that all of Longstrets command except one division which is stationed near Cumberland Gap passed over the Rail Road towards Richmond se[v]eral days ago.'" Telegram received, DNA, RG 107, Telegrams Collected (Bound). *O.R.*, I, xxxiii, 894. On the same day, Lt. Col. Orville E. Babcock, Cumberland, Md., telegraphed to Brig. Gen. John A. Rawlins. "Please inform the General that General Sigel has telegraphed to Genl Crook for some information but cannot obtain it before morning as the wires are down Soon as the information is received Genl Sigel will telegraph in full Genl Sigel reports that he needs at once at least twenty five hundred (2500) horses for the old regiments and soon as available some four thousand for the new and veteran regiments If the twenty five hundred cannot be obtained at once it will materially cripple the anticipated movement Genl Sigel asks if something cannot be done His Chief Quarter master has asked the Cavalry Bureau for permission to pay hundred fifty three (153) dollars and to purchase a portion of mares at proper prices." Telegram received, DNA, RG 107, Telegrams Collected (Bound). Printed as sent at 11:30 P.M. in *O.R.*, I, xxxiii, 894.
   On April 18, 10:30 A.M. and 9:00 P.M., Sigel telegraphed to USG. "Your dispatch in regard to Genl Ord is received. I am only waiting for an answer from

Genl Crook and will then report in full all the arrangements I think necessary" Telegram received, DNA, RG 107, Telegrams Collected (Bound); copy, Sigel Papers, OClWHi. "According to the latest reports received from Gen Ord and Gen Sullivan at Webster [as w]ell as from Gen Crook on the Kan[a]wha and Col Moor at Beverly, and following my [own conv]ictions I find the following measures the best and most promising under the present circumstances. They are: First, give up the Expedition by Beverly and leave only a small post of observation there with one Regiment of Cavalry to hold connection ~~with~~ between the force on the Kanawha and our lines on the Rail Road   Second: Form only two columns, one under Gen Crook on the Kanawha, strongest, and one ~~under~~ on the Shenandoah, which would make that on the Kanawha about ten thousand men—that in the Shenandoah Valley about seven thousand—Gen Averell will be ordered with one thousand Cavalry [to] Genl Crook to take command [of] his Cavalry Division which will consist of eight regiments, of which at least twenty five hundred will be effective immediately—Third: The other Cavalry Division and the rest of the Infantry with a strong force of Artillery in proportion to the other arms will assemble between Cumberland and the Shenandoah, and the Infantry and Artillery will be advanced to Cedar Creek with such Cavalry as can be made effective at the moment to threaten the force of the Enemy in Shenandoah Valley and to advance as soon, and as far as possible   Genl Crook will be ordered to take possession of Lewisburg ~~and~~ with part of his forces, and to march down the Tennessee R. R. to do as much damage as he can, to destroy the New Creek Bridge or the Salt works which are two ~~2~~ near objects, [or] to operate as you may think proper—I have spoken in detail with Col Babcock and he says that he will telegraph you his opinion"   Telegram received, DNA, RG 107, Telegrams Collected (Bound). *O.R.*, I, xxxiii, 901. On the same day, 9:00 P.M., Babcock telegraphed to Rawlins. "[I have] examined as fully as possible here the present state of the roads to Beverly, and from Beverly in all directions and believe them to be impassable for heavy trains. It was snowing there yesterday   Also that Gen Sigels transportation is still limited, too much so for a cavalry force—I think Genl Sigel's plan is the only one by which his force can be used to an advantage at present and not uncover the Baltimore and Ohio Rail Road. The forces [he] proposes to send to Gen Crook are at Clarksburg and Webster, and can be sent to Genl Crook within five (5) days   The Cavalry can march from Clarksburg   The concentration in the Shenandoah Valley can commence at once and progress as rapidly as horses and transportation can be supplied. Th[ere are] two hundred (200) wagons at Hagerstown now fitting out but cannot be sent in time [to] use at Beverly   They can be used in the Valley—" Telegram received, DNA, RG 107, Telegrams Collected (Bound). *O.R.*, I, xxxiii, 900–1.

On April 19, 12:30 A.M., Sigel telegraphed to USG. "The following telegram in answer to my inquiries is just received from Genl Crook. 'Charleston Va April 18 7 P M 1864   Maj. Gen SIGEL Cumberland. I don't know whether I can accomplish all Gen'l Grant expects or not by may acting independently as you suggest but will do my best. Success depends much on the weather; Roads are most impassable now. Send all to this point. Infantry by water and cavalry by land from Parkersburg. I wanted thirty five hundred Infantry, effective, if you can send them. I have sufficient Artillery. The demonstration towards Huntsville would do me no good unless the column could reach Covington. Can you send me one hundred (100) yards of pontoon? I ~~Send~~ have none. Send all the horses and mules you can at once by water. Your telegram was delayed f my line being down. I have plenty of provisions here. You need send none. (signed) GEO CROOK Br Genl' This is essentially in conformity with the telegrams which I have sent to you without awaiting the answer of Gen Crook because I thought it would take too long to receive his answer. The pontoons are being constructed and will be sent to him" Telegram received, DNA, RG 107, Telegrams Collected (Bound); copy, Sigel Papers, OClWHi. *O.R.*, I, xxxiii, 910–11. On the same day, 8:00 P.M., USG telegraphed to Sigel. "I approve your plan of operations, make your preparations for executing it with all dispatch" Telegram received, DNA, RG 107, Telegrams Collected (Bound); copies, *ibid.*, RG 108, Letters Sent; Sigel Papers, OClWHi; DLC-USG, V, 45, 59. *O.R.*, I, xxxiii, 911. On the same day, 10:00 P.M., Sigel telegraphed to USG. "Your answer to my telegram and that of Col. Babcock just received I will act accordingly—Col Babcock will leave to night—" Telegram received, DNA, RG 107, Telegrams Collected (Bound). *O.R.*, I, xxxiii, 911. Also on April 19, Sigel wrote to USG. "Latest information is this. Elzegy with 4 to 5000 men in the Shenandoah valley north and south of Stanton. The 12th Georgia rgt. 12 miles north of Stanton. It is reported by a deserter of this regt. that Gen. Early would take command in the valley, whether with his division or not, he could not say. Enemy is fortifying Bulls Gap and Strassburg. No news of special importance from the Kanowha. There are reported from 6 to 8000 men under Breckenridge between Liberty and Saltville and in front of this line. Breckenridge's Head quarters at Dublin station. Morgan is said to be with 4000 men at Abington. No troops of the enemy at Petersburg and Moorfield, but 150 between Romney and Winchester, on little Cacapon. Skirmishes took place between small parties in Wyoming Cy. Southwest of Gauley bridge, also at the Mouth of Seneca, S. W. of Petersburg and one in Loudon Cy, where Mosby has full sway. Col. Moor reports from Beverly. Two deserters just in from Franklin of Imboden's Brigade. They report Longstreet and Corps near Richmond after a battle in East Tenessee. Imboden intends to make a raid in this country with 10,000 men. Stanton pike heavily blockaded in on five places fifty miles from here (Beverly) Food and forage very scarce The deserters seem honest and intelligent. Since my last Cipher Telegram and that of Lt. Col. Babcock no changes have taken place in the position of our own troops. The infantry and artillery at Webster, Grafton and Beverly 5500 men; the cavalry at Clarksburg and Webster, 1700, and 300 on their way to Webster, will arrive there to night. General Averell passed through here and will be in Grafton to night, at Clarksburg to-morrow. We have now transportation for all these troops, also ammunition, forage and provisions for 15 days. I have sent all available infantry and one battery from Harpers-Ferry to Martinsburg as there are only 900 Cavalry left of Gen. Averill's Division, in a bad condition, with a line of 25 miles to guard, from the Shenandoah to Back Creek and beyond. The infantry at Martinsburg consists of three regiments under Col. Wells. This is the only movable force between Harpers Ferry and New Creek. I you wish, I can send them West, but have almost to give up the line from Harpers Ferry to Cumberland. A pontoon bridge is laid at Falling waters for the forces at Martinsburg." Copy, Sigel Papers, OClWHi.

On April 21, 6:00 P.M., Sigel telegraphed to USG. "The troops are mostly on their way west and east and the necessary arrangements [are m]ade at Parkersburg to ship the infantry The cavalry and trains will [go] from Parkersburg by land to Charlestown where Genl Crook wishes that all troops from [here] should be sent I sent him five infantry regiments and two Regts of Cavalry under Gen Averell, which will make him about ten thousand (10000) effective men. As soon as the troops at Martinsburg are assembled for the greater part I will go there   No information has been received in regard to important changes in the position of the enemy—Latest reports say that Elsey, ~~with~~ with four to five thousand men is in the vicinity & north and south of Staunton—The forces of Breckinridge are reported at Lafayette Station ten (10) miles west of New ~~Creek~~ River Bridge are [estima]ted at from six to eight thousand men   they are stationed from Lynchburg to Saltville and in front of this line to Greenbriar River; [Deserters] from Staunton say that Genl Early [w]ould take command in the Valley, they also report that they were left behind by Longstreet in June 1863 at Staunton and that they received orders at the commencement of this month to return to Tennessee to join Hoods division   They say that Longstreet in person was at Richmond but do not know whether his Corps has gone east. It may be that Hoods division has been left at or near Cumberland Gap as reported by Gen Crook and that the other divisions have gone to join Lee's Army. Genl Crook to whom I sent the report [of] Breckinrid[ge] says that this [report] is very correct as far as the country in hi[s] front is concerned. [Col] Babcock knows about this report [of which I] have sent a copy to the adjutant General at Washington." Telegram received, DNA, RG 107, Telegrams Collected (Bound); copy, Sigel Papers, OClWHi. *O.R.*, I, xxxiii, 936.

On April 22, 9:30 P.M., Sigel telegraphed to USG. "Colonel ~~Tailor~~ Taylor commanding Cav'y forces at Martinsburg, telegraphs the following. Scouts from up the Shenandoah report a large force concentrating near Front Royal. No force this side of the river. I believe that there is some truth in this Statement, as refugees have arrived at Harpers' Ferry, who say, that troops of the enemy were concentrating at Luray and that Longstreet had arrived at Charlotteville.— Farmers reports say that Rosser's Brigade of Cavalry, about 2000 strong was at Luray; it may be his troops who have moved to Front Royal. We have now 5 rgts. of inf'y at Martinsburg with one battery and 700 cavalry. 200 cavalry and two batteries are on theire way to that place. The troops for Gen. Crook have commenced embarking on transports at Parkersburg this morning." Telegram received (faded), DNA, RG 107, Telegrams Collected (Bound); copy, Sigel Papers, OClWHi. *O.R.*, I, xxxiii, 942. On April 23, 11:30 A.M., John I. Davenport, Fort Monroe, telegraphed to USG. "Our man reports Longstreet at Charlottsville   five thousand men from his own corps forwarded him a day   Think the no large but believe the information"   Telegram received, DNA, RG 108, Letters Received.

On April 24, USG telegraphed to Sigel. "Unless you receive orders from me to the contrary, start your column under Averill and Crook on the 2d day of May. I have telegraphed to Gen. Sherman to order your old Chief Q. M. of the 11th Corps to you, if he is not on duty from which he cannot be taken." Copies, DLC-USG, V, 45, 59; DNA, RG 108, Letters Sent; Sigel Papers, OClWHi. *O.R.*, I, xxxiii, 964. On April 23, 9:00 P.M., USG had telegraphed to Maj. Gen. William T. Sherman. "If Lt Col Meisenberg Chf. Q. M. Eleventh Corps (11th) can be dispensed with order him to report to Gen. Sigel." Telegram received (press), DNA, RG 107, Telegrams Collected (Bound); copies, DLC-USG, V, 94; DNA, RG 393, Military Div. of the Miss., Letters Sent. On April 25, Sherman telegraphed to USG. "Lt. Col. Meisenberg was ordered by Gen. Hooker some time ago to go to St. Louis and thence report to the Adjutant Genl at Washington— Col. Comstock left Nashville last evening for you with letter and figures"   Copies, *ibid.* On April 28, USG telegraphed to Maj. Gen. Henry W. Halleck. "Will you please order A Meysenburg, a. a. g. to report to Genl Sigel if he has not been otherwise assigned. I believe he is in St Louis awaiting orders." Telegram received, *ibid.*, RG 94, ACP, M778 CB 1863; *ibid.*, RG 107, Telegrams Collected (Bound); copies, *ibid.*, RG 108, Letters Sent; DLC-USG, V, 45, 59.

On April 24, 9:00 P.M., Sigel telegraphed to USG. "All the Infantry Cavalry and trains have been shipped to Parkersburg and should arrive in Charleston on the 26th. The 36th Ohio Infantry has also arrived at Charleston from Ohio but it numbers only 300 men, the rest is in Chattanooga   Six 6 Infantry regiments are now at Martinsburg. The last two which can be sent are on their way from Beverly to Webster and will be shipped to Martinsburg as soon as they arrive at Webster. I will leave for Martinsburg tomorrow morning and report from there"   Telegram received, DNA, RG 107, Telegrams Collected (Bound); copy, Sigel Papers, OClWHi. *O.R.*, I, xxxiii, 964.

On April 26, Sigel, Martinsburg, West Va., telegraphed to USG. "I left Cumberland yesterday after having made all arrangements for Genl Crooks command—All the troops sent to him will reach him today the 26th if nothing extraordinary happens, he telegraphed me that he would not be ready to move before two or three days which would be on the 28th or 29th—He requested me to advance a small force from Beverly toward ~~Leesburg~~ Huntersville which I have done in ordering the cavalry which was stationed at Beverly about 300 to Pocahontas county—This involved the necessity of reoccupying Beverly with at least one Regt of Infantry which I intended to send east—It is understood that Genl Crook will march down from Lewisburg to the Railroad and after having done all the damage he can to return to Lewisburg or to a point between Lewisburg and Staunton—From all information we have it appears to me that he will be successful as his forces will be stronger than any force the enemy can concentrate between Lewisburg and the Railroad at this moment. Here at Martinsburg I have now six Regts of Infantry with three Batteries and seven hundred available cavalry—In two or three days I will have five hundred cavalry more   this will then be the force on which I must rely—A party of one hundred & fifty of our cavalry sent out yesterday met 300 of the Enemy this side of Cedar Creek and were beaten back losing fifteen horses and one officer. The enemy were of Rosser's command—I will act according to circumstances with the forces I have and move them forward on the 28th or 29th"   Telegram received, DNA, RG 107, Telegrams Collected (Bound); copy, Sigel Papers, OClWHi. Printed as sent at 2:00 A.M. in *O.R.*, I, xxxiii, 986.

On April 27, 9:00 A.M., USG telegraphed to Sigel. "Did you receive my letter fixing date of departure of Expedition? Start it Second of May if not otherwise directed"   Telegram received, DNA, RG 107, Telegrams Collected (Bound); copies, *ibid.*, RG 108, Letters Sent; Sigel Papers, OClWHi; DLC-USG, V, 45, 59. *O.R.*, I, xxxiii, 997. On the same day, 8:00 A.M., Sigel telegraphed to USG. "Your letter of the 24th inst in regard to Genls Crook and Averill is just received and communicated to Genl Crook"   Telegram received, DNA, RG 107, Telegrams Collected (Bound); copy, Sigel Papers, OClWHi. *O.R.*, I, xxxiii, 997.

On April 28, 9:00 P.M. and 10:00 P.M., Sigel, Martinsburg, telegraphed to USG. "I will [move to-morrow] to Bunker Hill twelve miles [south] of Martinsburg   [No] further news received in regard to the enemy [except] that Longstreets forces are supposed to be in Page County   This [however] is only the [re]port of [a refugee] who [learned] it at Winchester on [his] way from Harrisonburg—There is an excellent road leading from Madison C H [by] Criglersville and Ragged Mountain to [Luray]. This road is not marked on Lloyds map—

I believe that if Longstreet is on the left of Lee's army he has sent a force on that road to Luray Page County   He may follow with his corps and either march to Front Royal or [throw] his troops from Luray across the Shenandoah   There are two or three fords by which he can pass from Luray into the Shenandoah Valley   I will report again tomorrow   It is difficult to [get much] positive information as the cavalry here is [in a wretched] condition [and] can hardly protect my scouting parties." "Genl Crook will be prepared to move on the Second of May, he telegraphs me so. I informed him that he shall move on that day"   Telegrams received, DNA, RG 107, Telegrams Collected (Bound); copies, Sigel Papers, OClWHi. *O.R.*, I, xxxiii, 1006.

On April 30, noon, Sigel, Bunker Hill, West Va., telegraphed to USG. "No news of special importance has been received since yesterday. There is no enemy of considerable force this side of Cedar Creek and no information of a strong movement of the enemy down the valley. It is reported but not fully reliable that Lees army had begun to move with seven (7) days rations yesterday and that he has sent his baggage trains to Scottsville due south of Charlottsville on James River. I am waiting here for one part of my troops ordered forward from Romney yesterday and will then move to Winchester. Strong scouting parties have been sent out today. The reports of those sent out yesterday morning have not come in yet. Please send all dispatches to Martinsburg"   Telegram received, DNA, RG 107, Telegrams Collected (Bound); *ibid.*, RG 108, Letters Received. *O.R.*, I, xxxiii, 1025–26. On the same day, USG transmitted this telegram by letter to Maj. Gen. George G. Meade. Copies, DLC-USG, V, 45, 59; DNA, RG 108, Letters Sent.

To Julia Dent Grant

Culpepper Apl. 17th 1864

DEAR JULIA,

Bowers will leave here on Teusday,[1] (Washington on Wednesday) for the West. If your mind is made up to accompany him telegraph me and I will go in to see you off. I dislike however very much going in again. In the first place I do not like being seen so much about Washington. In the second it is not altogether safe. I cannot move without it being known all over the country, and to the enemy who are hovering within a few miles of the rail-road all the time. I do not know that the enemy's attack on the road last Friday was with the view of ketching me, but it was well timed.[2] If you intend going either get Mr. Stanton or Mr. Chadwick[3] to telegraph me.

I understand Jess has been having a fight in the hall! How

is that?—Fred has said nothing about Helen[4] coming East. He told me that when you went out she would have to leave your fathers. Kisses for yourself and Jess. Gen. Hunter will deliver this and tell you how we are living. Plain and well, surrounded with mud. I do not say you must go but I see no particular reason for your remaining longer. I shall certainly go to Washington but once more and that will be to see you off. As soon as it is possible for me to settle I will send for you and the children. Should we be so fortunate as to whip the enemy well, I feel that after that there will be no campaigning that I cannot direct from some one place.

Kisses again.

ULYS.

ALS, DLC-USG.

1. April 18, 1864. On April 18, USG telegraphed to Secretary of War Edwin M. Stanton. "Will you please send Mrs Grant word that Col Bowers will not leave here for the west until wednsday to be prapared to leave on the wednsday Evening train"   Telegram received, USG 3.
2. For an account of the presence of C.S.A. Col. John S. Mosby near a train carrying USG on May 4, see *Memoirs*, II, 141–42.
3. Probably someone associated with Sykes, Chadwick, and Co., operators of Willard's Hotel in Washington. On Sept. 30, USG wrote to Maj. Gen. William T. Sherman. "The bearer of this, Mr. C. A. Chadwick, one of the proprietors of Willards Hotel, Washington, expects to visit Atlanta Ga. and is desirous of paying his respects to you whilst there. I am under obligations to Mr. Chadwick for many acts of personal kindness and commend him to your attention with pleasure. All attention shewn him amidst your many duties will be highly appreciated by him and me also." ALS, deCoppet Collection, NjP.
4. Mrs. Frederick T. Dent, the former Helen Louise Lynde.

To Edwin M. Stanton

————

Culpepper, Apl. 18th 1864

HON E. M. STANTON,
SEC. OF WAR,
SIR:

Your note of this date enclosing copy of M. Geoffroys[1] note to the Hon. Sec. of State, together with the reply he proposes to make, is just received. It is rather embarassing to know how to answer because to refuse to allow the French to go on bringing out their tobacco would indicate that we expect to use the line of the James River; to permit a continuance will give the enemy information of the very day we make any move from Fortress Monroe. Altogether I think it would be better to say that the time expiring on the 23d inst. for French vessels bringing out tobacco they will be allowed until that time, and no longer, until new stipulations are entered into, and which will not be entertained until after the Spring Campaign is over, or at least shall grant no privileges to enter rebel ports until such campaign is closed. This I give simply as my view. Any other arrangement entered into, with the sanction of the President, of course I shall not oppose.

Yours Truly

U. S. GRANT

Lt. Gen.

ALS, PPRF. *O.R.*, I, xxxiii, 896.

On April 12, 1864, Secretary of War Edwin M. Stanton had written to USG. "I communicate herewith a despatch, dated April 11, from Major General Butler, commanding at Fortress Monroe, in respect to the movements of French vessels about getting tobacco from Richmond, and request that you will give him such instructions touching the subject as the service may require." Copy, DLC-Edwin M. Stanton. See *O.R.*, I, xxxiii, 843. On the same day, 3:30 P.M., USG telegraphed to Maj. Gen. Benjamin F. Butler. "Your dispatch of the 11th inst. to the sec. of War in relation to the shipment of tobacco by the French Government has been refered to me for my orders. The agreement made by the Sec. of state, (Copy of which you have) will have to be carried out. But make no agreement to extend the time for doing so beyond the 23d inst. at which time the agreement expires by limitation. ~~This decision is of course subject to any~~ unless directed to do so by the President or Sec. of War." ALS (telegram sent), DNA, RG 107, Telegrams Collected (Bound); telegram received, *ibid.*; DLC-Benjamin F. Butler. *O.R.*, I, xxxiii, 849–50. On April 23, 11:00 A.M., Butler telegraphed to Maj. Gen. Henry W. Halleck, sending a copy to USG, concerning the expiration of the time for shipping tobacco. *Ibid.*, p. 956. On the same day, 5:00 P.M., USG telegraphed to Halleck. "Genl Butlers dispatch of this date suggests I think the right course to pursue in notifying the French to discontinue shipping their tobacco   Please direct him to adopt it"   Telegram received, DNA, RG 107, Telegrams Collected (Bound); copies, *ibid.*, RG 108, Letters Sent; DLC-USG, V, 45, 59. *O.R.*, I, xxxiii, 956. See *HED*, 38-1-1, vol. 2, p. 1327; Lynn M. Case and Warren F. Spencer, *The United States and France: Civil War Diplomacy* (Philadelphia, 1970), pp. 525–44.

1. Louis de Geofroy became chargé d'affaires of the French legation in Washington in Jan., 1864. On April 19, Col. Edward D. Townsend, AGO, tele-

graphed to USG. "The Secretary of War says please return the letter of M. Jeffroy to Secretary Seward, enclosed to you in his despatch of the seventeenth—Please acknowledge this." Telegram received, DNA, RG 107, Telegrams Collected (Bound). On the same day, 3:00 P.M., USG telegraphed to Townsend. "11 a. m. dispatch received. Papers refered to will be sent in the morning." ALS (telegram sent), Berg Collection, NN; telegram received, DNA, RG 94, Letters Received, 352A 1864; *ibid.*, RG 107, Telegrams Collected (Bound).

To Maj. Gen. Henry W. Halleck

Hd Qrs Culpepper C H
7 30 P. M. Apl. 18. 1864.

MAJ. GEN. HALLECK,
CHF. OF STAFF.

Except the regt which Gen. Augur[1] proposed to spare, I did not expect to order any troops from the Defences of Washington.

It was only such unassigned troops as may arrive that I expected to thus report to Gen. Burnside.

The regt which has been assigned to him please order to Alexandria to relieve troops now there from this army on special duty, the latter to join their proper commands at the front.

U. S. GRANT,
Lt. Genl.

Telegram received, DNA, RG 107, Telegrams Collected (Bound); copies, *ibid.*, RG 108, Letters Sent; DLC-USG, V, 45, 59. *O.R.*, I, xxxiii, 897. On April 16, 1864, 10:40 A.M., Maj. Gen. George G. Meade telegraphed to Brig. Gen. John A. Rawlins. "Please say to the Lt. Genl. Comd. that *Shaler's* brigade of the 6th Corps (sent to Sandusky in January last) which was ordered some time ago to return to this army, has not arrived nor any intelligence reached me of its movement.—Also two regiments of the Pa. Reserves ordered to the front from Alexandria, to be relieved there by a part of the Veteran Reserve Corps, have not come forward. I would be glad if any measures can be taken to expedite the movement of these troops.—" ALS (telegram sent), DNA, RG 107, Telegrams Collected (Unbound); telegram received, *ibid.*, RG 108, Letters Received. *O.R.*, I, xxxiii, 881. On the same day, Rawlins telegraphed to Meade. "An Inspector has been sent to Sandusky or Johnson's Island, with instructions to reduce the number of men for guards &c, to the lowest possible number, and to give his personal attention to the execution of orders for the sending of troops to their respective commands in the field. The order for the return of your brigade, is no doubt being executed. Gen Augur has been directed to releive the Penn. Reserves and send them forward." Telegram received, DNA, RG 107, Telegrams Collected (Unbound);

copies, *ibid.*, RG 108, Letters Sent; DLC-USG, V, 45, 59. On the same day, Rawlins telegraphed to Maj. Gen. Christopher C. Augur. "Please have the Penn. Reserves at Alexandria releived and ordered to the front." Telegram received, DNA, RG 107, Telegrams Collected (Unbound); (press) *ibid.*, Telegrams Collected (Bound); copies, *ibid.*, RG 108, Letters Sent; DLC-USG, V, 45, 59. *O.R.*, I, xxxiii, 882. Also on April 16, 11:00 A.M., USG telegraphed to Maj. Gen. Henry W. Halleck. "Order all troops that can be spared from the Defences of Washington either from New troops arriving or from those already there, to report to Genl Burnside for assignment to Brigades. Genl Augur mentioned to me the arrival of a regiment of heavy Artillery twenty nine hundred (2900) strong with which he could make such disposition as to give Genl Burnside a considerable force of Infantry." Telegram received, DNA, RG 107, Telegrams Collected (Bound); copies, *ibid.*, RG 108, Letters Sent; DLC-USG, V, 45, 59. *O.R.*, I, xxxiii, 879. On April 17, Halleck wrote to USG. "As I telegraphed this morning, I have ordered General Augur to organize an infantry regiment for Genl Burnside out of the 2d Penn Heavy Artillery. I asked him if he could not spare the 2d New York H'y. Art'y. also; but he thinks it would leave his line too weak. I therefore submit the matter for your decision, with the following remarks: The line of defences is about 37 miles in length; some of the works are not completed, and the recent heavy rains have so injured some of them as to require extensive repairs by working parties. They are now garrisoned by 10 regiments and 1 battalion of heavy artillery, effective force about 14,000, or deducting regiment ordered for Burnside, about 13,000. Very few of these men have ever been under fire, and one third are raw recruits. The public stores and buildings are guarded exclusively (with the exception of two or three special detachments) by Invalids (Veteran Reserves). General Tyler has in the front, on Rail Road and picketing Bull Run and the Accoquan about 2,000 infantry, 1.000 cavalry, and a battery of artillery. There are also a few companies of cavalry and infantry north of the Potomac guarding railroads and picketing the river to the mouth of the Monocacy. There is always at the Artillery Depôt a number of batteries being repaired and fitted out, and at the present time there are some 4.000 dismounted cavalrymen. All these in case of an emergency could be armed as infantry and placed in the trenches. The public stores are mostly in wooden sheds, and if not well guarded would be burned by the rebels in this city and Alexandria. The Board of Officers ordered by the Sec'y of War to report on the Defences, estimated that, with a covering army in front, they should be garrisoned by 25.000 men and 3.000 cavalry for reconnoitering in front. This was exclusive of the storehouse guards and military police. With no covering army, the complete garrisons should be 50,000   I think the estimates made to the President by the Generals under McClellan at the time of his Peninsula campaign were about the same. I have always considered this this line of defence too long, but very able officers are of a different opinion. The evil, if it exists, cannot probably be remedied now. Perhaps the Forts south of Annacosta Creek might be abandoned. If so, as they bear on the Arsenal and Navy Yard, they should be dismantled and the guns and ammunition removed. I submit herewith a list of the Heavy art'y regiments now here, with effective strength, in order that you may decide what forces shall be assigned to General Burnside's command.   1st Vermont 1460   1st Maine 1591   7th N. York 1560   9th N. York 1322   2d N. York 783   10th N. York 1278   1 Conn 1199   2d Conn 1442   1 Mass 1478   2 Penna 1846   1 Batt. Wis. 388"   ALS, DNA, RG 108, Letters Received. *O.R.*, I, xxxiii, 887–88. See telegram to Maj. Gen. Henry W. Halleck, April 16, 1864.

On April 18, 4:00 P.M, Meade telegraphed to USG. "The regiments belonging to the 5th Corps now on duty under Genl. Briggs at Alexandria & which it is desirable should rejoin their brigade are 44th N. Y. Vols. 5th Penna. Reserves 11th U. S. Infantry—Genl. Briggs reports present for duty with these regiments, one thousand & Sixty four officers & men.—" ALS (telegram sent), DNA, RG 107, Telegrams Collected (Unbound); telegram received, *ibid.*, RG 108, Letters Received. On April 20, Halleck wrote to Augur. "Lt Genl Grant directs that the Provisional Regt organised from 2d Penn. Heavy Arty be sent to Alexandria to relieve troops now there from Army of the Potomac, which will be sent to their proper comds." ALS, *ibid.*, Letters Sent (Press). *O.R.*, I, xxxiii, 925.

On April 25, 9:30 P.M., Meade telegraphed to USG. "I have not heard today from the Pa. Reserves—I published an order warning them of the consequences of refusing to do duty & promising to obtain a speedy decision from the War Dept in their case.—I also received & transmitted to them a telegram received today from Col. Townsend promising prompt action in their case—I will telegraph to the Comd. officer & advise you.—" ALS (telegram sent), DNA, RG 107, Telegrams Collected (Unbound); telegram received (dated April 26), *ibid.*, RG 108, Letters Received. Dated April 26 in *O.R.*, I, xxxiii, 982. See *ibid.*, 1032. On April 26, USG wrote to Meade. "Is there still excitement among the Pa. Reserves?" ALS, CSt.

1. Augur, promoted to maj., 13th Inf., as of May 14, 1861; appointed brig. gen. as of Nov. 12; promoted to maj. gen. as of Aug. 9, 1862. He commanded a div. of the 5th Army Corps, Army of the Potomac, until severely wounded during the battle of Cedar Mountain, Va., on Aug. 9, participated in the siege of Port Hudson, and was assigned to command the 22nd Army Corps and the Dept. of Washington on Oct. 13, 1863.

To Maj. Gen. Henry W. Halleck

———

Hd Qrs Culpepper C H.
8. P. M. Apl 18. 1864.

MAJ. GEN. H. W. HALLECK.
CHF OF STAFF.

There is such a call for Cavy horses from all parts of the army, that I would suggest the propriety of an order from the Secretary of War authorizing Dept. Commanders to convert forty (40) percent of all their Cavalry into Infy, selecting those regts who have [re]quired the greatest number of horses to keep them up, to be dismounted.

There is full that percentage of Cavy in service more than can be kept mounted & more than is required.

If it would be acting in bad faith to dismount them I would discharge them altogether.

U. S. GRANT

Lt Genl

Telegram received, DNA, RG 107, Telegrams Collected (Bound); copies, *ibid.*, RG 108, Letters Sent; DLC-USG, V, 45, 59. *O.R.*, I, xxxiii, 897.

On April 17, 1864, Brig. Gen. George Crook, Charleston, West Va., telegraphed to USG. "It will be impossible for me to be supplied with the requisite number of horses to mount my men, within the proper time, with the present facilities in this Department for will you authorize me to purchase & horses horses in Ohio for that purpose. deserters report all Longstreets Corps, gone in direction of Richmond except one division which is near Cumberland Gap" ALS (telegram sent), DNA, RG 107, Telegrams Collected (Unbound); telegram received (dated April 18, 2:30 P.M.), *ibid.*, Telegrams Collected (Bound); *ibid.*, RG 108, Letters Received. *O.R.*, I, xxxiii, 900. On April 18, USG telegraphed to Maj. Gen. Henry W. Halleck. "Gen Crook asks authority to purchase horses to fill his command Will you please ask the Secretary of War to grant it? Please order Genl Devens to report to Genl Meade." Telegram received, DNA, RG 107, Telegrams Collected (Bound); copies (2), *ibid.*, RG 92, Supplies and Purchases, Public Animals, Letters Received; *ibid.*, RG 108, Letters Sent; DLC-USG, V, 45, 59. On the same day, 9:00 P.M., Maj. Gen. George G. Meade telegraphed to USG. "Brig Genl. Devens is a good officer;—formerly belonged to the Sixth Corps, in which is Prince's brigade—He will do very well." ALS (telegram sent), DNA, RG 107, Telegrams Collected (Unbound); copies, *ibid.*, RG 393, Army of the Potomac, Telegrams Sent; Meade Papers, PHi. *O.R.*, I, xxxiii, 898. See telegram to Maj. Gen. Henry W. Halleck, April 19, 1864. Also on April 18, 11:15 P.M., Secretary of War Edwin M. Stanton telegraphed to USG. "Your telegram has been communicated to Mrs Grant. General Crook will be ordered authorized to supply himself with horses wherever he can procure them. The order for converting forty per cent of cavalry into infantry will be issued tomorrow." ALS (telegram sent), DNA, RG 107, Telegrams Collected (Bound).

On April 20, Brig. Gen. John A. Rawlins telegraphed to Halleck. "Gen Grant is on his way to Washington. will be there this afternoon" Telegram received, *ibid.* On April 21, Halleck wrote a memorandum for the Cav. Bureau. "Lt Genl Grant directs that one thousand horses be assigned to Genl Butler's command in preference. Next supply Army of Potomac from Cavalry Bureau." ANS, *ibid.*, RG 92, Supplies and Purchases, Public Animals, Letters Received.

To Maj. Gen. William T. Sherman

Culpepper
Apl 18 1864 7 P M

MAJ GEN SHERMAN
NASHVILLE TENN

Gen Smith has made requisition for thirty thousand (30000) cavalry horses   It will be impossible to supply half the number. Use dismounted cavalry to guard depots and Stations & relieve Infantry to go to the front   I have sent Gen Prince to command ~~West~~ West Kentucky   He will report to you[1]

U. S. GRANT
Lt Gen

Telegram received, DNA, RG 107, Telegrams Collected (Bound); copies, *ibid.*, RG 108, Letters Sent; *ibid.*, RG 393, Military Div. of the Miss., Letters Sent; DLC-USG, V, 45, 59. *O.R.*, I, xxxii, part 3, 398. On April 18, 1864, 7:00 P.M., USG telegraphed to Maj. Gen. William T. Sherman. "Have you any information of movement of troops from Johnstons Army [to] Lee's?" Telegram received, DNA, RG 107, Telegrams Collected (Bound); copies, *ibid.*, RG 108, Letters Sent; DLC-USG, V, 45, 59. *O.R.*, I, xxxii, part 3, 397. On April 18, 11:30 P.M., Sherman, Nashville, telegraphed to USG. "Genl Sooy Smith made his requisition for horses without consultation with me. I did not expect half the number you name & indeed had already ordered the dismounted cavalry to be used as you suggest   I have full accounts from Thomas up to date   None of Johnstons army has gone East   There was a talk in Johnstons camp about Hardee's Corps going east, mere camp talk and nothing more" Telegram received, DNA, RG 107, Telegrams Collected (Bound); *ibid.*, RG 108, Letters Received; copies, *ibid.*, RG 393, Military Div. of the Miss., Letters Sent; DLC-USG, V, 94. *O.R.*, I, xxxii, part 3, 398.
    Also on April 18, USG had telegraphed to Maj. Gen. Henry W. Halleck. "I will direct Genl Sherman to get what Cavalry horses he conveniently can & then use his dismounted Cavalry to guard Railroad & relieve Infantry to go to the front. Before ordering Gen Pope peremptorily to send off any troops he now has I will see the reason he assigns for retaining them—" Telegram received, DNA, RG 107, Telegrams Collected (Bound); copies, *ibid.*, RG 108, Letters Sent; DLC-USG, V, 45, 59.
    On April 19, midnight, Sherman telegraphed to USG. "Gen Thomas reports by telegraph to night that he has satisfactory intelligence that no troops have left Dalton for Richmond. His dates from Johnstons Camp are as late as the eighteenth" Telegram received, DNA, RG 107, Telegrams Collected (Bound); *ibid.*, RG 108, Letters Received. *O.R.*, I, xxxii, part 3, 410. On the same day, Sherman wrote to Brig. Gen. John A. Rawlins at length discussing

C.S.A. movements and his own plans. ALS, DNA, RG 108, Letters Received. *O.R.*, I, xxxii, part 3, 410–11.

On April 19, 4:30 P.M., Sherman telegraphed to USG. "General Hurlbut reports the Mobile and Ohio Railroad done from Mobile to Okalona and that it will be finished to Corinth in a week. I dont believe it but even if true when Banks strikes it near Mobile it will be worse than useless to the Enemy." Telegram received, DNA, RG 107, Telegrams Collected (Bound); *ibid.*, RG 108, Letters Received. *O.R.*, I, xxxii, part 3, 419.

On April 20, Sherman telegraphed to USG transmitting telegrams of April 19 from Maj. Gen. John M. Schofield and Maj. Gen. George H. Thomas concerning C.S.A. movements. Telegram received, DNA, RG 107, Telegrams Collected (Bound); *ibid.*, RG 108, Letters Received. See *O.R.*, I, xxxii, part 3, 411–12, 413–14. Also on April 20, Sherman telegraphed to USG. "I want to defer the destruction of that rail road on the bridges till the last ~~momt~~ moment as it will clearly reveal our plans not to operate up towards Virginia—but if your cavalry reach the Watauga bridge it is useless long to defer it and you may order its destruction. We are waiting for our troops from Red River for acting offensively ~~on~~ on the main line." Telegram received, DNA, RG 393, Dept. of the Ohio, Telegrams Received. On the same day, Sherman wrote to USG, telegraphing the same message at 7:00 P.M. "General Schofield reports positive information, that Longstreet has gone to Virginia and has not destroyed the Rail Road. I have ordered him to feel up as far as Watauga, and expect the enemy will break that bridge.—If they do not, I will order it done.—Hovey can occupy the Road above Hiwassee and Thomas will now collect his whole Command from Cleveland to Bridgeport, ready to unite at Chattanooga on a days notice and be all ready to advance. Schofield only awaits my orders to drop down with his complement to Hiwassee. Guntersville will in my judgment be the place of concentration for McPherson, but his two furloughed Divisions have not yet rendezvoused at Cairo, though all his transportation is there ready to come up the Tennessee, as soon as as the Regiments come in. No authentic news from Red River, although it seems the enemy will have had time to make a concentration at Shreveport. I have the rumor of a check at Mansfield, which must be partial, for Mansfield is back from Red River on the Texas Road. If Banks, Smith, Steele and the Gunboats all reach Shreveport in concert, they ought to make short work, still I have nothing satisfactory from that quarter. Hurlbut reports from Memphis, that Forrest has escaped South by way of Lagrange. It does seem, as though he had made not the least effort to stop him or molest him. He is on his way to Cairo, and I will bring him round to his Corps at Decatur. I have not yet heard of Washburn or Prince. If Forrest is below Memphis, ought we not to disturb him, by way of the Yazoo and Grenada?" LS, *ibid.*, RG 108, Letters Received. *O.R.*, I, xxxii, part 3, 422.

1. On April 17, USG telegraphed to Maj. Gen. George G. Meade. "Gen Prince has been relieved from the Army of Potomac and ordered to Sherman   the orders were sent to Genl Sedgwick tonight   copies will be sent to you in the morning" Telegram received, DNA, RG 94, War Records Office, Army of the Potomac; copy, Meade Papers, PHi. See *O.R.*, I, xxxii, part 3, 397. On April 30, Maj. Gen. Cadwallader C. Washburn telegraphed to USG. "Genls Hurlbut & Brayman think that the assignment of Genl Prince to Command District of Columbus does not give him command at Cairo   Genl Prince thinks

otherwise   Will you instruct them them and me at once"   Telegram received,
DNA, RG 107, Telegrams Collected (Bound); *ibid.*, RG 108, Letters Received;
copy, *ibid.*, RG 393, 16th Army Corps, District of West Tenn., Telegrams
Sent. On May 2, USG telegraphed to Washburn and Brig. Gen. Henry Prince.
"Genl. Princes command embraces all troops in the Department Of the Tenn
north of New Madrid"   Telegram received, *ibid.*, Letters Received; copies, *ibid.*,
Register of Letters Received; *ibid.*, RG 108, Letters Sent; DLC-USG, V, 45, 59.
O.R., I, xxxix, part 2, 8.

To Maj. Gen. Henry W. Halleck

Culpepper Apl. 19th 1864
MAJ. GEN. HALLECK, WASHINGTON D. C.

Gen. Meade did not apply for Gn. Devens.[1] The latter applied
for orders and Meade stating that he was a good officer I asked to
have him sent to the A. P.   Keep Gen. Devens where he is so long
as his services are needed. Order Gen. Seymour[2] some place to
await orders unless he can be profitably placed on such duty as
Gen. Devens is now doing.

U. S. GRANT
Lt. Gen.

ALS (telegram sent), DNA, RG 107, Telegrams Collected (Unbound); telegram received, *ibid.*, Telegrams Collected (Bound). *O.R.*, I, xxxiii, 907. On
April 19, 1864, 2:00 P.M., Maj. Gen. Henry W. Halleck telegraphed to USG.
"Genl Devins has been ordered through the northern & Eastern states to collect
together recruits & send them to regts & depots. The war Dept thinks his services
there almost indispensable for the next week or two. Men are still recruiting at
the rate of a thousand per day. Please see of Genl Meade cannot spare him a
little longer. Genl Seymour is relieved from Dept. of the south. Where shall I
send him?" ALS (telegram sent), DNA, RG 107, Telegrams Collected (Bound);
telegram received, *ibid.*; *ibid.*, RG 108, Letters Received. *O.R.*, I, xxxiii, 907.

1. Charles Devens, born in Mass. in 1820, graduated from Harvard in
1838, studied at Harvard Law School, and started to practice law in 1840. He
served in the Mass. Senate as a Democrat (1848–49) and was U.S. marshal for
the district of Mass. (1849–53), becoming involved in 1851 in the case of
Thomas Sims, a fugitive slave. Appointed col., 15th Mass., as of July 24, 1861,
and brig. gen. as of April 15, 1862, he participated in numerous battles with the
Army of the Potomac as a regt., brigade, and div. commander, being wounded
during the battles of Fair Oaks and Chancellorsville. See telegram to Maj. Gen.
Henry W. Halleck, April 18, 1864.

2. Truman Seymour of Vt., USMA 1846, served in the Mexican War, was promoted to capt., 1st Art., as of Nov. 22, 1860, and helped defend Fort Sumter. Appointed brig. gen. as of April 28, 1862, he served as a brigade and div. commander in the Army of the Potomac, then went to the Dept. of the South where, in March, 1864, he commanded the District of Florida. See telegram to Maj. Gen. Henry W. Halleck, April 30, 1864.

To Maj. Gen. Henry W. Halleck

Culpepper Va 8 30 P M
April 19th 1864

MAJ. GEN. H W. HALLECK
CHIEF OF STAFF.

Before ordering Genl Pope to send any troops from his Dept I was waiting to see his reasons for retaining the number he has. My own opinion has been that a small force of Cavalry with but very little Infantry was all that he required—I would advise that he be ordered to send all the Infantry he can possibly spare to Washington at once[1]

U. S. GRANT
Lt Genl

Telegram received, DNA, RG 107, Telegrams Collected (Bound); copies, *ibid.*, RG 108, Letters Sent; DLC-USG, V, 45, 59. *O.R.*, I, xxxiii, 907; *ibid.*, I, xxxiv, part 3, 235. On April 19, 1864, 3:00 P.M., Maj. Gen. Henry W. Halleck telegraphed to USG. "The Iowa delegation in House of Representatives and Senators Washburn and Wilkinson urged strenuously the withdrawal of all infantry force from the Northwest Dept. as needless and expensive there while the troops would be useful in active service which they are anxious to be engaged in   As you have the subject under consideration it is proper to apprise you of these opinions   They affirm that 1500 or 2000 is the whole force needed in that department" Telegram received, DNA, RG 108, Letters Received. *O.R.*, I, xxxiv, part 3, 234–35. The same telegram signed by Secretary of War Edwin M. Stanton is an ADfS, DNA, RG 107, Telegrams Collected (Bound).

1. See *O.R.*, I, xxxiii, 929, (misdated) 1008; *ibid.*, I, xxxiv, part 3, 243.

To Maj. Gen. Ambrose E. Burnside

Culpepper Va
April 19th 1864 [*11:45* A.M.]

MAJ GEN BURNSIDE
ANNAPOLIS, MD.

Divert all troops you may now have on the way to Annapolis or yet to start to Alexandria and send a General there to take charge of them. Crittenden ranking Parke makes no difference. Under no circumstances would he command the corps

U. S. GRANT
Lt Genl

Telegram received, DNA, RG 107, Telegrams Collected (Bound); copies, *ibid.*, RG 108, Letters Sent; DLC-USG, V, 45, 59. *O.R.*, I, xxxiii, 913. On April 19, 1864, 9:00 P.M., USG telegraphed to Maj. Gen. Ambrose E. Burnside. "Commence moving your troops according to the directions you have received, on the 23rd" Telegram received, DNA, RG 107, Telegrams Collected (Bound); copies, *ibid.*, RG 108, Letters Sent; DLC-USG, V, 45, 59. *O.R.*, I, xxxiii, 913. On the same day, 9:00 P.M., USG telegraphed to Maj. Gen. George G. Meade. "Send the ninth (9th) Army Corps to Washington as rapidly as their places can be filled by such other troops as you may designate to take their place—Let the shipment of such as can be spared before their places are filled, be commenced at once." Telegram received, DNA, RG 94, War Records Office, Dept. of the Cumberland.

On April 20, Burnside telegraphed to USG. "Lt Jno B. Parke 17th U. S. Infy Army Potomac is cousin of Maj Genl Parke   Cannot he be detailed as Aide De Camp for Genl Parke." Telegram received, *ibid.*, RG 108, Letters Received; copy, *ibid.*, RG 393, 9th Army Corps, Telegrams Sent. On the same day, USG telegraphed to Burnside. "To detail Lt. Parke as Aid to Gen Parke would be a violation of the law requiring Aides to Volunteer Generals to be taken from the Volunteer service and also of the order requiring Staff officers to be selected from the command of the officer ~~with wh~~ on whose staff they ~~serve~~ are called to serve." ALS (telegram sent), *ibid.*, RG 107, Telegrams Collected (Bound); telegram received, *ibid.*

To Maj. Gen. Benjamin F. Butler

———

Head Quarters, Armies in the Field,
Culpepper C. H. Va. Apl. 19th 1864

Maj. Gen. B. F. Butler,
Comd.g Dept. of N. C. & Va,
General,

I send Lt. Col. Dent, of my staff, with this not with the view of changing any instructions heretofore given, but more particularly to secure full co-operation between your command and that of Gen. Meade. I will, as you understand, expect you to move from Fortress Monroe the same day Gen. Meade starts from here. The exact time I will telegraph as soon as it can be fixed. At present the roads are in such condition that the time could not be fixed earlyer than the 27th inst. You can understand therefore you have fully to that date to make your preparations. You also understand that with the forces here I shall aim to fight Lee between here and Richmond if he will stand. Should Lee however fall back into Richmond I will follow up and make a junction with your Army on the James River. Could I be certain that you will be able to invest Richmond, on the south side, so as to have your left resting on the James, above the City, I would form the junction there. Circumstances may make this course advisable any how. I would say therefore use every exertion to secure footing as far up the south side of the river as you can and as soon as possible. If you hear of our advancing from that direction, or have reason to judge from the action of the enemy that they are looking for danger to that side, attack vigerously and if you cannot carry the City at least detain as large a force there as possible.

You will want all the co-operation from the Navy that can be got. Confer freely with Admiral Lee[1] your plans that he may make as much preparation as possible.

If it is possible to communicate with you after determining my exact line of march I will do so. If you can possibly get scouts through to me do it.

Inform me by return of Col. Dent your present situation and state of readiness for moving.

Very Truly, your obt. svt.

U. S. GRANT

Lt. Gen.

Instruct the Commanding officer at Plymouth[2] to hold the place at all hazards, unless it is of no importance to hold. Have transports there ready to carry off such troops as it was intended to bring off and place aboard of them all ba[ggag]es to be removed with the troops. Instruct the officer in command that the moment the enemy abandon their siege to put the force previously designed to draw from there aboard and start with them. If the enemy will continue to hold a force to threaten the place we can well afford to keep enough to resist them and make by the bargain. The enemy will unquestionably however bring every thing to Richmond the moment we begin to move.

When I telegraph we will start rain or shine we will start and hope that from all points there will be a responsive move.

I have made preparations, or am making them, for a full siege equipment to use if the enemy should fall ~~into~~ within the intrenchments at Richmond. Nothing of this kind need be looked after by Gen. Butler further than he expects to require such auxiliaries whilst acting separately.

Every effort is being made to draw troops from the Northern states to Washington so as to have reserves ready if they should be required at any point.

Speak to Gen. Butler particularly about the possibility, and for what I now see probability of my making my appearance on the south side of the river.

ALS, DLC-Benjamin F. Butler. Dated April 18, 1864, in *O.R.*, I, xxxiii, 904–5. The text following the signature, undated and unattached, appears to have been written for the guidance of Lt. Col. Frederick T. Dent but to have been delivered to Maj. Gen. Benjamin F. Butler. AL, DLC-Benjamin F. Butler.

On April 19, 11:00 A.M., Butler, Fort Monroe, Va., telegraphed to USG. "I have received communication that the Enemy have attacked Plymouth in considerable force, thus far have been repulsed, their Iron-Clads have not yet come into action. I have directed Gen Peck to make such disposition of the forces in his district as best to repel this movement. I have taken from him a single

Cavalry Reg't and a light battery   He must have ten thousand (10000) men under his command. Shall I do anything more?" Telegram received, DNA, RG 107, Telegrams Collected (Bound); *ibid.*, Telegrams Collected (Unbound); copies, DLC-Benjamin F. Butler; DLC-Robert T. Lincoln; USG 3. On the same day, 8:00 P.M., USG telegraphed to Butler. "Genl Peck should be able to hold Plymouth with the force he has—you however will have to be the judge of what is best to do   The moment you move from Ft Monroe, all rebel forces threatening along the North Carolina coast will be withdrawn and you can then bring away surplus troops to reinforce your moving Army"   Telegram received, DLC-Benjamin F. Butler; DNA, RG 107, Telegrams Collected (Bound); copies, *ibid.*, RG 108, Letters Sent; DLC-USG, V, 45, 59. *O.R.*, I, xxxiii, 914.

On April 20, Butler wrote to USG. "On monday evening I received a note from Genl. Gilmore by hand of Genl. Vodzes, who arrived here with two Regiments of troops from Hilton Head. The Letter contained the following Extracts, which are all that are ~~materially~~ specially material as to the time when Genl. Gilmore will probably be here. 'Brig: Genl. Vozdes bears this letter and is directed to report to you to take command of the 10 Corps as it arrives from time to time. Brig. Genl. Terry will follow in a day or two and will ~~leave~~ then command the Corps until my arrival. Genl. Turner will remain a few days longer still while I do not propose to leave here or turn over my command of this Department untill all my troops are in motion, and the last Regiment ready to embark. Great delay has occurred here in concentrating my scattered forces, but it could not be avoided—'   From the tone of his letter and my conversation with Genl. Vogdes, I am of opinion that he will not be able to be here or to even get his troops here until at least ten days from to day. I have directed those troops to assemble at Gloucester Point, opposite Yorktown under the immediate command of Gen Vozdes, assigning Gen. Smith to the Camp of Instruction at Yorktown and the command of the troops on both sides of the River—I have information upon which I most implicitly rely, that the enemy have three iron clads done near Richmond. One I am informed but of that I am not certain is up the Appomatox River—I shall take measures to make certain that fact—Neither of the iron clads to be furnished by the Navy have yet reported, nor do I beleive they will be here for sometime.—I have some two thousand of my Cavalry dismounted for want of horses, although the requisitions have been in, a long time and I have forwarded my Officers for the purpose of inspecting them. Genl Halleck telegraphs me that you will decide whether I shall be filled up or the other Armies and as you know my needs I am very well content to abide by your decision   I have no further news from Plymouth in addition to my telegram save the Report of Capt. Flusser the Naval Commander there, to Admiral Lee that he needed no reinforcements but was confident of success against the Rebels Ram"   Copy, DLC-Benjamin F. Butler.

On April 22, Butler wrote to USG. "I got your despatch this morning by the hand of Col. Dent of your staff with whom I have had a conference upon the matters which were entrusted to him by you. Upon the matter to which you seemed to place the most stress, whether I would move when ordered, I have to say, that I may not be as ready as I would because of the almost inevitable delays in assembling troops, especially from the front of the enemy and under the circumstances of the attack upon North Carolina and the delays in the concentration of the 10th Army Corps, which I suppose cannot be avoided, but when the word comes to go, I shall go if there are but ten men to go with me. You may reckon upon that as a certainty. That within twelve hours from the time indicated, I will be at the point agreed upon and will there bring everything under my control as fast as possible. I find from topographical surveys of the position, which I indicated to you that the ground is even more favorable for holding it, than I hoped. The only thing that can by possibility fail us, is the Navy. The Richmond iron clads, if they are able to check or force back the Navy will give us immensity of trouble, but even that I propose to provide for by sinking obstructions in the channel. General Smith is organizing his corps with activity and energy under the name of a camp of Instruction at Yorktown and Gloucester Point. My belief is from information I receive, that Lee intends to take the initiative and put himself across the Rapidan. Of course you could desire him to do no better thing, because if he is engaged with you on the northern side of the Rapidan, I shall not stop to entrench my position. The Ram has escaped the Navy at Plymouth and done us much harm, principally because Plymouth was fortified by General Foster upon the theory that the flanking fire of the gunboats would aid the works. The unfortunate death of Lieut. Commander Flusser commanding the Naval forces there, caused that force to retire without giving much battle, although still greatly superior in guns and strength. The gunboats retired into the sound. The Miami having a battery of four (4) nine (9) inch guns and a hundred pounder rifle, remained off the mouth of the river in the sound, the Whitehead was sent up for observation and the Ceres was sent to Roanoke Island with the body of Captain Flusser. This is the last reliable news we have from Plymouth. The Ram mounts but two guns 20 pdrs. Its speed scarcely over four miles to the hour. The Admiral can spare but a single boat to be sent down there which has gone. I have sent down my three Army gunboats which are very swift and strong with directions that if the Ram is in the sound where she can be got at, to run her down. The enemy have been repulsed twice at Plymouth in their attacks and at last accounts were attempting a siege. Wessels holds out as he has been ordered to at all hazards, having provisions for thirty days he will be doing the very best service by detaining a large number of troops there. I have already informed Admiral Lee of your plans and wishes and have advised with him as far as I care to be ready but I still think there is great doubt of our getting any iron clads down here in time. Pardon me for recurring to this again as I think it is the only danger of our movement. At the risk of violating a principle in the military correspondence that a communication should contain but one subject matter, I beg leave to refer to the question of Exchange of prisoners, while I shall implicitly follow your orders, and my judgement approves of them, yet in the matter of the sick and wounded, I feel a little embarrassment, as I had agreed with Ould to send him their sick in return for ours and I am fearful if I don't send theirs he may accuse me of breach of faith. I will not send him another well prisoner unless he agrees to the proposition which you suggested. Heretofore I have had authority to make special exchanges of man for man and officer for officer of equal rank in special cases. I understand that you desire this to be cut off and perhaps it may as well, because such cases are only brought to my attention through the intervention of influential friends and it causes heartburnings among the poor fellows who are left behind. All the officers that I have been expecting have reported except General Weitzel who is not up from New Orleans. As you are aware that my men are to be embarked before they can start, please give me forty-eight (48) hours if possible, or as much as possible notice of when the word go will certainly come. Then as I propose to start at night, I shall be at the points indicated at noon the following day. The moment we are substantially ready, I will notify you." Copy, USG 3.

1. S. Phillips Lee, born in Va. in 1812, and appointed midshipman, U.S. Navy, in 1825. After participating in the capture of New Orleans, he was appointed act. rear admiral as of Sept. 2, 1862, and placed in command of the North Atlantic Blockading Squadron. See *O.R.* (Navy), I, vii, 695–96.

2. Plymouth, N. C., at the mouth of the Roanoke River on Albemarle Sound, approximately fifty-five miles north of New Berne.

To Maj. Gen. William T. Sherman

Head Quarters, Armies in the Field,
Culpepper C. H. Va. Apl. 19th 1864

MAJ. GEN. W. T. SHERMAN,
COMD.G MIL. DIV. OF THE MISS.
GENERAL,

Since my letter to you I have seen no reason to change any portion of the general plan of Campaign if the enemy remain still and allow us to take the initiative. Rain has continued so uninteruptedly until the last day or two that it will be impossible to move however before the 27th even if no more should fall in the mean time. I think Saturday the 30th will probably be the day for our general move.

Col. Comstock, who will take this, can spend a day with you and fill up many little gaps of information not given in any of my letters.

What I now want more particularly to say is, that if the two main attacks, yours and the one from here, should promise great success the enemy may in a fit of desperation, abandon one part of their line of defence and throw their whole strength upon a single army, believing that a defeat with one victory to sustain them better than a defeat all along their line, and hoping too at the same time that the army meeting with no resistince will rest perfectly satisfied with their laurels having penetrated to a given point south thereby enabling them to throw their force first upon one and then on the other.

With the majority of Military commanders they might do this. But you have had too much experience in traveling light and subsisting upon the country to be caught by any such ruse. I hope my experience has not been thrown away. My directions then would be if the enemy in your front show signs of joining Lee follow ~~them~~ him up to the full extent of your ability. I will prevent the concentration of Lee upon your front if it is in the power of this Army to do it.

The Army of the Potomac looks well and so far as I can judge officers and men feel well.

Yours Truly
U. S. GRANT
Lt. Gen.

ALS, DLC-William T. Sherman. *O.R.*, I, xxxii, part 3, 409. On April 24, 1864, Maj. Gen. William T. Sherman, Nashville, wrote to USG. "I now have at the hands of Col Comstock of your staff the letter of April 19th, and am as far prepared to assume the offensive as possible. I only ask as much time as you think proper to enable me to get up McPhersons two Divisions from Cairo. Their furloughs all expire about this time and some of them should now be in motion for Clifton when they march to Decatur and join on to Dodge. McPherson is ordered to assemble the 15th Corps near Larkins and to get Dodge and Blair at Decatur at the earliest possible momt, and from those two points he will direct his forces on Lebanon, Summerville and Lafayette, where he will act against Johnston if he accept Battle at Dalton or move in the direction of Rome if he give up Dalton and fall behind the Ostanaula or Etowah. I see there is some Risk in dividing our forces but Thomas & Schofield will have forces enough to cover all the valley as far as Dalton, and should Johnston turn his whole force against McPherson, the latter will have his Bridge at Larkins and the Route to Chattanooga via Wills valley and the Chattanooga, and if Johnston attempts to leave Dalton Thomas will have force enough to push on through Dalton to Kingston which would checkmate him. My own opinion is Johnston will be compelled to hang to his Railroad, the only possible avenue of supply to his army estimated from 45 to 60000 men. At Lafayette all our armies will be together and if Johnston stand at Dalton we must attack him, in position. Thomas feels certain that he has no material increase of force, and that he has not sent away Hardee or any part of his army. Supplies are the great question. I have materially increased the number of cars daily—When I got here they ran from 65 to 80 per day—Yesterday the Report was 193, today 134 and my estimate is 145 per day will give us daily a days accumulation. McPherson is ordered to carry in wagons 20 days supply & rely on the Depot at Ringgold for the renewal of his bread Ration. Beeves are now being driven to the Front, and my Commissary Col Beckwith seems fully alive to the importance of the whole matter. Our weakest point will be from the direction of Decatur, and I will be forced to risk something from that quarter depending on the fact that the enemy has no force available with which to threaten our Communications from that direction   Col Comstock will explain much that I cannot commit to paper." ALS, DNA, RG 108, Letters Received. *O.R.*, I, xxxii, part 3, 465–66. The enclosed "Report of Effective Strength & Station" is *ibid.*, pp. 466–69.

To Abraham Lincoln

———

Culpepper, April 20th 1864.

A. LINCOLN PRESIDENT U. S.
WASHINGTON, D. C.

I would earnestly recommend the appointment of Wells W. Leggett, son of Brig. Gen. M. D. Leggett of Ohio, Cadet at large to the West Point Military Academy. He will be 17 years of age in June next. His education in the elementary branches has been thorough, as so far as I know, and can learn of him, his habits are correct. He has been with his father from the beginning of the war, though never enlisted, and has been in all the skirmishes and battles in which his father has participated. The appointment would be conferred upon a worthy young man and the son of one of our most gallant and meritorious officers.

U. S. GRANT.
Lieut. Gen.

Copies, DLC-USG, V, 45, 59; DNA, RG 108, Letters Sent. On Aug. 14, 1863, USG had endorsed a letter of Aug. 13 from Brig. Gen. Mortimer D. Leggett, Vicksburg, to Maj. Theodore S. Bowers requesting the appointment of his son to USMA. "Respectfully forwarded and recommended that Wells W. Leggett receive the appointment of Cadet to fill a vacancy from one of the Southern states." AES, *ibid.*, RG 94, Cadet Applications. On May 6, 1865, USG endorsed a letter of April 28 of Leggett repeating his request. "Respectfully forwarded to the Secretary of War, with the recommendation that Wells W. Leggett be appointed Cadet in the Military Academy at West Point." ES, *ibid.* An appointment followed.

To Maj. Gen. Henry W. Halleck

———

Culpepper, April 20th 1864

MAJ GEN. H. W. HALLECK
CH'F OF STAFF WASHINGTON, D. C.

I desire an order in substance as follows, for the purpose of facilitating the carrying of mails in that part of the insurectionary

States in the occupancy of our forces. Require all steamboats, no matter in what capacity employed, whether public or private, when called on to do so by duly authorized agents of the Post Office Department, or by Military commanders, to carry all mail matter including that from Cairo, free of charge in all navigable waters in the insurectionary States where navigation is protected by the Military or Naval forces of the United States. Such boats will furnish room with lock and key, where such mail matter may be securely kept, and will make all landings required for its proper delivery. In cases where mails are given in charge of Steamers, an officer of the boat will be required to deliver the same at all points on their route, to which it may be directed.

Special messengers in charge of such mails will not be charged for transportation, and will be furnished board at the cabin table at a price not exceeding 75 cents per day.

Commanders of boats, and the boats also, will be held responsible and liable for the faithful observance of this order.

U. S. GRANT,
Lieut. Gen.

Copies, DLC-USG, V, 45, 59; DNA, RG 108, Letters Sent. Dated April 21, 1864, *ibid.*, Register of Letters Received. On April 27, Maj. Gen. Henry W. Halleck wrote to USG. "I have omitted to say that on recieving your letter of the 21st in regard to an order for carrying Mail Matter I immediately submitted it to the Secty of War who replied that he knew of no law which authorized him to issue such an order for steamboats not in the employment of the government. It would appear very harsh to compel them to carry mails free of charge over routes where the Post office Dept can readily renew the Mail Service. The Secty therefore concluded to suspend any action till he could consult with you, or the matter was brought up by the Post Master Genl in the cabinet." ALS, *ibid.*, Letters Received.

On April 12, Postmaster Gen. Montgomery Blair had written to USG asking that U.S. Post Office agents "manage all postal affairs connected with the army in the insurectionary portions of the country occupied by Federal troops . . ." *The Collector*, LXXV, 1–2 (1962), r34. On April 25, Absalom H. Markland, U.S. Post Office Dept., wrote to USG. "Did you reply to the letter of Judge Blair Post Master Genl, or issue the order in reference to the Western steamers. Genl Sherman is in the best spirits of any man in America, I never saw him appear to so good an advantage. Please say to Rawlins that a package left Louisville to his address on Monday last, per Adams Express. Everybody in the West is looking to the Potomac. God bless and be with you all" ALS, USG 3.

To Edwin M. Stanton

Culpepper Va
4 30 P M Apl 21, 1864

HON EDWIN M STANTON
SECRETARY OF WAR,

As a rule I would oppose receiving men for so a short term, but if one hundred thousand (100,000) men can be raised in the time proposed by the time Governors of Ohio Indiana and Illinois & Iowa they might come at such a crisis as to be of vast importance I would not recommend accepting them in lieu of Quotas now due on any previous calls for three years troops. Otherwise I would.

U. S. GRANT
Lt Gen

Telegram received, DNA, RG 107, Telegrams Collected (Bound); copies, *ibid.*, Telegrams Received in Cipher; *ibid.*, RG 108, Letters Sent; DLC-USG, V, 45, 59. *O.R.*, III, iv, 239. On April 21, 1864, Secretary of War Edwin M. Stanton telegraphed to USG. "The Governors of Ohio, Indiana, Illinois, and Iowa are here, and propose to offer to the Government one hundred thousand men, to be ready for the field, clothed, armed, and fully equipped, within twenty days from date of notice, and to serve for the period of three months in fortifications, or wherever else their services may be required, and in any State. The Department would be glad to have your opinion as to whether this offer should be accepted or refused." LS (telegram sent), DNA, RG 107, Telegrams Collected (Bound). *O.R.*, III, iv, 238–39. For the proposal of the governors (including Wis.) and President Abraham Lincoln's favorable endorsement, see Lincoln, *Works*, VII, 312–13.

Also on April 21, Stanton telegraphed to USG. "General Canby reports that he will forward by Saturday or Sunday the 14th New York Heavy Artillery, the 4th U S Infantry 329—the 8th infantry 321 and the 14th Infantry 263—making in all twenty eight hundred and eighteen." ALS (telegram sent), DNA, RG 107, Telegrams Collected (Bound). On the same day, 8:30 P.M., USG telegraphed to Stanton. "With men of force like Canby to inspect, troops can be drawn out from all the northern Depts as he has done in N. York. I left directions to have all troops coming to Washington to be reported to Gen Burnside for assignment to brigades." Telegram received, *ibid.*; *ibid.*, RG 108, Letters Sent; DLC-USG, V, 45, 59.

To Maj. Gen. William T. Sherman

Culpepper Va
April 21st 1864 5. P M

MAJ GEN W. T. SHERMAN
NASHVILLE TENN.

Gen Washburne has gone to relieve Gen Hurlbut,[1] the latter to report from Cairo, where orders will reach him. I would not trust him with any further command   Prince has gone to West Kentucky. I would recommend leaving that portion of the 16th Corps in the field to the command of Dodge & Washburne to command from Cairo to Memphis   I would not spare Infantry intended for your main columns to go after Forrest, but if you can make the Cavalry force strong enough to cope with him it would be well. I have ordered Gen Rosecrans to send troops to Cairo intended to drive Forrest out of Tennessee and then go to Genl Steele. They have been so slow coming that they will be of no use for the first part of the purpose intended, order them where you think best.

U. S. GRANT
Lt Genl

Telegram received, DNA, RG 107, Telegrams Collected (Bound); copies, *ibid.*, RG 108, Letters Sent; *ibid.*, RG 393, Military Div. of the Miss., Letters Sent; DLC-USG, V, 45, 59, 94. *O.R.*, I, xxxii, part 3, 437–38.

On April 21, 1864, 7:40 P.M., Maj. Gen. William T. Sherman transmitted to USG a telegram of the same date from Maj. Gen. John M. Schofield. "Later reports confirm [w]hat I sent you on the 19th of the movements of Longstreets main force But indicate that Hayles Division about 2500 strong still remain near Bristol   The two divisions which have gone are Fields (formerly Hoods) and McLaws, They amount to about 10,000 men   Rail Road employees say these troops took the cars from Lynchburg for Orange Court House   They also report it as generally understood among the officers of Longstreets command that Lee is receiving reinforcements from Beauregard & Johnston   I go to Bulls Gap tomorrow" Telegram received, DNA, RG 107, Telegrams Collected (Bound); *ibid.*, RG 108, Letters Received; copy, DLC-John M. Schofield. *O.R.*, I, xxxii, part 3, 437.

1. On arriving at Memphis on April 23, Maj. Gen. Cadwallader C. Washburn wrote to Brig. Gen. John A. Rawlins at length, reporting his assessment of the command he had assumed. Copy, DNA, RG 393, Dept. of the Tenn., District of West Tenn., Letters Sent. *O.R.*, I, xxxii, part 3, 462–63.

To Julia Dent Grant

Culpepper C. H. Va Apl. 21st/64

DEAR JULIA,

I got through to-day without further difficulty than the locomotive getting off the track. I shall now stay with the Army unless called away for some reason not now seen. I hope you got as pleasantly, or more so, to New York. While there is no objection to your staying two or three weeks in New York I think you had better avail yourself of the first oppertunity of lady-company going to St Louis to get where the children are.

I can have nothing special to write about so soon after parting with you of course, and you must not expect long letters from me at any time. If I write often you must be satisfied. Kisses for yourself and Jesse. Write often to the children and me.

ULYS.

ALS, DLC-USG.
On April 19, 1864, 6:00 P.M., USG telegraphed to Maj. Gen. George G. Meade. "I will go to the City in the morning. You need not set the time for review before Saturday." Copies, *ibid.*, V, 45, 59; DNA, RG 108, Letters Sent. On April 21, 10:00 P.M. and 11:00 P.M., Meade telegraphed to USG. "Will it be agreable to you to inspect the 2d. Corps Tomorrow? I have only just learned of your return." ALS (telegram sent), *ibid.*, RG 107, Telegrams Collected (Unbound); copies, *ibid.*, RG 393, Army of the Potomac, Telegrams Sent; Meade Papers, PHi. "The 2d. Corps will be formed for inspection at 12. M tomorrow in the vicinity of Stevensburgh—I will meet you on the road from Culpeper to Stevensbugh in time to take you to the ground.—" ALS (telegram sent), DNA, RG 107, Telegrams Collected (Unbound); copy, Meade Papers, PHi.

To Maj. Gen. Henry W. Halleck

Culpepper Va
April 22nd 11. a m 1864

MAJ GEN H. W. HALLECK
CHIEF OF STAFF.

Admiral Lee's despatch to the Secretary of the Navy has been sent me for my information.[1] I do not know situation of affairs in

North Carolina well enough to give positive instructions, but it appears to me there is no us of our holding Washington[2] or Plymouth It would be better to have the force necessary to garrison those two places added to Gen Butlers column of attack, which if successful will give back to us not only the coast but probably most of the state. It may be that to evacuat now would compromise union men who have shown their unionism in full faith that the country would never be given up to Enemy. I wish you would inquire of Genl Butler if the two points above named can be abandoned as well as not and if so give the order

U S Grant
Lt. Gen'l

Telegram received, DNA, RG 107, Telegrams Collected (Bound); copies, *ibid.*, RG 108, Letters Sent; DLC-USG, V, 45, 59. *O.R.*, I, xxxiii, 947. On April 24, 1864, Maj. Gen. Henry W. Halleck wrote to USG. "I happened to be present at a discussion of a Board or commission of Army & Navy officers on the blockade or occupation of the coast of North Carolina about October 1861. It was then said the Navy could not blockade that coast so as to prevent contraband trade; on the contrary a very extensive trade was being carried by small vessels in Albemarle & Pamlico sounds which from the number & nature of the inlets & bays no blockade could possibly prevent. It was decided that, to prevent this, it was absolutely necessary to occupy & hold the mouths of Neuse, Tar & Roanoke rivers, & some point on the Chowan. Our gun boats which could enter the sounds being too small to resist those which the enemy could send down these rivers, the rebels would control, it was said, these waters unless Newberne, Washington, & Plymouth were fortified and garrisoned. Again, last year when it was very desirable to reinforce the Army of the Potomac, it was represented to me by Army & Navy officers that to abandon either of the above named places would be extremely injurious to our cause in North Carolina, fatal to union men who had accepted our protection, and destructive to our flotilla in the sounds. Admiral Lee has frequently represented that his fleet was barely sufficient for the blockade of Wilmington, and we know that even that is very imperfect. After a full consideration of the case, I could not decide to abandon these places, when the demand for troops elsewhere was even greater than at present. I, therefore, cannot advise it now, but will order it, if you so direct. It is useless for me to consult with Genl Butler on this subject, for his opinion would not change my judgement." ALS, DNA, RG 108, Letters Received. *O.R.*, I, xxxiii, 966.

On April 22, 2:30 P.M., Halleck telegraphed to USG. "I have ordered two new regiments of cavalry at the Depot to be equipped as infantry & turned over to Genl Burnside. After sending a thousand horses to Butler, it will not be possible to mount all of Burnside's cavalry in time. It has been suggested that a part of Genl Meade's cavalry now here could be equipped as Infantry & sent to the front. As the transports for artillery & horses can also carry men, would it not be well to send the fragments of the 10th corps to Fort Monroe without waiting further for Genl Gillmore's arrival?" ALS (telegram sent), DNA, RG 107, Telegrams Collected (Bound); telegram received, *ibid.*; *ibid.*, RG 108, Letters Received. *O.R.*, I, xxxiii, 940. On the same day, 7:30 P.M., USG telegraphed to Halleck. "It will be just as well to send Gen Gillmore's men to Fort Monroe as you suggest whenever vessels are going that can take them. I will answer you as soon as I can inquire of Gen Meade about sending his cavalry equipped as Infantry" Telegram received, DNA, RG 107, Telegrams Collected (Bound); copies, *ibid.*, RG 108, Letters Sent; DLC-USG, V, 45, 59. *O.R.*, I, xxxiii, 946.

Also on April 22, USG telegraphed to Maj. Gen. George G. Meade. "As it will be impossible to mount all your Cavalry in time for the Spring Campaign Gen Halleck suggests that part of that in Washington be equipped as Infantry and sent to the front. What shall I answer." ALS (telegram sent), DNA, RG 107, Telegrams Collected (Bound); copies, *ibid.*, RG 108, Letters Sent; DLC-USG, V, 45, 59. On the same day, Meade telegraphed to USG. "I have no objection to the dismounted Cavalry being equipped with Carbines & organized as infantry, indeed have so directed Gen Sheridan to use the large number of dismounted men now with the Cavaly Corps. To give them muskets & Convert them into infantry would I think produce discontent demoralize them & their numbers are not sufficient to make it a matter of great importance they can be used as dismounted Cavalry to protect trains & act as support to the mounted force." Telegram received, DNA, RG 108, Letters Received. On the same day, USG telegraphed to Halleck. "Genl Meade [would] prefer having [his] cavalry armed with carbines & sent [to] the front to be used [on] foot to support Cavalry guard trains &c. [He] has given orders to use all the dismounted cavalry in that way" Telegram received, *ibid.*, RG 107, Telegrams Collected (Bound); copies, *ibid.*, RG 108, Letters Sent; DLC-USG, V, 45, 59. *O.R.*, I, xxxiii, 940.

On April 23, 10:30 A.M., Meade telegraphed to USG. "On consultation with Genl. Sheridan, I am of the opinion any increase to our dismounted Cavalry (now three thousand) would not be desirable—I would therefore suggest the dismounted men of this army now in Washington being retained there till they can be mounted;—& not forwarded with carbines as I last night recommended." ALS (telegram sent), DNA, RG 107, Telegrams Collected (Unbound); telegram received, *ibid.*, RG 108, Letters Received. *O.R.*, I, xxxiii, 949. On the same day, 11:00 A.M., USG telegraphed to Halleck. "Genl Meade would prefer retaining his dismounted cavalry in Washington on duty to having them sent to the front before being mounted. He has now about three thousand (3000) dismounted cavalry on duty in the field" Telegram received, DNA, RG 107, Telegrams Collected (Bound); copies, *ibid.*, RG 108, Letters Sent; DLC-USG, V, 45, 59. *O.R.*, I, xxxiii, 949.

1. On April 21, 6:00 P.M., Act. Rear Admiral S. Phillips Lee, Fort Monroe, telegraphed to Secretary of the Navy Gideon Welles. "Official dispatches, principally military, from Roanoke Island and New Berne, state that at 3 a. m. on the 19th instant the rebels attacked Plymouth by land and with an iron-clad ram on the water. The Southfield was sunk and Miami disabled. Lieutenant-Commander Flusser was killed. The ram is below Plymouth and has possession of the river. Firing was heard at New Berne in the direction of Washington, N. C., and it was expected that Washington was attacked. An attack by land and water upon New Berne is apprehended. The ram I hope may not be able to pass Croatan Sound. Her draught is unknown. The Miami has much more power than any

wooden gun-boat that can be sent from here of suitable draught to enter the sound." *Ibid.*, pp. 938–39.

2. Washington, N. C., on the Pamlico River near the mouth of the Tar River, approximately twenty-five miles north of New Berne. On April 22, noon, USG telegraphed to Maj. Gen. Benjamin F. Butler. "Your despatch received.— You must not movements of the enemy interrupt carrying out your programme in the coming campaign. It would be better to evacuate Washington and Plymouth than to have your whole force neutralized defending them" Telegram received, DLC-Benjamin F. Butler; DNA, RG 107, Telegrams Collected (Bound); *ibid.*, Telegrams Collected (Unbound); copies, *ibid.*, RG 108, Letters Sent; DLC-USG, V, 45, 59. *O.R.*, I, xxxiii, 946. On April 21, 8:30 P.M., Butler telegraphed to Halleck, and a copy went to USG. *Ibid.*, pp. 278–79. See letter to Maj. Gen. Benjamin F. Butler, April 19, 1864.

To Maj. Gen. Henry W. Halleck

Culpepper Va
April 22nd 1864 12 m

MAJ GEN H. W. HALLECK
CHIEF OF STAFF.

You can see from Genl Brayman's despatch to me something of Gen'l Banks disaster[1]   I have been satisfied for the last nine months that to keep General Banks in command was to neutralize a large force and to support it most expensively. Although I do not insist on it I think the best interests of service demand that Genl Reynolds[2] should be placed in command at once and that he name his own successor to the command of New Orleans.

U. S. GRANT
Lt Genl

Telegram received, DNA, RG 107, Telegrams Collected (Bound); copies, *ibid.*, RG 108, Letters Sent; DLC-USG, V, 45, 59. *O.R.*, I, xxxiv, part 3, 252–53. On April 23, 1864, Maj. Gen. Henry W. Halleck endorsed this telegram. "This telegram shown to the President, by order of the Secretary of War. The President replied that he must delay acting on it for the present." *Ibid.*, p. 253. On April 26, 2:15 P.M., Halleck telegraphed to USG. "Your telegram of the 22nd asking for the removal of Genl Banks was submitted to the President who replied that he must await further information before he could act in the matter. Genl. Steele was at Camden on the 20th and was informed of Genl Banks disaster. An order to him to return to Little Rock would probably reach him in five or six days. One to Genl Banks would not reach him in less than two or three weeks. This would [cause] a conflict in your proposed instructions to these officers, if Banks [sh]ould have advanced on Shreveport, for Steele would then have returned to Little Rock. Would it not be better to send the instructions of your telegram to Banks & a copy of them to Genl [Ste]ele, with orders to communicate with Banks or his successor in command, & to carry out the spirit of your instructions as, in in his judgement, the condition of affairs at the time would require? I omitted to state that Admiral Porter says the failure of Banks expedition & [the] withdrawal of our forces from Red River will result in the loss [of] nearly all Louisianna, & a part [of Ar]kansas where there is already a pretty strong union sentiment. If Genl Banks is withdrawn from the field, Genl Franklin will be the senior officer left." ALS (telegram sent), DNA, RG 107, Telegrams Collected (Bound); telegram received, *ibid.*; *ibid.*, RG 108, Letters Received. *O.R.*, I, xxxiv, part 3, 293. See telegram to Maj. Gen. Henry W. Halleck, April 26, 1864.

1. On April 21, Maj. Gen. William T. Sherman transmitted to USG a telegram of the same date, 2:30 P.M., from Brig. Gen. John M. Corse, Cairo. " 'Banks was attacked by Kirby Smith near Mansfield La on the 8th instant and retreated to Grand Ecore á la "Bull Run" He refused to let Smith go for obvious reasons stating however that he had authority from both Genls Grant and Halleck to retain your troops longer' 'The admirals iron clads are caught by low water, some above the bar at Grand Ecore The rest above the falls and he not only refuses to consent to the removal of Smith but refused to allow him a transport to take him out of the river stating that to take Smith away would occasion the loss of his fleet—The utter destruction of Banks demoralized command and enable the enemy to crush Steele' 'I have communications from ~~Steele~~ Banks & Porter and will be with you as speedily as possible' " Telegram received, DNA, RG 107, Telegrams Collected (Bound); *ibid.*, RG 108, Letters Received. *O.R.*, I, xxxii, part 3, 437. Also on April 21, Brig. Gen. Mason Brayman, Cairo, telegraphed information from Corse to Secretary of War Edwin M. Stanton, sending a copy to USG. *Ibid.*, I, xxxiv, part 3, 244. On April 23, 8:30 P.M., USG telegraphed to Sherman. "Have you sent Steele information of Banks situation?" Copies, DLC-USG, V, 45, 59, 94; DNA, RG 108, Letters Sent; *ibid.*, RG 393, Military Div. of the Miss., Letters Sent. On the same day, midnight, Sherman telegraphed to USG. "Genl Corse says that Genl Banks and the fleet would again start for Shreveport to cover Steeles advance I will send a message round by Ft Smith but have no doubt ere this he knows everything By the 14th instant he must have been near Red River" Telegram received, *ibid.*, RG 107, Telegrams Collected (Bound); *ibid.*, RG 108, Letters Received. *O.R.*, I, xxxiv, part 3, 265. Also on April 23, 10:30 P.M., Lt. Col. Cyrus B. Comstock telegraphed to USG. "Arrived this evening Gen Sherman desires that I stay to morrow (Sunday) when he will go over his Returns, maps &c—Will leave on night train from here tomorrow All quiet. Gen Corse states that Genl Banks will be ready to move again on Shreveport about twenty eighth (28th) April" Telegram received, DNA, RG 107, Telegrams Collected (Bound).

2. Joseph J. Reynolds, an old friend of USG, promoted to maj. gen. as of Nov. 29, 1862, served as chief of staff, Army of the Cumberland, before being assigned to command the defenses of New Orleans in Jan., 1864.

To Maj. Gen. William T. Sherman

Culpeper Va
April 22d 1864

MAJ. GEN. SHERMAN
NASHVILLE

Despatch just recd from General Brayman satisfies me of what I always believed that forces sent to General Banks would be lost for our spring campaign. You will have to make your calculations now leaving A J. Smith out. Do not let this delay or embarras you Leave for him if he should return such directions as you deem most advisable   He may return in time to be thrown in some whre very opportunely

U. S. GRANT
[Lieut Genl]

Telegram received, DNA, RG 107, Telegrams Collected (Bound); copies (dated noon), *ibid.*, RG 108, Letters Sent; *ibid.*, RG 393, Military Div. of the Miss., Letters Sent; DLC-USG, V, 45, 59, 94. Printed as sent at noon in *O.R.*, I, xxxii, part 3, 443. On April 22, 1864, Maj. Gen. William T. Sherman telegraphed to USG. "I will calculate to leave Smiths command out   My chief trouble will be supplies but I am hurrying forward beef cattle"   Telegram received, DNA, RG 108, Letters Received. *O.R.*, I, xxxii, part 3, 443.

Also on April 22, Sherman forwarded to USG a telegram of the same day from Maj. Gen. George H. Thomas, Chattanooga, reporting C.S.A. movements in Ga. Telegram received, DNA, RG 108, Letters Received. *O.R.*, I, xxxii, part 3, 444.

To Maj. Gen. Ambrose E. Burnside

Head Quarters Armies in the Field,
Culpepper C. H. Va. Apl. 23d 1864

MAJ. GEN. A. E. BURNSIDE,
COMD.G 9TH A. C.
GENERAL;

March your troops with as little delay as possible taking position from Bull Run to the Rappahannock so as to perfectly guard the road between the two streams and releive the troops now there so as to enable them to come to the front and join the Corps to which they have been assigned. Get forward to the troops as rapidly as possible all their transportation and supplies to the 2d of May inclusive. When this is done send forward to Brandy Station a competant Asst. Q. M. & C. S. to take charge of stores. Forward also troops of your own, a Brigade if you think proper, to guard your stores at that place. Have brought up there fifteen days rations and ten days forage, of grain alone, to be held for use after you march from there. All supplies that you use whilst on the railroad is to be independent of these supplies.

Of the fifteen days supplies to be carried with you but four will be of Pork or bacon. The remainder will be beef on the hoof. Your men must carry seven days rations, without meat, in haversacks and Knapsacks. Baggage must be reduced to nothing in wagons or as near that standard as possible, all the transportation being reserved as far as possible for provisions and Ordnance stores.

One hundred & fifty rounds of Infantry Ammunition per man will be the amount required to be carried on the person and in wagons together. If it can be avoided no ammunition should be carried on the persons except what can be put in the cartridge boxes.

For the sake of uniformity you should adopt about the same orders go[v]erning transportation that Gen. Meade has. I have no copy of his order on the subject ~~to send you but you will be able to get one in time~~ but will have one sent to you.

Further details and instructions will be furnished you after your troops are in position.

> Very respectfully
> your obt. svt.
> U. S. Grant
> Lt. Gen.

ALS, DNA, RG 107, Telegrams Collected (Unbound). *O.R.*, I, xxxiii, 955.

On April 23, 1864, 4:00 p.m., Maj. Gen. Ambrose E. Burnside telegraphed to USG. "Troops all started from Annapolis   Second Ohio Cavalry not yet mounted   Is it intended that all the horses now here shall go to Genl Butler before the second is mounted   It has been waiting a long time and I have no cavalry except the third New Jersey"   ALS (telegram sent), DNA, RG 107, Telegrams Collected (Unbound); telegram received, *ibid.*, RG 108, Letters Received. On the same day, USG telegraphed to Burnside. "Gen Butler is to have the first thousand horses—His Cavalry force is small and this only half the number required by him   The Cavalry Bureau ought to supply these and supply you also in a short time"   Telegram received, *ibid.*, RG 94, Generals' Papers and Books, Burnside; copies, *ibid.*, RG 108, Letters Sent; DLC-USG, V, 45, 59. On April 24, 4:30 P.M., USG telegraphed to Maj. Gen. Henry W. Halleck. "Gen Meade will turn over to Gen Burnside the 13th Penna now on railroad between Bull Run and Rappahannock"   Telegram received, DNA, RG 107, Telegrams Collected (Bound); copies, *ibid.*, RG 94, Generals' Papers and Books, Burnside; *ibid.*, RG 108, Letters Sent; DLC-USG, V, 45, 59. On the same day, 11:30 P.M., Halleck telegraphed to USG. "Before recieving your d[i]spatch I [h]ad telegraphed to Genl Butler to use his own judgement as to the manner of giving notice to the French. The 22d New York cavalry now at the depot is undisiplined & unfit for the field. I have ordered them armed as Infantry & their horses to be given to the 2d Ohio (veteran) and to detachments of Army of the Potomac. I think at least a regt of the latter should be given to Genl Burnside as he will be deficient in cavalry on going to the field. The northern states are nearly exhausted of cavalry horses, and purchases will be small till after the crops are put in. When the mares have folded they will be used for summer farm work & more horses can be procured." ALS (telegram sent), DNA, RG 107, Telegrams Collected (Bound); telegram received, *ibid.* *O.R.*, I, xxxiii, 966–67.

On April 25, 10:30 P.M., Burnside telegraphed to USG. "The troops from Annapolis have arrived at Alexandria—Shall I organize these with the regiments that have gone to Alexandria by rail and arrange all the transportation before leaving Alexandria? It will take 24 hours to complete the organization or shall I move them on at once? I think time will be saved by completing the organization tomorrow   Please answer tonight—The Regiments from Washington are now on the way to Alexandria also others from New York"   Telegram received, DNA, RG 107, Telegrams Collected (Unbound); *ibid.*, RG 108, Letters Received. On the same day, USG telegraphed to Burnside. "You can remain a day at Alexandria or come immediately on as you deem best. I sent directions to you today by one of my Staff—"   Telegram received, *ibid.*, RG 94, Generals' Papers and Books, Burnside; *ibid.*, RG 107, Telegrams Collected (Bound); copies, *ibid.*, RG 108, Letters Sent; DLC-USG, V, 45, 59.

On April 27, 2:00 P.M., Burnside, Alexandria, telegraphed to USG. "The columns in motion will reach Fairfax tonight   Several regiments not reported; will leave orders for them to follow up. We have the requisite ammunition and supplies with the column"   Telegram received, DNA, RG 108, Letters Received.

On April 27, 8:30 A.M., USG telegraphed to Maj. Gen. George G. Meade. "Burnsides Command leaves Alexandria this morning to take position between Bull Run and Rappahannock   You can give orders to your troops to move to the front as soon as relieved and guards posted"   Telegram received, *ibid.*, RG 94, War Records Office, Army of the Potomac; copies, *ibid.*, RG 108, Letters Sent; DLC-USG, V, 45, 59; (2) Meade Papers, PHi. *O.R.*, I, xxxiii, 992. On the same day, Meade telegraphed to USG. "The following telegram just received from

Colonel McCandless Commanding Pa Reserves   The orders in reference to the relieving of the 5th Corps on the R. R. had been given when your telegram of this A. M. was received"   Copies, DNA, RG 393, Army of the Potomac, Telegrams Sent; Meade Papers, PHi.

To Maj. Gen. Benjamin F. Butler

From Culpepper April 23d 1864 *5 P. M.*
To MAJ GEN'L B F BUTLER COM'D'G
FT. MONROE VA

General Halleck telegraphs me that one iron clad reached Ft. Monroe this morning. One on way from Boston. One leaves New York today. One Philadelphia Monday. Will probably have six (6) there in course of a week.

Some of the prisoners paroled from Ft. Monroe are known to be in our front now.

I do not want to place you in a position to show bad faith in our dealings with the Rebels as they have done with us, but before sending another man, who by any possibility can do duty in the next three (3) months, I would have an explanation on what ground they have placed men on duty, released by you on parole.—

U. S. GRANT
Lieut. Gen'l

Copies, DLC-Benjamin F. Butler; DLC-USG, V, 45, 59; DNA, RG 108, Letters Sent; (incomplete) USG 3. *O.R.*, I, xxxiii, 957. On April 22, 1864, 11:00 P.M., USG telegraphed to Maj. Gen. Henry W. Halleck. "Genl Butler reports that no Iron clads have yet gone to Fort Monroe. Will you please have inquiries made of the Secretary of the Navy if they are yet ready and will go soon"   Telegram received, DNA, RG 107, Telegrams Collected (Bound); copies, *ibid.*, RG 108, Letters Sent; DLC-USG, V, 45, 59. *O.R.*, I, xxxiii, 946. On April 23, 11:30 A.M., Halleck telegraphed to USG. "Capt Fox says one iron-clad reached Fort Monroe this morning, one on the way from Boston, one leaves New York to day,—one Philadelphia monday—will probably have six there in course of a week. Says rebel ram in Albemarle Sound has only four small guns & that panic is unfounded. Near two thousand effective at Plymouth & same at Little Washington by last returns. To withdraw garrisons now would be difficult & sacrifice heavy artillery, and union people. Said to have thirty days supplies. Will write you the reasons of joint board of Army & Navy officers for occupying these places. To save time, have Genl Butler telegraph direct to you. Copies will always be taken off the wires here. The troops coming from New York have been assigned to Genl Burnside." ALS (telegram sent), DNA, RG 107, Telegrams Collected (Bound); telegram received, *ibid*. *O.R.*, I, xxxiii, 956.

On April 27, Maj. Gen. Benjamin F. Butler telegraphed to USG. "Col Rowley has arrived. but one iron clad here yet. three more to come. will not be here before Sunday. General Gilmore not before Saturday if then. Six regiments of his troops behind two of which are near Washington" DfS (telegram sent), DLC-Benjamin F. Butler; DNA, RG 107, Telegrams Collected (Unbound); telegram received, *ibid*., Telegrams Collected (Bound). *O.R.*, I, xxxiii, 1000.

To Maj. Gen. Benjamin F. Butler

By Telegraph from Culpepper C. H. *1.30 P. M.*
Dated April 24th *1864.*

To Maj Gen'l B F Butler Com'd'g

A Richmond paper of the 22nd brought in by a deserter, reports Capture of Plymouth with one General, 2500 prisoners, and all the stores.[1] I do not think it advisable to attempt the re-capture if this is true.

What are your preparations for for holding Washington N. C.? It will be much better to hold Newberne strongly, than to have little posts picked up in detail

U. S. Grant
Lieut General

Telegram received, DLC-Benjamin F. Butler; DNA, RG 107, Telegrams Collected (Bound); copies, *ibid*., RG 108, Letters Sent; DLC-USG, V, 45, 59. *O.R.*, I, xxxiii, 967. On April 24, 1864, 3:00 P.M., Act. Rear Admiral S. Phillips Lee, U.S.S. *Minnesota*, telegraphed to Secretary of the Navy Gideon Welles the news of the capture of Plymouth, N. C., and a copy was sent to USG. Telegram received, DNA, RG 108, Letters Received. *O.R.*, I, xxxiii, 967. See *ibid*., pp. 278–305.

On April 25, 11:30 P.M., USG telegraphed to Maj. Gen. Henry W. Halleck. "I want Genl Butler to hold Newbern at all hazards but would prefer him to remove every thing from Washington to having our little force in North Carolina picked up in detail, or to being forced to abandon our offensive operations to defend them" Telegram received, DNA, RG 107, Telegrams Collected (Bound); copies, *ibid*., RG 108, Letters Sent; DLC-USG, V, 45, 59. *O.R.*, I, xxxiii, 979. See *ibid*., p. 990.

On April 27, 11:00 A.M., Maj. Gen. Benjamin F. Butler telegraphed to USG. "Despatches from Newbern All quiet at Newbern & Little Washington. Deserter captured reports Martins Brigade of which he was a member and other troops being forwarded via Weldon ~~for that~~ to Richmond & railroad siezed for that purpous. Do not apprehend further demonstration in North Carolina"   DfS (telegram sent), DLC-Benjamin F. Butler; DNA, RG 107, Telegrams Collected (Unbound); telegram received, *ibid.*, Telegrams Collected (Bound). *O.R.*, I, xxxiii, 1000.

On July 12, Butler wrote to USG. "I have the honor to forward the sworn testimony of Saml. Johnson as to the occurrences at Plymouth after its capture— The man is intelligent, was examined by me and duly cautioned as to the necessity of telling the exact truth, and this, is his reiterated statement, in which I have confidence as to its main features and substantial accuracy—It seems very clear to me that something should be done in retaliation for this outrage—Many prisoners have been taken from the 8th N. C. Regt.—The 6th, is still at Plymouth— Were I commanding independently in the field I should take this matter into my own hands, but now deem it my duty to submit it to the better and cooler judgment of the Lieut Gen Com'dg—For myself, at the present moment, I am far too much moved by the detail of these occurrences, to act in the matter—" LS, DNA, RG 108, Letters Received. *O.R.*, II, vii, 459. Butler enclosed a statement of Sgt. Samuel Johnson, 2nd U.S. Colored Cav., who had recently entered U.S. lines. At the time of the capture of Plymouth, he had dressed himself in civilian clothes; he reported that all black troops found in uniform had been killed. DS, DNA, RG 108, Letters Received. *O.R.*, II, vii, 459–60. See *ibid.*, p. 468.

1. On April 24, 11:00 A.M., Maj. Gen. George G. Meade telegraphed to USG. "A Richmond paper of the 22d instant brought in by a deserter reports the capture of Plymouth N. C. with twenty five hundred prisoners one Brig General & a no. of pieces of artillery   Paper sent by orderly"   Telegram received, DNA, RG 108, Letters Received.

To Maj. Gen. Quincy A. Gillmore

Head Quarters, Armies in the Field,
Culpepper C. H. Va. Apl. 24th 1864

MAJ. GEN Q. A. GILLMORE,
COMD.G DEPT. OF THE SOUTH,
GENERAL,

Herewith I send you copy of letter from Adml. Dahlgren[1] to the Sec. of the Navy, and one from the latter to Military Authorities recommending certain movements near Charleston S. C. The letters explain themselves. Please read them and send me your views on the proposed movements.

Not knowing the situation of affairs about Charleston, and particularly since the withdrawel of so many of your forces, I can give no specific directions. I would state however that it ~~would~~ will be of great advantage to us if the force at Charleston ~~could~~ can be safely employed in keeping up a demonstration that will force the enemy to keep large numbers there to watch their movements.

> I am Gen. very respectfully
> your obt. svt.
> U. S. GRANT
> Lt. Gen.

ALS, DNA, RG 94, War Records Office, 10th Army Corps. *O.R.*, I, xxxv, part 2, 67. The enclosures, endorsed by Maj. Gen. Henry W. Halleck on April 22, 1864, still attached to the original letter, are *ibid.*, pp. 67–68. On April 24, Lt. Col. Theodore S. Bowers issued Special Orders No. 16. "Lieut Colonel W. R. Rowley, Military Secretary will proceed immediately to Fortress Monroe, as bearer of dispatches from the Lieut General commanding, to Major General Q. A. Gillmore, commanding Department of the South. Upon the execution of this order, he will rejoin these Headquarters." Copies, DLC-USG, V, 57, 62. On April 23, 5:00 P.M., USG telegraphed to Halleck. "Confidential letters from Admiral Dahlgren and Secy of the Navy just received. With the reduced state of the command at Charleston I do not know what can be done in the direction recommended by the Admiral but I will send the letters by special messenger to Genl Gilmore at Fort Monroe and ascertain from him the exact situation and give directions accordingly" Telegram received, DNA, RG 107, Telegrams Collected (Bound); copies, *ibid.*, RG 108, Letters Sent; DLC-USG, V, 45, 59. *O.R.*, I, xxxv, part 2, 64. On April 24, Halleck wrote to USG. "confidential . . . If the Iron-clads and the large number of troops off Charleston for the last year could not take & hold Sullivan's Island, how can they expect to do it with force diminished more than one half? Moreover, if taken it would simply result in the loss from active service of five thousand troops to garrison it, without any influence upon the coming campaign. It will require sixty thousand men three months to take Charleston. The capture of Sullivan's Island would not have much influence upon a siege of that place, as it can be conducted with greater advantage from other points. I am satisfied that Admiral Dahlgren's letter was intended simply as an excuse in advance for the inability of the Iron clads to accomplish anything against Charleston." ALS, DNA, RG 108, Letters Received. *O.R.*, I, xxxv, part 2, 68. On May 7, Maj. Gen. Quincy A. Gillmore drafted a reply to USG on the letter received. "I have to acknowledge the receipt from the hands of Maj. Gen. Butler of your communication ~~of Apr~~ the 24th Ult. transmitting copies of two ~~com~~ letters one from Rear Admiral J. A. Dahlgren to the Hon Secretary of the Navy— another enclosing the latter from the Secr of the Navy to the War Department recommending combined operations in Charleston Harber, having in view the Capture of Sullivans Island, by first occupying Long Island   Long Island can be taken ~~possession of~~ at any time without great difficulty, ~~without naval assistance~~ and without our incurring much loss; ~~but it would not place us~~ but its possession by us would not only not forward the object in view, but would diminish the ~~ch~~ chances of success.—A lodgement upon Sullivans Island must be made by a surprise. ~~party with boats~~   No other method promises sucess & the prior occupation of Long Island would at once ~~develop~~ publish our plans to the enemy, & enable them to the north end of ~~long Island~~ Sullivans Island is strongly fortified ~~efforts~~, & the wall there must be gained by open assaults from small boats & such a assault ~~which~~ can as well be made from Morris Id as from Long Island—" ADf, DNA, RG 94, War Records Office, 10th Army Corps. A letter of this date from Gillmore is registered in DLC-USG, V, 48.

1. John A. Dahlgren, born in Philadelphia in 1809, appointed act. midshipman in 1826, invented the Dahlgren naval gun in 1851. In April, 1861, he became commander of the Washington Naval Yard, and chief of the Bureau of Ordnance in July, 1862. He was appointed rear admiral as of Feb. 7, 1863, and assigned to command of the South Atlantic Blockading Squadron in July.

To Louisa Boggs

Culpepper C. H. Va. Apl. 24th/64

Dear Cousin,

Julia has gone to New York City and will probably remain a couple of weeks before going to St. Louis. In the meantime I shall not hear from the children unless they write to me direct. I wish you would urge them all to join in letters to me every week. I feel anxious to hear from them always and then it improves them quite as much to write letters as to study their lessons. How do Buck and Nellie progress in their German? I hope they will place me in their debt, the fine gold watches I promised when they learned to speak the language.

Jess has cut his eye teeth mingling with Washington society. He has become very independent and a great favorite with both ladies and gentlemen at Willard's hotel. He is still very anxious to get back to St. Louis to go to school.

Kiss all the children for me, and the young ladies too if you like. I should like to see you all very much but I have a big contract on hand to complete before I can expect to indulge in any such pleasure.

Please write to me yourself also.

Yours Truly
U. S. Grant

Partial facsimile and transcript, *Topeka State Journal*, April 22, 1905.

To Julia Dent Grant

Culpepper April 24th/64

DEAR JULIA,

I see by the papers you are having a good time in New York. Hope you will enjoy it. But don't forget Jess and loose him in the streets in all the excitement, New York is a big place and you might not find him.—A telegraph dispatch announces that the sword has been voted to me! I am rather sorry for it, or rather regret that my name has been mixed up in such a contest.[1] I could not help it however and therefore have nothing to blame myself for in the matter.

The weather has been very fine here for a few days and dried the roads up so as to make them quite passable. It has commenced raining again however, and is now raining so hard, that it will take a week to bring them back to what they were this afternoon.

Remember me kindly to Col. and Mrs. Hillyer and the children. Kisses for yourself and ~~children~~. Jess. I rather expected a letter from you this evening, but none came. I will write to the children to-morrow evening. Don't forget to send me any letters you receive from them. I know they must be anxious to see you back.

ULYS.

ALS, DLC-USG.

1. At the Sanitary Fair in New York City, each donor of one dollar was entitled to cast one vote for either USG or Maj. Gen. George B. McClellan as the recipient of an ornate sword. Julia Dent Grant voted for McClellan. *New York Herald*, April 23, 1864; John Y. Simon, ed., *The Personal Memoirs of Julia Dent Grant* (New York, 1975), pp. 130–31, 144.

To Maj. Gen. Henry W. Halleck

Culpepper C. H. Va
Apr. 25th 1864 8 P. M

Maj Gen H W. Halleck
Chief. of Staff.

A. J. Smith will have to stay with Gen Banks until the gunboats are out of their difficulty   Gen Banks ought to be ordered to New Orleans and have all further execution on Red River in other hands, I have just received two private letters, one from New Orleans and one anonymous from the 13th Corps[1] giving deplorable accounts of Gen Banks mismanagement   His own report and these letters clearly show all his disasters to be attributable to his incompetency. Send troops for Gen Sherman where he wants them

U. S. Grant Maj Genl

Telegram received, DNA, RG 107, Telegrams Collected (Bound); copies, *ibid.*, RG 108, Letters Sent; DLC-USG, V, 45, 59. *O.R.*, I, xxxiv, part 3, 279. On April 25, 1864, 3:00 p.m., Maj. Gen. Henry W. Halleck telegraphed to USG. "Genl Sherman requests that all u[n]assigned troops in Illinois and the Northwest rendezvous at Cairo. Your orders sent to those states were to rendezvous at Louisville. Shall I change the order as Sherman requests? Despatches just recieved from Genls Butler & Peck state that the garrison at Plymouth, after a small loss, surrendered to the Rebels on Wednesday the 20th   No particulars. [Genl] Butler says nothing about what he intends to do. [I] have just seen Admiral Porter's despatch, dated Grand Ecore, April 14th to the Navy Dept. He says whatever may be said, the Army there has met with a great defeat and is much demoralized. He speaks in strong terms of Banks' mismanagement & of the good conduct of A. J. Smith & his corps. He fears that if Smith is withdrawn Banks will retreat still further, & Steele's command & the gun-boats above the rapids (which, from fall of water cannot be withdrawn) will be greatly periled if not lost. He says Bank's army [w]as ten days behind the appointed time. He protests against the withdrawal [of] Smith at this time, as it would be fatal to us. The Navy Dept asks to know this, in order to telegraph instructions to Cairo for Admiral Porter. What shall I reply?" ALS (telegram sent), DNA, RG 107, Telegrams Collected (Bound); telegram received, *ibid.*; *ibid.*, RG 108, Letters Received. *O.R.*, I, xxxii, part 3, 489; (incomplete) *ibid.*, I, xxxiii, 979; *ibid.*, I, xxxiv, part 3, 278.

1. On April 10, "An old Iowa vetron," Alexandria, La., wrote to USG. "Permit an old, Iowa Soldier one that has fought many a hard battle under you & would be willing to fight many more to save this Goverment. But I must enter my solem protest against Gen Banks for the maner in which he has treated

Western troops in this Dep from their first enterence here after the fall of Vicksburgh.—never have we been permitted to meet the enemy in any thing like a fair
fight   we must fight them By detail one Bergade at a time   in the last fight on
Red River our Lees Cavelry was cut to peceis   Gen *Banks* sends one Bergade
forward to reinforce them   they to are repulsed   then comes another order for
another Bergade & they meet the same fate & then a Division all of the 13 army
Core and they hold the Enemy in check for 4 hours, & they to are compelled to
fall Back in the cover of Night to where the 19 Army Core are reclineing at Ease
and then the shatered Rank of the 13th must form in front of the 19th and meet
the advanceing foe and Just in time to gain the credit of the fight the 19 is called
into action where if the two fire of the 13 had been permited to have engaged the
Enemy at one time though inferior in No the result must have been Difrent. and
now after three most shameful Blunders of *Gen Banks* to wit sabane Pass, Carion
Crow Buyou & Pleasant Hill are we yet to be Compelled to serve under such a
man one in whom we have all Lost confidence (if ever there was any) & one
whom two thirds of the 13th army Core would *shoot* down sooner than the Reb
Gen Taylor or Muton for the sake of our Cause & the sake of the repotation that
we have won for our selves while under you do not Let us be thus Murdered &
Robed of our Just rights   we know no mutany or Rebelion or there would be
such a clash of arms as the world never knew   give us Hooker or Gives Rosen-
cranze or give us any Body in Preferance to *Gen Banks*. Give us the Gallant Warren of Iowa or or McClenard of your native state but do for the Love that we
know you Bare ~~to~~ your old soldiers of Vicksburgh fame give us sombody with
capasity to comand a Reg at Least. O we will ever Pray & fight"   AL, USG 3.
On April 23, Maj. Gen. William T. Sherman sent USG a copy of a letter of
April 14 from Rear Admiral David D. Porter to Sherman strongly critical of the
Red River campaign. Copy, DNA, RG 108, Letters Received. *O.R.*, I, xxxiv, part
3, 153–54.
        On May 2, "a *Private*" of the 13th Army Corps, Alexandria, La., wrote at
length to USG criticizing Maj. Gen. Nathaniel P. Banks. AL, DNA, RG 108,
Letters Received.

To Maj. Gen. Henry W. Halleck

Hd Qrs Culpeper
8 30 P M Apl 25. 1864

MAJ. GEN HALLECK,
CHF OF STAFF,

        I would send orders to Gen Steele to return to Little Rock—
to Gen Banks to return himself immediately to New Orleans and
make preparations to carry out his previous instructions the moment his troops returned; to place the senior officer under himself
in command of the troops in the field, with instructions to see the

gunboats safely out of Red River as soon as possible & then return all the troops rapidly, to where they belong—If before receiving these instructions he has taken Shreveport, then to leave Genl. Steele & the Navy in charge of the river giving Gen Steele if necessary all of Smith's troops—

U. S. GRANT
Lt. Genl

Telegram received, DNA, RG 107, Telegrams Collected (Bound); copies, *ibid.*, RG 108, Letters Sent; DLC-USG, V, 45, 59. *O.R.*, I, xxxiv, part 3, 279.

To Maj. Gen. William T. Sherman

Culpepper Va. April 25th 1864

MAJ. GEN. SHERMAN

The following dispatch has been received from Cairo. Cairo, Apl. 23rd   To. COL ANSON STAGER Washington. Capt Bush Comdg at Smithland, Ky reports rebels commenced crossing Tennessee at Birmingham and above at 8. P. M. yesterday and were still crossing when his informant left Chandits early this morning. wire is cut between Smithland and Fort Donelson. signed. MASON Have you received the information and taken measures to attend to them

U. S. GRANT. Lieut Gen.

Telegram received, DNA, RG 107, Telegrams Collected (Bound); copies, *ibid.*, RG 108, Letters Sent; *ibid.*, RG 393, Military Div. of the Miss., Letters Sent; DLC-USG, V, 45, 59, 94. *O.R.*, I, xxxii, part 3, 488. On April 25, 1864, 2:00 P.M., Maj. Gen. Henry W. Halleck telegraphed to USG. "Telegraph Manager at Cairo reports rebels crossing Tennessee river at Birmingham & above." ALS (telegram sent), DNA, RG 107, Telegrams Collected (Bound); telegram received, *ibid.*; *ibid.*, RG 108, Letters Received. On April 25, Maj. Gen. William T. Sherman twice telegraphed to USG. "No such information is received here as is reported by Col Anson Stager   Boats are constantly passing up & down both the Tennessee & Cumberland" "I have no account of any force crossing the Tennessee   The officer Comdg at Ft Donelson reports about one hundred men Committing depredations between the Cumberland & Tenn, boats are Constantly ascending & descending & Tenn is Closely watched—" Telegrams received, *ibid*. The second is in *O.R.*, I, xxxii, part 3, 488.

Also on April 25, 11:30 A.M., USG telegraphed to Sherman. "Will your Veterans be back to enable you to start on the second of May? I do not want to delay later." Telegram received, DLC-William T. Sherman; DNA, RG 107, Telegrams Collected (Bound); copies, *ibid.*, RG 108, Letters Sent; DLC-USG, V, 45, 59. *O.R.*, I, xxxii, part 3, 488. On the same day, 3:30 P.M., Sherman telegraphed to USG. "The veteran Division cannot be up by May 2d but I am willing to move with what I have   Col Comstock left for you last night & has facts and figures—As soon as you see them make your orders   I am now getting all in hand ready but every day but every day adds to my animals and men   If you can, give me till may fifth" Telegram received, DNA, RG 107, Telegrams Collected (Bound); *ibid.*, RG 108, Letters Received. *O.R.*, I, xxxii, part 3, 489.

Also on April 25, USG telegraphed to "Telegraph Operator Washington D. C" "Is the telegraph line working to Nashville"   Copy, DNA, RG 94, War Records Office, Dept. of the Cumberland.

On April 27, Sherman telegraphed to USG. "In view of the fact that I will have to take the initiative with twenty thousand less men in McPhersons army than I had estimated I intend to order all McPhersons displacable force twenty thousand and Garrards cavalry five thousand to Chattanooga to start from a common centre   I go forward tomorrow" Telegram received, *ibid.*, RG 108, Letters Received. *O.R.*, I, xxxii, part 3, 510.

On April 28, 11:00 P.M., USG telegraphed to Sherman. "Get your forces up so as to move by the fifth (5th) [of] May—" Telegram received, DNA, RG 107, Telegrams Collected (Bound); copies, *ibid.*, RG 108, Letters Sent; *ibid.*, RG 393, Military Div. of the Miss., Telegrams Received; DLC-USG, V, 45, 59. *O.R.*, I, xxxii, part 3, 521. On April 28, 11:00 A.M., Sherman had telegraphed to Halleck that he would be ready to move by May 5, and this telegram had been forwarded to USG. Telegram received, DNA, RG 107, Telegrams Collected (Bound); *ibid.*, RG 108, Letters Received. *O.R.*, I, xxxii, part 3, 521. On April 29, 11:00 A.M., Sherman telegraphed to USG. "I am here—Gen Thomas is already in position—Genl Schofield will be by May Second and McPherson is Marching for Lafayette via this place,   All my effective cavalry is breaking for Dalton and I will be all ready by May fifth (5.th)—I will write you fully to-night" Telegram received, DNA, RG 107, Telegrams Collected (Bound); *ibid.*, RG 108, Letters Received; copies, *ibid.*, RG 393, Military Div. of the Miss., Letters Sent; *ibid.*, Telegrams Sent. *O.R.*, I, xxxii, part 3, 531. On April 30, 6:30 P.M., Sherman telegraphed to USG. "I have news from Atlanta 24th & Dalton 27th   Some of Polks troops have arrived—By the fifth all of Gen Thomas and Gen Schofields troops will be within one march of Dalton and I doubt not Genl McPherson will be on time—All things work as smoothly as I could expect—Gen Rosecrans holds some of the Memphis dismounted Cavalry to guard against some secret plot in St Louis. I think the city Police and Militia could attend to all such machinations—and leave us all our troops at this critical time" Telegram received, DNA, RG 107, Telegrams Collected (Bound); *ibid.*, RG 108, Letters Received; copies, *ibid.*, RG 107, Telegrams Received in Cipher; *ibid.*, RG 393, Military Div. of the Miss., Letters Sent; *ibid.*, Telegrams Sent. *O.R.*, I, xxxii, part 3, 541.

On May 1, 8:00 P.M., Sherman telegraphed to USG. "Genl Schofield is now at Charleston and will move to Cleveland—Thomas will concentrate at Ringgold, and McPhersons troops are all in motion towards Chattanooga, and by the fifth (5th) I will group them at Rossville and Gordons Mills.—The first move will be

Thomas, Tunnel Hill, Schofield Catoosa Springs and McPherson, Villanow— Next move will be battle—I have Atlanta dates of April twenty ninth (29th)— Enemy has a general idea of our plans and are massing about Richmond and Dalton—Nothing new in the papers except Genl Polk reports officially under date Demapolis April twenty third (23d) that Wirt Adams had captured and burned a gunboat, at Yazoo City, taking on shore eight (8) twenty four (24) pounder guns—Weather fine—roads very good—I leave Gen Jno. E. Smith's Division at Huntsville and Decatur till Blair gets there with the Seventeenth (17th) Corps, when I will bring forward more men according to the issue of our first battle—A good deal of the enemy's Cavalry is hanging about North Alabama and Mc-Pherson is uneasy about Decatur but we must risk something—I have removed the bridge at Larkinsville, and will try and get one of the new gunboats to patrol the river from Bridgeport down—Thomas is here but we will all go out on the fifth (5th)—I will expect further notice from you, but agree to draw the enemy's fire within twenty four hours of May Fifth (5th)" Telegram received, DNA, RG 107, Telegrams Collected (Bound); *ibid.*, RG 108, Letters Received; copies, *ibid.*, RG 393, Military Div. of the Miss., Letters Sent; *ibid.*, Telegrams Sent in the Field. *O.R.*, I, xxxviii, part 4, 3. On May 2, 3:00 P.M., USG telegraphed to Sherman. "Move at the time indicated in my instructions, all will strike together" Telegram received, DNA, RG 107, Telegrams Collected (Bound); copies, *ibid.*, RG 108, Letters Sent; *ibid.*, RG 393, Military Div. of the Miss., Telegrams Received in the Field; DLC-USG, V, 45, 59. *O.R.*, I, xxxviii, part 4, 11. On the same day, 5:00 P.M., Sherman telegraphed to USG. "Despatch of today received. We will be on time" Telegram received, DNA, RG 107, Telegrams Collected (Bound); *ibid.*, RG 108, Letters Received; copies, *ibid.*, RG 393, Military Div. of the Miss., Letters Sent; *ibid.*, Telegrams Sent in the Field. *O.R.*, I, xxxviii, part 4, 11.

On May 4, 9:00 A.M. and 10:00 P.M., Sherman telegraphed to USG. "Genl Thomas has just started for Ringgold, all his command will be there tonight. Gen Schofield is at Cleveland moving down to Red Clay and closing on Thomas left. Gen McPherson is here and by night three 3 divisions will be at Rossville, the other two will be there tomorrow and all move to Thomas right. Thomas will have 45,000. Schofield 13,000 McPherson 20.000" "Genl Thomas center in Ringgold, Left at Catoosa, Right at Leet's Tan Yard. Dodge is here. 15th Corps at Whiteside—Schofield closing up on Thomas left. All move tomorrow but I hardly expect serious battle till the 7th. Everything very quiet with the Enemy— Johnston evidently awaits my ~~initiations~~ initiation. I will first secure the Tunnel Hill then throw McPherson rapidly on his line of communication attacking at same time in front continuously & in force" Telegrams received, DNA, RG 107, Telegrams Collected (Bound); *ibid.*, RG 108, Letters Received; copies, *ibid.*, RG 393, Military Div. of the Miss., Letters Sent; *ibid.*, Telegrams Sent in the Field. *O.R.*, I, xxxviii, part 4, 25. See *ibid.*, p. 34. Further reports from Sherman were telegraphed to Halleck, then transmitted to USG.

To Maj. Gen. Henry W. Halleck

Culpepper Va
Apr. 26.th 1864

Maj Gen H. W. Halleck
Chief of Staff,

The way you propose to communicate orders to Genl Steele and Gen Banks will be better than as I directed. Gen Franklin[1] is an able officer, but has been so mixed up with misfortune that I would not select him for a large separate command, but he is so much better than Gen Banks that I will feel safer with him commanding midst danger than the latter. I submit this however to the President and Secretary of War whether the change shall be made. I am in hopes the whole problem will be solved before orders reach

U. S. Grant
[Lt. Genl.]

Telegram received, DNA, RG 107, Telegrams Collected (Bound); copies, *ibid.*, RG 108, Letters Sent; DLC-USG, V, 45, (sent at 6:00 p.m.) 59. *O.R.*, I, xxxiv, part 3, 293–94. See telegram to Maj. Gen. Henry W. Halleck, April 22, 1864. See also *O.R.*, I, xxxiv, part 3, 306–7.

1. William B. Franklin of Pa., USMA 1843, a classmate of USG, fought in the Mexican War and was promoted to col., 12th Inf., as of May 14, 1861. Appointed brig. gen. as of May 17, and promoted to maj. gen. as of July 4, 1862, he commanded the 6th Army Corps, Army of the Potomac, during the peninsular campaign and the battle of Antietam. Blamed by Maj. Gen. Ambrose E. Burnside for the U.S. defeat at Fredericksburg, he was relieved from command. Assigned to command the 19th Army Corps, Dept. of the Gulf, in Aug., 1863, he was wounded at the battle of Sabine Crossroads, April 8, 1864.

To Brig. Gen. John E. Smith

Culpepper C. H. Va.
Apl. 26th 1864

Dear General,

Your kind congratulatory letter from Huntsville is just received. The subscription for E. B. you speak of I heartily approve and will subscribe my part, what ever it may be, cheerfully. I send all my money to Jones so you are authorized to say to him to pay for me $50⁰⁰, for Rawlins $20⁰⁰ and Rowley $10⁰⁰ and charge the whole amount to me. If a still further sum be necessary we are all willing to double this amt. The Army of the Potomac is in splendid condition and evidently feel like whipping some body. I feel much better with this command that I did before seeing it. There seems to be the very best feeling existing.

All join me in respects to you and the Armies composing the Military Division of the Miss.

Your Friend
U. S. GRANT

ALS, IHi. On April 17, 1864, Brig. Gen. John E. Smith, Huntsville, Ala., wrote to USG. "Thinking over the Various Changes that have taken place during the past three years I have Concluded to write you 'and first as I have not had an Opportunity to do so in person, I desire to Congratulate you upon the attainment of your present position, with the hope that you will Continue to be as successful as heretofore' while I know that *your* old army of the Tenn feel proud of your promotion yet it is Clouded by the inevitable Consequence 'your Separation' from us, beleiving however that it is for our Countrys good, the Army of the Tenn. will not fail you. we little thought when smoking our pipes three years ago in *Crooked Muddy Hilly Galena* (at least I did not) of the Changes that have occurred. In thinking over the Circumstances & influences that controlled at least those of our Section of the Country it must be our Friend E B Washburne has contributed most effectually, and I propose if it meets your approval that a subscription for a suitable Testimonial (Say a Service of Silver) be made up. I do not think it would be politic that it should be known that he recd or that any one in the Army had any thing to do with it but I think a handsome sum could be raised and sent to J R Jones, (as I beleive many in the Army would be glad to subscribe) if you favour the Idea let me know how much   Dr Kittoe is here inspecting the 15th A. C.   the men generally are in good condition   if we had Artillery Horses & Cav to & Could move at once   these it seems are hard to get   ought not to be" ALS, USG 3.

To Edwin M. Stanton

Head Quarters, Armies in the Field,
Culpepper C. H. Va. Apl. 27th/64

Hon. E. M. Stanton,
Sec. of War,
Sir:

Your letter of yesterday enclosing one from Gen. Sherman to the Q. M. Gen., one from the latter to yourself, and copy of a proposed order requiring the Quartermaster General of the Army to accompany these Hd Qrs. in the Field, and Gen. Allen to accompany the Comd.g officer of the Military Division of the Miss. in the same way, is just received.—I do not think the order should be made. Whilst personally I should like very well to have Gen. Meigs with me in the approaching campaign, I must say, when called on ~~officially~~ to speak officially of the necessity for it, that in the capacity of Quartermaster General of the Army he can render this Army no special service with it that he cannot render through his Agts. in the field, from his place in Washington.—The same is true with reference to Gen. Allen in the West. His duties as supervising Qr. Mr. of the West embrases several Departments besides those embrased in the Mil. Div. of the Miss. To go into the field himself, he must neglect these interests, or entrust them to subordinates.—If Gen. Meigs be authorized to take the field, I would say that it should be on the authority of the Sec. of War but not under orders making it obligatory.

Very respectfully
your obt. svt.
U. S. Grant
Lt. Gen.

ALS, DNA, RG 107, Letters Received from Bureaus, AG 1312 1864. On April 26, 1864, Secretary of War Edwin M. Stanton wrote to USG. "I refer to you a communication addressed to this Department by Quartermaster General Meigs, suggesting that he should be sent into the field with you in the approaching campaign, and also a proposed order in reference to sending General Allen into the field with General Sherman, which this Department is asked to sanction. It is my wish, in every thing, to conform to whatever you desire, and to subordinate everything else to the success of your impending military operations; and if you deem either or both of the propositions essential, or in any important degree as likely to facilitate the military operations under your immediate supervision, or those under General Sherman, I will, at whatever sacrifice of convenience, adopt them. In respect to Genl. Allen, I do not perceive that the proposed order would confer upon him any more power than he has exercised during this war, but would only relieve him from the post at which his supervision can most conveniently be exercised, and commit to subordinates that immediate control which the vast operations of the Quartermaster's Department in the West require. In this respect, while appreciating the desire of General Sherman to have an able Quartermaster attendant upon him, I cannot avoid the conclusion that very serious embarrassment may arise, and perhaps much hazard to the Government, in committing the vast outlays of the Department to subordinates, however well selected they may be. The same observation also applies in respect to General Meigs. The principal expenditures of the war, as you are aware, pass through the Quartermaster's Department, and no one, so well as yourself, understands the importance of having at their proper posts the officers exercising the power of Quartermaster General at Washington, and Chief Quartermaster in the West. If, however, in your judgment, their duties can be performed by these officers in the field, without injury to the service, and you deem their presence essential to yourself or to General Sherman, the order will be made. You will please favor me with your views upon this question. I ask it, not for the purpose of diminishing my own responsibility in the conclusion to which the Department will arrive—for that I am always ready to assume and bear—but for the sole purpose of benefiting by your judgment and conforming to your wishes. I have sent Mr. Dana specially, in order to have an immediate answer." Copy, DLC-Edwin M. Stanton. On April 29, Brig. Gen. Montgomery C. Meigs wrote to USG. "I send you a copy of the reply of the Secretary of War to my formal request to accompany you on the approaching campaign. It seems that the Secretary is of opinion that I cannot be spared from Washington & I must abandon the hope of seeing this great campaign in person. God grant you success & victory & enable you to restore by short sharp & decisive measures peace & unity to our distracted country. While the decision of the Secretary is a sore disappointment to me—I shall cheerfull[y] obey his orders & exert myself in this station for the success of our armies." ALS, DNA, RG 92, Miscellaneous Letters Sent (Press).

To Maj. Gen. Henry W. Halleck

Culpepper Apl 27 1864

MAJ GEN HALLECK
CHF OF STAFF

Cannot the Bridges between Bull Run & Rappahannock be held when we move from here by troops from Washington(?) Block house have been built so that two thousand (2000) men would be sufficient whilst the enemy is in front—They should be supplied with thirty days rations so that there would be no necessity of sending cars over the road

U S GRANT
Lt Genl

Telegram received, DNA, RG 107, Telegrams Collected (Bound); copies (sent at 1:00 P.M.), *ibid.*, RG 108, Letters Sent; DLC-USG, V, 45, 59. *O.R.*, I, xxxiii, 992.

On April 27, 1864, USG telegraphed to Maj. Gen. Henry W. Halleck. "Please order Col Porter to report here for duty by the end of this week" Telegram received, DNA, RG 94, Letters Received, 387A 1864; *ibid.*, RG 107, Telegrams Collected (Bound). On the same day, 11:10 A.M., Halleck telegraphed to USG. "~~What Col Porter do you want? Col Andrew 16th Infty, or Col Porter in command of heavy artillery at Baltimore? The former on being ordered to join his regiment under Genl Thomas sent his resignation to the Secty of War, who on recieving it said he should accept it or dismiss him.~~ Genl Curtis telegraphs that Quantrel with three hundred and twenty five men were on the Arkansas river threatening Kansas. He asks for authority to mount his Indian Brigade on Ponies. What answer shall be given?" ALS (telegram sent), *ibid.*; telegram received, *ibid.*; *ibid.*, RG 108, Letters Received. *O.R.*, I, xxxiv, part 3, 312. On the same day, 4:30 P.M., USG telegraphed to Halleck. "I see [no ob]jection to Genl Curtis mounting as many men on ponies as may be necessary" Telegram received, DNA, RG 107, Telegrams Collected (Bound); copies, *ibid.*, RG 108, Letters Sent; DLC-USG, V, 45, 59. *O.R.*, I, xxxiv, part 3, 313. See *ibid.*, pp. 302, 328.

On April 28, 1:30 P.M., USG telegraphed to Halleck. "Has any but the one Iron clad gone to Fortress Monroe Genl Butler states that but one has reached there" Telegram received, DNA, RG 107, Telegrams Collected (Bound); copies, *ibid.*, RG 108, Letters Sent; DLC-USG, V, 45, 59. *O.R.*, I, xxxiii, 1009. On the same day, 3:30 P.M., Halleck telegraphed to USG. "Genl Augur has been stript of almost everything available to give to Genl Burnside. When the trains cease to run the guards under Genl Briggs can be placed in the Block houses between Bull Run & the Rappahannock. I will also give him the Massachusetts detached artillery as soon as it arrives. No troops are yet available to replace Abbott's Artillery in the fortifications. Perhaps some Militia or Invalids from the West may arrive in time. If not, we must weaken the other garrisons. There is very little left, outside of Burnside's command, to use against any movement of Longstreet. The Navy Dept says that one iron clad left New York and one left Philadelphia on the 26th, and should reach Fort Monroe to-day. The one from Boston touched at New York & will leave there to-morrow." ALS (telegram sent), DNA, RG 107, Telegrams Collected (Bound); telegram received, *ibid.*; *ibid.*, RG 108, Letters Received. *O.R.*, I, xxxiii, 1002–3.

On April 28, Maj. Gen. Ambrose E. Burnside, Bristoe Station, Va., telegraphed to USG. "Arrived here this P. M. and will relieve all the troops this side of the Rappahannock tomorrow The Penna Reserves will start for the front early tomorrow Will have brigade at Brandy Sta day after tomorrow I need some good cavalry the 13th Pa is not good Have you any person at Warrenton" Telegram received, DNA, RG 108, Letters Received; copy (dated April 29), *ibid.*, RG 393, 9th Army Corps, Telegrams Sent. On April 28, 9:00 P.M., Maj. Gen. George G. Meade telegraphed to USG. "There are no troops now at Warrenton—Greggs Division of Cavalry has been there all winter but is now on the Warrenton R. Rd. 3 miles from the Junction—I proposed to move him tomorrow or next day across the Rappahannock. I see no occasion for the permanent occupation of Warrenton except to keep out Mosebys men   This can be done by Scouting parties from the junction.—I have telegraphed about Gregs to Genl Burnside.—" ALS (telegram sent), *ibid.*, RG 107, Telegrams Collected (Unbound); telegram received, *ibid.*, RG 108, Letters Received. *O.R.*, I, xxxiii, 1003. On the same day, 11:00 P.M., USG telegraphed to Burnside. "There are no troops [at] Warr[en]ton   Non[e are necessar]y" Telegram received, DNA, RG 107, Telegrams Collected (Bound); copies, *ibid.*, RG 108, Letters Sent; DLC-USG, V, 45, 59. *O.R.*, I, xxxiii, 1004.

An undated telegram from USG to Meade may have been sent on April 29. "Are you going out to-day? If not I will go over to see you." ALS (telegram sent), DNA, RG 107, Telegrams Collected (Unbound). On April 29, 10:30 A.M. and 8:00 P.M., Meade telegraphed to USG. "I will await you at these Head-Quarters" Copy, *ibid.*, RG 393, Army of the Potomac, Telegrams Sent. "Genl. Burnside has just been here—He will have relieved all my troops by 8. a. m. tomorrow. He has returned to Warrenton junction for the night & will take an engine & run up to Culpeper tomorrow if you desire it & so advise him by telegram.—" ALS (telegram sent), *ibid.*, RG 107, Telegrams Collected (Unbound); copies, *ibid.*, RG 393, Army of the Potomac, Telegrams Sent; Meade Papers, PHi. *O.R.*, I, xxxiii, 1013. On the same day, Burnside, Brandy Station, telegraphed to USG. "Have just seen Gen. Meade & will have all his troops relieved by 8. a. m. tomorrow   He says you spoke of sending for me tomorrow   I will at 11. a. m. or 1. P. m as you wish   my Headquarters are at Warrenton Junct with the advance troops at Bealton" Telegram received, DNA, RG 108, Letters Received.

To Maj. Gen. Henry W. Halleck

Culpepper Va
Apr 27th 1.30 P. M/64

Maj Gen H. W. Halleck
Chief of Staff.

There are rumors brought in by deserters that Longstreet reinforced by Beauregards troops will move down the Shenandoah Valley. Should they do so throw all the force you can to head them, taking, if Gen Burnside should still be north of the Rappahannock, all or as much of his force as necessary. If such a movement is commenced by the Enemy after we start from here I will follow him with force enough to prevent his return south

U. S. Grant
Lt Genl

Telegram received, DNA, RG 107, Telegrams Collected (Bound); copies, *ibid.*, RG 108, Letters Sent; DLC-USG, V, 45, 59. *O.R.*, I, xxxiii, 992. On April 26, 1864, 2:00 P.M., Maj. Gen. Henry W. Halleck had telegraphed to USG. "A spy, whose information has [here]tofore proved correct, reports on the 16th that Longstreets baggage was at Richmond & his artillery at Lynchburg, that Pickett was sending five or six thousand men from North Carolina to Lee, & that the latter had eighty days supplies at Gordonsville. Also that the rebels [w]ere planting torpedoes in the Rappahannock below Tappahannock" ALS (telegram sent), DNA, RG 107, Telegrams Collected (Bound); telegram received, *ibid.*; *ibid.*, RG 108, Letters Received. *O.R.*, I, xxxiii, 982.

On April 27, 1:30 P.M., USG telegraphed to Maj. Gen. Franz Sigel. "There are indications and rumors of an intention on the part of the enemy to move a force down the Shanandoah valley. Use every effort to get information as far up in that direction as you can, and report everything you learn." Copies, DLC-USG, V, 45, 59; DNA, RG 108, Letters Sent; Sigel Papers, OClWHi. *O.R.*, I, xxxiii, 997. On the same day, Sigel twice telegraphed to USG. "Your dispatch in regard to movement in the Shenandoah Valley received   I will do every thing to find out and report"   "Six Rebel prisoners of Gillmores Battallion were brought in yesterday. I examined them. They wish to be exchanged and go back to the Southern Army with the exception of an Irishma[n] a Sailor who wishes to take the oath of allegiance—I had a private interview with him and he says the following— 'Longstreets troops were encamped on last Saturday between Charlotte[s]ville and Gordonsville on his way to Lee. He says that two men cam[e] from Richmond to join Gillmores Battallion at Mount Jackson—They told him that Roland was on the peninsula and that Wise has taken command at Charleston. Opinion prevails in the south that we have got tired of Charleston. He assures me tha[t] there is no truth in the rumor of Johnson having joined Lees army, at least there was nothing known about it at Stanton and in the valley—He says that Genl Elsey at Stanton is authorized to strengthen his Division assisted by Marshal Kane of Baltimore from all Marylanders of Lees army and other commands but that Lee refused to let them go. Imboden has been made a Maj Genl and Gillmore is before a court martial for robbing citizens on the Railroad instead of destroying bridges and cars when he made his last raid—Our Cavalry had a successful skirmish yesterday at Springfield north of Romney" Telegrams received, DNA, RG 107, Telegrams Collected (Bound); copies, Sigel Papers, OClWHi. *O.R.*, I, xxxiii, 997, 998.

To Julia Dent Grant

Culpepper C. H. Va. Apl. 27th 1864

DEAR JULIA,

This is my forty second birth day. Getting old am I not?—I received a very short letter from you this evening scratched off in a very great hurry as if you had something much more pleasing if not more important to do than to write to me. I'll excuse you though.

It only gratifying a little desire to appear angry that I am indulging in. Your letter enclosed three horseshoes from Mrs. McDowell which I will wear—in my pocket—for the purposes named i e *to keep off witches*. I am still very well. Dont know exactly the day when I will start or whether Lee will come here before I am ready to move. Would not tell you if I did know. Give my kindest regards to Col. and Mrs. Hillyer. Kisses for yourself and Jess. I sent $1100⁰⁰ to J. R. Jones to day in liquidation of my indebtedness.[1]

Good night

ULYS.

ALS, DLC-USG.

1. On April 28, 1864, J. Russell Jones, Chicago, wrote to USG. "Yours of the 24th with Dft for $1097.00 is rcd and to your credit. From present indications I shall be able to make at least a 4% Divd 1st May which is pretty good considering all things. That will make 9% divided the past 9 months. I am delighted to know you feel so confident of success. The fact is the people have about settled down into the firm conviction that if you fail in the Spring Campaines the Country is gone up. I wish Banks had been kept in Mass—Have had no faith in him for a long time—From what Washburne wrote me a day or two since I inferred that we might expect almost any day now to hear of your having 'opened the ball'—He seems full of hope and Confidence in your success. Remember me to Rawlins, Bowers, the 'Big Injun,' and the other good friends around you. If you have a moment to spare occasionally, drop me a line" ALS, USG 3.

To Maj. Gen. Henry W. Halleck

Culpepper Va
April 28th 1864 11 P M

MAJ GEN H W HALLECK
CHF OF STAFF

Gen Banks dispatch of the Seventeenth (17th) received[1]—I do not see that better orders can be given than those sent a few days ago—If Gen Banks has not advanced on Shreveport and beaten the Enemy then Steele will be so exposed to a superior force as to make it necessary to reinforce him. I would order in this event Genl A J Smith's whole force t[o] Genl Steele—Genl Banks by his failure has absorbed ten thousand (10.000) veteran troops that should now be with Genl Sherman, and thirty thousand (30.000) of his own that would have been moving towards Mobile, and this without accomplishing any good result.

U S GRANT
Lt Genl

Telegram received, DNA, RG 107, Telegrams Collected (Bound); copies, *ibid.*, RG 108, Letters Sent; DLC-USG, V, 45, 59. *O.R.*, I, xxxiv, part 3, 316.

1. See letter to Maj. Gen. Nathaniel P. Banks, April 17, 1864.

To Maj. Gen. Benjamin F. Butler

Culpepper C. H. Va. Apl. 28th/64

MAJ. GEN. BUTLER,
COMD.G DEPT. OF VA. & N. C.
GENERAL,

If no unforeseen accident prevents I will move from here on Wednesday the 4th of May. Start your forces the night of the 4th so as to be as far up James River as you can get by daylight the morning of the 5th and push from that time with all your might for the accomplishment of the object before you. Should anything transpire to delay my movement I will telegraph you.

Acknowledge the receipt of this by telegraph.

Everything possible is now being done to accumulate a force in Washington from the Northern States, ready to reinforce any weak point. I will instruct General Halleck to send them to you should the enemy fall behind his fortifications in Richmond. You will therefore keep the Hd Qrs. in Washington advised of every move of the enemy so far as you know them.

I am Gen. very respectfully
Your obt. svt.
U. S. GRANT
Lt. Gen.

ALS, DLC-Benjamin F. Butler. *O.R.*, I, xxxiii, 1009; *O.R.* (Navy), I, ix, 713.
On April 28, 1864, Maj. Gen. Benjamin F. Butler, Fort Monroe, telegraphed

to USG. "~~Mr~~ Capt. Clark of my staff has just returned from North Carolina. Reports North Carolina relieved from rebel troops that have gone to Virginia" LS (telegram sent), DLC-Benjamin F. Butler; telegram received, DNA, RG 107, Telegrams Collected (Bound). *O.R.*, I, xxxiii, 1009.

On April 29, Lt. Col. Orville E. Babcock wrote to Maj. Gen. William F. Smith. "Your letter of 26th Yorktown reached me last night. I showed it to Comstock who entered into the spirit of it, and during the evening had a talk with the Genl upon the subject, though not mentioning your letter. The Genl is very fixed in letting Butler have his own way with all minutia. He was so firm in the matter that Comstock and I both think he would decline at once if asked direct to send such staff officer. The Genl thinks Genl Butler has sufficient number of able Genls to render him all necessary aid to execute the details—and he has indicated his starting points and objective points. I would send your letter to Wilson but I am sure Comstock has more influence than he (Wilson). The Genl is quite well— You did not speak of Bowen's being with you—He was ordered some time ago. I hope he is not sick again—Burnside is in his position this morning—Comstock came in from Nashville last night   Genl Sherman is feeling quite well and nearly ready. A Capt Montgomery a. a. g (Vol) wished me to ask for a place on your staff. I promised—but knowing you would not want that kind I have not done so before. No Chief Engr yet. Rumor says Halleck is to be the one intended by the President. We have no news. Banks official reports make out his battle a victory; but it was without doubt a disgraceful defeat, the first day, Banks retook 3 pieces only of Artillery—My kind regards to all of your Staff—Also to Madam Smith. I shall expect to meet you in Richmond if not before." ALS, DNA, RG 393, 24th Army Corps, Smith Papers, Letters Received (Unarranged). *O.R.*, I, xxxiii, 1019. On May 1, Butler forwarded to USG a telegram from Smith to Butler. "Will you do me the favor to telegraph to Gen Grant & ask that Capt Saml Wright A A G may be ordered to report to you If he can be spared from the Hd Qrs of the ninth (9) Corps. They have a large surplus of A A Gs there & Col Bowens health is so delicate I am anxious to get some one to assist him and take his place when he is absolutely unfit to do duty"   Telegram received, DNA, RG 107, Telegrams Collected (Unbound).

On May 1, 10:00 A.M., USG telegraphed to Butler. "Have any more ironclads reached you? Has General Gillmore arrived?"   Telegram received, DLC-Benjamin F. Butler; DNA, RG 107, Telegrams Collected (Bound); copies, *ibid.*, RG 108, Letters Sent; DLC-USG, V, 45, 59. *O.R.*, I, xxxvi, part 2, 326. On the same day, noon, Butler drafted his reply at the foot of USG's telegram. "One iron clad has arrived   two more now due. Four gunboats due besides. General Gilmore not yet arrived"   ADfS, DLC-Benjamin F. Butler; LS (telegram sent), *ibid.*; DNA, RG 94, War Records Office, Army of the Potomac; telegram received, *ibid.*, RG 107, Telegrams Collected (Bound). *O.R.*, I, xxxvi, part 2, 326.

Also on May 1, 2:30 P.M., USG telegraphed to Butler. "Have you received letter from me giving date for Commencing operations? If General Gillmore arrived by morning of the third (3d) those directions will be followed. Answer"   Telegram received, DLC-Benjamin F. Butler; DNA, RG 107, Telegrams Collected (Bound); copies, *ibid.*, RG 108, Letters Sent; DLC-USG, V, 45, 59. Printed as sent at 5:10 P.M. in *O.R.*, I, xxxvi, part 2, 327. On the same day, 4:30 P.M. and 7:00 P.M., Butler telegraphed to USG. "~~There is no record~~   Your confidential communication of the 28th of April received at this hours & contents noted—"   "Letter & telegram in regard to commencing operations received. Flag of Truce boat just in. All quiet. Siezed West Point to-day. Enemy fortifying fords on the Chickahominy. Have answered receipt of despatch before." LS (telegrams sent), DLC-Benjamin F. Butler; telegrams received, DNA, RG 107, Telegrams Collected (Bound); *ibid.*, Telegrams Collected (Unbound).

On May 2, 3:30 P.M., USG telegraphed to Butler. "What is the latest news from General Gillmore? State what number of his force is yet to arrive—" Telegram received, *ibid.*, Telegrams Collected (Bound); copies, *ibid.*, RG 108, Letters Sent; DLC-USG, V, 45, 59. Printed as sent at 4:00 P.M. in *O.R.*, I, xxxvi, part 2, 345. On the same day, 4:30 P.M. and 7:00 P.M., Butler telegraphed to USG. "~~I have just ree~~ Letter just recd from Gen Gilmore wh. states that he would start yesterday wh. wud bring him here to night or tomorrow morning. He comes with the last detachment." LS (telegram sent), DLC-Benjamin F. Butler; telegram received, DNA, RG 107, Telegrams Collected (Bound); *ibid.*, Telegrams Collected (Unbound). "Telgram as to probable time of General Gilmores arrival already sent—Will be here Tuesday night or Wednesday moring, with all his force not more than two Regiments and three batteries behind now   Three Iron Clads here—one more expected tomorrow—~~and~~ Three more Gunboats to arrive. Washington quietly evacuated bringing away every thing   Four Regime[nts] recieve from North Carolina   Shall be ready at time indicated   All quiet on the south Bank of James so far." ALS (telegram sent), *ibid.*; telegram received, *ibid.*, Telegrams Collected (Bound). *O.R.*, I, xxxvi, part 2, 345.

Also on May 2, 2:45 P.M., Butler telegraphed to USG. "The following has just been received from Point Lookout in addition to a despatch that there was a movement on the Rappahannock sent yesterday. 'Point Lookout 12 noon May 2nd 1864—Captain Hooker, Potomac Flotilla sends word that the force which crossed the Rappahannock is very heavy, composed of many thousand men, principally cavalry, probably intended as a flank movement against General Grant. (signed) A. G. DRAPER Col Com'd'g District'" LS (telegram sent), DLC-Benjamin F. Butler; telegram received, DNA, RG 107, Telegrams Collected (Bound). *O.R.*, I, xxxvi, part 2, 346. On the same day, 10:30 P.M., USG telegraphed to Butler. "Start on the date given in my letter. There will be no delay with this army. Answer that I may know this is received, and understood as regards date" Telegram received, DLC-Benjamin F. Butler; DNA, RG 107, Telegrams Collected (Bound); copies, *ibid.*, RG 108, Letters Sent; DLC-USG, V, 45, 59. *O.R.*, I, xxxvi, part 2, 346. On May 3, Butler telegraphed to USG. "Your Telegram is received this morning—Gen Gillmore has just arrived but has not yet landed—We understand the order to be on Wednesday the 4th at 8 o'clock P. M. and it will be obeyed" LS (telegram sent), DLC-Benjamin F. Butler; telegram received (dated May 4), DNA, RG 107, Telegrams Collected (Bound). Dated May 4 in *O.R.*, I, xxxvi, part 2, 391.

On May 2, 12:30 P.M., USG telegraphed to Butler. "I have ordered Brigadier General J. B. Carr to report to you. He is now Commanding a Division in this army, but the Senate refusing to confirm him with the date of his appointment, will make him Junior to the Brigade Commanders who have been serving under him. If it embarrasses you to give him a Brigade, you need not give it. His reputation as an officer is good" Telegram received, DLC-Benjamin F. Butler; DNA, RG 107, Telegrams Collected (Unbound). *O.R.*, I, xxxvi, part 2, 346. Orders for the transfer are *ibid.*

On May 3, 10:00 A.M., Butler telegraphed to USG. "I have seen my Chief Qr Master at Fortress Monroe, whom I had ordered there for consultation on another matter. I think the boats will not be ready at Fortress Monroe till tomorrow morning. Is that so understood by you. ~~It is better~~ Shall we move at once" ALS (telegram sent), DNA, RG 393, Dept. of Va. and N. C., Telegrams Sent (Press).

To Edwin M. Stanton

Culpepper C. H. Va.
Apl. 29th 1864

HON. E. M. STANTON
SEC. OF WAR,
DEAR SIR:

I would respectfully request that you would give J. Steinberger, late Colonel of the 1st Washington Territory Infantry, an interview and if it can be done, or if injustice has been done him, revoke the order mustering him out of service. He has the highest testamonials for good soldierly qualities from Gen. Wright,[1] who does not give those things lightly. I have been personally acquainted with Col. S. for the last twelve years and believe h[e] possesses qualities which would have made him now one of our best Citizen Generals had his lot been cast in the East, at the begining of the War, instead of on the Pacific Coast. I am sorry to see such men thrown out of service whilst we are obliged to retain so many inferior, so much inferior, to him.

Should Col. Steinberger be restored to ~~duty~~ service I have no doubt but he would be glad to accept duty on this side of the mountains where he can be brought into the field.

Truly yours
U. S. GRANT
Lt. Gen.

ALS, DNA, RG 94, Vol. Service Div., Letters Received, W2192 (VS) 1863. On July 9, 1864, Col. Edward D. Townsend, AGO, issued Special Orders No. 232 restoring Col. Justus Steinberger to his command. Copy, *ibid*. On the same day, Steinberger wrote to the AG through USG asking that his commission, due to expire on Oct. 19, be extended. ALS, *ibid*. On July 13, USG endorsed this letter. "I presume there is no doubt but Col. Steinburger will be continued as Col. of his regiment until the expiration of the term of service of his men without regard to the date of his own muster into service. If by reenlisting his men or by obtaining new recruits for his regiment he can keep it up to a fair organization I would recommend that he be notified that he and the regt. will be retained in the service to the expiration of the War, or so long as its services may be required." AES, *ibid.*

On April 27, Brig. Gen. Alvan C. Gillem, Nashville, had telegraphed to USG. "On my return to Nashville last night I recd your dispatch & Col Steinberger also yours to Gen Sherman, there is no vacancy in any Tenn Cavalry regt above the rank of Major, when the Command of a regt becomes vacant we shall be glad to avail ourselves of Col Steinberger experience & services" Telegram received, *ibid.*, RG 107, Telegrams Collected (Unbound).

1. George Wright of Vt., USMA 1822, appointed brig. gen. as of Sept. 28, 1861, then assigned to command the Dept. of the Pacific.

To Maj. Gen. Henry W. Halleck

Culpepper Va
Apr. 29th. 1864 10 30 a m

MAJ GEN H. W. HALLECK
CHIEF OF STAFF.

On due reflection, I do not see that anything can be done this spring with troops West of the Mississippi except on that side. I think therefore it will be better to put the whole of that territory into one military Division under some good officer and let him work out of present difficulties without reference to previous instructions. All instructions that have been given have been given with the view of getting as many of these troops East of the Mississippi as possible

U. S. GRANT Lt Genl

Telegram received, DNA, RG 107, Telegrams Collected (Bound); copies, *ibid.*, RG 108, Letters Sent; DLC-USG, V, 45, 59. *O.R.*, I, xxxiv, part 3, 331. On April 29, 1864, 2:30 P.M., Maj. Gen. Henry W. Halleck telegraphed to USG. "Your telegram of 10.30 A M has been recieved & submitted to the Secty of War. You do not name any officer for the Trans. Miss. command. Did you propose to leave Banks in the General command, or only of his present Dept, or to supercede him entirely? I will immediately write you confidentially the difficulties in the way of removing Genl Banks, as I understand them." ALS (telegram sent), DNA, RG 107, Telegrams Collected (Bound); telegram received, *ibid.*; *ibid.*, RG 108, Letters Received. *O.R.*, I, xxxiv, part 3, 331. On the same day, Halleck wrote to USG. "confidential . . . I fully agree with you that after Genl Banks long delays, it will hardly be possible to get his troops east of the Miss. in time to be of any use in the spring campaign. Moreover, to withdraw any of his forces at the present time might lead to serious disasters, & to a virtual closing of the navigation of the Miss. River. I submitted your telegram of 10.30 A. M. to the secty of War, who was of ~~the~~ opinion that, before asking the President for an order, I should obtain your views in regard to the extent of the proposed Division, the officer to command it, &c., and that I should write to you confidentially on the subject. Do you propose to include Pope's Curtis' & Rosecrans' commands, or only the present Depts of the Gulf and of Arkansas with the Indian Territory? Is it proposed to give Banks the command of the Division, or to leave him in the subordinate position of his present Dept, or to remove him entirely? In either case, the order must be definite. If Banks is superceded, Franklin will be the ranking officer in the field, and Rosecrans, Curtis or McClernand, in the Division. You have also heretofore spoken of Steele and Reynolds in connexion with this command. I think the President will consent to the order, if you insist upon Genl Banks removal as a military necessity, but he will do so very reluctantly, as it would give offence to many of his friends, & would probably be opposed by a portion of his cabinet. Moreover, what could be done with Banks? He has many political friends who would demand for him a command equal to the one he now has. The result would probably be the same as in the cases of Rosecrans, Curtis, Sigel, Butler & Lew. Wallace. Before submitting the matter to the President, the Secty of War wishes to have in definite form precisely the order you wish issued. Your last instructions to Genl Banks were telegraphed to Cairo on the 27th in as nearly as possible the words of your telegrams to me. Copies were also sent by mail. I enclose herewith a copy. The present proposed change should be decided upon and telegraphed to him & Steele as early as possible." ALS, DNA, RG 108, Letters Received. *O.R.*, I, xxxiv, part 3, 331–32. See following telegram.

To Maj. Gen. Henry W. Halleck

Culpepper Va
Apr. 29th 1864 6 P. M

MAJ GEN H. W. HALLECK
CHIEF OF STAFF.

Of the four Department Commanders West of the Mississippi I would far prefer Gen Steele to take the general charge, but he cannot be spared from his special command, there is no one to fully take his place. I would leave Gen Banks in command of his Department but order him to his Head Quarters in New Orleans. If you could go in person and take charge of the trans-Mississippi Division until it is relieved from its present dilemma and then place a commander over it or let it return to separate Departments as now, leaving Gen'l Canby[1] temporarily in your place. I believe it would be the best that can be done. I am well aware of the importance of your remaining where you are at this time and the only question is, which of the two duties is the most important, If a commander must be taken from out there to take general charge I would give it to Gen Steele, giving Gen Reynolds his place—

U. S. GRANT
Lt Genl

Telegram received, DNA, RG 107, Telegrams Collected (Bound); copies, *ibid.*, RG 108, Letters Sent; DLC-USG, V, 45, 59. *O.R.*, I, xxxiv, part 3, 331. See preceding telegram.

Also on April 29, 1864, USG telegraphed to Maj. Gen. Henry W. Halleck. "Send all the Horses for the Army of Potomac here instead of mounting men there—Horses are now worth more than men & horses" Telegram received, DNA, RG 107, Telegrams Collected (Bound); copy, *ibid.*, RG 92, Supplies and Purchases, Public Animals, Letters Received.

1. Edward R. S. Canby, born in Ky., raised in Ind., USMA 1839, appointed col., 19th Inf., as of May 14, 1861, commanded the Dept. of N. M. Appointed brig. gen. as of March 31, 1862, he served chiefly in the War Dept. until promoted to maj. gen. as of May 7, 1864, and assigned to command the Military Div. of West Miss. *O.R.*, I, xxxiv, part 3, 490. This effectively reversed the roles suggested by USG for Canby and Halleck. See Adam Badeau, *Military History of Ulysses S. Grant* (New York, 1868–81), II, 204; *Memoirs*, II, 238.

To Maj. Gen. Henry W. Halleck

Head Qrs. Armies in the Field,
Culpepper C. H. Va. Apl. 29th 1864

MAJ. GEN. HALLECK,
CHIEF OF STAFF OF THE ARMY,
GENERAL,

If General Gilmore reaches Fortress Monroe in time, and if four of the Iron Clads promised by the Navy are also there, our advance will commence on the 4th of May.[1] Gen. Butler will operate on the South side of James River, Richmond being his objective point. I will move against Lee's Army attempting to turn him by one flank or the other. Should Lee fall back within his fortification[s] at Richmond, either before or after giving battle, I will form a junction with Butler, and the two forces will draw supplies from the James River. My own notions about our line of march are entirely made up. But, as circumstances beyond my controll may change them I will only state that my effort will be to bring Butler's and Meade's forces together.

The Army will start with fifteen days supplies. All the country affords will be gathered as we go along. This will no doubt enable us to go twenty or twenty-five days, without further supplies, unless we should be forced to keep in the country between the Rapidan and Chickahominy, in which case supplies might be required by way of the York or the Rappahannock River. To provide for this contingency I would like to have about one million rations, and two hundred thousand forage rations, afloat to be sent wherever it may prove they will be required.

The late call for one hundred day men ought to give us all the old troops in the Northern States for the field. I think full two thousand of those in the West ought to be got to Nashville as soon as possible. Probably it would be as well to assemble all the balance of the reinforcements for the West at Cairo. Those that come to the East I think should come to Washington unless movements of the enemy, yet to develope, should require them elswhere. With all our reserves at two or three points you will know what to do with them when they come to be needed in the field.

If the enemy fall back it is probable General Butler will want all the force that can be sent to him. I have instructed him however to keep you constantly advised of his own movements, and those of the enemy, so far as he can.

General Burnside will not leave his present position, between Bull Run and the Rappahannock, until the 5th of May. By that time the troops to occupy the Blockhouses, with their rations, should be out. If they cannot be sent from Washington I will have to require Gen. Burnside to furnish the detail from his Corps. When we get once established on the James River there will be no further necessity of occupying the road South of Bull Run. I do not know even that it will be necessary to go even so far South as that.

In this matter your opportunity for knowing what is required being so far superior to mine I will leave it entirely to you.

> I am General, Very respectfully your obt. svt.
> U. S. GRANT
> Lt. Gen.

ALS, IHi. *O.R.*, I, xxxiii, 1017–18.

1. On May 2, 1864, 12:30 P.M., Maj. Gen. Henry W. Halleck telegraphed to USG. "Navy Dept reports five Iron clads now in Hampton Roads, viz: to Roanoke, Atlanta, Onondaga, Tecumsa & Saugus. Another, the Canonicus, passed Sandy Hook, 10 A. M. May 1st & will be at Hampton Roads on the evening of the 3d. Forage & provision rations will be ready in time as directed." ALS (telegram sent), DNA, RG 107, Telegrams Collected (Bound); (sent at 12:40 P.M.) telegram received, *ibid.*; *ibid.*, RG 108, Letters Received. Printed as sent at 12:40 P.M. in *O.R.*, I, xxxvi, part 2, 329.

To Maj. Gen. Henry W. Halleck

Culpepper Va
Apr. 30th 1864 10.30 a m

MAJ GEN H. W. HALLECK
CHIEF OF STAFF.

Please order General Seymour to report to Gen Meade to be assigned to command a brigade. Can the horses of the 22nd New York Cavalry be sent here, and how many other horses can the bureau send? I want to know so that Gen'l Sheriden can tell what number of equipments belonging to dismounted men to keep here

> U. S. GRANT
> Lt Genl

Telegram received, DNA, RG 92, Supplies and Purchases, Public Animals, Letters Received; *ibid.*, RG 107, Telegrams Collected (Bound); copies, *ibid.*, RG 108, Letters Sent; DLC-USG, V, 45, 59. On May 1, 1864, 2:45 P.M., Maj. Gen. Henry W. Halleck telegraphed to USG. "The 22d New York were not dismounted as Genl Burnside represented that they were required for his command. Four hundred & twenty five cavalry horses were shipped for Culpepper yesterday   Two hundred or more will be sent forward per day. Messenger just returned from Genl [Bank]s with despatches for you which have been forwarded. He left Grand Ecore on the 21st and represents condition of affairs more favorably. Admiral Porter sent verbal message that 'they were all right.' Navy Dept closed & I can get no further information about Iron clads to day. See in New York papers that two more have sailed from that city. Will order col McIntosh as soon as Genl Augur returns. I have just examined rebel officer whose statement made in Baltimore was sent you last night. He evidently believes what he says." ALS (telegram sent), DNA, RG 107, Telegrams Collected (Bound); telegram received, *ibid*. *O.R.*, I, xxxvi, part 2, 319–20.

On April 30, 8:00 P.M., Maj. Gen. George G. Meade telegraphed to USG. "Maj. Genl. Sheridan desires Col. McIntosh 3d. Pa. Cavalry to be ordered to join this army where his regiment is, that he may be assigned to a Cavaly Brigade— Col. McIntosh is at present on duty in Washington in charge of Cavalry depot at Giesboro' Point. I should be glad if this order could be given.—" ALS (telegram sent), DNA, RG 107, Telegrams Collected (Unbound); copies, *ibid*., RG 393, Army of the Potomac, Telegrams Sent; Meade Papers, PHi. On the same day, 10:30 P.M., USG telegraphed to Halleck. "Please order Col McIntosh to join his regiment to take command of the Brigade in which it is in. He need not come out until Gen Augur returns to the City and appoints his successor." Copies, DLC-USG, V, (2) 45, 59; DNA, RG 107, Telegrams Received in Cipher; *ibid*., RG 108, Letters Sent. Also on April 30, 9:00 A.M., Meade had telegraphed to USG. "Brig. Genl. Seymour expresses his willingness to take a brigade in this army, and I should like to have him, if you can order him here. Have you any reply to your telegram about the horses of the 22d. N. Yk. Cavalry that was said to be dismounted for the purpose of mounting A. P. men?" ALS (telegram sent), *ibid*., RG 107, Telegrams Collected (Unbound); telegram received, *ibid*., RG 108, Letters Received. On the same day, USG telegraphed to Meade. "I have received no reply to my dispatch about horses. I will ask for one and send it to you. Will also order Gen. Seymour to you." ALS (telegram sent), USMA; copies, DLC-USG, V, 45, 59; DNA, RG 108, Letters Sent.

On May 1, USG telegraphed to Maj. Gen. Ambrose E. Burnside. "Do you not think the Twenty-second New York Cavalry would be worth more to you on foot than mounted? Their horses would mount 1,000 veteran cavalrymen now with Meade's army and without horses." *O.R.*, I, xxxvi, part 2, 322. On the same day, Burnside telegraphed to USG. "I am satisfied the horses will be of more use to Meade than to me & I will dismount them as soon as they arrive but I fear I will be short of Cavalry—" Telegram received, DNA, RG 94, War Records Office, Army of the Potomac; copies, *ibid*., RG 108, Letters Sent; DLC-USG, V, 45, 59. *O.R.*, I, xxxvi, part 2, 322. See *ibid*., p. 324.

To Maj. Gen. Henry W. Halleck

Culpepper Va
Apr. 30th 1864. 5.30 P. M

MAJ GEN H. W. HALLECK
CHIEF OF STAFF.

My despatch to you of 6. P. M. yesterday answers the questions asked in your letter of the 29th. just received,[1] except as to extent of the trans Mississippi Division. I would not have it include Rose-crans and Curtis. An entire failure of the Banks Expedition may make operations requiring an increase of force necessary in either of those Departments. I see from my despatch I do not propose removing Gen Banks but would not increase his command. If you could not go to take temporary command until present difficulties are cleared up, I think Gen Steele would be the best man, and Gen Reynolds to take his place. The great objection to this, taking Genl Steele from where he is at this time

U. S GRANT
Lt Genl.

Telegram received, DNA, RG 107, Telegrams Collected (Bound); copies, *ibid.*, RG 108, Letters Sent; DLC-USG, V, 45, 59. *O.R.*, I, xxxiv, part 3, 357. On April 30, 1864, 3:15 P.M., Maj. Gen. Henry W. Halleck telegraphed to USG. "As some time may elapse before Trans-Mississippi affairs are definitively decided upon, had I not better telegraph to Cairo & Little Rock modifying my telegram of the 27th to the effect that no troops will be withdrawn from operations against Shreveport & on Red River and that those operations will be continued under direction of the officer senior in command in the field till further orders. It appears that Major Genl Hurlbut claims that special orders No 150, War Dept, do not relieve him from command of the sixteenth Army Corps, and that he is still exercising command over Genl Washburne. Shall I not telegraph to him that he is relieved from all command & will repair to his home in Illinois." ALS (telegram sent), DNA, RG 107, Telegrams Collected (Bound); telegram received, *ibid.*; *ibid.*, RG 108, Letters Received. *O.R.*, I, xxxiv, part 3, 357. On the same day, 6:00 P.M., USG telegraphed to Halleck. "Your suggestion to modify orders for troops on Red River so as to leave them to operate there until something definite is settled upon, I think advisable, please send the order. I wanted Gen Hurlbut relieved entirely from all connection with the 16th Corps" Telegram received, DNA, RG 107, Telegrams Collected (Bound); copies, *ibid.*, RG 108, Letters Sent; DLC-USG, V, 45, 59. Printed as sent at 6:30 P.M. in *O.R.*, I, xxxiv, part 3, 357. See telegram to Maj. Gen. William T. Sherman, April 15, 1864.

On May 2, 7:30 P.M., USG telegraphed to Halleck. "Has anything definite been done in regard to affairs West of the Mississippi?" Telegram received, DNA, RG 107, Telegrams Collected (Bound); copies, *ibid.*, RG 108, Letters Sent; DLC-USG, V, 45, 59. *O.R.*, I, xxxiv, part 3, 389. On May 3, 11:00 A.M., Halleck telegraphed to USG. "Your last instructions in regard to Trans Mississippi matters were telegraphed to Cairo and were sent by Genl Brayman down the river on May 1st. The President has seen your telegrams, but has said nothing to me on the subject since I last wrote to you. I will write to you immediately." ALS (telegram sent), DNA, RG 107, Telegrams Collected (Bound); telegram received, *ibid. O.R.*, I, xxxiv, part 3, 409. On May 2, Halleck wrote to USG. "I believe all the directions in your confidential dispatch of the 29th ultimo, have been carried out, so far as possible. It is a difficult matter to get troops out of the hands of some of the governors of states, but we are making considerable progress. The Asst Secty of War, Mr. Dana, has gone west with full powers to start them off, forcibly if necessary. The five cavalry regts, so long detained in Indianna, have started for Louisville just as they are, half-mounted and half on foot. We can regulate them when we get them away from the state authorities. The Gov. of Mass. opposes the dismounting of his half mounted colored Regt. & we cannot get their horses. I have to-day ordered the men *with* their horses here, where we can dismount them in spite of the Governor & send their horses to Genl Meade. Dont rely too much on any immediate assistance from the proposed western militia force. It will take some time to raise them & get them into position, even under the strongest pressure. As fast as I can get militia regts I will bring to the front the present guards at Johnson's Island, &c. A regt from Ohio has been ordered to relieve Sigel's troops which are guarding the Depot at Galipolis. In your calculations take into account the fact that all the water transportation we can get is absorbed by Genl Butler and by rations put afloat. In case troops are to be sent to Genl Butler, most of the transports must come from him. The north has been completely stript. Genl Canby has been assisting me in getting recruits, furloughed men & troops out of the northern states. He has been sick & his duties in the War Dept have nearly broken him down. He says his business is greatly behind in the office. Whatever you & the Secty of War think I can be of most use I am ready to go. I am willing to serve any where and every where. Just at the present crisis it might not be well to derange the machinery here. There must be some military head here to keep things from getting into a snarl. There must be some common head to make the different Bureau's act in concert & with promptness. It is impossible for the Secty of War or his Assts to attend personally to these matters." ALS, DNA, RG 108, Letters Received. *O.R.*, I, xxxvi, part 2, 328–29. On May 3, Halleck wrote to USG. "I enclose herewith a copy of my last telegram to Genls Banks & Steele in pursuance of your orders. In regard to changes in commanders West of the Mississippi, or the superceding of Genl Banks by placing Steele, Reynolds, or some other officer in general command, the secretary of war has copies of all your telegrams and I believe they have all been read by the President. I have not, however, heard him say any thing on the subject since his reply, which I sent you, to your first telegram immediately after the news of Banks defeat. Genl Banks is a personal friend of the President, and has strong political supporters in and out of Congress. There will undoubtedly be a very strong opposition to his being removed or superceded, un-less and I think the President will hesitate to act, unless he has a definitive request from you to do so, as a military necessity, you designating his successor or superior in command. On recieving such a formal request (not a mere suggestion) I believe, as I wrote you some days ago, he would act immediately. I have no authority for saying this, but give it simply as my own opinion formed from the last two years experience. And the reason I think is very obvious. To do an act which will give offense to a large number of his political friends, the President will require some evidence in a positive form to show the military necessity of that act. In other words he must have something, in a definite shape, to fall back upon, as his justification. You will percieve that the press in New Orleans and in the eastern states are already beginning to open in Genl Banks favor. The administration would be immediately attacked for his removal. Do not understand *me* as advocating his retention in command. On the contrary I expressed to the President months ago, my own opinion of Genl Banks' want of military capacity. Whatever order you may ask for on this subject, I will do my best to have issued. The reasons of my telegram in regard to the 22d New York artille cavalry was that the Ordnance Dept had four conflicting requisitions, 1st to arm the regt as cavalry, 2d as infantry, 3d then to leave them their cavalry arms, and 4th to send them infantry arms, and the matter was referred to me for decision. I did not know that they had been dismounted. All is now right & the last requisition will be filled." ALS, DNA, RG 108, Letters Received. *O.R.*, I, xxxiv, part 3, 409–10.

1. See telegram to Maj. Gen. Henry W. Halleck, April 29, 1864, 10:30 A.M.

To Maj. Gen. William S. Rosecrans

Culpepper Va. Apl 30th 1864

MAJ GEN W S. ROSECRANS

Genl Sherman has stripped his rear to get troops for the field, calculating on his furloughed men yet to return to take their place —His dismounted cavalry will have to be sent as he desires—send it without delay.

Should secret movements in Missouri require a greater force than you now have, you will be able to get any amount necessary from the one hundred day men now raising, and from the state militia

U S GRANT
Lt Genl

Telegram received, DNA, RG 107, Telegrams Collected (Bound); copies, *ibid.*, RG 108, Letters Sent; *ibid.*, RG 393, Dept. of Mo., Telegrams Received; DLC-USG, V, 45, 59; Rosecrans Papers, CLU. Printed as sent at 1:00 P.M. in *O.R.*, I, xxxiv, part 3, 363. On April 30, 1864, 3:00 P.M., Maj. Gen. William S. Rosecrans telegraphed to USG. "No 100 one hundred day men are being raised in this Department. The rebel raids have begun from the south in the Central District. The emergency cannot be met in that way and is a present one. If you order these troops away without replacing the disaster will follow   why should the grand depot be risked and such places as Columbus & Paducah be guarded" ALS (telegram sent), DNA, RG 107, Telegrams Collected (Unbound); telegram received, *ibid.*, Telegrams Collected (Bound); *ibid.*, RG 108, Letters Sent. *O.R.*, I, xxxiv, part 3, 363.

On April 25, 5:30 P.M., Rosecrans had telegraphed to USG. "Have rebel information that their plan is to send two Brigades of cavalry & two of mounted infantry to North Missouri, a column of Re guerillas and 7th Rebel Missouri on Rolla to operate with the conspirator organization here. Our troops are scattered over the State　　Please let me have the 17th Ill Cavalry. ~~and~~" ALS (telegram sent), DNA, RG 107, Telegrams Collected (Unbound); telegram received, *ibid.*, Telegrams Collected (Bound); *ibid.*, RG 108, Letters Received. *O.R.*, I, xxxiv, part 3, 283. On the same day, USG telegraphed to Maj. Gen. Henry W. Halleck. "If the 17th Ill. Cavalry is unassigned order it to St. Louis to report to Gen. Rosecrans." ALS (telegram sent), DNA, RG 107, Telegrams Collected (Bound); telegram received, *ibid.*; *ibid.*, RG 94, Vol. Service Div., E575 (VS) 1865.

On April 29, 11:00 P.M., Rosecrans telegraphed to USG. "Genl Sherman is urgent that the dismounted cavalry of his command should be sent forward without horses. I telegraph you direct that you may give such instructions as may be necessary. I repeat to you what I have already ~~said~~ stated. ~~It will not do~~ in presence of secret dangers which I know to exist and hope soon to circumvent, and the posture of affairs ~~of~~ in arkansas and Louisiana to leave this depot without adequate force would be most hazardous. If the ~~twoos~~ rgiments of infantry sent to garrison Columbus & Paducah were sent back I could send two or three of the dismounted cavalry regiments to the front. Theose regiments were eminently qualified by discipline and order for the work—while the ~~absence~~ lack of these qualities in the cavalry has given rise to frequent disorder and complaints already. Please direct—Rest assured that what I say about secret dangers is well considered and ~~and~~ based on facts" ALS (telegram sent), *ibid.*, RG 107, Telegrams Collected (Unbound); telegram received, *ibid.*, Telegrams Collected (Bound); *ibid.*, RG 108, Letters Received. *O.R.*, I, xxxiv, part 3, 344.

To Julia Dent Grant

Culpepper C. H. Va.
Apl. 30th 1864.

DEAR JULIA,

This is the last time I shall write to you—this month. We are not yet off as you see. I am growing impatient to be off but must wait completion of preparations. I have not a word to write you except to let you know that I am well. You are no doubt enjoying your visit very much but do you not think it would be better for you to be with the children? You can write me long letters telling me where you have been, who seen &c. &c.—Have you heard from the children lately? I wrote to Louisa Boggs to insist on the children writing me a joint letter every week.

Remember me to Col. & Mrs. Hillyer. Kisses for Jess and you.

ULYS.

ALS, DLC-USG.

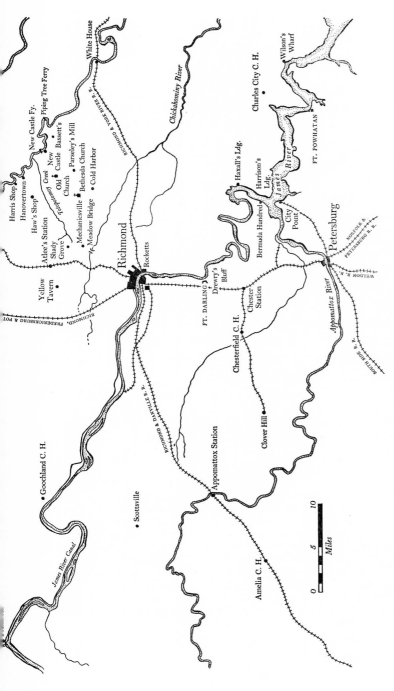

Harris Shop
Hanovertown
Haw's Shop
New Castle Fy.
Piping Tree Ferry
White House

Atlee's Station
Shady Grove
New Castle
Old Church
Parseley's Mill
Bassett's
Bethesda Church
Cold Harbor

Totapotomoy Creek

Yellow Tavern

Mechanicsville
Meadow Bridge

Chickahominy River

RICHMOND & YORK RIVER R. R.

Richmond
Rocketts

RICHMOND, FREDERICKSBURG & POT.

FT. DARLING
Drewry's Bluff

Chesterfield C. H.

Chester Station

RICHMOND & DANVILLE R. R.

Goochland C. H.

James River Canal

Scottsville

Clover Hill

Appomattox Station

Amelia C. H.

Charles City C. H.

Wilson's Wharf

Haxall's Ldg.
Harrison's Ldg.

FT. POWHATAN

James River

Bermuda Hundred
City Point

Petersburg

NORFOLK & PETERSBURG R. R.

WELDON R. R.

Appomattox River

SOUTH SIDE R. R.

0 5 10
Miles

Grant's Spring Campaign of 1864

To Abraham Lincoln

———

Culpepper C. H. Va. May 1st 1864

THE PRESIDENT,

Your very kind letter of yesterday is just received. The confidence you express for the future, and satisfaction with the past, in my Military administration is acknowledged with pride. It will be my earnest endeavor that you, and the country, shall not be disappointed.

From my first entrance into the volunteer service of the country, to the present day, I have never had cause of complaint, have never expressed or implied a complaint, against the Administration, or the Sec. of War, for throwing any embarassment in the way of my vigerously prossecuting what appeared to me my duty. Indeed since the promotion which placed me in command of all the Armies, and in view of the great responsibility, and importance of success, I have been astonished at the readiness with which every thin[g] asked for has been yielded without even an explaination being asked. Should my success be less than I desire, and expect, the least I can say is, the fault is not with you.

Very Truly
your obt. svt.
U. S. GRANT
Lt. Gen.

ALS, DLC-Robert T. Lincoln. On April 30, 1864, President Abraham Lincoln wrote to USG. "Not expecting to see you again before the Spring campaign opens, I wish to express, in this way, my entire satisfaction with what you have done up to this time, so far as I understand it. The particulars of your plans I neither know, or seek to know. You are vigilant and self-reliant; and, pleased with this, I wish not to obtrude any constraints or restraints upon you. While I am very anxious that any great disaster, or the capture of our men in great numbers, shall be avoided, I know these points are less likely to escape your attention than they would be mine—If there is anything wanting which is within my power to give, do not fail to let me know it. And now with a brave Army, and a just cause, may God sustain you." ALS, CSmH. Lincoln, *Works*, VII, 324.

To Edwin M. Stanton

Culpepper Va
~~Apr.~~ May 1st 1864 10 30 A M

HON EDWIN M STANTON
SECY OF WAR.

Your despatch giving information derived from rebel Lieu-ten[ant] received. It will not be necessary to send the Lieutenant here as th[e] despatch is very full. I do not place great reliance on the information because I do not see how an officer of that ran[k] comes to know so much of futur[e] plans, but I will watch

U. S. GRANT
Lt Genl

Telegram received, DNA, RG 107, Telegrams Collected (Bound); copies, _ibid._, RG 108, Letters Sent; DLC-USG, V, 45, 59. _O.R._, I, xxxvi, part 2, 319. On April 30, 1864, 10:35 P.M., Secretary of War Edwin M. Stanton telegraphed to USG. "A rebel Captain who came within our lines as a deserter was arrested in Baltimore today. General Wallace sends a long statement by him as to the po-sition of the enemies forces their condition &c the principal points of which will be telegraphed tonight and the whole statement by mail. I have ordered the prisoner here for examination and if you wish to see him will forward him to you. How much of his true and how much romance you can judge" ALS (tele-gram sent), DNA, RG 107, Telegrams Collected (Bound). _O.R._, I, xxxiii, 1022. On the same day, Stanton telegraphed to USG a detailed account of the inac-curate information supplied by the C.S.A. officer. LS (telegram sent), DNA, RG 107, Telegrams Collected (Bound). _O.R._, I, xxxiii, 1022–23.

To Edwin M. Stanton

Culpepper
May 1 _1864._

Private
HON E M STANTON
SECY WAR

Is there any objections to Lieut Worth remaining on the Staff of Gen H J Hunt[1]   He has been there a long time & Gen Hunt is desirous of retaining him   I have received no reply to my question as to the propriety of allowing Cadet Walker to Serve on the staff of some Genl during the approaching Campaign—I declined assigning him because he has been suspended from West Point as a punishment[2]

U. S. Grant
Lt Genl

Telegram received, DNA, RG 107, Telegrams Collected (Bound). On May 1, 1864, Secretary of War Edwin M. Stanton telegraphed to USG. "Your action in relation to Cadet Walker is approved. If the Cadets can get into the field as aids it will be a strong [t]emptation to get suspended. It Should he [b]e permitted to remain with the army? It seems to me he should be ordered away away and if you concur send him off. There is no objection to Lieutenant Worth remaining on General Hunts Staff and he has permission to do so if you do not think his services more valuable elsewhere." ALS (telegram sent), *ibid.*; telegram received, *ibid.*, RG 108, Letters Received. On the same day, USG telegraphed to hd. qrs., Army of the Potomac. "Authorizing Genl Hunt to retain Lt. Worth on his staff." *Ibid.*, RG 393, Army of the Potomac, Register of Letters Received.

1. William S. Worth, born in Albany, N. Y., in 1840, was appointed 2nd lt., 8th Inf., as of April 26, 1861, and promoted to 1st lt. as of June 7. He served on the staff of Brig. Gen. Henry J. Hunt from the summer of 1862.
2. See letter to Jesse Root Grant, April 16, 1864.

To Maj. Gen. William S. Rosecrans

Culpepper 10 a m May 1st 64

Maj Gen W S Rosecrans

Have you sent any troops from your department at any time in obedience to orders from me?

The troops which you are detailing without authority, and in violation of orders are a part of the garrison for keeping open the Mississippi. With the troops belonging to your department proper, with other commanders interposing between you and all organized forces of the enemy, I do not understand your threat of disaster as a consequence of permitting veterans to return to where they belong, unless it means that you must do as you please or be held in no way responsible.

You can bring troops from places where you now have more
than is necessary to hold your Depots safely

U S GRANT
Lt Genl

Telegram received, DNA, RG 107, Telegrams Collected (Bound); copies, *ibid.*,
RG 108, Letters Sent; *ibid.*, RG 393, Dept. of Mo., Telegrams Received; DLC-
USG, V, 45, 59; Rosecrans Papers, CLU. *O.R.*, I, xxxiv, part 3, 381. On May 1,
1864, 8:30 P.M., Maj. Gen. William S. Rosecrans telegraphed to USG. "Your
dispatch recieved. By your orders I have sent away the only two regiments of infantry I had at this post, one of which is put in garrison at Columbus the other
at Paducah   By your telegraphic order I armed the dismounted Calvalry and
put them on guard duty here in place of the infantry sent away. No further order
of yours came to me until yesterday. I telegraphed to say that if these guards
are sent away and not replaced the Eight thousand armed secret society ~~society~~
men whose intended rising has been postponed but the preparation for which
rebel cavalry from the south was already beginning, would seize that opportunity
burn our depots and do us irreparable damage—This matters of the secret society
must be kept ~~to yourself or~~ perfectly secret until I can secure names and evidence
which will enable me to seize and convict the ri~~e~~ng leaders and crush the organization which is wide spread—If you think it safe ~~with~~ after my statement of
these facts to risk sinding off these troops without bringing ~~others~~ some disciplined infantry to take their place your orders will be obeyed—" ALS (telegram
sent), DNA, RG 107, Telegrams Collected (Unbound); telegram received, *ibid.*,
Telegrams Collected (Bound); *ibid.*, RG 108, Letters Received. *O.R.*, I, xxxiv,
part 3, 381.
    On May 3, 2:30 P.M., Rosecrans telegraphed to USG. "All Shermans dis-
mounted cavalry save those on guard duty in the city has been ordered down the
river. For your information I report that three parties of from one to three hundred rebel cavalry are reported moving towards Missouri in the South west. There
are two or three rebel organizations in Illinois. Quantrel with eight hundred is
between the Illinois and Mississippi below Quincy. his second Todd was discovered making arrangements for the raid & captured near Independence—I
hope to bring these conspirators and raiders to grief But must remind you ~~not
only~~ of the importance of this depot with its steam boats arsenal and two large
prisons well stocked with desperadoes, and await your final orders on my telegram of the 2nd." ALS (telegram sent), DNA, RG 107, Telegrams Collected
(Unbound); telegram received, *ibid.*, Telegrams Collected (Bound); *ibid.*, RG
108, Letters Received. *O.R.*, I, xxxiv, part 3, 416. On the same day, 9:00 P.M.,
USG telegraphed to Rosecrans. "The troops you were ordered to return of the
Departments where they belong are needed there. I do not want you to endanger
the depots by sending them away before you can replace them from other parts
of your command, but with the force at your disposal it does seem to me, my
order might have been obeyed without all the correspondence which has en-
sued" Telegram received, DNA, RG 107, Telegrams Collected (Bound);
copies, *ibid.*, RG 108, Letters Sent; DLC-USG, V, 45, 59; Rosecrans Papers,
CLU. *O.R.*, I, xxxiv, part 3, 416–17.
    On May 1, Lt. Col. Cyrus B. Comstock wrote in his diary: "Rosecrans is

adroit: Like all generals he wishs to get all the troops he can & like Rosecrans does not obey an order if he can avoid it. The Gen. ordered him to spare 5000 troops—instead he seizes two regts of Shermans & cries that disaster will follow if they are taken away. His telegram is a model for quiet insolent disobedience of orders. If Grant had the power he would be mustered out of service." DLC-Cyrus B. Comstock.

On April 28, USG endorsed a letter of Brig. Gen. Montgomery C. Meigs submitting a report on the issue of tents. "Respy. returned. G. O. No. 160 series 1862 from the AGO. providing for the issue of shelter tents instead of common, wall or sibley tents will be strictly adhered to. Where troops refuse to accept of shelter tents they must go without tents. Quartermaster must be prohibited from issuing tents other than the kind provided for—no matter by whom the requisition are approved, or by whose order the issue is directed to be made, until otherwise ordered from the Adjutant Generals office Commanding officers of troops will be held responsible for the enforcement and due observance of the order from the adjutant Generals office in this particular and any order from them directing the issue of tents other than as prescribed will be a violation of orders subjecting them to trial by Court Martial, or summary dismissal from the service. Troops serving in detachments, in garrison, or at stations as are the enrolled Missouri Militia as shown in the com'n of M. G. W. S. Rosecrans to Genl Allen Chief Q. M. of the West can build huts if they prefer them to shelter tents" Copy, DLC-USG, V, 58. See *O.R.*, I, xxxiv, part 3, 399.

To Elihu B. Washburne

Culpepper C. H. Va.
May 1st 1864.

Hon. E. B. Washburn
Dear Sir:

Please permit me to call the attention of Congress, through you, to the fact that the law creating the grade of Lieut. Gen. and fixing the pay and allowances of Staff officers serving with the Lt. Gen. simply revived old laws. Under these his Aides, with the rank of Lieut. Col. receive only the pay and allowances of officers of their grade in the Infantry. Under more recent Acts of Congress all other staff officers receive the pay and allowances of Cavalry officers. Maj. Gens. comma[nding] Army Corps, have four Staff officers with the rank of Lieut. Col. who receive Cavalry pay. It certainly never was contemplated that the Staf[f] of a higher grade and command should receive less pay.

Hoping that Congress will correct this, I remain

> Your obt. svt.
> U. S. GRANT
> Lt. Gen.

ALS, IHi. On May 2, 1864, U.S. Representative Elihu B. Washburne introduced, and the House immediately passed, a joint resolution providing that staff officers of USG would be paid as much as staff officers of corps commanders. *CG*, 38-1, 2035. For Senate passage, see *ibid.*, p. 2324. See also *ibid.*, pp. 3501, 3514.

On April 14, USG had endorsed a draft of a bill concerning staff officers. "I fully concur in recommending the passage of the within. The Bill giving increased rank to some staff officers of Corps was defective in not including all." Copy, DNA, RG 107, Letters Received from Bureaus.

On April 29, Washburne telegraphed to USG. "M[r] Swinton, Chief Editor N. Y. Times wants your permission to visit your Army to correspond for his paper. He is a loyal and true man and a good friend. Please send what is necessary for me. Ans. by telegraph." ALS (telegram sent), *ibid.*, Telegrams Collected (Unbound). On the same day, USG telegraphed to Washburne. "Pass will be sent you by mornings mail" Telegram received (press), *ibid.*, Telegrams Collected (Bound). Washburne's account of his visit to USG during the Wilderness campaign is in Gaillard Hunt, *Israel, Elihu and Cadwallader Washburn* . . . (New York, 1925), pp. 207–20. For William Swinton, see telegram to Maj. Gen. George G. Meade, July 2, 1864.

To Brig. Gen. Lorenzo Thomas

> In field Culpeper Court House Va.
> May 2nd 1864.

ADJUTANT GENERAL. U. S. A.
WASHINGTON D. C.

In compliance with General Orders No. 244. War Department A. G. O. series 1863, I have the honor to report the following named officers as constituting my staff and that they are on duty as such.

Brig. Genl. *John A. Rawlins*, Chief of Staff.
Lieut Colonel, *T. S. Bowers*, Assistant Adjutant General.
Lieut. Colonel, *C. B. Comstock*, Senior Aide-de-Camp.

Lieut. Colonel, *O. E. Babcock*, Aide-de-Camp.

Lieut. Colonel *F. T. Dent*, Aide-de-Camp.

Lieut. Colonel, *Horace Porter* Aide-de-Camp.

Lieut. Colonel, *W. L. Duff* Assistant Inspector General

Lieut Colonel *W. R. Rowley* Secretary.

Lieut. Colonel, *Adam Badeau* Secretary.

Captain *E. S. Parker* Assistant Adjutant General

Captain *George K. Leet*, Assistant Adjutant General in charge of office at Washington.

Captain *P. T. Hudson* Aide-de-Camp

Captain *H. W. Janes* Assistant Quartermaster, on special duty at Headquarters.

1st Lieutenant, *W. M. Dunn* Jr. 83rd Indiana Volunteers acting Aide-de-Camp.

> Very Respectfully
> Your Obdt. Servt.
> U. S. GRANT
> Lieut. General.

LS, DNA, RG 94, ACP 4754/1885.

To Maj. Levi C. Turner

> Culpepper Va.
> May 2nd 3.30 P. M 1864

MAJ L. C. TURNER
JUDGE ADVOCATE.

The man Bell whom you telegraph about I know has been a scout under Gen'l Hurlbut and I believe has the full confidence of that officer. I cannot answer for him myself but believe he is all right   I would say let him go now   I saw him in Washington and know the object of his mission

> U S. GRANT
> Lt Genl

Telegram received, DNA, RG 107, Telegrams Collected (Bound); copies, *ibid.*, RG 108, Letters Sent; DLC-USG, V, 45, 59. Levi C. Turner was appointed judge advocate and maj. as of July 31, 1862, and assigned to matters of disloyalty. On May 2, 1864, Turner telegraphed to USG. "A man by name C. S Bell, was arrested yesterday in Maryland *en route* for Richmond. He says he has been fourteen (14) months a trusted scout of Genl Hurlbut—That he was on a mission now for him, and was furnished two Hundred Dollars ($200) by Genl Hurlbut.—His mission to go to Richmond and get Commissions from the rebel authorities for privateering, for certain rebels now in Canada.—then thirty or forty are to go to Boston and Capture a Steamer &c   He has the papers which verify this statement. But he says his real purpose is, to get these men to Boston, and then have them seized. That Genl. Hurlbut is fully advised of the plan. He proposes to return through Lee's army, and get all the information possible, and communicate it to you. He says that you know him, and about his valuable services as a scout: and that he saw you in this city last week   The Secretary of War directs me to send this telegram, and to ask you to reply, as to what you may know of this young man" LS (telegram sent), DNA, RG 107, Telegrams Collected (Bound); telegram received (incomplete), *ibid.*, RG 108, Letters Received. See letter to Maj. Gen. Stephen A. Hurlbut, June 11, 1863.

On Aug. 31, 1864, Capt. George K. Leet telegraphed to Lt. Col. Theodore S. Bowers. "A man named C. S. Bell, who says he was formerly a scout for Gen. Hurlbut and that Gen. Grant, about four months ago, sent him through Canada to Wilmington N. C., is here and wishes to go to City Point. Shall I send him." ALS (telegram sent), DNA, RG 107, Telegrams Collected (Bound). On Sept. 1, Bowers telegraphed to Leet. "Genl Grant did not send Bell to Wilmington & does not desire to see him—Let him furnish the War Dept any information he may have" Telegram received (press), *ibid.*

On Oct. 4, Maj. Gen. Stephen A. Hurlbut, New Orleans, wrote to USG. "I forward this communication by C. S. Bell the most intelligent and active of the scouts ever employed by me. You will remember him as the man who penetrated through Johnson's Army in rear of Vicksburgh and reported to you, and afterward returned through the same line to me at Memphis   I consider him a man of singular daring and fitness for his dangerous work. His family reside in Galesburgh Illinois & he has two brothers now in Illinois Regiments. I sent him some months since to Canada intending him to go thence to Richmond & report either to myself or Genl. Sherman. He has probably been denounced at Richmond by a Jew Spy Simon E. Adler. There are letters of Adler's in the possession of the War Dept which if Bell can obtain them will give him the means of obtaining absolute credence (together with others in his possession) and will enable him to obtain the most full & accurate information on the status of the rebel force—the roads water courses & other points of vital interest. If you do not specially desire him to make any particular line I wish him to make the trip from Richmond by Danville & Greensboro RRd through North Carolina—thence by Columbia S. C. Augusta & Macon Geo & Mobile where he will report to me. I have furnished him $500—   & would give him Confederate Scrip if I had it. He will require about $1000—   to do what I wish" ALS, *ibid.*, RG 94, Turner-Baker Papers, 630-B. On Oct. 14, USG endorsed this letter. "I would respectfully recommend that the Sec. of War furnish C. S. Bell with the means of carrying out the programe proposed within. Bell has heretofore been very successful as a scout." AES, *ibid.* Charles S. Bell mentioned his wartime services and connection with USG while testifying in 1876 against Bvt. Brig. Gen. Orville E. Babcock. *HRC*, 44-1-799. See *New York Times*, Feb. 24, 1879.

To Maj. Gen. Henry W. Halleck

Culpepper Va
May 2d 1864 10 30 P M

MAJ GEN H W HALLECK
CHF OF STAFF

The Twenty Second (22d) New York cavalry were dismounted at my suggestion that the horses were worth more to mount Veteran Cavalry who have no horses than men and horses together are   A new regiment will be worth something on foot but less than their forage on horseback   I did not give a preemptory order for dismounting the regiment however

U S GRANT
Lt Genl

Telegram received, DNA, RG 107, Telegrams Collected (Bound); copies, *ibid.*, RG 108, Letters Sent; DLC-USG, V, 45, 59. *O.R.*, I, xxxvi, part 2, 329. On May 2, 1864, 2:30 P.M., Maj. Gen. Henry W. Halleck had telegraphed to USG. "Have you given any orders direct to Genl Burnside to dismount the 22d N. Y. cavalry? There seems to be some misunderstanding." ALS (telegram sent), DNA, RG 107, Telegrams Collected (Bound); telegram received, *ibid. O.R.*, I, xxxvi, part 2, 329. See telegram to Maj. Gen. Henry W. Halleck, April 30, 1864.

To Maj. Gen. Ambrose E. Burnside

Culpeper C. H. Va. May 2d 1864.

MAJ GEN A. E. BURNSIDE
COMD'G 9TH A. C.

The movement of this Army will commence at 12 oclock to morrow night. The attempt will be made to turn the right flank of the enemy; that is to cross the Rapidann, East or below the railroad. Ely's Ford, Germania Ford & Culpeper Mine Ford will be the crossing places. At Ely's Ford a Pontoon train will be left for your use. You will send a suitable guard to take charge of this bridge and crossing by the morning of the 5th.

So soon as the crossing of Meades Army is perfectly assured,

I will notify you of the fact by telegraph, which will be the signal for you to start. Make all your preparations on the 4th inst. to move at a moments notice. Select your own route, or routes to the Rapidann. When you reach there if Meades trains should be in your way, do not interfere with them following his Army unless you should receive notice to push forward with your troops. In that case you will stop his trains until your troops are over, and a sufficient number of ammunition wagons and ambulances to enable you to go into battle with a supply.

In the absence of any further directions, your line of march, after crossing the Rapidann, will be in the rear of the right flank of the Army of the Potomac.

Being in the rear you will require very heavy guards with your trains.

My Headquarters, until further notice, will, as a rule be near the Hdqrs of the Army of the Potomac. On the night of the 4th this will be on the road to Germania Ford, and not far from the river.

Furnish me a copy of your order of march as soon as you can.—

I am General, Very Respectfully
Your Obdt Servt.
U. S. GRANT
Lieut Genl.

Copies, DLC-USG, V, 45, 59; DNA, RG 108, Letters Sent. *O.R.*, I, xxxvi, part 2, 337.

To Maj. Gen. Franz Sigel

Culpepper Va
May 2nd 11. P. M 186[4]

MAJ GEN FRANZ SIGEL
WINCHESTIR VA

I do not want you to move further south than Cedar Run to watch any movement the Enemy may attempt by the way of the

Shenandoah Valley. The army of the Potomac occupies nothin[g] between the Blue Ridge & Orange and Alexandria Rail Road. In the plan which I first gave, but which was modified at your sugges[tion] it was thought, taken in connection with the movement of this Army the force which was to start from Beverly might work ~~entirely~~ Easterly to Lynchburg and return by Staunton, then you would want to meet them with a train loaded with supplies. It is to be hoped the efforts making for raising troops will enable us to send any reinforcements you may require should the Enemy move down the Valley. Call on Genl Halleck for what may be necessary and report to him after the 3rd. To cut New River bridge and the road ten or twenty miles East from there would be the most important work Crook could do

U. S. GRANT
Lt Genl

Telegram received, DNA, RG 107, Telegrams Collected (Bound); copies, *ibid.*, RG 108, Letters Sent; DLC-USG, V, 45, 59. *O.R.*, I, xxxvii, part 1, 369. On May 1, 1864, noon, Maj. Gen. Franz Sigel, Bunker Hill, West Va., telegraphed to USG. "The following despatch just received, I also forward it to Genl Crook— 'Beverly Va Apr 30th 64 6 P. M   Just arrived. went to Green brier bridge Marlem bottom. attacked rebel pickets there and captured seven 7,   brought six 6 in   left one badly wounded. There were three 3 companies of the 19th Va Cavalry at Little Levels two companies ~~of the regt~~ at Huntsville & Jacks-town   Was between Sulphur Springs and the Warm Springs. There were three hundred of the 20th Va Cavalry at Crab Bottom. Very little forage in the country. Several horses gave out, did not think it prudent to go further. Col Harris says I took the right course under circumstanc[es]   (signed) J. B. GORE Capt Comdg Detachmen[t]'   I have no positive information yet whether a large force of the enemy is in the Shenandoah valley; from all reports received I believe that there is not. McNeil & Imboden with one thousand (1000) men and Rosser with two thousand (2000) men are near Front Royal and Woodstock. Their pickets at Cedar Creek and their scouts at Winchester. Gen Elzy has probably moved from Staunton to Woodstock with about three to four thousand Infantry & Artillery   We will occupy Winchester today with all our forces, consisting of about four-thousand Infantry one thousand Cavalry & three 3 Batteries and push our advance towards Cedar Creek" Telegram received, DNA, RG 107, Telegrams Collected (Bound); copy (incomplete), Sigel Papers, OClWHi. *O.R.*, I, xxxvii, part 1, 363–64. On May 2, 2:00 A.M., Sigel, Winchester, telegraphed to USG. "The following telegraph was received from Genl Crook— 'Charlestown Apl 30th 64   Not having a sufficient mounted force to make two demonstrations I shall only make a demonstration toward Lewisburg so as to keep the enemy from leaving there while I will march with the main body from Fayetteville on the bridge of New river. Gen Averill with two thousand (2000)

Artillery crossing pontoon bridges at Germanna Ford, Rapidan River.
Photograph by Timothy H. O'Sullivan. *Courtesy Library of Congress.*

Grant writes an order at Bethesda Church, June 2, 1864.
Photograph by Timothy H. O'Sullivan. *Courtesy Library of Congress.*

mounted men will go through Logan County to the vicinity of Saltville and if circumstances will not justify his attacking that place, to destroy the Railroad from that place towards the bridge so as to prevent troops from Tennessee. Should I be successful in taking the bridge I shall cross the bridge & move toward Lynchburg, destroy the road as far as I deem it prudent, then ~~take~~ fall back on Lewisburg. The officer who commands on the Lewisburg line is instructed to watch the enemy's movements well and if he retreat, to advance, occupy Lewisburg and collect the supplies of the country. On the contrary if the enemy should attack him, for him to retreat delaying the enemy all he can by contesting strong points blockading the roads &c' This plan of Genl Crook may prove successful and may have a very important result, but it is not in accordance with my views because it brings Genl Averill too far west and out of reach of Genl Crook. his Cavalry will be used up and therefore cannot assist Genl Crook in future operations. Secondly because this movement will allow the enemy to concentrate nearly all his forces which are between Staunton and Lewisburg at Staunton. Thirdly. because it makes all co-operation of forces here with those of Genl Crook impossible. My understanding was that all the forces of Genl Crook should operate between the James and New River and that the movement should end with a demonstration against Staunton with all the forces under Crook the Cavalry included, but I may be wrong and it is too late to interfere, I will therefore say nothing to Genl Crook but wish him success which he so well deserves, as he has done all in his power to be prepared and to act. As for me I would very much like to know what your expectations are. I understand that I am to occupy the line at Cedar Creek and to advance up the Shenandoah valley if circumstances will allow me to do so. To advance beyond Strausburg with my present force is hardly possible, if I cannot at the same time leave a pretty strong force opposite Front Royal to prevent the enemy from marching into my rear or cutting off my line of communication with cavalry. I have only a very vague idea about the position of the army of the Potomac and do not know whether there is any force of ours at or near Luray. If I am expected to make energetic and decisive movements I should have at least five thousand (5000) more of good Infantry with which I could march up the Shenandoah valley. The country here is an open country in which fifty thousand men can maneuvre. I would submit that under all circumstances a strong corps of observation should be formed here to maneuvre upon the enemys left flank. I do not however ask for more troops but simply state how things are and appear to me. The few troops I have here are excellent with the exception of the cavalry, but they are too weak and too near the main body of the enemy to be able to venture much especially as long as nothing is decided in regard to his movement. I also take leave to inform you that by the concentration of nearly all the troops of this Department in the Kanawha & Shenandoah valley, the interior of the state of West Va is laid open to Guerrillas and bands of raiders. Cannot the states of Penna and Ohio send a few Regiments of Militia to the assistance of the people who have sent nearly every available man into the field and those who are left are too poor and dependant upon their daily labor to organize and to defend themselves. I bring this subject to your knowledge because I do not know what military resources the Government has at present and what the people of West Virginia may expect" Telegram received, DNA, RG 107, Telegrams Collected (Bound); *ibid.*, RG 108, Letters Received; copy, Sigel Papers, OClWHi. *O.R.*, I, xxxvii, part 1, 368–69.

To Julia Dent Grant

_____

Culpepper May 2d 1864

DEAR JULIA,

The train that takes this letter will be the last going to Washington. This then is the last letter you can receive from me until the Army strikes some new base. The telegraph will be working for a few days however so that you will hear through the papers what the Army is doing.

Before you receive this I will be away from Culpepper and the Army will be in motion. I know the greatest anxiety is now felt in the North for the sucsess of this move, and that the anxiety will increase when it is once known that the Army is in motion. I feel well myself. Do not know that this is any criterion to judge results because I have never felt otherwise. I believe it has never been my misfortune to be placed where I lost my presence of mind, unless indeed it has been when thrown in strange company, particularly of ladies. Under such circumstances I know I must appear like a fool.

I received a letter from Buck this evening. It was very well written. He says he can speak German a little.

All your letters reach me the second day after they are written. If I do not get one to-morrow I shall not expect to hear from you for several weeks. All the letters you write however send to me directed to Washington and they will come to me by first opportunity.

Love and Kisses for you and Jess.

ULYS.

ALS, DLC-USG.

To Maj. Gen. Henry W. Halleck

Culpepper Va
May 3rd 1864. 12.30 P. M

MAJ GEN H. W. HALLECK
CHIEF OF STAFF.

This Army moves tomorrow morning. Will occupy Germanna, Ely's & Culpepper Ford by daylight the morning of the 4th. I will have to leave affairs West entirely with you. Gen Banks now proposes to keep Smith's force altogether so as to give him sufficient strength to operate against Mobile. It is now too late for Smith's force to return to be of any use in the Spring Campaign but I do ~~not~~ think it is a waste of strength to trust Gen Banks with a large command or an important expedition

U S. GRANT Lt. Genl

Telegram received, DNA, RG 107, Telegrams Collected (Bound); copies, *ibid.*, RG 108, Letters Sent; DLC-USG, V, 45, 59. *O.R.*, I, xxxiv, part 3, 408–9; (incomplete) *ibid.*, I, xxxvi, part 2, 351.

To Maj. Gen. Ambrose E. Burnside

Culpeper May. 3d 1864.

MAJ GEN BURNSIDE,
WARRENTON JUNCTION

The number of wagons you now have is all that can be supplied. If they are insufficient for what you have to take, send back your surplus in the morning. It is not designed to haul anything but, rations, forage, Ordnance and Medical Stores.

U. S. GRANT
Lieut Genl.

Copies, DLC-USG, V, 45, 59; DNA, RG 108, Letters Sent. *O.R.*, I, xxxvi, part 2, 363. On May 3, 1864, 1:30 P.M., Brig. Gen. Montgomery C. Meigs had telegraphed to USG. "Burnside has recd over six hundred wagons 7 or 8̶0̶0̶ medical wagons and over 180 ambulances   It was decided at Annapolis that 500 wagons would be enough for his force then estimated at 35.000 men   He now asks that 75 more wagons teams & drivers completely organized be sent to him by Rail road by tomorrow noon   This Depot can furnish them but they cannot be spared without injury to the service here   Shall they be sent"   Telegram received, DNA, RG 107, Telegrams Collected (Bound); *ibid.*, RG 108, Letters Received. *O.R.*, I, xxxvi, part 2, 352. On the same day, USG telegraphed to Meigs. "Send no more wagons to the 9th Corps. I have informed Burnside that he must send back everything his present supply of teams will not draw"   Telegrams received (2), DNA, RG 107, Telegrams Collected (Bound); copies, *ibid.*, RG 108, Letters Sent; DLC-USG, V, 45, 59. *O.R.*, I, xxxvi, part 2, 352.

Also on May 3, 3:30 P.M., USG telegraphed to Maj. Gen. Ambrose E. Burnside. "All of Gen Meades troops will be away from Brandy Station to morrow morning. You must have a force there to guard your stores. They should be started up at once." Copies, DLC-USG, V, (misdated 1865) 45, 59; DNA, RG 108, Letters Sent. *O.R.*, I, xxxvi, part 2, 362. On the same day, 6:00 P.M., Lt. Col. Frederick T. Dent telegraphed to Burnside. "Gen Grant directs that you leave as guard for the rail-road sufficient force to hold it until the rolling stock is removed—this will be done to-morrow—Order up your guards as fast as they are relieved by those of Gen Auger." Copies, DLC-USG, V, 45, (2) 59; DNA, RG 108, Letters Sent. *O.R.*, I, xxxvi, part 2, 363.

On May 3, noon, Maj. Gen. George G. Meade telegraphed to USG. "I have issued the orders for tomorrow—they can be suspended if desired   Genl Burnside has sent 400.000 rations to Brandy   I am a little nervous about them in case the enemy tomorrow should cross and advance   Had he not better send as large a force as ~~possible~~ he can spare to be at Brandy tomorrow soon after day light   Nothing new from the other side   No indication of disputing the passage of the lower fords" Telegram received, DNA, RG 107, Telegrams Collected (Unbound); *ibid.*, RG 108, Letters Received. *O.R.*, I, xxxvi, part 2, 352. On the same day, 3:30 P.M., USG telegraphed to Meade. "You will move according to the orders issued—Gen Burnside knows the fact and has certainly made arrangements for guarding his stores—I will telegraph him however Saturday" Telegram received, DNA, RG 94, War Records Office, Army of the Potomac; copies, *ibid.*, RG 108, Letters Sent; DLC-USG, V, 45, 59; (2) Meade Papers, PHi. *O.R.*, I, xxxvi, part 2, 352. On the same day, 8:00 P.M., Meade telegraphed to USG. "I shall leave these Hd. Qrs at 5. a m to morrow & proceed to Germanna ford via Stevensbugh   Should I leave Germanna ford before you arrive a staff officer will be left at that point to indicate where I may be found." Telegram received, DNA, RG 94, War Records Office, Army of the Potomac; copies, *ibid.*, RG 200, Letters Sent by Meade; *ibid.*, RG 393, Army of the Potomac, Letters Sent; DLC-Andrew Johnson; (2) Meade Papers, PHi. *O.R.*, I, xxxvi, part 2, 352.

To Maj. Gen. Henry W. Halleck

Germania Ford May 4th 1864

MAJ GEN H W. HALLECK
CHF OF STAFF

The crossing of Rapidan effected. Forty Eight hours now will demonstrate whether the enemy intends giving battle this side of Richmond   Telegraph Butler that we have crossed the Rapidan[1]

U S GRANT
Lt Genl

Telegram received, DNA, RG 107, Telegrams Collected (Bound); copies, *ibid.*, RG 108, Letters Sent; DLC-USG, V, 45, 59, 66. *O.R.*, I, xxxvi, part 1, 1; *ibid.*, I, xxxvi, part 2, 370.

On May 4, 1864, USG twice telegraphed to Maj. Gen. Ambrose E. Burnside, the second time at 1:15 P.M. "To be taken off by all operators from Brandy Station to Bull Run   Crossing effected. Put your troops in motion as soon as Gen Augur's relieves you and the trains are south of Bull's Run"   "Make forced march until you reach this place. Start your troops now in the rear, the moment they can be got off, and require them to make a night march. Answer"   Copies, DLC-USG, V, 45, 59, 66; DNA, RG 108, Letters Sent. *O.R.*, I, xxxvi, part 2, 380. On the same day, 3:58 P.M., Burnside telegraphed to USG. "Dispatch received; will start column at once." *Ibid.* Also on May 4, Brig. Gen. Robert O. Tyler telegraphed to USG. "I have placed guards upon the bridges between Bull Run and the Rappahannock as ordered by General Augur. The rolling-stock is expected to be off by 10 o'clock to-night." *Ibid.*, p. 381.

1. For USG's telegram transmitted verbatim by Maj. Gen. Henry W. Halleck to Maj. Gen. Benjamin F. Butler, see telegram received, DLC-Benjamin F. Butler.

To Maj. Gen. Ambrose E. Burnside

Germanna Ford May 5 1864 8 41. A. M.

MAJ GEN BURNSIDE
COM'D'G 9TH A. C.
GENL:

Place one Division of your Corps on the ridge south of the river and west or south west of the plank road. Leave it there until your entire command is over, then close up as rapidly as possibly with the 6th Corps following the Frederickburg Plank road. As ~~soon~~ your troops cross they can either pass the first Division that crosses or may take the place of that Division and let it pass on out of the way as you may choose

Yours &c

U S GRANT

Lt Genl

Copies, DLC-USG, V, 45, 59, 66; DNA, RG 108, Letters Sent. *O.R.*, I, xxxvi, part 2, 423–24.

On May 5, 1864, 6:00 A.M., 10:30 A.M., and 3:00 P.M., Lt. Col. Cyrus B. Comstock wrote to Maj. Gen. Ambrose E. Burnside. "Lieut. Gen Grant desires that all your baggage and supply trains not immediately needed with your Command Cross the Rapidan at Ely's Ford and join the trains of the Army of the Potomac. As soon as you can dispense with the Ponton Bridge at Ely's Ford you will have it rejoined the Army of the Potomac" "Lieut Genl Grant desires that you consult with Gen Ricketts and relieve the two brigades he has moved from the plank road toward Mine run and which were to move out about a mile & hold the roads. You should send some cavalry out in front of your two brigades. The General desires that you should then mass your command about a mile this side of Germania Ford on the Plank road and await orders." "Lt Gen Grant directs that if Gen. Sedgewick calls on you, you will give him a division." Copies, DLC-USG, V, 45, 59, 66; DNA, RG 108, Letters Sent. *O.R.*, I, xxxvi, part 2, 423–24. On the same day, Burnside wrote to USG. "General Stevenson was placed in position by an Aide from your Head Qrs. and Gen—Willcox was placed in accordance with your order this morning. Gen—Potter's Division will soon be up and I will hold him subject to Gen. Sedgwick's request." ALS, DNA, RG 108, Letters Received. *O.R.*, I, xxxvi, part 2, 424.

Also on May 5, 5:20 P.M. and 8:00 P.M., Comstock wrote to Burnside. "Lieut Gen. Grant understands that you guard the roads which Rickett was on this morning, and in addition have sent a Division to support Sedgewick's right   He desires that you at once move your third white Division to this place." "Lieut Gen Grant desires ~~you~~ that your start your two Divisions at 2 A. M. to morrow morning punctually for this place. You will put them into position between the Germanna plank road and the road ~~and the~~ leading from this place to Parkers Store so as close up the gap between Warren and Hancock, consulting both. You will move from this position on the enemy beyond fail at 4½ A. M. the time at which the Army of the Potomac moves,   If you think there is no enemy in Wilcox's front bring him also." Copies, DLC-USG, V, 45, 59, 66; DNA, RG 108, Letters Sent. *O.R.*, I, xxxvi, part 2, 425. On the same day, Lt. Col. William R. Rowley wrote to Burnside. "If you do not consider that your reserve artillery would be safe left where it now is, you will have it brought in this direction to a safe place and parked. Otherwise let it remain where it is,— as there is not room for it at this point—" Copies, DLC-USG, V, 45, 59, 66; DNA, RG 108, Letters Sent. *O.R.*, I, xxxvi, part 2, 425.

To Maj. Gen. George G. Meade

Germanna Ford, May 5th/64

GEN. MEADE

Your note giving movement of enemy and your [dis]positions rec'd.

Burnsides advance is now crossing the river. I will have Ricket's[1] Div. relieved and ad[v]anced at once and urge Burnsides crossing. As soo[n as] I can see Burnside I will go forward.

If any opportunity presents [it]self for pitching into a part of Lee's Army do so without giving time for [di]sposition.

U. S. GRANT
Lt Gen.

ALS, DNA, RG 107, Telegrams Collected (Unbound). Entered as written at 8:24 A.M. in USG's letterbooks and *O.R.*, I, xxxvi, part 2, 403. On May 5, 1864, 7:30 A.M., Maj. Gen. George G. Meade, Old Wilderness Tavern, wrote to USG. "The enemy have appeared in force on the Orange pike and are now reported forming line of battle in front of Griffins Divn 5. corps—I have directed Genl. Warren to attack them at once with his whole force—Until this movement of the enemy is developed, the march of the corps must be suspended a I have therefore sent word to Hancock not to advance beyond Todds tavern for the present.—I think the enemy is trying to delay our movement & will not give battle but of this we shall soon see—For the present I will stop here & have stopped our trains" ALS, DNA, RG 108, Letters Received. *O.R.*, I, xxxvi, part 2, 403. Meade endorsed USG's letter, probably to Maj. Gen. Gouverneur K. Warren. "I send you the above—Wright is advancing on the Spottwood road— Attack as soon as you can & communicate if possible with Wright—" AES, DNA, RG 107, Telegrams Collected (Unbound). *O.R.*, I, xxxvi, part 2, 404. On May 4, 7:15 P.M., Brig. Gen. Seth Williams, adjt. for Meade, had written to Brig. Gen. John A. Rawlins transmitting the order of march for the following day. Copies, DNA, RG 200, Letters Sent by Meade; Meade Papers, PHi; DLC-Andrew Johnson. *O.R.*, I, xxxvi, part 2, 370–71.

On May 5, 9:00 A.M., 9:20 A.M., 9:00 P.M., and 10:30 P.M., Meade wrote to USG. "A Mr Wychoff a northern miner, whom I had met & believe to be reliable, has sent me word that a person from Orange C H. yesterday told him that Breckenridge & Polk had joined Lee I send you this for what it is worth.— Warren is making his disposition to attack & Sedgwicke to support him—Nothing immediate from the front I think still Lee is simply making a demonstration to gain time—I shall if such is the case punish him if he is disposed to fight this side of Mine run at once he shall be accomodated." "I ordered Genl. Ricketts to hold the roads leading from the enemys line to our right flank—I am informed you have ordered him forward as one of Burnsides Divisions have arrived—I would suggest Burnsides Division relieving Ricketts on these roads—also a small party of cavalry I have in front of Ricketts   Ricketts having received my order after yours is awaiting your action on this suggestion" "Warren informs me that Wadsworth & Robinson got into action just in time to meet Wilcox's Division (Hills corps) and drove them handsomely for a mile   I have also just heard from Sedgewicke who reports Wrights right having been vigorously attacked at 8. P. M. the attack handsomely repulsed—" "After conversing with my corps commanders, I am led to believe that it will be difficult owing to the dense thicket in which their commands are located the fatigued condition of the men rendering it difficult to rouse them early enough & the necessity of some day light to properly put in re-inforcements   All these considerations induce me to suggest the attack should not be made till Six 6 o'clock instead of ½ past Four —I have ordered it for 4.30, but am of the opinion it will be more likely to be simultaneous if made at 6. Should you permit this change I will advise corps commanders. It appears to be the general opinion among prisoners that Longstreet was not in the action to-day, though expected, and that his position was to be on their right or our left. His force supposed to be about 12,000. He probably will attack Hancock to-morrow. I have notified Hancock to look out for his left, but think it will be well to have Willcox up as soon as possible." ALS, DNA, RG 108, Letters Received. *O.R.*, I, xxxvi, part 2, 404–5. The last is incomplete in RG 108. On the same day, Lt. Col. William R. Rowley wrote to Meade. "I am directed by the General Commanding to say that you may change the hour of attack to 5 o'clock, as he is afraid if delayed until 6, the enemy would take the initiative which he desires specially to avoid—Gen Burnside is directed to bring up Gen Wilcox's division with his other troops if they can possibly be spared, and will probably bring them—" Copies, DLC-USG, V, 45, 59, 66; DNA, RG 108, Letters Sent. *O.R.*, I, xxxvi, part 2, 405.

1. James B. Ricketts of N. Y., USMA 1839, served in the Mexican War with the 1st Art. Promoted to capt. as of Aug. 3, 1852, he was severely wounded and captured during the first battle of Bull Run. Appointed brig. gen. as of July 21, 1861, he was again wounded at the battle of Antietam, and his disability led to assignment to the court-martial of Maj. Gen. Fitz John Porter. In May, 1864, he commanded the 3rd Div., 6th Army Corps, Army of the Potomac.

To Maj. Gen. Henry W. Halleck

Headqrs Armies &c
Wilderness Town May 6th 11.30 A. M.

MAJ GEN HALLECK WASHINGTON

We have engaged with the enemy in full force since early yesterday. So far there is no decisive result, but I think all things are progressing favorably. Our loss to this time I do not think exceeds eight thousand of whom a large proportion, are slightly wounded. Brig Gen. Hays[1] was killed yesterday, and Gens Getty[2] and Bartlett[3] wounded. We have taken about fourteen hundred prisoners —Longstreets, Hills[4] and Ewells are all represented among the prisoners—

U. S. GRANT
Lt. Gen—

Copies, DLC-USG, V, 45, 59, 66; DNA, RG 108, Letters Sent. *O.R.*, I, xxxvi, part 1, 2; *ibid.*, I, xxxvi, part 2, 437.

1. Alexander Hays of Pa., USMA 1844, served in the Mexican War, resigned as of April 12, 1848, and worked as a civil engineer in Pa. Appointed maj., 12th Pa., as of April 25, 1861, and col., 63rd Pa., as of Aug. 25, he was severely wounded at the battle of Manassas, Aug. 30, 1862. Appointed brig. gen. as of Sept. 29, he was killed on May 5, 1864, while leading the 2nd Brigade, 3rd Div., 2nd Army Corps. See *PUSG*, 8, 564; *Memoirs*, II, 194; George Thornton Fleming and Gilbert Adams Hays, *Life and Letters of Alexander Hays* . . . (Pittsburgh, 1919), pp. 658–59.

2. George W. Getty of D. C., USMA 1840, served in the Mexican War. An art. officer with the Army of the Potomac during the peninsular campaign, he was appointed brig. gen. as of Sept. 25, 1862, and wounded on May 6, 1864, while commanding the 2nd Div., 6th Army Corps. See *O.R.*, I, xxxvi, part 1, 676–80.

3. Joseph J. Bartlett, born in Binghamton, N. Y., in 1834, began to practice law in 1858. Appointed maj., 27th N. Y., as of May 21, 1861, promoted to col. as of Sept. 21, and appointed brig. gen. as of Oct. 4, 1862, he participated in almost all of the battles of the Army of the Potomac. He remained in command of the 3rd Brigade, 1st Div., 5th Army Corps, after the battle of the Wilderness.

4. Ambrose P. Hill of Va., USMA 1847, served in the Mexican War and resigned from the U.S. Army as of March 1, 1861, to become col., 13th Va. Appointed C.S.A. brig. gen. as of Feb. 26, 1862, promoted to maj. gen. as of May 26, and to lt. gen. as of May 24, 1863, he led the 3rd Army Corps, Army of Northern Va., at the battles of Gettysburg and the Wilderness.

To Maj. Gen. Ambrose E. Burnside

Wilderness Tavern, May 6th 1864

MAJ GEN BURNSIDE,
COMDG 9TH CORPS,
GENERAL

General Hancock[1] has been severely engaged for some time the enemy having forced his line in one place, but being immediately repulsed. In consequence of this, orders have been sent Hancock suspending the order to attack at 6 p. m. In your movements for the balance of the day, or until you receive further orders, hold your own, and be governed entirely by circumstances. Should the enemy attack Hancock give such aid as you can. After dark, and all is quiet, put your men in a good position for defence and for holding our line and give your men all the rest they can get.

Yours

U. S. GRANT

Lt. Gen

ALS, USG 3. *O.R.*, I, xxxvi, part 2, 462.

On May 6, 1864, 6:00 A.M., Maj. Gen. George G. Meade wrote to USG. "Sedgwick and Warren are engaged; have been since 5 a. m. No news from Hancock. Would it not be well for Burnside's cavalry to watch our extreme right by the fords, letting them go out on all the roads toward the enemy; and if enough can be spared to cross the river, they might scout on the other side." *Ibid.*, p. 438. At 6:10 A.M., Lt. Col. Cyrus B. Comstock endorsed this message to Maj. Gen. Ambrose E. Burnside. "Lieutenant-General Grant desires that you adopt General Meade's suggestion." *Ibid.* At 6:20 A.M., Comstock wrote to Burnside. "Lt Gen Grant desires that you take but two of your Divisions to the front and place the third at this place near the crossing of the turnpike & Germania Plank road" Copies, DLC-USG, V, 45, 59, 66; DNA, RG 108, Letters Sent. *O.R.*, I, xxxvi, part 2, 460. At 10:00 A.M., Comstock wrote to USG. "Burnside has gained 1½ miles to his left to connect with Wadsworth, and now moves at once toward Hancock's firing, with Potter's division deployed, supported by a brigade. I should think Hancock's firing a mile away." *Ibid.*, p. 460. At 11:45 A.M., Brig. Gen. John A. Rawlins wrote to Burnside. "Push in with all vigor so as to drive the Enemy from Gen Hancock's front, and get in on the Orange and Frederick Plank Road at the earliest possible moment   Hancock has been expecting you for the last 3 hours and has been making his attack and disposition with a view to your assistance—" Copies, DLC-USG, V, 45, 59, 66; DNA, RG 108, Letters Sent. *O.R.*, I, xxxvi, part 2, 461. At 12:30 P.M., 1:55 P.M., and 2:45 P.M., Comstock wrote to USG. "Burnside put in one brigade behind another, holding the third in reserve. The leading brigade has been rather smartly engaged for fifteen minutes and the firing has now stopped. He must be near Hancock, as General Stevenson, who got cut off from Hancock with 100 men, came into Burnside's column." "As Willcox's brigade is withdrawn from its position, about 2 miles out the Parker Store road, General Willcox reports the enemy following it with skirmishers, but apparently not in great force. There are no troops now on the road except those about half a mile from the Lacy house. . . . Burnside is driving the enemy in his front, and has carried a small earth-work or log-work." "Warren's troops, now on the Parker's Store road, one-half or three-quarters of a mile from the Lacy house, don't connect with Wadsworth's right, and Burnside's whole force is three-quarters of a mile in front of the gap. Connection should be made. Potter, commanding leading division, reports enemy advancing at 2.25. Willcox is moving his brigade up to him. Some regiments had behaved badly, and Potter had been checked. . . . An officer who came in the Parker's Store road with Willcox's brigade reports seeing a force which he thought as large as a division moving from our left to right." *Ibid.* The first is also printed *ibid.*, I, xxxvi, part 1, 353. At 3:30 P.M., USG wrote to Burnside. "Gen Hancock is directed to make an attack at 6 o'clock this evening. Be prepared & aid him in it" Copies, DLC-USG, V, 45, 59, 66; DNA, RG 108, Letters Sent. *O.R.*, I, xxxvi, part 2, 462. At 3:45 P.M., Comstock wrote to USG. "Your note is received. Wilcox has orders to get through to Hancock if possible & attack again at once. He has nearly two brigades of fresh troops besides the other division which was severly checked, the new regiments breaking. He ~~brings~~ ~~Potters~~ will move to left of Potters ~~left~~ attack. Nothing new from the Parkers store road." ALS (undated), DNA, RG 94, War Records Office, Army of the Potomac. *O.R.*, I, xxxvi, part 2, 462. At 4:00 P.M., USG wrote to Comstock. "Immediately on receipt of your first note, the reserve Brigade of Gen Burside was sent out on Parkers store road. Gen Warren has also been instructed to keep a lookout, and if any troops moved out to attack them vigorously. Your last note is just ~~received~~ sent to Gen Warren with instructions to the same effect—" Copies, DLC-USG, V, 45, 59, 66; DNA, RG 108, Letters Sent. *O.R.*, I, xxxvi, part 2, 462.

1. Winfield S. Hancock, born in Pa. in 1824, USMA 1844, appointed brig. gen. as of Sept. 23, 1861, and maj. gen. as of Nov. 29, 1862, fought in all of the major battles of the Army of the Potomac, winning special acclaim at Gettysburg, where he was severely wounded. In May, 1864, he commanded the 2nd Corps. See *ibid.*, I, xxxvi, part 1, 318–28; *Memoirs*, II, 539–40.

To Brig. Gen. Edward Ferrero

HdQrs Armies of the U. States
Wilderness Tavern, May. 6/64 8. P. M.

GEN'L. FERRERO
GENERAL

The 6th Corps has been forced back from its position late this evening[1] and their is now every probability that before morning the enemy will intervene between you and this command. Should you learn such to be the case, move at once across Germania Ford and down the river to Ely's Ford. There cross to the south side and remain with the wagon train until you receive further orders.

Yours
U. S. GRANT
Lieut General

Copies, DLC-USG, V, 45, 59, 66; DNA, RG 94, War Records Office, 9th Army Corps; *ibid.*, RG 108, Letters Sent. *O.R.*, I, xxxvi, part 2, 465. Edward Ferrero, born in Spain to Italian parents in 1831, operated a dancing school in New York City before the Civil War. Previously a militia officer, he was appointed col., 51st N. Y., as of Oct. 14, 1861, and confirmed as brig. gen. on April 21, 1864, after an earlier appointment had expired for lack of Senate action. On April 19, he was assigned to command the 4th Div. (Colored), 9th Army Corps. *Ibid.*, I, xxxiii, 913.

On May 6, 7:10 A.M., Lt. Col. Cyrus B. Comstock wrote to Ferrero. "Lieut Gen'l. Grant desires that you report to Gen'l Sedgwick with your colored division and with (the White troops on the two roads leading west from the plank road) belonging to Gen'l Burnside" Copies, DLC-USG, V, 45, 59, 66; DNA, RG 94, War Records Office, 9th Army Corps; *ibid.*, RG 108, Letters Sent. *O.R.*, I, xxxvi, part 2, 463. At 8:00 A.M. and 2:30 P.M., Brig. Gen. John A. Rawlins wrote to Ferrero. "Releive Col. Marshalls Provisional Brigade and Heavy Artillery Regiments now guarding the roads leading to the Jacobs' Ferry road, by colored Troops, reserving enough of the latter to guard your trains and bridge move Col Marshall's command up the plank road to the intersection of the road leading to Gen. Sedgwick, to support him when called for. Report this disposition to Gen Sedgwick. Direct all your trains to be moved to this side of the river and park them Gen'l. Meade ordered all the troops to report to him" "Place a guard at the bridge and permit no Stragglers to pass over. Arrest them, and as fast as they amount to a sufficient number send them under guard to Genl Patrick, Pro. Marshal Gen. A. P. at this place" Copies, DLC-USG, V, 45, 59, 66; DNA, RG 94, War Records Office, 9th Army Corps; *ibid.*, RG 108, Letters Sent. *O.R.*, I, xxxvi, part 2, 464, 465. The first is entered in USG's letterbooks as written by USG. At 9:00 P.M., USG wrote to Ferrero. "Move your troop with every thing at the river up the plank road to this place. You must move immediately otherwise you may be cut off, should you not start before the enemy intervene, then go by Ely's Ford to Chancellorsville" Copy, DNA, RG 94, War Records Office, 9th Army Corps. *O.R.*, I, xxxvi, part 2, 465.

On May 7, 7:30 A.M., Comstock wrote to Ferrero. "Lt. Gen'l Grant directs that you move your colored Division alone to Dowdalls Tavern and Chancellorsville, a Brigade at each place to cover our trains now assembling between those points. You will move by the turnpike and inform Gen Burnside that you have received this order, on reaching Dowdalls Tavern you will report by a Staff Officer to Maj. Gen'l Sheridan Comd'g Cavalry, for further orders" Copies, DLC-USG, V, 45, 59, 66; DNA, RG 94, War Records Office, 9th Army Corps; *ibid.*, RG 108, Letters Sent. *O.R.*, I, xxxvi, part 2, 513.

1. On May 6, 7:00 P.M., Maj. Gen. George G. Meade wrote to USG. "Gen Sedgwicke has just reported the enemy having vigorously assualted his line & turned his right flank—I have sent the Pa. Reserves to him—Will report when more is heard—. . . Another officer just reported that Sedgwick's whole line has given way." ALS, DNA, RG 108, Letters Received. *O.R.*, I, xxxvi, part 2, 438. The final sentence appears only in *O.R.*

To Maj. Gen. Henry W. Halleck

———

Hd Qrs "Wilderness"
11 a. m. May 7. 1864.
By mail from Alexandria Va.

MAJ GEN. H. W. HALLECK,
CHIEF OF STAFF

We were engaged with the enemy nearly all day both on the 5th & 6th. Yesterday the enemy attacked our lines vigorously first at one point and then another from right to left. They were repulsed at all points before reaching our lines, except once during the afternoon on Hancock's front, and just after night on Sedgwick's[1] front In the former instance they were promptly and handsomely repulsed. The latter, Milroy's old brigade, was attacked & gave way in the greatest confusion almost without resistance, carrying good troops with them. Had there been daylight the enemy could have injured us very much in the confusion that prevailed, they however instead of getting through the break, attacked Gen Wright's[2] Div of Sedgwick's Corps & were beaten back.

Our losses to this time in killed, wounded & prisoners will not probably exceed 12.000. of whom an unusually large proportion are but slightly wounded. Among the killed we have to deplore the loss of Genls Wadsworth[3] & Hays, Genls Getty & Bartlett wounded & Genls Seymour & Shaler[4] taken prisoners. We have about 2.000 prisoners. They report Gen Jenkins[5] killed & Longstreet wounded. I think the loss of the enemy must exceed ours, but this is only a guess based upon the fact that they attacked & were repulsed so often.

I wish you would send me all the information you have of Gen Sherman by Bull Run & also care of Genl Butler. Send by way of Bull Run all the information from the James River expedition.

At present we can claim no victory over the enemy, neither have they gained a single advantage

Enemy pushed out of their fortifications to prevent their position being turned & have been sooner or later driven back in every instance.

Up to this hour enemy have not shown themselves in force within a mile of our lines.

U. S. GRANT

Lt Genl

Telegram received, DNA, RG 107, Telegrams Collected (Bound); copies (sent at 10:00 A.M.), *ibid.*, RG 108, Letters Sent; DLC-USG, V, 45, 59, 66. *O.R.*, I, xxxvi, part 1, 2; *ibid.*, I, xxxvi, part 2, 480.

1. John Sedgwick of Conn., USMA 1837, was appointed brig. gen. as of Aug. 31, 1861, and promoted to maj. gen. as of July 4, 1862. In May, 1864, he commanded the 6th Army Corps, Army of the Potomac. See letter to Maj. Gen. Ambrose E. Burnside, May 10, 1864, 3:20 P.M.

2. Horatio G. Wright of Conn., USMA 1841, was appointed brig. gen. as of Sept. 14, 1861, and promoted to maj. gen. as of July 18, 1862, but not confirmed by the Senate, reverting to brig. gen. as of March 12, 1863. In May, 1864, he commanded the 1st Div., 6th Army Corps, Army of the Potomac. See letter to Maj. Gen. Ambrose E. Burnside, May 10, 1864, 3:20 P.M.

3. James S. Wadsworth, born in Geneseo, N. Y., in 1807, a Democrat turned Republican in 1856, was appointed brig. gen. as of Aug. 9, 1861. He was mortally wounded and captured on May 6, 1864, while commanding the 4th Div., 5th Army Corps, Army of the Potomac, and USG reportedly remarked that he "would rather have lost an entire infantry brigade than this brave and wise man." *New-York Tribune*, May 10, 1864.

4. Alexander Shaler, born in Conn. in 1827, was educated in private schools in New York City. A member of the N. Y. militia, he was appointed lt. col., 65th N. Y., as of June 11, 1861, and promoted to col. as of June 17, 1862. Appointed brig. gen. as of May 26, 1863, he was captured on May 6, 1864, while commanding the 4th Brigade, 1st Div., 6th Army Corps, Army of the Potomac.

5. Micah Jenkins, born in S. C. in 1835, graduated from South Carolina Military Academy in 1855, and became col., 5th S. C., in 1861. Appointed C.S.A. brig. gen. as of July 22, 1862, he was mortally wounded on May 6, 1864, by his own men in the same incident in which Lt. Gen. James Longstreet was severely wounded.

To Maj. Gen. Ambrose E. Burnside

May 7th 1864, 5.15 a. m.

MAJ. GEN. BURNSIDE,
COMD.G 9TH CORPS,
GENERAL,

General Hancock reports indications of enemy moving in heavy force on his left. In case ~~there~~ he is ~~an~~ attacke you ~~can~~ will render him assistance either by an advance from your present front or leaving your line entirely and moving by the left flank to the point of attack. In the absence of further instructions you will exercise your judgement which will be the best.

After the falling back last night of Sedgewicks right fearing your Colored troops might be cut off I ordered them up here. They are now in front of my quarters. If there does not prove to be absolute need of retaining them here by 10 O'Clock a. m. you may order them to Chancellorsville where the trains have been ordered.

Respectfully yours
U. S. GRANT
Lt. Gen.

ALS, deCoppet Collection, NjP. *O.R.*, I, xxxvi, part 2, 511. On May 7, 1864, Maj. Gen. Ambrose E. Burnside wrote to USG. "The officer in command of pickets in front of our left connecting with 2d Corps reports that the wagons & troops of the enemy in front were moving quite busily during the night he thinks to the South—No rebels in front this morning—Some movements have been ordered from our front, that will draw the fire of the enemy if they occupy the ground they occupied yesterday, or the ground in the advance of it. A prisoner reports that Longstreet & Hill were present yesterday in our front—that Jenkins was killed, and Longstreet wounded." LS, DNA, RG 108, Letters Received. *O.R.*, I, xxxvi, part 2, 511.

On May 7, 7:30 A.M., Lt. Col. Cyrus B. Comstock wrote to Burnside. "Gen Grant desires that if you have not already done so, that you at once strongly fortify the hill where your personal Hdqrs were most of the day yesterday" Copies, DLC-USG, V, 45, 59, 66; DNA, RG 108, Letters Sent. *O.R.*, I, xxxvi, part 2, 511. At 1:00 P.M. and 2:00 P.M., Brig. Gen. John A. Rawlins wrote to Burnside. "It is definitely ascertained that Longstreet's corps—at least two divisions of it—is at Spotsylvania Court-House. General Warren's corps has engaged it near there, and the whole of General Sedgwick's corps has been ordered forward, one division of which has joined General Warren, with a view to crushing Longstreet, if possible. This leaves no troops at this point." *Ibid.*, pp.

511–12. "Gen. Sedgwick Corps will move immediately after dark. You will follow immediately upon his rear—taking the same road stopping at the Piney Branch Church. These movements must be made with the greatest promptitude possible Send your Cavalry by the Brock Road, where it will be relieved by Gen Meade A part of his forces go out on that road and the necessary orders will be given it by him—" Copies, DLC-USG, V, 45, 59, 66; DNA, RG 108, Letters Sent. *O.R.*, I, xxxvi, part 2, 512. At 2:45 P.M. and 7:15 P.M., Comstock wrote to Burnside. "Lt Gen Grant desires that you at once send either Potter or Wilcox's Division to reinforce Sedgwick on the plank road—" "Lt Gen Grant desires me to say that you will take your wounded men with you instead of sending them to Rappahannock Station—" Copies, DLC-USG, V, 45, 59, 66; DNA, RG 108, Letters Sent. *O.R.*, I, xxxvi, part 2, 512.

To Maj. Gen. George G. Meade

May 7th 1864. 6.30 a. m

MAJ. GEN. MEADE,
COMD.G A. P.
GENERAL,

Make all preparations during the day for a night march to take position at Spotsylvania C. H. with one Army Corps; at Todd's Tavern with one and another near the intersection Piney Branch & Spotsylvania road with the road from Alsops to Old C. H. If this move is made the trains should be thrown forward early in the morning to Ny River.

I think it would be advisable in making this change to leave Hancock where he is until Warren[1] passes him. He could then follow and become the right of the new line. Burnside will move to Piney Branch church. Sedgewick can move along the pike to Chancollorsville, thence to Piney Branch Church and on to his destination. Burnside will move on the plank road to the intersection of it with the O. F. plank road then follow Sedgewick to his place of destination.

All vehickles should be got out of hearing of the enemy before the troops move and then move off quietly.

It is more than probable the enemy will concentrate for a heavy attack on Hancock this afternoon. In case they do we must be prepared to resist them and follow up any success we may gain with

our whole force. Such a result would necessarily modify these instructions. All the hospitals should be moved to day to Chancellorsville.

Respectfully &c.

U. S. GRANT

Lt. Gen.

ALS, ICarbS. *O.R.*, I, xxxvi, part 2, 481. Brig. Gen. John A. Rawlins sent a copy
of this letter to Maj. Gen. Ambrose E. Burnside, omitting the words "on Hancock." *Ibid.*, pp. 481, 482.

On May 8, 1864, 6:40 A.M., Lt. Col. Cyrus B. Comstock wrote to USG.
"Two-thirds of Warren's corps is up and the head of Wright's. The country is
covered with stragglers and the tails of the columns. General Meade thinks it
will take half the day to get them up. Warren is trying to see in what force the
enemy is." *Ibid.*, p. 527. On the same day, 11:00 P.M., Maj. Gen. George G.
Meade wrote to USG. "Warren reports that Crawfords attack developed the fact
that the enemy were not very strongly entrenched, but he was not able to carry
their line—On withdrawing the enemy made a charge which was repulsed and
about 100 prisoners taken—one of them who represents himself as an ensign in
an Alaba regt—a northern man says Lee's army is not over 70,000, that they
have lost a good many in the recent battles and that the men are greatly exhausted
by fatigue—that they left their entrenchments soon after dark last night & traveled all night—that when we first attacked this morning their line of battle was
unformed, and that there were no rifle pits—that they have been since making
them & by tomorrow will have the usual rude breastworks—That Ewell & Longstreet are opposite Warren & Hill is said to be on the left.—Hancock has taken
prisoners in some skirmishing this P. M from Hills corps & is under the impression Hill is taking position in front of h[im] which I think not unlikely   A scout
has returned from Fredericks burgh who reports some of the enemy's cavalry
having come in from the N. side of the Rappahanock & capturing some of our
wounded—that the 3d N. Jersey were in pursuit on the N. side.—I have given
the orders for tomorrow & the preparatory orders agreed on for a move—
Sheridan reports he will move tomorrow at 4. a m to carry out his instructions—"   ALS, DNA, RG 108, Letters Received. *O.R.*, I, xxxvi, part 2, 527.

1. Gouverneur K. Warren of N. Y., USMA 1850, was appointed lt. col.,
5th N. Y., as of May 14, 1861, and promoted to col. as of Sept. 11. Appointed
brig. gen. as of Sept. 26, 1862, and promoted to maj. gen. as of May 3, 1863, he
commanded the 5th Army Corps, Army of the Potomac, in May, 1864.

To Maj. Gen. George G. Meade

Head Quarters Armies U. S.
May 7th 1864

MAJ GEN MEADE

Burnside has but two Divisions and rather a long line to hold so that I think it would not be prudent to remove any of his men, except to move to the front until our line is entirely changed. I will instruct him however to assist Hancock in case of an attack. Either as suggested above by an advance or to move round with his whole force in case there is evidence of the enemy massing on Hancock, leaving the line between Hancock and Warren as it was before Burnside came up.

If our line has been shortened as was directed last night, is there not a large surplus of troops on the right

Yours &c
U. S. GRANT Lt. Gen.

Copies, DLC-USG, V, 45, 59, 66; DNA, RG 108, Letters Sent. *O.R.*, I, xxxvi, part 2, 481. On May 7, 1864, 5:00 A.M., Maj. Gen. George G. Meade wrote to USG. "Hancock writes there are indications the enemy are massing on his *left* and he expects to be attacked. Has Burnside any reserve he can send to him—I suggest this because B is the nearest & I have not yet ascertained precisely the locality of the troops changing last night tho I know they are in position—I have told Hancock to call on Burnside—He now has I think Stevenson—" ALS, DNA, RG 108, Letters Received. *O.R.*, I, xxxvi, part 2, 480–81.

To Maj. Gen. Henry W. Halleck

Hd Qrs Piney Branch Church
11 a m May 8th 1864

MAJ GEN H W HALLECK

The army com[mence]d moving south at 9 p m yesterday and when close up to the position assigned one days march will stand thus—Genl Warrens Corps at Spotsylvania Court House—Hancocks' at Todds tavern—Sedgwicks on road from Piney Branch

Church to Spotsylvania and Gen Burnside at Aldrichs. It is not yet demonstrated what the enemy will do—but the best of feeling prevails in this army and I feel at present no apprehension for the result. My efforts will be to form a junction with Genl Butler as early as possible[1] and be prepared to beat any enemy interposing— The results of the three days fight at Old Wilderness was decidedly in our favor—The enemy having a strongly entrenched position to fall back on when hard pressed—and the extensive train we had to cover rendered it impossible to inflict the heavy blow on Lees army I had hoped—My exact route to the James River I have not yet definately marked out

U S GRANT
Lt Genl

Telegram received, DNA, RG 107, Telegrams Collected (Bound); DLC-Robert T. Lincoln; copies (sent at 11:30 A.M.), DLC-USG, V, 45, 59, 66; DNA, RG 108, Letters Sent. *O.R.*, I, xxxvi, part 1, 2–3; *ibid.*, I, xxxvi, part 2, 526.

1. On May 5, 1864, 9:00 P.M., Maj. Gen. Benjamin F. Butler, City Point, telegraphed to USG. "We have seized Wilson's Wharf landing a Brigade Wilds Col. Troops there   Fort Powhatan landing two Regiments of same Brigade. Have landed at City Point Hinks Division of Colored troops remaining Brigades and battery—Remainder of both 18th and 10th Army Corps are now being landed at Bermuda Hundreds above the Appomattox. No opposition thus far   Apparently a complete Surprise   Both Army Corps left Yorktown During last night   Monitors all over the bar at Harrisons landing and above City Point. The operations of the fleet have been conducted to day with energy and success. Genls Smith & Gilmore are pushing the landing of their men   Gen Graham with the Army Gunboats led the advance during the night Capturing the signal Stations of the rebels   Col. West with 1800 Cavalry made demonstration from Williams burgh yesterday Morning   General Kautz left Suffolk this morning with 3000 Cavalry for the service indicated in conference with the Lt General. The New York flag of truce Boat was found lying at the Wharf with four hundred rebel prisoners which she had not had time to ~~unload~~ deliver. She went up yesterday morning   Duplicate of this has been sent to the Secretary of War   We are landing the troops during the night a hazardous service in face of the enemy"   ALS (telegram sent), DNA, RG 393, Dept. of Va. and N. C., Telegrams Sent; telegram received, *ibid.*, RG 107, Telegrams Collected (Bound); DLC-Robert T. Lincoln. Incomplete in *O.R.*, I, xxxvi, part 2, 430. On May 6, 2:30 P.M., Butler telegraphed to USG. "In continuation of my telegram of yesterday I have to report that we have not been disturbed during the night, that all our troops are landed that we have taken the positions which were indicated ~~by~~ to the Comdg General at our last conference, and are carrying out that plan"   LS (telegram sent), DNA, RG 393, Dept. of Va. and N. C., Telegrams Sent; telegram received, *ibid.*, RG 107, Telegrams Collected (Bound). *O.R.*, I, xxxvi, part 2, 471.

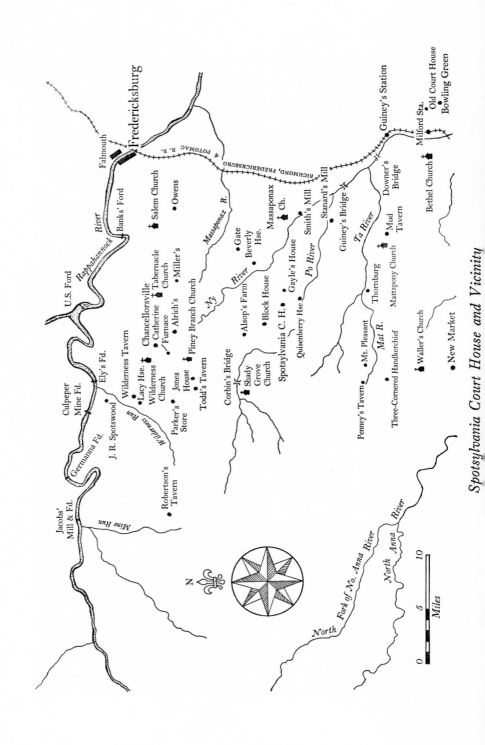

Spotsylvania Court House and Vicinity

To Maj. Gen. Ambrose E. Burnside

Camp Near Spotsylvania C. H. May 8th/64
MAJ. GEN. BURNSIDE,

The enemy have made a strong resistence here, so much so that no advance will be attempted to-morrow. You will not therefore move your advance beyond (south of) the Gate. If you have not already got two Divisions at the front get them up by 6 O'Clock a m to-morrow so that if they should be called for they can be marched from the Gate directly on Spotsylvania.

Respectfully yours
U. S. GRANT
Lt. Gen.

ALS, deCoppet Collection, NjP. Printed as written at 9:00 P.M. in *O.R.*, I, xxxvi, part 2, 548.

On May 8, 1864, 9:00 A.M. and 9:40 A.M., Lt. Col. Cyrus B. Comstock wrote to Maj. Gen. Ambrose E. Burnside. "Lt Gen Grant desires that you occupy a position as near Aldrichs as you can get to cover our trains from a possible attack down the plank road. Sedgwick will have a division at Piney Branch Church where these Hdqrs will be. You should connect with this Division . . . You should to day & tonight issue five days rations from tomorrow. You will probably remain in position till sometime tomorrow morning" "Lt Gen Grant desires that like Gen Meade, you send your wounded to Fredericksburg, where your Medical officers will act in conjunction with the Medical Director of the Army of the Potomac in establishing temporary hospitals and moving these wounded thence to Washington via Aquia Creek. If you are not able to move all your wounded at once, you will, keeping your ambulances with you, send your empty Qr. M. wagons under flag of truce to the battle field with supplies and get the rest of the wounded & move them to Fredericksburg" Copies, DLC-USG, V, 45, 59, 66; DNA, RG 108, Letters Sent. *O.R.*, I, xxxvi, part 2, 545. On the same day, Brig. Gen. John A. Rawlins wrote to Burnside. "We have no troops at Alsops Gate or Andersons. These three points are on the road which will be designated in future orders for your next march—Please get the five days rations, you were directed to issue this morning into the hands of your men at the earliest possible moment—" Copies, DLC-USG, V, 45, 59, 66; DNA, RG 108, Letters Sent. *O.R.*, I, xxxvi, part 2, 546. At 12:45 P.M., 1:00 P.M., and 3:00 P.M., Rawlins wrote to Burnside. "The following is a memorandum of the order of the next march. The time of starting will be given you hereafter. Hancock followed by Warren via Block House, Pennys Tavern, Mount Pleasant, Three-Cornered Handkerchief, Wallers Church and Dabney's Mill—Sedgwick followed by artillery reserve and such ammunition trains as are not taken with Corps, via Spottsylvinia C. H. Mattapony Church, Green Branch to New Market, to Davensport Ford, the main wagon train to be followed by Burnside, via Alsop, Gate, Anderson, Smith's Mill, Stannard's Mill, Mud Tavern, Round Oak Church and Childsburg—Each Corps to have a pontoon train. No guards for the main wagon trains from Corps, but disabled and extra duty men. The Cavalry has all been cut loose from the main Command, and directed to make its way to the James River and Communicate with Gen Butler—Your line of march will therefore be as hereinbefore indicated—with two divisions of your white troops in advance of main wagon trains, and the remaining two divisions in rear of the trains. The white, troops will form the rear guard. The greatest vigilance should be exercised in the protection of these trains and the keeping of them well up." "It has been definitely ascertained that Longstreets Corps—at least two divisions of it—are at Spottsylvania. Warrens whole Corps has engaged it. Sedgwick has been ordered up with a view of crushing it if possible. This leaves no troops at this place." "You will move forward to Childsburg the moment you can get the trains started. If you can find another road in supporting distance of the one you have been directed to move on, & by which other troops have not been ordered to march, so as to double your troops, you will do so—" Copies, DLC-USG, V, 45, 59, 66; DNA, RG 108, Letters Sent. *O.R.*, I, xxxvi, part 2, 546–47.

At 4:20 P.M., Lt. Col. Orville E. Babcock wrote to Rawlins. "General Burnside wishes to know whether a pontoon train has been ordered to report to him with engineers. He says he will follow the trains as quick as they can move. I shall start for headquarters in a little while, unless something turns up to keep me here." *Ibid.*, p. 547. Rawlins endorsed this letter to Burnside. "I have sent pontoon trains in the train you convoy, but you will not need one." *Ibid.*

At 7:30 P.M., Rawlins wrote to Burnside. "Dispose of your command so as to most easily and effectually to guard the trains in your convoy, and at the same time be in readiness on receipt of orders to send two Divisions of Infantry to help drive the enemy from Spottsylvania C. H. where he appears to have made a stand in very considerable force—" Copies, DLC-USG, V, 45, 59, 66; DNA, RG 108, Letters Sent. *O.R.*, I, xxxvi, part 2, 547.

To Maj. Gen. Henry W. Halleck

Near Spotsylvania Court House
1 p m May 9th 1864

MAJ GEN H W HALLECK
GENL IN CHIEF

If matters are at all favorable with Butler send him all reenforcements you can.[1]

Enemy are now moving from our immediate front either to interpose between us and Fredericksburg or to get the inside road to Richmond—

My movements are terribly embarrassed by our immense wagon trains. it could not be avoided however

U S GRANT
Lt Genl.

Telegram received, DNA, RG 107, Telegrams Collected (Bound); copies, *ibid.*, RG 108, Letters Sent; DLC-USG, V, 45, 59, 66. *O.R.*, I, xxxvi, part 1, 3; *ibid.*, I, xxxvi, part 2, 561. On May 9, 1864, 1:00 P.M., Secretary of War Edwin M. Stanton wrote to USG. "I enclose herewith all the information we have since Mr Dana started from here. May God bless you and crown you and your gallant army with victory. . . . .P S. Every thing that comes will be forwarded you by the first opportunities. The road is open to Rappahanock Station. Trains & Supplies are there to bring back the wounded. Provision is also made for bringing them from Aquia if that route should be preferred by you—" ALS, DNA, RG 108, Letters Received. *O.R.*, I, xxxvi, part 2, 560–61. Stanton enclosed an intercepted message from Gen. Robert E. Lee. Copy, DNA, RG 108, Letters Received. *O.R.*, I, xxxvi, part 2, 561. On May 10, Stanton twice wrote to USG, first at 8:20 P.M. "Your despatch of yesterday was received this evening. I send herewith despatches from Generals Sherman & Butler which contain all that we have from them to this date. This Department is now in telegraphic communication with Belle plain. The despatch boat Diamond will receive and deliver all despatches to and from you which will save some hours in transmission. It is reported that matters are not well organized at Fredericksburg & I send Brig Gen Slough an active & energetic man there for police duty as Military Governor subject to your orders" "General Abercrombie is ordered to Fredericksburg instead of General Slough. The whole nation is rejoicing in your achievements. God bless and preserve you." ALS, DNA, RG 108, Letters Received. The first is in *O.R.*, I, xxxvi, part 2, 595.

1. On May 7, Maj. Gen. Benjamin F. Butler, Bermuda Landing, telegraphed to Stanton. "We have no news from General Grant. If he has been in any degree successful there can we have here ten thousand (10.000) of the reserves? . . ." Copy, DNA, RG 108, Letters Received. *O.R.*, I, xxxvi, part 2, 517.

To Maj. Gen. Ambrose E. Burnside

May 9th/64

MAJ. GEN. BURNSIDE,

I will direct the Chief Q. M. to turn his trains back so as to fall towards Chancellorsville if necessary. The enemy have disappeared from our right moving in the direction of Gate's evidently which will enable us to follow from here. Direct Wilcox to entrench and hold his position strongly only falling back at the last extremity, expecting the enemy, if they have gone in force towards him, to be attacked from here.

Respectfully &c.

U. S. Grant

Lt. Gen

ALS, deCoppet Collection, NjP. Printed as written at 12:45 P.M. in *O.R.*, I, xxxvi, part 2, 582.

On May 9, 1864, 8:45 A.M., Brig. Gen. John A. Rawlins wrote to Maj. Gen. Ambrose E. Burnside. "Send out a small force from Gate towards Spottsylvania to reconnoitre the woods and enemy's position in that direction and especially have all roads leading to your right between Gate & Spottsylvania examined and their condition ascertained, and whether they lead to the positions occupied by Genl Meade's forces near Spottsylvania or to roads immediately in their rear,   Have these cross roads marked on a map which you will send to these Hdqrs. In these reconnoissances, use your cavalry as far as practicable. Move the Division of white troops forming your rear guard to Piney Branch church, leaving the colored troops where they now are, but so disposed as to guard your rear. Let all your troops, not used as herein directed get all the rest possible during the day. Please send in by 5 o-clock P. M. ~~to morrow~~ or sooner if you can, the effective strength of your forces"   Copies, DLC-USG, V, 45, 59; DNA, RG 108, Letters Sent. *O.R.*, I, xxxvi, part 2, 580. At 9:25 A.M., Burnside wrote to USG. "The enclosed dispatch just received from Gen Wilcox—I have received your dispatch of 8:45 this morning and have sent the necessary instructions to Gen Wilcox—I am glad to learn from Maj Lydig that you will visit these Headquarters this morning—The division will be sent to Piney Branch at once." LS, DNA, RG 94, War Records Office, Army of the Potomac; *ibid.*, RG 393, 9th Army Corps, Telegrams Sent. *O.R.*, I, xxxvi, part 2, 580–81. The enclosed message from Brig. Gen. Orlando B. Willcox stated that he had encountered C.S.A. forces at Gayle's house. *Ibid.*, p. 581. On the same day, Rawlins wrote twice to Burnside, first at 10:00 A.M. "You will please direct the General commanding the Division of your troops ordered to Piney Branch church, to send out Staff officers at once to learn and aquaint themselves with the roads leading from Piney Branch Church to the positions of Genl's Warren & Sedgewick near Spottsylvania, and to Gen Hancock's at Todd's Tavern. Also to hold his Division in readiness at Piney Branch church to move to the support of either Warren & Sedgewick or to Gen. Hancock, as he may be directed on the receipt. When the Division receives orders to moves it must be conducted by one of these Staff officers who have familiarized themselves with the roads on which it is to move, that there may be no delay." "If after going to Gates in person, you deem it necessary, move up your three White Divisions without hesitancy or reference to previous orders." Copies, DLC-USG, V, 45, 59; DNA, RG 108, Letters Sent. *O.R.*, I, xxxvi, part 2, 581. At 11:20 A.M., Burnside wrote to USG. "The enclosed dispatch has just been received from Genl Wilcox—I have directed him to hold his own as long as it is possible & to keep out a sharp watch for his flanks"   LS, DNA, RG 108, Letters Received. The enclosed message from Willcox, 11:45 A.M., described heavy fighting. Copy, *ibid. O.R.*, I, xxxvi, part 2, 584.

At 12:30 P.M. and 12:45 P.M., Burnside wrote to USG. "The note from Genl Wilcox to me, stating that he was heavily engaged with equal or superior numbers, was by mistake sent you without an accompanying note. I have taken the responsibility of halting the division ordered to Piney Church at Aldrichs about a mile this side of that place with a view to sending" Copy (incomplete), DNA, RG 393, 9th Army Corps, Telegrams Sent. "Genl Wilcox reports himself heavily engaged with equal or superior numbers—This was prior to Stevenson's joining him. I have sent a staff officer to him with instructions to report to me the state of affairs—I have ordered Genl Wilcox to hold his position if possible & have directed Genl Potter to halt a mile this side of Piney church where he was ordered with a view to supporting Genl Wilcox if it becomes necessary. He can easily be moved to Piney Branch church in a few minutes—Genl Wilcox reports Genl Longstreet & Hill Corps at Spottsylvania   Please send me word by bearer if I have done right in retaining Genl Potter, if not I will send him at once to Piney Branch Church—" LS, *ibid.*, RG 108, Letters Received. *O.R.*, I, xxxvi, part 2, 582.

At 1:15 P.M., USG wrote to Burnside. "I hear artillery firing in the direction of Gates. I think it will be advisable for you to go there and take general charge in person" Copies, DLC-USG, V, 45, 59, 66; DNA, RG 108, Letters Sent. *O.R.*, I, xxxvi, part 2, 582. On the same day, Rawlins wrote to Burnside. "Dispatches enclosing Gen Wilcox's of 1.15 P. M. received and communicated to Gen Meade   Order up the other Division at once to support of Wilcox—" Copies, DLC-USG, V, 45, 59, 66; DNA, RG 108, Letters Sent. *O.R.*, I, xxxvi, part 2, 582. At 2:00 P.M., USG wrote to Burnside. "Your dispatch of 12.45 is just rece'd. You will see from dispatch sent from these Hd Qrs. you have done right in stopping Gen. Potter's Div. and holding in readiness to go to Gen. Wilcox." ALS, deCoppet Collection, NjP. *O.R.*, I, xxxvi, part 2, 583. At 10:30 P.M., Burnside wrote to USG. "I have the honor to send you two orderlies who know the way to my present Head Qrs—The position occupied by Genl Wilcox is at Mr Gales house, there being no such place as *Gate* in this section and is 3 miles farther from Aldrich than we supposed—in fact his position is within mile & a half of Spottsylvania C. H. and there seems to be no ~~with~~ way of connecting with Genl Meade—I mention this so that you may see whether or not the position is not too much isolated—I have a strong guard at Tabernacle Church, and have directed Genl Ferrero as to the roads leading out of Chancellorville. I will await here such orders as you may send by the orderlies" LS, DNA, RG 393, 9th Army Corps, Telegrams Sent; (incomplete) *ibid.*, RG 108, Letters Received. *O.R.*, I, xxxvi, part 2, 583. On May 10, 1:30 A.M., Rawlins wrote to Burnside. "Your note of 10.30 last evening just received—A division of Hancocks Corps has been ordered to ~~report~~ take position to night between you and the present left of Gen Meades army. If you should need its aid, make no hesitation in ordering it to your assistance—If you can hold your position at Mr Gates do so   if you ascertain that you cannot hold it, quietly withdraw to the head of the column near Alsop's—" Copies, DLC-USG, V, 45, 59, 66; DNA, RG 108, Letters Sent. *O.R.*, I, xxxvi, part 2, 610.

To Maj. Gen. George G. Meade

_____

10.15 a. m.
Aldrich's May 9th/64

GEN. MEADE;

You will see by Gen. Wilcox dispatch that he has met a force
not far from the Gate. Under these circumstances I think it advisable to send out scouts at once to the left of the road from Piney
Branch church, say from Sedgwicks position to work their way
over to the road from the Gate to Spotsylvania C. H. to discover if
there is any considerable movement of force in that direction.
Should there prove to be it would become necessary to recall the
troops and push the enemys left flank vigerously.

Yours,
U. S. GRANT
Lt. Gen.

ALS, DNA, RG 393, Army of the Potomac, Telegrams Received. *O.R.*, I, xxxvi,
part 2, 561–62. See preceding letter. On May 9, 1864, 12:45 P.M., USG wrote
to Maj. Gen. George G. Meade. "The enclosed dispatch, together with the report from Gen. Hancock, would indicate the enemy to be moving towards Gate.
If this is the case we must follow and attack vigerously. The trains should all be
turned back so as to get them back of Alsops and headed so that we may, if it
should be decided upon, make a rapid march on Gordonsville." ALS, deCoppet
Collection, NjP. *O.R.*, I, xxxvi, part 2, 562. See preceding letter.

To Maj. Gen. Henry W. Halleck

_____

Head Q'rs Army U. S.
Near Spotsylvania C. H.
May 10th. 9 30 A. M. '64

MAJ GEN H. W. HALLECK
CHIEF OF STAFF.

Enemy hold our front in very strong force and evince strong
determination to interpose between us and Richmond to the last.
I shall take no backward step but may be compelled to send back
to Bell Plain for further supplies   Please have supplies of forage

and provisions sent there at once and fifty (50) rounds of Infantry ammunition for one hundred thousand (100.000) men. Send Genl Benham[1] with the necessary bridge train for Rappahannock. We can maintain ourselves at least and in the end beat Lee's Army I believe.

Send to Bell Plain all the Infantry you can rake and scrape. With present position of the Army ten thousand (10.000) men can be spared from the Defences of Washington besides all the troops that have reached there since Burnside's departure   Some may also be brought from Gen Wallace' Department.

We want no more wagons nor Artillery

U. S. GRANT
Lt Genl

Telegram received, DNA, RG 107, Telegrams Collected (Bound); copies, *ibid.*, RG 108, Letters Sent; DLC-USG, V, 45, 59. *O.R.*, I, xxxvi, part 1, 3; *ibid.*, I, xxxvi, part 2, 595–96. On May 11, 1864, Maj. Gen. Henry W. Halleck wrote to USG. "Yours of 9½ A M. yesterday is recieved. Acting on your previous despatches I have sent about three thousand men from here to Genl Butler. I hope to send to Belle Plain to day from three to four thousand, and more as soon as they arrive. None of the western militia nor of the troops relieved by them in the west have yet reached here. Genl Benham has promised to have the bridge at Fredericksburg completed by night. Your orders on this matter & in regard to supplies have been anticipated. Everything with Sherman looks well, but no general engagement yet. All despatches recieved for you will be sent forward from War Dept. Please keep us advised of your position & the condition of affairs, and we shall probably be able to anticipate most of your wants." ALS, DNA, RG 108, Letters Received. *O.R.*, I, xxxvi, part 2, 628.

1. Henry W. Benham of Conn., USMA 1837, was promoted to maj., Corps of Engineers, as of Aug. 6, 1861. Appointed brig. gen. as of Aug. 13, he commanded the Pontoon Depot in Washington in May, 1864.

To Maj. Gen. Ambrose E. Burnside

May 10, 1864—10.30. a. m.

MAJ GEN BURNSIDE

A General attack will be made on the enemy at 5 p. m. to-day. Reconnoitre the enemy's position in the mean time, and if you have any possible chance of attacking their right do it with vigor and

with all the force you can bring to bear. Do not neglect to make all
the show you can, as the best co-operative effort

U S Grant
Lieut. Gen'l

Copies, DLC-USG, V, 45, 59, 66; DNA, RG 108, Letters Sent. *O.R.*, I, xxxvi,
part 2, 610. Earlier on May 10, 1864, USG wrote to Maj. Gen. Ambrose E.
Burnside. "A Division of troops were sent from here last evening to interpose
between what was the left of Meades position and yours. They are now working
up towards you and will, I think, soon connect. ~with~ ~you~." ALS, deCoppet Collection, NjP. *O.R.*, I, xxxvi, part 2, 610. On the same day, "12 o'clock," Burnside
wrote to USG. "I have the honor to enclose you this morning a Dispatch received
from Genl Ferrero near Chancellorville thinking the information therein may be
unknown to you—I would add that Capt Marsh Chief of Ambulance Corps for
my Command was in Fredericksburg last night, and reports to me that the sick
& wounded were being cared for, but there was necessarily some confusion, attendant upon the arrival of so many wounded at the same time—" LS, DNA,
RG 108, Letters Received. Enclosed was a letter of the same day from Brig. Gen.
Edward Ferrero, "Camp near Chancellorsville" to Burnside's adjt. "I have the
honor to report that my Cavalry have scouted for five or six miles around my
entire lines, and can find no signs of the enemy—It is reported to me that affairs
at Fredericksburg are in great Confusion, and they are sadly in need of some one
to Superintend & arrange matters—" Copy, *ibid.*
      Also on May 10, Burnside telegraphed to USG. "What disposition shall be
made in the present movement of Gen Ferrero's Division and the Cavalry Brigade" Telegram received, *ibid.*, RG 107, Telegrams Collected (Unbound).
See letter to Maj. Gen. Ambrose E. Burnside, May 11, 1864, 8:15 A.M.

To Maj. Gen. Ambrose E. Burnside

May 10th/64 3.20 p. m.

Maj. Gen. Burnside,

Your dispatch of 2.15 p. m just received. It will now be too
late to bring up your third Division. I will have to leave it to your
judgement whether it will be best to attack with your two Divisions
as they are or whether one of them should be sent to Mott.[1] As the
attack is to be general however I incline to the opinion you will be
secure in attacking as you are. I want the attack promptly made
in one or other of the modes proposed.

U. S. Grant
Lt. Gen.

ALS, deCoppet Collection, NjP. *O.R.*, I, xxxvi, part 2, 611. On May 10, 1864, 2:15 P.M., Maj. Gen. Ambrose E. Burnside, Alsop House, wrote to USG. "By concentrating the three divisions of the Corps at Gales I can make a very heavy attack upon the right flank of the enemy or I can ~~instead~~ have the two divisions at Gales make a demonstration and put the other division in rear of Mott's division who is on the left of Wrights Corps—I write this because I do not know if you would care to run the risk of allowing the enemy to break through ~~Here~~ Mott's on the road from alsop's to Spottsylvania. Which do you think had best be done. I have directed the bearer to proceed with greatest possible haste & he will bring your answer—" LS, DNA, RG 108, Letters Received. *O.R.*, I, xxxvi, part 2, 611.

On the same day, 11:00 P.M., USG wrote to Burnside. "A survey of the positions occupied by the different Corps made today shows your Corps entirely isolated and without support. You must get up at once so as to connect on your right with Wrights Command. To do this bring up your third Division, if it is not already up, and place it to the right of the two now at Gales." ALS, deCoppet Collection, NjP. *O.R.*, I, xxxvi, part 2, 611–12.

Also on May 10, 9:30 A.M., noon, 12:40 P.M., and 3:30 P.M., Maj. Gen. George G. Meade wrote to USG. "Genl Wright reports the enemy on his left moving rapidly to his right—I have ordered him to push forward his left, and gain as much ground as possible so as to save Hancocks distance—" "A scout just in from the right says there is no infantry beyond Barlows right, but a cavalry force at Corbins bridge—Under these circumstances, I have directed Gen. Hancock to send Birneys Division to Wrights left, where with Motts Division (now there) he will press forward at once between Wright & Burnside & endeavor to rectify our lines—This will leave our right as it now is.—" "From what Comstock reports of the change of position of Burnside and of his (C's) interview with Wright, I have concluded not to move Birney as with Mott there, Wright ought to make a complete connection with Burnside and it is better to have some force here available for contingencies." "Genl Warren having made progress and taken some prisoners indicating the enemy were shaky, I have ordered him to attack at once—This will probably relieve Barlow, and may assist Wrights & Burnsides attack later." ALS, DNA, RG 108, Letters Received. *O.R.*, I, xxxvi, part 2, 596. On May 9, Lt. Col. Theodore S. Bowers issued Special Orders No. 21. "Maj Gen Horatio G Wright U. S. Vols. is hereby temporarily assigned to the command of the 6th Army Corps and will assume command at once—" Copies, DLC-USG, V, 57, 62, 66. *O.R.*, I, xxxvi, part 2, 577. On that day, Maj. Gen. John Sedgwick, commanding 6th Army Corps, had been killed in battle.

On May 10, Bowers wrote to the commanding officer, Aldrich's. "The enemy is moving in force on our right. Is supposed to be advancing rapidly. Prepare to protect trains and attack him if he comes within your reach." Copies, DLC-USG, V, 45, 59; DNA, RG 108, Letters Sent. *O.R.*, I, xxxvi, part 2, 615.

1. Gershom Mott, born in N. J. in 1822, was appointed 2nd lt., 10th Inf., as of April 23, 1847, and was discharged as of Aug. 22, 1848. Working in a bank on the eve of the Civil War, he was appointed lt. col., 5th N. J., as of Aug. 17, 1861, and col., 6th N. J., as of May 7, 1862. Appointed brig. gen. as of Sept. 7, he commanded the 4th Div., 2nd Corps, Army of the Potomac, in May, 1864.

To Edwin M. Stanton

———

Head Qrs. in the Field, Va
8 a m May 11th 1864.

HON. E. M. STANTON,
SEC. OF WAR. WASHINGTON D. C.

We have now entered the sixth day of very hard fighting. The result to this time is much in our favor. Our losses have been heavy as well as those of the enemy. I think the loss of the enemy must be greater. We have taken over five thousand prisoners, in battle, while he has taken from us but few except stragglers. I propose to fight it out on this line if it takes all summer.

U. S. GRANT
Lieut. Gen. Comdg Armies

ALS, DLC-USG, I, B. See following letter.

To Maj. Gen. Henry W. Halleck

———

Near Spotylvania C. H. Va.
May 11th 1864. 8.30 a. m.

MAJ. GEN. HALLECK,
CHIEF OF STAFF OF ARMY,
GENERAL,

We have now ended the sixth day of very heavy fighting. The result to this time is much in our favor. But our losses have been heavy as well as those of the enemy. We have lost to this time eleven General officers killed, wounded or missing, and probably twenty thousand men. I think the loss of the enemy must be greater we having taken over four thousand prisoners, in battle, whilst he has taken from us but few except stragglers. I am now sending back to Belle Plaines all my wagons for a fresh supply of provisions, and Ammunition, and propose to fight it out on this line if it takes ~~me~~ all Summer.

The arrival of reinforcements here will be very encouraging to the men and I hope they will be sent as fast as possible and in as great numbers. My object in having them sent to Belle Plaines was to use them as an escort to our supply train. If it is more convenient to send them out by train to march from the rail-road to Belle Plain or Fredericksburg send them so.

I am satisfied the enemy are very shaky and are only kept up to the mark by the greatest exertion on the part of their officers, and by keeping them entrenched in every position they take.

Up to this time there is no indication of any portion of Lee's Army being detached for the defence of Richmond.

> Very respectfully
> your obt. svt.
> U. S. GRANT
> Lt. Gen.

ALS, DNA, Treasure Room. *O.R.*, I, xxxvi, part 1, 4; *ibid.*, I, xxxvi, part 2, 627–28. This letter (and possibly the one preceding) was carried to Washington by U.S. Representative Elihu B. Washburne, who arrived at the War Dept. at 10:00 P.M. Adam Badeau, *Military History of Ulysses S. Grant* (New York, 1868–81), II, 169n; Horace Porter, *Campaigning with Grant* (New York, 1897), pp. 97–98; Gaillard Hunt, *Israel, Elihu and Cadwallader Washburn* . . . (New York, 1925), p. 219.

To Maj. Gen. Ambrose E. Burnside

> Near Spotsylvania C. H. Va.
> May 11st/64 8.15 a m.

MAJ. GEN. BURNSIDE,
COMD.G 9TH A. C.
GENERAL,

Make immediate preparation to send back to Belle Plain every team you have empty or can empty to bring up fresh supplies. Unload from your present supplies two days rations to be issued to men and ammunition enough to fill all the cartridge boxes. All the trains of the A. P. will go back at the same time.

Send as escort to the trains your Cavalry and Colored Division.

There will be arriving at Belle Plain reinforcements for this Army sufficient to make, with this escort, a strong Column to protect the train on its return.

> Very respectfully
> your obt. svt.
> U. S. GRANT
> Lt. Gen.

ALS (facsimile), USG 3. *O.R.*, I, xxxvi, part 2, 642–43. Lt. Col. William L. Duff was unable to deliver this message to Maj. Gen. Ambrose E. Burnside until 1:00 P.M., May 11, 1864. *Ibid.*, p. 643. At 12:15 P.M. and 8:00 P.M., Brig. Gen. John A. Rawlins wrote to Burnside. "After the departure of the trains with the Colored troops and Cavalry of your command for Belle Plains, as per orders to day, there will be but small trains remaining here, and each Corps will guard its own. You can guard yours by sending back your provisional brigade to where it now is. You may bring your trains up closer to you as you may deem most prudent." Copies, DLC-USG, V, 45, 59; DNA, RG 108, Letters Sent. *O.R.*, I, xxxvi, part 2, 643. "Only so much of Gen Ferreros Division will be sent as convoy to our empty wagons, ordered to Belle Plain as the Quartermaster in charge may ~~direct~~ deem sufficient. The remainder will be continued in its present duty of guarding roads to our rear, and on which our trains move. Gen. Ferraro has been so instructed. This will enable you to use your Provisional Brigade, if you need it." LS, DNA, RG 107, Telegrams Collected (Unbound). *O.R.*, I, xxxvi, part 2, 644; (misdated May 10) *ibid.*, p. 611. At 8:00 P.M., Rawlins wrote to Brig. Gen. Edward Ferrero. "You will furnish only such escort for trains going to Belle Plains as the Quarter Master in charge of same may require, retaining the remainder of your command in its present position, guarding the roads in our rear and on which are our trains. Communicate this order to Genl Burnside" Copies, DLC-USG, V, 45, 59; DNA, RG 94, War Records Office, 9th Army Corps; *ibid.*, RG 108, Letters Sent.

To Maj. Gen. Ambrose E. Burnside

> Headqrs Armies U. S.
> May 11th/64 4 P. M.

MAJ GEN A. E. BURNSIDE
COMD'G 9TH A. C.

Maj Gen Hancock has been ordered to move his Corps under cover of night to join you in a vigorous attack against the enemy at 4 o'clock a. m. of tomorrow. You will move against the enemy with your entire force promptly and with all possible vigor at precisely 4 o'clock a. m. tomorrow the 12th inst. Let your preparations for this attack be conducted with the utmost secrecy and veiled entirely from the enemy—

I send two of my Staff Officers, Cols Comstock & Babcock in whom I have great confidence and who are acquainted with the direction the attack is to be made from here, to remain with you and Gen Hancock with instructions to render you every assistance in their power—Gens Warren and Wright will hold their Corps as close to the enemy to take advantage of any diversion caused by your and Hancocks attack, and will push in their whole force if any opportunity presents itself—

U. S. GRANT
Lt. Gen.

Copies, DLC-USG, V, 45, 59, 66; DNA, RG 108, Letters Sent. *O.R.*, I, xxxvi, part 2, 643. On May 11, 1864, 8:00 P.M., Maj. Gen. Ambrose E. Burnside wrote to USG. "I have the honor to report that my troops occupy their old line of works we had withdrawn to this side of the Nye but on receipt of order have reestablished our former line without opposition" Telegram received, DNA, RG 108, Letters Received; copy, *ibid.*, RG 393, 9th Army Corps, Telegrams Sent.

To Maj. Gen. Ambrose E. Burnside

May 11th 1864 9. P. M.

MAJ GEN BURNSIDE
COMD'G 9TH A. C.

Scout just in from Gen Sheridan with dispatches. He has reached the South Anna as is followed by the rebel Cavalry. He has cut ten miles of the Orange and Richmond rail road, destroyed two locomotives & three trains—and a very large quantity of provisions. He has recaptured five hundred of our men including two Colonels and Lee's papers.

U. S. GRANT.
Lt. Gen—

Telegram received, DNA, RG 107, Telegrams Collected (Unbound); copies, *ibid.*, RG 108, Letters Sent; DLC-USG, V, 45, 59. *O.R.*, I, xxxvi, part 2, 644. On

March 12, 1864, USG telegraphed to Maj. Gen. Henry W. Halleck a telegram
of March 10 from Maj. Gen. Philip H. Sheridan to Maj. Gen. George G. Meade.
"I returned the Enemy's right and got into their rear—Did not meet sufficient of
Cavalry. Destroyed from eight 8 to ten 10 miles of Orange Rail Road two locomotives, three 3 trains and a very large amount of supplies   The Enemy were
making a depot of supplies at Beaver Dam. Since I got into their rear there has
been great excitement among the inhabitants and with the Army. The citizens
report that Lee is beaten. Their Cavalry has attempted to annoy my rear and
flank but have been run off. I expect to fight their cavalry south of South Ann
river. I have no forage. Started with half rations for one day and have found none
yet. Have recaptured five hundred of our men. Two Colonels." Telegram received,
DNA, RG 107, Telegrams Collected (Bound). *O.R.*, I, xxxvi, part 1, 776.

To Maj. Gen. George G. Meade

Near Spottsylvaina C. H. Va
May. 11th 1864—8:15 a. m.

MAJ GEN MEADE
COMD'G A. P.
GENERAL

Send back to Bell Plain every wagon that can be spared, retaining here only sufficient to move what ammunition and other
stores that cannot be carried on the person. Two days of the present
supply of rations should be unloaded to issue to the men, and ammunition enough to fill all the cartridge boxes. These wagons can
go back with a small escort relying on reinforcements expected to
give them a strong escort back. All the wagons should start back
with a heavy load, say from twenty five to thirty five hundred
pounds, the amount depending on the strength of the team—

I would advise also the sending back to Bell Plain of all the
reserve Artillery. This however I leave to your own discretion

Gen Burnside will be instructed to send back as an escort to
the wagon all his Cavalry and, if necessary, his Division of Colored
Troops

Very Respectfully Your Obt Svt
U. S. GRANT
Lt. Gen

Copies, DLC-USG, V, 45, 59, 66; DNA, RG 108, Letters Sent; (2) Meade Papers, PHi. *O.R.*, I, xxxvi, part 2, 628. On May 11, 1864, 12:20 P.M., Brig. Gen. John A. Rawlins wrote to Maj. Gen. George G. Meade. "As the trains remainging here will be small after the compliance with orders sending all empty wagons to Belle Plain, and as Gen Burnside sends his Colored troops and Cavalry with the empty wagons, each Corps must furnish guards for its own train. You will please give directions accordingly—Gen Burnside has been notified that he will have his own train only to guard—" LS, DNA, RG 94, War Records Office, Dept. of Va. and N. C., Army of the James. *O.R.*, I, xxxvi, part 2, 629. Meade endorsed this letter. "Issue necessary orders   Corps Comdr can learn from Chf QM where their trains are—" AE, DNA, RG 94, War Records Office, Dept. of Va. and N. C., Army of the James. *O.R.*, I, xxxvi, part 2, 629.

Also on May 11, USG wrote to Meade. "The movements of the enemy may be explained by the position Burnside has assumed. Comstock is over with Burnside and will not loose a chance to push the enemy. ~~and~~ He has probably made such developments as to induce the enemy to give up his right if it was weak." ALS, DNA, RG 393, Army of the Potomac, Telegrams Received. *O.R.*, I, xxxvi, part 2, 629.

To Maj. Gen. George G. Meade

May 11th/64. 3 p. m.

MAJ. GEN. MEADE,

Move three Divisions of the 2d Corps by the rear of the 5th & 6th Corps under cover of night so as to join the 9th Corps in a vigerous assault on the enemy at 4 O'Clock a. m. to-morrow. I will send one or two staff officers over tonight to stay with Burnside and impress him with the importance of a prompt and vigerous attack. Warren and Wright should hold their Corps as close to the enemy as possible to take advantage of any diversion caused by this attack and to break in if the opportunity presents itself. There is but little doubt in my mind but that the assault last evening would have proven entirely sucessful if it had commenced one hour earlyer and had been heartily entered into by Mott's Division and the 9th Corps.

Respectfully
U. S. GRANT
Lt. Gen.

ALS, DNA, RG 393, Army of the Potomac, Telegrams Received. *O.R.*, I, xxxvi, part 2, 629.

To Maj. Gen. Henry W. Halleck

Near Spottsylvania Court House, Va.
May 12th 1864—6:30 p. m.

MAJ GEN. HALLECK, WASHINGTON

The eighth day of battle closes, leaving between three and four thousand prisoners in our hands for the days work, including two General Officers, and over thirty pieces of Artillery. The enemy are ~~obtaining~~ obstinate and seem to have found the last ditch. We have lost no organizations, not even that of a Company whilst we have destroyed and captured one Division, (Johnsons)[1] one Brigade (Dole's)[2] and one Regiment entire of the enemy.

U S GRANT
Lieut Gen'l

Telegram, copies, DLC-USG, V, 45, 59, 66; DNA, RG 108, Letters Sent; *ibid.*, Letters Received; DLC-Robert T. Lincoln. *O.R.*, I, xxxvi, part 1, 4; *ibid.*, I, xxxvi, part 2, 652.

On May 12, 1864, USG wrote to Maj. Gen. Henry W. Halleck. "Send Gen. Augur if possible with ten thousand of the best Infantry from the defences of Washington" ALS, Schoff Collection, MiU-C. *O.R.*, I, xxxvi, part 2, 652. On the same day, Halleck wrote to USG. "One officer and some hundred or more men, deserters have arrived here with the wounded under pretence of wounds which on examination is found to be false. They are unquestionably cowardly deserters, and deserve the death penalty. The Secty of War has directed that the officer be placed in irons and the men under strong guard & sent back to your head. Qrs to be disposed of as you may deem proper. He directs me to say that he advises and authorizes you to have these deserters tried by a drumhead court &, if guilty, executed without delay as an example. Prompt & severe punishment is deemed necessary to prevent straggling & desertion. A considerable number of our deserters are said to be on the Rappahannock, robbing for subsistance, and waiting to get through our lines or to be picked up by rebel cavalry. Some are said to have reached the Potomac & crossed into Maryland. Your action in this matter, whatever it may be, will be sanctioned by the War Dept. I hope to be able to send you ten thousand reinforcements by to-morrow night & three or four thousand more in a few days. I have ordered every thing from the Rappahannock Station inside of Bull Run which will be our outer line. This will enable me send you some fifteen hundred men from there. A battery of artillery & some companies of Invalids have ordered to Belle Plain as guards for depot & supplies. When you break off communication with that place & the wounded are all withdrawn, the depot will be broken up and removed to such place as you may direct. Heard from Sherman to yesterday. His operations delayed by non-arrival of Stoneman's cavalry. No general engagement yet. Buzzard's Roost found too strong & he will now attempt to turn it. Nothing new from Butler. Steele returned to Little Rock on the 2d, badly cut up. Genl Rosecrans after repeated orders still retains 9th Iowa cavalry. Genl Canby has been authorized by Secty of War to *take* troops from Dept of Missouri. Ohio militia is organising pretty rapidly, but not a regiment yet raised in Inn. Ill. or Iowa. No recent news from Banks. By last accounts his army was nearly in a state of mutiny. He abandoned Admiral Porter in his retreat & many of the gun-boats were destroyed or lost. The enemy did not pursue except in small detachments, Kirby Smith's main force being sent to reenforce Price against Steele. . . . P. S. This will be sent by the escort of deserters." ALS, DNA, RG 108, Letters Received. *O.R.*, I, xxxvi, part 2, 652–53.

Also on May 12, USG telegraphed to Halleck. "I send this evening to Belle Plain all the prisoners captured to this time. Please direct the commanding officer there what disposition to make of them." ALS (telegram sent), DNA, RG 107, Telegrams Collected (Unbound); telegram received, *ibid.*, Telegrams Collected (Bound). *O.R.*, I, xxxvi, part 1, 4; *ibid.*, I, xxxvi, part 2, 653. On the same day, 2:00 P.M. and 6:15 P.M., Brig. Gen. John A. Rawlins wrote to the commanding officer, Belle Plain, Va. "Have all troops coming to the front from Belle Plain provided and furnished with five days rations on their person's; exclusive of the day on which they start forward. You will give your personal attention to the execution of this order." Copies, DLC-USG, V, 45, 59; DNA, RG 108, Letters Sent. "You will take charge of and closely guard all prisoners of War sent from here to Belle Plain until you receive directions as to what disposition to make of them from the authorities at Washington, who have been requested to give the necessary directions concerning them. Send troops forward to the front as fast as they arrive at Belle Plain, retaining there no greater force than is absolutely required to garrison the place and guard the prisoners" LS, *ibid.*, RG 393, Army of the Potomac, Miscellaneous Letters Received.

On May 13, Halleck twice wrote to USG. "Yours of 6.30 P. M. yesterday is just recieved. We have already got under way, at Belle Plain, in the river & on the road not less than ten thousand men, and I hope to add three or four thousand more within the next two days. Before recieving your despatch, I had ordered Genl Robt. O Tyler to go down in command of these troops. We can also spare Genl Augur as soon as we get all the troops under way. At this moment he is most useful in organizing & getting them off. I have sent some five hundred Rail Road operatives & Genl Benham's brigade of Engr troops to Belle Plain to construct wharfs & repair roads to Fredericksburg There is much delay now in landing troops & stores. Transports are also short, but more have been ordered from Butler. I have sent all dismounted cavalry men to Belle Plain as guards for prisoners of war. All Invalids are sent down for same purpose & to guard depot & trains. The moment a militia regt reaches Baltimore, Porters Heavy Artillery, armed as infantry will be sent to the front. I ordered every thing ~~in front of~~ beyond Bull Run to be brought in and the Irish Brigade to go to Bell Plain. Genl Abercrombie has been placed in charge of that depot with orders to push forward the troops & stores with all possible despatch. I estimate that we shall have sent forward by Sunday night about fiften thousand men, three thousand to Butler & 12,000 to Army of Pot. Possibly I may be able to collect more. You may be assured that no effort will be spared to reinforce you. You have had some experience in this way before. Nothing of importance from Butler or Sherman for the last two days. The former was strengthening his position & the latter was moving on Snake Gap. McPherson found Resaca too strongly fortified to attempt a coup de main. I wrote you yesterday most of the foregoing details, but you may recieve this first. Your despatch of the 7th did not reach me till this morning being telegraphed from Alexandria. Perhaps it may be well to ascertain what the messenger was doing the intermediate time. I need not say how great is the general satisfaction at your successes:" "Since writing to you this afternoon I have obtained detailed reports of troops forwarded & to be forwarded by to-morrow evening to you & Genl Butler, viz: . . . Making in all sent & to be sent within the next 48 hours to Belle Plain 24,500 men, & to Genl Butler 3,000, Total 27,500. I shall not fall much short of this, but it is about as much as I can do. I have generally under estimated rather than over-estimated." ALS, *ibid.*, RG 108, Letters Received. *O.R.*, I, xxxvi, part 2, 695–97.

Also on May 13, USG telegraphed to Halleck. "Please telegraph Gen. Butler to have the Richmond & Danville road cut if possible." ALS (telegram sent), DNA, RG 107, Telegrams Collected (Unbound); telegram received (6:30 P.M., May 14), *ibid.*, Telegrams Collected (Bound). *O.R.*, I, xxxvi, part 2, 697. On May 14, 9:12 P.M., Halleck telegraphed to USG. "Despatch for Genl Butler sent forward. Telegram from Sherman to-day near Resaca, saying that he had turned enemy's position & forced him to evacuate Dalton. Reinforcements mentioned in my letter of last night will not all reach Belle Plain before [T]uesday, for want of transportation." ALS (telegram sent), DNA, RG 107, Telegrams Collected (Bound); telegram received, *ibid.*; *ibid.*, RG 108, Letters Received. *O.R.*, I, xxxvi, part 2, 746.

1. Edward Johnson, born in Va. in 1816, raised in Ky., USMA 1838, resigned from the U.S. Army as of June 10, 1861, to serve as col., 12th Ga. Appointed brig. gen. as of Dec. 13, and maj. gen. as of Feb. 28, 1863, he was captured while commanding a div., 2nd Army Corps, Army of Northern Va., at the battle of Spotsylvania. *Ibid.*, I, xxxvi, part 1, 1079–80.

2. George P. Doles, born in Ga. in 1830, a militia capt. before the Civil War, rose to col., 4th Ga., and was appointed brig. gen. as of Nov. 1, 1862. At Spotsylvania he commanded a brigade in the div. of Robert E. Rodes, 2nd Army Corps, which was overrun. *Ibid.*, I, xxxvi, part 2, 982. He was killed on June 2, 1864.

To Maj. Gen. Ambrose E. Burnside

May 12th 7.10 a. m.

GEN. BURNSIDE,

Hancock has captured about 3000 prisoners among them three General officers and also about fifteen guns.[1] Push your troops so as to keep up the connection with Hancock. Wright is now attacking and Warren is in readiness to push in also.

U. S. GRANT
Lt. Gen

ALS, ICHi. *O.R.*, I, xxxvi, part 2, 677. On May 12, 1864, 5:45 A.M. and 6:00 A.M., Brig. Gen. John A. Rawlins wrote to Maj. Gen. Ambrose E. Burnside.

"Gen. Hancock reports that he has carried the enemy's first & second line of Works, and taken many prisoners. He is still pressing on ~~The telegraph operator adds in a note that he has taken the Second line~~" "Gen. Hancock is pushing forward vigorously. He has captured three Generals. Push in with all possible vigor." ALS, DNA, RG 107, Telegrams Collected (Unbound). *O.R.*, I, xxxvi, part 2, 676, 677. In a message received at 6:40 A.M., Burnside wrote to USG. "Our ~~advance is~~ forces are full ~~to~~ two miles ~~of in the~~ in ~~advance~~ advance of our position this morning and driving the enemy all the time—Hope to make junction with Hancock soon—We have capture[d] some prisoners—" ALS, DNA, RG 107, Telegrams Collected (Unbound). *O.R.*, I, xxxvi, part 2, 677.

At 7:40 A.M., Burnside wrote to USG. "We had established communication with Gen Hancock It was broken on the advance We are seeking to make connection now" Copy, DNA, RG 108, Letters Received. *O.R.*, I, xxxvi, part 2, 678. USG endorsed this message to Maj. Gen. George G. Meade. "I have notified General Burnside that he will have to allow your two corps to use a portion of his artillery until theirs can be got up." *Ibid.* An undated message, 5:30 A.M., from Lt. Col. Cyrus B. Comstock, Burnside's hd. qrs., to USG, was probably written on May 12. "An aide from Gen. Potter reports him sharply engaged but the musketry has now ceased. An order has gone to him & Crittenden to push on rapidly as possible." ALS, DNA, RG 107, Telegrams Collected (Unbound). Another undated message, 6:30 A.M., from Comstock to USG apparently dated from May 12. "Potter & Crittenden heavily engaged and going ahead Wilcox just going in with Crittenden, & on his left." ALS, *ibid.* At 7:00 A.M., Comstock wrote to USG. "Potters connection with Hancock is reported broken, he is thinks he can re establish it & tries at once. Wilcox & Crittenden just attacking again. Every thing looks well" ALS, *ibid.* At 8:00 A.M., USG wrote to Burnside. "Push the enemy with all your might. That is the way to connect. We must not fail." ALS, *ibid. O.R.*, I, xxxvi, part 2, 678. Burnside then sent two messages to USG, the second at 9:15 A.M. "Genl Potter sends in word he has made connection with second Corps." LS, DNA, RG 108, Letters Received. *O.R.*, I, xxxvi, part 2, 678. "Connection with General Hancock is established." *Ibid.*

At 10:00 A.M., USG wrote to Comstock. "How are things progressing on the left? Tell Burnside to push hard with everything he can bring into the fight: If his provisional Brigade is not in, bring that up." Copies, DLC-USG, V, 45, 59; DNA, RG 108, Letters Sent. *O.R.*, I, xxxvi, part 2, 679. At 10:30 A.M., Comstock wrote to USG. "Burnside connects ~~practicly~~ within one or two hundred yards with Hancock. Potter has tried once with a small force to carry a work of the enemy but without success and is now attacking his lin[e] of rifle pits. . . . P S Burnsides now connects with Hancock he proposes to send his trains round in rear of Hancock and in case of any failure in the attack to day not to cover the Fredericksburg road in force. Do you wish that road covered? Dispatch just received and every thing will be put in." ALS (telegram sent), DNA, RG 107, Telegrams Collected (Unbound). At 11:10 A.M., USG wrote to Comstock. "Let Gen. Burnside send his trains as he proposes." ALS, *ibid.* At 1:45 P.M., Comstock wrote to Burnside. "Lt Gen Grant desires that such disposition of your colored troops be made as best to cover the main supply train. He does not deem it necessary to hold the Spoottsylvania & Fredericksburg road if that would absorb any but an insignificant part of your present command, as the three White divisions and provisional brigade must be used where they are. You should to night open a wagon road to connect with Hancock." Copies, DLC-USG, V, 45, 59; DNA, RG 108, Letters Sent. *O.R.*, I, xxxvi, part 2, 679.

1. On May 12, Maj. Gen. Winfield S. Hancock reportedly wrote to USG. "I have captured from thirty to forty guns. I have finished up Johnson, and am now going into Early." *New York Times*, May 14, 1864. This may have been the correspondent's summary of a dispatch from Hancock to Meade printed in *O.R.*, I, xxxvi, part 2, 657.

To Maj. Gen. Ambrose E. Burnside

Hd qrs Armies U. S. May 12th 1864 10-20 a. m.

Maj Gen Burnside comd'g 9th a. c.

Move one division of your troops to the right to the assistance of Hancock, and push the attack with the balance as vigorously as possible. Warren & Wright have been attacking vigorously all day.

See that your orders are executed.

U. S. Grant
Lieut Genl.

Copies, DLC-USG, V, 45, 59; DNA, RG 108, Letters Sent. *O.R.*, I, xxxvi, part 2, 679.

On May 12, 1864, 1:25 P.M., Brig. Gen. John A. Rawlins wrote to Lt. Col. Orville E. Babcock. "Our whole force is now engaged. If Gen Burnside cannot hold his present line he must shorten it. Strengthening his centre and right towards Gen Hancock." Copies, DLC-USG, V, 45, 59; DNA, RG 108, Letters Sent. *O.R.*, I, xxxvi, part 2, 679. In an undated message, written at 4:30 P.M., Babcock wrote to Rawlins. "Genl Burnsides lines are reestablished a little in advance of the points occupied before his last advance. Unless the enemy force him to fall back he will hold his present position—His men to night—" ALS, DNA, RG 107, Telegrams Collected (Unbound).

At 3:15 P.M., USG wrote to Maj. Gen. Ambrose E. Burnside. "The 5th Corps is now moving up to the 6th and will together form a heavy column of assault. Keep your Division Commanders on the lookout to take advantage of any weakening on your front, to meet it." Copies, DLC-USG, V, 45, 59; DNA, RG 108, Letters Sent. *O.R.*, I, xxxvi, part 2, 679.

At 6:10 P.M., Rawlins wrote to Burnside. "You will strengthen your position so as to hold it against any attack of the enemy, and give your men as much rest as possible.—you can consistent with your work in fortifying your position. Act on the offensive with your Artillery during to-morrow, and annoy the enemy all you can. Send all the prisoners you have to Tabernacle church that they may go to Fredericksburg to-night by the same escort that accompanies the prisoners being sent by Gen Meade from here." LS, DNA, RG 107, Telegrams Collected (Unbound). *O.R.*, I, xxxvi, part 2, 680. At 6:20 P.M., USG wrote to Burnside. "Do you not think there may be danger of the enemy moving on your position and attacking you in the morning? If so, would you not be strengthened by throwing your left back on to the Ny river and removing your Artillery to the East side? I want you to make your position secure. Answer as soon as possible—Let the regiment whose time is up go as Escort to your prisoners—" Copies, DLC-USG, V, 45, 59, 66; DNA, RG 108, Letters Sent. *O.R.*, I, xxxvi, part 2, 680. At 8:00 P.M., Burnside wrote to USG. "I have the honor to report that my troops occupy their old line of works. We had withdrawn to this side of the Ny, but on receipt of order have re-established our former line without opposition." *Ibid.*

At 8:15 P.M. and 9:00 P.M., Rawlins wrote to Burnside. "The prisoners will not be sent from here until tomorrow morning. Have yours meet them at Tabernacle church" Copies, DLC-USG, V, 45, 59; DNA, RG 107, Telegrams Collected (Unbound); *ibid.*, RG 108, Letters Sent. *O.R.*, I, xxxvi, part 2, 680. "You will notify your Division Commanders to have their men wake up and under arms by half-past three oclock to-morrow morning (3:30 a m) for it is not unlikely the enemy will take the initiative, and if so, your position he will most probably attack." Copies, DLC-USG, V, (misdated March 12) 45, 59; DNA, RG 108, Letters Sent. *O.R.*, I, xxxvi, part 2, 681.

To Maj. Gen. George G. Meade

May 12th 10.40 a m

MAJ. GEN. MEADE,

If Warren fails to attack promptly send Humphreys[1] to command his corps and relieve him. I have ordered Burnside to push on vigerously and to send a Division to Hancock.

U. S. GRANT
Lt. Gen.

ALS, DNA, RG 393, Army of the Potomac, Telegrams Received. *O.R.*, I, xxxvi, part 2, 654. On May 12, 1864, Maj. Gen. George G. Meade wrote to USG. "Warren seems reluctant to assault. I have ordered him at all hazards to do so, and if his attack should be repulsed to draw in the right and send his troops as fast as possible to Wright and Hancock. Tell Hancock to hold on." *Ibid.*; *ibid.*, I, xxxvi, part 1, 360.

On the same day, 3:00 P.M., Meade wrote to USG. "I have ordered the 5th Corps to move down to Wrights support. He will at once organize a heavy column of assault from both corps which I trust will break through the enemys line Hancock will press forward at the same time & I trust Burnside will do the same. Every thing is working well on the field by my reports." ALS, DNA, RG 108, Letters Received. *O.R.*, I, xxxvi, part 2, 656.

1. Andrew A. Humphreys, born in Philadelphia in 1810, USMA 1831, resigned from the U.S. Army in 1836 to practice engineering, then was appointed to the U.S. Topographical Engineers in 1838. During the Civil War he served as engineer, staff officer, and commander with the Army of the Potomac before his

appointment as chief of staff to Meade with the rank of maj. gen. as of July 8, 1863. He later wrote *The Virginia Campaign of '64 and '65* . . . (New York, 1883).

To Edwin M. Stanton

Spotsylvania C. H. Va.
May 13th 1864.

HON E. M. STANTON SEC. OF WAR
WASHINGTON.

I beg leave to recommend the following promotions to be made for gallant and distinguished services in the last eight days battles, towit: Brig. Gens. H. G. Wright and John Gibbon to be Maj. Gens. Col. S. S. Carroll 8th O. V. Col. E. Upton 121 N. Y. V. Col. Wm McCandless 2d Pa. Reserves and Col. S. C. Griffin 6th N. Hampshire[1] to be Brigadiers. I would also recommend Maj. Gen. W. S. Hancock for Brig. Gen. in the regular Army. His services and qualifications are eminently deserving of this recognition. In making these recommendations I do not want the claims of Gen. Dodge for promotion forgotten but recommend his name to be sent in at the same time. I would also ask to have Gen. Wright assigned to the command of the 6th A. C. I would further ask the confirmation of Gen. Humphreys to the rank of Maj. Gen.[2]

General Meade has more than met my most sanguine expectations. He and Sherman are the fittest officers for large commands I have come in contact with. If their services can be rewarded by promotion to the rank of Maj. Gen. in the regular army the honor would be worthily bestowed and I would feel personally gratified. I would not like to see one of these promotions at this time without seeing both.

Very respectfully
U. S. GRANT
Lt. Gen

ALS, ICHi. *O.R.*, I, xxxvi, part 2, 695. On May 12, 1864, Secretary of War Edwin M. Stanton wrote to USG. "By this bearer of dispatches I transmit to you all the military intelligence which has been received by this Department since the dispatch forwarded to you night before last. An officer will be sent to day to Belle Plain to receive and transmit telegraphic messages that may be forwarded from your Headquarters for Washington, and such as may be transmitted from here to you. His name will be designated to you, and thus a more frequent and early communication can be established. Major General Halleck, Chief of Staff, will inform you what measures are taken to furnish you with reinforcements, and to relieve you from the burthen of the wounded and prisoners that are now on your hands. Colonel Hoffman Commissary General of Prisoners will be sent to Belle Plain today and if necessary to your Headquarters to make the proper arrangements. I have communicated with Mrs Grant, while she remained in New York. I received yesterday a letter from Mr Hillyer, at whose house she was staying informing me that she had returned in good health to St. Louis. I shall communicate with her to day. I also enclose you a note received from Lieut General Scott, which he desired to have transmitted to you. . . . P S General Kautz nomination is confirmed. General Wright will be confirmed as Major General today   Please favor me with any other nominations you desire to have made." LS, DNA, RG 108, Letters Received. *O.R.*, I, xxxvi, part 2, 651–52.

On May 13, 6:00 A.M., Stanton telegraphed to Col. William Hoffman, Belle Plain, Va. "I send herewith an important despatch for General Grant which ~~you will dup~~ I have directed the operator to ~~duplicate~~ triplicate to be sent by three several couriers. You will send it forward ~~in~~ quickly and safely. Report the receipt of this and the hour received." ALS (telegram sent), DNA, RG 107, Telegrams Collected (Bound). At the same time, Stanton telegraphed to USG. "A despatch has just been recieved from General Butler dated [in] the field near Chester Station Va May [12]. 3.30 P M. He states that he is now pressing the enemy near Fort Darling [a]nd has before him all the troops from North and South Carolina that have yet come up. A captured despatch from Beauregard to General Hoke Commanding at Drewrys bluff states that Beauregard will join him as some as the rest of his troops come up. General Gilmore is left to hold the intrenchments while Smith demonstrates upon Drewry and the enemies lines. General Kautz has been sent with cavalry force to cut the Danville rail road near Appamattox Station and perhaps can advance on James River. Will do all I can but ~~thise~~ Country is a terrible one to operate in. Nothing has been heard from General Sherman since the despatches sent to you yesterday which stated him to be in front of the Buzzard roost waiting for ~~his forces~~ Stoneman and that McPherson had fallen back from Resaca to Snake creek gap. General Steele is at Little rock having whipped Kirby Smith and a superior force at Saline river. A boat reached Cairo ~~with~~ yesterday with dates to May 2. All was quiet at Alexandria only a small force of the enemy in front of Banks and re inforcements going up the Red river to Banks. Canby left Cairo to Red river two days ago. He wanted Buel to be assigned him. But Buel thinks it 'degradation.' May God bless you." ALS (telegram sent), *ibid.*; telegram received, *ibid.*, Telegrams Collected (Unbound); *ibid.*, RG 108, Letters Received. *O.R.*, I, xxxvi, part 2, 694–95.

On May 14, 2:00 P.M., Stanton telegraphed to USG. "[C]are of Captain Collins to be forwarded immediately in duplicate by ~~separate~~ different couriers. Your note of yesterday has just reached me the courier having come on to Washington. General Wright was nominated two days ago & confirmed by the Senate for Major General. General Humphries, General Schofield General Wilson and all before the Senate have been confirmed except General Carr whose nomination was not acted upon. There is at present no vacancy for Major Generalship. But I will muster out some [o]ne for Gibbons. The Brigadiers in volunteer service

you name shall be appointed. If there be any vacancies in regular army for Brigadier Hancock shall have it, ~~immediately~~. There is one regular Major General
ship vacant. But Brevets can be given without limit. Dodge has been designated
for some time for the first vacant Major Generalship in the Volunteers. Buell objects to serving under Canby. Wright will be assigned to Sixth Corps. Your
reccommendations in favor of Meade and Sherman will be carried out. We have
heard nothing from Sherman for three days nor from Butler. Sigel is at Wood-
stocks, reports Breckenridge at Staunton ~~with~~ on the 10th of May and that a
portion of his force was in Sigels front. Crooks had not been heard from since the
Sixth of this month and was then at Princeton." ALS (telegram sent), DNA, RG
107, Telegrams Collected (Bound); telegram received, *ibid.*, RG 108, Letters
Received. *O.R.*, I, xxxvi, part 2, 746; (incomplete) *ibid.*, I, xxxvii, part 1, 453.

On May 15, 10:00 P.M., Stanton telegraphed to USG. "There are eight
vacancies for Brigadier Generals. If you deem it expedient to promote any officer
on the field for gallant conduct you are authorized to do so provisionally and your
appointment will be sanctioned by the President and sent ~~onto~~ to the Senate."
ALS (telegram sent), DNA, RG 107, Telegrams Collected (Bound); copy, *ibid.*,
RG 108, Letters Received. *O.R.*, I, xxxvi, part 2, 781. On May 16, Maj. Gen.
George G. Meade wrote to Lt. Col. Theodore S. Bowers. "I have the honor to
request that the following-named officers be appointed brigadier-generals in the
volunteer service for distinguished gallantry on several occasions in the face of
the enemy: Col. J. R. Brooke, Fifty-third Regiment Pennsylvania Volunteers;
Col. N. A. Miles, Sixty-first Regiment New York Volunteers; Col. Joseph Hayes,
Eighteenth Regiment Massachusetts Volunteers. Independent of the conspicuous
bravery they have exhibited on the field of battle, the above-named officers are in
all other respects well qualified for the position for which they are recommended.
Colonels Brooke and Miles have for a long time past commanded brigades with
marked ability, and have repeatedly been recommended for promotion." *Ibid.*,
p. 812.

On May 16, Maj. Gen. Henry W. Halleck wrote to USG. "I think that you
will concur with me that Meade and Sherman should be made Major Generals
of the Army, and Hancock and H. G. Wright should be made Brig. Genls. of the
Army in their places. Of the four I think Wright has the most solid intellect, but
as he has before won less distinction than the others he should be put at the foot
of the list. If you would write a letter to the Secty of War urging these promotions
I think they would be made. I do not wish to see these vacancies left so long un-
filled, lest outside political influences may cause the President to fill them by the
promotion of persons totally unworthy. I know that influences have been exerted
in favor of a man utterly unfit to hold *any* commission in the Army. After your
splendid victories almost anything you ask for will be granted. The case may be
different if you should meet with reverses. I therefore ask that, if you concur with
me in the recommendation, you will urge them *now*. I think you would fully appreciate the importance of doing so, if I were at liberty to tell you who is a candidate for one of the vacancies." Copy, DNA, RG 108, Letters Sent. *O.R.*, I, xxxvi,
part 2, 810–11. Halleck's last sentence referred to Maj. Gen. Benjamin F. Butler.
See Lincoln, *Works*, VII, 346–47. See letter to Maj. Gen. Henry W. Halleck,
May 20, 1864.

1. USG interlineated the name of Col. Simon G. Griffin, 6th N. H., which
does not appear in letterbook copies. On May 13, Brig. Gen. John A. Rawlins
wrote to Maj. Gen. Ambrose E. Burnside. "Have you a Colonel that ought to be

promoted for competency & meritorious conduct at if so the Lt Gen Comd'g will send in his name on being furnished with it—" Copies, DLC-USG, V, 45, 59, 66; DNA, RG 94, War Records Office, Miscellaneous War Records. *O.R.*, I, xxxvi, part 2, 730. On the same day, 9:00 A.M., Burnside telegraphed to Rawlins. "Col Hartraft of the 51st Penna has I presume been confirmed as Brig Genl. If his confirmation is not hazarded I would strongly urge the promotion of Col S G Griffin of the 6th New Hampshire who has for the last five few days been conspicuous for his bravery and gallantry" Telegram received, DNA, RG 108, Letters Received; copies, *ibid.*, RG 107, Telegrams Collected (Unbound); *ibid.*, RG 393, 9th Army Corps, Telegrams Sent. *O.R.*, I, xxxvi, part 2, 730. Griffin was confirmed on May 28 to rank from May 12.

2. On May 13, Meade wrote to Bowers. "I beg leave to present the following names of officers in this Army for immediate promotion, for distinguished services in the battles of the 'Wilderness' and 'Spottsylvania C H'—Brig-Genl H G Wright to be Major-General (6th Corps) Brig-Genl Jno. Gibbon to be Major-General (2d Corps) Colonel S S Carroll, 8th Ohio Vols to be Brigr-Genl. (2d Corps) Colonel E. Upton, 121st N. Y. Vols to be Brigr-Genl. (6th Corps) Colonel W McCandless, 2d Pa Res. to be Brigr-Genl. (5th Corps) I would also ask the influence of the Lieut.-Genl. Comd'g to have confirmed, the nomination, now pending, of Major-Genl. A A Humphreys—" Copies, Meade Papers, PHi; DLC-Andrew Johnson. *O.R.*, I, xxxvi, part 2, 698.

To Col. William Hoffman

Hdqrs Armies of the U. S.
Near Spottsylvania C. H. Va. May 13th 1864

COL WM HOFFMAN
COM. GEN. MUS.
COL

Your communication of this date is just received. I forwarded this morning all the prisoners then on hand with directions for the Commanding officer at Belle Plain to take charge of them and to communicate with the authorities at Washington as to the disposition to be made of them. On this subject I have nothing to add— We now have more prisoners to forward which will probably be sent tomorrow—At present the road to Fredericksburg is open to travel, and whilst reinforcements are arriving will easily be kept open. If you have men to put on the line between the army & Fredericksburg or Belle Plain, they might leave here say at 12 M & 6 P. M, daily—If you have not got men for this purpose, I can detail

Cavalry as they are required, and will communicate at all times
when there is any thing to communicate—

All troops coming to the front should carry all the rations they
can on their persons, but we want no more wagons here. I am now
sending back an additional number of wagons after supplies—

I want the very smallest number of men possible retained at
Belle Plain for duty. Stragglers and slightly wounded men going
to the rear, I think will form sufficient guard for prisoners and
stores—

> Very Respectfully Your Obt Svt
> U. S. GRANT
> Lt. Gen.

Copies, DLC-USG, V, 45, 59, 66; DNA, RG 108, Letters Sent. *O.R.*, I, xxxvi,
part 2, 697–98. On May 13, 1864, Col. William Hoffman, Belle Plain, Va., twice
wrote to USG. "I have the honor to report my presence at this place under instructions from the War Department, to communicate with you, and to take
charge of the prisoners of war in your hands. I am also instructed to arrange a
line of despatch bearers to and from your Hd. Quarters. I respectfully request
your instructions on these points. There is now at this landing transportation in
readiness to receive and carry to such points as may be selected, the prisoners of
war in your hands. The troops now landing will furnish guards for them if required. There is no transportation at this point for troops moving to the front
and they can take with them only four days rations which they carry in their
haversacks. Between four and five thousand are here and on the way to the front.
General Abercrombie is moving them forward as rapidly as possible." ALS, PHi.
"I had the honor to report my presence at this place this morning, but lest my
communication should be delayed by the way, I take the liberty of addressing
you again, I received from the Secretary of War, a packag of despatches addressed to you, which, fearing to intrust them in charge of an individual, I have
placed in the hand of Col. Byrne who marched this morning in command of
troops, I am here under instructions from the War Department to communicate with you, and to receive the prisoners of War captured by the army of the
Potomac. I am also instructed to arrange with Col. Sharp of the Army of the
Potomac a line of despatch bearers, to and from your Hd. Quarters and I respectfully request any instructions you may please to give on this matter, Col.
Sharp has not arrived, Despatches may be sent from this point to Washington
by telegraph, There is transportation at this place ready to receive the prisoners
of War as they arrive, And the troops now here, or arriving, can furnish the
nescessary guard if required, Some four to five thousand troops are here, on the
way to the front, They take with them no transportation and carry four days
rations in their haversacks, Genl. Abercrombie is sending them forward as
rapidly as possible, and when the facilities for landing, which are now very
limited, are enlarged as he hopes soon to have them, their movements will be
much expedited, Small mounted Pickets have been Established between this

place and Fredericksburg, to protect teams and despatch bearers against Gueril-las,   The bearer of this Pt. McEneany 2nd U. S. Cavalry is entrusted with a despatch for the Hon. C A Dana Asst. Secty of War, which he is directed to de-liver to the Comdg Officer at Fredericksburg to be forwarded by an officer and escort." LS, DNA, RG 108, Letters Received.

Also on May 13, 4:00 P.M., Brig. Gen. John J. Abercrombie, Belle Plain, wrote to USG. "The prisoners of war have just arrived; until more troops arrive the detachments which guarded them to this place will necessarily have to re-main with them as I have dispatched all but a sufficient number to protect the depot, and for this purpose I have retained the most inefficient. As soon as they arrive I will relieve them. The rebel officers will be shipped this p. m. for Fort Delaware. Colonel Hoffman, commissary-general of prisoners, is here with in-structions to send them on." *O.R.*, I, xxxvi, part 2, 736–37.

Also on May 13, Lt. Col. Theodore S. Bowers issued Special Orders No. 22. "The Commanding Officers at Fredericksburg and Belle Plain are specially di-rected to use every possible effort to collect and put under guard all straggling soldiers who make their way from this Army to either place or vicinity, and keep them until they can be sent to the front with troops coming forward, or under suitable guards—Soldiers slightly wounded, or such as are disabled for active duty may be retained for garrison duty at the respective posts named—"   Copies, DLC-USG, V, 57, 62, 66.

On May 14, Hoffman twice wrote to USG. "I have the honor to acknowledge the receipt of your note of yesterday. The prisoners forwarded from the Army of the Potomac in charge of Col. Gates arrived last evening, and the officers were immediately embarked for Fort Delaware. The enlisted men will be detained a day or two until the troops coming forward from Washington have all been brought down. Genl. Abercrombie will making arrangements for forwarding despatches from this point to Fredericksburg, twice a day, at 12 M. and 6 P. M. as you suggest. From Fredericksburg to your Hd. Quarters the Escort will have to be furnished from the Army of the Potomac. The General has written to you in reference to the character of his command and the nature of the duties they have to perform. At present a considerable force of efficient troops is required. The prisoners require reliable guards whether in camp or on transports, for which service the Veteran Reserves will answer very well. They are too feeble to per-form the labor required at this post at this time,   There are few stragglers here, and the medical officers have not detained any of the wounded men. I have com-municated your wishes on this subject to Genl. Abercrombie." ALS, ICU. "I have the honor to inform you that I have made all the necessary arrangements for the forwarding from this point all the prisoners of War who may be sent in from the Army of the Potomac, and as this was the chief object of my visit here, and there is no necessity for my remaining longer I shall return to Washington this evening or to morrow morning. By direction of the Secretary of War Capt A. D. Collins V. R. C. will remain here to receive, and forward by telegraph, despatches received from the War Department, or from your Hd Quarters. The wires will be laid to this point by this evening and in two days it will probably be laid to Fredericksburg." LS, DNA, RG 249, Letters Sent (Press).

To Maj. Gen. Ambrose E. Burnside

May 13th/64 9.10 p. m.

GENERAL. BURNSIDE 9TH A. C.

The two Corps moving to the left march by the road cut out immediately to the rear of Hancocks and your Corps. The roads are so bad that I fear they will find difficulty in moving Artillery and therefore will want your reserve or such as yoy do not require in your line. The only instructions I now have is for you to keep up a threatning atitude ready to attack if the enemy weakens in your front or to reinforce Warren or Wright if necessary. ~~No Aides will be sent to you.~~ My Aides will be sent in the morning to the left and if there is any further instructions then I will send it.

U. S. GRANT
Lt. Gen.

ALS, DNA, RG 107, Telegrams Collected (Unbound). *O.R.*, I, xxxvi, part 2, 732.

On May 13, 1864, 1:35 A.M., USG wrote to Maj. Gen. Ambrose E. Burnside. "The enemy seem to have abandoned his position in front of General Wright's troops. Send out to see if the same is the case in your front." *Ibid.*, p. 730.

At 12:40 P.M., Lt. Col. Frederick T. Dent wrote to Burnside. "The lieutenant-general desires to know the news you may have of the movements of the enemy. Are they in force, where, and how moving?" *Ibid.*, p. 731. At 1:00 P.M., Burnside telegraphed to USG. "The telegram just sent you, ~~is not my own~~ does not convey my own impression—I think the enemy are retreating; but their movement is so well protected, as to make [it] ~~impossible~~ very hard to determine—I will send you more definite information as soon as possible—" ALS (telegram sent), DNA, RG 393, 9th Army Corps, Telegrams Sent; telegram received, *ibid.*, RG 108, Letters Received. *O.R.*, I, xxxvi, part 2, 731. An undated telegram from Burnside to USG is probably the message referred to above. "The enclosed despatch has just been received from our extreme left, and is sent for your information   (insert dispatch from W C Raulston)" ALS (telegram sent), DNA, RG 393, 9th Army Corps, Telegrams Sent.

At 5:00 P.M., Burnside telegraphed to USG. "I have just ordered an advance upon the enemy's lines which has demonstrated that they are there in sufficient force to make it doubtful whether we can carry ~~him~~ them or not—but I am still under the impression that they are making arrangements to fall back—My left as it now stands is very weak and in case ~~Genl. Burnside~~ we are attacked ~~we would~~ that part of the line [would] need support—if there is a surplus division near this point, it might be well to let me have it—" ALS (telegram sent), *ibid.*, RG 107, Telegrams Collected (Unbound); *ibid.*, RG 393, 9th Army Corps, Telegrams Sent (Press); telegram received, *ibid.*, RG 108, Letters Received. *O.R.*, I, xxxvi, part 2, 731. At 6:20 P.M., USG telegraphed to Burnside. "There will be a night movement of two Corps from the right to your left. They will attack immediately on getting into position if the chance offers. Be ready to support them if required—" Copies, DLC-USG, V, 45, 59, 66; DNA, RG 108, Letters Sent. *O.R.*, I, xxxvi, part 2, 731. At 8:15 P.M., Burnside telegraphed to USG. "Your dispatch of 6.20 is received, and will recieve immediate attention—If possible I I will make more definite arrangements as soon as I hear from you the time & route the troops will take, which will be brought I presume by one of your aide de camps" ALS (telegram sent), DNA, RG 393, 9th Army Corps, Telegrams Sent; *ibid.*, RG 107, Telegrams Collected (Unbound); telegram received (misdated May 12), *ibid.*, RG 108, Letters Received. *O.R.*, I, xxxvi, part 2, 731; (misdated) *ibid.*, p. 681. At 8:15 P.M., Lt. Col. Orville E. Babcock telegraphed to Burnside. "The Lieut Genl desires to know how many batteries with you and where the remainder are." ALS (telegram sent), DNA, RG 107, Telegrams Collected (Unbound); copies, *ibid.*, RG 108, Letters Sent; DLC-USG, V, 45, 59, 66.

Also on May 13, Lt. Col. Theodore S. Bowers issued Special Orders No. 22. "Brig Gen James H Ledlie U. S. Vols. will report to Maj. Gen. A E Burnside Commanding 9th Army Corps for orders" Copies, DLC-USG, V, 57, 62, 66. *O.R.*, I, xxxvi, part 2, 732.

To Maj. Gen. George G. Meade

May 13th/64 8.40 a. m.

MAJ. GEN. MEADE,

From the dispatches just shown me by Capt. Meade[1] I do not infer the enemy are making a stand but simply covering a retreat which must necessarily have been slow with such roads and so dark a night as they had last night. I think it advisable to push with at least three good Divisions to see beyond doubt what they are doing.

Respectfully &c
U. S. GRANT
Lt. Gen.

ALS, Berg Collection, NN. *O.R.*, I, xxxvi, part 2, 698. Also on May 13, 1864, USG endorsed a letter forwarded to him by Maj. Gen. George G. Meade. "I do not desire a battle brought on with the enemy in their position of yesterday but want to press as close to them as possible to determine their position and strength. We must get by the right flank of the enemy for the next fight." Copy, Meade Papers, PHi. *O.R.*, I, xxxvi, part 2, 716. See *ibid.*, p. 715.

1. Meade's son George attended USMA (1860–62), served as 2nd lt., 6th Pa. Cav. (1862–63), then joined his father's staff as aide when the elder Meade assumed command of the Army of the Potomac.

To Brig. Gen. Edward Ferrero

———

Headquarters Armies of the United States,
Near Spotsylvania Court-House, May 13, 1864.
BRIGADIER-GENERAL FERRERO,
COMDG. FOURTH DIVISION, NINTH ARMY CORPS:
GENERAL: The enemy have crossed the Ny to the right of our line in considerable force, and may possibly detach a force to move on Fredericksburg. Keep your cavalry pickets well out on the plank road and all other roads leading west and south of you. If you find the enemy moving infantry and artillery toward you report it promptly. In that case take up strong positions and detain him all you can, turning all trains back to Fredericksburg, and whatever falling back you may be forced to do, do in that direction. I do not think the enemy will detach in that direction, but give you this warning in time in case they should. Require all trains coming to the front to come by the Massaponax Church road.

Very respectfully,
U. S. GRANT,
Lieutenant-General.

O.R., I, xxxvi, part 2, 732.

To Brig. Gen. Edward Ferrero

———

Headqrs Armies of in the Field
Near Spottsylvania C. H. Va May 13th/64
GEN,

Your letter of this evening is received. I enclose you with this the position our troops will hold tomorrow morning. The only Fords necessary to hold will be Ely's & United States. Dowdalls

Tavern is far enough west for you to picket. You can give up therefore the guard at Todds Tavern and Banks Ford—No more troops need be taken from you to guard trains, and those sent already you may send for to return—

Communicate this to Gen Burnside Comd'g 9th Corps through whom it would be sent, but for the delay that would occur in so sending it.

Very Respectfully
U. S. GRANT Lt Gen

P. S. The black lines on the map show the position of our troops

Copies, DLC-USG, V, 45, 59, 66; DNA, RG 108, Letters Sent. *O.R.*, I, xxxvi, part 2, 733. On May 13, 1864, Brig. Gen. Edward Ferrero, Chancellorsville, wrote to Brig. Gen. John A. Rawlins. "I wish to make the following report of my position. My lines extend from Todds Tavern, Furnaces, Dowadalls Tavern, Ely's Ford, U. S. Ford, Banks' Ford, the road to Fredericksburg, and patrol Six (6) miles down the Telegraph road. The lines are very much extended and I cannot spare any more troops to accompany trains to Belle Plains without endangering trains at this place. If the General Commanding desires any change in my position, I should be happy to hear from him. I would like to know the exact position of our troops at the front that I may be able to conform with their changes." LS, DNA, RG 108, Letters Received. *O.R.*, I, xxxvi, part 2, 733. On the same day, Rawlins wrote to Ferrero. "On a closer examination of the map you are directed to withdraw only the guards at Todds Tavern back to Piney Branch Church— The order sent you this evening is modified accordingly" Copies, DLC-USG, V, 45, 59, 66; DNA, RG 108, Letters Sent. *O.R.*, I, xxxvi, part 2, 733.

To Julia Dent Grant

Near Spotsylvania C. H. Va.
May 13th 1864

DEAR JULIA,

The ninth day of battle is just closing with victory so far on our side. But the enemy are fighting with great desperation entrenching themselves in every position they take up. We have lost many thousand men killed and wounded and the enemy have no doubt lost more. We have taken about eight thousand prisoners and lost likely three thousand. Among our wounded the great majority are but slightly hurt but most of them will be unfit for service in this battle. I have reinforcements now coming up which will greatly encourage our men and discourage the enemy correspondingly.

I am very well and full of hope. I see from the papers the country is also hopeful.

Remember me to your father and Aunt Fanny. Kisses for yourself and the children. The world has never seen so bloody or so protracted a battle as the one being fought and I hope never will again. The enemy were really whipped yesterday but their situation is desperate beyond anything heretofore known. To loose this battle they loose their cause. As bad as it is they have fought for it with a gallantry worthy of a better.

ULYS.

ALS, DLC-USG.
On May 13, 1864, William S. Hillyer, New York City, telegraphed to Julia Dent Grant, St. Louis. "Letter recd this morning from your husband dated May 11th He says we have ended the sixth day of very hard fighting with a fair prospect of having at least a week more yet to do So far the advantages have been on our side, & I feel no doubt about the result in the end We as well as the enemy have lost very heavily We have taken in battle over four thousand prisoners & I should think, killed & wounded at least twenty thousand of the enemy I never felt better in my life Will forward the letter today" Telegram received, OClWHi. On the same day, Secretary of War Edwin M. Stanton telegraphed to Mrs. Grant. "A despatch from General Grant dated yesterday near Spotsylvania Court House at half past six in the evening has just been received. He was quite well. The eighth day of hard fighting was just over resulting for the days work in the capture of between three and four thousand prisoners including one Major General, one entire division, brigade, and regiment and over thirty cannon. I will keep you advised of events & hoping you have reached home safely" ALS (telegram sent), DNA, RG 107, Telegrams Collected (Bound).
On May 8, Hillyer telegraphed to Stanton. "Mrs Genl Grant my House this City requests you telegraph her any information not improper from her husband" Telegram received, *ibid.* On the same day, Stanton telegraphed to Mrs. Grant. "No reports have been recieved directly from General Grant since Wednesday. But it is known that he is well and the Government has perfect confidence in his success. There have been two days hard fighting. The enemy are reported to be retiring, whether this is true or not can not be certainly known until official reports are received which are hourly expected. It is known that he is continuing his preparations to advance. I will keep you advised as events transpire" ALS (telegram sent), *ibid.* For the next few days, Stanton telegraphed to Mrs. Grant the latest news of her husband. ALS (telegrams sent), *ibid.*

To Maj. Gen. Henry W. Halleck

———

Head Qrs Near Spotsylvania
May 14th 1864 [*7:10* A.M.]

MAJ GEN H. W. HALLECK
CHIEF OF STAFF.

The heavy rains of the last forty eight hours have made it almost impossible to move trains or Artillery—Two Corps were moved last night in the night from our right to the left with orders to attack at four a. m., but owing to the difficulties of the road have not fully got into position. This, with the continued bad weather may prevent offensive operations today. Yesterday but little was done, only from one hundred to one hundred and fifty prisoners falling into our hands without, or almost without, loss on our side

U S. GRANT.
Lt Genl

Telegram received, DNA, RG 107, Telegrams Collected (Bound); copies, *ibid.*, RG 108, Letters Sent; DLC-USG, V, 45, 59, 66. *O.R.*, I, xxxvi, part 1, 5; *ibid.*, I, xxxvi, part 2, 746.

To Maj. Gen. George G. Meade

———

May 14th/64 9.30. p. m.

MAJ. GEN. MEADE,

You may move Hancock's Corps to the left as you suggest leaving one Division in rear of and for the support of Burnside's right until I can send officers there in the morning to fix his position to feel it secure.

Very respectfully
U. S. GRANT
Lt. Gen.

ALS, DNA, RG 94, War Records Office, Army of the Potomac. *O.R.*, I, xxxvi, part 2, 747. On May 14, 1864, 9:00 P.M., Maj. Gen. George G. Meade wrote to USG. "Warren reports the enemy moving troops to the left—He also says the force that attacked Upton came from the south on the road from Geiuneys Station —Dont you think Hancock had better move around starting before day tomorrow—I would like to get the A. P. together & Burnside would have the right flank—" ALS, DNA, RG 108, Letters Received. *O.R.*, I, xxxvi, part 2, 747.

At 6:00 A.M., Meade wrote to USG. "General. Warren reports the head of his column, just arrived.—The column broken and scattered.—he doubts the practicability of getting his command into a condition to do anything to day. General. Wright has also just reached here, and I have directed him to move over to the Massaponax Church road, and mass out of sight of the enemy." Copies (2), Meade Papers, PHi; DNA, RG 200, Letters Sent by Meade; *ibid.*, RG 393, Army of the Potomac, Letters Sent; DLC-Andrew Johnson. *O.R.*, I, xxxvi, part 2, 747. Meade apparently enclosed a letter of 4:00 A.M. from Maj. Gen. Gouverneur K. Warren to Maj. Gen. Andrew A. Humphreys, readdressed to USG. Copy, DNA, RG 108, Letters Received. See *O.R.*, I, xxxvi, part 2, 755. At 7:45 A.M., Meade wrote a note possibly addressed to USG. "I propose to place my headquarters in the vicinity of this place, the Beverly house, on north side of the Ny." *Ibid.*, p. 747.

At 7:00 P.M., Brig. Gen. John A. Rawlins telegraphed to Maj. Gen. Ambrose E. Burnside. "What is the state of affairs in your front? Please give any news you have" Copies, DLC-USG, V, 45, 59; DNA, RG 107, Telegrams Collected (Unbound); *ibid.*, RG 108, Letters Sent. *O.R.*, I, xxxvi, part 2, 764. At 7:20 P.M., Lt. Col. Lewis Richmond, adjt. for Burnside, telegraphed to Rawlins. "Your despatch received General Burnside is just leaving for General Grants Head Qrs and will give the report in person—" ALS (telegram sent), DNA, RG 107, Telegrams Collected (Unbound); copy, *ibid.*, RG 393, 9th Army Corps, Telegrams Sent. *O.R.*, I, xxxvi, part 2, 764.

To Maj. Gen. Henry W. Halleck

May 15th/64 7. a. m.

MAJ. GEN. HALLECK, WASHINGTON

The very heavy rains of the last three days have rendered the roads so impassable that but little will be done ~~unless the enemy should attack wh~~ until there is a change of weather, unless the enemy should attack which they have exhibited but little inclination to do for the last week. On reflection I believe it will be better to strengthen the Corps here with all reinforcements coming to having them a separate command. You need not therefore send Augur. Please order Maj. Morton Eng. to report to Gen. Burnside.[1]

U. S. GRANT
Lt Gen.

ALS (telegram sent), Lackawanna Historical Society, Scranton, Pa.; telegram received, DNA, RG 107, Telegrams Collected (Bound). *O.R.*, I, xxxvi, part 1, 5; *ibid.*, I, xxxvi, part 2, 781. This telegram reached Washington on May 15, 1864, 10:00 P.M. On the same day, 1:30 P.M. and 8:30 P.M., Maj. Gen. Henry W. Halleck telegraphed to USG. "Telegram from Genl Sherman dated 8 P. M. yesterday. Had hard fighting all day near Resaca but drove the enemy. His forces are all united and he will attack at all points to-day. Six thousand splendid Infantry embark to-day for Belle Plain with orders to push forward to your Head Qurs. Each man carries on his person five days rations and one hundred & fifty rounds of [c]artriges." "Genl Butler says that Genl Kautz was sent on the 12th with orders to cut the Danville R. R. and also the James River Canal. Genl Augur estimates that the reinforcements which will be at Belle Plain by to-morrow night for Army of Potomac will be at least twenty four thousand   I hope in a few days to increase the number to thirty thousand." ALS (telegrams sent), DNA, RG 107, Telegrams Collected (Bound); telegrams received, *ibid.*; *ibid.*, RG 108, Letters Received. *O.R.*, I, xxxvi, part 2, 781–82. See letter to Maj. Gen. Ambrose E. Burnside, May 16, 1864.

1. James St. C. Morton of Pa., USMA 1851, appointed brig. gen. as of Nov. 29, 1862. On Nov. 3, 1863, 5:00 P.M., Asst. Secretary of War Charles A. Dana, Chattanooga, had telegraphed to Secretary of War Edwin M. Stanton. "Bridge here still unfinished and little progress with it. Genl. Morton who has charge of this important work, grossly neglects his duty—" Telegram received, DLC-Edwin M. Stanton. On Nov. 4, 11:00 A.M., USG telegraphed to Halleck. "I would respectfully ask that Br. Gen. St. C. Morton be assigned to duty elsewhere   Whilst a fine Engineer, he is reported by Gen Thomas as unsuited for the kind of work we have in the field, or to command troops. He might do well on the Pacific where more time can be allowed." Telegram received, DNA, RG 107, Telegrams Collected (Bound); *ibid.*, RG 94, Letters Received; copies, *ibid.*, RG 107, Telegrams Received in Cipher; *ibid.*, RG 393, Military Div. of the Miss., Hd. Qrs. Correspondence; DLC-USG, V, 40, 94. On Nov. 5, Halleck wrote to Stanton. "I respectfully recommend that Capt Morton be mustered out as a Brig Genl of Vols, & ordered to report to the Chf Engr. for duty on fortifications." AES, DNA, RG 94, Letters Received. Morton was mustered out as brig. gen. of vols. as of Nov. 7, retaining his regular rank of capt. Assigned in May, 1864, as USG requested, Morton was killed on June 17 in the assault on Petersburg.

To Maj. Gen. George G. Meade

[*May 15, 1864*]

Would it not be well for Gen. Birney[1] to drive the enemy from the Brown house refered to in this dispatch and hold the place until somithing is decided upon? My opinion now is that our next attack should be from Wrights position he supported by

Hancock with Warren & Burnside ready to advance from where they are if any strong impression is made by our attack. Preparitory for such a movement Wright's & Hancocks staff officers should now be gathering all the information they can of the approaches to the enemys line from Wright's front and left.

U. S. GRANT

Lt. Gen.

AES, DNA, RG 94, War Records Office, Army of the Potomac. *O.R.*, I, xxxvi, part 2, 794. Entered as written as 12:30 P.M., May 15, 1864, in USG's letterbooks. Written on a telegram of 11:36 A.M. from 1st Lt. Frederick Van Vliet, 3rd Cav., act. aide to Maj. Gen. Ambrose E. Burnside, to Brig. Gen. John A. Rawlins. "The enemys skirmishers are in possession of the Brown House and have a battery in position which enfilades our line to a point about opposite my head-qrs I have directed Genl Birney to hold the Landrum House with one brigade & a section of artillery if possible If he is driven out it will make it very hard to hold the line which we now occupy ~~but~~ if the enemy attacks in force. ~~in force~~ Col Babcock will soon be at your hd-qrs and explain the position There are not sufficient indications yet to determine in what force the enemy is advancing As soon as it is determined I will let you know" Telegram received, DNA, RG 94, War Records Office, Army of the Potomac. *O.R.*, I, xxxvi, part 2, 794.

At 8:10 P.M., Burnside telegraphed to Rawlins. "I have the honor to report ~~all~~ no particular change along my lines—all seems quiet—is there any information of importance from the other portions of the line—" Copy, DNA, RG 393, 9th Army Corps, Telegrams Sent. *O.R.*, I, xxxvi, part 2, 793. On the same day, Rawlins telegraphed to Burnside. "Nothing new. all is quiet along our entire lines so far as heard from" ALS (telegram sent), DNA, RG 107, Telegrams Collected (Unbound). On the same day, Lt. Col. Orville E. Babcock telegraphed to Burnside. "The Lt Gen Comd'g directs that you at once commence the line of entrenchments on your right flank, preparatory to the withdrawal of Gen Birney's Divn. You will be notified of his withdrawal—" Copies, DLC-USG, V, 45, 59, 66; DNA, RG 108, Letters Sent. *O.R.*, I, xxxvi, part 2, 795.

1. David B. Birney, born in Ala. in 1825, son of the prominent abolitionist James G. Birney, educated at Andover, was a Philadelphia lawyer and lt. col. of a militia regt. on the eve of the Civil War. Appointed lt. col., 23rd Pa., as of April 21, 1861; brig. gen. as of Feb. 17, 1862; and maj. gen. as of May 20, 1863, Birney commanded the 3rd Div., 2nd Army Corps, in the battle of the Wilderness and on May 13, 1864, was assigned to command the 4th Div. also. *Ibid.*, p. 709.

To Maj. Gen. George G. Meade

Head Qrs. of the Army, In Field
Near Spotsylvania C. H. Va. May 15th/64

MAJ. GEN. MEADE.
COMD.G A. P.
GENERAL,

I have written to the Commander at Fredericksburg and also to General Ferrero, Comd.g Division of Colored troops, putting them on their guard about Hampton's Cavalry.[1] We now have a large force between here and Fredericksburg which, if it does its duty, can prevent any serious disaster to our trains.

General Burnside just now informs me that the enemy are moving on his right in conciderable force but he does not know yet in what force or for what object.[2] If they move on him the best possible relief will be to move the whole Army of the Potomac forward from Wrights and Warrens front.

U. S. GRANT
Lt. Gen.

ALS, Jensen Collection, WHi. *O.R.*, I, xxxvi, part 2, 782. On May 15, 1864, 3:30 P.M., Maj. Gen. George G. Meade wrote to USG. "Your note in reference to Burnsides right being threatened is received—Warren & Wright have been ordered to be prepared to advance on the receipt of orders & Hancock has been directed to hold his command (Birney excluded) ready to move at a moments notice—" ALS, DNA, RG 108, Letters Received. *O.R.*, I, xxxvi, part 2, 782.

1. Wade Hampton, born in Charleston, S. C., in 1818, graduated from South Carolina College in 1836, and owned plantations in both S. C. and Miss., which produced over 5,000 bales of cotton in 1861. During the 1850s, he served in both the House and Senate in S. C., and opposed secession in 1861. He was appointed C.S.A. brig. gen. as of May 23, 1862, becoming commander of the 1st Cav. Brigade, Army of Northern Va., in July. Promoted to maj. gen. as of Aug. 3, 1863, he assumed command of the Cav. Corps, Army of Northern Va., after Lt. Gen. James E. B. Stuart was mortally wounded on May 11, 1864, at the battle of Yellow Tavern, Va. See letter to Maj. Gen. Ambrose E. Burnside, May 16, 1864.

On May 15, 2:30 P.M., Meade wrote to USG. "Asst. Surgeon Sinclair 1st Mich Cav. who has been employed in bringing our wounded off the Wilderness battle field, reports that Hampton's Divn. of Reb. Cavalry is on our right & rear threatening our communications   Dr. S. has had several interviews with the

Rebel officers, and they claim that Sheridan has been worsted in a fight near Richmond with the loss of 1500 men.—I have given Dr. S. a letter to Genl. Hampton asking for the body of Genl. Wadsworth, which Gen. H, said he might have if he brought a request from me." ALS, DNA, RG 108, Letters Received. On the same day, USG wrote to Brig. Gen. Edward Ferrero. "The enemys cavalry under Wade Hampton is said to be in our rear between Old Wilderness Church, Fredericksburg and your position. Do you hear through your pickets any thing of it? Keep a sharp lookout for this Cavalry, and if you can attack it with your Infantry and Cavalry do so." Copies, DLC-USG, V, 45, 59, 66; DNA, RG 108, Letters Sent. *O.R.*, I, xxxvi, part 2, 797. On the same day, Ferrero, "Millers House on Plank Road East of Aldrich's," wrote to Brig. Gen. John A. Rawlins. "I have the honor to report, that at 12½ P. M. this day, the 2d Ohio Cavalry, stationed at Piney Branch Church, were compelled to fall back, being attacked, by superior forces, consisting of one Brigade of Cavalry with two pieces of Artillery. I immediately ordered the 4th Division in readiness, and marched the 23d U. S. C. T. to support the Cavalry. On arriving at Aldrich's on the Plank Road, I found the 2d Ohio, driven across the road and the enemy occupying the Cross Roads. I ordered the Colored regiment to advance on the enemy in line of battle, which they did, and drove the enemy in perfect route. Not being able to pursue with Infantry, the 2d Ohio formed and gave them chase to Piney Branch Church which they (the 2d Ohio) now occupy. All quiet elsewhere. Our loss amounted to about Eight (8) or Ten (10) wounded. The enemy lost some Five (5) horses killed. I have changed my position to a more secure one to protect the trains, and roads leading to the Army. I have since learned from one of my scouts that Hamptons Brigade are in full retreat in perfect disorder, towards Todds Tavern" LS, DNA, RG 108, Letters Received; copy (dated May 16), *ibid.*, RG 393, 9th Army Corps, 4th Div., Letters Sent.

Also on May 15, USG wrote to the commanding officer, Fredericksburg. "The rebel Cavalry under Wade Hampton being now in our right rear, in the neighborhood of Old Wilderness Tavern, and having no Cavalry here to send out to meet it, you will picket with the Cavalry at your disposal as far in that direction as possible. If you can meet this with yours or with a mixed of Infantry and Cavalry, do so   Report to Gen Meade or myself all you learn and as soon as possible, the movements of the enemy in our rear—" Copies, DLC-USG, V, 45, 59, 66; DNA, RG 108, Letters Sent. *O.R.*, I, xxxvi, part 2, 800–1. On the same day, Col. Edmund Schriver, Fredericksburg, wrote to Rawlins. "I have to acknowledge the receipt of Lieutenant-General Grant's communication of this date, informing me of the presence of the Hampton cavalry on our right, and directing me to picket in that direction, and to meet it with a mixed force of infantry and cavalry. In reply I beg to assure the general that all proper measures shall be taken, but I must say I have but 120 infantry, and the cavalry are not to be depended on. A force appeared this morning on the Telegraph road (horsemen), and I have been obliged to keep quite a large number to watch the movement in that direction. The demands on me for escorts, patrols, messengers, &c., are numerous, so that the available force at my disposal is very small for other purposes." *Ibid.*, p. 801.

2. At 2:40 P.M., Maj. Gen. Ambrose E. Burnside telegraphed to USG. "Our pickets on the right report a strong Column of the enemy moving to my right—It is yet impossible to say in what strength ~~of~~ or with what object" Telegram received, DNA, RG 108, Letters Received. *O.R.*, I, xxxvi, part 2, 795. At

3:05 P.M., USG telegraphed to Burnside. "Is the enemy crossing the Ny? If not, you will no doubt be able to hold your position or at least the position marked out by the Engineers this morning by bringing Birney within it." Copies, DLC-USG, V, 45, 59, 66; DNA, RG 108, Letters Sent. *O.R.*, I, xxxvi, part 2, 795. At 3:20 P.M. and 3:30 P.M., Burnside telegraphed to USG. "Dispatch received— There are no indications at present that the enemy are crossing nye—we will probably be able to hold our own—Gen Birney's right strikes the Nye river at a point opposite the deserted house on the other side of the river, which house is about or nearly on a line from your Headquarters to Landram House   If that point can be occupied by a brigade & a battery it would be of great service to us in case of an attack—I mean the point on which the deserted house stands; ~~it is possible that the force passing by on our right may be moving in the direction of Alsops or Piney Church~~" "~~I am inclined to think that if the line to be lengthened it should~~   I am inclined to think that the point designated as the deserted house in my last despatch should be occupied as soon as possible   It is reported that the enemy are passing to our right, and aiming for that place. There is supposed to be about a brigade passing—" Copies, DNA, RG 393, 9th Army Corps, Telegrams Sent. *O.R.*, I, xxxvi, part 2, 796. At 4:20 P.M., Lt. Col. Cyrus B. Comstock endorsed the second telegram. "Lieutenant-General Grant refers the within dispatch of General Burnside to General Meade, with the suggestion that it might be well to watch from the deserted house with cavalry, and if a brigade moves on that point, to attack it with a division." *Ibid.* Meade later endorsed the same telegram. "Major-General Hancock will occupy the deserted house with such force as he may deem necessary to comply with the within suggestion of the general commanding." *Ibid.*

Also on May 15, Meade wrote to USG. "Burnside has been advised that Birney is under his orders, and to remain there so long as in his judgment the security of his line requires it, but that so soon as he can dispense with him he is to be sent back. I fancy it is only the enemy's cavalry feeling our position." *Ibid.*, p. 782. On the same day, USG telegraphed to Burnside. "The Army of the Potomac except Birney's Div which is with you have all been notified to advance and attack the enemy in case you are attacked by him." Copies, DLC-USG, V, 45, 59, 66; DNA, RG 108, Letters Sent. *O.R.*, I, xxxvi, part 2, 796.

To Maj. Gen. Henry W. Halleck

Near Spotsylvania C H
May 16th 8 a m 1864

MAJ GEN H. W. HALLECK
CHIEF OF STAFF.

We have had five 5 days almost constant rain without any prospect yet of it clearing up. The roads have now become so impassable that ambulances with wounded can no longer run between here & Fredericksburg. All offensive operations necessarily cease until we can have twenty four hours of dry weather.

The army is in the best of spirits and feel greatest confidence in ultimate success. The promptness with which you have forwarded reinforcements will contribute greatly to diminishing our mortality list and insuring a complete victory   You can assure the President and Secretary of War that the elements alone have suspended hostilities and that it is no manner due to weakness or exhaustion on our part

U. S. Grant
Lt Genl

Telegram received, DNA, RG 107, Telegrams Collected (Bound); copies, *ibid.*, RG 108, Letters Sent; DLC-USG, V, 45, 59, 66. *O.R.*, I, xxxvi, part 1, 5; *ibid.*, I, xxxvi, part 2, 809–10.

To Maj. Gen. Henry W. Halleck

Near Spottsylvania C H
May 16th 1864 5 P M

Maj Gen Halleck
Chf of Staff

Private letters[1] and Official statements from the Department of the Gulf, show such a state of affairs there as to demand (in my opinion) the immediate removal of Genl Banks—The Army has undoubtedly lost confidence in him—I would suggest the appointment of Franklin to the command of the Nineteenth 19th Corps, and Reynolds or Hunter to the command of the Department. This is sent on the supposition that Canby has gone in command of the Military Division of the Trans-Mississippi—If Canby has simply relieved Banks in command of the Department, then the change will be satisfactory

U. S. Grant
Lt Gnl

Telegram received, DNA, RG 107, Telegrams Collected (Bound); copies, *ibid.*, RG 108, Letters Sent; DLC-USG, V, 45, 59, 66. *O.R.*, I, xxxiv, part 3, 615. On

May 17, 1864, 11:30 A.M., Maj. Gen. Henry W. Halleck telegraphed to USG. "Your telegram of yesterday [in] relation to Genl Banks [h]as been recieved. Nearly all your wishes in this matter have [be]en anticipated. Canby has general command of Depts of the [Gu]lf & Arkansas. Banks was [or]dered to New Orleans & Franklin [p]ut in command of the Army. It [is] rumored that Franklin is wounded, [if] so Reynolds or A. J. Smith [will] take his place. The latter has been made a Major Genl. for [th]at purpose. Canby has full authority to make any change in commanders he may desire. It is also arranged with Sherman that Canby shall use any troops or transportation belonging to the former on east bank of the Miss. Telegram from Sherman last night saying that he had captured Resaca & Johnston [w]as in full retreat; expects to reach Kingston to-night." ALS (telegram sent), DNA, RG 107, Telegrams Collected (Bound); telegram received, *ibid.*; *ibid.*, RG 108, Letters Received. *O.R.*, I, xxxiv, part 3, 631.

On May 19, 8:30 P.M., Asst. Secretary of War Charles A. Dana telegraphed to USG. "It is Canby and not Hurlbut who commands the combined departments of the Gulf & Arkansas. Hurlbut is not on duty. Banks is to be relieved & Reynolds appointed to command the department. The order will be issued tomorrow." ALS (telegram sent), DNA, RG 107, Telegrams Collected (Bound); telegram received, *ibid.*, RG 108, Letters Received.

On May 27, Halleck wrote to USG. "Major Genl Rosecrans' report of May 20th, just recieved, shows that he has in Dept of Mo., 20 regiments, 235 companies, & an aggregate present of 16,034, of which 14,718 are for duty. In the Dist. of St Louis alone he has 5,877 present for duty. Of these (in Dist. of St Louis) there are 54 companies of cavalry. In the whole Dept. he has 179 companies of cavalry. What particular troops you ordered away, I do not know; but I hardly think that all, if any of your orders have been executed. In addition to the forces above enumerated there are always at the cavalry depot at St Louis a considerable number of dismounted & partly mounted cavalrymen who could be of service in case of any local disturbance. But from all I can learn there is no more danger now of a disturbance in St Louis than in Chicago or Springfield or Cincinnati. Indeed the danger is less, because no prisoners are kept there. I have therefore ordered from that place down the Miss. River to Genl Canby: the 7th Kansas Cavalry, 10 companies; the 12th Mo. Vols Cavalry, 12 companies; the 68th U. S. colored Inf'ty, 10 companies; & 10th Kansas Vol. Inf'ty, 10 companies. If the cavalry cannot be fully mounted, they will go as Infantry. I mean to follow up this order by telegraph till it is executed. More troops can well be spared from that Dept. if we succeed in getting these away. When Genl Canby went west he was authorized to order in the name of the Secty of War any troops from Mo. & Genl Rosecrans was directed to obey such orders. Canby ordered him in the name of the Secty to send from four to six thousand men down the Mississippi; but Rosecrans refused to do so on the ground that the Secty of War could not authorize Canby to use his name, and that you had decided that he had no troops to spare. The President has now placed Missouri in the Military Division of West Mississippi & directed that Genl Canby's orders must be obeyed. Whether Genl Rosecrans will obey these orders remains to be seen." LS, *ibid. O.R.*, I, xxxiv, part 4, 64.

1. On May 11, Marie M. Lathrop, Schenectady, N. Y., wrote to USG. "While all longing and loving eyes in our Country are turned anxiously upon you, I, a woman, come to humbly implore you to do justice to the Mothers and Sisters of those brave men, who have been most cruelly, most shamefully sacri-

ficed, and slaughtered, to atone for the gross mismanagement of Major General Banks, in his late battles. Perhaps I am acting very unwomanly. That may be, but *you* will pardon it. I have a right to write to you, for my young Brother has just fallen a victim to this wretched General, in the battle of Cane River. Had my brave Brother died, while fighting under a loyal, an able General, one who loved his men, and knew how to guide them in a fair field, like yourself, and Burnside, his two idols, I could endure his death. But, I *will not* bear the thought that he should be so slaughtered. I but speak to you the voice of the Land, and of General Banks' officers and men, when I tell you that he has *never* shown himself competent to fill his post, when I tell you that he has recklessly squandered their valuable lives, and that he is despised and detested by them all. *They* will confirm my words. I beseech you, General Grant, in the midst of your glorious career, to listen to my words! For your Mother's sake, I beg you to avenge us women! Recall General Banks. You are all powerful. Have him tried by Court-Martial, and punished as he deserves. A grateful Nation, a loving Army will sustain you in this act of justice, and I, mourner as I am, will bless you evermore." ALS, DNA, RG 108, Letters Received.

To Maj. Gen. Ambrose E. Burnside

[*May* 16, 1864]

GEN. BURNSIDE,

I have official notice that up to yesterday 24 700 men had sailed and were ready to sail from Washington to reinforce this Army. This number is exclusive of about 3000 for the Garrison of Belle Plain. Butler had carried the outer works at Fort Darling. Sheridan has cut both rail-roads leading from Richmond had whipped Stuards Cavalry and had carried the outer works at Richmond besides whipping the Infantry sent out to drive him away. Thinks he could have gone into the city but not knowing our operations nor those of Butler did not know that he could stay. Therefore went on in pursuance of his orders. Crook has cut the New River Bridge and destroyed all the stores at Dublin.[1] I am in hopes he is now in Lynchburg. Sherman flanked the enemy and drove him out of Dalton. He was South and Southwest of Johnston at 8 p. m. the 14th and intended to attack him at all points yesterday.

U. S. GRANT
Lt. Gen.

ALS, DNA, RG 107, Telegrams Collected (Unbound). *O.R.*, I, xxxvi, part 2, 825. See telegram to Maj. Gen. Henry W. Halleck, May 15, 1864. A copy of the letter to Maj. Gen. Ambrose E. Burnside fell into the hands of Gen. Robert E. Lee. Clifford Dowdey and Louis H. Manarin, eds., *The Wartime Papers of R. E. Lee* (Boston and Toronto, 1961), p. 750. On May 16, 1864, Burnside telegraphed to USG. "Thanks for your dispatch and congratulate you upon your glorious successes. We will do every thing possible to arrange this line so as to hold it with one Corps If every thing remains quiet I should like to visit your Hd Qrs this P M" Telegram received, DNA, RG 107, Telegrams Collected (Unbound); *ibid.*, RG 108, Letters Received. *O.R.*, I, xxxvi, part 2, 825.

On May 16, USG wrote to Maj. Gen. George G. Meade. "I have heard from Sherman to 8 P. M. the 14th. He then occupied Dalton and Resacca having turned Johnstons position There was fighting all day on the 14th resulting in contracting the ground occupied by the rebels and in bringing all of Shermans forces togather The battle was to be renewed yesterday. Sherman says he is ready to attack at all points: I have returns of troops sent from Washington and ready for shipment. The re-inforcements to this Army to this time is 24.700 men. This is exclusive of about 3.000 for the garrison of Belle Plain" Copies, DNA, RG 200, Letters Sent by Meade; *ibid.*, RG 393, 2nd Army Corps, 1st Div., Letters Received; DLC-Henry J. Hunt; (2) Meade Papers, PHi. Meade transmitted this message to his corps commanders. Copies, *ibid.* *O.R.*, I, xxxvi, part 2, 812–13.

1. On May 14, Maj. Thomas T. Eckert, U.S. Military Telegraph, telegraphed to USG. "Rebel Papers State that Averill has destroyed New River Bridge an Va & Tenn R R Together with all Supplies &C at Dublin" Telegram received, DNA, RG 108, Letters Received. See telegram to Maj. Gen. Franz Sigel, May 2, 1864.

To Maj. Gen. Ambrose E. Burnside

Hdqrs Armies U. S.
May 16th 1864 12 M.

Maj Gen Burnside
Comd'g 9th A. C.

Your dispatch of this date just received. You are authorized to make the reconnoissances you suggest. I See no objections to your visiting these Hdqrs this P. M.

U. S. Grant
Lt. Gen.

Telegram received, DNA, RG 107, Telegrams Collected (Unbound); copies, *ibid.*, RG 108, Letters Sent; DLC-USG, V, 45, 59, 66. *O.R.*, I, xxxvi, part 2, 825. See preceding telegram. On May 16, 1864, Maj. Gen. Ambrose E. Burnside had telegraphed to USG. "We have been making some reconnoisances this morning in our front—If not inconsistant with your plans I propose to find the position of the enemy with Artillery and feel him with small columns of attack." Telegram received, DNA, RG 107, Telegrams Collected (Unbound). *O.R.*, I, xxxvi, part 2, 825.

At 9:50 A.M., Burnside telegraphed to Brig. Gen. John A. Rawlins. "We have no change to report on our line—The line is intrenched from our right to the river opposite the Deserted House but it too long to occupy without the assistance of Birney. Is it the intention that the line should be still further contracted so as to occupy the whole of it with the 9th Corps in doing so the line which we would have to take would be very weak. Are there any material changes in the other parts of the army—Our Corps is in good condition" Telegram received, DNA, RG 107, Telegrams Collected (Unbound); *ibid.*, RG 108, Letters Received. *O.R.*, I, xxxvi, part 2, 826. At 10:40 A.M., USG telegraphed to Burnside. "Gen. Birney will not be taken from you until it is intended to make another attack.—You should prepare to hold the right by yourself when that takes place All quiet on all parts of the line" Copies, DLC-USG, V, 45, 59, 66; DNA, RG 108, Letters Sent. *O.R.*, I, xxxvi, part 2, 826; (misdated May 15) *ibid.*, p. 793.

At 12:35 P.M., Maj. Gen. Gouverneur K. Warren wrote to Maj. Gen. George G. Meade. "As any further advance will most probably bring on a shelling from the enemy's batteries I require a little delay to get out my wagons which are issueing supplies to the troops having but a short time ago arrived. If I may refer to it, Col Comstock was just here & thought we had already developed the condition of affairs in our front. I shall make immediate preparation to advance my skirmish line as ordered." Copy, Meade Papers, PHi. *O.R.*, I, xxxvi, part 2, 816. This message was endorsed by Meade, then by USG. "As Lt Col Comstock is of the opinion an advance on Genl Warrens front unnecessary, the question is referred to the Lt Genl Comdg. His orders here are to advance" "All I wanted was to be assured that the enemy retained their old position or if they had taken up a new one, to find where it was" Copies, Meade Papers, PHi. *O.R.*, I, xxxvi, part 2, 816.

At 3:30 P.M., Meade wrote to USG. "I have ordered Gibbon to move out to the right far enough to withdraw our hospitals uncovered yesterday by Hancocks withdrawal I hear some firing in that direction which is probably his—He was instructed to move with caution & if the enemy was found in heavy force to with draw" ALS, DNA, RG 108, Letters Received. *O.R.*, I, xxxvi, part 2, 811–12. On the same day, Burnside telegraphed to USG. "The firing from our front is merely to cover a reconnasance which was replied to by a few shots only I have not as yet heard the result" Telegram received, DNA, RG 107, Telegrams Collected (Unbound); *ibid.*, RG 108, Letters Received. The same message, as sent to Meade, is in *O.R.*, I, xxxvi, part 2, 827.

At 4:00 P.M., Meade wrote to USG. "The Medical Director of this Army reports an accumulation at Fredericksburgh of over Six thousand wounded—for whom some provision must be made, as the condition of the road to Belle Plain renders it out of the question to transport them there as originally designed— General hospitals must be established unless there is some probability of the navigation of the Rappahanock being opened, in which case they could be carried away. If the army should be detained any time in this vicinity, it might be well to put in order the Fredericksburgh R. Rd. to do which to Hamiltons Crossing will

take per estimate of Chief Qr. Msr from Ten to Twelve days—If the enemy dispute the passage of the Pamunkey or either of the Annas this road would be
useful.—" ALS, DNA, RG 108, Letters Received. *O.R.*, I, xxxvi, part 2, 812.

At 3:00 P.M., Rawlins wrote to Burnside and Meade. "You will send to
Belle Plaine, early to-morrow morning all your Reserve Artillery, and ammunition
belonging to it." Copies, DLC-USG, V, 45, (2) 59; DNA, RG 108, Letters Sent.
O.R., I, xxxvi, part 2, 811, 826. On the same day, Meade wrote to Rawlins. "Your
note requiring the Artillery Reserve of this Army to go to Belle Plain has been
recieved—Do you intend to include the Six batteries of Horse Artillery which are
the reserve of the cavalry artillery—There are now Six batteries with the
cavalry, but it has been the practice hitherto to exchange them thus giving the
horses rest and increasing their efficiency—Please let me know as soon as convenient.—" ALS, DNA, RG 108, Letters Received. *O.R.*, I, xxxvi, part 2, 811.

On May 17, 6:00 P.M., Rawlins telegraphed to Burnside. "If your Reserve
Artillery has not yet started back, send it at once. Most of the Reserve Artillery,
of the Army of the Potomac has been distributed to Divisions, and other artillery
has been sent back in lieu of it." Copies, DLC-USG, V, 45, 59; DNA, RG 108,
Letters Sent. *O.R.*, I, xxxvi, part 2, 849. At 5:20 P.M. or 6:20 P.M., Burnside
telegraphed to Rawlins. "My Reserve artillery was ordered to accompany the
reserve artillery of the Army of the Potomac back to Fredericksburgh" Copy,
DNA, RG 393, 9th Army Corps, Telegrams Sent. Printed as sent at 6:20 P.M.
in *O.R.*, I, xxxvi, part 2, 849. An undated telegram from Burnside to Rawlins
was probably sent on the same day. "The reserve artillery of 9th Corps left for
Fredericksburg about noon—" Telegram received, DNA, RG 107, Telegrams
Collected (Unbound); copy, *ibid.*, RG 393, 9th Army Corps, Telegrams Sent.
At 6:00 P.M. or 6:30 P.M., USG telegraphed to Maj. Gen. Henry W. Halleck.
"I have ordered back to Belle Plain all the reserve Artillery over one hundred
(100) pieces   This I think had better go back to Washington" Telegram re-
ceived, *ibid.*, RG 107, Telegrams Collected (Bound); copies, *ibid.*, RG 108,
Letters Sent; DLC-USG, V, 45, 59, 66. *O.R.*, I, xxxvi, part 2, 840.

To Brig. Gen. Robert O. Tyler

Headqrs Armies of the U. S.
Near Spottsylvania C. H. Va. May 16th/64 6.30 P. M.
BRIG GEN R. O. TYLER[1]
COMD'G REINFORCEMENTS
BELLE PLAIN VA
GENERAL

Enclosed find copy of a communication to Brig Gen Abercrombie.[2] I want and must have the whole of your command here by
tomorrow night at fartherest. If your troops have not yet all ar-

rived at Belle Plain, you must bring forward by that time, without fail, such as have arrived, leaving the remainder to follow as fast as they land—

Very Respectfully
U. S. GRANT
Lt. Gen.

Copies, DLC-USG, V, 45, 59, 66; DNA, RG 108, Letters Sent. *O.R.*, I, xxxvi, part 2, 829. On May 16, 1864, USG had written to Brig. Gen. John J. Abercrombie, Belle Plain. "Direct Gen Tyler to forward such of his troops as have reached Belle Plain immediately and forward all others arriving as fast as they land. Small bodies get along more conveniently than large ones, and then too we get the benefit of reenforcements from day to day" Copies, DLC-USG, V, 45, 59, 66; DNA, RG 108, Letters Sent. *O.R.*, I, xxxvi, part 2, 828.

On May 17, USG wrote to Abercrombie. "Directs Brig Genl Abercrombie Comdg at Belle Plain to ascertain and report to these Hd Qrs by what authority Capt A. D. Collins assumes to open letters addressed to officers at Washington and take out and examine their contents" DNA, RG 393, Dept. of Washington, Register of Letters Received. On the same day, Abercrombie replied. "States that Captain A D Collins was sent there by War Dept; and was releived from duty by same authority" DLC-USG, V, 48. See *O.R.*, I, xxxvi, part 2, 856. On the same day, Abercrombie wrote to Brig. Gen. John A. Rawlins. "Your telegram of the 17th, in relation to the First Maryland Volunteers, is received. It was absolutely necessary to stop Colonel Dushane and his command, as at that time the guerrillas were making demonstrations on us. Our trains of wounded had been fired on, and horses had been captured on the road from here to Fredericksburg. A large body of rebel prisoners were also expected at the time. Colonel Dushane and his command are ordered forward." *Ibid.*, p. 857.

Also on May 17, Rawlins wrote to Brig. Gen. Seth Williams. "The preceding order has been sent to Colonel Murphy, who last evening encamped with his command about 3 miles out from here on the Fredericksburg road." *Ibid.*, p. 854. On the same day, Rawlins wrote to Col. Mathew Murphy, 69th N. Y. National Guard. "You will report with your command to Maj Gen Geo G. Meade Comdg army of the Potomac for orders & assignment" Copies, DLC-USG, V, 45, 59, 66; DNA, RG 108, Letters Sent. *O.R.*, I, xxxvi, part 2, 853.

On May 19, Capt. Robert L. Orr, adjt. for Abercrombie, wrote to Rawlins. "The Twenty-third and Eighty-second Pennsylvania Volunteers arrived at this post just as we were in receipt of over 7,500 prisoners. It was indispensably necessary that the provost guard, Army of the Potomac, who brought them, should be relieved and sent to the front. The two Pennsylvania regiments (who had been on duty at Johnson's Island over prisoners) were substituted in the emergency. The last of the rebels left here yesterday, and the Twenty-third and Eighty-second have been ordered forward." *Ibid.*, p. 934.

1. Robert O. Tyler, born in Hunter, N. Y., in 1831, USMA 1853, was appointed col., 4th Conn., as of Sept. 17, 1861, and brig. gen. as of Nov. 29, 1862. An art. commander with the Army of the Potomac through much of the war, he

commanded a div. of art. fighting as inf., 2nd Army Corps, in late May, 1864, until severely wounded at Cold Harbor on June 1.

2. Abercrombie, born in Md. in 1798, raised in Tenn., USMA 1822, promoted to col., 7th Inf., as of Feb. 25, 1861, and appointed brig. gen. as of Aug. 31, fought in the peninsular campaign, then served mostly around Washington until assigned to command the depots at Belle Plain and Fredericksburg, Va., in May, 1864. *Ibid.*, p. 685.

To Maj. Gen. Henry W. Halleck

Spottsylvania 8 45 a m
May 17th 1864

MAJ GEN H W HALLECK
CHF OF STAFF

Send all cavalry horses here to mount men who are without horses—I think it will be advisable to repair the Rail road from Aquia Creek at once—Sheridans dismounted men ought to return from James River by boat—I want him to get back here as soon as possible—If Sheridan has not started back he had better turn over all his weak artillery to Butler

U S. GRANT
Lt Genl

Telegram received, DNA, RG 107, Telegrams Collected (Bound); copies, *ibid.*, RG 108, Letters Sent; DLC-USG, V, 45, 59, 66. *O.R.*, I, xxxvi, part 2, 840. On May 16, 1864, 1:00 P.M. and 9:30 P.M., Maj. Gen. Henry W. Halleck had telegraphed to USG. "A new regt of Pa. cavalry ordered here. I propose to dismount the men & send them forward as Infantry. Shall I give the horses to veteran cavalry Army of the Potomac, or send them to Genl. Sheridan who asks for a thousand horses? Rail Road from Aquia Creek to Falmouth can be repaired in 8 days. Shall it be done? Genl Sherman defeated the rebels yesterday & a part of his force has [c]rossed the Oostanaula river. Our loss about three thousand in all. A messenger just arrived from Genl Sheridan. He is at Haxall's Landing on James River & has recieved supplies for men & horses." "There is considerable dissatisfaction in the artillery & cavalry regts sent forward as infantry, especially in the latter. I respectfully recommend that they be put in old brigades & divisions in the front. One successful fight will remove all dissatisfaction; [an]d if not it will do no harm there. Sherman still successful." ALS (telegrams sent), DNA, RG 107, Telegrams Collected (Bound); telegrams received, *ibid.*; *ibid.*, RG 108, Letters Received. *O.R.*, I, xxxvi, part 2, 810.

On May 17, USG telegraphed to Halleck. "Cannot Gen'l Sigel go up Shenandoah Valley to Staunton? The Enemy are evidently drawing supplies largely from that source and if Sigel can destroy the road there it will be of vast importance to us. The weather is still cloudy & threatening, as if the rain was not yet over." Telegram received, DNA, RG 107, Telegrams Collected (Bound); copies (misdated May 18), *ibid.*, RG 108, Letters Sent; DLC-USG, V, 45, 59, 66. Dated May 17 in *O.R.*, I, xxxvi, part 2, 840; *ibid.*, I, xxxvii, part 1, 475. On the same day, 11:30 P.M., Halleck telegraphed to USG. "Sheridan has anticipated your orders & moves to day on his return to Army of the Potomac. All the horses we can collect will be put in the hands of veteran cavalry men & sent to Army of the Potomac. I have sent the substance of your despatch to Genl Sigel. Instead of advancing on Staunton he is already in full retreat on Strausburg. If you expect anything from him you will be mistaken. He will do nothing but run. He never did anything else. The Secty of War proposes to put Genl Hunter in his place. Send him up immediately. Bridges at Harpers Ferry carried away. I have sent Pontons to day to replace them   Butler has fallen back to day. Dont rely on him. Sherman is doing well. I will push forward rail road from Aquia creek with all possible despatch. More reinforcements will leave here to-morrow. I will run them up in a few days from twenty five to thirty thousand." ALS (telegram sent), DNA, RG 107, Telegrams Collected (Bound); telegram received, *ibid.*; *ibid.*, RG 108, Letters Received. *O.R.*, I, xxxvi, part 2, 840–41.

To Maj. Gen. Ambrose E. Burnside

Hd. Qrs. Armies of the United States
Near Spottsylvania C. H., May 17, 1864

Maj Gen. Burnside
Comd'g 9th Army Corps
General:

A reconnoisance of the ground over which it was intended to attack to-morrow morning proves the ground entirely impracticable to pass troops over. The attack therefore will not be made as ordered. In lieu of that Hancock and Wright will move back during the night to the old position of the 2d Corps and attack there at 4 A. M. in the morning. Warren will commence with his Artillery, which is so placed as to enfilade the enemy's rifle-pits in your front, being prepared however to follow Hancock and Wright, if they should succeed in breaking through or to strengthen Warren if they enemy should move on him

U. S. Grant, Lieut Gen.

Copies, DLC-USG, V, 45, 59, 66; DNA, RG 108, Letters Sent. *O.R.*, I, xxxvi, part 2, 850.

To Maj. Gen. Ambrose E. Burnside

Headqrs Armies of the United States
Near Spottsylvania May 17th/64

MAJ GEN BURNSIDE
COMD'G 9TH A. C.
GENERAL

If the Div. of reinforcements under Genl Tyler arrive tonight as is expected an attack will be made at 4 a. m. tomorrow morning to the left of the position now held by Warren's Corps. Hancocks and Wrights Corps will commence the attack and Warren's Corps will support batteries which will be established during the night—I want you to hold your command in readiness to move out of their present place at half past three in the morning to move by the left flank to follow up the two attacking Corps and support them. If you move leave your pickets, to remain until driven in or recalled—

I will let you know in the evening if the attack is to be made. Send out some of your Staff officers to reconnoitre the roads over which you will have to pass when you do move, and parties to make such repairs or new roads as may be required—

My Hdqrs will be removed in the course of an hour or so to near the Anderson House

U. S. GRANT
Lt Gen.

P. S.—I have just received news from Sherman. On the 15th he had whipped J. Johnston with a loss of 3,000 men on our side. Sherman was then crossing the Oostenaula. Johnston has evidently given up.

U. S. G.

Copies (incomplete), DLC-USG, V, 45, 59, 66; DNA, RG 108, Letters Sent. *O.R.*, I, xxxvi, part 2, 849–50. On May 17, 1864, 7:40 P.M., Maj. Gen. Ambrose E. Burnside telegraphed to USG. "According to your instructions of this morning further instructions were to be sent to me this evening. Is the programme spoken of to be carried out? If" Copy (incomplete), DNA, RG 393, 9th Army Corps, Telegrams Sent. A notation "no" may indicate that the telegram was never completed or sent. A telegram of the same date, 6:15 P.M., from Burnside to Brig. Gen. John A. Rawlins is marked "Not Sent." Copy, *ibid.*

To Commanding Officer, C.S.A. Forces

Head Qrs. Armies of the U. States
Near Spotsylvania C. H. Va.
May 18th 1864

COMD.G OFFICERS CONFED. FORCES
NEAR OLD WILDERNESS TAVERN VA.
SIR:

To secure proper medical supplies and care for wounded soldiers who I understand are still left in hospitals near Old Wilderness Taver I would request that all who are still in your hands be delivered to Asst. Surg. Edwd. Breneman, U. S. A. who is authorized to receipt the rolls of the same.

I will state that all Confederate wounded who have fallen into our hands are receiving good care and abundance of supplies of all discriptions. Such however as have not ~~have~~ been sent beyond Fredericksburg will be delivered into your hands, at Chancellorsville, if you desire it.

I have the honor to be
Very respectfully
your obt. svt.
U. S. GRANT
Lt. Gen. Com

ALS, ICHi. *O.R.*, I, xxxvi, part 1, 221; *ibid.*, I, xxxvi, part 2, 865. On May 17, 1864, Asst. Surgeon Platt R. H. Sawyer, Fredericksburg, wrote to Surgeon Edward B. Dalton stating that some 400 wounded U.S. troops remained in the hands of C.S.A. forces near the Wilderness. ALS, DNA, RG 108, Letters Received. *O.R.*, I, xxxvi, part 2, 841–42. On the same day, Asst. Surgeon Edward De W. Breneman wrote to Surgeon Thomas A. McParlin, medical director, Army of the Potomac. "I was instructed by surgeon E. B. Dalton U. S. V. to report to you the fact that about four hundred of our wounded, from different Corps of the Army, are yet in the hands of the enemy at 'Robertson's Tavern'; that they decline to deliver them under flag of truce from Major Genl. Meade, and require that a flag of truce be sent by order of Lieut. Genl. Grant before their delivery can be effected." ALS, DNA, RG 108, Letters Received. *O.R.*, I, xxxvi, part 2, 841. On May 18, Maj. Gen. George G. Meade endorsed this letter. "Respectfully forwarded to Lieut: General Grant, for his information & action—" ES, DNA, RG 108, Letters Received.

On May 19, Brig. Gen. John A. Rawlins issued an unnumbered Special

Order. "The Commanding Officers at Fredericksburg or Officer in Command of troops at any point of our lines, will furnish the bearer Asst. Surg. Brenerman U. S. A. on his application, all facilities he may require as bearer of a Flag of Truce, from the Lieut. Gen. Comd'g to the Confederate authorities for the purpose of bringing in our wounded or for the purpose of furnishing them supplies—" DS, PHi.

On May 21, Breneman, Fredericksburg, wrote to Rawlins. "I have the honor to report that in obedience to instructions from Head Quarters Army of the United States, dated May 18th, and received last evening, authorizing me to receive wounded soldiers of the U. S. A. left in Hospitals on recent battle fields, from the Confederate authorities, I this morning proceeded to the 'Old Wilderness Tavern' with twenty-five Ambulances, under flag of truce. The Major commanding the forces at that point declined receiving any communications, under instructions from his superiors unless addressed to General Robert E. Lee, and I returned with empty ambulances. Supplies were sent to the wounded yesterday, of whom more than six-hundred remain in the hands of the enemy, at different points—viz. 'Wilderness,' 'Robertson's Tavern' and elsewhere in those vicinities. They were represented to be comfortably situated. The Major commanding the Confederate forces stated that Genl. Lee would be notified that I appeared to-day, while I agreed to meet again, under flag of truce to-morrow at twelve O'clock, at the 'Old Wilderness.' I have the honor to await instructions from you at this point, after which I hope to successfully accomplish their recovery." ALS, DNA, RG 108, Letters Received.

On May 22, 11:30 P.M., Breneman wrote to Rawlins. "I have the honor to report that I again proceeded to the Confederate lines on the plank road, at a point near Parker's Store, this morning, with a flag of truce, and two unarmed orderlies, for the purpose of learning the condition of our wounded and the number in their hands, and was met by Capt. James C. Borden, Company H, First North Carolina Cavalry, commanding the pickets, by whom I was courteously received, and the desired information obtained. Supplies were represented by a Confederate surgeon, who accompanied the captain, as becoming scarce, but the patients comfortable and well treated. I agreed to furnish supplies to-morrow, while a communication from your headquarters, under date of 18th instant, 'To the officer commanding the Confederate forces at the Old Wilderness,' was transferred to be forwarded to General Lee. On my return, with the flag of truce flying, and when in the neighborhood of Old Wilderness Tavern, on the turnpike, I was met and halted by 6 men, dressed in Confederate uniform, fully armed, who represented themselves as an 'independent command of scouts' acknowledging no authority. The flag of truce was disregarded, my horse taken from me, person fully searched, official and private papers and other articles removed, and after much insult and delay I was permitted to return to this point without further molestation. Some of the official papers were returned. I deem it unquestionably unsafe to forward supplies under existing circumstances, and in consultation with Colonel Schriver, inspector-general, military governor, and Surg. Edward B. Dalton, U. S. Volunteers, medical director, they coincided. As I found these independent bands in force between our lines and Wilderness Tavern bent on plunder of whatever description, as one of the six met informed me, an armed escort will subject the train to certain capture, while an unarmed one will be useless to repel any attack that may be made by guerrillas before it could reach the enemy's picket-line. I hasten to represent these matters fully and properly, and await instructions from your headquarters." O.R., I, xxxvi, part 3, 136–37.

On May 31, Breneman wrote to Rawlins. "I have the honor to report that, protected by an armed force of cavalry and infantry (in obedience to instructions from headquarters Armies of the United States to Brigadier-General Abercrombie), under command of Colonel Di Cesnola, Fourth New York Cavalry, I proceeded to Jones' field, in the Wilderness, on the 27th instant; recovered all the wounded at that point, 86 in number, mostly from the Second Corps; brought them safely to Fredericksburg, Va.; had them placed on board of a transport the same night, and they are probably by this time in general hospital, Washington. From a few prisoners captured belonging to the Ambulance Corps of the so-called Confederate Army, it was learned that the enemy were removing the wounded, our own and theirs, from their hospitals at Parker's Store and Robertson's Tavern, to Gordonsville and Richmond. I hope that in the performance of these duties I have met the approbation of the lieutenant-general commanding the Armies of the United States," *Ibid.*, p. 415.

To Maj. Gen. George G. Meade

Headqrs Armies of the United States—
Near Spottsylvania Va. May 18th/64

MAJ GEN MEADE
COMD'G A. P.
GENERAL

Before daylight tomorrow morning I propose to draw Hancock & Burnside from the positions they now hold and put Burnside to the left of Wright. Wright and Burnside should then force their way up as close to the enemy as they can get, without a general engagement, or with a general engagement if the enemy will come out of their works to fight, and entrench. Hancock should march and take up a position as if in support of the two left Corps. Tomorrow night at twelve or one o'clock, he will be moved Southeast with all his force, and as much Cavalry as can be given to him, to get as far towards Richmond on the line of the Fredericksburg rail road, as he can make, fighting the enemy in whatever force he may find him. If the enemy make a general move to meet this, they will be followed by the other three Corps of the Army and attacked if possible, before time is given to entrench—

Suitable directions will at once be given for all trains and surplus Artillery to conform to this movement.

U. S. GRANT Lt Gen—

Copies, DLC-USG, V, 45, 59, 66; DNA, RG 108, Letters Sent; Meade Papers, PHi. *O.R.*, I, xxxvi, part 2, 864–65.

On May 18, 1864, 2:00 P.M., Brig. Gen. John A. Rawlins wrote to Maj. Gen. Ambrose E. Burnside. "Enclosed please find copy of instructions from the Lieutenant General Commanding to Maj Gen Meade, which embraces the directions for your next movement, and by which you will be governed—In moving from your present position to your new, march your Infantry by the rear of Generals Warren & Wright, keeping on the same side of the Ny, you now are, if practicable, and send your artillery and wagons around by the road. Commence your movement immediately after Gen Hancock takes up his line of march—" Copies, DLC-USG, V, 45, 59, 66; DNA, RG 108, Letters Sent. *O.R.*, I, xxxvi, part 2, 880.

At 9:00 A.M. and 6:10 P.M., USG wrote to Burnside. "No vulnerable point presenting itself in the front now occupied, there will be no attack to-day. You will therefore assume a defensive position, holding yourself in readiness for being withdrawn to your left at short notice" Copies, DLC-USG, V, 45, 59, 66; DNA, RG 108, Letters Sent. *O.R.*, I, xxxvi, part 2, 880. "The same road will be used from here to Fredericksburg after our first move as now, so that the position of Ferrero's command will not be changed at present. Warren does not move." *Ibid.*

To Maj. Gen. Henry W. Halleck

May 19th/64 10 p. m.

MAJ. GEN. HALLECK, WASHINGTON

The enemy came out on our right late this afternoon and attacked but were driven back until some time since dark. Not knowing their exact position and the danger our trains at Fredericksburg will be in if we move I shall not make the move designed for to night until their designs are fully developed. We captured men from three different Divisions of the enemy all from Ewells Corps.

U. S. GRANT
Lt. Gen.

ALS (telegram sent), DNA, RG 107, Telegrams Collected (Unbound); telegram received, *ibid.*, Telegrams Collected (Bound). *O.R.*, I, xxxvi, part 1, 6; *ibid.*, I, xxxvi, part 2, 906.

On May 19, 1864, 1:00 P.M., USG telegraphed to Maj. Gen. Henry W. Halleck. "I shall make a flank movement early in the morning and try to reach Bowling Green and Milford Station If successful Port Royal will be more convenient as a depot than Fredericksburg. I wish you would stir up the Navy to see if they cannot reach there" Telegram received, DNA, RG 107, Telegrams

Collected (Bound); copies, *ibid.*, RG 108, Letters Sent; DLC-USG, V, 45, 59, 66. *O.R.*, I, xxxvi, part 1, 6; *ibid.*, I, xxxvi, part 2, 906. On May 20, 2:00 P.M., Halleck telegraphed to USG. "There are three thousand wounded men in Fredericksburg who cannot be removed except by water transportation. Genl Meigs will send transports to day to ascend the Rappahannock to-morrow for that purpose. The south bank of the river above Port Royal should be held by our cavalry in ordr to enable the transports to pass up. Supplies of forage will accompany the fleet. Large amounts of property have been sent to Fredericksburg. If that place is to be abandoned, this property should first be removed. Moreover, the repair of the Aquia Creek Railroad should cease. The navigation of the Rappahannock above Port Royal is difficult & will cease when the river falls." ALS (telegram sent), DNA, RG 107, Telegrams Collected (Bound); telegram received, *ibid.*; *ibid.*, RG 108, Letters Received. *O.R.*, I, xxxvi, part 3, 4.

On May 19, USG telegraphed to Halleck. "The furloughs of the 2nd Maryland forty sixth N. Y. & twenty ninth Mass. Veterans are now out. Please order them to join the 9th Corps," Telegram received, DNA, RG 94, Vol. Service Div., A428 (VS) 1864; *ibid.*, RG 107, Telegrams Collected (Bound); copies, *ibid.*, RG 108, Letters Sent; DLC-USG, V, 45, 59, 66. *O.R.*, I, xxxvi, part 2, 907.

To Maj. Gen. Ambrose E. Burnside

May 19th/64

MAJ. GEN. BURNSIDE, 9TH A. C.

After occupying the Quesenbury House push pickets out to the Po River if you can and drive in the rebel pickets until you find the end or right of the enemys main line. You want to get if possible where their movements can be observed and if they move away we want to follow close upon them. Push pickets also good distances on the roads East & Southeast from you.

U. S. GRANT
Lt. Gen.

ALS, deCoppet Collection, NjP. *O.R.*, I, xxxvi, part 2, 928. On May 19, 1864, 5:45 A.M., Maj. Gen. Ambrose E. Burnside, "Myers House," telegraphed to USG. "The head of the Column reached here some time ago but cannot move further until Gen Wrights troops get out of the way   The whole Corps is now massed here" Telegram received, DNA, RG 107, Telegrams Collected (Unbound); *ibid.*, RG 108, Letters Received. *O.R.*, I, xxxvi, part 2, 927. At 1:45 P.M., Burnside telegraphed to USG. "The result of the reconnoisances & observations made this morning is as follows, at a point one mile & a quarter due south from the Myers house is a house owned by Quesenberry   taking that as a starting point and going a half a mile due south you strike the Po River drawing a line south west from spottsylvania C. H. you strike the Po again then drawing a line from the Quesenberry house a little south of west one mile you strike the Po again and at that point the enemys entrenchments seem to end & to run from that point directly to spottsylvania C H   All accounts agree that there are no entrenchments south of the Po at a point two miles south East of Smiths Mill. The Po & Ny unite   the four points on the Po given in this dispatch will give the General direction of that River   from all the information given by our pickets left behind this morning the enemy evacuated their works in our front before we left this morning" Telegram received, DNA, RG 107, Telegrams Collected (Unbound); *ibid.*, RG 108, Letters Received; copy, *ibid.*, RG 393, 9th Army Corps, Telegrams Sent. *O.R.*, I, xxxvi, part 2, 927–28.

On the same day, USG sent to Burnside a telegram received at 4:15 P.M. "Can you not occupy the Quesenberry house with a brigade? It will be a good point from which to observe the movements of the enemy." *Ibid.*, p. 928. At 3:40 P.M., Burnside telegraphed to USG. "I had one brigade at the Queensbury house but withdrew it   will have it replaced at once" Telegram received, DNA, RG 107, Telegrams Collected (Unbound); *ibid.*, RG 108, Letters Received. Printed as sent at 4:30 P.M. in *O.R.*, I, xxxvi, part 2, 928.

At 9:15 P.M., USG telegraphed to Burnside. "What news with you this evening? The enemy crossed the Ny, to our right, this evening, in considerable force. We having taken prisoners from three different divisions. Quite a sharp engagement has taken place, in which we have lost probably 1,500 men, killed and wounded." *Ibid.*, p. 929. See following letter.

To Brig. Gen. Edward Ferrero

Head Quarters Armies of the U. S.
Near Spottsylvania C. H. Va May 19th/64

BRIG GEN FERRERO
COMD'G 4TH DIV. 9TH A C.
GENERAL

The enemy have crossed the Ny to the right of our lines in considerable force and may possibly detach a force to move on Fredericksburg. Keep your Cavalry pickets well out on the plank road and all the roads leading west and south of you. If you find the enemy moving Infantry and artillery towards you report it promptly—In that case take up strong positions and detain him all you can turning all trains back to Fredericksburg, and whatever falling back you may be forced to do do in that direction. I do not think the enemy will detach in that direction, but give you this warning in time in case they should—

Require all trains coming to the front to come by the Massaponax church road—

Very Respectfully
U. S. GRANT Lt. Gen.

Copies, DLC-USG, V, 45, 59, 66; DNA, RG 108, Letters Sent. *O.R.*, I, xxxvi, part 2, 930.

To Maj. Gen. Henry W. Halleck

Head Q'rs of the Army
In the field
May 20th 1864. 8 30 a m

MAJ GEN H. W. HALLECK
CHIEF OF STAFF.

The attempt to turn our right last evening was by Ewells Corps wholly. They were promptly repulsed by Birney's & Tylers divisions and some of Warrens troops that were on the extreme right. About three hundred (300) prisoners fell into our hands besides many killed and wounded. Our loss foots up little over six hundred wounded and about one hundred and fifty killed & missing. This is as near an accurate report as can be given at this time, probably the killed and missing is over stated

U. S. GRANT
Lt General

Telegram received, DNA, RG 107, Telegrams Collected (Bound); copies, RG 108, Letters Sent; DLC-USG, V, 45, 59, 66. *O.R.*, I, xxxvi, part 1, 6; *ibid.*, I, xxxvi, part 3, 3.

On May 20, 1864, 7:30 P.M., USG telegraphed to Maj. Gen. Henry W. Halleck. "Our casualties for yesterday foot up 196 killed, 1090 wounded and 249 missing. We buried nearly an equal number of rebel dead besides what they buryed or carried off and retain 472 prisoners exclusive of wounded. Send all new Cavalry equiped as Infantry and mount veterans on their horses." ALS (telegram sent), DNA, RG 107, Telegrams Collected (Unbound); telegram received, *ibid.*, Telegrams Collected (Bound). *O.R.*, I, xxxvi, part 1, 6; *ibid.*, I, xxxvi, part 3, 3. USG's figures apparently came from a report of May 20 submitted by Maj. Gen. George G. Meade, but omitting ten officers killed and forty-five officers wounded. DS, DNA, RG 108, Letters Received.

To Maj. Gen. Henry W. Halleck

Near Spotsylvania C. H. Va.
May 20th 1864

MAJ. GEN. H. W. HALLECK,
CHIEF OF STAFF OF THE ARMY,
GENERAL,

In regard to the operations it is better for General Hunter to engage in with the disposable forces at his command I am a little in doubt. It is evident that he can move south, covering the road he has to guard, with a larger force than he can spare to be removed, to reinforce armies elswhere. Then too under the instructions to Gen. Sigel Crook was to get through to the Va & Ten. rail-road, cut New River Bridge and move Eastward to Lynchburg if he could, if not to ~~Fyncastle~~ Finn Castle, Staunton and down the Shenandoah Valley. Sigel was to collect what force he could spare from the rail-road and move up the valley with a supply train to meet him.

The enemy is evidently relying for supplies greatly on such as are brought over the branch road running through Staunton. On the whole therefore I think it would be better for Gen. Hunter to move in that direction. Reach Staunton and Gordonsville, or Charlottesville if he does not meet too much opposition. If he can hold at bay a force equal to his own he will be doing good service.[1]

In a letter to the Sec. of War written about one week ago[2] I recommended Gens. Sherman and Meade for promotion to Maj. Gen. in the regular army and Hancock for Brig. I wish you would urge this again. The Secretary replied that there was but one vacan[cy] for Maj. Gen. I think this must be a mistake. I was appointed before Gen. Wool was retired or at least was notified of the fact that an original vacancy existed before his retirement.

Gen. Wright is one of the most meritorious officers in the service, and with opportunity will demonstrate his fitness for any position. But at present I doubt whether Sheridan has not most entitled himself to the other vacaneyt Brigadier Generalcy. This however I would leave open for a time.

> I am General, very truly
> your obt. svt.
> U. S. GRANT
> Lt. Gen.

ALS, Schoff Collection, MiU-C. *O.R.*, I, xxxvi, part 3, 3–4; (incomplete) *ibid.*, I, xxxiv, part 1, 20; *ibid.*, I, xxxvi, part 1, 24; *ibid.*, I, xxxvii, part 1, 500; *ibid.*, I, xxxviii, part 1, 13.

1. On May 18, 1864, 5:30 P.M., USG telegraphed to Maj. Gen. Henry W. Halleck. "By information just received I judge Genl Crook is going back to Gauley by the same route he went—If so all the surplus force in Gen Sigels Department had better be collected at Harpers Ferry, so that it can be brought here, or sent up the Shenandoah as may then seem most advantageous—" Telegram received, DNA, RG 107, Telegrams Collected (Bound); copies, *ibid.*, RG 108, Letters Sent; DLC-USG, V, 45, 59, 66. *O.R.*, I, xxxvii, part 1, 485–86. On the same day, 4:00 P.M., Halleck telegraphed to USG. "The Secty of War directs me to say that the President will appoint Genl Hunter to command Dept of West Virginia, if you desire it. Please answer as early as possible." ALS (telegram sent), DNA, RG 107, Telegrams Collected (Bound); telegram received, *ibid.*; *ibid.*, RG 108, Letters Received. *O.R.*, I, xxxvii, part 1, 485. On May 19, 10:30 A.M., USG telegraphed to Halleck. "By all means I would say appoint Genl Hunter or any one else to the command of West Virginia" Telegram received, DNA, RG 107, Telegrams Collected (Bound); copies, *ibid.*, RG 108, Letters Sent; DLC-USG, V, 45, 59, 66. *O.R.*, I, xxxvii, part 1, 492. On the same day, 11:00 A.M. and 10:00 P.M., Halleck telegraphed to USG. "If Genl Crook falls back to Gauley, I will dispose of his troops as directed. A telegram in the newspapers of this morning dated Gauley Bridge the 17th says that Genl Crookes was at Newbern on the 13th having gained three victories [o]ver the rebels, destroyed bridge [o]ver New River & several miles of [ra]il road track. Nothing further [fr]om Sigel or Sherman. If Genl Hunter should be given [the] command in West Va, please [se]nd me Substance of your instructions for operations in that Dept, I do not know what your orders [to] Sigel & Crook have been; [b]ut I presume they have looked mainly to the destruction of the rebel rail roads & the protection of the B. & O. Road. The destruction of the Bridge at Harpers Ferry by the flood has delayed the arrival of western troops." "Genl Hunter placed in command of Dept of West Virginia. The Navy will work up the Rappahannock even to Fredericksburg if you protect the South Bank from Guerrillas. The land is so high they can fire down upon the decks without danger to themselves. More troops will be sent to Fredericksburg to-morrow. I shall continue [to] send there all I can raise till [o]therwise ordered. The 21st Penn Cavalry arrived to-night fully mounted. Shall I send them forward as cavalry or arm them as Infantry & give their horses to veterans of Army of the Potomac? They are raw recruits & of little use as cavalry." ALS (telegrams sent), DNA, RG 107, Telegrams Collected (Bound); telegrams received, *ibid.*; *ibid.*, RG 108, Letters Received. *O.R.*, I, xxxvii, part 1, 493. The second is also *ibid.*, I, xxxvi, part 2, 907.

2. See letter to Edwin M. Stanton, May 13, 1864. On May 23, Halleck wrote to USG. "Private & Confidential." "What you say in your note of the 20th about the Major Genls. is correct—There are *two* vacancies. The law allows five. You filled an original vacancy, and I last year urged Sherman's name for Wool's place; but could not get him appointed. Your promotion makes a second vacancy, and I have urged the names of Meade and Sherman, and Hancock for Meade's place as Brig. There is some obstacle in the way and I cant remove it. I am not certain what it is, but can *guess*. Perhaps you will be enlightened a little by knowing what are some of the outside influences. I understand that the names of Butler and Sickles have been strongly urged by politicians, in order, they say, to break down 'West Point influence.' It will not be difficult to draw conclusions— This is *entre nous*." Copy, DNA, RG 108, Letters Sent. *O.R.*, I, xxxvi, part 3, 115. On June 15, Secretary of War Edwin M. Stanton wrote to USG. "Mr. Washburne called on the President this morning—as he represented, at your instance—to urge the appointment of General Meade and Genl. Sherman to the rank of Major General in the regular army; and said that you entertained some apprehension that the Government were holding back these appointments with a view of giving them to Genl. Butler & Genl. Sickles. Some weeks ago Genl Halleck showed me a letter from you, recommending Generals Meade and Sherman for promotion, and stating that you did not want one appointed until both could be appointed. It has been the design to comply with your request in this respect, but it was deemed expedient not to make the appointments until the operations of the respective armies of Genl. Meade & Genl. Sherman should develope some final result; and it was thought that when the Army of the Potomac should reach Richmond and Sherman reach Atlanta, these events would be a fitting occasion to confer upon the distinguished officers named the highest rank to which, under existing laws, they could be appointed. For this reason, and not with the design of appointing any other persons, the matter has laid over. If, however, for any reason, you deem immediate appointments desirable, they will be made. Congratulating you upon the unexampled ability and brilliant success of the operations under your charge," Copy, DLC-Edwin M. Stanton. On June 19, USG wrote to Stanton. "Your Letter of the 15th inst in relation to the promotion of Gens Meade and Sherman to the same rank in the regular Army they now hold in the volunteer service is received. I see no objection to defering their promotion to the end of the Campaign as you propose" Copies, DLC-USG, V, 45, 59, 67; DNA, RG 108, Letters Sent.

To Maj. Gen. Ambrose E. Burnside

May 20, 1864. 8 20 a m

MAJ GEN. BURNSIDE
COM'D'G 9TH ARMY CORPS

Push out a heavy line of skirmishers in connection with Gen. Wright to feel for the enemy and to keep him employed. It is not designed to attack him behind his entrenchments, but to find out all that can be learned of his position and the nature of his works and the intervening ground

U. S GRANT, Lt. Gen.

Copies, DLC-USG, V, 45, 59, 66; DNA, RG 108, Letters Sent. *O.R.*, I, xxxvi, part 3, 18. On May 20, 1864, Maj. Gen. Ambrose E. Burnside telegraphed to USG. "The reconnoisances have already been pushed down the roads from my position this morning for a mile & a half discovering no signs of the enemy,   The skirmish line will be pushed forward as you order. it is now forming in conjunction with Gen Wrights"   Telegram received, DNA, RG 107, Telegrams Collected (Unbound); *ibid.*, RG 108, Letters Received; copy, *ibid.*, RG 393, 9th Army Corps, Telegrams Sent. *O.R.*, I, xxxvi, part 3, 18.

Also on May 20, USG telegraphed to Burnside. "On the removal of Gen. Warren from the Right, Gen Wright and yourself will take the line marked out to-day by the Engineer officers. Make all the necessary preparations in advance for this change"   Copies, DLC-USG, V, 45, 59, 66; DNA, RG 108, Letters Sent. *O.R.*, I, xxxvi, part 3, 19. At 7:30 P.M., Burnside telegraphed to USG. "Gen Wright recvd the telegram in reference to the line after Morton saw him and is now laying out the line direct from Myers House to Quesenberry House & I will conform to his line by extending towards the Po certainly as far the Quesenberry House and farther if you wish"   Telegram received, DNA, RG 107, Telegrams Collected (Unbound); *ibid.*, RG 108, Letters Received. *O.R.*, I, xxxvi, part 3, 19. At 9:00 P.M., Lt. Col. Horace Porter telegraphed to Burnside. "Extend your line no farther than the Quesenberry House, unless it can be done with perfect security. Of this you must be the judge." Copies, DLC-USG, V, 45, 59; DNA, RG 108, Letters Sent. *O.R.*, I, xxxvi, part 3, 19.

Also on May 20, 5:30 A.M., 10:30 A.M., and 5:30 P.M., Maj. Gen. George G. Meade wrote to USG. "Birney reports the enemy having disappeared from his front of last night—He has followed them down to the rive at the deserted house taking several prisoners from their stragglers and all seem to indicate the presence of Ewells corps yesterday & their withdrawal in the night to their entrenchments, I propose now to withdraw *Birney* & *Tyler* & leave Russell with Warren's people —to keep watch against the return of the enemy—" ALS, DNA, RG 108, Letters Received. *O.R.*, I, xxxvi, part 3, 4. "I have sent directions to General Wright to prepare himself to hold the right flank of the army with his corps on the withdrawal of Warren. I have also directed two engineer officers to report to him to assist him in laying out his lines. I think it would be well if you should send either Comstock or Babcock to consult and advise with him. He is now rather advanced from the river to throw back his right flank, hold to the river, and have any force to hold the Anderson house, but this will depend greatly on the nature of the ground. Over 470 prisoners have reached the provost-marshal-general from the Second Corps. Warren says Crawford picked up a number. As soon as they come in and I get returns of casualties ordered, I will report." *Ibid.*, p. 5. "Genl. Ingalls has advices from the Gun boats announcing the Rappahanock river free from all obstructions up to Fredericksburgh.—This will enable steamers to take away all our wounded & secures Port Royal for a base in case it should be required.—" ALS, DNA, RG 108, Letters Received. *O.R.*, I, xxxvi, part 3, 5.

To Brig. Gen. Edward Ferrero

———

Headqrs of the United States
Near Spottsylvania C. H. Va May 20th/64

BRIG GEN FERRERO
COMD'G 4TH DIV 9TH A. C.
GENERAL

Yours of this date just received.[1] All our troops it is expected will be moved to the left so as to bring into use the road near the Fredericksburg and Richmond rail road. When this takes place you will move east so as to best cover it—In the mean time I think your troops had better remain substantially as they now are.

It is impossible to give you more Cavalry now, but Sheridan is now in his fourth day from Richmond and may be looked for today or tomorrow. When he arrives his Cavalry will be so disposed as to materially releive you.

Your Obt Svt
U. S. GRANT Lt. Gen

Copies, DLC-USG, V, 45, 59, 66; DNA, RG 108, Letters Sent. *O.R.*, I, xxxvi, part 3, 21. On May 20, 1864, Brig. Gen. John A. Rawlins wrote to Brig. Gen. Edward Ferrero. "You will make such disposition of your forces to-morrow morning, the 21st inst. as to best cover Fredericksburg and the road leading from there to Bowling Green. In doing this take up and maintain a line from Banks Ford, via Tabernacle Church road to the Port Royal road, letting your Cavalry Pickets extend as far as Tabernacle Church. Make your Headquarters at or near Owen's, where you will keep concentrated your main force." LS, DNA, RG 94, War Records Office, 9th Army Corps. *O.R.*, I, xxxvi, part 3, 21–22. On May 21, 8:30 A.M., Rawlins wrote to Ferrero. "Since the writing of instructions to you last evenings, the whole of our supply trains have been ordered forward from Fredericksburg to Guiney's Station. Immediately in the rear of these trains passing your line, you will follow them with your Command, and take up such position at Guiney's Station as to best protect and cover them from the enemy at that point" Copies, DLC-USG, V, 45, 59; DNA, RG 94, War Records Office, 9th Army Corps; *ibid.*, RG 108, Letters Sent. *O.R.*, I, xxxvi, part 3, 65. On the same day, Lt. Col. Cyrus B. Comstock wrote to Ferrero. "Stating to Gen'l Ferrero, that the Lieut Gen'l Com'd'g does not desire him to wait for wagons from Belle Plains, but to make such dispositions as to cover the main Trains of the Army" DNA, RG 393, 9th Army Corps, 4th Div., Register of Letters Received. On May 23, Rawlins wrote to Ferrero. "All organized troops not of your Command, or specially assigned to escort trains by Gen. Meade, you will please send forward to report to Gen. Meade without delay. It is of the greatest importance to get to the front every available man possible Your Command will be sufficient guard for trains" Copies, DLC-USG, V, 45, 59; DNA, RG 94, War Records Office, 9th Army Corps; *ibid.*, RG 108, Letters Sent. *O.R.*, I, xxxvi, part 3, 135.

On May 20, Lt. Col. Theodore S. Bowers issued Special Orders No. 23. "Fredericksburg and the forces there stationed together with the troops guarding the line of communications between there and Belle Plain is assigned to the command of Brig Gen. J. J. Abercrombie Commanding Belle Plain, and the Commanding officer, of the troops so assigned will report accordingly—Gen Abercrombie will promulgate this order & assume Command at once—" Copies, DLC-USG, V, 57, 62, 66. *O.R.*, I, xxxvi, part 3, 25. On the same day, 8:00 p.m., Rawlins telegraphed to Brig. Gen. John J. Abercrombie. "Send as guards to Trains from Fredericksburg to-morrow the 21st inst, all troops coming to or under orders for the front. Order troops already on the way to halt where they are until trains come up and then to accompany them as guards. Let these guards be as strong as possible. As soon as the Army gets on to the Fredericksburg Railroad, Belle Plain and Fredericksburg will be abandoned and Port Royal made the base for our supplies. You will therefore make preparations to this end. On the evacuation of Fredericksburg the work on the railroad will cease. Boats are now on their way to Fredericksburg for our wounded and to protect them from being molested by the enemy's roving Cavalry and guerillas. you will as far as practicable use your Cavalry along the banks of the river." LS, DNA, RG 107, Telegrams Collected (Unbound). *O.R.*, I, xxxvi, part 3, 26. On May 21, Abercrombie telegraphed to USG. "Telegraph of May 20th received about 2 A M. this date. Troops coming to you guard trains en route" ALS, DNA, RG 107, Telegrams Collected (Unbound). *O.R.*, I, xxxvi, part 3, 67. See letter to Brig. Gen. John J. Abercrombie, May 31, 1864.

1. On May 20, Ferrero wrote to Rawlins. "I have the honor to report that I was attacked by a strong force of Cavalry and Artillery at Five (5) P. M. last evening; at the same time heard heavy firing on my left and rear. The Enemy were defeated in their attempt to break through my lines. Captured several prisoners belonging to Ewell's Corps. I have given instructions for all trains proceeding to take the Massaponax Church Road. I would suggest that my lines be drawn back closer to Fredericksburg, as my left is too open, and I have not troops enough to cover the extent of country intervening between Salem Church and Massaponax Road. I await orders with reference to this change. I would add that we are constantly menaced by the Enemy, both in small and large parties. The amount of Cavalry that I have, being about 700, men is insufficient to do the duty." LS, DNA, RG 108, Letters Received. *O.R.*, I, xxxvi, part 1, 986.

To Maj. Gen. Henry W. Halleck

Head Qrs Armies U S
In the field
May 21st 7 a m 1864

Maj Gen H W. Halleck
Chief of Staff.

I fear there is some difficulty with the forces at City Point which prevents their effective use—The fault may be with the commander, or, it may be with his subordinates. Gen'l Smith, whilst a very able Officer, is obstinate and is likely to condemn whatever is not suggested by himself. Either those forces should be so occupied as to detain a force nearly equal to their own, or the garrison in the entrenchments at City Point should be reduced to a minimum and the remainder moved here. I wish you would send a competent officer there to inspect and report by Telegraph what is being done and what in his judgement it is advisable to do

U. S. Grant
Lt Genl

Telegram received, DNA, RG 107, Telegrams Collected (Bound); copies, *ibid.*, RG 108, Letters Sent; *ibid.*, Letters Sent (Press); DLC-USG, V, 45, 59, 66. *O.R.*, I, xxxvi, part 3, 43. On May 21, 1864, 1:40 P.M., Maj. Gen. Henry W. Halleck telegraphed to USG. "Orders in accordance with your letter of yesterday have been sent to Genl Hunter. Genls Meigs and Barnard have [b]een sent to James River to make the investigations and reports directed in your telegram of 7 A M today." ALS (telegram sent), DNA, RG 107, Telegrams Collected (Bound); telegram received, *ibid.*; *ibid.*, RG 108, Letters Received. *O.R.*, I, xxxvi, part 3, 44. See *ibid.*, pp. 68–69.

To Maj. Gen. Ambrose E. Burnside

Hd. Qrs. Armies of the U. S.

Mass [*Massaponax*] Church May 21. 1864

Maj Gen Burnside.

Com'd'g 9th A C.

General,

You may move as soon as practicable upon receipt of this order, taking the direct Ridge road to where it intersects the Telegraph road, thence by the latter road to Thornsburg Cross roads. If the enemy occupy the crossing of the Po in such force as to prevent your ~~crossing~~ using it then you will hold the north side at Stannard's Mills until your whole column is past and move to Guiney Bridge. Gen Wright will follow you and will cover the crossing of the Po for his own Corps. At Guinney Bridge you will receive further directions if you ~~are~~ are forced to take that road. If successful in crossing at Stannards Mill your march will end at Thornburg

U. S Grant

Lt Gen

Copies, DLC-USG, V, 45, 59, 66; DNA, RG 108, Letters Sent. *O.R.*, I, xxxvi, part 3, 64–65.

On May 21, 1864, 7:00 A.M., USG wrote to Maj. Gen. Ambrose E. Burnside. "The 13th Pa. and 5th New York Cavalry under Col Hammond, are now on your left   I know nothing of Capt Pikes Company—No order having been given it from these Headquarters" Copies, DLC-USG, V, 45, 59, 66; DNA, RG 108, Letters Sent. *O.R.*, I, xxxvi, part 3, 63. On the same day, Burnside telegraphed to Brig. Gen. John A. Rawlins. "Have you any news that you can communicate this morning from Sheridan or other armies—" Telegram received, DNA, RG 107, Telegrams Collected (Unbound); copy, *ibid.*, RG 393, 9th Army Corps, Telegrams Sent. *O.R.*, I, xxxvi, part 3, 63. On the same day, Rawlins telegraphed to Burnside, drafting his reply at the foot of the telegram from Burnside. "No news except that Sheridan is on his way ba[c]k, last heard from at Baltimore Store." ADfS, DNA, RG 107, Telegrams Collected (Unbound). *O.R.*, I, xxxvi, part 3, 64.

At 8:25 A.M. and 9:30 A.M., USG wrote to Burnside. "If Gen. Warren's movement is successful, your corps and Wright's will move to-night the latter following Hancock and you following Warren on the Telegraph road. The actions of the enemy may change or modify this.—You want to keep as close to the enemy as possible, and report any movement of his you may observe. At 10

A. M. my Hd. Qrs. will be removed to Mattaponax's church." "The route to be taken by Warren has been changed from the Telegraph road. He will move by Massaponax Church to Guiney Bridge. Your route has not been changed. It will be the Telegraph road by Stannards Mills, unless otherwise directed. Wright will follow you." Copies, DLC-USG, V, 45, 59, 66; DNA, RG 108, Letters Sent. *O.R.*, I, xxxvi, part 3, 64.

To Maj. Gen. Henry W. Halleck

Bethel Church
May 22nd 1864 6 30 p. m

Maj Gen H W Halleck
Chf of Staff

The enemy have evidently fallen ~~back~~ behind North Anna— Prisoners have been captured to day from Picketts[1] Division and there is [e]vidence of other troops having been sent from Richmond also—Besides these Breckinridge is said to have arrived

The force under Genl Butler is not detaining ten thousand (10.000) men in Richmond, and are not even keeping the road ~~cut~~ south of the city cut—Under these circumstances I think it advisable to have all ~~the~~ of it here except enough to keep a foothold at City Point   If they could all be brought at once to Tappahannock, or West Point by water, that would be the best way to bring them—They might march across, but if the enemy should fall back of the South Anna this might become hazardous—

Send Smith in command, and send neither Artillery or Cavalry, unless it is deemed expedient to march over to West Point, thence up north side to join this command—I shall be on the Anna to morrow, or meet the enemy this side. Notify me which way they will be sent—

U S Grant Lt Gen

Telegram received, DNA, RG 107, Telegrams Collected (Bound); copies (sent at 8:00 p.m.), *ibid.*, RG 108, Letters Sent; DLC-USG, V, 45, 59, 66. *O.R.*, I, xxxvi, part 1, 7; *ibid.*, I, xxxvi, part 3, 77.

On May 21, 1864, 9:40 p.m., Maj. Gen. Henry W. Halleck telegraphed to USG. "If the depots at Fredericksburg Belle Plain & Aquia Creek are to be transferred to Port Royal, please let me know immediately, as troops & supplies are being sent every hour to the former places & much delay will be caused by landing re-embarking." ALS (telegram sent), DNA, RG 107, Telegrams Collected (Bound); telegram received, *ibid.*; *ibid.*, RG 108, Letters Received. *O.R.*, I, xxxvi, part 3, 44. On May 22, 8:30 A.M., USG telegraphed to Halleck. "We now occupy Milford Station and South of the Mattapony on that line   I will transfer our Depot to Port Royal at once   Please direct the transfer of everything there"   Telegram received, DNA, RG 107, Telegrams Collected (Bound); copies, *ibid.*, RG 108, Letters Sent; DLC-USG, V, 45, 59, 66. *O.R.*, I, xxxvi, part 1, 7; *ibid.*, I, xxxvi, part 3, 77. On May 23, Halleck wrote to USG. "Your despatch from Bethel Church, dated 6.30 P. M. yesterday is recieved. In accordance with your previous directions Genls Meigs & Barnard were sent to the James River with orders to report by telegraph how many troops could be spared & on the means of water transportation. The moment I recieve it, I will give the orders for the proposed movement. If the enemy retreats behind the South Anna West Point would be the proper place to occupy, but until he does so, I think it would be unwise & exceedingly hazardous to attempt to hold both City Point & West Point, as the enemy might concentrate on either and crush it out. I shall therefore order any troops that Meigs and Barnard think can be spared from Butler's command to Tappahannock or Port Royal,—to the latter if you are still in the vicinity of Bowling Green or the North Anna. Whatever I can raise here will be sent to same place till further orders. Permit me to repeat, what I have so often urged, that, in my opinion, every man we can collect should be hurled against Lee, wherever he may be, as his army, not Richmond, is the true objective point of this campaign. When that army is broken, Richmond will be of very little value to the enemy. Demonstrations on that place exhaust us more than they injure the rebels, for it will require two men outside to keep one in Richmond. I once thought that this could be more than compensated for by destroying their lines of supply, but experience has proved that they can repair them just about as fast as we can destroy them. Such at least was the case under Dix and Foster, and I think Butler's operations will have no better result. I have no doubt we shall soon have loud calls for reinforcements in West Va., but I shall not send any unless you so order, for I have very little faith in these collateral operations. The little good they accomplish seldom equals their cost in men & money. If you succeed in crushing Lee, all will be well; if you fail, we immediately lose whatever we may have gained in West Va or around Richmond. I therefore propose to send to you everything I can get, without regard to the calls of others, until you direct otherwise." ALS, DNA, RG 108, Letters Received. *O.R.*, I, xxxvi, part 3, 114.

1. George E. Pickett, born in Richmond, Va., in 1825, USMA 1846, resigned from the U.S. Army as of June 25, 1861. Appointed C.S.A. brig. gen. as of Jan. 14, 1862, and maj. gen. as of Oct. 10, he led a famous charge at Gettysburg and in Sept., 1863, was assigned to command the Dept. of N. C. Pickett's div. moved from Petersburg to join the Army of Northern Va. on May 21, 1864. *Ibid.*, I, xxxvi, part 1, 1058.

To Maj. Gen. George G. Meade

Head Quarters Armies of the United States.
New Bethel Va. May. 22nd 1864

MAJ GEN MEADE
COMD'G A. P.
GENERAL

Direct Corps Commanders to hold their troops in readiness to march at 5. A. M. tomorrow—At that hour each command will send out Cavalry and Infantry on all roads to their front leading South and ascertain if possible where the enemy is—If beyond the South Anna the 5th and 6th Corps will march to the forks of the road, where one branch leads to Beaver Dam Station, the other to Jericho Bridge; then south by roads reaching the Anna as near to and east of Hawkins ~~bridge~~ creek as they can be found —The 2nd Corps will move to Chesterfield Ford—The 9th Corps will be directed to move at the same time to Jericho Bridge—The map only shows two roads for the four Corps to march upon, but no doubt by the use of plantation roads and pressing in guides others can be found to give one for each Corps—

The troops will follow their respective reconnoitering parties. The train will be moved at the same time to Milford Station—

Head Quarters will follow the 9th Corps—

U. S. GRANT
Lieut Genl—

LS, DNA, RG 393, Army of the Potomac, Telegrams Received. *O.R.*, I, xxxvi, part 3, 81–82.

On May 21, 1864, 6:15 P.M., Maj. Gen. Winfield S. Hancock, Coates' House near Milford, wrote to Brig. Gen. Seth Williams, adjt. for Maj. Gen. George G. Meade, reporting movements of the 2nd Corps, especially those of Brig. Gen. Alfred Torbert. *Ibid.*, pp. 49–50. This message was received at 4:00 A.M., May 22, and endorsed by Meade to USG. "The within just received. The officer bringing it says it is 16 miles to Hancock. I have retained him to send orders back. Warren was ordered to hold all he had gotten yesterday and to send support to his cavalry at the Ta. I have not ordered him to move till you shall so direct, and indicate the road. If he does move, he had better have another corps in rear in support." *Ibid.*, p. 50.

On May 22, 7:00 A.M. and 9:00 P.M., Brig. Gen. John A. Rawlins wrote to Maj. Gen. Ambrose E. Burnside. "Move forward your Corps promptly at 9 o'clock A. M to day by Downers Bridge to New Bethel Church and seize and hold the crossing of the Ta river on the roads from there to Colmans Old Academy and on the road to Carrots Tavern—You will also get up and issue to your men tonight six days rations from and including tomorrow—Gens Warren & Wright are under orders to move this morning to Harris Store—Gen Hancock is at Milford Station. You will open communication with each of these places from New Bethel Church, holding your Corps in readiness to move to the support of either—Please keep these Headquarters advised from time to time of your progress—" Copies, DLC-USG, V, 45, 59, 66; DNA, RG 108, Letters Sent. *O.R.*, I, xxxvi, part 3, 96. "The great number of men straggling from their commands on the march render it necessary that strong and efficient rear guards be detailed to prevent it You will therefore detail a regiment of your command as rear guard to your corps; one that will execute, strictly and to the letter, your orders, with instructions to summarily punish all men faling behind or stragling from their ranks, and especially those who may be found going to farm houses for the purpose of pillaging. This is not to be construed into an order prohibiting foraging, but foraging must be done under direction's of Division Commanders." Copies, DLC-USG, V, 45, 59; DNA, RG 108, Letters Sent. *O.R.*, I, xxxvi, part 3, 96.

To Maj. Gen. Henry W. Halleck

Hd Quarters U S. Armies
11 p m May 23d 1864

Maj Gen H W. Halleck
Chf of Staff

The army moved from its position of this morning to the North Anna following closely Lees army—The 5th & 6th Corps marched by way of Harris Store to Jerico Ford and the 5th Corps succeeded in effecting a crossing and getting position without much opposition. Shortly after however they were violently attacked but handsomely repulsed the assault without much loss to us.

We captured some prisoners. The 2nd Corps holds the Bridge just above the Railroad and the 9th Corps is between that and Jerico Ford on the North Bank in face of the enemy—It is doubtful whether troops can be crossed except where the 5th and 6th Corps are. Every thing looks exceedingly favorable for us

U S Grant
Lt Genl

Telegram received, DNA, RG 107, Telegrams Collected (Bound); copies, *ibid.*, RG 108, Letters Sent; DLC-USG, V, 45, 59, 66. *O.R.*, I, xxxvi, part 1, 7; *ibid.*, I, xxxvi, part 3, 113–14.

To Maj. Gen. Ambrose E. Burnside

Hd Qrs. Armis of the U States
10.30 p m
Near N. Anna May 23d/64

MAJ. GEN BURNSIDE
COMD.G 9TH A. C.
GENERAL,

Hold your Corps as a reserve to reinforce the 2d Corps (which is to force a crossing of the Anna at daylight) or to effect a crossing at Ox Ford as may be deemed most advisable.—Gen. Hancock is directed to effect the crossing at New Bridge and has been authorized to call on you for such assistance as he may require. You will therefore if called on by him send all the assistance he may ask for.

If your troops are not required at New Bridge get them as well in line ~~as~~ in front of the ford ~~to your~~ f between you and the enemy as possible and effect a crossing if you can. You had better see Gen Hancock, or communicate with him, to night and ascertain whether you can give the best ~~assistance~~ support by crossing with him or by operating over your present front.

My Hd Qrs. will be moved in the morning to Mt Carmel Church.

U. S. GRANT
Lt. Gen.

ALS, IHi. *O.R.*, I, xxxvi, part 3, 134. On May 24, 1864, 6:30 A.M., Maj. Gen. Ambrose E. Burnside wrote to USG. "Your despatch of last night was received— ~~and~~ after which the necessary orders were given—I proceded before daylight to Genl Hancocks to arrange with him as to the disposition of my forces—He is of the opinion that a demonstration in my front would be of more service to him than the reinforcements I could send him—I then left Genl Potter's division to his disposal, and went to the position occupied by Genl Wilcox in front of Oxford as soon as it was light enough to reconnoiter the position, and have arranged for an effort to carry the ford by the other two divisions of the 9th Corps—The prospects of success are not at all flattering but I think the attempt can be made without any very disastrous result, and we may possibly succeed we did not get into the position last night until after night fall so that we knew nothing of the nature of the ground and it would of been impossible to make an intelligent attack at daylight—The Enemys ~~bank~~ side of the river is densely wooded, along its banks, with high ground in rear with one battery in position flanked by rifle pits, and it is reported that there is another line of rifle pits in front—The ford is said to be about knee deep I think we can approach very near to it on this side under cover The men are now being placed in the woods, and in a few minutes we shall have 18 guns bearing on the enemy's battery—" LS, DNA, RG 108, Letters Received. *O.R.*, I, xxxvi, part 3, 166.

On May 23, 3:00 P.M., Lt. Col. Orville E. Babcock wrote to Burnside. "The lieutenant-general commanding desires you to follow General Hancock with your corps. The bearer will show you the road." *Ibid.*, p. 133. At 9:00 P.M., Burnside telegraphed to USG. "Genl Wilcox Division is in position at Oxford ford with pickets connecting with Genl Hancock—We have not yet been able to connect with the pickets of Genl Warren Genl Crittendens Division is in the rear of Genl Wilcox, and Genl Potter's Division which came in a few moments ago is placed on the right hand side of the telegraph road in the rear of Genl Crittenden My Head Qrs are immediately on the right of Genl Potters Division it can be found by coming down the Telegraph roads about a ¼ of a mile this side of Carmel Church at the end of the woods then across the open space to the right about Six or Seven hundred yards, to the only house in sight—" Copies, DNA, RG 393, Army of the Potomac, Telegrams Sent; *ibid.*, 9th Army Corps, Telegrams Sent. *O.R.*, I, xxxvi, part 3, 134.

To Maj. Gen. George G. Meade

Headquarters of the Army
Moncure House Va. May 23rd 1864. 2. P. M.

MAJ GEN MEADE
COMD'G A. P.
GENERAL—

The 2nd Corps will proceed to suitable Camping ground on the banks of North Anna near to New Bridge which is the crossing of the Telegraph road over the Anna. If possible the bridge and crossing will be secured. This Corps will also extend east to hold the rail road bridge. The 9th Corps will take position to the right of the 2nd Corps, and will seize Ox Ford, a ford over the Anna next west of New Bridge. If practicable this ford will also be held—The 5th Corps will occupy the bank of the river to cover and hold Jericho Ford—The 6th Corps will take place on the right of the 5th Corps—If any bridge or ford is found to their front it will be seized and held—If none is found efforts will be made to open roads to the river at points where crossings to the river may be effected to their front.

U. S. GRANT
Lieut Genl—

LS, DNA, RG 393, Army of the Potomac, Telegrams Received. *O.R.*, I, xxxvi, part 3, 115.

On May 23, 1864, 3:00 P.M., USG wrote to Maj. Gen. George G. Meade. "By all means I would have Warren cross all the men he can to-night and entrench himself strongly. There is but little likelyhood that he will be pushed by the enemy and if he is he can be reinforced or could fall back by the same road as necessity might require." ALS, DNA, RG 393, Army of the Potomac, Telegrams Received. Printed in *O.R.*, I, xxxvi, part 3, 119, as an endorsement on a letter of 2:35 P.M. from Maj. Gen. Winfield S. Hancock to Brig. Gen. Seth Williams discussing plans to cross the North Anna River, endorsed by Meade to USG. "I have ordered Warren to cross his whole corps and intrench. Wright, I think, had better take position on this side, to support Warren. Shall Hancock force a crossing?" *Ibid.*

At 4:15 P.M., USG wrote to Meade. "If Hancock can secure a crossing he should do so   If however the bulk of the Enemy appears to be to the left of him, our Cavalry should picket well down to see that no detachment of the enemy gets in on our left"   Copies, DLC-USG, V, 59, 66. Printed in *O.R.*, I, xxxvi, part 3, 120, as an endorsement on a letter of 3:15 P.M. from Hancock to Williams discussing the crossing of the North Anna River, endorsed by Meade to USG. "Hancock has three regiments across. I should think, from present indications, Lee is going to hold the Pamunkey and South Anna. Shall Hancock cross his whole force, if practicable?" *Ibid.*

To Maj. Gen. Henry W. Halleck

Head Qrs Army U. S.
North Anna
May 24th. 8. a m 1864

MAJ GEN H. W. HALLECK
CHIEF OF STAFF.

The Enemy have fallen back from North Anna, we are in pursuit—Negroes who have come in state that Lee is falling back to Richmond—If this is the case Butler's forces will all be wanted

where they are—Notify him to hold Smith in readiness to be
moved but to await further orders—I will probably know today
if the Enemy intends standing behind South Anna

U. S. GRANT
Lt Genl

Telegram received, DNA, RG 107, Telegrams Collected (Bound); *ibid.*, Dept.
of Va. and N. C., Telegrams Received; copies (misdated May 25, 1864), *ibid.*,
RG 108, Letters Sent; DLC-USG, V, 45, 59, 66. Dated May 24 in *O.R.*, I, xxxvi,
part 1, 8; *ibid.*, I, xxxvi, part 3, 145. On May 24, 8:20 P.M., Maj. Gen. Henry
W. Halleck telegraphed to USG. "When I recieved your telegram of 8 A M
yesterday, I had prepared orders for Genl Smith to join you with twenty thousand
men. Genl Butler is now ordered to hold him in readiness to move. I wish everything was away from south side of the James & with you; it would be much better.
I dont like these divided commands, with the enemy intervening. I would rather
see them all [t]ogether under your own eye." ALS (telegram sent), DNA, RG
107, Telegrams Collected (Bound); telegram received, *ibid. O.R.*, I, xxxvi, part
3, 145.

To Maj. Gen. Ambrose E. Burnside

Jericho Ford, Va. May 24th/64 8.20 p. m.

MAJ. GEN. BURNSIDE
COMD.G 9TH CORPS,
GENERAL,

The situation of the enemy appearing so different from what
I expected I do not deem it advisable for you to move your wagon
train to the South side of the river to-night, or not any more of it
than may now be on the South side. The enemy holding the South
bank of the river at Ox Ford I think it important that you should
hold the North side at the same place. You will therefore leave at
least a battery supported by a regiment of Infantry will stationed
for that purpose.

I understand you are moving two Divisions to connect with
Hancock and one above Ox Ford to connect with Warren! This
will be the best arrangement that can be adopted and if it is not
already carried out you will carry it out.

Bridges will be laid above and below the point on the river held by the enemy, and as near to it as possible, to-morrow morning, and roads opened between them, so at to bring our right and left as near supporting distance as possible. The only portion of this work you will be charged with will be opening the road near the river between the two bridges. The upper bridge will be laid near Carl's [*Quarles'*] Mill. The place for the lower one cannot be determined ~~and it~~ to-night. It ~~is not probable~~ may not be practicable to lay a bridge above the one Hancock now has. You may therefore regard the points to be connected by new roads as being that bridge and Carl's Mill.

U. S. GRANT
Lt. Gen.

ALS, IHi. *O.R.*, I, xxxvi, part 3, 168–69.

On May 24, 1864, 9:30 A.M., Maj. Gen. George G. Meade wrote to USG. "I find Warren holds down to Quarles' Mills and Ford, which is just above Burnside. I have directed Warren to push Crawford's division down the river beyond Quarles' Mills till he meets some enemy, and uncovering Ox Ford if possible. It seems to me Burnside might send up to Quarles' Mills and cross a few there. Crawford is directed to communicate with Burnside as he goes down. Will you inform Burnside of this." *Ibid.*, p. 146. At 1:00 P.M., Brig. Gen. John A. Rawlins, Mount Carmel Church, wrote to Maj. Gen. Ambrose E. Burnside. "You will move your entire Corps with trains to the South side of the North Anna this afternoon. Gen Warren has sent a Division on the South side to drive the enemy away from his position opposite you, and Gen Hancock has sent a Brigade for the same purpose. The ford must be open by the time this reaches you. If not, there is one about one mile further up between you and Warren, that is open, at least it is so reported. You can cross at this one, and also at the bridge where Hancock crossed, marching your troops thus crossed to a point opposite to where you now are on the South side. You must get over and camp to night on the South side. To night these Hdqrs will be on the South side of the river on the Telegraph road." Copies, DLC-USG, V, 45, 59; DNA, RG 108, Letters Sent. *O.R.*, I, xxxvi, part 3, 167. On the same day, Burnside wrote to USG. "Your Dispatch of one P M is received   We have been endeavoring all the morning to drive the enemy from his position opposite us, have had a road cut through intersecting the road which leads to the Ford of which you speak and General Crittendens Division started sometime since over that road with instructions to cross and come down in rear of the position occupied by the enemy at Ox Ford—General Crawford who is in Command of the Division sent by General Warren ~~from~~ to the Upper Ford informs one of my Staff that he is to remain there until further orders and I have just received a note from General Hancock stating that he had halted his Brigade lest there might be some confusion by meeting Gen Warren's Division which he had understood was coming down in that direction—Gen Crittenden will continue to cross and if possible move down in rear of the enemy's position   the Ford is very rough and deep and a considerable portion of the men fall in crossing thus spoiling their ammunition   Crittenden has crossed two Regts and a third is now crossing. ~~you~~ You may be sure that I will do all in my power to gain this Ford, and if I do not succeed I will cross by Hancock's or Warren's crossing—If it is desirable I will stop the crossing of Crittendens Command and cross the whole at one of these places—Lt Col Babcock can tell you something of the difficulties of taking this position" LS, DNA, RG 108, Letters Received. *O.R.*, I, xxxvi, part 3, 167. On the same day, Rawlins, Jericho Ford, wrote to Burnside. "These Hdqrs, instead of being on the Telegraph road, as you were notified it would be, will be at this Ford." Copies, DLC-USG, V, 45, 59; DNA, RG 108, Letters Sent. At 6:45 P.M., Burnside wrote to USG. "In accordance with your instructions I commenced movements with a view to throwing the entire corps on the South side of the river & making a junction in front of the position opposite to Genl Wilcox—Genl Crittenden Corps was thrown across the river just above Genl Wilcox   I described the ford to you in a former note—Since I wrote you Genl Crawford reports that the Enemy's line of Skirmishers ~~had~~ has cut off his communication with Genl Warren, and Genl Critttenden, has not been able to form a junction with Genl Potter who was thrown across over Hancocks bridge— They are back at work now to effect this object—Genl. Crittenden has had quite a sharp fight, and met with quite a loss, the ~~result~~ amount is not yet known: His aide represents that the enemy were repulsed and he has sent in some ten to twenty prisoners—Inasmuch as neither Genl Crawford or Genl Crittenden have any artillery I feel quite anxious about their position, and have therefore directed a bridge capable of passing artillery & Infantry to be built, & have taken the responsibility of retaining Genl Wilcox on this side of the river—I shall move my own Head Qrs to the South side in a few minutes, near to those of General Hancock—unless something should occur to detain me ~~here~~, on this side—in which case I will notify you—I hope the course I have pursued will meet your approbation—I am pretty well satisfied that the enemys works are such as I indicated to Col Comstock this morning—" LS, *ibid.*, Letters Received. *O.R.*, I, xxxvi, part 3, 168.

Also on May 24, Burnside wrote to USG. "Your despatch of this evening is received—and I believe I have anticipated your wishes, except that I have thought it best to keep the whole of Wilcox division on this side, in consequence of the trouble that has fallen upon Crittenden, who lost nearly half a brigade in attempting to move down to connect with Genl Potter, who crossed on Hancocks bridge—The brigade was small, and I think the loss will not be over 600—Both Crittenden and Crawford are well entrenched, and I hope to have a good bridge built by morning, so that we may give them some artillery if necessary—Would it not be well for Warren to try to open communication with Crawford—Potter attacked at the same time with Crittenden, but he was fortunate in having light losses—I am glad to get the order assigning the Corps to the Army of the Potomac because I think good will result from it—" ALS (incomplete), DNA, RG 108, Letters Received; *ibid.*, RG 393, 9th Army Corps, Telegrams Sent (Press). *O.R.*, I, xxxvi, part 3, 169. On the same day, Lt. Col. Theodore S. Bowers issued Special Orders No. 25. "To secure the greatest attainable unanimity in co-operative movements, and greater efficiency in the administration of the Army, the 9th Army Corps, Maj Gen. A. E. Burnside Comd'g, is assigned to the Army of the Potomac, Maj Gen. G. G. Meade Commanding, and will report accordingly—" Copies, DLC-USG, V, 57, 62, 66. *O.R.*, I, xxxvi, part 3, 169.

At 10:20 P.M., USG wrote to Burnside. "You have done quite right to retain Gen. Wilcox where he is under the circumstances. Gen. Warren has been informed of the contents of your note and will endeavor to open communication with Gen. Crawford. If you can get a bridge across to Gen. Crittenden it will serve to send Artillery or reinforcements over to him or will give him the means of withdrawing as necessity may require." ALS, deCoppet Collection, NjP. Printed as sent at 10:00 P.M. in *O.R.*, I, xxxvi, part 3, 169. On the same day, Maj. Gen. Winfield S. Hancock wrote to Maj. Gen. Andrew A. Humphreys reporting strong C.S.A. forces in his front and requesting that Burnside support his right. ALS, DNA, RG 393, Army of the Potomac, Letters Received. *O.R.*, I, xxxvi, part 3, 155. USG endorsed this letter. "I have directed Gen. Burnside to retain Wilcox where he is, (on North side of the river covering Ox Ford) for the night and to get his bridge over to Crittenden & Crawford. Potter's Div. is now with Hancock and he can direct him as he may deem best." AES, DNA, RG 393, Army of the Potomac, Letters Received. *O.R.*, I, xxxvi, part 3, 155.

To Maj. Gen. Henry W. Halleck

Jerico Ford Va
May 25th 1864
12. Noon

MAJ GEN H W HALLECK
CHF OF STAFF

The enemy are evidently making a determined stand between the two Annas   It will probably take us two days to get in position for a general attack or to turn their position, as ma[y p]rove best—

Send Genl Butlers forces to White House to land on north side, & march up to join this Army—The James River should be held to City Point, but leave nothing more than what is absolutely necessary to hold it, acting purely on defensive—Enemy will not undertake any offensive operations there but will concentrate everything [here]   Breckinridge is unquestionably here—Sixty six officers and men have been captured who were with Hoke[1] in the capture of Pl[ymou]th—

If Genl Hunter can possibly get to Charlottesville and Lynchburg he should do so, living on the country   The Railroads and Canals should be destroyed beyond possibility of repair for

[wee]ks—Completing this he could find his way back to h[is]
original base, or from about Gordonsville, to join this Army

U. S. GRANT
Lt Genl

Telegram received, DNA, RG 107, Telegrams Collected (Bound); copies, *ibid.*,
RG 108, Letters Sent; DLC-USG, V, 45, 59, 66. *O.R.*, I, xxxvi, part 1, 8; *ibid.*,
I, xxxvi, part 3, 183; *ibid.*, I, xxxvii, part 1, 535–36; (incomplete) *ibid.*, I, xxxiv,
part 1, 20; *ibid.*, I, xxxvi, part 1, 24; *ibid.*, I, xxxviii, part 1, 13. On May 26,
1864, 10:30 A.M., Maj. Gen. Henry W. Halleck telegraphed to USG. "Your instructions of yesterday 12 M. have been sent to Genl Butler & Genl Hunter. I
hope to send you some four or five thousand reinforcements to Port Royal to-day
& to-morrow. We are somewhat embarrassed for want of water transportation,
while moving Smith's command. Nothing recently from Sherman." ALS (telegram sent), DNA, RG 107, Telegrams Collected (Bound); telegram received,
ibid.; *ibid.*, RG 108, Letters Received. *O.R.*, I, xxxvi, part 3, 207.

1. Robert F. Hoke, born in 1837 in Lincolnton, N. C., educated at Kentucky
Military Institute, was a manufacturer before the Civil War. Appointed 2nd lt.,
1st N. C., he rose to col., 21st N. C., was nominated as brig. gen. on Jan. 23,
1863, and received both the thanks of the C.S.A. Congress and promotion to maj.
gen. for his capture of Plymouth, N. C., on April 20, 1864. In May, he brought
his div. to the defense of Richmond.

To Maj. Gen. George G. Meade

Quarles Mills, Va. May 25th/64

MAJ. GEN. G. G. MEADE,
COMD.G A. P.
GENERAL,

Direct Gens. Warren and Wright to withdraw all their teams
and Artillery not in position to the North Side of the river to-
morrow. Send that belonging to Gen. Wrights Corps as far on
the road to Hanover Town as it can go without attracting attention to the fact. Send with it Wrights best Division or Division
under his ablest commander. Have their place filled up in the line
so if possible the enemy will not notice their withdrawal   Send
the Cavalry to-morrow afternoon, or as much of it as you may
deem necessary, to watch, and seize if they can, Littlepages Bridge
and Taylors Ford and to remain on one or the other side of the

river at those points until the Infantry and Artillery all pass. As soon as it is dark to-morrow night start the Division which you withdraw first from Wrights Corps to make a forced march to Hanover Town taking with them no teams to impede their march. At the same time this Division starts commence withdrawing all of the 5th & 6th Corps from the south side of the river and march them for the same place.

The two Divisions of the 9th Corps not now with Hancock may be moved down the North bank of the river where they will be handy to support Hancock if necessary, or will be that much on their road to follow the 5th & 6th Corps. Hancock should hold his command in readiness to follow as soon as the way is clear for him To-morrow it will leave nothing for him to do but as soon as he can he should get all his teams and spare artillery on the road or roads which he will have to take.

As soon as the troops reach Hanover Town they should get possession of all the crossings they can in that neighborhood.

U. S. Grant
Lt. Gen

I think it would be well to make a heavy Cavalry demonstration on the enemy's left to-morrow afternoon also.

U. S. G.

ALS, DNA, RG 393, Army of the Potomac, Telegrams Received. *O.R.*, I, xxxvi, part 3, 183.

On May 25, 1864, noon, Maj. Gen. Gouverneur K. Warren wrote to Maj. Gen. George G. Meade reporting strong C.S.A. positions in his front. *Ibid.*, pp. 192–93. Meade endorsed this letter to USG. "I should judge from the within that unless Warren attacks not much more can be done in his front.—" AES, DNA, RG 393, Army of the Potomac, Telegrams Received. *O.R.*, I, xxxvi, part 3, 193. USG also endorsed this letter. "I do not think any attack should be made until preparations are made to use our whole force. The best Warren can do now is to cover his men well in their advanced position and rest them all he can ready for active service If you think proper to send a Div. of Wrights force across Little River do so. But I think unless there is some reason for it that I do not know it would be better not to send them over until the Cavalry gets around," AES, DNA, RG 393, Army of the Potomac, Telegrams Received. *O.R.*, I, xxxvi, part 3, 193.

Also on May 25, 11:30 A.M., Maj. Gen. Horatio G. Wright wrote to Maj. Gen. Andrew A. Humphreys advising against sending his forces across Little River. *Ibid.*, p. 196. Meade endorsed this letter to USG. "Do you think it advisable or necessary for General Wright to cross the Little River?" *Ibid.*

To Maj. Gen. Henry W. Halleck

Quarles Mills, Va. May 26th/64

MAJ. GEN. HALLECK, WASHINGTON,

GENERAL,

The relative positions of the two Armies is now as follows. Lee's right rests on a swamp East of the Richmond & Fredericksburg road and South of N. Anna, his center on the river at Ox Ford and his left on Little river with the crossings of Little River guarded as far up as we have gone. Hancock with his Corps, and one Division of the 9th Corps, crossed at Chesterfield Ford and covers the right wing of Lees Army. One Division of the 9th Corps is on the North bank of the Anna, at Ox Ford, with bridges above and below at points nearest to it where both banks are held by us, so that it could reinforce either wing of our Army with equal facility. The 5th & 6th Corps, with one Division of the 9th Corps, run from the south bank of the Anna, from a short distance above Ox Ford, to little river, and paralel with and near to the enemy. To make a direct attack from either wing would cause a slaughter of our men that even success would not justify. To turn the enemy by his right, between the two Anna's, is impossible on account of the swamp upon which his right rests. To turn him by his left, leaves Little River, New Found River, and South Anna River, all of them streams presenting considerable obstacles to the movement of an Army, have to be crossed. I have determined therefore to turn the enemy's right by crossing at or near Hanover Town. This crosses all these streams at once and leaves us still where we can draw supplies.

During the night, last night, the teams and Artillery not in position, belonging to the right wing of our Army, and one Division of that Wing, was quietly withdrawn to the North bank of the river and moved down to the rear of the left. As soon as it is dark, this Division with most of the Cavalry, will commence a forced march for Hanover Town, to sieze and hold the crossing. The balance of the right wing will withdraw at the same hour and follow as rapidly as possible. The left wing will also with-draw from the South bank of the river to night and follow in the rear of the right wing.

Lees Army is really whipped. The prisoners we now take show it, and the actions of his Army shows it unmistakeably. A battle with them outside of intrenchments, cannot be had. Our men feel that they have gained morale over the enemy and attack with confidence. I may be mistaken but I feel that our success over Lees Army is already insured.

The promptness and rapidity with which you have forwarded reinforcements has contributed largely to the feeling of confidence inspired in our men, and to break down that of the enemy.

We are destroying all the rails we can on the Central and Fredericksburg roads. I want to leave a gap in the roads north of Richmond so big, that, to get a single track they will have to import rails from somewhere.

> I am General, very respectfully,
> Your obt servt.
> U. S. GRANT.
> Lt. Genl.

P. S. Even if a crossing is not effected at Hanover Town it will probably be necessary for us to move on down the Pamunky un-til a crossing is effected. I think it advisable therefore to change our base of supplies from Port Royal to the White House. I wish you would direct this change at once, and also direct Smith to put the railroad bridge there in condition for crossing troops and Artillery, and leave men to hold it.

> U. S. G.

ALS (incomplete facsimile), Parke-Bernet Galleries, Inc., Catalogue 1683, May 22, 1956, no. 77; copies, DLC-USG, V, 45, 59, 66; DNA, RG 108, Letters Sent; *ibid.*, Letters Received. *O.R.*, I, xxxvi, part 1, 8–9; *ibid.*, I, xxxvi, part 3, 206–7.

On May 27, 1864, Maj. Gen. Henry W. Halleck wrote to USG. "It appears from returns just handed in by Genl Augur that I have sent to Fredericksburg and Port Royal, since you crossed the Rapidann, May 4th, a little over forty thousand troops. I have within a few days to send you between five and ten thousand more. As before stated, I have sent to Genl Butler within the same period, about three thousand. He telegraphs to me to-day that he will send with Smith to White House seventeen thousand Infantry. Some cavalry & artillery will go with them to cover the landing, escort trains, &c. I think he will make the entire force about twenty thousand. This will make your entire reinforcements since you crossed the Rapidann between sixty and seventy thousand men. This includes about one thousand returned veterans and a thousand stragglers & deserters who have been arrested & sent back. In a telegram from Capt. Pitkin to Genl Rucker, which I have just seen, it is stated on the authority of Genl Ingals that you propose to break up your depots on the Rappahannock about the first of next month & remove them to West Point, the White House or some other place on the Pamunkey. This would indicate that when Lee falls back behind the South Anna you propose to make the Pamunkey your base of operations on Richmond. Permit me to repeat to you the opinions which have been expressed to me within the last two years by officers who are thoroughly acquainted with the country and who had much experience with Genl McClellan in his Peninsular operations. They say that any campaign against Richmond based on the Pamunkey with West Point, White House, or even New Castle as the point of supplies will involve the defence of the line of the York & Pamunkey rivers, and the passage of the Chickahomony & its swamps. This will leave Lee, if he falls back upon Richmond, the James River Canal & one or more of the Railroads south of that river as communications by which to recieve reinforcements & supplies. Even if your cavalry should cut these communications they will soon be reopened. But should you occupy the sector, less than ninety degrees, between the James and the Chickahomony, your right resting on the former and your left on the Horse Pond or Meadow Bridge, your flanks will be pretty safe, your line of advance will be over favorable ground, you will hold the canal, and can, with your cavalry, control the Railroad lines south of the James River. Moreover, they say this point is the most favorable for an attack, as the Tredegar Iron works, the Arsenal, the Water Works, & all the flouring mills lie on the north west side of the city, exposed to a bombardment from that direction. By advancing on this line, you will, when within ten miles of Richmond, be about equi-distant from Fredericksburg, Port Royal, Tappahannock & West Point. At Ashland, or on the South Anna, the latter will be the most distant as well as the most inaccessible point of supplies. The navigation to White House is said to be difficult & precarious. If you keep up three points of supply, viz: Port Royal or Tappahannock by the Rappahannock, White House or West Point by the York, & City Point by the James, you will have three lines of communication to guard, which will require a large number of troops & gunboats. Moreover, three lines seriously affects our water transportation which is much reduced by keeping so many vessels loaded with ordnance & commissary stores. If consistent with your plan of operations it would be safer & more economical to keep up only a single line. It is especially inconvenient to keep so many vessels & supplies in the James river. Moreover, many of the commissary stores will be seriously injured by keeping them in vessels. The general impression among the Staff officers with whom I have conversed is that the Tappahannock line is preferable to West Point or Port Royal. Our larger transports cannot reach the latter place or White House. Why not, when Smith's forces have joined you, break up either the York or the Rappahannock line, & bring out of James river all transports with stores not required there? I think it would simplify the supplying of your army & greatly economize transportation. Is it not safer to have your depot of supplies in your rear towards Washington, than on the James or the York? I presume there were good reasons for abandoning the Fredericksburg road at the time you did, but if you should wish to resume that line it can be immediately put in operation. It is completed to Falmouth & the bridge to Fredericksburg can be restored in a few days. Although a little longer for land transportation than either of the others, it is much shorter & more convenient by water, & with our railroad facilities supplies could be forwarded much more rapidly. And I hardly think a larger force would be required to guard it. I simply make these suggestions for your consideration, but shall make no changes without your orders. I however must urge you not to put the Chickahomony between your army & its supplies, nor between you & Richmond. It is a most serious obstacle to be passed by a large army or by its supplies. Moreover in the summer months it is exceedingly unhealthy, as is also the James river below Richmond." LS, DNA, RG 108, Letters Received. *O.R.*, I, xxxvi, part 3, 245–46.

On May 28, 4:30 P.M. and 10:10 P.M., Halleck telegraphed to USG. "Your letter of the 26th is recieved, and measures taken to immediately carry out your wishes." "Nothing will leave here for Port Royal after 12 o'clock to-morrow. It is expected that everything for the army of the Potomac, and everything from that army will have reached that point by the 1st of June when Genl Abercrombie has been directed to break up the depot & transfer it to the Pamunkey. It is presumed that Genl Smith will have reached there by that time." ALS (telegrams sent), DNA, RG 107, Telegrams Collected (Bound); telegrams received, *ibid.*; *ibid.*, RG 108, Letters Received. *O.R.*, I, xxxvi, part 3, 267.

On May 26, 10:00 A.M., Maj. Gen. George G. Meade wrote to USG. "Would it not be well in view of all contemplated movement to direct Gen Smith at the White House to repair & put in order for the passage of troops the R. Rd. bridge at that point—Also make some arrangements for the transfer of our depot from Port Royal to that place.—I send you a despatch just received.—" ALS, DNA, RG 94, War Records Office, Army of the Potomac. *O.R.*, I, xxxvi, part 3, 207. USG endorsed this letter. "I will direct Smith, as you suggest, to secure us a crossing at the rail-road bridge, White Hous, and also have our depot moved to that place." AE, DNA, RG 94, War Records Office, Army of the Potomac. *O.R.*, I, xxxvi, part 3, 207. On May 28, 1:00 P.M., Brig. Gen. John A. Rawlins wrote to Maj. Gen. William F. Smith. "The Army of the Potomac is now crossing to the south side of the Pemunkey river, and massing at this place. The most of it has already crossed it You will leave a garrison at the White House, until it is releived by Gen. Abercrombie's Command from Port Royal, and with the remainder of your Command move direct to Newcastle, on the south side of the Pamunkey, and then await further orders. Order the garrison left by you at White House on being relieved, to follow after and join you" LS, DNA, RG 393, 24th Army Corps, Letters Received (Unarranged). *O.R.*, I, xxxvi, part 1, 998; *ibid.*, I, xxxvi, part 3, 285. At 10:30 P.M., Smith telegraphed to USG. "Am now embarking—I will proceed as rapidly as possible to West Point or White House according as I find it best to land to secure the Rail Road bridge at White House I have three (3) batteries, all I deem necessary and all certainly that I ha[ve] transportation for—I will telegraph my progress from time to time, but I shall send a brigade on fast Steamer and a battery of Artillery to secure the bridge in advance of my arrival, with the main body—" Telegram received, DNA, RG 107, Telegrams Collected (Bound). *O.R.*, I, xxxvi, part 3, 285.

To Maj. Gen. Henry W. Halleck

Hanover Town May 29th/64

MAJ. GEN. HALLECK, WASHINGTON

The Army has been successfully crossed over the Pamunky and now occupies a front about three miles south of the river. Yesterday, two Divisions of our Cavalry had a severe engagement with the enemy south of Harris ~~store~~ shop driving him about a mile upon ~~his Infantry~~ what appears to be his new line. We will find out all about it to day. Our loss in the Cavalry engagement was three hundred & fifty killed and wounded of whom but forty-four are ascertained to have been killed. Having driven the enemy most of their killed and many of their wounded fell into our hands. ~~besides other prisoners.~~

U. S. GRANT
Lt. Gen.

ALS (telegram sent), DNA, RG 107, Telegrams Collected (Unbound); telegram received, *ibid.*, Telegrams Collected (Bound). *O.R.*, I, xxxvi, part 1, 9–10; *ibid.*, I, xxxvi, part 3, 289. Received in Washington at 11:20 A.M., May 30, 1864, according to the telegram received and *O.R.*, I, xxxvi, part 1, 9; received at 12:10 P.M., May 31, as printed *ibid.*, I, xxxvi, part 3, 289.

To Maj. Gen. George G. Meade

May 29th/64 4 p. m.

MAJ. GEN MEADE, 2D CORPS HD QRS.

It will be well to keep the troops that have gone in search of the enemy to the front and close up on them in the morning, or, if you think their positions unsafe, ~~it might be partially done~~ strengthen the front tonight. If the enemy have gone behind the Chicahominy the trains should all be brought to the South side of the Pamunky in the morning. Your dispatch of 3.30 just received since writing the above. If the enemy is found in the position described by Gen. Barlow[1] he had better be supported before making an attack. They are probably only covering whilst getting everything well ready to receive us on the South side of the creek

U. S. GRANT
Lt. Gen

ALS, deCoppet Collection, NjP. *O.R.*, I, xxxvi, part 3, 290.

On May 29, 1864, 3:00 P.M., 3:30 P.M., and 5:15 P.M., Maj. Gen. George G. Meade wrote to USG. "Genl Barlow has advanced three miles on the road from this point and has reached the forks leading to Hanover C. H. and to Coal Harbor   He has passed the scene of yesterdays cavalry fight one and a half miles   He neither sees or hears anything of the enemy. From all I can learn I am under the impression the enemy has withdrawn behind the Chickahominy but as yet this is only surmise   Nothing reported from Genls Wright or Warren   No firing heard"   "Gen Barlow reports meeting a skirmish line of the enemy supposed to be cavalry—The people in the vicinity tell him there is a line of battle one mile ahead on Southards branch. Barlow is advancing to ascertain the true state of the case."   "Genl Barlow has met the enemy in force about 4 miles from this point   He reports Artillery in position & Infantry in rifle pits. In accordance with your dispatch I have directed Genl Hancock to support him & he is now moving out with his Corps   Gen. Griffin met the Enemy about one mile from the Tolopotamy on the road to shady grove and is now skirmishing with him   Genl Warren is prepared to support him   Genl Wright reports his reconnoissance being within one fourth (¼) mile of the R. R.   Hanover C. H. in sight   only cavalry pickets encountered   He will be directed to hold his advanced position & support them if necessary"   ALS, DNA, RG 108, Letters Received. *O.R.*, I, xxxvi, part 3, 290.

1. Francis C. Barlow, born in Brooklyn in 1834, graduated from Harvard and practiced law in New York City before the Civil War. Enlisting as a private, he was appointed lt. col., 61st N. Y., as of Nov. 9, 1861; col. as of April 14, 1862; brig. gen. as of Sept. 19. Wounded so severely at Gettysburg that he was thought dead, he recovered to rejoin the Army of the Potomac in 1864, assuming command of the 1st Div., 2nd Corps.

To Maj. Gen. Henry W. Halleck

———

Two Miles S. W. of
Hawes Shop 4 p m.
May 30th 1864

MAJ GEN H W HALLECK
CHF OF STAFF

There seems to be some prospect of Lee making a stand north of the Chickahominy his right near Shady Grove. I have heard nothing yet of Smiths troops reaching White House. If I can get up to attack will not wait his arrival. I wish you would send all the Ponton bridging you can to City Point to have it ready in case it is wanted

U S GRANT
Lt Genl

Telegram received, DNA, RG 107, Telegrams Collected (Bound); copies, *ibid.*, RG 108, Letters Sent; DLC-USG, V, 45, 59, 66. *O.R.*, I, xxxvi, part 1, 10; *ibid.*, I, xxxvi, part 3, 322. On May 31, 1864, 3:00 P.M., Maj. Gen. Henry W. Halleck telegraphed to USG. "It is understood that Genl Benham took to Fort Monroe nearly every available ponton. If any more can be found they will be sent immediately. Two steamers have left New York for this place with sixty pontons on board. I have telegraphed to Fort Monroe to intercept them if possible. If they come here they will be sent back immediately. Please say about how many pontons—or what length of bridge—is wanted so that I can make arrangements accordingly. If Genl Hunter meets with no serious disaster, I think a part of Sigel's force at Harper's Ferry & on road to Ohio River can be safely withdrawn. It is too late to send more troops to Hunter, but I can send them to you, if you want them. I think four regts of infantry can be spared." ALS (telegram sent), DNA, RG 107, Telegrams Collected (Bound); telegram received, *ibid.*; (incomplete) *ibid.*, RG 108, Letters Received. *O.R.*, I, xxxvi, part 3, 375. On June 1, Brig. Gen. Richard Delafield, chief engineer, wrote to Brig. Gen. John A. Rawlins. "In pursuance of instructions received from Major Genl Halleck this Department has ordered to be sent to Bermuda Hundred subject to the orders of Lt Genl Grant one train consisting of 60 French Bateaux with the equipage forming a bridge of 1200 feet in length   The train is now on its way in two steamers one of which left here this morning   Please to communicate this information to the General-in-Chief"   LS, DNA, RG 108, Letters Received.

To Maj. Gen. George G. Meade

May 30th/64 6 40 P. M.

MAJ GEN MEADE

Gen Smith will debark his force at the White House tonight and start up the south bank of the Pamunkey at an early hour, probably at 3 a. m. in the morning. It is not improbable that the enemy, being aware of Smith's movement may be feeling to get on our left flank for the purpose of cutting him off, or by a dash, to crush him and get back before we are aware of it. Sheridan ought to be notified to watch the enemys movements well out towards Coal Harbor and also on the Mechanicsville road. Wright should be got well massed on Hancocks right, so that if it becomes necessary he can take the place of the latter readily whilst troops are being thrown east of the Tolopatomoy if necessary.

I will want Sheridan to send a Cavalry force of at least half a brigade, if not a whole brigade at 5 a. m. in the morning to communicate with Smith and to return with him. I will send orders for Smith by the messenger you send to Sheridan with his orders

U S Grant Lt Gen

Copies, DLC-USG, V, 45, 59, 66; DNA, RG 108, Letters Sent; Meade Papers, PHi. *O.R.*, I, xxxvi, part 3, 323.

On May 30, 1864, 1:30 P.M., Lt. Col. Orville E. Babcock wrote to Brig. Gen. John A. Rawlins. "General Warren's skirmishers are still advancing. He is in advance of the troops on his right. He has taken some more prisoners of Ewell's corps. They report earth-works about three-fourths of a mile from Griffin's line." *Ibid.*, p. 339.

At 4:00 P.M., Maj. Gen. George G. Meade wrote to USG. "A dispatch from Sheridan reports, he drove the enemy's Cavalry this afternoon & now occupies *Coal Harbor—Parselys* & the *cross roads* from *Coal Harbor* & *Parselys*, connecting with Warren's left—I have advised him of Smiths movement, and told him to keep a sharp look out for any movement of the enemy in that direction—I have not moved Wright.—" ALS, DNA, RG 108, Letters Received. *O.R.*, I, xxxvi, part 3, 323. USG endorsed this letter. "Maj Gen W. F. Smith, Com'd'g 18th Army Corps will report to and receive orders from Maj. Gen. George G. Meade Com'd'g Army of the Potomac, until otherwise ordered." AE, DNA, RG 108, Letters Received. *O.R.*, I, xxxvi, part 3, 323. On June 1, Lt. Col. Theodore S. Bowers issued Special Orders No. 25½. "Maj. Gen. W. F. Smith, Commanding 18th Army Corps, will report to, and receive orders from Maj. Gen. Geo. G. Meade, Commanding Army of the Potomac until further orders." Copy, DLC-USG, V, 62. *O.R.*, I, xxxvi, part 3, 466. Designated Special Orders No. 25 in DLC-USG, V, 57.

On May 30, 5:20 P.M., USG wrote to Meade. "Is it not evident that the enemy's line is entirely to the left of Gen Wright? If he is not already doing so it seems to me he should push forward his right as far as possible, holding connection with Hancock with his left" Copies, *ibid.*, V, 45, 59, 66; DNA, RG 108, Letters Sent; Meade Papers, PHi. *O.R.*, I, xxxvi, part 3, 323.

At 8:45 P.M., Maj. Gen. Ambrose E. Burnside wrote to Meade stating the position of his troops. *Ibid.*, pp. 359–60. Meade endorsed this letter, presumably to USG. "I send this dispatch received since leaving you. It appears the whole of Burnside's corps is across the Totopotomoy, and that he has relieved General Griffin as Warren desired. If Wright is now moved it will leave only Hancock on this side of the creek. Do you think this alters the condition, or had Wright still better be moved." *Ibid.*, p. 360.

On May 31, Meade wrote to USG that C.S.A. forces were entrenched on the road from Bethesda Church to Cold Harbor. Thomas F. Madigan, Inc., *Autograph Letters, Manuscripts and Historical Documents* (New York, 1937), p. 38.

To Maj. Gen. William F. Smith

Near Haws Shop, Va. May 30th/64 7,30 p m
MAJ. GEN. W. S. SMITH,
COMD.G 18TH A. C.
GENERAL,

Triplicate orders have been sent to you to march up the South bank of the Pamunky to New Castle there to await further orders. I send with this a Brigade of Cavalry to accompany you on the march. As yet no further directions can be given you than is contained in your orders. The movements of the enemy this evening on our left, down the Mechanicsville road, would indicate the possibility of a design on ~~the~~ his part ~~of the enemy~~ to get between you and the Army of the Potomac. They will be so closely watched that nothing would suit me better than such a move. Sheridan is on our left flank with two Divisions of Cavalry with directions to watch as far out as he can go on the Mechanicsville and Cold Harbor roads. This, with the care you can give your left flank with the Cavalry you have and the Brigade sent to you, and a knowledge of the fact that any movement of the enemy towards you cannot fail to be noticed and followed up from here, will make your advance secure.

The position of the A. P. this evening is as follows; The left of the 5th Corps is on the ~~Mechanicsville road about four~~ Shady Grove road extending to the Mechanicsville road and about three miles south of the Tolopotomoy. The 9th Corps is to the right of the 5th then comes the 2d & 6th forming a line being on the road from Hanover C. H. to Cold Harbor and about six miles south of the C. H.

U. S. GRANT
Lt. Gen

ALS, DNA, RG 393, 24th Army Corps, Letters Received (Unarranged). *O.R.*,
I, xxxvi, part 3, 371.

On May 30, 1864, Brig. Gen. John A. Rawlins wrote to Maj. Gen. George
G. Meade. "Please order two Companies of Cavalry to proceed to White House
at 5 o-clock to-day as escort for bearer of dispatches." Copies, DLC-USG, V, 45,
59; DNA, RG 108, Letters Sent.

On May 31, 2:30 A.M., Maj. Gen. William F. Smith, White House, wrote
to Rawlins. "Capt Hudson arrived here at 1 a. m to day with the copy of dispatch
—the first copy having reached me two hours before—On Saturday evening the
28th inst between 6 and 7 O'clock I received my orders to march my command
to the landings to embark for this place—By 11 a. m. on Sunday the infantry force
was mostly on board, but an insufficiency of transportation for wagons and artillery, detained a great many steamers that were to take tows. My advance arrived at 11 a m. yesterday and things have been coming in all day—There have
as yet arrived only parts of three divisions and a part of three batteries—The
wagons only of one brigade have arrived—As soon as I can land & get issued
three days rations for the men's haversacks I shall move with what force I can
collect to comply with the orders of the Lieut General, leaving the remainder of
my command and supplies to follow as soon as possible—I left City Point with
16000 infantry, 16 pieces of artillery and a company of cavalry the latter having
been sent ~~this~~ yesterday A M early from West Point to communicate with your
Head Quarters via the N. side of Pamunkey River" ALS, *ibid.*, Letters Received. *O.R.*, I, xxxvi, part 3, 410. At 9:00 P.M., Smith, "Bassetts," wrote to
USG. "I have the honor to report the head of my column at this place—I shall
encamp to night between the New Castle ferry road and the Piping tree ferry
road, par~~r~~allel to the Old Church road and along it—Finding the New Castle
Ferry ~~Road~~ picketed, I shall save the command the extra march unless I receive
~~positive~~ orders from you to go there—I have twenty four (24) wagons to this
command, three days rations in haversacks and two days beef on the hoof. Between forty (40) and sixty (60) rounds of infantry ammunition, and no artillery ammunition save what is in the caissons—Three thousand men under Gen'l
Ames were left as a garrison at White House with orders to join me as soon as
Genl Abercrombie commences to disembark—I trust the remainder of my wagons
will be up to-morrow. They are ordered to join me with supplies of forage, ammunition and subsistence" ALS, DNA, RG 108, Letters Received. Printed as
written at 9:00 A.M. in *O.R.*, I, xxxvi, part 3, 410.

On June 1, 2:00 A.M., Lt. Col. Orville E. Babcock wrote to Smith. "Your
communication dated Bassetts 9 P. M. May 31st is at hand. In reply the Lieut
Gen. directs that you move your command to New Castle and take a position
on the right of Maj Gen Wright Comd'g 6th A. C. who moved to this position
since last night   You will place yourself between Genl Wright & Gen Warren—" Copy, DLC-USG, V, 66. The copy has slash lines indicating it may not
have been sent.

To Maj. Gen. Henry W. Halleck

————

6 a. m.

Haws Shop May 31st/64

MAJ. GEN. HALLECK, WASHINGTON.

The enemy came out on our left last evening and attacked. They were easily repulsed and with very conciderable slaughter. To releive Gen. Warren, who was on the left, speedily ~~Gens. Hancock~~ Gen. Meade ordered an attack by the balance of our line. Gen. Hancock was the only one who received the order in time to make the attack before dark. He drove the enemy from his intrenched skirmish line and still holds it. I have no report of our losses but suppose them to be light.

U. S. GRANT
Lt. Gen.

ALS (telegram sent), DNA, RG 107, Telegrams Collected (Unbound); telegram received, *ibid.*; *ibid.*, Telegrams Collected (Bound); *ibid.*, RG 393, Dept. of Va. and N. C., Telegrams Received; *ibid.*, 10th Army Corps, Official Records. *O.R.*, I, xxxvi, part 1, 10; *ibid.*, I, xxxvi, part 3, 375.

To Brig. Gen. John J. Abercrombie

————

Headqrs Armies of the U S—
Near Haws shops May 31st/64

BRIG GEN J. J. ABERCROMBIE
COMD'G U. S. FORCES WHITE HOUSE VA
GENERAL

I have no special directions for you at present further than to say that you will forward all reinforcements for this Army as rapidly as possible, give every facility for the ~~loadin~~ loading of trains with supplies, and when it is practicable send reinforcements along to guard the trains—I want all stragglers who go to the rear apprehended and sent back under guard to the Provost Marshal General Gen Patrick.[1] When commissioned officers are so apprehended cause their buttons and shoulder straps to be publicly cut from their coats, and send them with their hands bound here for trial—

Very respectfully

U. S. GRANT Lt. Gen

Copies, DLC-USG, V, 45, 59, 66; DNA, RG 108, Letters Sent. *O.R.*, I, xxxvi, part 3, 414.

On May 22, 1864, 9:00 A.M., Brig. Gen. John A. Rawlins had written to Brig. Gen. John J. Abercrombie. "Have all the empty teams that have returned to Fredericksburg and Belle Plain loaded with supplies, and send them forward with such supply trains as are now at these places to Bowling Green at once. Transfer without delay all other supplies to Port Royal which place will be made our base until further orders. March the garrisons of Belle Plain and Fredericksburg by the Port Royal road to Port Royal, leaving, however, a sufficient force at Fredericksburg to protect the wounded and transportation for same until they can be moved north, after which the force thus left will follow to Port Royal, and Fredericksburg abandoned." LS, DNA, RG 393, Army of the Potomac, Miscellaneous Letters Received. *O.R.*, I, xxxvi, part 3, 100. On the same day, Abercrombie wrote to USG. "I have the honor to report that from information derived from my Cavalry scouts, and contrabands daily arriving here, that I have reason to believe there are more guerillas between this point and Port Royal, than the small Cavalry force at my disposal can look after: having but six companies of the 8th Ills. Mtd. Cav. which, after deducting escorts, messengers, and details for the Engineers, Telegraph, Road & Bridge contractors, leaves me with a comparatively small force for other purposes—If I had mounted troops sufficient to clear the country between the Rappahannock and Potomac Creek of these marauders and arrest all disloyal persons, a small Cavalry force could then (with due diligence) keep them out—All the Cavalry that I can send out with safety to the Depot are constantly employed, notwithstanding their excursions extend but a few miles in circuit—scarcely ever returning without having a skirmish and bringing in from 2 to 8 Dismounted rebel Cavalry—" LS, DNA, RG 108, Letters Received. Printed as addressed to Rawlins in *O.R.*, I, xxxvi, part 3, 100. At 7:00 P.M., Rawlins telegraphed to Abercrombie. "The road from Bowling Green to Fredericksburg is now uncovered, and it will not be safe for anything to pass over it without escort. You will therefore permit nothing to Come forward from Fredericksburg unless when troops are passing to give the necessary protection." Telegram received, DNA, RG 107, Telegrams Collected (Unbound); copies, *ibid.*, RG 108, Letters Sent; DLC-USG, V, 45, 59. *O.R.*, I, xxxvi, part 3, 139. At 8:30 P.M., Abercrombie telegraphed to USG. "This P M the telegraphic Communication was interupted between hear and your Head Quarters. men have been sent to mend the wires. I have your order to abandon this place and go to Port Royal. Am I to draw in all Guards of Aquia Rail Road, Telegraph and road to Fredericksburgh. What disposition am I to make of six Batterys of reserve Artillery from A of P. I will send every thing off as fast as possible, and will leave here as soon as Rebel Prisoners are shipped. is it intended by your order the garrison of Belle Plain, should march by way of Fredericksburgh or, direct from here to Port Royal. There are Three engines and Sixty Cars now on the Aquia and Fredericksburgh Rail Road—150 bales straw are here that could be used in the Cars for wounded." Copy, DNA, RG 108, Letters Received. *O.R.*, I, xxxvi, part 3, 101. On May 23, 5:00 P.M., Rawlins telegraphed to Abercrombie. "The work on Rail road will cease and all guards for rail road and telegraph be drawn in. The 6 batteries Reserve artillery if convenient send to Washington, otherwise send it across with the garrison to Port Royal. The garrison from Belle Plain may march from there direct to Port Royal, or by Fredericksburg as you deem best. The engines and cars on rail road, ship to Washington. The one hundred & fifty bales of straw send to Port Royal with the other supplies. Port Royal must be garrisoned and made our base with the least possible delay. Act in this matter with the greatest dispatch—" LS (telegram sent), DNA, RG 107, Telegrams Collected (Unbound); copies (with briefer text), *ibid.*, RG 108, Letters Sent; DLC-USG, V, 45, 59. *O.R.*, I, xxxvi, part 3, 135–36.

Also on May 23, 4:15 P.M., Rawlins wrote to Abercrombie. "Enclosed find communication from Asst Surg. Edwd Breneman relating to our wounded on the Wilderness Battle field, and the treatment of officers by guerrilas who attempt to look after their welfare—You will send a sufficient ~~force~~ number of wagons and ambulances, with a competent force of Infantry Cavalry and Artillery to drive away any force of the enemy that may be found in the neighborhood of the Hospitals at that place, and remove all our wounded men from there to Fredericksburg. If necessary you can order for this purpose some of the reinforcements coming forward, but it is thought you have force enough without this. Attend to this at once—" Copies, DLC-USG, V, 45, 59, 66; DNA, RG 108, Letters Sent. *O.R.*, I, xxxvi, part 3, 136. For the enclosure, see letter to Commanding Officer, C.S.A. Forces, May 18, 1864.

On May 28, 7:00 A.M., Rawlins wrote to Abercrombie. "The Army is now at and near Hanover Town, and everything coming forward to it, you will please send to that place and by way of that place." Copies, DLC-USG, V, 45, 59; DNA, RG 108, Letters Sent. *O.R.*, I, xxxvi, part 3, 275. On the same day, Abercrombie wrote to Rawlins. "I have your communication of 26th inst. in relation to Officers of the 4th U. S. Infty. I expect to leave this place on 30th inst. for White House Va. There shall be no delay in forwarding these Officers to their regiment. 750 men went forward to the Army this morning guarding a train—2650 men in battalions and detatchments, leave here in the morning for the front with a large train—This leaves me for the protection of the Depot about 1400 Infantry, 700 of whom are from the Vet. Res. Corps and cannot march, the rest are detatchments from many regiments that I have organized and made serviceable. Also two Batty's of Artillery and 2000 Cavalry mounted and dismounted; The latter serving as Infantry—All will be mounted at White House and sent forward to you. The garrison of Fredericksburg has just arrived, about 3000 strong—1000 Cavalry and 2000 Infantry. Stragglers, squads from Camp Distribution, &c. these will be forwarded upon the abandonment of this depot." LS, DNA, RG 108, Letters Received. *O.R.*, I, xxxvi, part 3, 276.

On May 29, Abercrombie, Port Royal, wrote to USG. "Upward of 400 contrabands were shipped last evening for Washington. I have also apprehended over 2,500 stragglers, whom I shall send to-day or to-morrow under guard to the army. I have received no instructions myself as to abandoning Port Royal. From information derived through the Quartermaster's Department, however, I understand the basis to be the White House, on the Pamunkey, where I shall proceed with the Invalid Battalion, all of whom are completely knocked up by a short march from Belle Plain to this place, and are fit for nothing but garrison duty, and not very reliable for that. On my arrival at White House I will report for further instructions." *Ibid.*, p. 313.

On May 30, Abercrombie wrote to USG. "I have 6,140 men here, two-thirds of whom leave to-day for the army. This includes some 800 cavalry and a battery of artillery. The remainder go to you to-morrow, all according to your telegraphic order, by way of Hanovertown. To-morrow (May 31) everything will have been removed. I shall then leave for the White House. All unable to march will go by transport. Your brother is here, and will accompany me to the White House. I have collected from 1,500 to 2,000 stragglers, and between 500 and 600 contrabands. The stragglers go to their commands under guard, and the contrabands have gone to Washington." *Ibid.*, p. 364. On May 31, Rawlins endorsed this letter. "Respectfully referred to Major-General Meade, who will send back a pontoon bridge to the Mattapony, to enable these troops to cross." *Ibid.*, p. 365.

1. Marsena R. Patrick, born in N. Y. in 1811, USMA 1835, resigned from the U.S. Army in 1850 to take up farming, and on the eve of the Civil War was president of the New York State Agricultural College at Ovid. After serving as inspector gen. for N. Y., he was appointed brig. gen. as of March 17, 1862, and served with the Army of the Potomac, of which he was appointed provost marshal on Oct. 6. See David S. Sparks, ed., *Inside Lincoln's Army: The Diary of Marsena Rudolph Patrick*, . . . (New York, 1964).

Calendar

1864, JAN. 4.   Capt. Marcus D. Tenney, 1st Kan. Battery, to USG. "I have the honor to represent that privates Wm Bruce, Richard Ormsby Geo Vanbenthusen Mark Renfro Ahiza Cosho and John Witts of the 1st Kansas Battery were in Oct last tried by Gen Court Marshal and sentenced to 12 months Confinement and are as I understand undergoing the punishment at the Military prison at Alton Illinois. These Men have served in my Battery since July 1861, with Credit to themselves and the Governmet, but were in a Moment of excitement, entraped by their Enemies. I would respectfully ask that in consideration of their past good behavior, the unexpired portion of the term of imprisonment be remitted, and they Ordered to their Battery for duty especially as I believe that their sentence was the culmination of *political hatred.* I have been furnished with any Order promulgating their sentence."—ALS, DNA, RG 393, Military Div. of the Miss., Provost Marshal, Miscellaneous Records.

1864, JAN. 6.   Asst. Surgeon John C. G. Happersett, Memphis, to USG requesting the assignment of thirty-eight privates to hospital duty.—Copy, DNA, RG 393, Dept. of the Tenn., Unbound Materials.

1864, JAN. 8.   Brig. Gen. Grenville M. Dodge, Pulaski, Tenn., to [USG]. "One of the scouts has got back from Savannah. Smith got in Tuesday night. Crossed the Seventy-second Indiana on Wednesday. The reports there seemed to be that a part of Forrest's command was still in West Tennessee, but nothing was known certain. My scouts crossed over to go to Jackson Monday night, but the country was full of guerrillas. I think Forrest has gone out of Tennessee, leaving Newsom, Wilson, and Norton's [?] regiments, which were raised in West Tennessee. Roddey started to Forrest, but got word from Forrest that he had got out, and he returned. Spent New Years' at Russellville. This is reliable. He has now 20 boats at Little Bear, and has 100 men detailed all the time building."—*O.R.,* I, xxxii, part 2, 48. On Jan. 16, Dodge telegraphed to USG. "One of our men got in from Selma via Atlanta Dalton Rome & Decatur—At Selma they are at work on a line of fortifications also at Atlanta   at and near Dalton Johnson has from twenty five to thirty Thousand men—Wheeler & Horton had been ordered back from east Tenn or a part of their forces—Martins Div of Cavalry are at Dalton & Cove springs—at Rome are state Militia—all stores Hospitals Machinery &c have gone south—at Crossville a lot of state Militia—at Gadsden one brigade of state Militia—the rest of Quarles Brig that was left at Mobile have joined him at Ressecca   Roddy is guarding River from Flint river to Bear Creek has twenty flats in mouth of little Bear & is building them all time   he has about sixteen hundred effective men—Three of his officers deserted & reported to me   it is now twelve (12) days since the men left Rome"—Telegram received, DNA, RG 94, War Records Office, Military Div. of the Miss.; copies, *ibid.,* RG 393, Military Div. of the Miss., Telegrams Received; *ibid.,* 16th Army Corps, Left Wing, Telegrams Sent.

On Jan. 20, Dodge telegraphed to USG. "Co'l Johnson with about eight hundred men is down in the Colbert reserve west of Florence   part of his force was in Lexington and Lawrenceburg yesterday—I think they are mostly after Stock and forage. I have no mounted force except those left from the Volunteers and they are too small to do much good. I will watch them pretty close"—Copies, *ibid. O.R.,* I, xxxii, part 2, 155. On Jan. 22, Dodge telegraphed to Lt. Col. Theodore S. Bowers. "One of my scouts left Rome on Sunday last. he went by way of Decatur Sewerville & returned by Turktown and Whitesides—all quiet on south side of Tenn. At Rome in addition to State Militia are the 8th 11th and 4th Texas Cavalry 7th Georgia Cavalry and Biffles Brigade Consisting of 9th Tenn. Cavalry and 9th and 20th Ala. Infy Mounted   all below to Martins Division on Coosa River the Steamboat Curtis Peaks—Laura Moore and Albert Bitler play between Greensport and Rome transporting Corn and Meat to the Army. Martins Cavalry connect with Roddy between Courtland and Summerville—Roddy with Lee between Russellville and Vincents Cross roads—Lee and Forrest in and about Okalona and Columbus Miss—"—Copies, DNA, RG 393, Military Div. of the Miss., Telegrams Received; *ibid.,* 16th Army Corps, Left Wing, Telegrams Sent. *O.R.,* I, xxxii, part 2, 179. On the same day, Bowers telegraphed to USG. "The following is a copy of telegram rec'd by Maj. Gen. Rosseau from Co'l. Misner   Fourteen hundred men of Roddys Com'd. under Johnson and Moran crossed the Tenn. between Florence & Clifton on Monday designing raid upon railway line and destruction of bridges. I have advised Gen'l Dodge at Pulaski. I shall watch closely   (Signed) H. R. MISNER Co'l Comdg. Post Columbia Tenn."—Copy, DNA, RG 393, Military Div. of the Miss., Telegrams Received. *O.R.,* I, xxxii, part 2, 179.

1864, JAN. 9.   Harriette N. Lander, Fox Lake, Wis., to USG asking if her late husband, William H. Lander, had held a military commission.—ALS, DNA, RG 94, Letters Received, 285L 1864. Accompanying endorsements indicate that he had not.—*Ibid.*

1864, JAN. 10.   Brig. Gen. Robert Allen, Louisville, to USG. "I am instructed by Genl. Meigs to request that you will, by a General Order, reduce the ration of hay to one half its present amount throughout the States of Kentucky, Tennessee and Alabama, Georgia and Mississippi. I fully agree with the Quarter Master General in the necessity of this measure, since it will be impossible to supply the full ration of hay."—LS, DNA, RG 393, Military Div. of the Miss., Letters Received.

1864, JAN. 12.   President Abraham Lincoln to USG or Maj. Gen. George H. Thomas. "Let execution of the death sentence upon William Jeffries, of Co. A. Sixth Indiana Volunteers, be suspended until further order from here."—ALS (telegram sent), RPB. Lincoln, *Works,* VII, 122.

1864, JAN. 12.   Asst. Surgeon Gen. Robert C. Wood, Louisville, to USG. "The Situation of the insane Soldiers in the Military Division of the Mississippi having been reported to me as requiring attention, I made the necessary inquiries whether they could not be received in the Government Insane Asylum at Washington, and have been informed that there are accommodations for them in that Institution.—Their transfer will relieve the army and medical Staff from much embarrassment. I have detailed Surgeon Cooper to repair to Nashville, and make all necessary arrangements for their removal to this City, and transfer to Washington, and to ask of the military authorities all needful aid and assistance.—I have the honor to transmit this together with the enclosed copy of my instructions to Surgeon Cooper, for your information, and for such orders as may be necessary."—LS, DNA, RG 393, Military Div. of the Miss., Letters Received.

1864, JAN. 13.   USG endorsement. "Approved and respectfully forwarded to Head Quarters of the Army Washington D. C."—ES, DNA, RG 94, ACP, 671H CB 1863. Written on a letter of Dec. 11, 1863, of Brig. Gen. Marcellus M. Crocker recommending Col. Cyrus Hall, 14th Ill., for appointment as brig. gen.—ALS, *ibid.* An identical letter of Crocker was endorsed on Jan. 12, 1864, by President Abraham Lincoln. "Submitted to the Sec. of War, & Genl-in-Chief."—AES, *ibid.* No appointment followed.

1864, JAN. 13.   Maj. Gen. Henry W. Halleck to USG. "Complaints have been recieved from the 32d Iowa, and other regiments, that they have been divided and that parts of the same regiment are now serving in different Depts. It is presumed that this resulted from the exigencies of the service during the past year and was probably at the time unavoidable. It should, however, be remedied as promptly as possible by uniting in the same military Dept., the regiments so divided. For example, six companies of the 32d Iowa are reported at Columbus, Union City & Island 10, and four companies at Little Rock Arkansas. The entire regiment should either be sent to Arkansas or the four companies there sent to the Dept of the Tennessee. As Members of Congress from the Districts and States in which the regiments are raised are urgent in their protests against such division, it is hoped that you will give the matter your early attention."—LS, DNA, RG 108, Letters Sent (Press).

1864, JAN. 13.   Governor Andrew Johnson of Tenn. to USG discussing the case of Anselm Brown.—Copy, DLC-Andrew Johnson. A slave convicted of poisoning his owner's family and sentenced to death by hanging, Brown eventually was freed and served in the 16th U.S. Colored.—Johnson, *Papers,* V, 287–88, 289–90.

1864, JAN. 13.   Elizabeth F. Leggett, Ripley, Ohio, to USG. "Permit me to introduce myself to you, by saying—I am the daughter of the late Francis

Taylor of Maysville Ky, and wife of Archibald Leggett of Ripley Ohio. You will please excuse the liberty I have taken of addressing a letter to you, on a subject that lies near my heart, it is, the future of my son, Henry F. Leggett who is now in command of Company "A" 9th Ky Infantry. I want to know if you will take him on your Staff. I am anxious to have him out of the place he is, as both his, & his Company's time will expire, in about June, I think. And he wishes to remain in the Army—If you will take the trouble to inquire something about him of his Regimental & Brigade Commanders, you will find him highly spoken of. If you will only have a little patience with me, I will give you a short account of his present position: But will say first, that out of four sons, three of them in their zeal volenteered as *privates* in the 12th O. V. I. and each one was promoted for their gallant behavior—the oldest, Algernon Sidney (who attended school in Ripley at the same time you did) to a Lieutenantcy, for his bravery at the battle of Pittsburg Landing. And Wirt our second son to a Captaincy in the 12 Regt in Western Virginia   Henry was appointed 1st Lieutenant in the 59th Ohio, by Gov Tod— was afterwards taken on the Staff of Genl Boyle, & after the battle of Pittsburg Landing, was offered & accepted, the Captaincy of Co "A" 9th Ky Infantry—Sidney was killed at the battle of Stone River & Wirt at South Mountain Md.—For Henry I feel the greatest solicitude, and if it will be at all pleasant & practicable, I will urge you to take him on your Staff—or in some way, which you know better than I, have him placed where he can remain in the service, until the close of the war—I will close, by begging you to allow me the privelige of congratulating you, on your many *grand successes*, since you entered the Army, I assure you, that *Brown County* is very proud of you; If not asking too much, I will be glad to hear from you, at your earliest convenience."—ALS, USG 3.

1864, JAN. 15. Brig. Gen. Montgomery C. Meigs to USG. "I have consulted with the Navy Department in regard to Gun-Boats for the Upper Tennessee. I think the prospect of getting boats from the lower to the upper River doubtful, and I have instructed Col. Easton, Chief Quartermaster of the Army of the Cumberland, to have two or more of the larger class of steamboats now building at Bridgeport, Alabama, prepared to receive a light armament on the plan of certain light-draft armed transports built by W. Norman Wiard for this Department, and now in service on the Atlantic bays and rivers. I am informed at the Navy Department that if you desire it, not only armament boat howitzers and rifles on sliding carriages, but crews to man these boats will be supplied by Admiral Porter. If you desire that more than two steam[ers] shall be fitted for such armament it will be done. While in Louisville, I ordered six more engines to be constructed, making in all thirteen new engines, of which seven were nearly ready for delivery. Five steamers were at work on the Upper Tennessee; one hull was ready to launch; one was partly in frame; four more would be set up at Bridgeport immediately, and at Kingston Gen. Foster was making arrangements for constructing three; all to be sent to Bridgeport to receive their engines. Two boats had been purchased and were being fitted to ascend the Tennessee River and run over the Muscle-Shoals if the water rises. I fear they will not succeed."—LS, DNA, RG 92, Miscellaneous Letters Sent (Press). *O.R.* (Navy), I, xxv, 699. See *ibid.*, pp. 699–700.

1864, JAN. 15. Maj. Gen. Ambrose E. Burnside, New York City, to USG. "I have had with me two orderlies of the 77th Ohio for some time they are now at home on a furlough—Can I retain them with me for the present—I was sorry not to be able to return by way of Chattanooga as I was anxious to see you but there were good reasons for not doing so, which I will explain by letter. Please answer at once"—ALS (telegram sent), DNA, RG 393, 9th Army Corps, Telegrams Sent.

1864, JAN. 15. To Augustus Lemcke, Evansville, Ind. "Yours of January 11th is received. In reply I have to state that the fuel seized March 23d '62 for the use of the Steamer 'Fanny Bullitt' on her way from Pittsburgh Landing to the mouth of the Tennessee River, was seized by my order and for the use of the U. S. and that any claim for compensation should be made against the United States."—Copies, DLC-USG, V, 34, (dated Jan. 14) 35; DNA, RG 393, Military Div. of the Miss., Letters Sent. On Feb. 23, Lemcke wrote "In reference to fuel used by steamer 'Fanney Bullitt,' while in Government employ, and for which judgment has been rendered against him, by the County Court at Smithland, Ky."—Copy, DLC-USG, V, 37. On March 3, USG endorsed this letter. "Respectfully forwarded to the Secretary of War. The within letter fully explains all the facts referred to. The Fanny Bullitt among other steamers was taken to transport troops for the capture of Forts Henry and Donelson. Fuel was taken to run them by my order and the Smithland Court was fully advised of that fact."—Copies, *ibid.*, V, 39; DNA, RG 393, Military Div. of the Miss., Endorsements.

1864, JAN. 16. USG Special Orders No. 11. "The Quartermaster's Department within this Military Division, on application of authorised agents of the Western Freedmen's Aid Commission, will furnish public transportation for all goods they may desire to send to the freedmen in this Military Division, and the agents of the commission, in charge of such goods to and from the points of their departure and destination. Public transportation will in like manner be furnished persons engaged as teachers of freedmen. The Commissary Department will also issue rations to the teachers, voluntarily laboring for the benefit of these freed people, on the approval of the Post Commander, where they may be so employed."—Copies, DLC-USG, V, 38; DNA, RG 94, Letters Received, Q29 1864.

1864, JAN. 16. To Maj. Gen. George H. Thomas. "Please send the bearer of this, Mrs. Bransford, under 'Flag of Truce,' to the Confederate lines."— ANS (facsimile), *Confederate Veteran*, XIII, 5 (May, 1905), 216.

1864, JAN. 16.   Governor Andrew Johnson of Tenn. to USG. "I herewith enclose to you papers relating to the case of Jno C Newman & others now in Prison by order of Gen Rousseau. The facts as stated are taken from statement filed by each party before any action was taken. There have been many such suits brought, towards the close of last year and the beginning of this. The judgments of the Justices were disregarded in so many of such cases, by parties who happened to be in possession by contract or otherwise that it became oppressive, upon the owners   My Commission, authorizes me to establish Tribunals, and abolish existing Tribunals, and create offices and officers and in the exercise of this power. I thought this a proper case to exercise that power, as manifest injustice was being done, as I have done in several other cases of like nature, only though after a thorough examination of the case by ~~disinterested~~. I desire your interference in behalf of these men"—ADf, DLC-Andrew Johnson.

1864, JAN. 16.   Governor Oliver P. Morton of Ind. to USG. "I have appointed Lt. Co'l James Burgess Seventieth Regt. Ind. Vols. as Commander of this Congressional District to organize a new regt. under orders of War Dept. and request you grant him leave of absence for three weeks—answer hasty"—Copy, DNA, RG 393, Military Div. of the Miss., Telegrams Received. On Jan. 17, Morton telegraphed to USG. "I desire especially that Lieut Col Burgess, 70th Ind. Vols. now here may have special orders to report to me. I want him to take charge of recruiting in this District unders orders of War Department."—Copies, *ibid.*; Morton Papers, In. On Jan. 28, Lt. Col. Theodore S. Bowers telegraphed to Morton. "Lieut. Col. James Burgess 70th Regiment Indiana Vols. Infantry, will report in person and without delay to His Excellency, O. P. Morton, Governor of the State of Indiana, at Indianapolis, Indiana for recruiting service under the orders of the War Department."—Copy, *ibid.*

1864, JAN. 17.   USG endorsement. "Respectfully returned to Head Quarters of the Army, Washington D. C., with the recommendation that Brig. Gen. Kiernan's name be dropped from the list of appointments presented to the Senate for confirmation. I have good reason to believe that the *wounds* of which he complains were not received in battle but were caused by a fall from his horse whilst in a state of questionable sobriety"—ES, DNA, RG 94, Letters Received, 248K 1864. Written on a letter of Dec. 7, 1863, from Brig. Gen. James L. Kiernan, Cincinnati, to Brig. Gen. Lorenzo Thomas stating that he had left Milliken's Bend, La., suffering from old wounds and malaria, and asking assignment "in a more healthy locality."—ALS, *ibid.* On Feb. 3, 1864, Lt. Col. James A. Hardie, AGO, ordered Kiernan mustered out of service.—ES, *ibid.*

1864, JAN. 18.   To Maj. Gen. George H. Thomas. "Relieve Capt. Dickson, A. A. G., to enable him to report to Gen'l Foster for duty."—Copy, DNA, RG 393, Dept. of the Cumberland, Telegrams Received.

1864, JAN. 18. To Col. Sanders D. Bruce, 20th Ky., Louisville. "Your attention is respectfully directed to the enclosed copy of General Orders No 10 of date Dec. 12th from these Headquarters, under the provisions of which you will release such deserters as are now confined in the military prisons of your command You will exercise with care the discretion that this order confers."—Copies, DLC-USG, V, 34, 35; DNA, RG 393, Military Div. of the Miss., Letters Sent.

1864, JAN. 18, 4:10 P.M. Maj. Gen. George H. Thomas, Chattanooga, to USG. "Frank Marshall Co. C. 57th O. V. I. for whom you ordered 60 days furlough, is not within my command. The Regt. belongs to Genl. Sherman."—Copy, DNA, RG 393, Dept. of the Cumberland, Telegrams Sent.

1864, JAN. 18. Governor John Brough of Ohio to USG. "I find the second and third O.o. C. are not yet fully equipped though requisition were made thirty days since. I am advised they have been forwarded I will press forward the movement of these battalions as rapidly as possible"—Copy, DNA, RG 393, Military Div. of the Miss., Telegrams Received.

1864, JAN. 19. C.S.A. Gen. Joseph E. Johnston, Dalton, Ga., to USG. "I have the honor to send to your lines by Flag of Truce, Surgn, Hunt of the 9th Tenn (Federal) Cavalry, who was captured by some of our (Confederate) scouts, near Harrison, East. Tenn."—Copy, DNA, RG 109, Army of Tenn., Letters Sent.

1864, JAN. 19, 10:20 A.M. Col. Edward D. Townsend, AGO, to USG. "Please cause to be detailed two officers and four men from each of the Iowa Regiments under your command, to report to Lieut. Col. W. N. Grier Commanding Rendezvous at Davenport, Iowa. A like detail from each Minnesota Reg't. to report to Lieut. Col. George Andrews at Fort Snelling, and a like detail from each Missouri Reg't to report to Lieut Col. Pitcairn Morrison, Benton Barracks, St Louis, Mo. for duty conducting recruits to Regiments."—LS (telegram sent), DNA, RG 107, Telegrams Collected (Unbound); copies, *ibid.*, RG 393, Military Div. of the Miss., Hd. Qrs. Correspondence; DLC-USG, V, 40, 94. On the same day, 12:40 P.M., Townsend again telegraphed to USG. "Please cause to be detailed one officer and four men from each of the Illinois Regiments under your command, to report to Brig Gen Corse Commanding Rendezvous at Springfield, Illinois, for duty, conducting recruits to regiments."—LS (telegram sent), DNA, RG 107, Telegrams Collected (Unbound); copies, *ibid.*, RG 393, Military Div. of the Miss., Hd. Qrs. Correspondence; DLC-USG, V, 40, 94. On Jan. 25, Lt. Col. Theodore S. Bowers issued Special Orders No. 20 sending Brig. Gen. William Vandever to Iowa to assist in organizing both new and veteran regts.—Copies, *ibid.*, V, 38; DNA, RG 94, Letters Received, 67V 1864. *O.R.*, I, xxxii, part 2, 216. On Feb. 2, 1:30 P.M., Townsend telegraphed to USG a sentence similar to the first sentence of his first telegram of Jan. 19.—LS (telegram sent), DNA, RG 107, Telegrams Collected (Unbound); copies, *ibid.*, RG 393, Military Div. of the Miss., Hd. Qrs. Correspondence; *ibid.*, Letters Received; DLC-USG, V, 40, 94. On the same day, 1:30 P.M., Townsend telegraphed to USG. "Please cause to be detailed, one Officer and four men from each of the Ohio regiments under your command to report to Col. S. Burbank, 2d U. S. Inf. Comdg Draft Rendezvous, Columbus, Ohio—, for duty conducting recruits to regiments." —LS (telegram sent), DNA, RG 107, Telegrams Collected (Unbound); copies, *ibid.*, RG 393, Military Div. of the Miss., Hd. Qrs. Correspondence; DLC-USG, V, 40, 94.

1864, JAN. 19.   Samuel C. Reed, N. Y. Assembly, to USG transmitting a resolution of thanks.—ALS, USG 3.

1864, JAN. 20.   Col. William Hoffman, commissary gen. of prisoners, to USG. "I have the honor to enclose herewith a roll of prisoners of War, received from Tullahoma Tenn. It is a fair specimen of the rolls usually received at this office, and is so incomplete, as to occasion much embarassment. The heading of the rolls is not filled up, it does not state where they were sent from, not where they were sent to, and it was not accompanied, by a letter of advice, to clear up these doubtful points. It appears from the order of Maj. Genl. Slocum that the prisoners were sent from a Hospital at Tullahoma. May I request of you General, to direct that in future, officers in the Milty. Disct. of the Mississippi, in charge of Prisoners of War, shall make prompt reports to this office of all prisoners received by them, transferred &c. &c. giving all required details to make up a full history of each individual case. It is necessary to state, the rank, regiment, and Company; the time and place of capture, where held, to what place transferred, and when, date of release and authority therefore, and date of escape or death. I rarely receive rolls on which some of these items of information are not omitted, and I would be greatly obliged to you, if you give this matter your early attention. I had the honor of addressing you a letter in relation to prisoners of War, on the 6th of Nov. last which I hope was recieved."—Copy, DNA, RG 249, Letters Sent. See telegram to Maj. Gen. Henry W. Halleck, Sept. 25, 1863, note 1.

1864, JAN. 21.   USG endorsement. "Respectfully forwarded. I would recommend the appointment of Private H. W. Schmidt and his assignment to duty with Gen. Sherman who has need of another Adj. Gen. now having but one."—AES, DNA, RG 94, ACP, S1535 CB 1863. Written on a letter of Nov. 29, 1863, from Private H. W. Schmidt, Co. E, 12th Mo., to Brig. Gen. Lorenzo Thomas requesting an appointment as capt. and asst. adjt. gen. on the basis of twenty months of experience as army clerk.—ALS, *ibid.* No appointment followed.

1864, JAN. 21.   Brig. Gen. Edward R. S. Canby, War Dept., to USG. "REFERRED To Major General U. Grant, U. S. A., for his information and such acti action as he may deem necessary and proper."—ES, DNA, RG 110, Correspondence Relating to Scouts. Written on a letter of Jan. 19 from E. Bourlier, secret service agent, to Secretary of War Edwin M. Stanton stating that U.S. troops were protecting the property of rebels in northern Ala.—LS, *ibid.*

1864, JAN. 21.   Col. Edward D. Townsend, AGO, to USG. "No Returns of the Milt. Divn. of the Miss have been recd. at this Office. The Monthly and Tri-monthly Returns are much needed for the transaction of business. If regular Returns cannot at once be forwarded, please send Monthly & Tri-monthly returns of your personal Staff & Commd   This is very necessary as a matter of Justice to the Officers of your command, who are not reported regularly to this Office, and are liable to be reported absent if not heard from within a reasonable length of time"—Copy, DNA, RG 94, Enlisted Branch, Letters Sent.

1864, JAN. 21.   Ind. AG Lazarus Noble to USG. "We have in the service from this State Four Regiments Six months Volunteers now in the vicinity of Knoxville Tenn whose terms of service will expire between the middle of Feby & 20th of March,   There were among them a large number of very young men who broke down and are now here in Convalescent Camp,   From reliable information received we believe that a very considerable proportion of those in the field will reenlist if under favorable influences. I have been instructed by the Governor to address you and request that the Four Regiments be sent to this place to be mustered out and paid off. They are the 115th 116th 117th & 118th Regts. Ind. Vols."—ALS, DNA, RG 393, Military Div. of the Miss., Letters Received. On Dec. 30, 1863, Col. George W. Jackson, 118th Ind., Tazewell, Tenn., wrote to Governor Oliver P. Morton of Ind. requesting permission to organize a cav. regt. for three years service.—Copy, *ibid.* On Jan. 23, 1864, Noble endorsed this letter. "Respfy. forwarded to Maj. Gen. Grant Comdg. &c, and refering to letter of recent date the application is again made for the Four Regiments Inda. Vols. Six Mo. Troops to be sent to Indianapolis to be mustered out and paid. It is believed it would insure the re-enlistment of a large number of them"—AES, *ibid.* On Jan. 28, Lt. Col. Theodore S. Bowers wrote to Noble. "I am directed by Maj Genl U S Grant to acknowledge the receipt of your communication of date 21st inst and to respectfully inform you in reply that Maj Genl J. G. Foster com'dg Dept of the Ohio with whom the regiments are serving, telegraphs that some of these regiments are now on their way home and the remaining ones about leaving"—Copies, DLC-USG, V, 34, 35; DNA, RG 393, Military Div. of the Miss., Letters Sent.

1864, JAN. 22.   To Lt. Col. James A. Hardie. "my signature and all the signatures with which I am familiar, on the paper are forgeries." Written in

answer to a request to verify signatures on an application for promotion.—
Carnegie Book Shop, Catalogue 39, No. 615.

1864, JAN. 24.   USG endorsement. "Approved and respectfully recommended to the favorable consideration of the President."—AES, DNA, RG
94, ACP, T118 CB 1864. Written on a letter of the same day from Capt.
John Mendenhall, 4th Art., also judge advocate vols. with the rank of maj.,
to Brig. Gen. Lorenzo Thomas requesting an appointment as asst. inspector
gen.—ALS, *ibid.* Mendenhall was assigned as inspector gen. and lt. col.,
Dept. of the Cumberland, May 2–Sept. 7, 1864.

1864, JAN. 24.   To Governor Andrew Johnson of Tenn. "Can Stokes
cavalry be sent Immediately to clear out the country between Carthage &
sparta of guerillas   The work is Important & nearly all the cavalry of this
department is now in distant service"—Telegram received, DLC-Andrew
Johnson. Col. William B. Stokes, 5th Tenn. Cav., began the requested
operation on Jan. 29.—*O.R.,* I, xxxii, part 1, 162–63.

1864, JAN. 25.   Commander Thomas H. Stevens, U.S.S. *Patapsco,* to
USG. "I received some time since a letter from Mrs. Grant, in regard to my
indebtedness to you, growing out of our business connection in California,
which I have not replied to, because I was in hopes daily to have had the
money to send her, from the distribution of prize money, in some of the
nine or ten cases, in which I am interested, but there seems to be no more
probability of a settlement now, than there was six months ago & I write you
for the purpose of apoligising for my silence, and to assure you that as soon
as I can raise the means, from the source refered to or by any other means I
shall forward the amount with great satisfaction to you—Since the war commenced I have been actively engaged on this coast, & upon the York &
Pamunkey & James River cooperating with McClellans Army & in the West
Indies but wherever I have been I followed with pride & pleasure your distinguished career, & from my heart I congratulate you upon your splendid
triumphs & successes—While you are a tower of strength to our holy cause,
I know you are a terror to our common enemies, & I hope that under your
control the Armies of the Republic may soon succeed in restoring the authority of the Govt & the laws over the would be Confederacy—We are at
a dead-lock here—our hopes of doing something have been so often disappointed, that we can hope no longer, & if you can only make my services in
the field available to you, in any way, I should only be too proud & gratified
to find myself under your command, with a prospect of serving our Country,
in its time of need—I hope you will find time to answer this brief letter—
that my application for service may not be forgotten. Please make my kindest regards to Mrs Grant & believe me"—ALS, USG 3. See *Calendar,* Jan.
5, 1854. On April 28, 1864, Stevens wrote to a friend that he had been
"out to the front with Grant while I was in Washington . . ." and that he

had a letter from USG which "contains some matters I would not like to parade before the world—" —ALS, Wayde Chrismer, Bel Air, Md.

1864, JAN. 25.   James Q. Smith, Nashville, to USG recommending a cav. raid toward Selma, Ala.—ALS, DNA, RG 393, Military Div. of the Miss., Letters Received. *O.R.*, I, xxxii, part 2, 214–16.

1864, JAN. 26.   Brig. Gen. Grenville M. Dodge, Pulaski, Tenn., to Lt. Col. Theodore S. Bowers. "Monday morning A. M. my mounted force which included most of Garrisson at Athens moved on Roddys force west of Florence. Last night Co'l. Hannon with about six hundred men and two pieces of Artillery crossed River at Browns Ferry which is 10 Miles below Decatur and 12 miles ~~be~~ from Athens and at Four o'clock A. M. attacked Athens and some of my bridge parties near Athens—We had about one hundred men   after two hours fight the rebels were repulsed and retreated on wood Ferry. Our loss is twenty (20) the enemys much larger—The bridge parties are all right and before this the enemy is South of Tenn. They got news some way of our move and no doubt expected to take Athens, Stores & trains but they have gone back to day whipped   our trains all safe"—Telegram, copy, DNA, RG 393, Military Div. of the Miss., Telegrams Received. *O.R.*, I, xxxii, part 1, 118. On Jan. 27, Dodge telegraphed to Bowers. "Co'l. Miller had a severe fight this side of Florence yesterday. Our loss 15 killed 25 wounded   the enemy were repulsed and several prisoners taken   Prisoners say Corinth has been abandoned and burned   I think all the mounted force we can raise should be immediately sent to Florence and Colbert reserve and clear out the enemy, they are getting to Strong in there for our safety on the Rail Road and unless we get them out and keep them employed they will pick up some of our working parties   if we could take and hold Decatur it would make us all safe and keep them at proper distance"—Copy, DNA, RG 393, Military Div. of the Miss., Telegrams Received. Dated Jan. 26 in *O.R.*, I, xxxii, part 1, 118.

On Jan. 29, Brig. Gen. John A. Rawlins telegraphed to Col. John C. Kelton. "On the morning of the twenty fifth (25th) the Enemy six hundred (600) strong attacked our garrison of about one hundred (100) at Athens. After a two (2) hours fight the Enemy was repulsed and driven   Our loss twenty (20), the Enemy's much greater. On the twenty [se]venth (27) Col Miller had a severe fight on this side of Florence repulsing the Enemy. Our loss fifteen (15) killed twenty five (25) wounded"—Telegram received, DNA, RG 107, Telegrams Collected (Bound); copies, *ibid.*, RG 393, Military Div. of the Miss., Hd. Qrs. Correspondence; DLC-USG, V, 40, 94. *O.R.*, I, xxxii, part 1, 117.

On Jan. 27, Dodge telegraphed to Bowers. "Gen'l Roddy. desires to make an exchange with me man for man   will I be allowed to do it"—Copy, DNA, RG 393, Military Div. of the Miss., Telegrams Received. *O.R.*, II, vi, 884. On Jan. 28, Bowers telegraphed to Dodge. "You are authorized to make the exchange as proposed."—Copies, DLC-USG, V, 34, 35; DNA, RG 393, Military Div. of the Miss., Letters Sent.

1864, JAN. 26.　　Absalom H. Markland, Louisville, to USG. "Can you consistently write the President recommending me for a position in the revolted states, or rather the late revolted states. I desire to locate permanently in some one of them with the hope that I may, as a citizen, and an officer of some experience be of service to the Federal Govt. Having followed your fortunes for the past two years, and having been more prominently identified with the Army in the West than any other civil officer it is reasonable to presume that you are somewhat acquainted with my qualifications to do good for the administration and the governmt. My conduct as an officer of the P. O Dept since the beginning of the rebellion are well known at Washington. My reputation as a gentleman of integrity &c is known to all who have been so *un*fortunate as to cultivate my acquaintance. Since the rebellion this is the first personal favor I have asked of any one."—ALS, USG 3.

1864, JAN. 27.　　President Abraham Lincoln to USG. "Your note of the 14th Inst., asking the appointment of J. D. C. Hoskins as Cadet at large to West Point was handed me by Mr. Washburne three or four days ago— It shall be done—There being no vacancy now we must wait for one: but the Secretary of War and myself, between us, will not let the case be forgotten—Meantime I suggest that if you can you send us the boys *full* Christian name, instead of merely the initials."—ALS, USMA. Lincoln, *Works (Supplement)*, p. 221. See Lincoln, *Works*, VII, 139; letter to Elihu B. Washburne, Dec. 12, 1863. USG endorsed Lincoln's letter to Mrs. Jennie Deane Hoskins. "Please write to the President giving your sons name in full or write to me and I will do so."—AES, USMA. The son of 1st Lt. Charles Hoskins, killed at the battle of Monterey, Mexico, Sept. 21, 1846, John D. C. Hoskins was appointed at large to USMA, entering on July 1, 1864. On April 13, Mrs. Hoskins, New Rochelle, N. Y., wrote to USG acknowledging the appointment.—ALS, USG 3.

1864, JAN. 27.　　Brig. Gen. William F. Smith, Nashville, to USG. "From information derived from a Citizen of North Alabama I judge it to be of great importance that a permanent footing be obtained as soon as possible across the river in Logan's front and that Copies of your order be furnished to Citizens there for distribution."—ALS (telegram sent), NHi. On Jan. 28, USG, St. Louis, telegraphed to Smith. "Tell Bowers to make the order suggested in your dispatch of yesterday—I will leave here on Monday"—Copy, DNA, RG 393, Dept. of Mo., Telegrams Sent.

1864, JAN. 27.　　Sgt. George S. Morris, Nashville, to USG. "I take this opportunity to inform you that I am a Prisoner of War, and wish to be allowed to take the Oath of Allegiance to the U. S. I am a member of the 4th Tenn Rebel Inft. I have been in the Rebel service nearly three years. My home is in Weakley County in this State. Since my imprisonment I have, for the first time, seen a copy of the Amnesty Proclamation of Pres.d. Lincoln and am very anxious to accept it and return to my home. I have no ties to bind me to the South. All my Relatives live *North* and many are in the Federal Army."—ALS, DNA, RG 249, Letters Received. The letter was favorably endorsed on Jan. 27 by Governor Andrew Johnson of Tenn., and on Feb. 8 forwarded to Secretary of War Edwin M. Stanton by Maj. William R. Rowley, provost marshal, Military Div. of the Miss.—*Ibid.*

1864, JAN. 28. Maj. Robert Williams, AGO, to USG. "Your attention is invited to the expediency of granting furloughs to as many soldiers of the Regular Army who may re-enlist before the first of March as possible—"— Df (telegram sent), DNA, RG 107, Telegrams Collected (Unbound). Williams sent the same telegram to other commanders.

1864, [JAN. 28]. David Hirsch to USG. "Your petitioner would respectfully represent that in the year 1854 he became a naturalized citize[n] of the United States that he is at present sojourning in the City of New York but is and has been for the past seventeen months a citizen of Memphis Tennessee. That at the breaking out of the present rebellion he resided in the City of St Louis Missouri. That on the 23rd day of June 1861 he was commissioned as Captain of Company C 1st Regiment of Missouri Volunteers and in that capacity served in the armies of the so-called Confederate States for the period of thirteen months. That in the month of October 1861 he tendered to the proper authorities the resignation of his said Captain's commission assigning among others as a reason therefor that he desired to proceed to St Louis Missouri where his family resided and required his attention   That his resignation was returned to him with the endorsement thereon by the Secretary of War of the so-called Confederate States that 'upon the filing of Captain Hirsch in this office of his parole that he will not during the present war take up arms against the Government of the Confederate States his resignation will be accepted'   That in compliance with the terms of this endorsement he gave the required parole and his resignation was accepted. That about the 7th of June 1862 he came within the federal lines at Memphis Tennessee and reported himself to the Provost Marshal at the post that from that time to the time of the orders hereinafter complained of he has resided with his family in said City of Memphis   That he has there during this time been engaged in the business of a merchant   That during his said residence in Memphis he conducted himself in all things as a loyal and law abiding citizen of the United States and obeyed all orders of the military authorities having taken all the oaths of allegiance required by said authorities   That while so residing in said City of Memphis on the 15th day of December 1863 he was ordered by Brigadier Gen. Veatch Comdg. the Dist. of Memphis to pay a fine of five hundred dollars for non-compliance with orders requiring him to enroll and muster in the Militia of District of Memphis and to leave the district within thirty days. That in pursuance of said orders he paid said fine and left said district. A copy of said orders and receipt for the money are herewith filed   Your petitioner would further state that on the 28th Day of January 1864 he took and filed in the office of Brigadier General Hays A. A. Provost Marshal General for the District of New York the oath prescribed by the President of the United States in his Amnesty Proclamation of date December 8th 1864 a copy of which is hereto annexed   Your petitioner would further state that he admits that he did refuse to muster and enroll in the militia of the Dist of Memphis, he would further state that his refusal was not based on any disloyal feeling to the Government of the United States nor to any unwillingness on his part to perform his obligations as a citizen but solely of his having given the parole aforesaid to said Confederate States and his regard for the binding obligation of said parole upon his conscience and the penalty which would be attached to its violation should he be made a prisoner by the Confederate military authorities   Your petitioner would therefore respectfully request that in consideration of the premises the said order by which he was banished from Memphis be revoked and that the fine of five hundred dollars paid by him as aforesaid be remitted."—LS, DNA, RG 94, Letters Received, 422H 1864. On Jan. 28, William S. Hillyer, New York City, wrote to Brig. Gen. John A. Rawlins supporting Hirsch's petition.—LS, *ibid.*, RG 109, Union Provost Marshals' File of Papers Relating to Individual Civilians. On July 9, Asst. Secretary of War Charles A. Dana endorsed Hirsch's letter approving the fine and banishment.—ES, *ibid.*, RG 94, Letters Received, 422H 1864.

1864, JAN. 30.   John C. Farmington, Memphis, to USG. "This will be handed to you by Mr Peebles. He has been ordered away from here by Genl Veatch for having been in the Confederate service, and I think unjustly. He left that service before the arrival of the Federal forces in Memphis and has been here since that time. He has taken *no part* on either side since that time, nor has he been engaged in any business that would aid the Confederates. I think his sentence an unjust one, and hope you will allow him to return to Memphis. I *know* that no injury would result from it."—ALS, DNA, RG 109, Union Provost Marshals' File of Papers Relating to Individual Civilians. On the same day, D. Cockrell wrote a similar letter to USG in behalf of Robert A. Peebles.—LS, *ibid.*

1864, JAN. 31.   To President Abraham Lincoln. "I have the honor to enclose you letters just received from the Superintendent and Principle of the High School in relation to William Rawson, a boy of this city, who is extremely desirous of obtaining a Cadets appointment.—Mr Rawson is a young man of fine appearance and evident intelligence and with his anxiety to get to West Point I have no doubt he would succeed well as a student, and afterwards would prove an ornament to the service."—ALS, DNA, RG 94, USMA Applications. USG enclosed letters of Jan. 27 from C. F. Childs, principal of St. Louis High School, and of Jan. 28 from Ira Divoll, superintendent of public schools, recommending William Rawson.—ALS, *ibid.* Rawson, USMA 1869, died while on graduation leave.

1864, JAN.   Maj. Thomas M. Vincent, AGO, to USG. "I am directed to invite your attention to the fact that certain papers in the case of 1st Lieutenant Albert Coles, 13th Iowa Volunteers, were referred to you nearly six months since for report, and have not been returned. Lieutenant Cole appears to have been discharged for incompetency, while a prisoner of War in the hands of the Enemy."—Copy, DNA, RG 393, Military Div. of the Miss., War Dept. Correspondence.

1864, FEB. 1.   Maj. Samuel Breck, AGO, to USG. "I have the honor to enclose herewith the Descriptive List of Pvt. Edward H. Long, Co. G. 45th Inda. Vols. (3d Cavalry) who is at present on detached service in the Q. M. Depmt, Nashville, Tenn, and to suggest that as he has been in that position for a long period, he should be returned to his comm'd. in the field."—Copy, DNA, RG 94, Enlisted Branch, Letters Sent.

1864, FEB. 2.   Brig. Gen. Grenville M. Dodge, Pulaski, Tenn., to Brig. Gen. John A. Rawlins. "Co'l. Spencer stayed in Decatur last night under a flag of truce   Says that Roddy only knows that Johnson has fallen back and sent troops to Mobile. Roddy says Sherman is moving to take it. Roddy has moved his command to the vicinity of Decatur—Decatur only two (2) companies two Regts and a battery at mouth of Limestone"—Telegram, copies, DNA, RG 393, Military Div. of the Miss., Telegrams Received; *ibid.*, 16th Army Corps, Left Wing, Telegrams Sent. *O.R.*, I, xxxii, part 2, 313. On Feb. 4, Dodge telegraphed to Rawlins. "There are indications of some kind of a move South of the Tennessee at all the ferries and in the streams great activity in repairing and building boats is observed. Citizens have been suddenly stopped from Crossing and those retained. The report of my Scouts from every ferry south from Decatur is the same. It may be to cover a sudden departure"—Copy, DNA, RG 393, Military Div. of the Miss., Telegrams Received. *O.R.*, I, xxxii, part 2, 325. On Feb. 6, Dodge, Athens, Ala., wrote to Rawlins. "The Tennessee is rising rapidly. A regiment of mounted infantry went to Florence to-day to come up with boats. I think by to-morrow or next day boats can get over shoals. Troops are passing through Montgomery daily, going to Atlanta."—*Ibid.*, p. 339. On the same day, Dodge, Pulaski, twice telegraphed to Rawlins. "Rebel mail just brought in has letters dated Rome Ga Jan 29th   speak of movement of cavalry force to front &c; also says that all Tennesseeans have reenlisted for 30 yrs or the war &c. All speak of movement of their army and of cavalry to front. Will send few letters up tomorrow"—Copy, DNA, RG 393, 16th Army Corps, Left Wing, Telegrams Sent. *O.R.*, I, xxxii, part 2, 339. "A Scout just in from south side of river says Tenn. only guarded by small picket   Johnson regiment opposite Florence. All rest of Roddys Com'd has gone up towards Parkins Ferry to oppose force of ours said to be crossing: there   he also

says it is the common report in Roddys Camp that Johnson is now in Atlanta
that they have sent two divisions to Longstreet. this last is report among
officers soldiers & Citizens. Forrest at Okalona and his force is not represented near as strong as formerly"—Copies, DNA, RG 393, Military Div.
of the Miss., Telegrams Received; *ibid.*, 16th Army Corps, Left Wing,
Telegrams Sent. *O.R.*, I, xxxii, part 2, 339–40. On Feb. 14, Dodge telegraphed to Rawlins. "Gen'l Roddy with most of his command and part of
Davidsons Brigade have moved south toward Godsend [*Gadsden*]. the
last left day before yesterday and crossed mountains on Godsend road. Only
few men in Tuscumbia Valley—Scout in from Montgomery left the 5th
says on the fourth four Regts passed through going towards Meridian and
also says that this is all that have passed except the Division and Brigade
that went through about a month ago   he also says that the troops are
parts of three or four divisions   the last came from Atlanta   the conscription is being enforced every-where and sending to the Army good many
men   Scout was in Montgomery only five days"—Copies, DNA, RG 393,
Military Div. of the Miss., Telegrams Received; *ibid.*, 16th Army Corps,
Left Wing, Telegrams Sent. *O.R.*, I, xxxii, part 2, 391. On Feb. 16, Dodge
telegraphed to Lt. Col. Theodore S. Bowers. "R. R. is finished and in running order   Trains are safely run to this place   one of my mounted squads
while out obtaining Cattle in Lewis Co. captured the noted guerilla chief
Co'l Danc. Cooper and two of his men. He was on his way so he says to burn
Bridges on R. R."—Copies (dated Feb. 17), DNA, RG 393, Military Div.
of the Miss., Telegrams Received; *ibid.*, 16th Army Corps, Left Wing,
Telegrams Sent. *O.R.*, I, xxxii, part 2, 404. On Feb. 19, Dodge telegraphed
to Rawlins. "A considerable Cavalry force has got back into the tuscumbia
Valley   in an attempt to Cross to day were repulsed at three ferries   the
force arrived on river yesterday. We lost a few men wounded   the enemy
also lost some in wounded, prisoners and some 9 boats Skiffs & Flat-boats"—
Copies, DNA, RG 393, Military Div. of the Miss., Telegrams Received;
ibid., 16th Army Corps, Left Wing, Telegrams Sent. *O.R.*, I, xxxii, part 1,
408–9. On Feb. 20, Dodge telegraphed to Rawlins. "Lt. Co'l Phillips on
river sends following. 'I am informed by a party who crossed River yesterday that it is reported and the report credited on on other side of River that
Sherman is in Meridian that Hardee commands the Confederate forces before him and that the enemy are falling back before him moving up towards
Columbus Mississippi. I send it just as reported"—Copies (undated), DNA,
RG 393, Military Div. of the Miss., Telegrams Received; *ibid.*, 16th Army
Corps, Left Wing, Telegrams Sent.

1864, FEB. 3.   USG endorsement. "Col. Bruce rendered important service
under my command whilst his regiment was being recruited and before it
was mustered into service. Gen. Sherman is better acquainted with the
merits of Col. Bruce than I am but I can with safety endorse his recommendations knowing they are not lightly made."—Typescript, Atwood Collec-

tion, InU. Written on a letter of Jan. 26 from Maj. Gen. William T. Sherman to Secretary of War Edwin M. Stanton. "I wish to make a brief emphatic statement concerning Colonel J. D. Bruce Col. 20th Kentucky Inf. He espoused our cause early when men of his social position were nearly all against it. And at my request he cheerfully went on duty in a post of danger before his Reg. could be properly organized and equipped. I think he is an excellent soldier and a fine gentleman, and would like to see him advanced." —Typescript, *ibid*. On March 17, President Abraham Lincoln endorsed this letter. "Excellent recommendations."—Typescript, *ibid*. Col. Sanders D. Bruce, 20th Ky., received no appointment before his resignation due to ill health in the summer of 1864.

1864, FEB. 3. USG endorsement. "Respectfully forwarded to Hd Qrs. of the Army Washington, D. C. Capt. Jenkins is represented to be one of our most efficient and correct Quartermasters. If there is no charge against him of which I have not been informed I would respectfully request that he be restored to duty and ordered to repor[t] to Gen. Allen for assignment."— AES, DNA, RG 108, Letters Received. Written on a letter of the same day from Capt. Walworth Jenkins, Louisville, to Brig. Gen. Robert Allen stating that he had been relieved of duty as q. m. on Nov. 20, 1863, with no reasons given.—ALS, *ibid*. Allen added an undated endorsement. "Capt Jenkens appears to have fallen under the displeasure of the Hon Secretary of War as it was by his order that he was relieved from duty Capt Jenkens ~~appears~~ seems to be ignorant of the cause of his offence, and I have not been advised of it As Capt J. is a very competent officer, if he has not offended past pardon, I would be gratified to see him restored to duty; for we need the services of experienced and efficient Quarter Masters"—AES, *ibid*. On March 17, 1864, USG telegraphed to Secretary of War Edwin M. Stanton. "Is there any objections to placing Capt Jenkins a q m on duty His services are much needed"—Telegram received, *ibid*., RG 107, Telegrams Collected (Bound); copies, *ibid*., RG 108, Letters Sent; *ibid*., RG 393, Military Div. of the Miss., Hd. Qrs. Correspondence; DLC-USG, V, 40, 45, 59, 94. On March 18, Stanton telegraphed to USG. "The operations of Captain Jenkins at Louisville require investigation, and he should not be put on duty until they are satisfactorily overhauled. The Quarter Master General can now assign as large a force as the service requires from new appointments. ~~Let~~"—ALS (telegram sent), DNA, RG 107, Telegrams Collected (Bound). Jenkins spent the remainder of the Civil War awaiting orders.

1864, FEB. 3. Maj. Samuel Breck, AGO, to USG. "A communication from Major Wm Allen Pay master U S A at Louisville Ky, received at this Office states that men are discharged from the Volunteer service to reenlist as Veterans in the Regular Army. I am directed to inform you that such reenlistments are contrary to existing ~~Regulations and orders~~—Laws."—LS (telegram sent), DNA, RG 107, Telegrams Collected (Unbound); copies, *ibid.*, RG 94, Enlisted Branch, Letters Sent; *ibid.*, RG 393, Military Div. of the Miss., Hd. Qrs. Correspondence; DLC-USG, V, 40, 94.

1864, FEB. 3.   Maj. Thomas M. Vincent, AGO, to USG. "I have the honor to acknowledge the receipt of your endorsement of the 16th ulto, on report of Leiut Col. W. H. Thurston Asst Insp. Genl 16th Army Corps relative to the condition of the 7th Tennessee Cavalry commanded by Lieut Col. J. R. Hawkins. In reply I am directed to inform you that the same has been submitted to the General in Chief, who directs that the Regiment be consolidated to a Battalion and the supernumerary officers mustered out of the service. The selection of the officers to be retained in service will be under the control of Major General Hurlbut commanding 16th Army Corps."—Copies, DLC-USG, V, 40, 94; DNA, RG 393, Military Div. of the Miss., Hd. Qrs. Correspondence.

1864, FEB. 4.   USG endorsement. "Respectfully refered to Hd Qrs. of the Army with the request that Capt. J. P. Pope be restored to his position as C. S. and ordered to report to Gen. Hovey. Capt. Pope has served with distinction on the staff of Gen. Hovey ~~who~~ and has been recommended by him for promotion for his services."—AES, DNA, RG 94, ACP, P330 CB 1864. On Jan. 22, Capt. Joseph P. Pope wrote to Brig. Gen. Alvin P. Hovey that he had withdrawn his resignation because the "Cause (Hemmorrhoids) that induced my decision had been removed . . ."—ALS, *ibid.* Pope served through the war.

1864, FEB. 4.   To Col. Lewis B. Parsons. "One more tug will be sufficient" —Telegram received (undated), Parsons Papers, IHi; copies (dated Feb. 5), *ibid.*; (dated Feb. 4) DLC-USG, V, 34, 35; DNA, RG 393, Military Div. of the Miss., Letters Sent. On Feb. 4, Parsons, Louisville, had telegraphed to USG. "One tug is already down the river two more are in St Louis   do you desire more than one of them sent to Col Bingham   if not necessary one of them is now used & desired in St Louis to protect boats from fire"—Telegram received, *ibid.*, Dept. of the Tenn., Telegrams Received; copy, *ibid.*, Military Div. of the Miss., Telegrams Received.

1864, FEB. 4.   Brig. Gen. Montgomery C. Meigs to USG. "I enclose a copy of a law of congress providing for a medal—for officers & soldiers   Some have been given to the navy—but I have heard of no general distribution to the army—Is it not worth while to move in the matter by naming some of the officers & men who have passed through important battles as worthy of the medal—It would be highly prised by every officer & man fortunate enough to be thought worthy of wearing it—"—ALS, DNA, RG 393, Military Div. of the Miss., Letters Received. Meigs enclosed an extract from a law of March 3, 1863, which provided that the Congressional Medal of Honor could be awarded to officers as well as enlisted men.—Copy, *ibid.*

1864, FEB. 4. Col. Edward D. Townsend, AGO, to USG requesting him to send recruiting details from Conn., N. J., and Pa. regts.—LS, DNA, RG 393, Military Div. of the Miss., Letters Received.

1864, FEB. 5. To Col. William Hoffman, commissary gen. of prisoners. "I have the honor to acknowledge the receipt of your communication of date January 20th in relation to the appointment of a Provost Marshal at Louisville Ky, to take charge of Prisoners of War at that place, and in reply to respectfully inform you that I have appointed Captain S. E. Jones, A A d C. to that position"—LS, DNA, RG 249, Letters Received. On Jan. 28, Hoffman had written to USG. "I have the honor to request that a suitable officer may be detailed as Prov Marshal at Louisville to have charge of the prisoners of War held in that city. Capt S. E. Jones, A. A. D. C. temporarily on the staff of Brig Gen'l Boyle has been performing the duty for some months past, and the General recommends that he be assigned to the position permanently. He has performed the duties very satisfactorily and I will be pleased if he can be continued in the office. But any efficient reliable officer that you may see proper to detail for the place will be acceptable to me. The duties require close attention, energy and integrity on the part of the officer detailed."—LS, *ibid.*, RG 109, Unfiled Papers and Slips, Jones, Stephen E.

1864, FEB. 5. Col. Edward D. Townsend, AGO, to USG. "The Secretary of War directs that in accordance with the recommendation of the Acting Surgeon General, General Orders No 77, Head Quarters Dept of the Cumberland April 11th 1863, prescribing regulations for conducting a Hospital, remain in force, with the following addition thereto. 'Whenever an officer leaves the Hospital from any cause, either by resignation, or leave of absence, or to rejoin his regiment, the Surgeon in charge will immediately send to the Cheif Paymaster, and the Commanding officer of the regiment, to which the officer belongs, a statement of his indebtedness to the Hospital.' "—Copies, DNA, RG 94, Letters Sent; *ibid.*, RG 393, Military Div. of the Miss., Letters Received.

1864, FEB. 5. Maj. Thomas M. Vincent, AGO, to USG. "The General in Chief directs that the three companies of the 10th Maine Volunteers, now serving in the 12th Army Corps, which companies have been assigned to the 29th Maine Volunteers, be ordered to New Orleans, there to join that Regiment upon its arrival in the Department of the Gulf. The companies are to be sent whenever in your opinion the exigencies of the service will permit   The 29th Maine Volunteers was reported to have left the state on the 31st ultimo."—LS, DNA, RG 393, Military Div. of the Miss., Letters Received.

1864, FEB. 5. Maj. Robert Williams, AGO, to USG. "The Secretary of War authorizes regular recruiting officers to be instructed to enlist men for 3 three years under the joint resolution of January 13th 1864, Gen Order

No 20 1864, you will at once instruct the officers under your command"—
Copies, DLC-USG, V, 40, 94; DNA, RG 393, Military Div. of the Miss.,
Hd. Qrs. Correspondence. This telegram was sent to many other officers.—
DfS, *ibid.*, RG 107, Telegrams Collected (Unbound).

1864, FEB. 6. USG endorsement. "Approved and respectfully forwarded
to Hd Qrs of the Army, Washington D C"—ES, DNA, RG 94, ACP, O158
1864. Written on a letter of Jan. 14 from Maj. Gen. Oliver O. Howard to
Secretary of War Edwin M. Stanton recommending Maj. Thomas W. Osborn, 1st N. Y. Light Art., and chief of art., 11th Army Corps, for command of a brigade of colored troops.—LS, *ibid.* No appointment followed.
After the war, Howard wrote to USG and to Stanton urging that Osborn be
appointed bvt. brig. gen., again without success.—*Ibid.*

1864, FEB. 6, 1:30 P.M. To Brig. Gen. James H. Wilson, Cav. Bureau,
Washington, D. C. "Send all the cavalry horses for my command to Nashville   Full twelve thousand (12000) horses will be required here"—Telegram received, DNA, RG 107, Telegrams Collected (Bound); copies, *ibid.*,
RG 393, Military Div. of the Miss., Hd. Qrs. Correspondence; DLC-USG,
V, 40, 94. *O.R.*, I, xxxii, part 2, 337. On Feb. 5, 2:50 P.M., Wilson had
telegraphed to USG. "Contracts have been awarded at Indianapolis St.
Louis, Chicago & Columbus for eleven thousand five hundred 11500 Cavalry horses, mostly for the use of your cavalry—Shall I have them forwarded
as they come in—If so to what points and in what number. Please answer"—
ALS (telegram sent), DNA, RG 107, Telegrams Collected (Unbound);
copies, *ibid.*, RG 393, Military Div. of the Miss., Hd. Qrs. Correspondence;
DLC-USG, V, 40, 94. *O.R.*, I, xxxii, part 2, 330. On Feb. 8, Maj. Gen.
Henry W. Halleck telegraphed to USG. "Genl Banks is urgent to have more
cavalry. There are several regiments nearly organized in Minn. and other
northern states which can be sent to him by the Miss. river, unless you ab-
solutely need them. The Qr Mr Genl reports that it will be difficult to supply horses & forage to any additional cavalry in Tennessee, and that ocean
transports cannot be obtained to send much cavalry from the north to New
Orleans. Please answer."—ALS (telegram sent), DNA, RG 107, Telegrams
Collected (Bound); copies, *ibid.*, RG 393, Military Div. of the Miss., Hd.
Qrs. Correspondence; DLC-USG, V, 40, 94; DLC-Andrew Johnson. *O.R.*,
I, xxxiv, part 2, 269. On the same day, 5:30 P.M., USG telegraphed to Hal-
leck. "Let Genl Banks have the Cavalry now ready for the field   That be-
longing [to this Mil. Div.] if filled up will be quite as much as can be fed"—
Telegram received, DNA, RG 107, Telegrams Collected (Bound); copies,
ibid., Telegrams Received in Cipher; *ibid.*, RG 393, Military Div. of the
Miss., Hd. Qrs. Correspondence; DLC-USG, V, 40, 94; DLC-Andrew
Johnson. *O.R.*, I, xxxiv, part 2, 269.

1864, FEB. 6. To Maj. Gen. John M. Schofield. "Let the 2nd Michigan
Infantry reenlisted Volunteers, take their furlough."—Telegram, copies,

DLC-USG, V, 34, 35; DNA, RG 393, Military Div. of the Miss., Letters Sent.

1864, FEB. 6.   To Brig. Gen. Robert S. Granger. "Respectfully returned. General Granger has no right to assume the official acts of Lieut Col. Bowers to be other than my own. Although absent from Nashville at the date of the endorsement complained of, the command of this Military Division was not relinquished for a day by me, and during this absence some very important orders, involving great responsibility were published over the signature of Lt Col Bowers A. A. G. These orders were dictated by me over the telegraph wires   Until I deny the official act of my Asst. Adj't. General Gen. Granger cannot hold him responsible."—Copies, DLC-USG, V, 39; DNA, RG 393, Military Div. of the Miss., Endorsements. Granger's letter has not been found, but other documents concerning the matter are *ibid.*, RG 109, Union Provost Marshals' File of Papers Relating to Individual Civilians, Henry Sanfield.

1864, FEB. 6.   Col. Edward D. Townsend, AGO, to USG. "I have the honor to inform you that 1000 copies of the 'Proclamation' by the President, dated December 8 1863, have been sent to your address. In a few days instructions will be given you as to how they are to be used. Meantime please retain them in your possession."—Copies, DLC-USG, V, 40, 94; DNA, RG 393, Military Div. of the Miss., Hd. Qrs. Correspondence.

1864, FEB. 8.   Maj. Gen. George H. Thomas, Chattanooga, to USG. "Have received Capt. Chenoweith's communication. His explanation satisfactory."—Telegram, copy, DNA, RG 393, Dept. of the Cumberland, Telegrams Sent.

1864, FEB. 8.   Brig. Gen. Alfred T. A. Torbert to USG. "Enclosed please find a copy of instructions for reviews &c which I send for your inspection that you may give me your views on the subject. They have been approved and recommended for adoption by the Corps Commanders of this Army."—ALS, USG 3.

1864, FEB. 9.   USG endorsement. "Respectfully forwarded to Head Quarters of the Army with the recommendation that the detail be made"—Copies, DLC-USG, V, 39; DNA, RG 393, Military Div. of the Miss., Endorsements. Written on a letter of Jan. 22 of Governor Thomas Carney of Kan. asking the detail of Private Alfred Capper, 8th Kan.—*Ibid.* On Feb. 19, Maj. Samuel Breck, AGO, wrote to USG. "I have the honor to acknowledge the receipt of a communication of the 22nd ult from His Excellency, Thomas Carney, Governor of Kansas, and by you forwarded to this Office requesting that Private Alfred Capper, Company "A" 8th Kansas Volunteer Infantry, may be detailed and ordered to report to the Adjutant Genl. of Kansas for duty as clerk, and to inform you, that the interests of the service will not admit of the request being granted."—Copies, *ibid.*, RG 94, Enlisted Branch, Letters Sent; *ibid.*, RG 393, Military Div. of the Miss., War Dept. Correspondence.

1864, FEB. 11. To Brig. Gen. Stephen G. Burbridge. "The 26th Kentucky is an Infantry regiment and all men going into it must understand they are liable for duty wherever ordered as infantry. It is probable they will be mounted, but the right to be, they must not claim or expect."—Telegram, copies, DLC-USG, V, 34, 35; DNA, RG 393, Military Div. of the Miss., Letters Sent. On the same day, Burbridge, Louisville, had telegraphed to USG. "Twenty sixth 26 Kentucky the Regt. mentioned by Dr. Bailey and myself when here has returned—Will it be remounted and kept in Southern Kentucky. Information important in recruiting"—Copy, *ibid.*, Telegrams Received.

1864, FEB. 11. Maj. Samuel Breck, AGO, to USG. "I have the honor to inform you, that the appointment of 2nd Lieut George Harrington 3rd U S Cavalry, as Asst Commissary of Musters of 3rd Division 15th Army Corps, formerly 2nd Division 17th A. C.—Vice—Captain N. W. Osborne, 13th U. S. Infantry relieved, is approved by this Office, and the pay Master General has been notified   The appointment will date February 9th 1864."— Copies, DNA, RG 94, Enlisted Branch, Letters Sent; *ibid.*, RG 393, Military Div. of the Miss., War Dept. Correspondence.

1864, FEB. 12. Brig. Gen. James H. Wilson to USG. "Will you be good enough to direct Genl. W. F. Smith to select a half dozen honest and capable Cavalry officers for horse inspectors and direct them to repair to Louisville as soon as possible and report to me by telegraph for orders. I will have proper orders issued here as soon as their names are recd."—ALS (telegram sent), DNA, RG 107, Telegrams Collected (Unbound); copies (garbled), *ibid.*, RG 393, Military Div. of the Miss., Hd. Qrs. Correspondence; DLC-USG, V, 40, 94.

1864, FEB. 13. Dr. Charles A. Pope, St. Louis, to USG. "My brother & sister-in-law, Mr. & Mrs. Dox have determined to avail themselves of the pass-port you kindly gave them, and expect to leave us for Huntsville in a few days. They are both most loyal, being devoted Unionists, but this has not saved their property, which, (consisting as it did, mainly of slaves) has nearly all been lost under the influence of the President's proclamations and other causes connected with this War. It seems hard that such loyal people should suffer in this way, and I am sure you will do what lies in your power to aid Mr. Dox in some way in making good his losses. He thinks if he had permission to buy Cotton that he might do something to make up for what he has lost. If it be possible therefore for you to help Mr. Dox, by giving him a permit to buy Cotton—should he apply for one—or in any other way, we will all acknowledge any kindness you may show to him as a great personal favor. Of one thing we feel certain, and that is, that any thing done for Mr. Dox calculated to add to his influance will be advantageous to the Union cause."—ALS, USG 3. See John Y. Simon, ed., *The Personal Memoirs of Julia Dent Grant* (New York, 1975), pp. 124, 143n.

1864, FEB. 14. To Brig. Gen. Robert Allen. "Ship at Government expense all Sanitary Stores delivered to the Quartermaster at Louisville consigned to United States, Western or Indiana State Sanitary Commission"—Telegram, copies, DLC-USG, V, 34, 35; DNA, RG 393, Military Div. of the Miss., Letters Sent.

1864, FEB. 14. Brig. Gen. Morgan L. Smith, Larkinsville, Ala., to USG. "The following is a copy of dispatch captured on Sand mountain last night. Head Quarters Rome Ga. Feby. tenth 1864. To Lt. J. W. COLLIER Com'dg Scouts   Your dispatch by courier reached me this morning and was quite satisfactory. I hope Enquiries to the river without delay so that no doubt may exist of the enemys position about Larkins Landing. When that is satisfactorily done if no enemy is found on this side of the Tennessee you can report to me with your detachment   should you find the enemy still on this side of the river observe his movements narrowly and report them by Courier   I am Lieut. Most Respy Your Obt. Servant   Singed JNO. G. BROWN—Brig Gen."—Copy, DNA, RG 393, Military Div. of the Miss., Telegrams Received.

1864, FEB. 15. USG endorsement. "Respectfully forwarded to the General-in-Chief of the Army, Washington D. C. for his information"—ES, DNA, RG 108, Letters Received, 24 O 1864. Written on statements of C.S.A. deserters, one from the 6th Ga. describing in detail the defenses of Charleston, S. C., and two from the 43rd Ga. briefly discussing movements south of Chattanooga.—Copies, *ibid.*

1864, FEB. 15, 4:00 P.M. Maj. Gen. Henry W. Halleck to USG. "The Secty of War directs that, if you have under your command any persons under sentence of death for desertion only, you will report their cases to the War Dept, and suspend the execution till further orders."—ALS (telegram sent), DNA, RG 107, Telegrams Collected (Bound); copies, *ibid.*, RG 94, Letters Received, 102A 1864; *ibid.*, RG 393, Military Div. of the Miss., Hd. Qrs. Correspondence; DLC-USG, V, 40, 94. *O.R.*, I, xxxii, part 2, 395. A copy of this telegram was sent to Maj. Gen. Benjamin F. Butler, Fort Monroe, Va.

1864, FEB. 15. Bvt. Lt. Col. James L. Donaldson, Nashville, to USG. "I have the honor to enclose for your information, a copy of a telegram I have this day received from Lt Comdg. Glassiford of Naval Gun Boats convoy to Burnsides Point."—ALS, DNA, RG 393, Military Div. of the Miss., Letters Received. On Feb. 14, Lt. Henry A. Glassford, Camp Burnside, Tenn., telegraphed to Donaldson. "all here, but about four hundred (400) tons freight, and that is coming up fast. as possible. Had to lighten at Carthage & on every bar thence to this point. Road hence to Knoxville reported almost impassable. supplies must go by Pack Mules. Navigation from Carthage to this post is extremely uncertain & difficult, when at the best, and I respectfully recommend a consideration of the route, before the steamers now coming from cincinnati are ordered forward to this place. saw Briggs yesterday & will probably convoy about twenty (20) barges of his coal to Nashville. Every thing depends upon the River, which must rise here twelve (12) feet to let them over the shoals above."—Copy, *ibid.*

1864, FEB. 15.   Governor Oliver P. Morton of Ind. to USG. "The furlough of the 38th Indiana has expired, and return to the field. I desire that Col. Scribner remain here on recruiting service till 1st March, together with such officers as he may select   He can do more at recruiting than any one else"—Copies, DNA, RG 393, Military Div. of the Miss., Telegrams Received; Morton Papers, In.

1864, FEB. 16.   To Rear Admiral David D. Porter, Mound City, Ill. "The following dispatch is just received from Gen Dodge: 'Pulaski February 16th 64   Gen JOHN A RAWLINS, Chief of Staff. There is a Steamboat running on Tennessee river trading in Cotton, paying, Salt, Sugar, Coffee and gold. It runs to Eastport and Waterloo. On the boat is a relative of Gen Roddy and the boat has his protection. The points it runs to, are all in rebel lines. G M DODGE Brig Genl' "—Telegram, copies, DLC-USG, V, 34, 35; DNA, RG 393, Military Div. of the Miss., Letters Sent. *O.R.* (Navy), I, xxv, 761. See *ibid.*, pp. 765–66. Brig. Gen. Grenville M. Dodge's telegram is in *O.R.*, I, xxxii, part 2, 405.

1864, FEB. 17.   USG endorsement. "Respectfully forwarded to Head Quarters of the Army Washington D. C. and special attention invited to the statements in relation to Camp Douglas."—Copies, DLC-USG, V, 39; DNA, RG 393, Military Div. of the Miss., Endorsements. *O.R.*, II, vi, 851. Surgeon Edward D. Kittoe's report of the unhealthy state of Camp Douglas, Chicago, is *ibid.*, pp. 848–51.

1864, FEB. 17.   To Governor Oliver P. Morton of Ind. "Col. Spooner will be detailed as you desire"—Copy, Morton Papers, In. On the same day, Morton had telegraphed to USG. "I desire that Col Spooner of Eighty third (83d) Ind Vols be detailed on recruiting service till tenth of March"—Telegram received, DNA, RG 94, Compiled Service Records, Benjamin J. Spooner; copy, Morton Papers, In. On the same day, Capt. Ely S. Parker telegraphed to Maj. Roswell M. Sawyer, adjt. for Maj. Gen. William T. Sherman. "You will please detail Col Spooner 83d Ind Vols on recruiting service until 10th of March   Let him report to Gov Morton"—Telegram received, DNA, RG 94, Compiled Service Records, Benjamin J. Spooner; copies (entered as signed by USG), *ibid.*, RG 393, Military Div. of the Miss., Letters Sent; DLC-USG, V, 34, 35.

1864, FEB. 17. Lt. Col. James A. Hardie, AGO, to USG. "By direction of the Secretary of War, I have the honor to transmit herewith a copy of the Additional Regulations of the Treasury Department for trade with States declared in insurrection, dated January 26. 1864, also a Copy of an Additional Regulation dated February 2d 1864"—LS, DNA, RG 393, Military Div. of the Miss., Letters Received.

1864, FEB. 17. Col. Daniel C. McCallum, gen. manager, military railroads, Nashville, to USG. "When the track of the Nashville and Chattanooga Railroad is relaid, we will have on hand Three hundred and two (302) miles of old rails, weighing eleven thousand eight hundred and sixty four (11864) gross tons. At present rates new rails delivered at Chattanooga will cost one hundred and forty five (145) dollars per ton.—There is at Chattanooga a Rolling Mill, partially built by the Rebels, which if completed, say at a cost of Thirty thousand (30.000) dollars, these old rails can be rerolled at a cost of about Fifty (50) dollars per ton coal being contigous, and abundent.—This would not only be a large saving to the Government, but what in my opinion is of greater importance, the rails would be on hand ready for use when, and where required. The following figures represents the case   11864 Tons of new Rails delivered at Chattanooga at $145.00 per ton 1.719.250   11864 Tons of old rails rerolled at a cost of $50.00 per ton   593.200   Cost of Mill estimated at 30.000   623.200   In favor of Rolling Mill 1.096.80   By advices recently received the stock of Railroad iron in the market is small and demands large. In fact should an emergency arise requiring a large amount of iron, it is doubtful whether it could be had at any price. I therefore respectfully ask, unless military reasons forbid, your permission to complete the Rolling Mill at Chattanooga."—LS, DNA, RG 393, Military Div. of the Miss., Letters Received. On the same day, USG endorsed this letter. "Make Spl. order for Col. McCallum to proceed at once to complete and set at work Rolling mill at Chattanooga."— AE, *ibid.* See *O.R.*, I, lii, part 1, 521. See also *ibid.*, I, xxxii, part 2, 420–21.

1864, FEB. 17. J. B. Anders, sutler, 55th Ill., Louisville, to USG. "Will you allow chaplain Haneys Wife of fifty fifth Illinois Regt. & my wife to pass to Nashville, and I will report to your Head Quarters on arrival   Answer to night."—Telegram, copy, DNA, RG 393, Military Div. of the Miss., Telegrams Received.

1864, FEB. 18. USG endorsement. "Respectfully forwarded to Headquarters of the Army, Washington D C."—ES, DNA, RG 94, ACP, F540 CB 1864. Written on a letter of Jan. 20 from Brig. Gen. Marcellus M. Crocker,

Hebron, Miss., to Secretary of War Edwin M. Stanton recommending Lt. Col. Cassius Fairchild, 16th Wis., for appointment as brig. gen.—LS, *ibid.* No appointment followed.

1864, FEB. 18.   To Maj. Gen. Henry W. Halleck. "Cannot Cavalry arms and equipments be sent to Ordnance officer here to be drawn as required   This course would save much time in fitting recruits for the field" —Telegram received, DNA, RG 107, Telegrams Collected (Bound); copies, *ibid.*, RG 393, Military Div. of the Miss., Hd. Qrs. Correspondence; DLC-USG, V, 40, 94. On Feb. 24, 12:55 P.M., Halleck telegraphed to USG. "The chief of ordnance reports that 5,300 carbines & accoutrements, 2,000 extra sets of accoutrements, and 5,000 sets of horse equipments have been sent to Nashville since January 18th, in addition to more than 3,000 sets then on hand there. No more can be spared at present without interfering with the arming of the new regiments now being organized."—ALS (telegram sent), DNA, RG 107, Telegrams Collected (Bound); copies, *ibid.*, RG 393, Military Div. of the Miss., Hd. Qrs. Correspondence; DLC-USG, V, 40, 94. *O.R.*, I, xxxii, part 2, 456.

1864, FEB. 18.   Brig. Gen. Hugh T. Reid, Cairo, to USG. "The late Treasury order removes all restrictions from trade in Kentucky and Missouri, and goods going from Cairo, Paducah, and Hickman, will undoubtedly reach Tennessee if unrestricted, as I have not sufficent force to guard the whole Border,   What shall I do about it."—Telegram, copies, DNA, RG 393, District of Columbus, Telegrams Sent; *ibid.*, Military Div. of the Miss., Telegrams Received. *O.R.*, I, xxxii, part 2, 427. On Feb. 23, Lt. Col. Theodore S. Bowers telegraphed to Reid. "Make such Disposition of your forces as to guard & protect the river   give yourself no trouble concerning goods going into Kentucky   Treasury agents will be held responsible for the quantity that goes"—Telegram received, DNA, RG 94, War Records Office, Remount Station; copies, *ibid.*, RG 393, Military Div. of the Miss., Letters Sent; DLC-USG, V, 34, 35. *O.R.*, I, xxxii, part 2, 453.

1864, FEB. 18.   Col. Daniel C. McCallum, Nashville, to USG. "I learn from Mr W. J. Stevens that the Memphis & Little Rock Railroad is now operated by Capt. Carr A. Q. M. This road is five, and a half (5½) feet guage, and I understand Capt Carr has made a requisition upon Col Myers Q. M St. Louis for Rolling stock to operate the same.—I would respectfully suggest that the gauge be altered to five (5) feet by moving one (1) rail, and thus preserve uniformity of track south of this point.—If necessary a portion of the Rolling stock now at Memphis, can be transferred to the line referred to. I would be glad to be informed whether it is essential that this line should be operated at present, and whether it is your wish that, that portion of the line in the middle, still unfinished, should be completed. I am informed that there is at Grand junction Memphis & Charleston Railroad some machinery, left by the Rebels, and intended to be forwarded to Chattanooga Rolling Mill.—I respectfully ask permission to remove, and use the same."—LS, DNA, RG 92, Military Railroads, Nashville, Letters Sent by McCallum (Press). On Feb. 19, Lt. Col. Theodore S. Bowers wrote to Mc-Callum. "You have permission to use any machinery from the Memphis and Charleston Railroad that you may require."—Copies, DLC-USG, V, 34, 35; DNA, RG 393, Military Div. of the Miss., Letters Sent.

1864, FEB. 19. To Maj. Gen. John A. Logan. "Dismount the 3rd U. S. Cavalry, and order them to St Louis to recruit. The horses may be turned over to any cavalry troops requiring them."—Telegram, copies, DLC-USG, V, 34, 35; DNA, RG 393, Military Div. of the Miss., Letters Sent. On the same day, noon, Brig. Gen. James H. Wilson had telegraphed to USG. "The Third (3d). U. S. Cavalry has been ordered to be dismounted and sent without delay to recruit and act as a nucleus of organization and instruction to the Cavalry Depot at St Louis. Will you be good enough to send it as soon as possible, as it is very much needed there"—LS (telegram sent), *ibid.*, RG 107, Telegrams Collected (Unbound); telegram received, *ibid.*, RG 393, Dept. of the Tenn., Telegrams Received.

1864, FEB. 19. USG endorsement. "Lieut Coln. Ducat—leaves the service in consequence of ill health alone—His services have been valuable and fully appreciated by all those under whom he has served, as is shown by the fact that he rose from the position of 1st Lieut & Adjt of his regiment to Lt Col of it, and finally Asst: Inspector Genl: of the Department of the Cumberland"—Copy, Records of 12th Ill., I-ar. Written on a copy of Special Orders No. 45 discharging Lt. Col. Arthur C. Ducat, 12th Ill.—Copy, *ibid.*

1864, FEB. 19. To Governor Oliver P. Morton of Ind. "Lieut. P. F. Wiggins, 36th Indiana Vols., has permission to remain"—Copy, Morton Papers, In. On Feb. 18, Morton had telegraphed to USG. "Please authorize Lieut P. F. Wiggins Quarter Master 36th Ind. to remain a few days. His wife is very low and cannot survive long."—Copies, *ibid.*; DNA, RG 393, Military Div. of the Miss., Telegrams Received.

1864, FEB. 19. Brig. Gen. Edward R. S. Canby, War Dept., to USG. "The Secretary of War directs me to transmit to you, herewith enclosed a copy of the Quartermaster General's remarks, upon a communication of Major General Thomas, relating to the condition of the Nashville and Chattanooga rail road, and to rail road matters in his Department in general. So much of these remarks as relates to the Superintendence and management of the rail roads by Colonel McCullum has been approved by the Secretary, but the propriety of employing soldiers upon the roads, to a greater extent than heretofore, or the necessity for an impressment of white and colored persons for that purpose, are matters which must be left to your own judgment and discretion, and, in a great measure, be governed by transpiring events."—Copy, DNA, RG 107, Letters Sent, Military Affairs. A slightly different version of the same letter is dated Feb. 20.—Copy, *ibid. O.R.*, I, xxxii, part 2, 436–37. The lengthy report of Brig. Gen. Montgomery C. Meigs is *ibid.*, pp. 437–39. On Feb. 26, 10:45 A.M., Secretary of War Edwin M. Stanton telegraphed to USG. "The Superintendant and General Manager of Military Rail Roads in the Departments under your command is hereby authorized 'to make such additions to ordinery rations to his employees when actually at work as he may deem necessary' provided that such additions be first approved by you, and notice thereof given to this Department"—ALS (telegram sent), DNA, RG 107, Telegrams Collected (Bound); copies, *ibid.*, RG 393, Military Div. of the Miss., Hd. Qrs. Correspondence; DLC-USG, V, 40, 94.

1864, FEB. 19. Brig. Gen. Robert Allen to USG. "I have the honor to enclose herewith, a copy of a letter from the Quarter Master Genl. together with a statement of the means of transportation, Cavalry and Artillery horses at the principal depots within our reach. After examining this statement, will you please favor me with your views as to the expediency or necessity of increasing the present supply, and to what extent and in what items. There is a wide difference between Gen. Meigs' estimates, and those of the Quarter Masters in the field, and this difference can only be reconciled by your order. I refer more particularly to the number of wagons, mules and Cavalry horses. It is understood that the Cavalry Bureau has out large contracts for horses. Artillery horses will be purchased at St. Louis, Indianapolis, Chicago and Columbus Ohio."—LS, DNA, RG 393, Military Div. of the Miss., Letters Received.

1864, FEB. 19. Abram Houghtaling, Washington, D. C., to USG. "I beg leave to ask your action upon the petition herewith enclosed, and earnestly hope that it may accord with your views of public duty to grant it   Any communication by mail will reach me at 38 Front Row Memphis"—ALS, DNA, RG 109, Union Provost Marshals' File of Papers Relating to Individual Civilians. Houghtaling enclosed a letter of Feb. 17 from T. Lyle Dickey to USG. "I find my old friend A. Houghtaling here & trying to get from the Secretary of War—a permit to do all the ferrying from Memphis to the Arkansas Shore opposite—The Sec. of War, I am informed refers him to Gen. Grant—& I take the liberty of writing you on the Subject—I doubt not much smuggling of contraband goods & passing of improper persons has been practised at that point & it occurs to me that if the whole ferry business at that point was in the hands & control of one intelligent, honest, reliable & truly loyal man that *most* of *that evil* would be prevented—Such a man is Mr Houghtaling—I have known him for years—He was Sutler to my old regiment & I *never* heard of a single instance in which either officer or soldiers ever suspected—that Houghtaling had in any respect dealt unfairly or oppressively with him—I don't know a better man for the proposed position   Mr Houghtaling has had some hard luck withal—& on that ground

—(where it can be done without injury to the service)—ought to be cared for   In May last (3rd day) he was going down the Mississippi river—on Steamer Minnesota—with over thirteen thousand dollars worth of goods—under a permit from you—for the use of the Army—when the boat & cargo & passengers were captured at Greenville by the rebels & thereby he lost his goods—& some two thousand dollars money & notes & was personally made a prisoner & taken to Vicksburg & thence through Dixie to Richmond & did not get out of Libby prison until the 3rd day of July—I hope you may find it consistent with right to allow Mr Houghtalings request—& you know I would not wish you to do so unless you did think it right & I know Houghtaling would not ask it on any other hypothesis   Accept the expression of my warmest regards & believe me ever your sincere friend . . .P. S. It occurred to me at first that such a permit might more appropriately come from the Commandant of the Post at Memphis—but when it is considered that *that officer* in the ordinary course is likely to be occasionally changed—& when it is remembered that to do the ferrying properly will require a pretty large investment in property, the value of which would in a great measure depend upon permit—it seems plain to me that to give the necessary stability to the interprise—it would be more appropriate that the permit should come from your Head Quarters—& that the business should be regulated by the Post Commander—subject to the General orders—"—ALS, *ibid.* Also enclosed was a petition of Feb. 18 to USG favoring Houghtaling, signed by ten congressmen from Ill. and one from Mo.—DS, *ibid.*

1864, FEB. 19.   A. N. Read, inspector, U.S. Sanitary Commission, Nashville, to USG. "I would respectfuly ask of you an order authoriseing the issueing of forage for horses used by the agents of the U. S. Sanitary Commission while engaged in their Official business in your Command   Such an order would by save us much trouble and aid us vastly in our work"—ALS, DNA, RG 393, Military Div. of the Miss., Letters Received.

1864, FEB. 20.   To commanding officer, Louisville. "Is there a british consul in Louisville   answer"—Telegram received, DNA, RG 393, Military Installations, Louisville, Telegrams Received. On the same day, Col. Sanders D. Bruce, Louisville, telegraphed to USG. "There is no British Consul in this City"—Copy, *ibid.*, Military Div. of the Miss., Telegrams Received.

1864, FEB. 20.   To Governor Oliver P. Morton of Ind. "Chaplain Lakin is authorized to remain absent until tenth (10th) of March"—Telegram, copy, Morton Papers, In. On Feb. 19, Morton had telegraphed to USG. "Chaplain A. S. Lakin, 39th Ind. Vols., is doing much recruiting service, please authorize him to remain until 10th of March   I ask this specially"—Copy, *ibid.* On March 7, Morton telegraphed to USG. "I respectfully request that the leave of Chaplain A. S. Lakin, 39th Ind. Vols. be extended to April 1st" —Copy, *ibid.*

1864, FEB. 20.   Col. Lewis B. Parsons, Louisville, to USG. "The two boats purchased by order of Genl. Meigs to go above Muscle Shoals are lying at Paducah with gunboat as convoy, all ready and waiting a rise in the river, to start up. They are boats well adapted for the Cumberland, and would now be very useful there in taking Forage from Cairo. I should have put them into this service except for the fear that if a rise came they might be at Nashville and would not be ready to start up in time to take advantage of a rise in the river. If you think these boats may not be demanded on the Upper Tennessee, or that it would be prudent to put them into service on the Cumberland, I shall be very glad to do so and will start them as soon as I get dispatch from you authorizing it. We are loading a fleet of Canal boats and barges at Saint Louis for Nashville, which will come out as soon as Ice admits and continue in that service. You are aware I believe that that over forty (40) boats have been loaded with Forage and C. S. and have gone to Genl. Banks."—LS, DNA, RG 393, Military Div. of the Miss., Letters Received.

1864, FEB. 21.   To Col. Edward D. Townsend, AGO. "It is reported in the newspapers that Col. Wager Swayne forty third (43) Ohio Regt. has been dismissed the service by order of War Dept. Please inform me if such is the fact and for what Cause?"—Telegram received, DNA, RG 107, Telegrams Collected (Bound). On Feb. 22, Townsend telegraphed to USG. "Colonel J. B. Swain New-York Volunteers is the officer dismissed"—Copies, DLC-USG, V, 40, 94; DNA, RG 107, Telegrams Collected (Unbound); *ibid.*, RG 393, Military Div. of the Miss., Hd. Qrs. Correspondence.

1864, FEB. 22.   Brig. Gen. Montgomery C. Meigs to USG. "Please order steps to be taken by the commander at Vicksburg to protect any persons sent by Gen Allen to raise & save the machinery of the steamers sunk by the rebels in the Yazoo River & give to Gen Allen orders to make the necessary arrangements for the purpose."—ALS, DNA, RG 393, Military Div. of the Miss., Letters Received.

1864, FEB. 22.   Maj. Thomas M. Vincent, AGO, to USG. "I have the honor to enclose herewith a report of Captain L. E. Yorke 17th U. S. Infantry Commissary of Musters 15th Army Corps giving lists of various regiments in which the names of commissioned officers have been taken up in grades into which they have not been musters: this is in violation of General Orders No. 48 series of 1863 from the War Department. The pay of the Commanding Officers of the regiments and companies has been stopped until further orders. Upon receipt hereof, I am directed to instruct you to summon the officers concerned before Boards or Commissions which you will please cause to be"—Copy, DNA, RG 393, Military Div. of the Miss., War Dept. Correspondence.

1864, FEB. 23.   Maj. Gen. William S. Rosecrans endorsement. "Respectfully referred to Maj Genl Grant, Thomas and such other officers as it may be presented to   Col. Donephans—standing is such that I consider his recommendation ample voucher for the loyalty of Mr. Hugh J. Robertson of Clay Co. Mo. who wishes to go to our front to see if he can get his brother brought home"—Copy, DLC-USG, V, 102. Written on a letter of Tenn. Senator John Doniphan introducing "Hugh J. Robertson of Clay Co. Mo.— states that he is a Loyal and desires to go to Maury Co. Ala. to get his brother —who has been in the rebel army—but now is very low with consumption, requests that Mr. R., be permitted to go, if consistant with regulations"— *Ibid.* On Feb. 27, Maj. William R. Rowley, provost marshal, endorsed this letter. "Disapproved. such permits cannot be granted—"—Copy, *ibid.*

1864, FEB. 23.   Brig. Gen. Grenville M. Dodge, Pulaski, Tenn., to Brig. Gen. John A. Rawlins. "A Negro that left Dalton a week ago reported to our picket on Tenn. River   says that Hindmans Div. was going to Miss and that one the Miss. Div's was to come to Dalton, that Bragg was to command in Miss. and he wanted part of his old Army"—Telegram, copy, DNA, RG 393, Military Div. of the Miss., Telegrams Received. On the same day, Dodge telegraphed to Rawlins. "One of my Scouts arrived at Larkinsville, Ala. to day just from Atlanta and Rome. Telegraphs that he found Roddy at Godsend with Twenty five hundred men. Gen'l L. C. Brown at Rome fortifying extensively and has five thousand men—Atlanta was fortified and has three thousand men—Gen'l Brown went to Rome Feby. 1st from Dalton —Wheeler is is releived   Buckner takes command and is making extensive preperations for raid to Kentucky. Gen'l Grigsby is at Blue Mountain— Hume is between Rome & Dalton—Scouts bring dispatches from scout at Montgomery.   well send as soon as he arrives"—Copy, *ibid.*; *ibid.*, 16th Army Corps, Left Wing, Telegrams Sent. On Feb. 25, Dodge telegraphed to Rawlins. "Dispatch from Scout at Montgomery dated 19th says Sherman has reached Mobile and Ohio R. R. that Polk has evacuated that part of his force is North and part South of Sherman that bulk of it has gone towards Mobile and fallen back behind Tombigbee River that great consternation exists in all the town that all troops from there has been sent to Polk leaving only Provost guard at Montgomery, Selma and Tuscumbia that no troops have gone from Johnsons Army, last report but that everything that can be raked together is being hurried to Mobile and to Polk that our Iron Clads have attacked forts at Mobile   says rebels have no idea of Shermans destination that he is destroying everything and Negroes Mules and Citizens are flocking east. he sent a messenger through to Sherman. No battle up to that date had occurred"—Copies, *ibid. O.R.*, I, xxxii, part 2, 467. On Feb. 26, Dodge wrote to Rawlins. "I send some of the minor details from the report of Scouts sent to Atlanta and Rome, Ga., and Montgomery, Alabama.—The scout is one of our best men and very inteligent. The fortifications around Atlanta are simply three lines of Rifle pits; Surrounding the place; and on the Chattahootchie river—eleven miles north of Atlanta—Commencing at the Island they are putting up works running down to the Rail Road bridge. These works have been lately commenced and every tenth negro has been impressed to work upon them. At Rome General Brown with a Brigade of Infantry is at work on fortifications. Capt. Green is Engineer—near the bridge on Oastanaula River. On east side of river a large fort is being built; which commands approach from Alabama or the west. Near it are some 'thirty two-pound' guns, not mounted.—This line of fortifications is laid out but only partially built, runs up this river to the mountains north of town, and connects with another fort, laid out but not built; that Commands the Road running in from the north, between the two rivers.—From this fort four lines of Rifle-pits, now being worked on; run to the Etowah River. Some distance above the bridge over this river,—near the bridge, a battery is built that covers the bridge—and a Small village on South side of the river Called Lickskillet   During the first part of February troops (mostly Tennessee— North Alabama—Kentucky and Arkansas—regiments) were moved to Mississippi to prevent desertions, and Southern Alabama and Mississippi troops were brought up to supply this place.—This movement lasted till about the 12th; At Kingston; Cave Springs, Marietta—White River and Cross Plains are some 6000 Cavalry horses,—~~with~~ and some Cavalry with them.—The Stock is in very poor Condition.—Grigsby's Brigade was relieved at the front by Hume's, 1500 Strong, and went to Oxford, Benton County, Alabama, the terminus of the Railroad running toward, Rome, Ga. from Selma. Forage is very scarce everywhere except in Cross Valley, where there is plenty of Corn—Meat also is very scarce everywhere,—And the army at Dalton which, he says, is about 25000 men strong, is on half rations.— Where he was the new Conscript act has not as yet been very vigorously enforced—but ~~that~~ preperations were being made to rake up everybody.— All the State troops of Georgia have been turned over to the Confederacy— and on the 21st of January they were given twenty days furlough.—Alabama has not yet turned over her State troops. He gives troops Stationed as follows: Atlanta 5000, Rome 3000; Oxford 1500, Grigsby's Brigade, Gadsen 2500 under Roddy—& White Plains—three Companies. In Wills Valley about 300 State troops—The Scout from Montgomery says all troops have been hurried to Mobile and Polk. Corroborates the Change of troops in the two armies—but thinks perhaps three Brigades more went west than returned. Most all the Planters in Floyd Polk and Paulding Counties Ga. have moved their Stock, Negroes, and valuables South.—They have no faith in the ability of their Army to hold that portion of country. The Scout Says the work at Rome does not look like a vigorous effort to make the place a very formidable one, but north of Atlanta he says they are very buisy   He Saw advertisements of General Wheeler Calling upon refugees to join him and enlist, as he should operate in Tennessee and Kentucky this summer. Breckinridge and Buckner are collecting together all the Cavalry in East Tennessee and scout says that Humes, Roddy and Grigsby's Brigades are all he could hear of with Johnson."—Copies, DNA, RG 393, 16th Army

Corps, Letters Sent; *ibid.*, Left Wing, Letters Sent. *O.R.*, I, xxxii, part 2, 476–77. On Feb. 27, USG forwarded this report to Washington.—DNA, RG 94, Register of Letters Received. On Feb. 29, Dodge telegraphed to Rawlins. "One of the Scouts captured a mail from Rome Ga. Letters show that they have plenty to eat are pretty well clothed—That Conscripts brought there at point of bayonet generally desert—that Browns Brigade only is there and that they have generally reenlisted—One letter written by a Co'l says that they expect Longstreets troops to join them"—Copy, *ibid.*, RG 393, Military Div. of the Miss., Telegrams Received; *ibid.*, 16th Army Corps, Left Wing, Telegrams Sent. On March 4, Dodge, Decatur, Ala., telegraphed to Rawlins. "The scouts report that Sherman is falling back towards Vicksburg that his advance only reached Tombigbee but he did not cross and that the troops sent to reinforce Polk on their return that Roddy has moved a week ago from Goddard to Montville on Selma & Rome R. R."—Copy, *ibid.*, Military Div. of the Miss., Telegrams Received. See telegram to Brig. Gen. Grenville M. Dodge, March 4, 1864.

1864, FEB. 23. Lt. Col. Theodore S. Bowers to Col. Lewis B. Parsons. "Your letter of date yesterday is just received. I thank you for it. It affords me pleasure to assure you that Gen. Grant is fully alive to the importance of the early construction of the Northwestern Railroad. He has directed that the work be pushed forward with all possible vigor, and Col. McCallum is confident that he will have the road running within Sixty days. A large force is now at work in the vicinity of Reynoldsburg, and every effort will be made to complete the road at the earliest possible day. I imagine that Gen. Rawlins has given me credit for what he really is entitled to. But I can assure you that in him and myself you will *you* will always have defenders against the machinations of the public plunderers who pursue every man who discharges his public duties honestly and fearlessly. But such men can no longer harm you and should give you no annoyance. For integrity and efficiency you have established a reputation second to no officer in the government, and your services are and will continue to be appreciated."—ALS, Parsons Papers, IHi.

1864, FEB. 23. Governor Thomas E. Bramlette of Ky. to USG. "You will herewith receive a Memorial of citizens in the Western part of Ky to which your attention is respectfully invited. I will add by way of suggestion, that at the present Session of the Legislature upon my recommendation a law has been enacted giving civil redress for all the class of cases embraced in your military order. Knowing the difficulties as well as the hardships which necessarily arise in the execution of military orders for redress of grieveances, & believing it always better when practicable to enforce law to give legal redress I urged the adoption of a law, which has now become operative & fully covers the purposes con[template]d by the Military a[uthorities.]"—ALS (torn), DNA, RG 393, Military Div. of the Miss., Letters Received.

1864, FEB. 24.   Maj. Gen. John A. Logan, Huntsville, Ala., to Lt. Col. Theodore S. Bowers. "I have information from a scout just in from Atlanta and Rome to this effect   the reb'ls are building strong fortifications at Rome —One Brigade stationed there under Genl Brown—Atlanta is well fortified and strong fortifications are being erected North of on the Ostauaula river   about 5000 troops at Atlanta. Hardee with some troops has gone in the direction of Sherman. Roddy with 2500 Cavalry is at Gadsden preparing to make a raid on bridges across Tennessee &c   Johnstons forces in bad condition for want of clothing   Citizens about Atlanta looking for Long-streets forces to come to that point. This I dont give any weight to   a large force is being collected at some point for a raid into Kentucky Wheelers Morgans and others Cavalry. Jno. C. Breckenridge is to have command of the expedition. Gen'l Buckner one of his generals to command one column— this information was gathered from Citizens in the vicinity of Atlanta and also from the Engineer officers now at Oosteraula River—I give you this that you may compare with what other information you may have."—Telegram, copy, DNA, RG 393, Military Div. of the Miss., Telegrams Received. *O.R.*, I, xxxii, part 2, 462.

1864, FEB. 25.   Maj. Gen. Henry W. Halleck endorsement. "Respectfully referred to Genl. Grant"—Copy, DNA, RG 393, Military Installations, Nashville, Letters Received. Written on an unsigned letter of Feb. 21, Louisville, addressed to Halleck stating that gamblers of Louisville and Nashville preyed on army officers.—Copy, *ibid*. On March 1, Lt. Col. Theodore S. Bowers endorsed this letter to Maj. Gen. George H. Thomas.—ES, *ibid*.

1864, FEB. 25.   Brig. Gen. Hugh T. Reid, Cairo, to USG. "Reports just received from Vicksburg of the 19th inst, believed to be reliable, state that Genl Sherman entered and holds Selma after a severe fight. No particulars given"—Copies, DNA, RG 393, District of Columbus, Telegrams Sent; *ibid*., Military Div. of the Miss., Telegrams Received. *O.R.*, I, xxxii, part 2, 469.

1864, FEB. 26.   USG endorsement. "Respectfully refered to Brig. Gen. Ramsey, Chief of Ordnance, Washington D. C."—AES, DNA, RG 156, Correspondence Relating to Inventions. Written on a letter of Jan. 25 from Capt. William F. Patterson, 1st Ky. Engineers and Mechanics, Matagorda Bay, Tex., to USG describing an improvement in fuses for shells for Parrott rifled cannons.—ALS, *ibid*.

1864, FEB. 26.   To Maj. Gen. Samuel P. Heintzelman, Columbus, Ohio. "Capt S Perkins A Q M at Cincinnati is required as a witness before court martial here in case of Capt Stubbs A Q M   will you please order him here for that purpose"—Telegram received, DNA, RG 393, Northern Dept., Letters Received.

1864, FEB. 26.   To Maj. Gen. William F. Smith. "You will please say to the agent of the Louisville and Nashville Railway it is my request that he send an extra car with you on the three P M train today"—Telegram received, Smith Papers, Vermont Historical Society, Montpelier, Vt.

1864, FEB. 26.   To Brig. Gen. Hugh T. Reid, Cairo. "Suspend collections from citizens of West Kentucky until the matter can be refferred to General Sherman comdg Dept."—Copies, DLC-USG, V, 34, 35; DNA, RG 107, Letters Received; *ibid.*, RG 393, Military Div. of the Miss., Letters Sent; *ibid.*, Dept. of Ky., Correspondence Relating to Claims Against the U.S.

1864, FEB. 26.   To George H. Stuart, U.S. Christian Commission. "I have seen the letter addressed to you by the Rev. J. C. Thomas of Feb 23 1864 in reference to furnishing our officers and soldiers with the most valuable English and American periodicals. I heartily approve the scheme of furnishing our armies with such reading material at reduced prices and trust that with your organization you may be able to carry it into successful operation."— LS, DLC-George H. Stuart. See *Philadelphia Inquirer*, March 12, 1864. On March 22, Stuart wrote to USG. "It affords us very great pleasure to express to you, on behalf of the members and officers of the U. S. Christian Commission, the profound satisfaction your appointment as Lieutenant General commanding the armies of the nation, has afforded us. The uniform Kindness and courtesy—shown by you to our agents and delegates, and especially your order No. 32 issued December 12. 1863, have impressed us with gratitude to God that one so highly esteemed for heroism and generalship should so fully appreciate efforts for the bodily and especially for the religious benefit of the noble men under his command   Our gratitude has been still more enhanced by the distinct acknowledgment of God by you in accepting the high trust of your present position, and we assure you that to the extent of our power, you shall have moral support at home, and in [—] and benefitting those under your command in the field, and daily remembrance before God in prayer. In turn permit us to commend to your kindness in the future as it has been so well shown in the past, our agents and delegates as occasion may require. John A. Cole Esq. our field Agent for the Army of the Potomac, like Revd. E. P. Smith in the Army of the Cumberland you will find a Christian gentleman worthy of all confidence. Our arrangements both for times of rest, and for relief in times of heavy marches and battles, you will find much more complete than in any Western Department."—LS, DNA, RG 94, U.S. Christian Commission, Letters Sent (Press).

1864, FEB. 27.   USG endorsement. "Respectfully forwarded to the Sec. of War for his orders and directions. I have no suggestions to make further than to state that I think a fu[ll] and fair account between the Govt. and the Nashvil[le] & Chattanooga R. R. and betwe[en] man & man, would [bring] the road out so irre[trievably] in debt to the Govt. [that] the latter would become sole owner."—AES, DNA, RG 92, Letters Received Relating to

Railroads. Written on a lengthy letter of Feb. 22 from Michael Burns, Nashville, president, Nashville and Chattanooga Railroad, to USG asking for an accounting for the period since the seizure of the railroad on March 7, 1862, so that the co. could pay interest on its bonds, and requesting that the U.S. return the railroad to the control of the owners.—ALS, *ibid.*

1864, FEB. 27.   Lt. Col. Cyrus B. Comstock, Nashville, to Lt. Col. Theodore S. Bowers reporting an inspection of that part of the Army of the Ohio near Knoxville.—*O.R.*, I, xxxii, part 2, 484–85. On Feb. 29, Bowers forwarded this report to Maj. Gen. John M. Schofield.—DNA, RG 393, Army of the Ohio, Register of Letters Received.

1864, FEB. 27.   Lt. Col. Theodore S. Bowers to Maj. Gen. Lovell H. Rousseau. "It has been reported to these Headquarters that two negro women with their hands tied or chained have been taken to your Headquarters to day. You will please report to these Headquarters immediately by whose authority these persons were taken through the city in this condition."—Copies, DLC-USG, V, 34, 35; DNA, RG 393, Military Div. of the Miss., Letters Sent.

1864, FEB. 27.   Capt. Asher R. Eddy to USG. "Upon two different occasions citizens have reported to me with orders from your Hd Qrs. for the purpose of *superintending* the shipments to Nashville of R. R. Cars & locomotives—In each case these gentlemen have been unable to do anything as all was being done that could be to move the property, by the *proper officer* —These ajents have no means whatever at their disposal to carry out their orders and of course can exercise no control over the officer whose duty it is to attend to such matters—I need not assure you that any order or request of yours will be promptly executed without the aid of any ajents—"—ALS, DNA, RG 92, Letters Sent by Asher R. Eddy (Press).

1864, FEB. 27.   Brig. Gen. John A. Rawlins to U.S. Representative Elihu B. Washburne. "Your letter relating to Col. Beckwith, Commissary of Subsistence was duly received. The Colonel is now here and virtually on duty with the General in this, that he is busily engaged in inspecting the Commissary Department and making provisions for future supplies. He is certainly one of the most energetic officers I have ever met, and it was with pleasure I brought the contents of your letter to the notice of the General, but the General prefers to let Department Commanders see specially to their own supplies, holding them responsible for the same; hence I am not at liberty to say he desires his assignment. One thing, however, I can say: the General is pleased with the Colonel, and appreciates the valuable services he is now rendering."—LS, DLC-Elihu B. Washburne. Col. Amos Beckwith later served as chief commissary, Military Div. of the Miss.

1864, FEB. 27.   Charles W. Ford, St. Louis, to USG. "I have just read the Telegraph report from Washington. Glorious enough. Lieut, Genl! I fear I shall have to go on a *small bender* today. I give you my most hearty congratulations. God help you to confirm that appointment, by a glorious victory over the enemy."—ALS, USG 3.

1864, FEB. 29.   USG endorsement. "Respectfully forwarded to the Commissary General of Prisoners Washington D. C. recommending that the within named B. A. Tothy be released. I am satisfied that he was forced into the Confederate service against his own will and made repeated efforts to leave it. His mother is a poor, decrepid, old woman whose loyalty has been conspicuous and who from the loss of her property by Guerillas is solely dependent upon him. He is now at Hospital at this place wounded."—Copies, DLC-USG, V, 39; DNA, RG 393, Military Div. of the Miss., Endorsements. Written on a letter of B. A. Tothy, 5th Tenn., C.S.A., asking to take the amnesty oath.—*Ibid.*

1864, MARCH 1.   Maj. Samuel Breck, AGO, to USG. "I have the honor to acknowledge the receipt of a communication of Sep't 12. 1863, from Col. L. A Sheldon commd'g 42d Reg't Ohio Volunteers, and by you forwarded to the office, requesting the return to duty of Private Domingos Pereira Co "F" of his command, on duty as cook in Gen'l Hosp'l at Lexington Ky. and to inform you, that he is unfit for field duty, and has been examined with a view to his discharge or transfer to the Invalid Corps."—Copies, DNA, RG 94, Enlisted Branch, Letters Sent; *ibid.*, RG 393, Military Div. of the Miss., War Dept. Correspondence.

1864, MARCH 1.   Maj. Robert Williams, AGO, to USG. "I am directed to inform you that until further orders, disbursing officers of the funds for collecting & drilling Volunteers will pay any person who presents the certificate of regular recruiting officer, that he has furnished an accepted Veteran the sum of fifteen dollars, an accepted recruit the sum of ten (10) dollars."—Telegram, copies, DLC-USG, V, 40, 94; DNA, RG 393, Military Div. of the Miss., Hd. Qrs. Correspondence. This telegram was sent to many other officers.—DfS, *ibid.*, RG 107, Telegrams Collected (Unbound).

1864, MARCH 2.   To Brig. Gen. Robert Allen, Louisville. "Please direct the cars to be used daily for the transportation of beef cattle until further orders."—Telegram, copies, DLC-USG, V, 34, 35; DNA, RG 393, Military Div. of the Miss., Letters Sent.

1864, MARCH 2.   Asst. Secretary of War Charles A. Dana to USG. "An association for the relief of those citizens of East Tennessee, who have been reduced to destitution by the events of the war; has been formed in Philadelphia, & a considerable fund has been raised to procure supplies   The association has appointed as its comme for the distribution of these supplies Messrs. Frederic Collins, Col N E Taylor & Lloyd P Smith   I beg to commend them to your kindness, and to request that you will render them any assistance which may be in your power. They should have free transportation for themselves, their agents and the articles which they desire to distribute, upon all govt. railroads & chartered vessels"—LS, DNA, RG 107, Letters Received, T170. *O.R.*, I, xxxii, part 3, 8.

1864, MARCH 2.   B. Embry, Nashville, to USG. "I am in receipt of a letter informing me of (9) nine Horses taken by the Federal commander from my Farm about 6 miles above Fort Pillow depriveing me of the means of makeing a crop   among them are three mares, in foal, one 3 year old poney   I respectfully appeal to you to protect me in my private property as far as you may think I am justly entitled to   I have been previously deprived of my means of support myself & Family Refugees from our home since May 1861   I refer you to Gen Rousseau City officers and prominant Citizens generally not having the Pleasure of your Personal acquaintance—"—ALS, DNA, RG 109, Union Provost Marshals' File of Papers Relating to Individual Civilians.

1864, MARCH 3.   To Brig. Gen. Lorenzo Thomas. "I have the honor to transmit herewith ten copies, each, of all General Orders issued by me from Head Qrs. Dept. Tenn., during the year 1863. Copies of my General Orders for 1861-2 will be forwarded soon as they can be reprinted."—Copies, DLC-USG, V, 40, 94; DNA, RG 393, Military Div. of the Miss., Hd. Qrs. Correspondence.

1864, MARCH 3.   Lt. Col. William A. Nichols, AGO, to USG. "A board of three Cavalry officers will convene at an early day in this city for the purpose of considering and reporting upon the equipment and armament of the cavalry of the United States Army and such other matters as may refer to the improvement of that arm of the service. The General in Chief requests that you designate two suitable officers for the board"—Copies, DLC-USG, V, 40, 94; DNA, RG 94, Letters Sent; *ibid.*, RG 393, Military Div. of the Miss., Hd. Qrs. Correspondence. A similar letter went to Maj. Gen. George G. Meade.

1864, MARCH 4.   Maj. Thomas M. Vincent, AGO, to USG. "Congress has extended time for payment of the bounties heretofore authorized to first of April next. Re-enlisted Veterans will receive them accordingly to that date."—Telegram, copies, DLC-USG, V, 40, 94; DNA, RG 393, Military Div. of the Miss., Hd. Qrs. Correspondence. On March 5, Maj. Robert Williams, AGO, telegraphed the same information to USG and many other officers.—DfS, *ibid.*, RG 107, Telegrams Collected (Unbound).

1864, MARCH 4.   Brig. Gen. Hugh T. Reid, Cairo, to USG. "By directions of Adjt Genl Thomas I send You Report of force of this District. Send Detailed report by mail. Total effective force twenty two hundred and ninety four. (2294) Stationed at Paducah, Cairo, Columbus, Union City, Hickman and Island Ten."—Copies, DNA, RG 393, District of Columbus, Telegrams Sent; *ibid.*, Military Div. of the Miss., Telegrams Received.

1864, MARCH 4.   Col. Lewis B. Parsons, Louisville, to USG. "The within letter of Admiral Porter relative to Transpn. on the Arkansas is respectfully refered for your information. The views expressed by him are those I have entertained ever since our experience on the Ark. last Winter & I should not if left to my own judgement have advocated sending Stores for Little Rock by that river. The demands of Officers, however, have been so urgent that I did some months since order Transports to the Arkansas to go up that river which owing to long detention at very large expense resulted in very little advantage. With the short Road from Duvals Bluff to Little Rock put in complete order & white River, which is a navigable stream for almost the entire year, there should be little trouble in supplying all the Stores necessary for Little Rock."—AES, Parsons Papers, IHi. Written on a letter of Rear Admiral David D. Porter, White River, discussing problems of convoys in Ark.—Copy, *ibid. O.R.* (Navy), I, xxv, 784–85. On April 4, Maj. Gen. William T. Sherman endorsed this letter. "General Steele is the proper officer to judge of the mode and route of supply for his troops in Arkansas." —AES, Parsons Papers, IHi.

1864, MARCH 4.   U.S. Representative Lucian Anderson of Ky. and Lt. Carey [?], Washington, to USG. "Dont interfere in the tax levied on Farmers in the first District in Kentucky until you hear from the Union men in that dist. and from us"—Telegram, copy, DNA, RG 393, Military Div. of the Miss., Telegrams Received.

1864, MARCH 4.   Charles A. Fuller, asst. special agent, U.S. Treasury Dept., Nashville, to USG. "Your attention is respectfully called to the enclosed advertisement, 'Sale of Confiscated Goods.' An order is requested that the Goods specified be turned over to the Agent of the Treasury Department, or if the sale is allowed to take place that the proceeds be so turned over."—ALS, DNA, RG 366, Nashville District, Letters Received. Endorsements indicated that the goods were seized from sutlers rather than rebels, and thus did not fall under U.S. Treasury jurisdiction.—*Ibid.*

1864, MARCH 8.   Governor Oliver P. Morton of Ind. to USG. "Will you please send Capt. A. W Prather, 6th Ind Vols. here. he has been appointed Lieut. Colonel of 120th Ind. Vols., now ready for the field. Also Assistant Surgeon Max Hoffman 9th Ind. Vols. appointed Surgeon 128th Ind Vols. ready for the field"—Telegram, copy, Morton Papers, In.

1864, MARCH 9. Maj. Gen. George Stoneman, "Camp on Mossy Cr. Tenn.," to USG. "Allow me the pleasure and privelege of congratulating you upon the promotion you have recieved from a grateful people, for services rendered them, to the highest position ever bestowed upon an American citizen. The 23d Corps if it could be collected together might be made one of the finest in the service and I am much pleased with the material of which it is composed. We are all in hopes that it will not be found necessary to spend much time in merely occupying a now exhausted country, but will be sent to the front the farther the better—If you have any important Cavly operations in view, and it is probable that the 23d Corps will remain comparatively idle in the mean time, I should be glad to take a hand temporarily —I have now but one Divn Genl Judah's under my Comd numbering about thirty two hundred effective men—The Corps at one time numbered upwards of forty one thousand aggregate—With the exception of two days rain the weather has been very fine since I came here and the roads generally excellent. Trusting as a friend that your promotion will not take you from us to Washington"—ALS, USG 3.

1864, MARCH 12. Maj. Gen. James B. McPherson, Vicksburg, to USG. "I have the honor to enclose herewith a copy of letter to Maj Gen'l Sherman Com'd'g, Deptmt of the Tenn, requesting to be transferred to the Field of Operations in Southern Tenn, and Northern Alabama and Georgia. Also list of Reg'm'ts in my command which have re-enlisted as '*Veterans.*' I desire you to have a full and complete understanding of the case, as many of the officers and enlisted men in these Regiments are beginning to feel that they are not fairly dealt by. I write this in no spirit of complaint, as I am now, as I always have been ready and willing tol do everything in my power to bring this war to a successful termination, and to obey the orders of my superiors. When the Orders and instructions from the War Deptmt, relating to the enlistment of Veterans were received here, the officers and enlisted men of my command entered into the spirit of the matter with commendable zeal, influenced by motives of patriotism, the prospect of getting a furlough, of receiving the liberal bounty offered by the Gov'm't, and the chances of getting home to recruit their Regm'ts and thus keep up their organization after their original three years had expired. About the middle of January instructions were received from the Maj Gen'l Com'd'g the Dep'tm't that a certain portion of my command would be required about the first of February to make a short campaign into the interior of this State. I had then furloughed only two Regiments. I immediately informed the command that their services would be required in the Field and that I could furlough no more of them at present. Without a dissenting voice they expressed their readiness to go on the expedition, expecting a furlough shortly after their return. Immediately after getting back I furnished 2500 men for the Red River expedition, and am still, without any additional force being sent me, expected to protect and keep open the Mississippi River, and exercise my discretion about furloughing Veteran Regiments. Without some change many of the Regiments will not be able to get their Furloughs for months to come; the men will be disappointed in their well founded expectations, and disheartened, and one great object the Officers had in view, viz, getting home to recruit their Regiments defeated. Already we are beginning to feel the effects as Regiments have been sent home, from other commands and are being filled up with recruits, while the Regiments of my command not having the same opportunities are getting comparatively none. As there is a prospect of a good deal of hard fighting before the war is over I think it is of the utmost importance that the *strength* and *esprit* of the Army be kept up."—LS, Schoff Collection, MiU-C. *O.R.,* I, xxxii, part 3, 60.

1864, MARCH 12. Augusta M. Tilghman, Clarksville, Tenn., to USG. "The widow of Genl. Tilghman would ask protection at your hands that she may be permitted to remain unmolested in the retirement of her home— I have lived at this place from the opening of the *'war'* and until recently have been treated with respect by those who have at various times commanded the *'Post.'*—It has always been my wish and intention while within your lines, to avoid every thing at variance with existing rules of the Department, nor would I now ask any thing at your hands, but what humanity and the laws of the Country would accord to me—You may be aware of the calamities which the war has brought to my *'hearth-stone'* the loss of my *Husband,* & eldest son—eno' surely to satisfy the most unfeeling—recently however my *Household Furniture* has been recorded for *'Confiscation'*—I need hardly say it is not the 'intrinsic' value of the things—but 'tis all that is left me of my once 'happy home'—every article endeared by so many cherished associations.—If you have it in your power and in your heart, my dear Sir, to accord to me the protection I have asked you will ever be held in grateful remembrance."—ALS, DNA, RG 109, Union Provost Marshals' File of Papers Relating to Individual Civilians.

1864, MARCH 14. To Maj. Gen. Benjamin F. Butler. "If you still hold Col Howard D Smith of John Morgans command do not exchange him until further orders"—Telegram received, DLC-Benjamin F. Butler; (press) DNA, RG 107, Telegrams Collected (Bound). On March 16, Butler telegraphed to USG. "Col Howard D. Smith of Gen John Morgan's Command is still at Johnson's Island"—Telegram received, *ibid.,* Telegrams Collected (Unbound). See *O.R.,* II, vi, 1015.

1864, MARCH 16. USG endorsement. "Approved and respectfully forwarded to Headquarters of the Army Washington D C"—ES, DNA, RG 94, ACP, B1026 CB 1863. Written on a letter of March 10 from Brig. Gen. Davis Tillson, Knoxville, to Brig. Gen. Lorenzo Thomas asking the assignment of Asst. Surgeon William A. Banks, his brother-in-law, to his command.—ALS, *ibid.* Endorsements indicate that the request was denied.

1864, MARCH 16.   USG endorsement. "Gen. Buckland has been instructed to revoke his order No 2, of date Memphis Jan 30 1864, so far as the same relates to aliens and also to report fully the reasons for his issuing the same"—ES, DNA, RG 107, Letters Received from Bureaus. Written on a letter of Feb. 25 from Secretary of State William H. Seward to Secretary of War Edwin M. Stanton referring a question concerning aliens in Memphis.—Copy, *ibid. O.R.*, III, iv, 136. See *ibid.*, p. 200.

1864, MARCH 16.   Governor Oliver P. Morton of Ind. to USG. "I desire that Lieut Col Mank 32d Ind Vols. may be relieved from recruiting service and ordered to his regiment for the purpose of inducing it to re-enlist. He has great influence with the regiment"—Telegram, copy, Morton Papers, In.

1864, MARCH 17.   To Brig. Gen. Robert Allen, Louisville. "Are there not Quartermasters at Memphis that might be relieved and ordered here to report to Col Donaldson? At least three good A. Q. M's, one of whom can be trusted with large disbursements, are needed."—Copies, DLC-USG, V, 34, 35, 45, 59; DNA, RG 108, Letters Sent; *ibid.*, RG 393, Military Div. of the Miss., Letters Sent.

1864, MARCH 17, 11:30 A.M.   Maj. Gen. Henry W. Halleck to USG transmitting intelligence from the Army of the Potomac.—Telegram received, DNA, RG 108, Letters Received; copies, *ibid.*, RG 393, Military Div. of the Miss., Hd. Qrs. Correspondence; DLC-USG, V, 40, 94. See *O.R.*, I, xxxiii, 681–82.

1864, MARCH 18.   Lt. Col. Theodore S. Bowers to Maj. Gen. John M. Schofield. "Col Frank Wolfolk, 1st Kentucky Cavalry has this day been ordered to report to you in person in arrest. You will cause your Judge Advocate or some other Staff Officer to prepare charges against him based on his recent speech in Kentucky, and cause as soon as practicable, a General Court Martial to be convened for his trial."—Copies, DLC-USG, V, 34, 35, 45, 59; DNA, RG 108, Letters Sent; *ibid.*, RG 393, Military Div. of the Miss., Letters Sent. *O.R.*, I, xxxii, part 3, 88. On March 10, Lt. Col. John H. Hammond had telegraphed to Brig. Gen. John A. Rawlins. "Col Wolford is making seditious speeches counselling resistance to enrolling negroes & accusing the President tyranny   mischief will result. Make inquiry"—Telegram received, DNA, RG 107, Telegrams Collected (Bound). On March 14, Brig. Gen. Samuel D. Sturgis, Mount Sterling, Ky., telegraphed to USG. "Have recvd your dispatch from Louisville & ordered Col Wolford to report to you at Nashville as directed"—Telegram received, *ibid.*, RG 108, Letters Received; copy, *ibid.*, RG 393, Military Div. of the Miss., Telegrams Received. On June 28, Brig. Gen. Stephen G. Burbridge, Lexington, Ky., telegraphed to USG. "Ex-Col Frank Wolford has been arrested and is now on his way to Washington under guard."—Telegram received, *ibid.*,

RG 109, Union Provost Marshals' File of Papers Relating to Individual Civilians. See *O.R.*, I, xxxii, part 3, 146–47; *ibid.*, I, xxxix, part 2, 98, 116; *ibid.*, I, lii, part 1, 529; *ibid.*, II, vii, 302; *SED*, 38-2-16; Hambleton Tapp, "Incidents in the Life of Frank Wolford . . . ," *Filson Club History Quarterly*, 10, 2 (April, 1936), 82–99.

1864, MARCH 18.   1st Lt. Gilbert H. Clemens, 8th Tenn. Cav., Nashville, to USG. "I have the honor to inform you that I received an order on the 9th inst to report here to be mustered out of the service of the late 8th Tenn— Cavalry, which has been consolidated with the 10th Tenn Cavalry. I have been upon detached duty at Kingston Tenn as Post Q Master since the 11th of December. There had been no Post Q. M. at that point previous to my entering upon said duty, and I found the Q. M. Dpt. in a most disorganised condition. I have just succeeded in organising the Dept. and can, in ten or twenty days transfer all the Public property in my hands, and then, if the Goverment does not require my services longer I can be mustered out. I have been actively engaged in the Q. M. & Comms. Dpt. since April 1861— & labored most zealously in organising the 1st & 2nd Kintucky Infty   I was formerly in the 2nd Ky Infty, but resigned the service from disability, caused by vaccination, and some months afterwards was mustered in as Reg. Q. M. of the 8th Tenn Cavalry. I have communicated officially with Genl A. Gillam Adgt. Genl. of Tenn, and called upon the Astnt Commsy of Mustre, from whom I learn that I cannot be mustered out, until I have transfered all the Public Property in my possession. I most respectfully request that the date of my muster out be deferred until the 1st or 10th of April. My name is before the Senate of the U. S. as Captn A. Q. M; for confirmation, being endorsed by Maj Genl A. E. Burnside, Col Thomas Swords A Q M Genl, Honbls. Ben F. Wade & John Sherman—senators from Ohio—, Hon. Green Clay Smith Senator from Kentucky & Brig. Genl M C Meigs Q M Genl U S A. With the hope that you may feel disposed to give me the benifit of your recommendation . . ."—LS, DNA, RG 393, Military Div. of the Miss., Letters Received.

1864, MARCH 19.   E. F. Carter, Nashville, to USG. "I was notified by Rebel military in 1862 to leate my home and business (to leave the *County* farm) no other charges but because I was a Union Woman   I was Soon after Captured by the Rebel authorities and Sent South   I left in Hickman County my land and home with housekeeping eutencils. During my military imprisonment Rebel Citizen taken possession of my home—braking locks— and mooving my house Furniture Just where they pleased   In January 1864 I requested the Fedral authorities to comply with Genl Grants Order no 4   Genl Gillum promised me he would do so—but he and his Officers have failed to comply with Genl Grants Order in full—Gen Gillum notified the parties who were occupying my home through maj Thompson of the 8 Iowa Cavl. and Capt Evans Co B 8th Iowa Cavl to leave my home and property in good condition—but the parties did not comply with that notice in full—they left my land but carried of my housekeeping furniture—they are now living ⅓ of a mile of my home—and doing me the Same injuris they did when living on my lands—that is they keep me from living at home   Would you please have them Sent farther from me—. . . Will you investigate my claims and have me Justice done."—ALS, DNA, RG 109, Union Provost Marshals' File of Papers Relating to Individual Civilians.

1864, MARCH 23.   USG endorsement. "Respectfully forwarded to Hon. E. M. Stanton, Secretary of War, and the request of Maj. Gen. W. T. Sherman for the appointment of Major Sawyer to the rank of Lieut. Colonel in the Adjutant Generals Department approved."—ES, DNA, RG 94, ACP, 419S CB 1864. Written on a letter of March 19 from Maj. Gen. William T. Sherman, Cincinnati, to Secretary of War Edwin M. Stanton. "I ask that Maj R. M. Sawyer be promoted from Major to Lt Col in the Adjt. Genl Dept. I also ask that my Aid Capt L. M. Dayton be promoted in Same way, either by Appointmt in the Regular army, or made an aid-de Camp with Rank of Lt Col, if allowable under the Law."—ALS, *ibid.* Roswell M. Sawyer held the rank of lt. col. assigned from March 25; Lewis M. Dayton was promoted to maj. as of Jan. 12, 1865.

1864, MARCH 24.   Q. M. Sgt. William S. Toland, 83rd N. Y., Culpeper, Va., to USG. "I deem it my duty to communicate to you the following facts. I have been a prisoner of War on Belle Isle for four months past, and during a portion of that time was employed by our officers to assist in delivering clothing sent thither by the United States, which gave me frequent opportunities of being outside the enclosure and conversing with rebel soldiers and citizens there. It was a a matter of boasting amongst them that that they had frree communication with Culpepper. A member of the rebel Congress or Legislature named 'Rixie' in whose house you have your head Quarters came from our lines in Culpepper to Richmond while I was there, and it is my belief that he frequently makes such excursions, and that his family are very dangerous characters. I am not acquainted with any of them personally and am actuated solely in making this communication by a sincere desire to warn you against rebel spies and traitors. I endeavoured to notify Major Genl. Newton commanding 1st Corps of these facts but was unable to obtain an audience, and his Adjutant General did not appear to consider them worthy of attention. I refer to Col Moesch commanding 9th Regiment N. Y. S. M. (83d N. Y. V) who will guarentee that I am a citizen of respectability and that my statements are worthy of belief"—ALS, DNA, RG 108, Letters Received. See *O.R.*, II, vii, 80–81. On the same day, Luther A. Rose, U.S. Military Telegraph, Culpeper, wrote in his diary. "Lt Gen Grant & Staff arrived here making his Head Quarters in Bixeys House on Colman Street—"—AD, DLC-Luther A. Rose.

1864, MARCH 24.   John D. Hall, Philadelphia, to USG. "In accordance with an understanding arrived at when I met you in the Continental Hotel of this city some two days since I inclose herewith sketches and brief descriptions of my inventions for the 'Destruction of Harbor Obstructions' I have not deemed it necessary to obtain elaborate drawings as the inventions are so simple and so evidently practicable that the bare leading idea being suggested the details will at once occur to any practical mechanicel mind. These devices may be readily applied to *any* monitor whether in process of construction or already afloat and in service though it is worthy of consideration that they may be better applied to vessels in process of construction. Now if there be any present occasion for using these inventions or any *possibility* that there will come an occasion it would seem to me of great importance that their construction be ordered as soon as practicable. And should this be done I claim the right and pirvelege of superintending their construction. Should you or your engineers wish any further explanations it will give me pleasure to communicate them either in person or otherwise, as you may direct. . . . P. S. I am about procuring an illustrative engraving of my invention for Harbor Defence and shall defer the description of it until that is complete unless it be sooner desired."—ALS, DNA, RG 108, Letters Received.

1864, MARCH 26. Barr and Young, photographers, to USG. "We herewith transmit to you an Album, which we hope you will accept not for its pecuniary value, but for the many familiar faces which you will reccognize and which in after years you will refer to with pride and pleasure—not unmixed with pain, You will please Remember us to Genl Rawlins, Cols. Bowers & Duff and others—Most devoutly wish you success in putting down this wicked Rebellion . . . P. S. Please acknowledge Receipt Address Dr. Jno W Young Vicksburg Miss Box 235"—LS, USG 3.

1864, MARCH 27. George W. Bissell, Rarden, Ohio, to USG. "I beg you to excuse me, for Intruding, for a few moments, on your much occupied time, but boldness has at last taken the predominence over ever thing else, and I will venture on your time a little. I wish to know if theer is any chance or any Situation that you can give me whereby I can better my self. I am alone. I have buried my wife, and I want excitement. I would like a birth some where near you, if I could get it, or will take any position that you will give me if it is low you will confer a great favour on me by writing to me and let me know. if you can do no better can you not give me a post Sutlers position some where. pardon me for intruding on your time & Patience from your humble servant—(keep this private for me"—ALS, USG 3.

1864, MARCH 28. Col. Edward D. Townsend, AGO, to USG. "Please acknowledge receipt of this telegram containing General Orders No. 123, of this date. One Circular No. 23 of March 9th in relation to transfer of enlisted men of the Army to the Naval service is revoked. Two—Every Department and Army commander will cause to be transferred as speedily as possible to the nearest Naval station named in General Orders 91, all enlisted men who desire to enlist in the Navy, and who fulfill the conditions required in General Orders ninety one—without regard to the restriction in the said orders as to reduction of regiments and companies below the minimum organization, which restriction is removed. Three. Daily reports by telegraph will be made to the Adjutant Genl. of the number of men transferred and the station to which they are sent."—Copy, DNA, RG 94, Letters Sent. The same letter went to other commanders.

1864, MARCH 28.   Brig. Gen. Montgomery C. Meigs to USG. "Dispatches from the West inform me that there are three months' supply of forage, and still more of commissary stores at Nashville. That (20,000) twenty thousand tons were ~~loaded~~ landed there in one week. Dispatches of the 26th from Col. Easton at Chattanooga, however, inform me that he has not one days' supply of forage.—Animals improving, though many lost by glanders. The Railroad is apparently unable to accumulate at Chattanooga, while supplying East Tennessee. On Friday Gen. Sherman, in company with Gen. Allen, left Nashville for Huntsville, and they are expected at Bridgeport, on a tour of observation, to-day."—LS (telegram sent), DNA, RG 107, Telegrams Collected (Unbound); copy, *ibid.*, RG 108, Letters Received.

1864, MARCH 30.   USG statement. "I fully concur in the proposition to place the Chief Engineer of an Army Corps (or higher command) on the same footing as to rank and pay as the heads of the other staff departments of the Corps, deeming it essential to the efficiency of the officer in question." —DS, DNA, RG 94, Letters Received, 531M 1864. Prepared for Capt. George H. Mendell, who submitted it, other letters from gen. officers, and a proposed bill, to Brig. Gen. Lorenzo Thomas on April 7.—ALS, *ibid.*

1864, MARCH 30.   USG statement. "Contributors to the Sanitary Fair subscribe to the perpetuation of Independence and Freedom to govern them selves."—ANS, MHi. Written on the stationery of "The Great Central Fair for the Sanitary Commission, Philadelphia." On the same day, USG signed a card for the same fair.—ES, NN. USG also signed two undated statements commending this fair.—NS, Roberts Collection, Haverford College, Haverford, Pa.

1864, MARCH.   Reverend William H. Andrews and others, Lawrenceville, Pa., to USG on a printed form letter requesting money for a monument to "the young females who perished by the explosion at ALLEGHENY ARSENAL, on the 17th of September, 1862."—USG 3.

1864, [MARCH?].   USG statement. "I see nothing in it to oppose, but on the other hand everything to commend."—DLC-Joseph C. Thomas. Included in a printed statement of Thomas, dated April 1, comprising statements from twenty gen. officers commending "A Reading-System for the Army and Navy."

1864, [MARCH-APRIL].   Adam Gurowski to USG urging the removal of Maj. Gen. George G. Meade.—George Gordon Meade, ed., *The Life and Letters of George Gordon Meade* . . . (New York, 1913), II, 188. See Le-Roy H. Fischer, *Lincoln's Gadfly, Adam Gurowski* (Norman, Okla., 1964), pp. 151–52.

1864, APRIL 4.   Maj. Gen. Henry W. Halleck endorsement. "Lieut General Grant suggests that instructions be issued by the Treasury Dep't prohibiting all trade in arms and munitions of war in Kentucky and on the Mississippi River below Cairo."—AES, DNA, RG 107, Letters Received from Bureaus. Written on a letter of March 17 from Secretary of the Treasury Salmon P. Chase to Secretary of War Edwin M. Stanton enclosing letters from Treasury agents discussing trade in Ky.—LS, *ibid.*

1864, APRIL 4.   Maj. Gen. Benjamin F. Butler, Fort Monroe, Va., to Brig. Gen. John A. Rawlins. "You will remember that I spoke to you this morning about some men from the parole camp being ordered to me for special duty. I send you a memorandum of their names and a form of order. The sooner we can have them the better. Send me the order and I will send for the men."—*O.R.*, II, vii, 10. See *ibid.*, pp. 41–42.

1864, APRIL 4.   Maj. Gen. William T. Sherman endorsement. "I forward this to Lieut. Genl Grant—when at Vicksburg, Genl Hawkins complained of this same excess of work—you remember that in February, I took to Meridian, nearly all the white troops—now those troops marched 360 miles in February, and did fighting and work besides. I know the negro garrison left behind did not do as much work as the white troops—as to making a Corps of them, I tried in vain to make a Division, and there were not enough."—Copy, DNA, RG 393, Military Div. of the Miss., Endorsements. Written on a letter of Brig. Gen. John P. Hawkins "in reference to the Colored troops of his Command—states they are used by other Generals to do fatigue duty and dirty work. asks they may be concentrated and consolidated—"—*Ibid.* On the same day, Sherman endorsed a letter of Capt. James H. Burdick, act. ordnance officer, 16th Army Corps, requesting a commission to command a regt. of heavy art. of African Descent. "Respectfully referred to Lieut Genl. Grant. I hope more care will be taken in the matter of these Black Regiments, we have already too many skeleton Reg'ts—Let us fill up those we have before attempting to make new ones." —Copy, *ibid.*

1864, APRIL 4.   Erastus Wright, Springfield, Ill., to USG. "Permit a stranger now passed 65 years and one that Loves and fears God, and his

Holy and Blessed Word, to suggest a few thoughts touching this Great Rebellion . . ." Wright then denounced slavery at great length.—ALS, USG 3. Born in Mass. in 1799, Wright moved to Springfield in 1821 and was a friend of Abraham Lincoln.

1864, APRIL 6. USG endorsement. "Respy. returned to the A G. of the Army Washington D C. The resignation of Lieut T. F. Strong Co "H" 21st Wisconsin Volunteers was presented at my office at Chattanooga Tenn. on the 30th November 1863 and on the statement of Ex Maj Gen C. S. Hamilton that the officer was unfit for duty and that it was desirable that the paper should be acted on without delay necessary to its passing through the proper military channels was accepted by enclosed copy of sp orders No 20. Subsequently the statements of Generals Starkweather and Thomas regarding Strongs were received and am willing that an officer on staff duty, guilty of conduct such as was charged against him, should go out of the service honorably. I revoked the s. o. directing the resignation and requested the Provost Marshal of the state of Wisconsin to arrest him and forward him to me for trial by Court Martial. All I know of the charges against Lieut Song is derived from the statements of General Starkweather and Thomas and to which I invite special attention. I recommend that Lieut Strong be sent to General Thomas at Chattanooga for trial by Court Martial."—Copy, DLC-USG, V, 58. Written on a letter from the AGO concerning 1st Lt. T. F. Strong, 21st Wis.—*Ibid.*

1864, APRIL 6. USG endorsement. "Respy. forwarded to Brig General R. Allen Chief Quarter master Louisville Ky. The boat referred to was taken possession of by the Military at Youngs Point for the use of government, and was made to answer a good purpose. It is supposed to be worth from fifteen hundred to two thousand dollars. The owner is entitled to reasonable compensation for the time the boat was in service and her return to him"—Copy, DLC-USG, V, 58. Probably written on a letter of Feb. 22 from Col. Lewis B. Parsons, Louisville, to Brig. Gen. John A. Rawlins. "Dr. Leftrick of Memphis claims the ownership of the *celebrated* Str. 'Rawlins'—formerly the 'Lelia'—and has sent an Agent here asking compensation for the use of the said boat and its return, or payment for the value of the boat. You will recollect that I ordered this craft into service on instructions from Head Quarters at Young's Point Feby '63—What become of her after the advance into Lake Providence I was never before advised. Are you aware of any reason why a fair compensation should not be given to the owners as desired? I ask this as I have a recollection of some allegations of her being engaged in Cotton speculations or something of the kind, though I believe there was nothing definite and am inclined to think it was a mere rumor. Your early reply will oblige all parties."—LS (press), Parsons Papers, IHi.

1864, APRIL 7. USG endorsement. "Respectfully returned to the Secretary of War. Crafts J. Wright was formerly Colonel of 13th Missouri Vols. The Mr. Crafts of whom he writes I have no recollection of ever having seen consequently cannot speak as to his loyalty or recommend protection to his property. I know of but one man of unquestioned loyalty in Holly Springs and his name *is not Craft.* If further information is desired I recommend that this application be forwarded to Maj. Gen'l W. T. Sherman in whose command Holly Springs is"—Copies, DLC-USG, V, 58; DNA, RG 107, Letters Received. On April 26, Maj. Gen. William T. Sherman endorsed this letter. "I know all the parties to this transaction and I know well the sad influence cotton has had on our cause, developing the insatiate thirst for profit that has at times palsied our Armies. I would not sacrifice one life for all the cotton on earth and to send an expedition to Holly Springs and haul out Mr. Craft's cotton would cost us a thousand lives every one of which is as precious to us as Mr. Crafts. I can make no order in the case"—Copy, *ibid.* Written on a letter of March 17 from Crafts J. Wright, New Orleans, to Maj. Gen. Robert C. Schenck stating that H. Craft, a loyal citizen of Holly Springs, Miss., owned cotton in Miss. and Ala. for which he wanted military protection and permission to market. Wright was part owner.— Copy, *ibid.*

1864, APRIL 7, 4:35 P.M. Secretary of War Edwin M. Stanton to USG. "Mrs ~~General~~ Grant &. Mrs Stanton being in the telegraph office with the Secretary of War send their compliments to General Grant and hope he is very well today"—ALS (telegram sent), DNA, RG 107, Telegrams Collected (Bound). On the same day, Lt. Col. Adam Badeau telegraphed to Stanton. "Lt Genl Grant is not in his office but riding and of course well, even compliments cannot be acknowledged without orders or those of Mrs Grant & Mrs Stanton would be by . . ."—Copy, USG 3.

1864, APRIL 7. Lt. Col. Cyrus B. Comstock to Maj. Gen. George G. Meade. "Gen Grant desires me to ask for the estimated force of the enemy at Fredericksburg."—ALS (telegram sent), DNA, RG 107, Telegrams Collected (Unbound). On the same day, 9:00 P.M., Meade telegraphed to Comstock. "At the last accounts—there was no force of the enemy at Fredericksburgh nearer than Hamiltons Crossing, where there was said to be a brigade of Hampton's Cavalry Division—This command patrolled the lower fords of the Rappahanock & Rapidann—I have scouts out expected in tonight or tomorrow, from that derection who will bring in later intelligence."—ALS (telegram sent), *ibid.*; copy, Meade Papers, PHi. Printed as sent at 9:05 P.M. in *O.R.,* I, xxxiii, 816.

1864, APRIL 7, 12:15 P.M. Maj. Gen. George G. Meade to USG. "The troops are authorized to practice with their fire arms on Tuesdays Thursdays and Saturdays between 10 a m and 12. M."—Copies (telegram sent), DNA, RG 107, Telegrams Collected (Unbound); Meade Papers, PHi.

1864, APRIL 8. USG endorsement. "Respectfully returned to the Secretary of War—Disapproved"—ES, DNA, RG 94, ACP, 366E CB 1864. Written on a letter of March, 1864, from Maj. Gen. Nathaniel P. Banks to Brig. Gen. Lorenzo Thomas. "I beg leave to call the attention of the Department to the recommendation I have heretofore had the honor to make for the promotion of Brigadier General William H. Emory, to be Major General of Volunteers. Enclosing a copy of that recommendation, I can only add to it that the valuable and important services performed by General Emory, since its date, confirm my opinion that his promotion will be not only an act of justice to a gallant and deserving officer but an advantage to the public service"—LS, *ibid.* On Dec. 12, 1864, President Abraham Lincoln nominated William H. Emory as bvt. maj. gen. to rank from July 23, 1864. On Jan. 13, 1866, at the time he was mustered out of vol. service, Emory was nominated by President Andrew Johnson as maj. gen. to rank from Sept. 25, 1865.

1864, APRIL 8. USG endorsement. "It was under instructions from Head quarters of the Army to encourage the organization of troops from the loyal portions of the inhabitants of seceded states—that authority for the raising and equiping of this regiment was given—and Cavalry being at that time in demand—it was directed to be mounted. The letters and telegrams on this subject having been left at Head quarters Military Division of the Mississippi—I cannot refer to them by date—or state particularly their condition. Before leaving Nashville directions were given for dismounting mounted Infantry—and turning over their horses & Cavalry arms and equipments in order to supply the wants of the Cavalry."—Copy, DLC-USG, V, 58. Written on a letter of Capt. Samuel Gilbert, 1st Miss. Mounted Inf., concerning pay for his troops.—*Ibid.*

1864, APRIL 8, 9:00 P.M. Maj. Gen. George G. Meade to USG. "Maj. Genl. Hancock will have his corps ready for inspection near Stevensburgh tomorrow at Two P. M.—He will send a staff officer to show you the road & I will meet you on the ground. Of course if it rains the inspection will not take place.—"—ALS (telegram sent), DNA, RG 107, Telegrams Collected (Unbound); copies, *ibid.*, RG 393, Army of the Potomac, Telegrams Sent; Meade Papers, PHi.

1864, APRIL 9, 2:30 P.M. To Maj. Gen. Henry W. Halleck. "Letters from Secy of the Interior and Commissioner of Indian affairs endorsing letters from P. Chateau & Co—of St Louis requesting to be furnished means of defense and protection in transporting Indian goods up Missouri River have been recieved from the Secretary of War. Please direct the officer in charge of St Louis Arsenal to furnish them two twelve pounder howitzers and five hundred rounds of ammunition and Genl Curtis to furnish them a detail of thirty men from troops nearest the Missouri river to protect government property. Telegraph copies of each order to P. Chateau and Company St Louis"—Telegram received, DNA, RG 107, Telegrams Collected (Bound); copies, *ibid.*, RG 108, Letters Sent; DLC-USG, V, 45, 59. *O.R.*, I, xxxiv, part 3, 112. The letters received by USG are in DNA, RG 108, Letters Received.

1864, April 11.　Theophilus R. Kyes, Fort Smith, Ark., to USG. "About twenty months ago I left. N. W. Texas just after the conscript law passed　had I remained one day more at home I should have been hung for being a union man . . . will leave here the first of May with about 100 Texians & cross Red River & apply for a commission to form a regiment of Loyal Texians. . . . if we get arms you will here of some good fighting　at least 10,000 good union men would take up arms this moment if they had leaders from here to get them to gether. . . . there is not Gold enough in the South to make me a Rebel not even for a moment. Gens Rains offered me the contract to furnish his Bragade with cloathing &c　I could have cleared 10,000$ pr mo by—taking it.　but I would prefer to be a true man & make Rails, for a living"—ALS, USG 3.

1864, April 13.　To Maj. Gen. William T. Sherman. "Order Mr Croney clerk to report here in person at once"—Telegram received (press), DNA, RG 107, Telegrams Collected (Bound); copies, *ibid.*, RG 393, Military Div. of the Miss., Letters Sent; DLC-USG, V, 94. On May 13, Capt. George K. Leet telegraphed to the provost marshal, Alexandria, Va. "Charles A. Croney, a clerk at these Head Quarters, is in arrest at Annapolis. Release & return him to this place at once."—ALS (telegram sent), DNA, RG 107, Telegrams Collected (Unbound).

1864, April 14.　Maj. Gen. George G. Meade to USG. "Respectfully forwarded for the information of the Lt. Genl. Comd.—The transportation of this army is a subject which has engaged my attention most particularly and every effort made to reduce it to the minimum—It is believed a careful perusal of the within statement will satisfy the Lt. Genl. that with the number of men now in the army no reduction is practicable *unless* the amounts, of ammunition subsistence, forage, are all diminished—There are now 25 *wagons* carrying subsistence for contingencies with these Hd. Qrs—also 100 for the Qrs Mrs. *repair depot* & possibly some of the Prov. Mar. Genls. train that might be dispensed with, if deemed necessary—"—AES, DNA, RG 108, Letters Received. *O.R.*, I, xxxiii, 855. Written on a report of April 13 from Brig. Gen. Rufus Ingalls, q. m., Army of the Potomac, to Meade about available wagon transportation.—DS, DNA, RG 108, Letters Received. *O.R.*, I, xxxiii, 852–55.

1864, APRIL 15. USG endorsement. "Respectfully forwarded. As a rule I would recommend honest and intelligent officers who have been retired from active service in consequence of Physical disability for all the vacancies in the Pay Dept. and for such other necessary offices as they can fill. I believe Capt. Bates to be an officer qualified for the kind of duty he askes to be appointed to"—AES, DNA, RG 94, ACP, B129 CB 1870. Written on a letter of April 13 from Capt. Francis H. Bates, U.S. disbursing officer for N. J., Trenton, to Secretary of War Edwin M. Stanton asking an appointment as paymaster, stating that he could fill this position although he was on the retired list for disability.—ALS, *ibid.* No appointment followed.

1864, APRIL 16. Col. James A. Hardie, inspector gen., to Maj. Gen. Henry W. Halleck. "When Lieutenant General Grant was here night before last, he desired an order to issue breaking up three Companies of the 7th Infantry in New Mexico, and assigning them to the 5th Infantry, and that the officers of the companies broken up and such non-commissioned officers, as there may not be v[a]cancies for in the 5th Infantry, be ordered to report for duty at Fort Schuyler for recruiting service. The proposition received the sanction of the Secretary of War, who has directed me to refer the matter to you for the necessary order."—LS, DNA, RG 108, Letters Sent (Press). On April 17, Halleck endorsed this letter. "Adjt Genl will order as directed"—AES, *ibid.*

1864, APRIL 17. USG endorsement. "Respectfully forwarded to the Secretary of War, and attention invited to the endorsement of Maj. Gen. Meade hereon"—ES, DNA, RG 94, ACP, 302M CB 1864. Written on a copy of a letter of Feb. 29 from Maj. Gen. John A. McClernand, New Orleans, to Secretary of War Edwin M. Stanton requesting that Capt. Grantham I. Taggart be assigned as chief commissary, 13th Army Corps.—Copy, *ibid.* On April 13, Maj. Gen. George G. Meade endorsed this letter. "Respectfully returned. Captain Taggart can be spared for the duty within indicated—" —ES, *ibid.* On March 19, Brig. Gen. Joseph P. Taylor, commissary gen., endorsed the original letter. "Respectfully returned to the Secretary of War. Capt. Taggart, C. S. Vol's, was the chief C. S. of 13th Corps, was reported by Gen. Ord as inefficient—Was ordered by Gen Ord under instructions from Gen Bank[s] to report in person to this Office,—and is now on duty with the 2nd Division of the 6th Army Corps. From the knowledge of this Officer obtained from those with whom he has served and from his own accounts, I could not recommend him for the position asked for him"—AES, *ibid.* On April 21, Col. James A. Hardie forwarded the original letter with Taylor's endorsement to USG.—AES, *ibid.*

1864, APRIL 17. H. M. Dean, St. Louis, to USG. "On the Thirtieth or Thirty First of March, I wrote you, directed the Letter to Head Quaters Army of the Potomac Washt'on, marked *Private*, the Letter contained inqueries concerning John Dent; and a request in relation to Cornelias Husband; thinking it possible, the missal *might have been lost* I merely write to say how it was directed—We are in great trouble or rather dout & astonishment. Capt. Tillford receive Orders (last Evening) to repair immediatey to Willmington Delaware & to report to General McDowall; he has not the slightest Idea for what reason having always performed the Duties of his Profession *faithfully* & *Loyally*; never having lost *One* Day of active Service, Since the War commenced We are of course, Ignorant of what charges may be brought against him by Enemies *Open* or *concealed* and can only pray to the all merciful God to raise him up a *Friend*; to see that justice is done him: and the Efforts of his Enemy, defeated; If I could only see you for a few moment, ask and *receive* your valuable Advice I could rest content; as it is I can hae no rest untill I hear some thing definite God! have mercy upon us all! What ought to be done whom hae we to appeal to; if you write me let it be under care to J G McClelland, Attorny at Law St Louis. I am in great tribulation, May God protect you alway from the smarts of Enemies & the *Bullets* of Our Foes."—ALS, USG 3.

1864, APRIL 18. To Brig. Gen. Edward R. S. Canby. "Please release David P. Stallard on parole & permit him to return to his home. He is confined in the old capital which I believe is within your control."—Telegram received (press), DNA, RG 107, Telegrams Collected (Bound). On April 23, David P. Stallard of Culpeper Court-House, Va., signed a parole promising not to "give aid or information to the enemies of the United States, whether citizens or soldiers . . ."—DS, *ibid.*, RG 109, Union Provost Marshals' File of Papers Relating to Individual Civilians.

1864, APRIL 18. Col. Edward D. Townsend to USG. "General Court Martial in session in this city requires the testimony of General J. H. Wilson in an important case. The Secretary of War desires him to be ordered to appear if he can be spared. Please acknowledge receipt."—ALS (telegram sent), DNA, RG 107, Telegrams Collected (Unbound). On the same day, USG telegraphed to Townsend. "Gen. Wilson will be ordered to the City. Do you want him to-morrow?"—ALS (telegram sent), CSmH; telegram received, DNA, RG 94, Letters Received, 340A 1864; *ibid.*, RG 107, Telegrams Collected (Bound). On April 19, Townsend telegraphed to USG. "Brig. General J H. Wilson will not be needed befor the Court until Thursday the twenty first (21st) inst."—ALS (telegram sent), *ibid.*, Telegrams Collected (Unbound). On the same day, USG telegraphed to Maj. Gen. George G. Meade. "Order Brig. Gen. Wilson to Washington to appear as witness on Thursday next before the Court now in session there on Thursday next."—ALS (telegram sent), *ibid.*; telegram received, *ibid.*, RG 94, War Records Office, Army of the Potomac. See James Harrison Wilson diary, Historical Society of Delaware, Wilmington, Del.; DNA, RG 94, Letters Received, 439C, 443C, 1864.

1864, April 19. USG endorsement. "Respectfully returned to the Secretary of War. I concur in the opinions expressed by Mr. Gallagher in the within communication, and would recommend a rigid adherence to the Treasury Regulations and laws on this subject and urge their strict enforcement. No person has been authorized by me to give permits for the violation of them"—ES, DNA, RG 56, Div. of Captured and Abandoned Property, Letters Received .Written on a letter of March 2 from William D. Gallagher, surveyor, Louisville, to Secretary of the Treasury Salmon P. Chase protesting the shipment of gold into Tenn.—ALS, *ibid.* Apparently the same letter returned to USG, and on April 23 he endorsed it by repeating his endorsement of April 19.—ES, *ibid.*, RG 107, Letters Received from Bureaus.

1864, April 19. Maj. Gen. Benjamin F. Butler to Brig. Gen. John A. Rawlins. "I enclose to you the examination of a messenger from Richmond. He comes to me from a reliable source, and I have no doubt of the reliability of the information he brings so far as the knowledge of the person who sends it extends. Miss Eliza mentioned, is a lady from Richmond of firm Union principles, with whom I have been in correspondence for months, on whose loyalty I would willingly stake my life. The information which she sends is what is known to the Union people of Richmond. Thinking it may be useful to the Commdg. General, I take the liberty of sending it to you."—*Private and Official Correspondence of Gen. Benjamin F. Butler* . . . (n. p., 1917), IV, 94. Elizabeth Van Lew of Richmond continued to furnish information to U.S. commanders.

1864, April 20, 4:35 p.m. To Maj. Gen. George G. Meade. "Set Engineers to building Block houses at all the bridges between Bull Run and the Rappahannock both included   They should be put up with all rapidity"—Telegram received, DNA, RG 107, Telegrams Collected (Bound). *O.R.*, I, xxxiii, 918.

1864, April 21. USG endorsement. "I would respectfully recommend Private Robert Hedges, 84th Vol. Inf.y ~~to fill a va~~ for a cadetship at West Point Military Academy to fill any vacancy from any of the Southwestern states where he has been serving with so much credit to himself."—AES, DNA, RG 94, Cadet Applications. Written on a statement of April 11 of Col. Louis H. Waters, 84th Ill., Blue Springs, Tenn., recommending Private Robert W. Hedges.—DS, *ibid.* No appointment followed.

1864, April 21. USG endorsement. "Respectfully forwarded to Col. W. Hoffman, Commissary Gen'l of Prisoners, Washington D. C."—ES, DNA, RG 249, Letters Received. Written on a letter of April 14 from Diantha M. Weston or Wyton, Cleveland, Ohio, to USG. "please Remember my Brother Fr Vanrensaler Mace that made his Escape from the South and Reported himself to you at Chatanogia—my Brother wrote to me that he was a citizen-

Prisoner at Camp Chase Columbus and was to remain there until he could be Identified as a Loyal Citizen of the United States—my Brother was born in the state of New York and Raised there to man hood—my house was his house   I had the care of him from a little boy   he was a good moral young man—taught military tactics in the Principal cities   I have had my affidavit taken and sent to my Brother—he can hand it to the officers when called for—please have the goodness to order his case to be Investigated soon and you wil confer a grate favor—"—ALS, *ibid.* A statement of Nov., 1863, of Francis V. R. Mace concerning the defenses of Atlanta is *ibid.*, RG 109, Union Provost Marshals' File of Papers Relating to Individual Civilians.

1864, APRIL 21.   To Maj. Gen. Philip H. Sheridan. "You will give John Phlieger Co. "E" 10th N. Y. Cav'y. 2 Brig. 2nd Div. a furlough for 10 days. ~~you~~"—Telegram received, DNA, RG 94, War Records Office, Army of the Potomac; copy, *ibid.*, Dept. of the Cumberland.

1864, APRIL 21.   Maj. Gen. Benjamin F. Butler to USG. "The following extract from a letter of Genl Wessels at Plymouth on the 16th inst. is forwarded for your information—'Longstreet's army is in motion for Richmond. Genl Pemberton and many officers passed up to Richmond last week & talked freely of the opening campaign. It is Lee's intention to anticipate Lt Genl Grant's combinations and take the initiative—' "—LS (telegram sent), DLC- Benjamin F. Butler; DNA, RG 107, Telegrams Collected (Unbound); telegram received, *ibid.*, Telegrams Collected (Bound). Dated April 30 in *O.R.*, I, xxxiii, 1029.

1864, APRIL 21.   Private Otto Merfield, Co. G, 16th N. Y. Heavy Art., Gloucester Point, Va., to USG offering to provide his secret of writing with invisible ink.—ALS (in German), USG 3.

1864, APRIL 22.   Maj. Gen. Henry W. Halleck to USG. "Respectfully forwarded to Lt Genl Grant"—AES, DNA, RG 108, Letters Received. See *O.R.*, I, xxxii, part 3, 436. Written on a copy of a telegram of April 21 from Maj. Gen. William T. Sherman to Brig. Gen. Lorenzo Thomas asking about a command for Maj. Gen. Carl Schurz.—Telegram received, DNA, RG 107, Telegrams Collected (Bound); copy, *ibid.*, RG 108, Letters Received. *O.R.*, I, xxxii, part 3, 436. See *ibid.*, p. 505.

1864, APRIL 23.   USG endorsement. "Respectfully returned to the Secretary of War. After a careful reading of the within proposed order I would recommend that it be issued with this change in paragraph 2nd. Instead of reading: 'These officers shall be Captains in the line of the Army, selected' &c., &c.—that it be made to read: 'These officers shall be Captains and Lieutenants in the Regular or Volunteer service, selected,' &c., &c.—Such an order would not increase the number of officers on detached service, for so far as my experience goes every Brigade and Division have officers acting in this capacity."—ES, DNA, RG 94, Letters Received, 156O 1864. Written on a letter of April 7 from Brig. Gen. George D. Ramsay, chief of ordnance, to Secretary of War Edwin M. Stanton discussing the need for ordnance officers.—LS, *ibid.* On April 19, Maj. Gen. Henry W. Halleck referred this letter and his own recommendation to USG.—ES, *ibid.*

1864, APRIL 23, 5:00 P.M.   To Maj. Gen. George G. Meade. "Note from Gen. Humphreys giving copy of despatch to Gen. Sheridan, stating on information from a rebel deserter, that all of Stewarts Cavalry are at Fredericksburg, and intend to surprise Post of Grove Church. Prepare for it and let them come on."—Copies, DLC-USG, V, 45, 59; DNA, RG 108, Letters Sent. See *O.R.*, I, xxxiii, 952.

1864, APRIL 24.   Surgeon Madison Mills, St. Louis, to USG. "An Effort is about to be made to get increased rank for Medical Directors. It is proposed to ask Congress to pass a law giving to the Medical Director of a Department, or an army, the rank, pay, and all allowances of a Colonel of Cavalry; and to the Director of an Army Corps, the rank, pay &c of a lieut. Colonel of Cavalry. It requires no argument from me to show you that such rank is necessary, and that it will be only justice to the Medical officer who may be called on to perform these duties to give it to him. The office is not only an important one, but a very responsible one; and if its duties are faithfully performed, a very laborious one. It requires much professional experience and great administrative ability, as well as integrity of character   If you can find time to write a few lines stating the necessity and justice of this increased rank, and recommend that a bill be passed by Congress *granting* it, you will confer a favor on a class of officers who work hard, receive little pay, less thanks and no honor"—ALS, USG 3.

1864, APRIL 26, 3:00 P.M.   To Maj. Gen. William T. Sherman. "The third Iowa Cavalry can be mounted at St. Louis. Its last orders were for Vicksburg. Where shall it go."—Telegram, copies, DLC-USG, V, 94; DNA, RG 393, Military Div. of the Miss., Letters Sent. On the same day, Sherman telegraphed to USG. "The third Iowa should stop at Memphis   I will be at Chattanooga May 1st but will leave Gen. Webster and other Staff Officers at Nashville"—Copies, *ibid.* As printed in *O.R.*, I, xxxii, part 3, 498, this is an exchange between Maj. Gen. Henry W. Halleck and Sherman. Since USG was not in Washington on April 26, where his alleged telegram is datelined, the attribution to USG appears to be erroneous.

1864, APRIL 26.   William H. C. Bartlett, professor, USMA, to USG. "I have just seen in the public prints, a notice of your letter to the Chairman of the Committee on Military Affairs of the Senate, in behalf of Genl. Schofield,—and the purpose of this note is to beg you to accept therefor my hearty thanks. Genl. Schofield has been pursued by a set of party politicians, in

Missouri and Kansas, with a spirit of vindictiveness which, I really believe, has heretofore never had a parallel in this Country; and his Offence has been, to have discharged his duty to the Country, in these most trying times, with ability and fidelity; to have kept his own hands from 'picking & stealing,' and enforcing that policy which his official superiors have deemed the best suited to break down this unholy rebellion. I made him two visits during his military administration in Missouri, and can bear the most ample testimony to his never flagging zeal. To work all night as well as all day was with him a common occurrence, and I only wonder he had the physical and mental ability to stand it. His treatment at the hands of the Military Committee, is one of the saddest Commentaries I have known, and must appear so to all who know any thing of his case. Your noble and generous efforts in his behalf were well timed and well deserved, and all his friends will feel most grateful to you for them. What I now fear is that action on his nomination will be postponed till the senate at its close will lose a quorum and thus put it in the power of a single objector to defeat, it this session, as it was at the last. It has been a long time since I had the pleasure to see you & hope you may be able to recall me. I have seen your success with real gratification and trust that the God of battles may continue to prosper and bless your efforts."—ALS, USG 3. For a report of a letter from USG urging the confirmation of John M. Schofield as maj. gen., see *New York World* quoted in *Missouri Democrat*, April 25, 1864.

1864, APRIL 27.   To Maj. Gen. Henry W. Halleck. "Relative to officers recieving appointment of Br Gen. and failure of Senate to confirm said appts" —DNA, RG 108, Register of Letters Received. See Stan. V. Henkels, Catalogue No. 946, April 3–4, 1906, p. 37.

1864, APRIL 29.   To Lt. Col. Theodore S. Bowers. "Look in my desk and find to of my photographs and send them by an orderly to Miss Botts. You will find them in a pidgeon hole on right hand side of the desk."—Chicago Book & Art Auctions, Inc., Sale No. 4, Feb. 19, 1931, p. 13. On April 28, John M. Botts, prominent Va. Unionist, had entertained a group of U.S. gens., including USG, at his farm in Culpeper County.—*New-York Tribune*, April 30, 1864; diary of Frederick T. Dent, typescript, ICarbS.

1864, APRIL 30.   To Alexander Bliss. "The slippers worked by one of the Ladies of the 'Union Central Relief Association,' Baltimore, and through you presented to me, are recieved. Extend to the Ladies of the Association my thanks for this kind satin assurance of their approval of my efforts in the same cause in which they are so nobly working."—ALS, DLC-Alexander Bliss.

1864, MAY 1.   To Maj. Gen. Ambrose E. Burnside. "If the services of Capt Saml. Wright, a a. G. can be spared by you, will you please order him to Maj Gen Butler, for duty.—If his services cannot be spared you of course will retain him."—Telegram, copies, DLC-USG, V, 45, 59; DNA, RG 108, Letters Sent. On the same day, Burnside telegraphed to USG. "Captain Wright is one of our best ad'gt Genls and I would be glad to keep him unless he is necessary to Genl Butler"—Copy, *ibid.*, RG 393, 9th Army Corps, Telegrams Sent.

1864, May 1.   To Maj. Gen. George G. Meade. "Would you like to have Col Myer of the Signal Corps with you during the Campaign   He is desirous of coming and if you wish him I will ask the order"—Telegram received, DNA, RG 94, War Records Office, Army of the Potomac; copies, *ibid.*, RG 108, Letters Sent; DLC-USG, V, 45, 59. On the same day, 10:30 P.M., Meade telegraphed to USG. "I am perfectly satisfied with Capt Fisher who is at present my chief signal officer—If however you desire Col Meyer to be here I have no objection to his coming—"—ALS (telegram sent), DNA, RG 107, Telegrams Collected (Unbound); telegram received, *ibid.*, RG 108, Letters Received.

1864, May 2.   To Maj. Gen. George G. Meade. "You are hereby autherised to make the necessary orders for Brig Gen Rowley"—Telegram received, DNA, RG 94, War Records Office, Army of the Potomac; copies, *ibid.*, RG 108, Letters Sent; DLC-USG, V, 45, 59; Meade Papers, PHi. *O.R.*, I, xxxvi, part 2, 330. On the same day, 9:00 A.M., Meade had telegraphed to USG. "Brig. Genl. Rowley has been tried by Court Martial & is now awaiting the promulgation of proceedings—the record having been transmitted to Washn. He is without command & desires to go to Harrisburgh Pa to await further action   I would be glad if an order to that effect can be issued, or authority to that effect given to me.—"—Telegram received, DNA, RG 94, War Records Office, Army of the Potomac; copies, *ibid.*, RG 393, Army of the Potomac, Telegrams Sent; Meade Papers, PHi. *O.R.*, I, xxxvi, part 2, 330. On June 21, Lt. Col. Theodore S. Bowers issued Special Orders No. 40. "Brig Gen Thomas A. Rowley U. S. Vols, having reported for duty in pursuance of orders, and it being deemed inadvisable to place him on duty because of the feeling in the Army of the Potomac of distrust of his fitness to command troops in the field, he will therefore proceed to Washington D. C. and report to the Adjutant of the Army for orders."—Copies, DLC-USG, V, 57, 62, 67. *O.R.*, I, xl, part 2, 270. Brig. Gen. Thomas A. Rowley had been convicted by court-martial on charges including drunkenness at the battle of Gettysburg.—Edwin B. Coddington, *The Gettysburg Campaign: A Study in Command* (New York, 1968), pp. 308, 706; Ezra J. Warner, *Generals in Blue* (Baton Rouge, 1964), p. 655.

1864, May 2, 9:30 A.M.   Maj. Gen. George G. Meade to USG. "A deserter who crossed the Rapidan at Mortons Ford night before last reports up to that time everything quiet within the enemys lines and no indications of any immediate movement   I will be at your Hdqrs about 2 P M today"—Telegram received, DNA, RG 108, Letters Received.

1864, MAY 3.   Lt. Col. James A. Ekin, Washington, D. C., to USG. "A very fine horse, presented to you by Mr. H. Williams, of Little Falls, N. Y., has been sent here consigned to me. Please say how I shall dispose of this horse."—Telegram, copy, DNA, RG 92, Supplies and Purchases, Public Animals, Telegrams Sent (Press). On the same day, USG telegraphed to Ekin. "Turn over the horse presented by Mr Williams to Capt. Leet my adjt Genl. in Washington to use until I can send for him. Please tell Capt Leet to acknowledge the receipt of the horse & say to Mr Williams that he arrived too late for me to bring him into the field but as soon as I can do so I will send for him & ackn[ow]ledge the receipt of him."—Telegram received (press), *ibid.*, RG 107, Telegrams Collected (Bound). Also on May 3, USG telegraphed to Capt. George K. Leet. "There is a very fine horse in the hands of the Q. M Cav. Bu. belonging to me. Take the horse & use him as your own until I can send for him."—Telegram received, *ibid.*

1864, MAY 3.   Louis Cousin, Paris, to USG. "When I have reading your nomination as Lieutenant General of the Army, I have transported with great joy, because in my opinion the Submission of the South is only an question of time but undoubted. I am living twelve years in the United States (1850 to 1862), and I am Citizen by naturalization. I ha[ve] been Professor in the Rensselaer Polytechnic Institute for Several years, in the City of Troy, and I Submit my certificate in that letter. Ancien pupil of the Military School of St Cyr, in France, I was Captain in 1848. (Light Infantry). When the War was beginning, immediately I am going to Albany, and I proposed my services to Governor Morgan, who authorized the formation of regiment Called 'Les Chasseurs de Vincemer' (9 ber 1861)   But in January 1862, by order of the Minister of the War, that organization was stopped. In consequence of a serious illness, and having lossed all my property in the great fire, in the city of Troy (May 10th 1862), I am returning in France.—At present time, I am in good health and in the great wish to participate in the restablishment of the Union. My ambition is to be in the army near you, in your Staff, or in the federal corps. I propose to go at my own expenses, and I ask you for a single word: Coming."—ALS, USG 3.

1864, MAY 5.   Maj. Gen. George H. Thomas, Ringgold, Ga., to USG. "The Asst Adjt Genl of the State telegraphs that Col Jordan Ninth (9th) Penna Cavalry now on Veteran furlough desires to mount, arm and equip Regt before leaving. The State authorities rendering every facility practicable   Please have it authorized"—Telegram received, DNA, RG 107, Telegrams Collected (Bound); copies, *ibid.*, RG 393, Dept. of the Cumberland, Telegrams Sent; *ibid.*, Letters Sent.

1864, MAY 6.   Maj. Gen. Cadwallader C. Washburn, Memphis, to USG. "On the 30th Ulto I sent from here three thousand three hundred (3,300) Cavalry and two thousand (2000) Infantry in pursuit of Forest, under

Brig Gen Sturges—On the day following Forrest left Jackson Tenn in force retreating south. My advance met a Brigade of his in the p m of the 2nd near Bolivar and after a sharp engagement of two hours, drove them from their entrenchments with considerable loss. They retreated across the Hatchie destroying the Bridge behind them. Our loss two (2) killed ten (10) wounded. Forrest with his whole force encamped on night of 2nd at Purdy and continued his retreat the day following toward Pocahontas. He crossed the Hatchie at Pocahontas on the fourth (4th) & Sturges was in hot pursuit —A co-operating force which I expected from Tennessee to be at Purdy on the night of thirtieth (30th) failed me or I should have captured his whole force. The Hatchie was very high and impassable any where below Bolivar I still hope to punish him severely before he gets out of reach"— Telegram received, DNA, RG 107, Telegrams Collected (Bound); *ibid.*, RG 108, Letters Received. *O.R.*, I, xxxii, part 1, 693–94. On May 8, Washburn telegraphed to USG. "Forrest is driven out of West Tennessee—My forces followed him as far as East Mississippi—but his swift horses rendered further pursuit unavailing—There is no organized enemy in West Tennessee or Kentucky You will next hear of Forrest near Decatur Ala"—Telegram received, DNA, RG 107, Telegrams Collected (Bound); *ibid.*, RG 108, Letters Received.

1864, MAY 9. A. J. Brown, Washington, D. C., to USG. "Will you please forward through Maj Genl Halleck a statement of the services rendered by Spencer Kellogg, (executed at Richmond Va Sept 25 1863) in an expedition upon which he was sent by Com W. D Porter in Jany 1862, to obtain information in regard to rebel fortifications at Island No 10 Fort Pillow Columbus & other points. Said Kellogg reported to yourself on the morning of the 2d days fight at Pittsburg Landing. Were these services thus rendered of any value to the Gov't & of what did they consist? Would Governmt be justified in rendering any additional compensation for said services?—"—ALS, DNA, RG 108, Letters Received. See *Calendar*, Jan. 2, 1863; George Gardner Smith, ed., *Spencer Kellogg Brown: His Life in Kansas and his Death as a Spy* (New York, 1903). Brown enlisted in both the U.S. Army and U.S. Navy under the name of Kellogg.

1864, MAY 11. M. D. Howell, San Francisco, to USG. "Have bet ten thousand (10.000) dollars you capture Richmond forty five days"—Telegram received, DNA, RG 107, Telegrams Collected (Bound).

1864, MAY 16. USG endorsement. "Permission to send granted, subject to Secy of War"—Copy, DNA, RG 107, Telegrams Collected (Unbound). Written on a telegram of the same day from Brig. Gen. Orlando B. Willcox, Spotsylvania Court House, to Governor Austin Blair of Mich. "Michigan Regiments of this Division have been engaged in several skirmishes, and three general engagements They have all done well, some of them splendidly.—Their losses since crossing the Rapidan, to this date have been—

killed, one hundred sixty one (161)—[wo]unded, seven hundred twenty two (722) [mi]ssing, five hundred forty (540)—[t]otal loss fourteen hundred twenty [t]hree (1423)—Will you please use every ~~measure~~ means in your power to hurry up all reinforcements to these regiments,   I think we are on the high road to success"—Telegram received, *ibid.* *O.R.*, I, xxxvi, part 2, 827.

1864, MAY 19.   To President Abraham Lincoln. "Dr Winston may be of great service to us, please send him along."—Telegram received, DLC-Robert T. Lincoln; (2) DNA, RG 107, Telegrams Collected (Bound). On May 18, Lincoln had telegraphed to USG. "An elderly gentleman—Dr. Winston—is here, saying he is well acquainted with the ground you are on, and trying to get on, and having letters from Gov. Morton, Senator Lane, and one from your Father, and asking to be allowed to go to you—Shall we allow him to go to you?"—ALS (telegram sent), *ibid.*; telegram received, *ibid.*, RG 108, Letters Received. Lincoln, *Works*, VII, 350.

1864, MAY 29.   USG endorsement. "Respectfully forwarded to the Secretary of War for his information"—ES, DNA, RG 94, Letters Received, 1864. Written on a letter of April 28 from Brig. Gen. Thomas E. G. Ransom, Cairo, to Brig. Gen. John A. Rawlins defending Brig. Gen. Charles P. Stone against charges printed in the *Missouri Republican.*—ALS, *ibid.*

1864, MAY 29.   Annie L. Ash, Philadelphia, to USG. "In my deep sorrow I hasten to acknowledge your favor of the 21. inst. of which I have the honor to be in receipt, and to send you the following, which has just been received in a communication from Surgeon George L. Porter U. S. A. 'Capt. Joseph P. Ash, Fifth Regular Cavalry, was killed in battle, upon Sunday May 8. on the road leading from Todd's Tavern to Spottsylvania Court House. He was taken to the Cavalry Hospital, on the road from Todd's Tavern to Fredericksburg, at a Mrs M. R. Jones'   Three officers were buried on the South West side of the house. Capt. Ash's grave is the centre of the three. Mrs Jones knows about his grave and will give any information.' General, allow me, altho' at a very early age, to tender you the heartfelt and lasting gratitude of my bereaved Mother and myself, for granting my request to have the body of my most precious and only Brother, one who filled a Father's place, sent to us at the earliest moment possible. *Your* assurance, General, that it shall be immediately forwarded, has thrown a light upon the darkest hour of my life. Now that I can give you the Spot where my Brother is buried, I can be comforted, and will confidently trust that the body of one whom my Mother loved more dearly than her own life, and in whose invaluable character as Son and Brother, all her fondest hopes were realized will very soon reach her that she may rise from her low state. My Mother is constantly repeating, when I receive my Son's body I can rise from my bereavement. General, I am sure you can appreciate my sad and lonely condition, altho' I am resigned to my Brother's death for his Country, at the age of twenty three, after having been through all the battles of the Army of the Potomac, receiving in them, at different times, eight wounds without a murmur; and that you can understand that it devolves upon me to tell you that the speedy arrival of my Brother's remains will be, in my Mother's critical condition, a life-giving consolation. . . . General May I ask you to do us the kindness to send the particulars of my dear Brother's death." —ALS, DNA, RG 94, War Records Office, Army of the Potomac. On June 3, Lt. Col. Adam Badeau wrote to Maj. Gen. Andrew A. Humphreys. "I have the honor to forward you the accompanying lettre from Miss Ashe which contains information that may prove useful in the efforts made to obtain the body of Capt. Ashe"—ALS, *ibid.* On June 4, Badeau wrote to Humphreys. "Lt. Gen. Grant directs me to state that the circumstances mentioned by you in your note of this date, relative to the removal of Capt. Ashe's remains, are such as to render it inexpedient at present to take any further steps looking to their disinterment"—ALS, *ibid.*

1864, MAY 30.   Brig. Gen. James H. Carleton, Santa Fé, N. M., to USG. "Amidst all your great and responsible duties I hope you will have time to read a line or two which I take pleasure in writing in behalf of one of our old comrads, Major Henry D. Wallen, U. S. Army, who has just been relieved from duty in this Department and ordered East. I have known and served with Major Wallen at various times for nearly a quarter of a century. We were second Lieutenants together three years, even, before you left the Academy. There is no officer in the Army who is a purer patriot, or who brings as a guide in the discharge of his duty a more conscientious mind than himself. For a long time he was the Inspector General of this Department, and I had occasion frequently to call the attention of the War Department to the efficient manner in which he discharged the varied and laborious duties of that office. When relieved from this duty by Lieut. Col. Davis, Asst. Inspector General, Maj. Wallen was assigned to the command of Fort Sumner, and has had charge of the colonization of the Navajo prisoners located upon a reservation at that post. The labor of organizing and locating these Indians, so that regard should be had to their health, comfort, and the systematic employment of their time and labor in opening up farms for their support, has been very great. Yet this has been done in a manner to meet with praise and commendation on every hand. I regret deeply to lose Major Wallen's services, but feel that it is better for himself as a soldier to go where more can be done to reward him for a lifetime of faithful service than I have power to do for him. I hope, General, that he will receive that promotion which he so well has earned, and which as a patriot and as an efficient and able soldier, he so well merits."—Copy, DNA, RG 94, ACP, 1328W CB 1865. On Jan. 27, 1865, President Abraham Lincoln wrote to Maj. Gen. Henry W. Halleck, enclosing a copy of Carleton's letter. "Herewith are papers presented to procure the promotion of Major Henry D. Wallen. I do not forget that there is a good deal of 'opinion' not to say 'prejudice' against Major Wallen, among the officers of the old Army. I remember what Gen.

Grant once said to you and me in the carriage on the way to the Navy Yard
—Still as he seems to have acted faithfully during the war, it is rather hard
that he shall get no promotion, while so much is given to others—What say
you?"—ALS, *ibid.*

1864, MAY 30.   Maj. William P. Rucker, 13th W. Va., Wheeling, to
USG urging a promotion for Brig. Gen. George Crook, for whom Rucker
served as vol. aide.—ALS, DLC-John Sherman. Sent to U.S. Senator John
Sherman of Ohio to be forwarded if proper, its present location indicates that
USG never received it.

1864, [MAY?].   USG statement. "This sash, worn by me through all my
battles and campaigns, from and including the surrender of Vicksburg, July
4th, 1863, is presented to Brigadier General John A. Rawlins, my chief of
staff, in evidence of my appreciation as an officer and friend."—*Galena
Weekly Gazette*, May 17, 1864. Written with indelible ink on a silk sash
and signed by USG.

Index

All letters written by USG of which the text was available for use in this volume are indexed under the names of the recipients. The dates of these letters are included in the index as an indication of the existence of text. Abbreviations used in the index are explained on pp. xvi–xx. Individual regts. are indexed under the names of the states in which they originated.

189n, 190, 195 and n, 208, 213n; praises Thomas E. G. Ransom, 41; has dispute about cipher, 48–49, 49n, 79–80, 80n–81n; son ill, 48n, 74, 75n; suggested as presidential candidate, 53n, 133, 148–49, 166–67, 167n, 183, 183n–84n; regulates trade, 54, 105–6, 108n, 120, 121n, 528, 553, 555, 560; biographical sketch of, 54n; at St. Louis, 65n, 66, 69–70, 70n–71n; early life of, 67n, 90n, 133n, 341n, 356n, 510, 516, 568–69; makes speeches, 70n–71n, 195, 214; finances of, 100, 215, 357, 363 and n, 516, 517; horses of, 121, 123n, 138–39, 565; health of, 122, 133, 139, 155, 297, 363, 365n, 394, 444 and n, 555; staff of, 122, 159, 160n–62n, 220, 220n–22n, 226, 259, 259n–60n, 261–62, 384–86, 385n, 569; in Nashville, 123n; praises Grenville M. Dodge, 126; plans to visit Galena, 128; praises Frederick Steele, 132; praises David D. Porter, 133; distrusts John A. McClernand, 140; upset by father, 148–49; deals with prisoners, 155–56, 301–2, 302n, 345, 429n, 437–38, 513, 525, 560; William T. Sherman describes, 187n–88n; deals with civilians, 206–7, 528–29, 563; presented sword, 214, 214n–15n, 351; and newspaper correspondents, 221n; criticizes Stephen A. Hurlbut, 284–85, 286n, 374n; purchases home, 297; sister of, 297n; safety of, 315, 316n; suggests command for Henry W. Halleck, 369–70, 370n; and Abraham Lincoln, 380 and n; angry with William S. Rosecrans, 382–83, 383n–84n; campaigns in Va., 397–503 passim, 566–69 passim; brother of, 503n; and liquor, 512; forged signature of, 515–16; in Culpeper, 550

Grant, Ulysses S., Jr. (son of USG), 7, 349, 394

Grant, Ulysses S., 3rd (grandson of USG): documents owned by, 36n–37n, 37n–39n, 48n, 52–53, 54n, 61n–62n, 70n, 133n–34n, 134n, 142n, 142n–43n, 166–67, 180n, 183n–84n, 195n (2), 196n, 208n–9n, 218n–19n, 293n–94n, 305n, 316n, 328n–29n, 329n–30n, 334n, 345, 351n–52n, 357n, 363n, 401–2,

423–24, 509–10, 514, 516, 518 (2), 527, 528–29, 543, 546, 551 (2), 552, 553–54, 555, 557, 558–59, 561, 562, 562–63, 565

Grant, Virginia (sister of USG), 297

Graves County, Ky., 180

Grear, Jesse (Tenn. Vols.), 155, 156n

Greeley, Horace (newspaper editor), 38n

Green, John W. (C.S. Army), 538

Greenbrier River (Va.), 313n, 390n

Greeneville, Tenn., 157n, 168n

Greensboro, N.C., 18n, 387n

Greensport, Ala., 508

Greenville, Miss., 191, 535

Greenwood, Miss., 22n, 143n

Gregg, David M. (U.S. Army), 361n

Grenada, Miss., 20n, 22n, 267n, 277, 323n

Gresham, Walter Q. (Ind. Vols.), 145

Grier, William N. (U.S. Army), 513

Grierson, Benjamin H. (U.S. Army), 146, 229 and n, 230n, 285n, 286n

Griffin, Charles (U.S. Army), 399n, 495n, 497n

Griffin, Simon G. (U.S. Army), 434, 436n, 437n

Grigsby, J. Warren (C.S. Army), 88n, 537, 538

Grove Church, Va., 562

Guiney's Bridge, Va., 476, 477n

Guiney's Station, Va., 446n, 473n

Guntersville, Ala., 251n, 323n

Gurowski, Adam (journalist), 553

Guthrie, Jacob F. (of Mount Pleasant, Tenn.), 4n

Guthrie, James V. (railroad president), 178n

Hagerstown, Md., 311n

Haines, Thomas J. (U.S. Army), 74 and n

Hale, John P. (U.S. Senator), 259n, 260n

Hall, Cyrus (Ill. Vols.), 509

Hall, John D. (of Philadelphia), 550–51

Hall, Theron E. (U.S. Army), 93n, 94n

Hall, Willard P. (Gov. of Mo.), 299n

Halleck, Henry W. (U.S. Army): handles personnel problems, 6n, 34n–35n, 56n, 57n, 78n–79n, 85n, 86n, 94, 124 and n, 127n, 141n, 165n, 189n, 204n, 212n, 217n, 222, 223n,